ELSE/WHERE: MAPPING NEW CARTOGRAPHIES OF NETWORKS AND TERRITORIES

JANET ABRAMS + PETER HALL, EDITORS

published by
UNIVERSITY OF MINNESOTA DESIGN INSTITUTE

distributed by
UNIVERSITY OF MINNESOTA PRESS

Else Where
Mapping
Jeremy Wood
002
1/8
ITS

NOT
DOWN

Else/Where
Mapping
Jeremy Wood
005

ANY
MA

TRUE
PLACES

7/8
Transco
NEVER
ARE

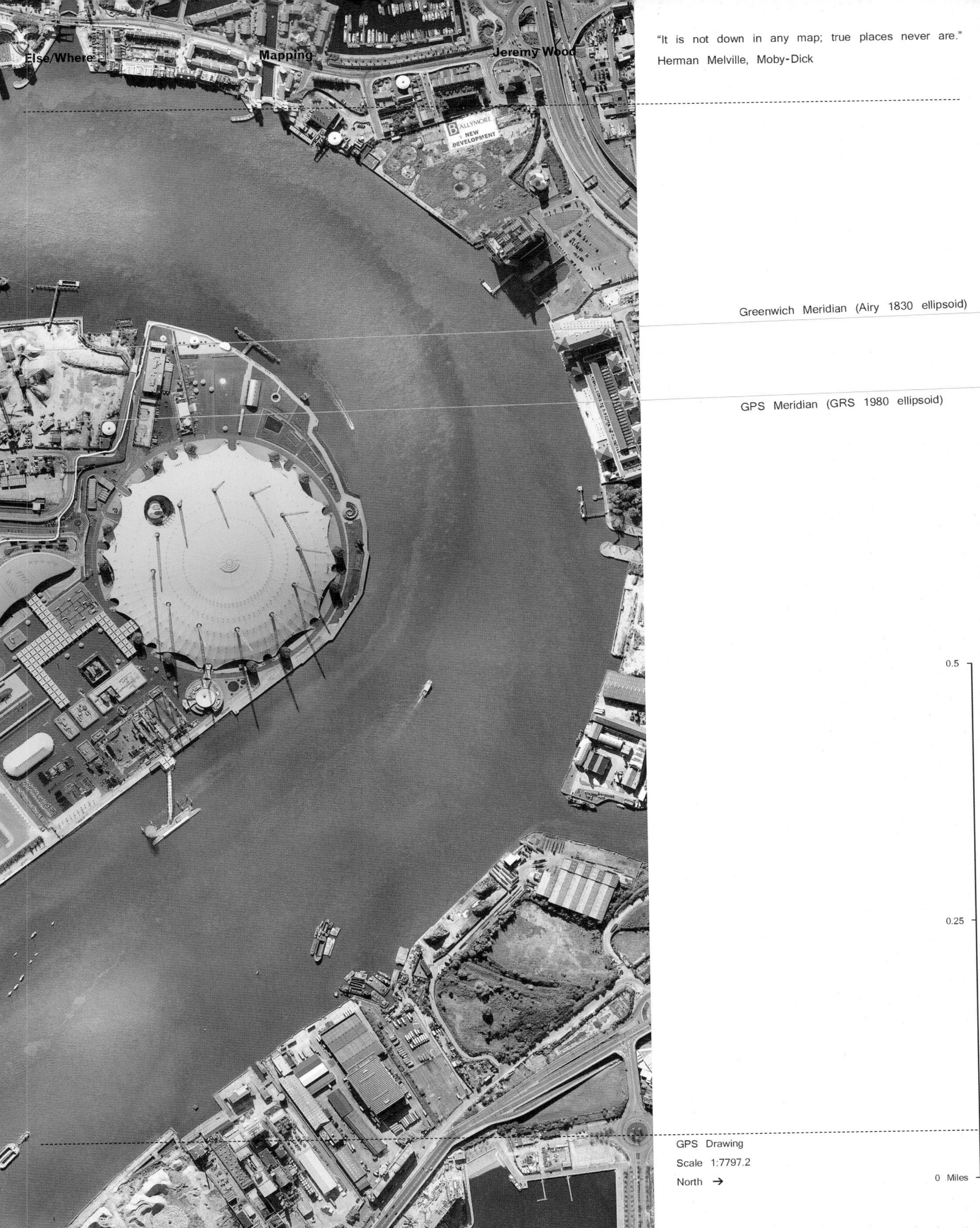
Else/Where
Mapping
Jeremy Wood
"It is not down in any map; true places never are."
Herman Melville, Moby-Dick
BALLYMORE
NEW DEVELOPMENT
Greenwich Meridian (Airy 1830 ellipsoid)
GPS Meridian (GRS 1980 ellipsoid)
0.5
0.25
0 Miles
GPS Drawing
Scale 1:7797.2
North →

Else/Where: Mapping

Contents

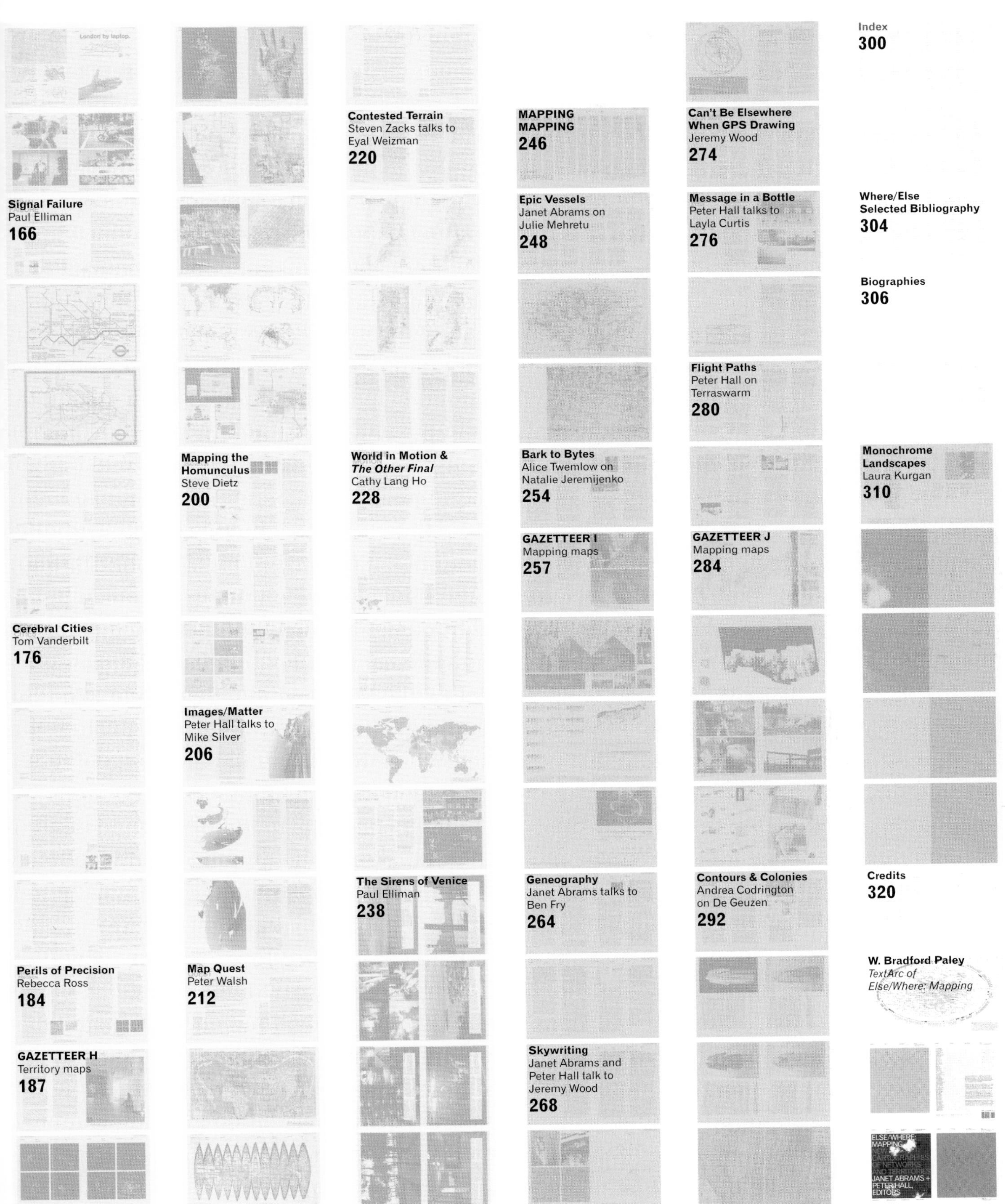

WHERE/ABOUTS

Mapping has emerged in the information age as a means to make the complex accessible, the hidden visible, the unmappable mappable. As we struggle to steer through the torrent of data unleashed by the Internet, and to situate ourselves in a world in which commerce and community have been redefined in terms of networks, mapping has become a way of making sense of things.

This book contends that mapping is an increasingly vital activity, one that undergirds diverse disciplines and transcends the supposed physical/digital divide. It is the conceptual glue linking the tangible world of buildings, cities and landscapes with the intangible world of social networks and electronic communications. Mapping is also a core aspect of what designers do. To design is to invent strategies for visualizing information that make new interpretations possible.

The late J. B. Harley—who is credited with bringing a cross-disciplinary approach to cartography—argued that maps are social constructions of the world: "Far from holding up a simple mirror of nature that is true or false, maps redescribe the world—like any other document—in terms of relations of power and of cultural practices, preferences, and priorities."[1]

With this in mind, we chose the activity *mapping* rather than the noun *map* (which tends to connote paper artifacts) for the title and theme of this book. If a map is a completed document, mapping refers to a process—ongoing, incomplete and of indeterminate, mutable form. Mapping refers to plotting points and finding common terms of reference with which to analyze data; it benefits from the lack of finality denoted by the word *map*. Where maps measure and notate the world, mapping is, in the words of landscape architect James Corner, a "collective enabling enterprise," a creative act that describes and constructs the space we live in, a project that "reveals and realizes hidden potential."[2]

DATA/SPACE

The mapped "space" under consideration here ranges from information space (grasping patterns within vast quantities of data) to physical space (navigating the city, region or globe) to social space (representing power relations within and between organizations, whether corporate cultural, political or even covert). But what has propelled the recent surge in mapping—in gathering and arraying data in visual form—which can be observed in such a wide array of disciplines?

In his recent chronicle, *The Mapmakers*, John Noble Wilford notes that digital technology has brought about a revolution in the way maps are created and used that is without precedent since the Renaissance. Wilford identifies two areas of growth that are of particular relevance to the kind of projects that appear here.

First, the democratization of Geographic Information Systems (GIS) has spawned a new generation of "user cartographers" who are not necessarily trained mapmakers in the traditional sense, and are more likely to be working in groups than alone. Second, where the printed map functioned as both database and visualization in one medium, computerization has had a bifurcating effect. With storage functions largely transferred to digital databases, maps themselves can be easily customized, their content quickly streamlined. "Unburdened by archival responsibility, individual maps can be more pictorial," says Wilford.[3]

From a user-interface design perspective, the term "pictorial" is a massive understatement. In effect, mapping technology has split the interface from the database, a split comparable to the liberating effect photography had on the development of painting. Before the advent of aerial photography, satellite tracking and computerized data-gathering, a map was expected to represent its territory with comprehensive accuracy. Freed of that responsibility, cartographers can manipulate their data into any number of visual representations—an act so potent it has attracted the attention of other disciplines. As Harley remarked, "Maps are too important to be left to cartographers alone."[4]

So, who are the new cartographers of networks and territories? In *Else/Where: Mapping*, we set out to identify some of the most significant practitioners and projects, which we have organized in four sections addressing, respectively: the rise of the network as an organizing trope (Mapping Networks); the emerging languages of interactive, screen-based mapping (Mapping Conversations); shifting notions of the cartographer's domain, *terra firma* (Mapping Territories); and how a new generation of mapmakers is using technology to challenge and stretch the notion of what a map can be (Mapping Mapping).

TOP DOWN/BOTTOM UP

Mapping Networks looks at various visual representations of the "Network Society," both in terms of its backbone infrastructure, the Internet, and the social formations enabled by global communications. The network, when viewed from above, faces the same charges of misrepresentation that Harley and a generation of critical cartographers leveled at the bird's eye

1. J. B. Harley, "Text and Contexts in the Interpretation of Early Maps," in *The New Nature of Maps: Essays in the History of Cartography*. Baltimore and London: Johns Hopkins University Press, 2001, p. 35.

2. James Corner, "The Agency of Mapping: Speculation, Critique and Invention," in Denis Cosgrove, ed., *Mappings*. London: Reaktion Books, 1999, p. 213.

3. John Noble Wilford, *The Mapmakers*. New York: Alfred A. Knopf, 2000, p. 417.

view — a view that has reigned supreme in cartographic tradition. As Harley said of the aerial map: "Here technology has suppressed social relations." He called for a new strategy of map-reading: "Instead of picking up social messages that the map emphasizes, we must search for what it de-emphasizes; not so much what the map shows, as what it omits."[5] Although Harley wrote this in the late 1980s, network mapping has yet to become the subject of an equivalent critical cartography. The first section of this book is an attempt to establish some footwork in that direction.

J. J. King argues here that networks are inherently resistant to such a synoptic "aerial" view. He surveys both corporate and contestatory examples of "knowledge mapping" and finds an irreconcilable contradiction between the desire for comprehensiveness in representing the "space of flows" of the networked economy, and the impossibility of representing something so vast and infinitely subjective. The network "at once inspires and thwarts the cartographer," says King, who advocates instead a "node-centric" organization of information that acknowledges its own incompleteness and focuses only on how each node relates to other nodes: with whom each interacts and why.

CRITICAL/MASS

Writing in the 1980s, the critic Fredric Jameson argued that the notion of "cognitive mapping," as outlined by Kevin Lynch in his 1960 *The Image of the City*, needed to be extrapolated from the spatial to the social realm.[6] Brian Holmes assesses the status of today's "critical and dissident cartography" in the light of Jameson's challenge, and offers a compass-like schema of four types of mapping corresponding to different spheres of social organization: hierarchical power (cultural, military, economic) at one apex, contrasting with swarms of "self-organizing singularities" at the opposite pole, such as the activist groups that converge at political and economic summits.

The former (such as the "organigrams" by the French artists Bureau d'études) can be so overwhelming in their complexity as to make the beholder feel puny, almost disarmed of individual agency. The latter mappings constitute a kind of "cartography with your feet,"[7] constructing an alternative future rather than confirming the status quo. Holmes confronts the paradox that many "dissident" mapping projects nonetheless rely for their implementation on "the very tools that consolidate the control society."

Dirk van Weelden argues that although network mapping often appears preoccupied with an hermetic world constituted within and by digital communication, its real subject is always and inevitably the physical world. Reviewing recent trends in social software and network mapping, van Weelden rebuts the prevailing view of a split between virtual and physical space. In the now-familar efforts to map and aestheticize the "traffic of bits," and in the social network mapper's desire to render the physical world according to their image of network relations, van Weelden finds a common failure to acknowledge their true reciprocity.

Social networks need not be represented by pixels alone. Robert Horn uses a visual vocabulary closer to children's cartoons in his maps of "Complex Social Messes" which are intended as tools for social change, rather than as refined and conclusive graphic artefacts. The collaborative process of their assembly is where their value lies, Horn explains. On these "mess maps," the rough-edged boxes and swirly arrows are meant to convey the provisional nature of the connections; once "cross-boundary causalities" between social entities are disentangled, relationships can be realigned.

AS/WITH

Mapping Conversations evolved out of our realization that a dumb-bell relationship exists between two types of "conversations" we have with maps. On the one hand, there is a growing body of work in visualizing multi-party online dialogue — sometimes among a few people, sometimes many. Such "Conversations As Maps" allow the participants to perceive their "place" within the community and chronology of electronically-mediated conversations, which may take place in Internet chat rooms, news groups, email, blogs or web-to-web discourse. On the other hand, as individuals, we increasingly find ourselves interacting with dynamic database-driven maps, whether for practical purposes of A-to-B wayfinding or for more playful psychogeographic meanderings in urban space. Again, such "Conversations With Maps" may be experienced in a variety of environments, and on a range of platforms: desktop computer, in-car navigation system, hand-held PDA, giant interactive table.

For the first part, "Conversations As Maps," we curated an online conversation *about* online conversation, by bringing together six people who are actively developing new visualizations of collective digital discourse, through experimental software and interface designs that offer capabilities beyond those offered by their current mass-market counterparts. Conversing at first via email, and then in a chat session straddling several time zones, the invited participants — Judith Donath, Mark Hansen, Valdis Krebs, Warren Sack, Marco Susani and Richard Rogers — begin by debating whether traditional notions of navigation still apply to

4. J. B. Harley, "Deconstructing the Map," in T. J. Barnes and J. S. Duncan, eds., *Writing Worlds: Discourse, Text and Metaphor in the Representation of Landscape*. London and New York: Routledge, 1992, p. 213.

5. J. B. Harley, "Text and Contexts," *op. cit.*, p. 45.

6. Kevin Lynch, *The Image of the City*. Cambridge, MA: The MIT Press, 1960.

7. Brian Holmes, email to *Else/Where: Mapping* editors, May 28, 2005.

the electronic arena, then go on to explore various questions: how Internet browsers might enhance rather than inhibit "self-governance"; how to indicate when the data presented is uncertain, rather than definitive; different ways to convey active involvement versus more passive "spectator" status; how the mapping of communicative links between individuals or websites reveals constellations of political and social affiliation; the latent ideological tensions discernible in the layout algorithms used to perform social network analysis; and whether such maps can be considered descendants of Taylorism, intent on presenting people as efficient — or inefficient — nodes.

BODY/MEMORY

As statistician Mark Hansen notes, merely by making a "map" of something (by clustering or grouping objects in a certain way) the resulting image "tends to take on a life of its own." Participants caution that visual metaphors, and seemingly minor interface design decisions — such as line-thickness and orientation, straight versus curving nodal connections — dramatically affect users' perceptions of electronically-mediated conversation. In this realm, bereft of everyday spatial cues and body language, the way to register one's presence is to keep on "speaking" and leave a visible trail. As Judith Donath puts it: "persistent history is the information world's version of the body."

The chat wraps up on Warren Sack's point, following Marshall McLuhan, that "each new medium displaces the old." And whereas "old media" (newspapers, radio, television) offer neat pre-packaged, seemingly-authoritative parcels of information, the "new media" (blogs, newsgroups and the emerging array of news- and issues-gathering and delivery tools) offer an open-source, messier and more fragmentary version of events. If "Conversations As Maps" ultimately frustrates the reader's wish for a convenient set of conclusions, then our transcribed and edited conversation (and its three visualizations, by Donath, Hansen and Sack) at least reverberates with the spirit of the new media. It leaves us not with easy answers but, as Valdis Krebs says, capable of asking better questions.

The second part of Mapping Conversations, entitled "Conversations with Maps," takes the form of case studies of recent experimental projects — practical, whimsical and sometimes subversive — that have emerged out of the use of formerly military technologies, such as the Global Positioning System (GPS). This creative flourishing can be traced back, as Alex Terzich points out, to the Clinton-era decision to end the intentional degradation of GPS signals available to the public (a decision less easy to imagine being made in a post 9/11 world, and one that is, as Terzich notes, easily reversed, granting the thrill of what may be a temporary creative zone). In this same section, Andrea Moed sees the promise of predictive maps in a Penn State University interactive prototype, and identifies the unexpected appeal of military technologies to artists and hobbyists as that of an orderly game space in which treasure can be hidden, drawings can be rendered, and one need never be unwillingly lost.

LOST/FOUND

Indeed, the art of getting lost seems, itself, to be in danger of getting lost, as more and more devices are conceived to provide easy access to geo-spatial information, thus re-anchoring data obtained in virtual space to the "wet rock" (as David Weinberger has pithily termed it) of the earth.[8] Dutch information designer Paul Mijksenaar contends that "cartofreaks are also cartophobes" who collect maps because they are "frightened of their environment...and don't want to be lost." Paul Elliman, in the course of a reverie about an audio-guide to Venice (supplied by the the ubiquitous voice of the technological castrato *Salvatore*) notes similarly that "most planners and designers regard the experience of being lost or disoriented as the urban equivalent of a fatal disease."

A prototype in-car navigation system, designed by Antenna Design with Nissan Design America, proposes something more like a personal journal, an enticement to get lost in the city for the sheer pleasure of it. Antenna's "Enhanced Navigation System" would allow the driver (or front-seat passenger) to add personal annotations to the electronic map, rather than simply serving as an on-board destination-management tool.

Antenna's *Civic Exchange* project, which appears at the end of Mapping Conversations, also has an interactive map at its center, but this time a multi-user touch-screen table. The winning entry in a 2004 competition, this design is a hybrid of tourist information kiosk and community notice-board, and melds industrial design, urban design and interaction design into a new species of street furniture for the public realm. We juxtapose the *Civic Exchange* project with another interactive mapping table, launched commercially in 2004: the *Touch Table*, a joint venture of Applied Minds, Inc. and Northrop Grumman. Each of these projects reconceives the printed map as a large-scale interactive surface, with obvious advantages over the limited screen real-estate of the PDA or desk-top computer.

Though conceived in markedly different contexts and for different primary users (the workers, visitors and residents of downtown Manhattan, in the case of *Civic*

8. David Weinberger, "The Semantic Earth," *Release 1.0*, 22:1, January 28, 2004, p. 2. New York: EDventure Holdings, Inc.

Exchange; officials in federal and local urban management, in the case of the *Touch Table*), both tables aspire to enable collective conversation around layers of database-driven information, whether presented in maps, graphics, aerial photographs, or some combination thereof. They reveal that essentially the same mapping platform might be used to achieve quite different ends: the sharing of public information toward strengthening of community and enhancement of tourist experiences, or the deployment of restricted-access information by authorized officials, for the purposes of spatial and social control in urban or other environments.

TOPOGRAPHIES/TOPOLOGIES

In **Mapping Territories**, we turn our attention to the more traditional focus of cartography—the surface of the known and as-yet-unknown (or un-named) world—taking several canonic maps of physical terrain as texts ripe for re-reading. They range widely in scale, era, location, style, and technique of reproduction, from a 500-year-old woodcut of the globe, to late 20th-Century MRI scans of London taxi drivers' brains, and a bird-shaped journey drawn using GPS.

Denis Cosgrove provides a magisterial survey of the historical interrelationships between cartography and urbanism, exploring landmarks of "scientific" versus "celebratory" mapping, from almost every continent. He shows how recording and measuring techniques, and cartographic point-of-view have influenced the way cities are represented, and thus enabled or constrained their future form and the social experiences therein. Peter Walsh explores the etymological debates inspired by the first maps to show America as an independent continent—in a volume published by an early 16th-Century French think-tank, using the then cutting-edge technology of the printing press.

The electrification of cities in the early 20th century was the technological driver behind Harry Beck's London Underground system map of 1933; inspired by an electrical circuit diagram, it dispensed with fidelity to ground-level topography in favor of network clarity. Paul Elliman investigates the mythology that has grown up around this influential map, emulated by transit systems worldwide. He points out that Beck's elimination of topographical features should be viewed less as a stroke of genius than as part of a wider cultural glorification of the efficient utopian city.

Contemporary digital mapping techologies such as LIDAR (Light Detection and Radar) could radically change the way the built environment is conceived and constructed, according to architect Mike Silver. This data-intensive mapping technique—capable of recording objects, buildings and whole environments in 3D in unprecedented detail—may shatter the dichotomy between the "Duck" and "Decorated Shed" that has held sway within architectural discourse since Robert Venturi *et al* coined these terms in the 1960s.

Aerial photography and AutoCAD were among the technologies employed, along with deliberate choices of color, to create the 2002 B'Tselem map of Israel's West Bank settlements, as Stephen Zacks finds out in talking to its designer, Israeli architect Eyal Weizman. In endeavoring to reveal the "facts on the ground" of the settlements' actual and prospective dimensions, this map provoked renewed debate over issues of land, religious identity, and nationhood at the heart of the Israeli/Palestinian conflict, and vividly demonstrates the political "agency of mapping."[9] (A map shown in Mapping Conversations addresses this conflict from a different perspective: *Occupied and Unoccupied Media Spaces*, by govcom.org, lays out a linguistic geography of the various terms for the Israeli "Security Fence" as used in Israeli, Palestinian and Western news outlets.)

LINES/TRACES

Echoing Judith Donath's remarks (in "Conversations As Maps") on the impact of seemingly trivial decisions about line thickness and orientation, Weizman also notes how apparently incidental inflections of a line drawn on a geographic map can dramatically affect people's lives, carving through property, shifting the balance of power to one side of the line or the other. Once translated to the built world, lines become hard scorings, etched into territory.

By contrast, consider the filigree of evanescent lines that gradually formed a familiar set of concentric rings in *Amsterdam RealTime*, a project cited by several authors, which emerges as a paradigm of contemporary "bottom-up" mapping, the kind of collaborative cartography that Steve Dietz discusses in his essay on psychogeography, urbanism and emergent systems. Questioning the tendency to privilege precision over blur, technical fidelity over the messiness of experienced reality, Rebecca Ross contrasts *Amsterdam RealTime* (compiled in 2002) with two utopian mappings of New York: the 1960s scale model *Panorama of the City of New York* and the recent digital *NYCMap*.

Ross compares the richness of the personal geographies collected in *Amsterdam RealTime* to the top-down authority of the Robert Moses-era *Panorama*, whose aspiration toward exhaustive accuracy is forever thwarted by the constant changes in a living organism as complex as New York City. Faced with this paradox, Ross, adapting Bruno Latour's question, asks: "What

9. Corner, *op. cit.*

would it mean to say that a map is more human-made because it incorporates the participation of many people? Might it even *increase* its claim to accuracy?"

BIT/MAP

The issue of scale threads through this book, in both form and content. Sometimes it has seemed faintly quixotic to be attempting to document projects that were made to be experienced digitally, on the pages of a *book*—grappling with issues of image-size and pixel resolution to which we are more or less oblivious as we nonchalantly shift, in daily life, back and forth between screens of various size/resolution, and the printed page. We have resolved (sic) this dilemma by establishing a strict system of text-only double-spreads for the essays, with the very occasional facing-page image; sandwiched in between are visual "gazetteers" whose grid accommodates images of different sizes, including those plucked from websites, which cannot be shown larger than an eighth of a page without degrading into a bit-map blur.

Zooming back to a much larger scale, questions of image resolution shade into issues of surveillance, as a smaller and smaller footprint of the earth's surface becomes susceptible to the panoptic eye of satellite photography. These issues are addressed visually and philosophically in several essays and visual contributions, especially in the two artists' projects that start and end the book.

Laura Kurgan has been making art for over a decade that critically examines the implications of surveillance technologies such as GPS, and the political dimensions of geo-spatial information. Her suite of images, *Monochrome Landscapes*, which provides the book's closing sequence and also graces its covers, is explicitly concerned with the limits of satellite vision. For this work, Kurgan commissioned four images of particular locations on the earth's surface from satellite imaging companies; at first sight, these images appear to be innocuous swatches of a single hue, but turn out to be sites freighted with geo-political significance. (Kurgan's 1995 *You Are Here Museu* is featured in "Conversations With Maps," while her 2001 map of Ground Zero is discussed in Mapping Territories.)

NOT/NOUGHT

The play of scale is most exuberantly manifested by the work of the young British artist Jeremy Wood, the inventor of GPS drawing, whose *Meridian Drawing* was commissioned for the book's opening pages; his account of making it appears in Mapping Mapping. Wood brings satellite perspective down to earth by using GPS receivers to draw outsize letterforms, figural shapes or purely abstract patterns that correspond to the different types of movement used to produce them. Walking the words of Herman Melville with GPS receiver in hand, Wood finds that a line taken to be a reliable benchmark—zero degrees longitude, the Count Zero of mapping—has two distinct versions: the Greenwich Meridian and its GPS doppelgänger are some 343 feet apart at the Royal Observatory, thanks to the discrepancy between two models of global measurement. As they say on the London Underground: "Mind the Gap."

In early 2005, as this book approached completion, the release of Google Maps and Google Earth sparked an explosion of popular interest in satellite imagery and digital cartography, and a rash of U.S. conferences dedicated to the commercial potential of "location-based technologies." In Europe, meanwhile, the phrase "locative media" has emerged to describe the kind of exploratory art/technology projects that we cover in the fourth section of this book, **Mapping Mapping**. Here we present the work of a new generation of artists—many in their 20s and 30s—who are engaging mapping technologies self-reflexively, questioning their social and cultural effects, or inventing dynamic visualizations that offer fresh perspectives on scientific information. As Denis Cosgrove wrote in his anthology *Mappings*: "The most challenging mappings today are found in the creative and imaginative work of artists, architects and designers, neither seeking absolute empirical warranty for their maps nor claiming for them any metaphysical revelation."[10]

CLONES/GENOMES

In both Natalie Jeremijenko's *OneTrees* project and in Ben Fry's group of studies collectively entitled *Genomic Cartography*, mapping techniques are used to explore frontiers of development in biological sciences. For the former, Jeremijenko deploys cloned Paradox trees as organic beacons that, over time, will map—in their progressive physical changes—the variations in environmental conditions at their planting sites all around the Bay Area. The differences between cloned pairs planted at the same spots also visibly challenge popular perceptions of genomics—complicating, according to Jeremijenko, the notion of simple genetic causality that dominates the public imagination.

On the opposite coast, in Cambridge, Massachusetts, Fry is working at a leading genomics research institute, the Broad Institute of MIT and Harvard, adapting principles of traditional cartography for the age of bio-informatics, and finding ways to navigate in exponential landscapes of genomic data. Again, the issue of scale is paramount: Fry emphasizes the need for different approaches to representation according to

10. Cosgrove, *op. cit.*, p. 19.

the level of information under scrutiny, rather than a "one-size-fits-all" approach. Eric Lander, director of the Broad Institute, even borrows a spatial metaphor to explain the transformation of biology into an information science. Twenty years ago, says Lander, it was as if biologists were "studying the earth from ground level," but with the advent of genomics, they "have been able to pull up to the 100,000 feet level and see the entire world of biology in one glance."

GLOBAL/REVISIONING

While much of Fry's work has already proven useful to the scientists with whom he collaborates, many other projects in the Mapping Mapping section have something of the character of follies: mapping experiments with no immediate practical application. Of what real use, you might ask, is a GPS drawing, a message in a GPS-equipped bottle, or an aerial "map" produced by a pigeon-mounted camera? In what way could a silk dress made from British World War II parachutists' maps help illuminate the Netherlands' relationship to its former colonies in the East Indies and its immigrant community today? The connective threads are traced by Andrea Codrington, in her reflections on a project by Dutch artists De Geuzen, which can be seen as the sartorial counterpart to Cathy Lang Ho's study of the global diffusion of football, in Mapping Territories.

In a similar spirit to the practice of "critical design" advocated by British designers Anthony Dunne and Fiona Raby,[11] the artists presented in Mapping Mapping (and elsewhere in this book) aim to expose and critique the cultural and professional assumptions embedded in the technologies they co-opt. As Marc Tuters has remarked, "the self-conscious locative artist treats the technology tactically — starting from an assumption that mobile technology 'will not only track you, but in fact *is* tracking you — and works backwards from a frank acceptance of the existing Society of Control to develop useful hacks'... I would contend that the socially-aware locative artist is experimenting with a new field of techno-cognition of potentially utopian dimensions."[12] Whether or not they are implemented with a full awareness of the "fundamental contradiction" to which Tuters refers, these sometimes satirical, sometimes absurdist artworks nonetheless bring to light intriguing and troubling possibilities. They draw attention to the undemocratic nature of maps (and, by extension, of much urban design) by asking: what gets missed in our preoccupation with top-down, scientifically accurate measurement?

At different places in this book, Steve Dietz and Warren Sack both point out that all interface designs (like all maps) implicitly have an agenda, in terms of how they determine a user's path through a body of information and permit or constrain awareness of our relationships to others in virtual space. It is easy to overlook how our maneuvers in the digital realm are directed by social and cultural assumptions — rules of engagement — that are built in to the software. Two different interfaces might facilitate very different experiences of the same body of information, yet the dominant paradigms have quickly gained an uncontested status akin to that of cartographic conceits. The predominance of the two-dimensional "desktop" metaphor has arguably become the interface equivalent of the Mercator projection. But just as Arno Peters' equal-area projection of the world (1974) challenged the Mercator's authority, so too new interface paradigms can offer alternative perspectives; they can reveal territory *between* territory, thereby opening up new possibilities.

HERE/NOW

In contrast with the mutable digital map, every printed map is already out of date, as soon as it is published. So too, this book is, inevitably, already a period-piece. We go to press at a moment of extraordinary efflorescence in the field of mapping, a creative proliferation we merely glimpsed a couple of years ago when we embarked on this journey, armed with some hunches that mapping was about to become foregrounded as a cultural concern — a mode of gathering, presenting, perceiving and reconceiving knowledge of the world and our place in it. Perhaps *mapping* may even come to surpass *designing* as the term to express the complex but related practices underlying fields as seemingly disparate as architecture, biology, geography, interaction design, social network analysis, statistics, art, cartography, wayfinding design and urban studies.

Like the borders of ancient mariners' maps, festooned with icons of the fantastical creatures that lurked beyond in *terra incognita*, we can only guess at the scope of the landscape ahead as networks, territories and communities are mapped and reimagined using digital technologies. We offer this collection in the belief that Mapping Mapping is a work in progress, and that these projects are the leading indicators of a sphere of intellectual and practical endeavor whose true dimensions are only just coming into view.

Janet Abrams and Peter Hall

11. Anthony Dunne, *Hertzian Tales: Electronic Products, Aesthetic Experience, and Critical Design*. London: Royal College of Art, 1999/Cambridge, MA: The MIT Press, 2006. Anthony Dunne & Fiona Raby, *Design Noir: The Secret Life of Electronic Objects*. Basel/London: Birkhäuser/August Media, 2001.

12. Marc Tuters, "The Locative Utopia," in *TCM Locative Reader*, 2004. Tuters quotes from a posting to the CRUMB new media discussion list. <http://locative.net/tcmreader/index.php?endo;tuters>

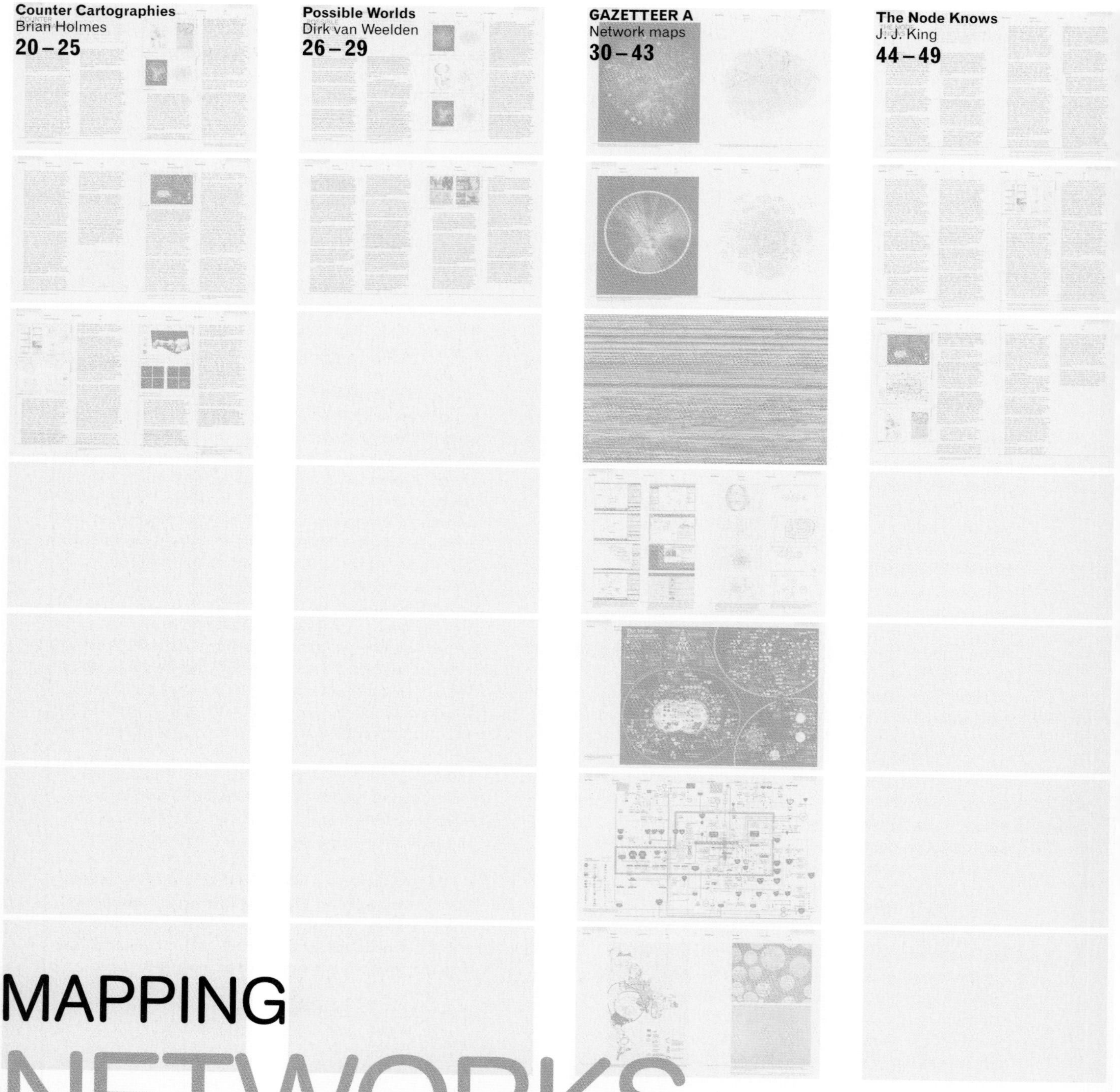

MAPPING NETWORKS

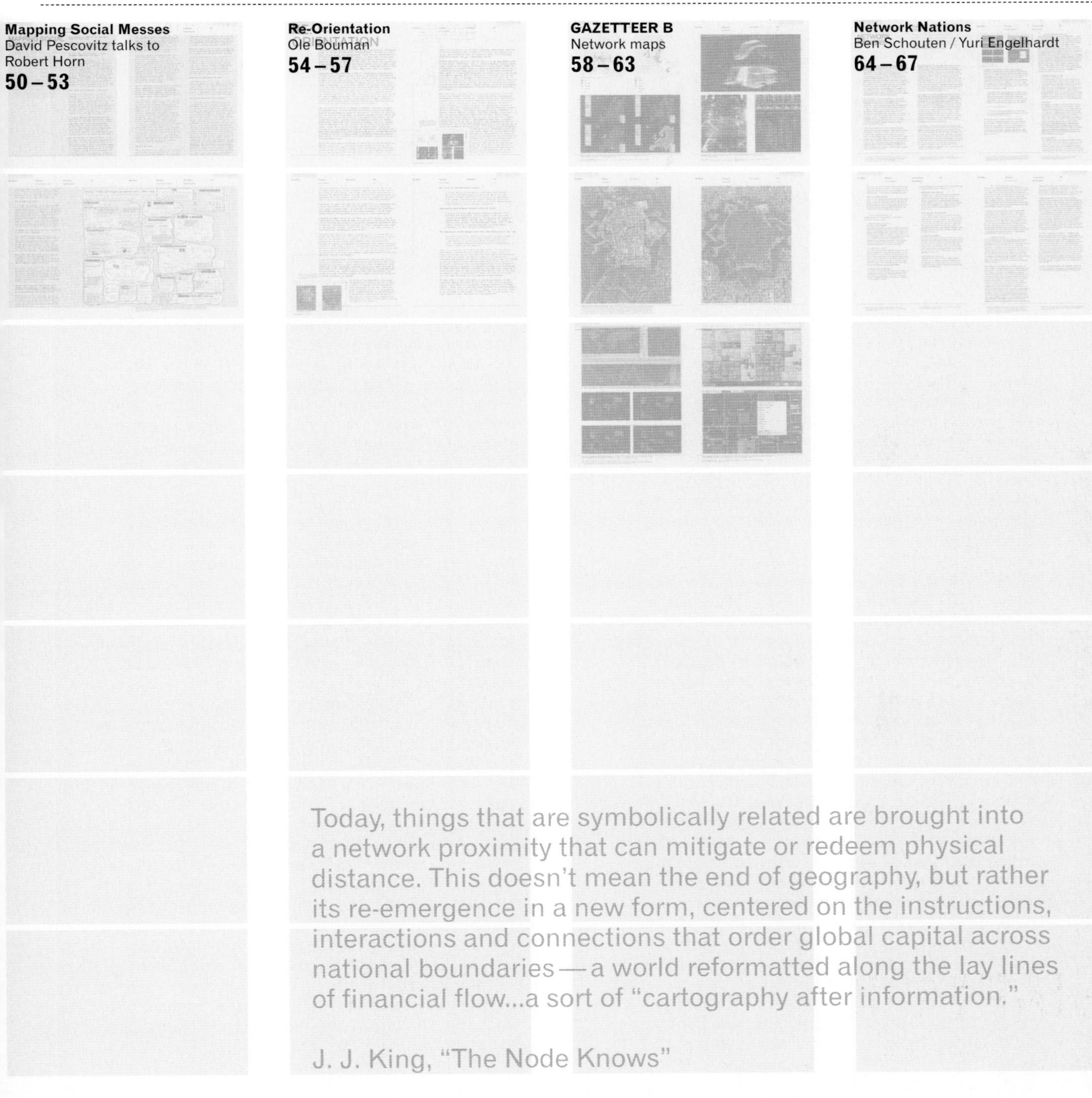

Today, things that are symbolically related are brought into a network proximity that can mitigate or redeem physical distance. This doesn't mean the end of geography, but rather its re-emergence in a new form, centered on the instructions, interactions and connections that order global capital across national boundaries—a world reformatted along the lay lines of financial flow...a sort of "cartography after information."

J. J. King, "The Node Knows"

COUNTER CARTOGRAPHIES

CAN THE NETWORK SOCIETY BE RE-ENVISIONED? HOW DO FORCES OF RESISTANCE OPERATE IN AN ERA OF PLANETARY MANAGEMENT? **BRIAN HOLMES** EXPLORES THE CARDINAL POINTS OF A DISSIDENT CARTOGRAPHIC AESTHETIC, WHOSE NETWORK MAPS AND ENERGY DIAGRAMS ARTICULATE CONTEMPORARY SOCIAL STRUCTURES, FROM HIERARCHICAL POWER TO SELF-ORGANIZING SWARMS.

The Internet is the vector of a new geography—not only because it conjures up virtual realities, but also because it shapes our lives in society, transforms our cities, and shifts our perception along with the ground beneath our feet. Networks have become the dominant structures of cultural, economic and military power. Yet this power remains largely invisible. How can the networked society be represented? And how can it be navigated, appropriated, reshaped in its turn?

Reflecting in the early 1980s on the spatial chaos that technological and financial developments had impressed upon contemporary cities, Fredric Jameson pointed to the need for "an aesthetics of cognitive mapping" to resolve "the incapacity of our minds, at least at present, to map the great global multinational and decentered communicational network in which we find ourselves caught as individual subjects." He conceived this cartographic aesthetics as a collective pedagogy, whose challenge would be to correlate the abstract knowledge of global realities with the imaginary figures that orient our daily experience. Epistemological shifts, pushed forward by the use of sophisticated technical instruments, would need to be paralleled by the deployment of radically new visual vocabularies in order to produce a clearer understanding of contemporary symbolic relations (social roles, class divides, hierarchies) and a fresh capacity for political organization in the postmodern world. Only by inventing "some as yet unimaginable new mode of representing" could we "again begin to grasp our positioning as individual and collective subjects and regain a capacity to act and struggle which is at present neutralized by our spatial as well as our social confusion."[1]

Twenty years later, what has become of the mapping impulse Jameson foretold? What new forms of cartography have arisen to chart the virtual/real spaces of the present? What kinds of agency do they permit? What modes of social organization do they foster? Can critical and dissenting maps be distinguished among the established and dominant ones?

Let's start by looking at an impressive technical and aesthetic feat: the *Skitter Graph* by the Cooperative Association for Internet Data Analysis (CAIDA)—an academic offshoot of the military-industrial complex, based in the city of San Diego. This map shows a record of peering sessions between some 12,500 autonomous systems (basically equivalent to Internet Service Providers, or ISPs). To produce it, 25 different monitoring points run a traceroute program known as *Skitter* over a period of two weeks, following packets from over 1.1 million IP addresses. The researchers analyze the path of the packet stream, which is only considered significant when it goes outside its autonomous system of origin. Information from the Border Gateway Protocol database is used to track each message back to a localized ISP. The graph displays the major link lines between the autonomous systems, and represents the quantity of outgoing connections per ISP, placing the lower values on the edges, in light blue, with higher intensities as you move toward the center, in dark blue, violet, orange, and finally yellow. But to give all this data the form of a world map, it is also organized by the geographical location of the ISPs—or, at least, their head offices—which are distributed around the circle according to longitude.

<http://www.caida.org/analysis/topology/as_core_network/pics/ascoreApr2003.gif>

1. Fredric Jameson, "The Cultural Logic of Late Capitalism," in *Postmodernism, or The Cultural Logic of Late Capitalism*. Durham: Duke University Press, 1991, p. 44.

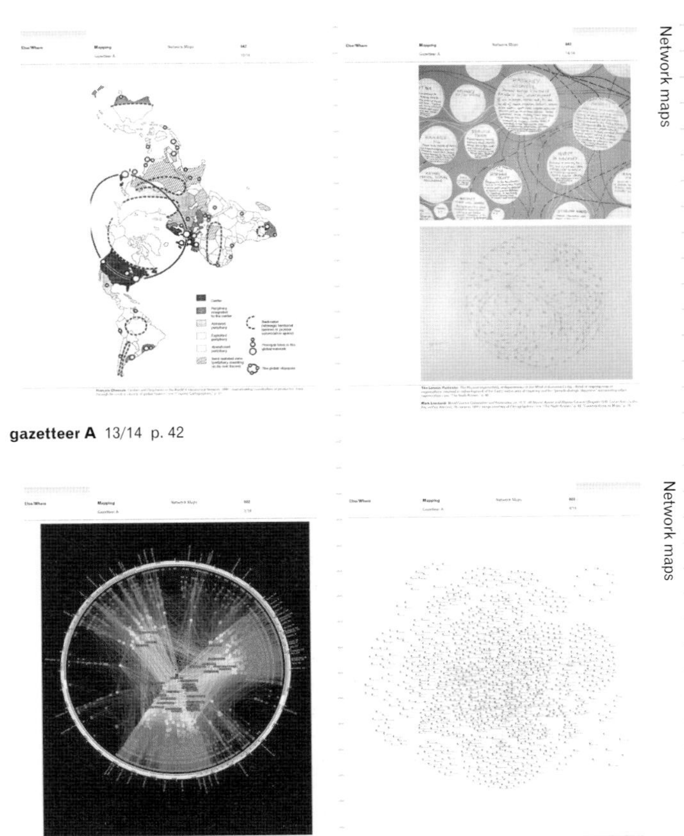

gazetteer A 13/14 p. 42

gazetteer A 3/14 p. 32

The autonomous systems fall into three major groups. At the bottom are those in North America—from San Jose and Vancouver to the Eastern seaboard—clearly dominating the Western hemisphere. Slightly further west are two exceptions: Buenos Aires and São Paulo/Rio de Janeiro, indicating the only significant connectivity in South America. Next comes Europe, with a great arc of ISPs stretching from London to Moscow; Pretoria falls in the middle, the one African city to be mentioned. On the upper left is Asia, with peak intensities in Tokyo, Seoul and Hong Kong, and lower values in Singapore, Perth and Sydney. The immensely productive population of mainland China barely shows up on this map of outgoing connections.

The *Skitter Graph* presents the raw facts of location and transmission: a geography of unqualified information flow. But what does it tell us about social relations? It can be compared to the map of *Centers and Peripheries*, published in a 1994 volume on the globalization of capital by the economist François Chesnais.[2] This map shows three things. First, a circuit linking the United States, Western Europe and Japan, the so-called Triad regions, which form a global oligopoly accounting for the majority of industrial and financial exchanges. Second, the major nodes of the world network, represented by densely outlined circles. And third, the hierarchical relations between the regions, as described with these categories: *center; periphery integrated to the center; annexed periphery; exploited periphery; abandoned periphery*. Chesnais performs a Marxist analysis, showing how globally fragmented production lines are coordinated through the computerized circuits of the financial sphere. His map describes the hierarchy of social relations in a post-national era, when no political formation can erect any substantial barrier to the dictates of capital. And it reveals the near-perfect correlation between the graph of virtual flows and the geography of human exploitation.

So having identified a dominant map, I now want to ask the political question: Where do the forces of resistance come from, and how do they gain agency in an era of planetary management and control?

To find out, you can log onto the Net and look at an animated version of exactly the same information used in the *Skitter Graph*. Each frame of this movie-map is a snapshot of Internet usage; five different images are recorded per day. The result is an extraordinary visual experience. The ISPs turn green and advance toward the center as their connectivity increases; the link lines shift as the routing structure reconfigures to meet each moment's demands. We watch the diurnal flux of the Internet, and feel the complex, disjunctive rhythm of the global information machine. It's like the pulsing of a hive, a planetary brain: the cognitive and imaginary activity of untold millions of individuals, establishing far-flung connections. What the activation of the *Skitter Graph* reveals—as though despite itself—is the micro-political dimension of the global production system: not a stratified representation, but an energy diagram.

<http://www.caida.org/outreach/resources/animations/active_monitoring/animAS.20000702-20020120.gif>

2. François Chesnais, *La Mondialisation du Capital*. Paris: Syros, 1994, p. 26. Map adapted from M. F. Durand, J. Levy and D. Retallé, *Le Monde: espaces et systèmes*. Paris: Presses de la Fondation des sciences politiques, 1992.

This animated map can be seen as a *diagram of power* in the sense described by Gilles Deleuze: a cartography that is coextensive with the whole social field.[3] The notion of the diagram, derived from Michel Foucault's work on the microphysics of power, does not simply designate a static grid, a preconceived template for the application of a unified force. Rather, it describes a productive matrix: a dynamic field where tensions are maximized at an almost infinite number of heterogeneous points. Each of these points—human beings, but also their material objects and inventions—is entwined in singular and evolving relations to others, relations of power that involve both constraint and freedom. From the interplay of such relations, functional patterns and statistical averages emerge. These can be codified as stratified laws within the social sciences. They can be represented in a synoptic table, by works like the *Skitter Graph* or the map of centers and peripheries. But beyond the stratified structures, the vital dynamics of each period arise from what Deleuze calls *strategies*, which can also be understood as the generative moves of social experimentation.

Thus we can distinguish between a determinate *network map*—a geographical representation of structures of networked power, which attempts to identify and measure the forces at play—and an undetermined *energy diagram*, which opens up a field of possible agency. Deleuze describes the diagram of power as "highly unstable or fluid...constituting hundreds of points of emergence or creativity." His aim is to indicate the openness, the possibility for intervention that inheres to every social relation, because of the limited but real power that flows through each of the participants. Thus, at its point of application, where individual behavior is molded into functional patterns by the convergence of mutually reinforcing constraints, power can also fold in upon itself, producing resistance and alterity through its own redoubling and subsequent dispersal.

This understanding of the way that social hierarchies can be dissolved—by a deliberate twisting or counter-application of the very forces that make them cohere—was the fundamental breakthrough of French critical thinking in the late 1970s and early 1980s, going beyond the deterministic schemas of traditional Marxism, but without abandoning the description of dominant structures. Two decades later, that epistemological breakthrough has lent momentum to an aesthetics of critical and dissident cartography, capable of twisting the techniques and visual languages of network maps away from their normalized uses, thereby pointing to a place for autonomous agents within the global information society.

Jameson saw the correlation of abstract knowledge and imaginary figures as key to understanding contemporary symbolic structures, and regaining the capacity to act within them. A range of recent mapping projects, all dealing with the forms of social organization, will serve as exemplars of this process. They can be arrayed within a circle marked by four cardinal points, and traversed by two major oppositions. At the top of the compass, a first group offers critical depictions of hierarchically concentrated cultural, economic and military power. At its polar opposite, another group invokes swarms of self-organizing singularities. In the right-hand quadrant are diagrams of social networks, represented either in their tendency toward the concentration of power, or in their moment of dispersion into all-channel meshworks. And in the left-hand quadrant, opposite these constitutive diagrams, we find the cartography of dissemination, which traces and effaces the footfalls of wanderers in the global labyrinth.

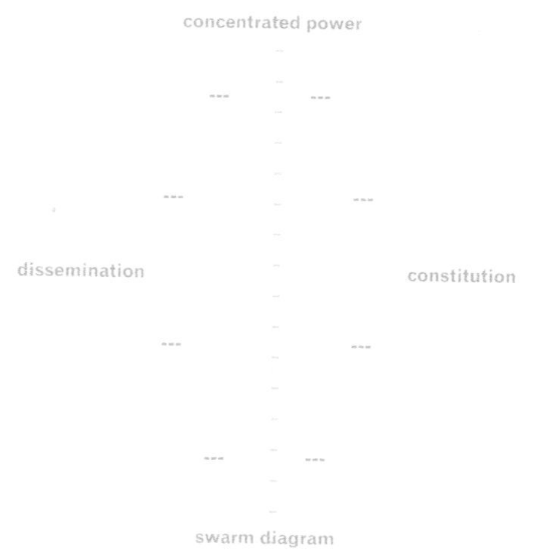

concentrated power

dissemination constitution

swarm diagram

3. Gilles Deleuze, *Foucault*. London: Athlone Press, 1988, p. 34.

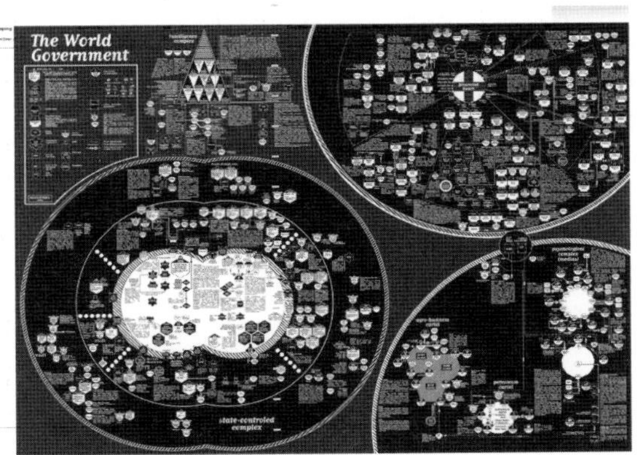

Network maps

gazetteer A 9–10/14 pp. 38–39

The cardinal examples of the first group are the flowcharts by Bureau d'études, such as *The World Government* (2003), which can be seen as a culmination of the critical analysis of globalization carried out by scholars and social movements since the early 1990s. This information map uses pictograms to represent over 40 different categories of actors, linked into a continuous and contradictory network. At the center is a financial core, populated by transnational investment groups. Around them, in a structure of nested rings, are nation-states subsumed under regional or strategic ensembles. Major industries, service providers and transnational organizations appear in direct or ambiguous relations to these blocs. The effect is one of arresting detail, compelling the eye to a seemingly endless iteration of links. But if you draw back, this extraordinarily complex map reveals rounded, almost cosmological forms, small enough to be seen in a single gaze.

<http://ut.yt.t0.or.at/site/index.php?option=com_content&task=view&id=52&Itemid=117>

"To understand a real thing in its totality we always tend to work from its parts. The resistance it offers us is overcome by dividing it," writes the anthropologist Claude Lévi-Strauss. He compares this analytic process to the effect of artistic miniatures: "Reduction in scale reverses this situation. Being smaller, the object as a whole seems less formidable. More exactly, this quantitative transposition extends and diversifies our power over a homologue of the thing, and by means of it the latter can be grasped, assessed and apprehended at a glance. A child's doll is no longer an enemy, a rival or even an interlocutor. In and through it a person is made into a subject."[4] Through miniaturization, the aesthetics of cognitive mapping becomes a way for an individual to grasp the complexity of the networked world.

The shift from object to subject propels us from one pole of the compass to its opposite, from hierarchies of power to self-organizing swarms. Howard Rheingold has convincingly described this new organizational form, showing how "smart mobs" use mobile devices to coordinate actions in real time.[5] The best examples of what might be called "swarm cartography" have come from activist groups in Spain. *Transacciones/ Fadaiat* is a "geography of the geopolitical territory of the Straits of Gibraltar," compiled in 2004 by independent media producers of the group Hackitectura, with collaborations from Tangiers and the Canary Islands. On a Mercator projection turned upside-down, the map shows sea-going migration routes, refugee camps, destination zones, electronic surveillance systems, military installations, and internment centers. The other side traces a meshwork of activist groups on both sides of the Straits, showing aspects of their evolution over time. The aim is to catalyze a range of interventions by autonomous agents, from direct action protests to immigrant support networks, legal cases, satire, subversion and the production of dissident knowledge. A comparable project was completed in 2004 by activist groups in Barcelona who created a sophisticated city map to help spark protests against the Universal Forum of Cultures event, widely perceived as a mere prop for real-estate speculation along the waterfront.

<http://mcs.hackitectura.net/tiki-browse_image.php?imageId=592>

<http://sindominio.net/mapas/ing/index_ing.htm>

This strategy of diverse, punctual, recurrent interventions was defined by John Arquilla and David Ronfeldt in their study, *The Zapatista "Social Netwar"*: "Swarming occurs when the dispersed nodes of a network of small (and perhaps some large) forces can converge on a target from multiple directions. The overall aim is *sustainable pulsing*—swarm networks must be able to coalesce rapidly and stealthily on a target, then dissever and re-disperse, immediately ready to recombine for a new pulse."[6] But the ambiguity of an activist strategy defined by military experts asks us to consider how organizational forms emerge and dissolve in contemporary society. The question shifts us to the right-hand quadrant of our hypotheti-

4. Claude Lévi-Strauss, *The Savage Mind.* Chicago: University of Chicago Press, 1966, p. 23.
5. Howard Rheingold, *Smart Mobs.* Cambridge, MA: Perseus Books, 2002.
6. John Arquilla, David Ronfeldt, *et al*, *The Zapatista "Social Netwar" in Mexico.* Rand Corporation, 1998, chapter 2, available at <www.rand.org/publications/MR/MR994>.

Network maps

gazetteer A 8/14 p. 37

Conversation maps

gazetteer C 5–6/12 p. 84

cal map of maps to explore the constitutive processes that lie between swarm phenomena and hierarchical structures. Social network analysis yields insights here, especially when combined with computerized research and visualization techniques. The maps by govcom.org use an *Issue Crawler* to analyze a group of websites, discovering common outgoing links (two included sites both linking to a third one, outside the initial group). Thus they identify a larger network of issues. For example, *Ruckus Camp* starts with the websites of forty-nine organizations, whose common links reveal a remarkably consistent set of almost 300 activist groups. A more complex document entitled *Climate Change* displays a densely interlinked cluster of major international organizations at upper right, relatively isolated from the broader meshwork of NGOs, businesses and domestic governmental agencies concerned with the issue. The map illustrates the difficulty for bureaucratic hierarchies to interface with ad hoc civil-society initiatives. But can social network analysis be used to portray the dynamics of network formation?

<http://govcom.org/publications/drafts/ruckus_camp.gif>

<http://govcom.org/publications/drafts/climate_existing.pdf>

An intriguing sequence of govcom.org diagrams titled *The case of Sklyarov versus Adobe on the Web* shows how a constellation of ephemeral allies comes together to defend a Russian programmer's hack of a proprietary software application. We see the timeline of a small-scale swarm phenomenon, from constitution to dispersal. Unfortunately, few network analyses deal with such dynamics. More characteristic is Josh On's ingenious database project, *They Rule*, which uses a friend-of-a-friend algorithm to generate charts of overlapping membership on the boards of America's Fortune 100 companies, revealing what are arguably the most robust networks of power in the contemporary world. But the weakness of such studies is precisely to focus on what sociologists call "strong ties"—eliminating the play of chance encounters and the insurgency of events that continually reshape social existence.

<www.govcom.org/maps/map_set_2.0/GCO_Maps_set_2.0_Sklyarov.pdf>

<www.theyrule.net>

When power structures coalesce and harden, the specific opposite of network constitution becomes an issue. The last quadrant of our metamap deals with the cartography of dissemination. The idea of a dispersed, subjective cartography is inspired by Michel de Certeau's opposition between the representational grid of the modern map and the "spatial practices" of walkers in the city, their "opaque and blind mobility," narrated through word and step. "One can follow the swarming activity of these procedures that, far from being regulated or eliminated by panoptic administration, have reinforced themselves in a proliferating illegitimacy."[7] That phrase can perfectly introduce the *Geograffiti* proposal, which involves spontaneously recording waypoints with a GPS device and associating them with impressions about what's on the spot—all to be inscribed on a website accessible to the mobile devices of other passers-by.

<www.gpster.net/geograffiti.html>

The dream is to retell the story of the world with your ideas and emotions, even while moving through it. Christian Nold gives that dream another twist, with his *Biomapping* project. A galvanic sensor is wrapped around a person's finger, to regis-

<www.biomapping.net>

7. Michel de Certeau, *The Practice of Everyday Life*. Berkeley: University of California Press, 1984, pp. 91–96.

Mapping maps

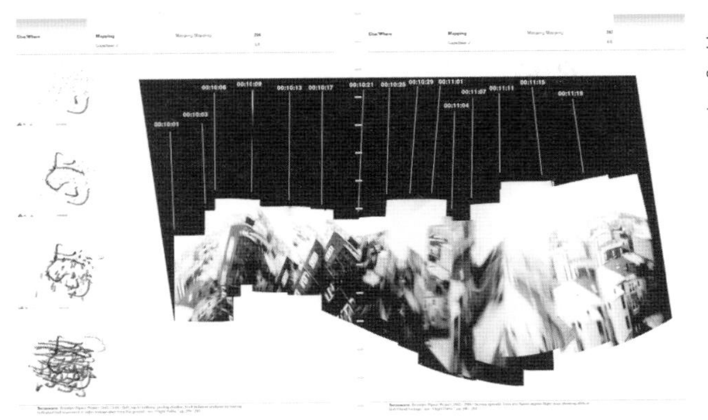

gazetteer J 3–4/8 p. 286–287

Territory maps

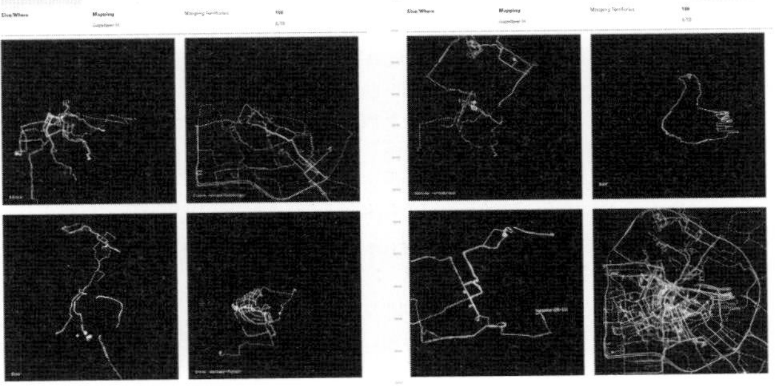

gazetteer H 2–3/13 pp. 188–189

ter the so-called startle response that provokes a drop in the electrical resistance of the skin. That information, coupled with continuous waypoint recording by a GPS device, produces a map of the participant's route through the city in cool green dots, punctuated by bursts of stress or excitement marked in red: psychogeography goes automatic. But Nold foresees critical applications too: the *Biomapping* unit could be connected to additional sensors correlating stress response with pollution, radiation, noise levels and so forth.

The most beautiful example of cartography in motion is Esther Polak's *Amsterdam RealTime/Diary in Traces*, where GPS-equipped pedestrians sketched out the city plan of Amsterdam as a record of their everyday itineraries. Their paths appear as lines of light on a black ground, only to be gradually effaced, giving way to the traces of other walkers. But the work is a fragile gesture, fraught with ambiguity: the individual's wavering life-line appears at once as testimony of human singularity in time, and proof of infallible performance by the satellite mapping system.

<www.waag.org/realtime>

The increasing use of Geographic Information Systems to profile the habits and desires of consuming populations makes clear the ways that corporate networks can now reach in to seize the very flux of subjective difference. A company like iMapData sorts such consumer profiles into precise geographic envelopes on a digitized city plan (such as a political jurisdiction, an infrastructure service zone, an area impacted by a major sports facility, a tourist attraction, or a natural disaster). Web access to these maps is sold to businessmen who want to make strategic marketing decisions on the go. Even more impressive is the integration of such private-sector archives to government databases, themselves keyed to the new biometric passports with which security forces seek to track entire populations caught up in the frenetic mobility of the present. An International Campaign Against Mass Surveillance has been mounted to warn the public of the dangers that may lie ahead.[8]

<http://imapdata.com>

<http://i-cams.org>

Critical and dissident cartographies arise against the background of these dominant mapping technologies. They appear as counter-behaviors in Michel Foucault's sense: deliberately denormalized refusals of the reason of State, elaborated with the very tools that consolidate the control society.[9]

<http://terraswarm.com/traffic_primer/bpp/index.html>

Beyond the constituted maps, on the unraveling edges of the energy diagrams, the jumbled, careening views of the skyline as seen by a wheeling flock of birds in Terraswarm's *Brooklyn Pigeon Project* might be a good way to remind ourselves that a poetics of flight can still be inscribed in the architectonic structures of Twenty-First Century power.

See "Perils of Precision," pp. 184–186.

See "Flight Paths," pp. 280–283.

8. For examples of commercial and governmental surveillance, see <www.imapdata.com> and the report at <www.i-cams.org>.
9. See Michel Foucault, *Sécurité, Territoire, Population.* Paris: Gallimard/Seuil, 2004, pp. 195–219 and pp. 362–365.

POSSIBLE WORLDS

Attempts to map the Internet range from the strategic to the encyclopedic to the socially utopian. But whatever issues are explored, network mapping inevitably addresses the reciprocities between digital and physical worlds, says DIRK VAN WEELDEN.

In that Empire, the Art of cartography attained such Perfection that the map of a single Province occupied the entirety of a City, and the map of the Empire, the entirety of a Province. In time, those Disproportionated Maps no longer satisfied, and the Cartographers Guilds built a Map of the Empire whose size was that of the Empire, and which coincided accurately with it.
—Jorge Luis Borges, Del rigor en la ciencia, *1960.*

INTRODUCTION

Maps are interfaces between knowledge and experience. Always more than descriptions, they represent what we usually experience as a series of impressions in the form of an image seen from an extra-corporeal viewpoint—that of shared knowledge.

Maps can be studied and interpreted, and used to generate new metadata so we can recognize otherwise undiscovered opportunities. By representing knowledge about the world graphically, we climb above our normal earthbound position and gain an eagle's eye view—visually as well as intellectually.

With a map, we can extrapolate from what we know to what's possible, what's not yet accomplished. The value of every map lies in its potential to generate a vision for attacking the terra incognita it portrays—not just literally, in uncharted white space, but also metaphorically, in an abstract sense. A good map automatically produces the possibility of a surprise attack, a decisive march, the likelihood of identifying the perfect site to strike the mother lode, or finding an elusive, almost extinct species.

Mapping the Internet poses numerous problems. The challenge is not just that it contains a staggering amount of extremely complex, rapidly-changing information, but also that it exists nowhere and yet operates simultaneously in the physical world.
To be more precise: the Internet produces a new type of space-time that bears a loose and flexible relationship to the physical world. The word "space" in "cyberspace" is highly metaphoric and cannot be separated from the activity conducted within it because the activity is what produces this "space."

Yet the reality of the data and the immediacy of the communication is so strong that we can only describe it as a "space."

The first attempts to visualize the Internet as a fuzzy cloud of connectivity came in the late 1990s. Barrett Lyon's visualization looked mysterious—much like an abstract Bob Ross painting—but was of very limited use, since it generated little metadata. Lyon described his Opte Project as a way of showing the growth of the Internet, of monitoring disasters (in the physical world) and as a work of art. Lyon's Internet maps make an interesting comparison with those by Bill Cheswick and Hal Burch of Lumeta.

<www.opte.org>

THE MAP AS INSTRUMENT

The most efficient way to make a map is to be single-mindedly instrumentalist and uncritical: ignore the discrepancies and possible conflicts between your infographic logic and any unintended consequences of using the map in the physical world. In other words, don't ask questions about the political, social and moral issues raised by this new and powerful interplay between digital space and the physical world.

Network mapping projects produced by military, commercial, technical and administrative entities are therefore the most successful. At Orgnet's website, a long list of applications of network mapping to the intelligence, commercial and managerial sectors can be found. The latest version of InFlow (3.0), the software developed by Orgnet founder Valdis Krebs, facilitates projects with such titles as "What emergent purchasing patterns on the WWW may reveal." Similar applications are used to undertake email and phone traffic analysis of Al Qaeda cells. At CAIDA's website, similar techniques are offered for the graphic visualization of Internet traffic in relation to routing, bandwidth and new trends in network usage: cold, hard, extremely useful metadata for generals, spies, terrorists, corporations and politicians. Beautiful, powerful and innovative results are logged when network mapping overlooks the social and moral dimension.

<www.orgnet.com>

<www.caida.org>

See "Counter Cartographies," pp. 20–25.

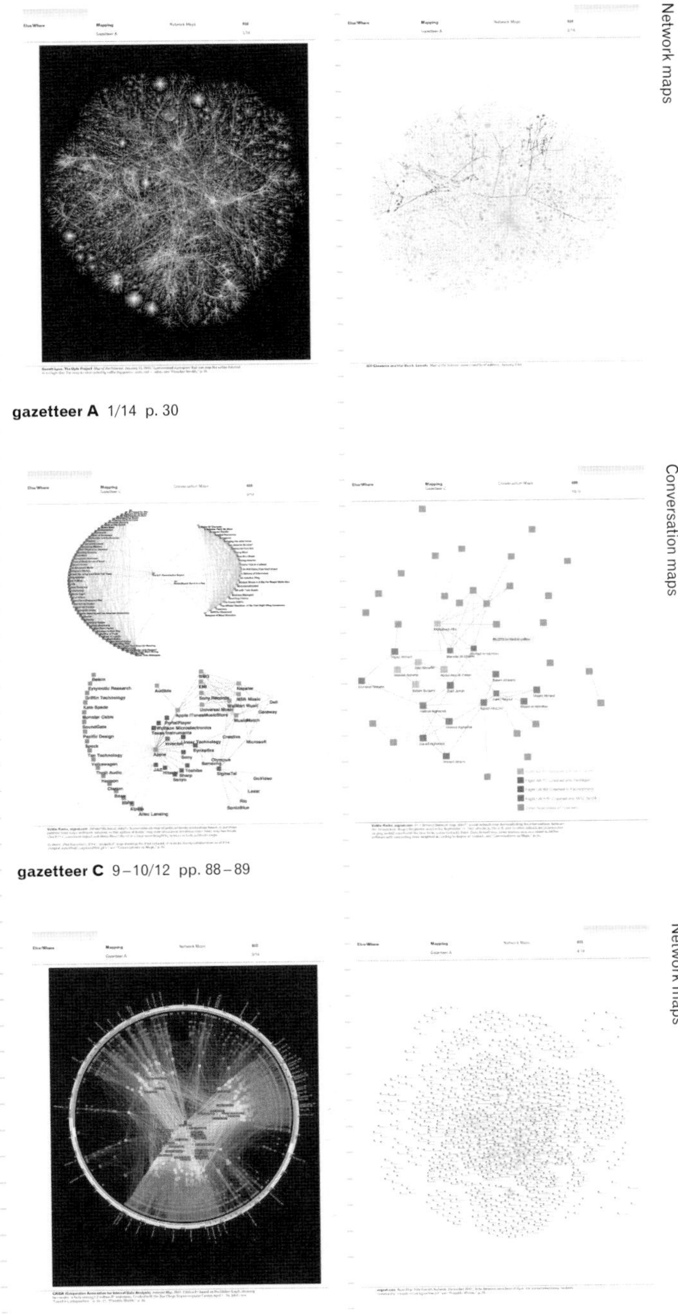

gazetteer A 1/14 p. 30

gazetteer C 9–10/12 pp. 88–89

gazetteer A 3–4/14 p. 32

THE ENCYCLOPEDIC MAP

The thorniest aspect of network mapping is the still poorly understood relationship of digital space to the physical world. As soon as this dilemma is acknowledged, the task ceases to be just a matter of intelligently visualizing the traffic of bits. Rather, it becomes a question of graphically visualizing the Internet as a specific part of human society. How do you depict connectivity as a special kind of social activity? The most straightforward model of network maps is as encyclopedic tools, which undertake a form of data mining geared toward the critical study of the world, harnessing the specific realities of cyberspace. Universities, non-governmental organizations, activists and political parties' scientific institutes all try to map the Internet from the perspective of their own particular social agenda, exploring digital space as a way of understanding how it may change social reality in the physical world. To them, mapping is more than a useful tool; it is proof that the Internet provides a new method to improve the world.

<www.uia.org/db>

<www.uia.be/trapproaches/trappcom_bodies.php?kap=13>

An ambitious example is to be found at the website of the Union of International Associations, which has developed a special kind of network visualization tool to get an overview of 10,000 world problems, the 15,000 international organizations that are trying to solve them, and the hundreds of thousands of relations between them. What differentiates the UIA's Netmap project from those of Orgnet is the belief that superior insights can be gained by accessing metadata that transcends the boundaries of disciplines, objectives and interests. The UIA regards the Internet as an archive of data, people, organizations, ideas and relationships whose potential can be better realized if a less formal, more socially beneficial overview can be constructed of its constituent parts. Designed as a dynamic map, an infographic interface, Netmap works as an oracle. It sets out to present policymakers, activists and academics with metadata that open up new transformative ways of tackling social or ecological problems.

This kind of network mapping aims at reconciling cyberspace and the physical world, on the assumption that connectivity can remove the blind spots that hamper our efforts at improvement. Netmap is designed as an automatic way of tapping this holistic extra dimension of the digital network. Behind it lies the humanistic notion that all knowledge is ultimately produced for the survival and development of the species, and that cyberspace is likewise to be valued and used in that way. Netmap aspires to humanize and domesticate the inhuman power and metadata stored in digital space.

SOCIAL SOFTWARE AND GEOGRAPHY

Bloggers are essentially socially-minded individualists. So when they began to form communities (e.g. BlogTribe) and blogging became integrated into the business world, it didn't take long before bloggers wanted maps of activity in their corner of the digital world, to see who were the opinion leaders, the silent originators, the most active among them, as well as to streamline the software they were working with.

<blog-tribe.ryze.com>

This kind of network mapping goes hand in hand with the production of social software, including not just programs that tell you the geographical location of URLs or local communication tools that some people believe have the potential to restore social cohesion and political awareness, but also products made by companies like Socialtext that are basically adaptations of the Wiki — a web page to which anybody with network access can write and send comments to the corporate environment. Socialtext's Eventspace software, for example, fuses email, blogs, background information and reporting in the same digital space, for use before, during and after a conference.

<www.ercim.org/publication/Ercim_News/enw47/persson.html>
<http://geonotes.sics.se> <www.geoURL.org> <www.upmystreet.com>
<www.socialtext.com>

Social software mapping shares with the encyclopedic approach the notion of a relationship between the physical and the digital world. But it is less focused on data-mining, on the cognitive side, and more focused on communication. Social software wants to turn a part of the physical world into a digital network. Or, more accurately, the coupling of the digital and the physical takes place resolutely according to patterns of digital communication. Geography comes into it, but in a diffuse way.

As one reads about this type of software, one gets the impression that its makers consider digital communication and digital community superior to community and communication in the physical world. The former is more open, active, democratic, sharing, productive and beneficial to all involved. At least, that's what's implied.

THE NET, THE WORLD, THE MAP

In every folk culture, there's a joke about the king who wanted better and better maps of his kingdom, and ended up commissioning a map as large as the land it represented; literati know this story from Borges, quoted in the epigraph to this essay. It is the classic tale of misunderstanding the use of a map, which is not a copy of space, but a way of opening up space through information. With GPS (Global Positioning System), mobile phones, mobile computing, online refrigerators, online storage rooms, online heating systems and even online groceries, maybe the world and the map will finally fit in one and the same lived environment. This is a radically different way of looking at the relation between cyberspace and physical space. Though it may sound like science fiction or magic, there is a scientific name for it: Augmented Reality (AR). Research being done under this rubric falls into two main categories: the wearable online computer, which enables us to navigate the physical world and automatically see or hear information linked to people, objects or spaces; and intelligent environments, which involve embedding networked computers into urban structures.

AR aims to blend all things digital (from phones, Internet access, to 3D projections) into the physical environment, making digital information directly accessible and present as physical objects, persons and images. The ultra-fast nowhere space-time of cyberspace is no longer confined to the experience of sitting in front of a computer screen, but is theoretically everywhere — a magical notion for sure, something like the digital re-enchantment of the world.

As magic goes, AR is fiercely practical and useful. All the big computer science universities have such projects underway, and it comes as no surprise that many of them are supported by military research institutes. An immense list is to be found at the website of the Rochester Institute of Technology's Software Engineering Program. Among other things, MIT's Project Oxygen is developing AIRE (Agent-based Intelligent Reactive Environments), while the University of South Australia's AR research, initially made possible by the Defence Science Technology Organisation, is developing its wearable computer as a tool in city planning — mixing designs and reality on site in real time — and medical applications.

<www.se.rit.edu/~jrv/research/ar/>
<http://oxygen.lcs.mit.edu/Overview.html>
<www.tinmith.net>

The real-time transmission of information from satellites, planes, spies, databases and experts, to soldiers in the field — seamlessly interwoven with their experience of physical reality — is a long-standing military dream. When Napoleon said that every Private carried a Field Marshal's staff in his backpack, he was speaking metaphorically, but his remark was perhaps the first intimation of developments whereby soldiers in the field operate with increasing amounts of data.

Now, thanks to mobile, wireless technology and the ever-cheaper GPS chip, the networked world and the physical world can be seamlessly enmeshed, for better and for worse. Imagine AR-spam: as you pass a tree, it starts singing about maple syrup, while pancakes sing and dance in front of your eyes courtesy of your earphones and digital spectacles.

Howard Rheingold sees socially liberating aspects

Conversation maps

gazetteer E 8/10 p. 123

to the intermixing of atoms and bits. In his 2002 book Smart Mobs, he envisions unique possibilities for activism and spontaneous forms of resistance, protest and civil disobedience. He cites situations in which SMS texting, mobile phones and wireless Internet access enabled Smart Mobs to materialize that had considerable success in influencing public opinion and even politics.

Visionary possibilities for the radical mixing of digital space and the physical world are presented by Headmap, whose focus is less on developing the technology and more on tracking its cultural fallout. Based in London, Paris, Kathmandu, and San Francisco, Headmap "examines the social implications and applications of location-aware devices, augmented social networks, wearable computers, thinking tools and semantic network interfaces." The participants in this "informal guerilla (distributed) think tank" gathered reviews, thoughts, quotations, notes, essays and designs, and antecedents in literature, architecture, philosophy and art history, for their Headmap Manifesto (first version 1999, updated since).

<www.headmap.org>

With a keen eye for the cultural and social side of Augmented Reality, Headmap's associations range from psychedelic theory and AR's hallucinatory qualities — references to 'magick' included — to the Situationists' ideas about psychogeography and the city. One of Headmap's stronger themes is that maps and infographics about places are becoming increasingly a directly-experienced part of place itself. Not only do users know where they are, they also know the location of the buildings, phones, machines and devices and who is using them.

CONCLUSION

William Gibson envisioned cyberspace in the early 1980s as an electronic consensual hallucination in which the user's body was online and on the line: his console cowboys could be killed while cutting through black ice. That was literature, a metaphor. But technology has a way of making metaphors alarmingly physical.

Network mapping shows us more than the terra incognita of the Internet, the untapped potential of digital networks; it provides insight into the specifics of digital connectivity. Network mapping focuses our attention on the reciprocity between digital and physical-social worlds. The more it tells us about connectivity, the more we find we are actually studying versions of metadata — economic, political, cultural, religious — that describe how we intentionally and unintentionally run our physical world. Network mapping reveals that connectivity is not virtual at all. It is real, like religion, beauty or the American Dream. Real in the sense that it encapsulates properties of power, communication, community on the Net, and historical, social and political realities in the physical world.

The world we live in has always been a world full of signs, ghosts, knowledge, stories and dreams. We thought that the mechanisms with which these immaterial realities were integrated into our social world were stable and eternal: churches, libraries, clubs, schools, theatres and concert halls. But electronic and digital communication has changed the way in which knowledge, ghosts, dreams and stories become part of the social world and circulate. Mass media and the Internet turn metaphors, fictions, theories and illusions into instant social realities faster than we can comprehend. On top of that, they seem to be able to mutate rapidly into weird, uncontrollable phenomena in digital networks.

We still understand very little about the turbulent and powerful relationship between the digital and social worlds. In this respect, network mapping is an indispensible method for research. It is as if our world becomes fluid and malleable amid the speed and illusory quality of digital media. For our ancestors, the world didn't change much, if at all: they lived in dream time, in which ghosts, gods, family memories, animals and the weather were equally real. If in some ways that reminds us of our digital world, it is far less spooky than what is happening to us today.

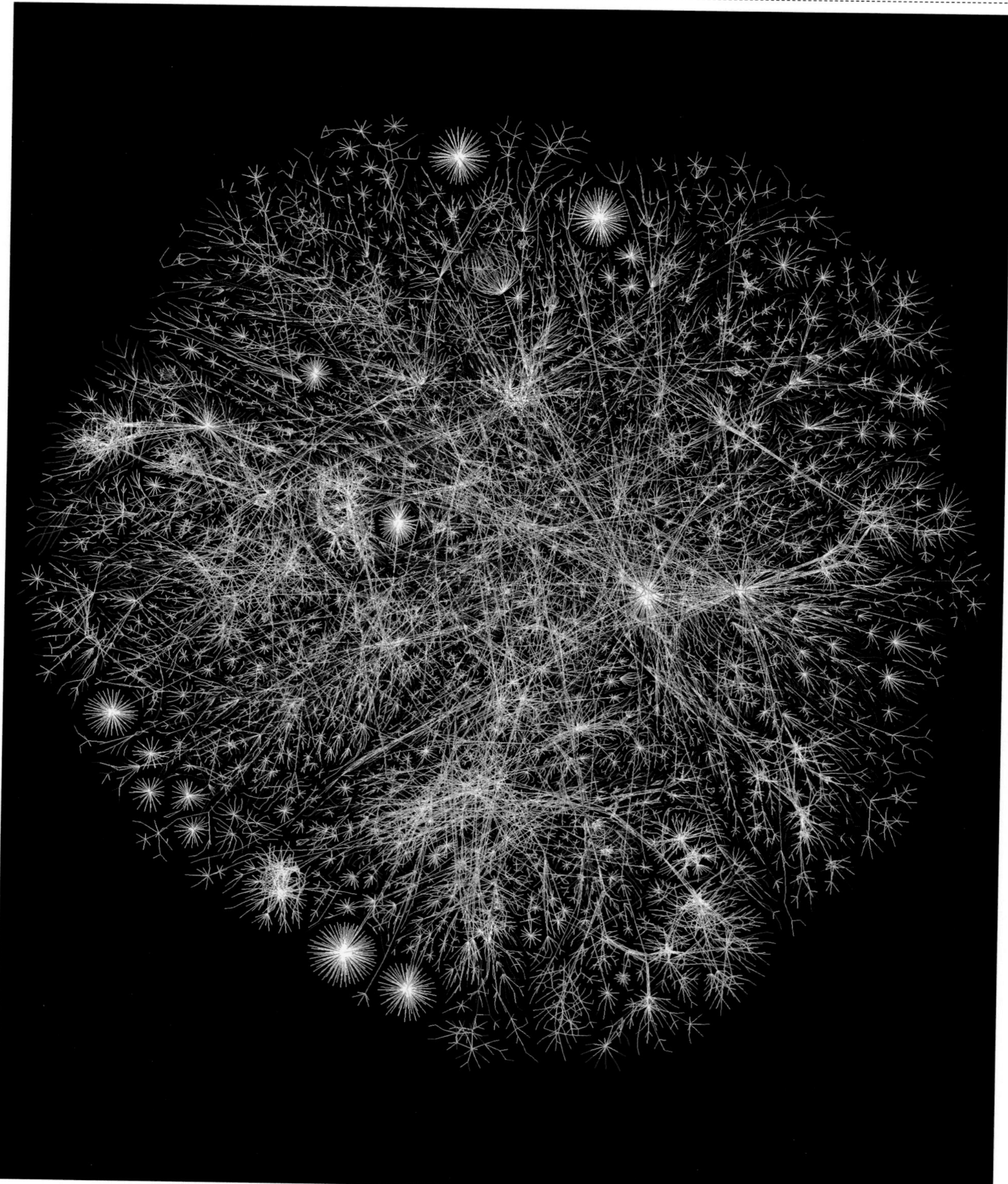

Barrett Lyon, The Opte Project *Map of the Internet*, November 23, 2003 / Lyon set himself the goal of mapping the entire Internet in a single day using a single computer and a single Internet connection. The Opte Project's first full Internet map, above, was created using the LGL graph engine, and color-coded according to class A allocation of Internet Protocol (IP) space to registrars around the world (red = Asia Pacific; green = Europe/Middle East/Central Asia/Africa; blue = North America; yellow = Latin America and Caribbean; cyan = RFC1918 IP addresses; white = unknown) / image courtesy of Barrett Lyon / see "Possible Worlds," p. 26.

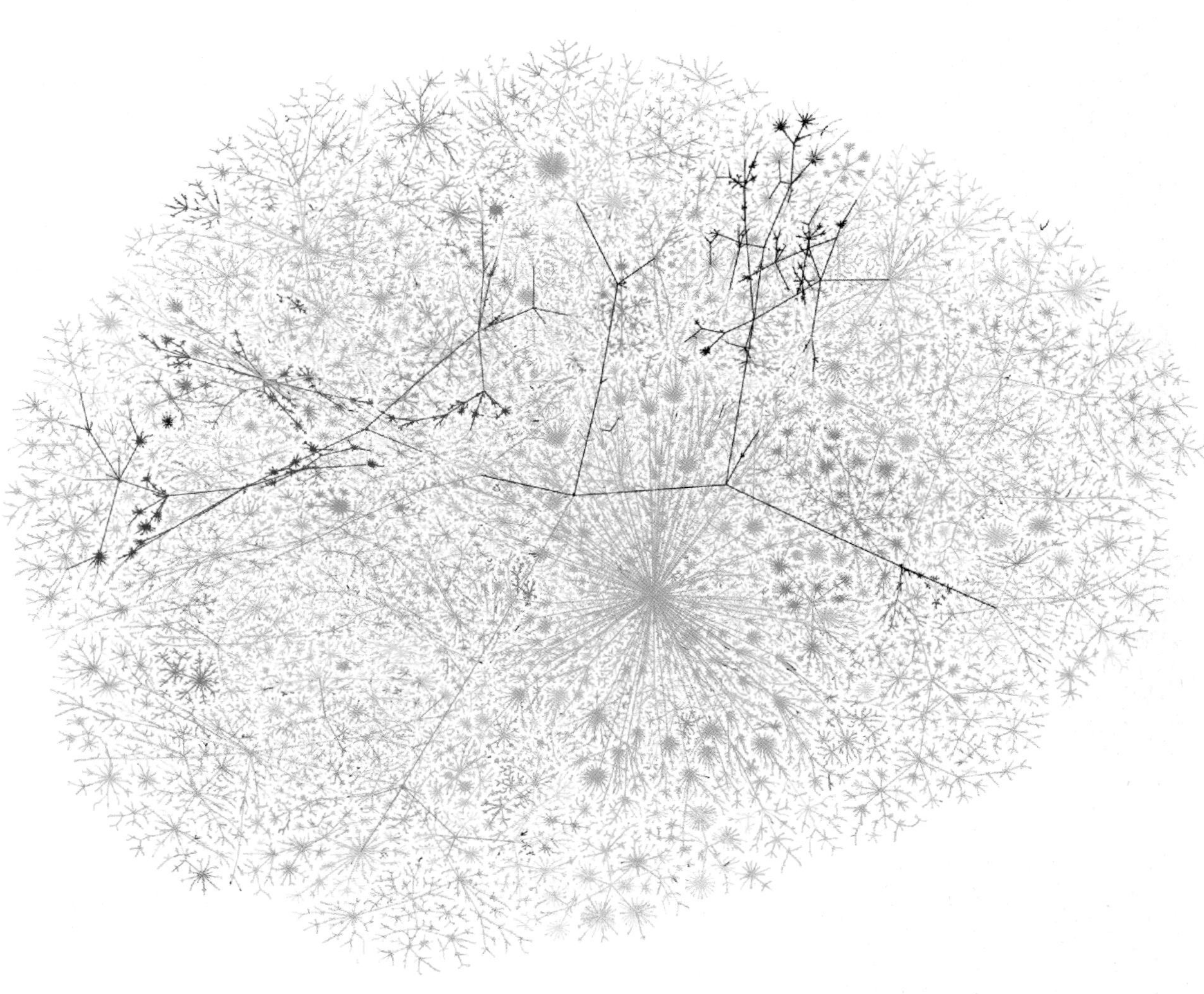

Bill Cheswick and **Hal Burch, Lumeta** *Map of the Internet, color-coded by IP address*, January 1999 / using a traceroute program, Burch and Cheswick (then working at Bell Laboratories) recorded the pathways taken by packets to all existing networks in the central registry of assigned Internet addresses. The resulting tree-like form is independent of geography; clusters of nodes are positioned by the layout algorithm according to various attraction/repulsion criteria. Other Lumeta Internet maps highlight factors such as distance from test-host, network capacity and ISPs—the "city-states of the Internet" / image courtesy of Lumeta. Patent(s) pending. <http://www.lumeta.org>.

CAIDA (Cooperative Association for Internet Data Analysis) *Internet Map*, 2003, Edition 2 / based on the *Skitter Graph*, showing two weeks' activity among 1.2 million IP addresses. Created with the San Diego Supercomputer Center, April 1–16, 2001 / / see "Counter Cartographies," p. 20–21, "Possible Worlds," p. 26.

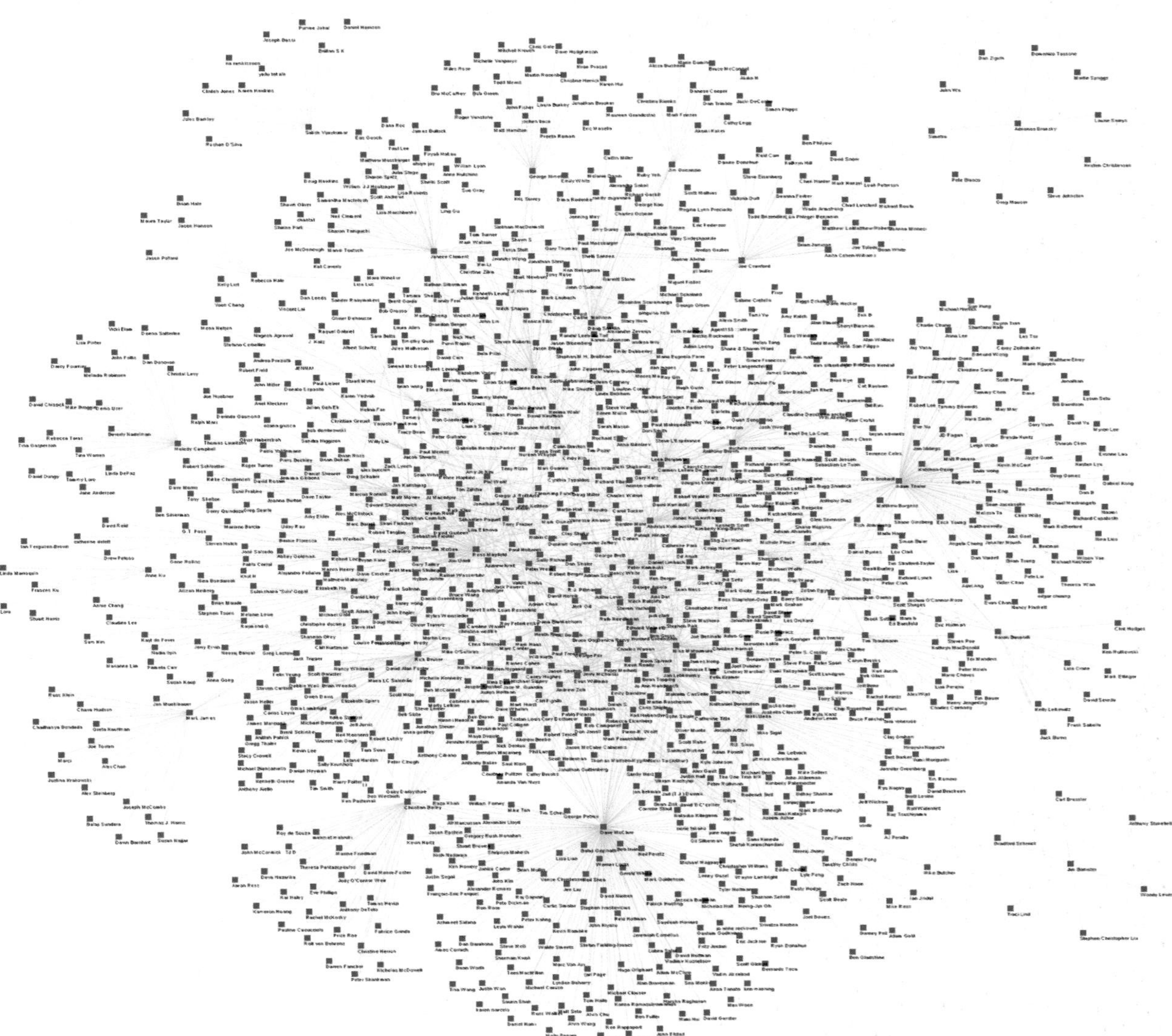

Valdis Krebs, orgnet.com *Ryze Blog Tribe Friends Network,* December 2002 / links between members of Ryze, the social networking "website community," visualized using *InFlow* 3.0 / see "Possible Worlds," p. 28.

Lisa Jevbratt *1:1 – Interface Every*, 1999 / Jevbratt used a robot crawler to catalogue over 200,000 Internet Protocol (IP) addresses from a database of all possible addresses from 000.000.000.000 to 255.255.255.255. A pixel of color was assigned to each IP address, with red, green and blue mixed according to the parts of the address / image courtesy of Lisa Jevbratt <http://jevbratt.com/1_to_1/>

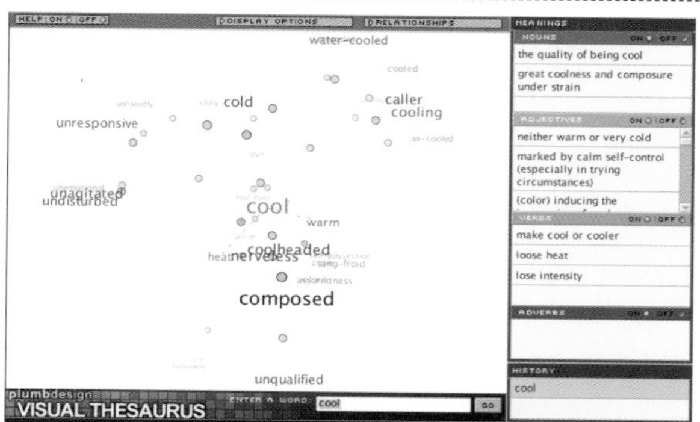

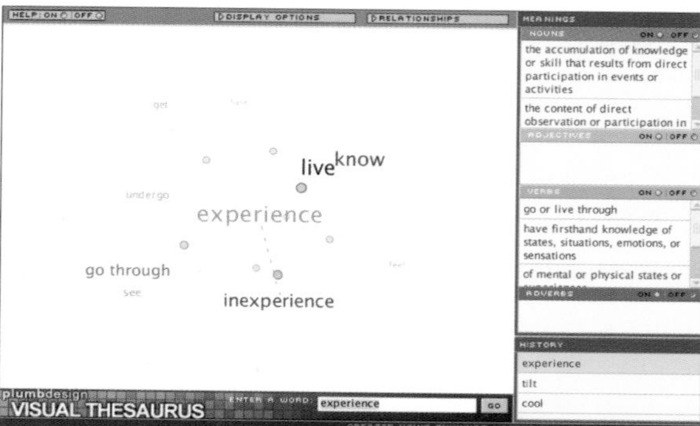

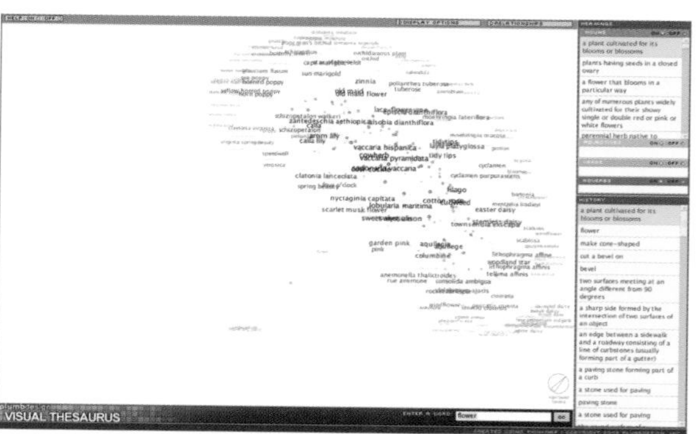

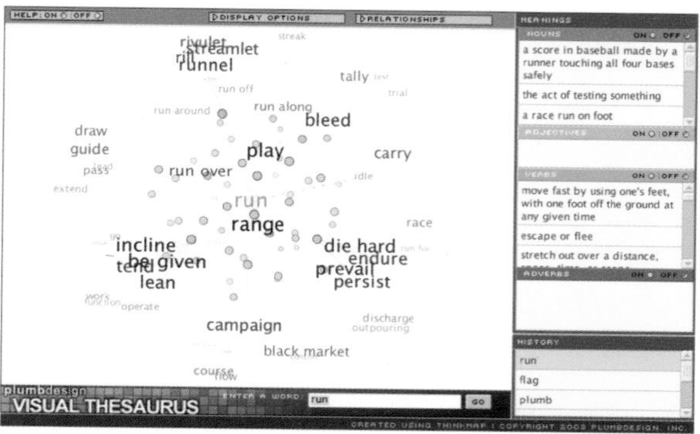

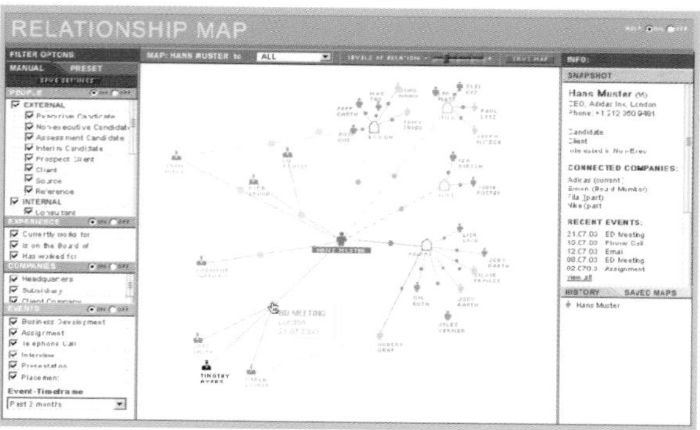

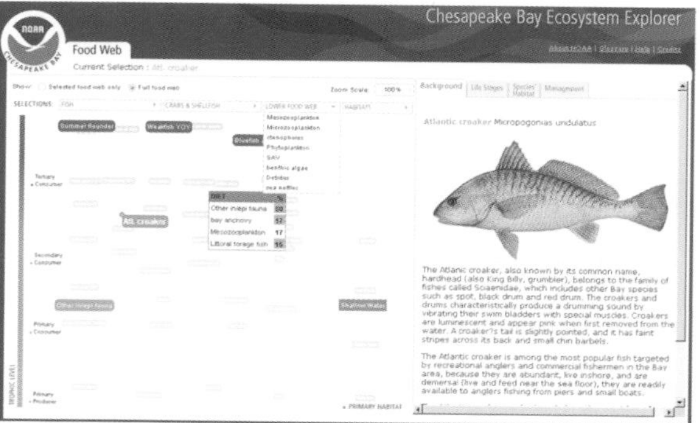

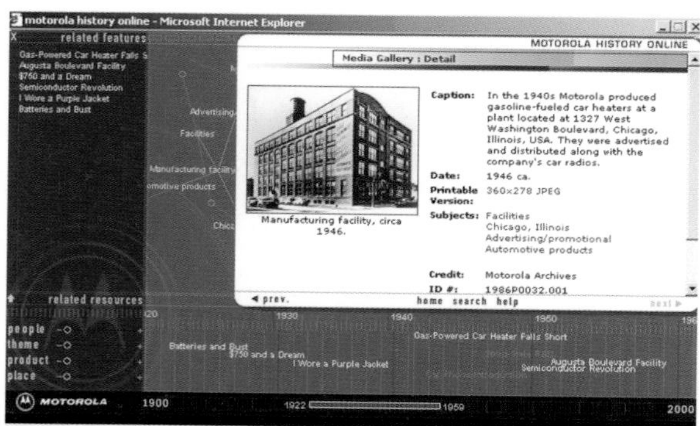

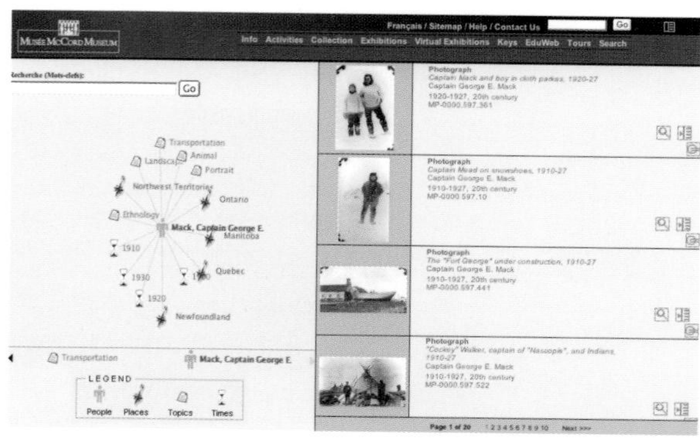

Thinkmap (top to bottom): *Visual Thesaurus*, an interactive reference tool created with *Thinkmap*, which places a word entered center screen, in a relational, 3D space with its synonyms and antonyms / images this page courtesy of Thinkmap / see "The Node Knows," p. 46.

Thinkmap (top to bottom): *Relationship Map*, an exercise in the depiction of business relationships; prototype application created for the National Oceanic and Atmospheric Association to explain the Chesapeake Bay ecosystem; Motorola Museum and Archives application as part of *Motorola History Online*; Musée McCord Museum website / see "The Node Knows," p. 46.

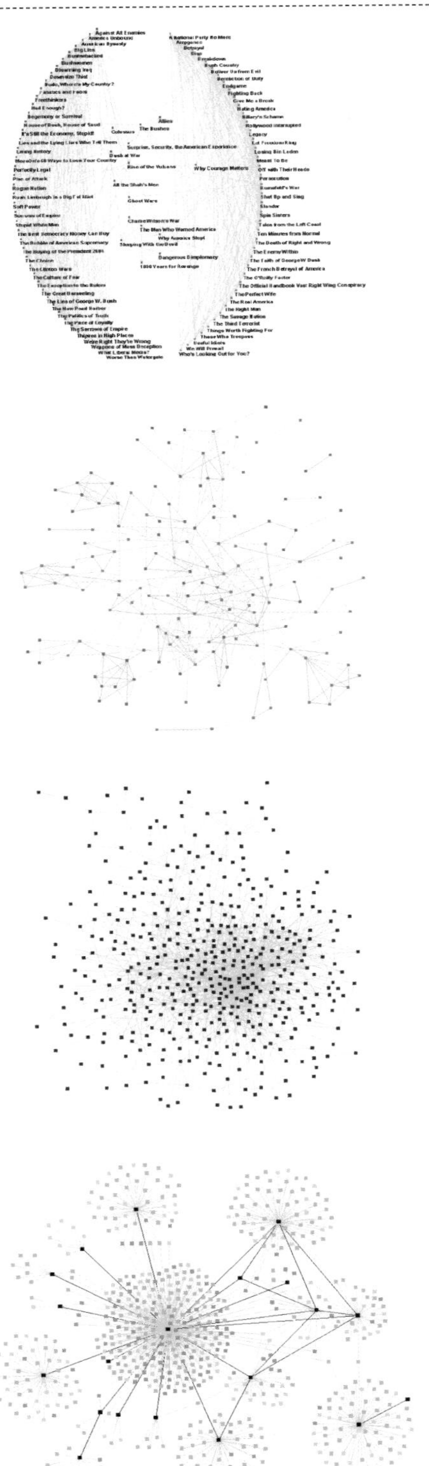

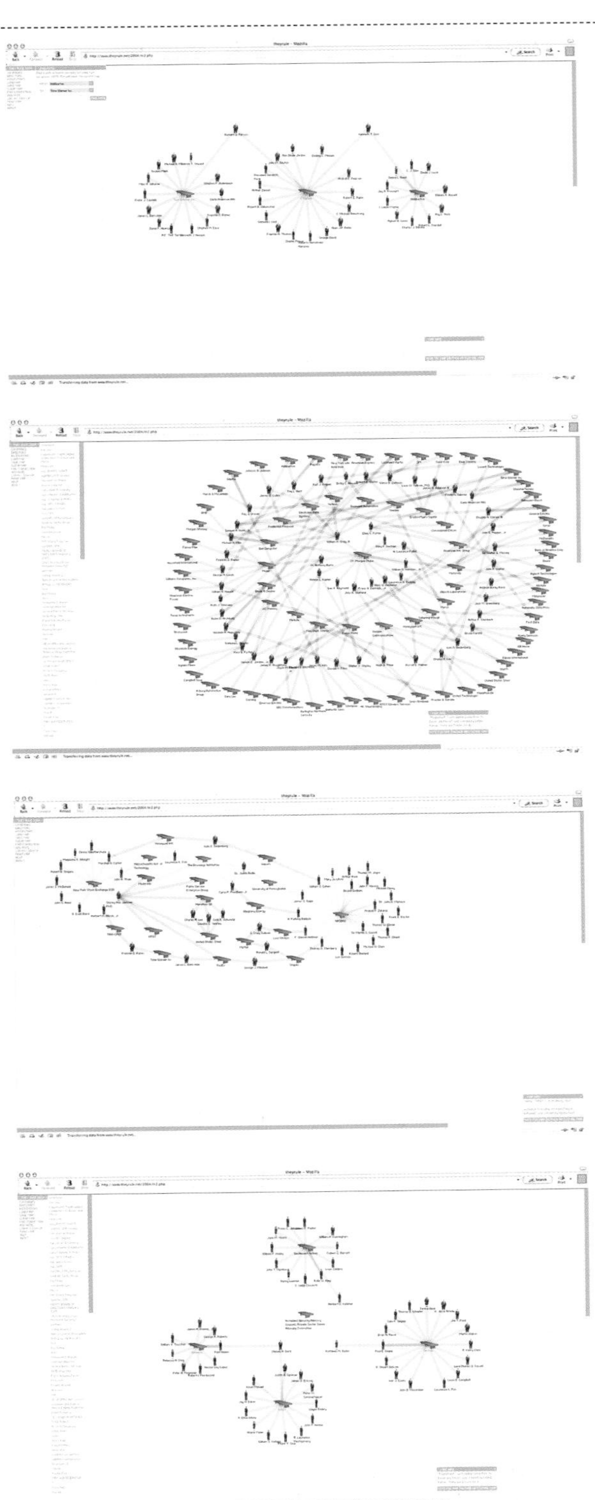

Valdis Krebs *orgnet.com* social network maps / (top to bottom): *Divided We Stand*, 2004, political book readerships, using data from major web retailers (see p. 88); *Post-Merger Integration*, 2002, showing executives from acquiring (red) and acquired (green) firms; *Social Networking in Academia: The Collaboration Network of Paul Erdös*; *Mapping the Spread of Contagions via Contact Tracing*, spread of airborne infectious diseases / see "The Node Knows," p. 46.

Josh On *theyrule.net* / (top to bottom): *Haliburton vs. TimeWarner; The Magnificent Seven*; *NYSE vs. NASD*; *Who Profits from Homeland Security?* / images courtesy of Josh On / see "Counter Cartographies," p. 24, "The Node Knows," p. 48.

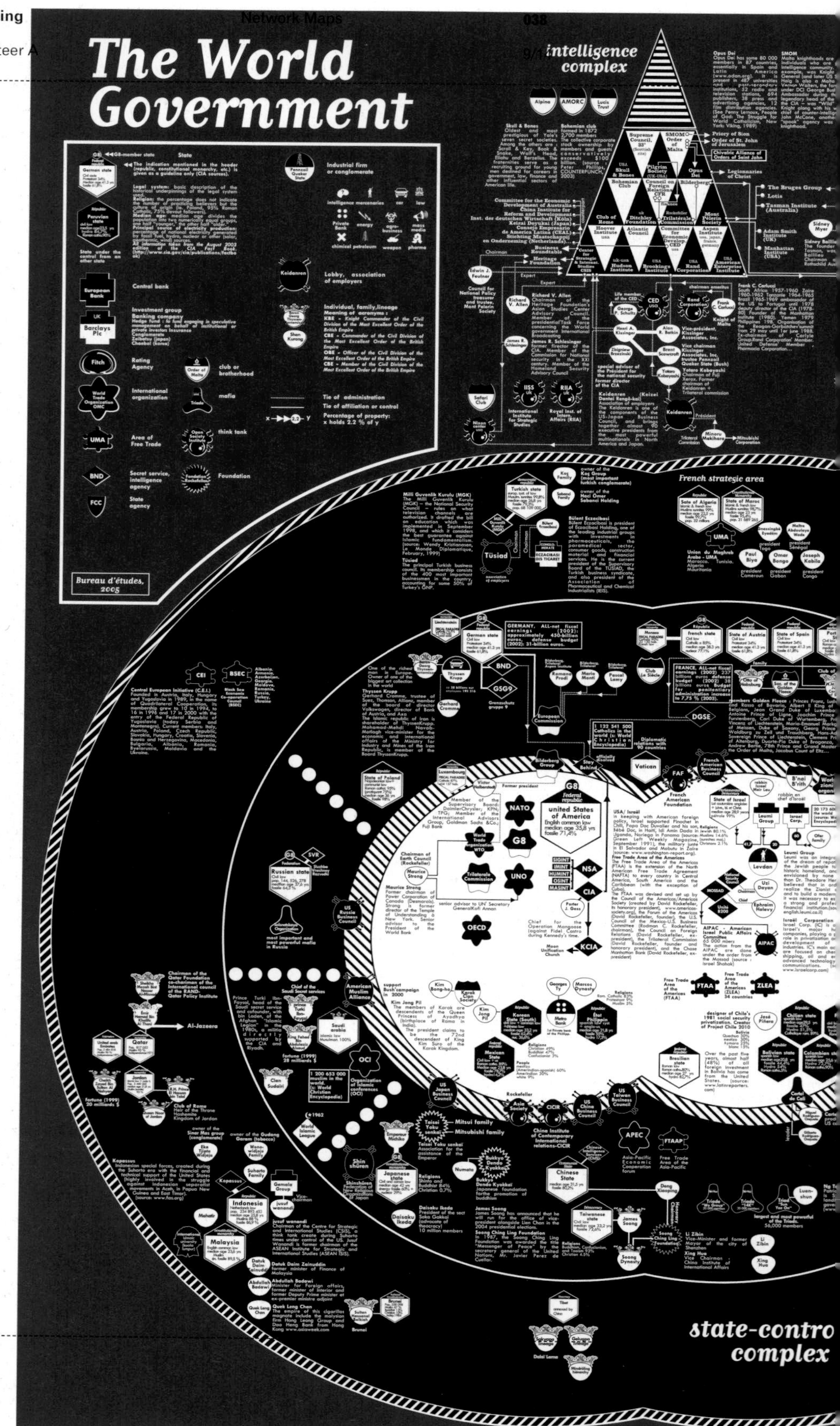

Bureau d'études *The World Government*, 2003 / image courtesy of Bureau d'études / see "Counter Cartographies," p. 23, "The Node Knows," pp. 47 – 48.

financial heart
Vatican
Bush Clan
Rothschild Clan
Rockefeller Clan
Windsor Clan
Al Saud Clan
Bin Laden Clan
Li Ka-Shing family
Soong family
Mitsubishi Clan
Mitsui Clan
Sumitomo Clan
Matsushita Clan
Hitotsubashi Clan
Mori Clan
Fitch
Moody's
Standard & Poor's
Carlyle Group
Rothschild Group
Warburg Dillon Read
Rockefeller Group
Fidelity
State Street Corp.
Merrill Lynch
citigroup Inc.
Goldman Sachs
Lehman Brothers
Barclays Plc
HSBC
Lloyds
Royal Bank of Scotland
NatWest
Société Générale
Crédit Agricole
BNP Paribas
AXA
Allianz
deutsche bank
Bank of Japan
European Bank
Bundesbank
Banque de France
Bank of England
World Bank
CLUB DE PARIS
Hutchison Whampoa
Citic pacific
China Life
Power Corporation
Keizei Doyukai
Nikkeiren
TABD
ERT
Davos Economic Forum
psychological complex (medias)
TV Globo
abril
Comcast
ABC
Disney Corp.
FOX
News Corporation
Viacom
CBS
MTV
Bertelsmann
Hachette
Reuters
AFP
BBC
Berlusconi
RAI
Voice of America VOA
FCC
USIA
MPA
MEMRI
agro-business cartel
Tradax
Cargill
ContiGroup
grain cartel
meat cartel
food cartel
Nestlé
Unilever
Kraft Food
Walmart
Louis Dreyfus
Toepfer
petroleum cartel
Rockefeller
Bush
Queen Beatrix
Desmarais
Albert Frère
Exxon
Total
Rio Tinto
Chevron Texaco
Royal Dutch Shell
Sir Mark Moody-Stuart

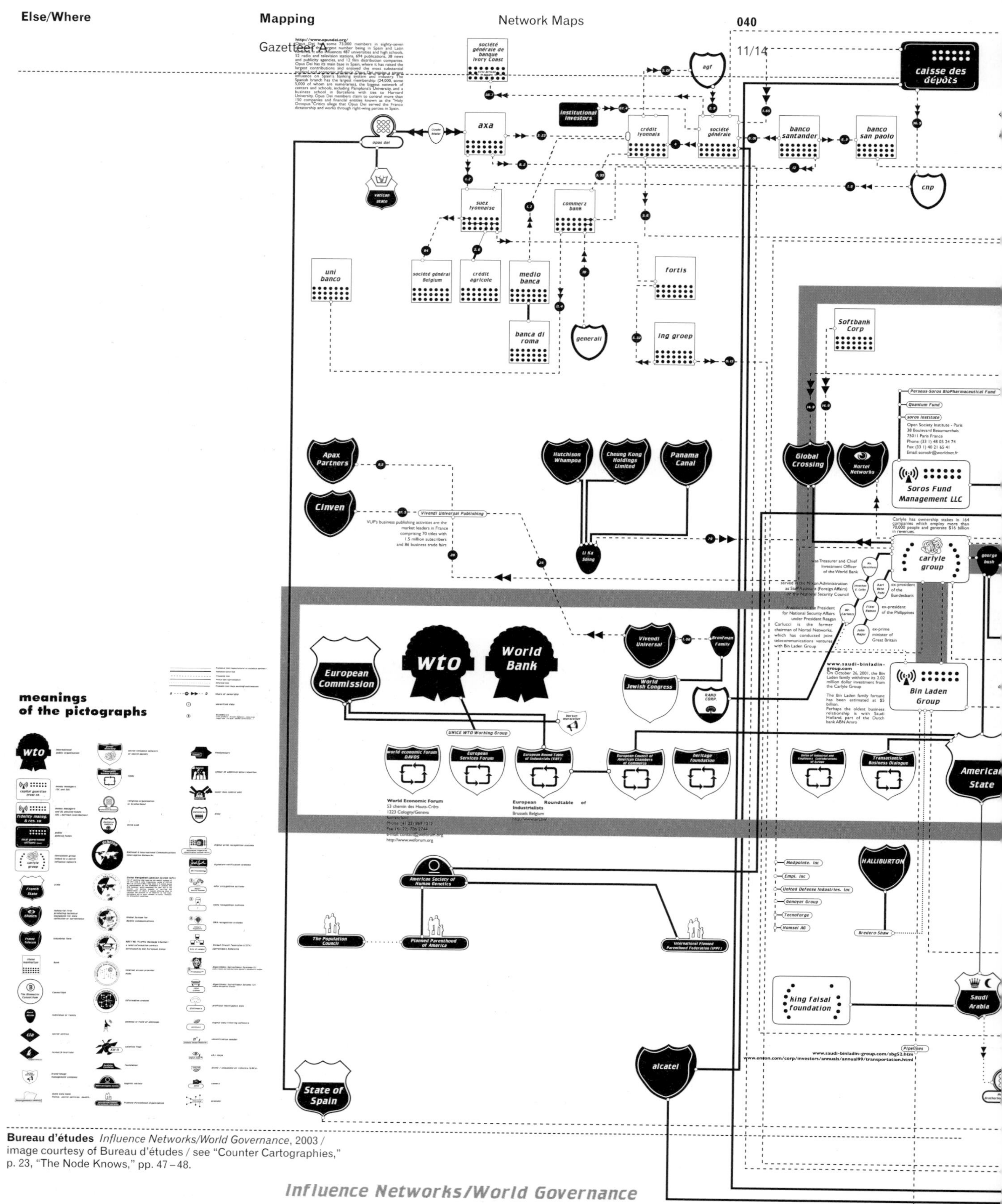

Bureau d'études *Influence Networks/World Governance*, 2003 / image courtesy of Bureau d'études / see "Counter Cartographies," p. 23, "The Node Knows," pp. 47–48.

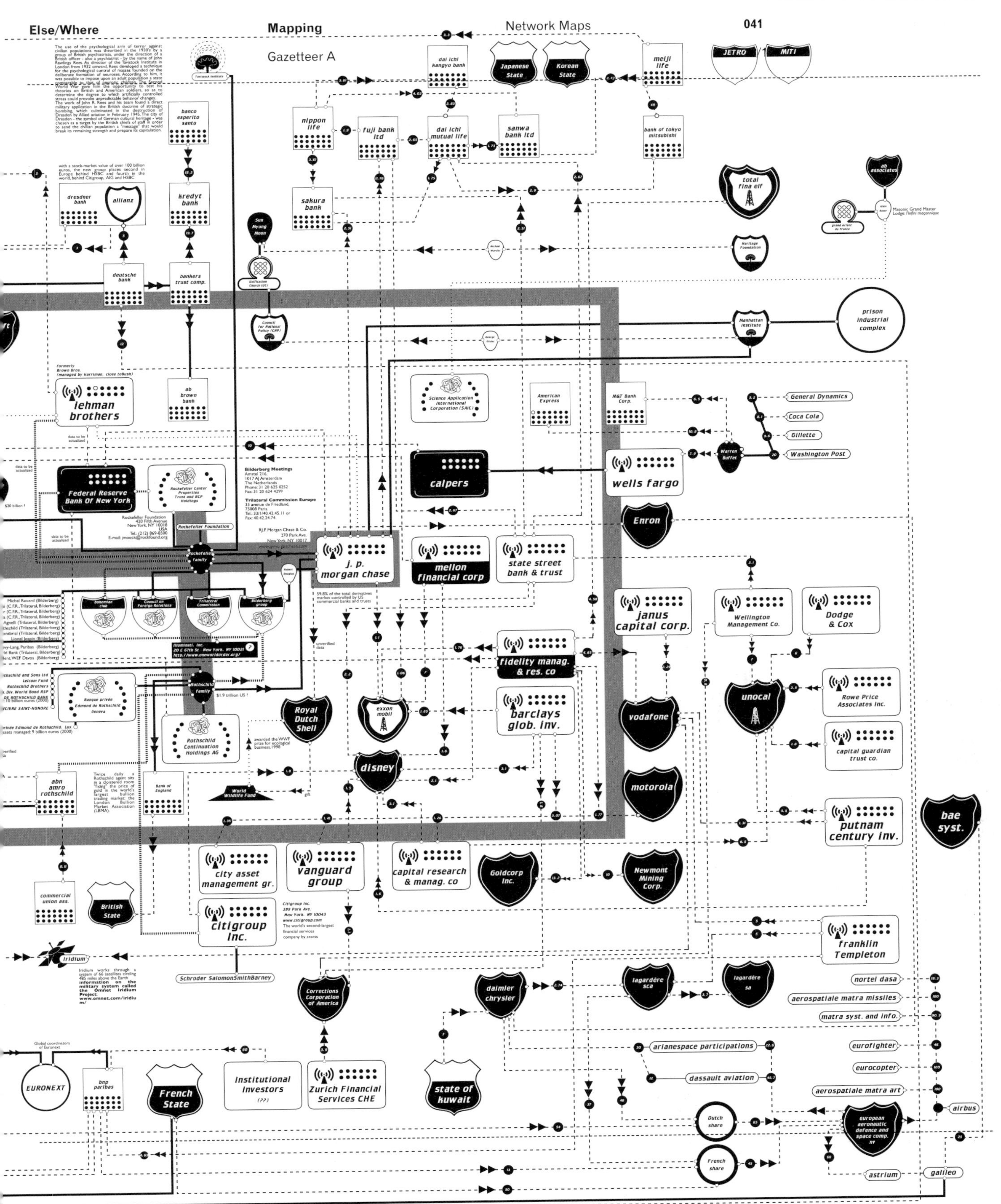
The use of the psychological arm of terror against civilian populations was theorized in the 1930's by a group of British psychiatrists, under the direction of a British officer - also a psychiatrist - by the name of John Rawlings Rees. As director of the Tavistock Institute in London from 1932 onward, Rees developed a technique for the psychological control of masses founded on the deliberate formation of neuroses. According to him, it was possible to impose upon an adult population a state comparable to that of neurotic children. The Second World War gave him the opportunity to test his theories on British and American soldiers, so as to determine the degree to which artificially controlled stress could provoke unpredictable behavior changes.
The work of John R. Rees and his team found a direct military application in the British doctrine of strategic bombing, which culminated in the destruction of Dresden by Allied aviation in February 1945. The city of Dresden - the symbol of German cultural heritage - was chosen as a target by the British chiefs of staff in order to send the civilian population a "message" that would break its remaining strength and prepare its capitulation.
Tavistock Institute
with a stock-market value of over 100 billion euros, the new group places second in Europe behind HSBC and fourth in the world, behind Citigroup, AIG and HSBC
dresdner bank
allianz
banco esperito santo
kredyt bank
deutsche bank
bankers trust comp.
ab brown bank
Formerly Brown Bros. (managed by Harriman, close toBush)
lehman brothers
nippon life
sakura bank
fuji bank ltd
dai ichi kangyo bank
dai ichi mutual life
sanwa bank ltd
Japanese State
Korean State
meiji life
bank of tokyo mitsubishi
JETRO
MITI
total fina elf
ab associates
Masonic Grand Master Lodge: l'infini maçonnique
grand orient de france
Sun Myung Moon
Unification Church (UC)
Heritage Foundation
Council for National Policy (CNP)
Manhattan Institute
prison industrial complex
Science Application International Corporation (SAIC)
American Express
M&T Bank Corp.
General Dynamics
Coca Cola
Gillette
Washington Post
Warren Buffet
Federal Reserve Bank Of New York
Rockefeller Center Properties Trust and RCP Holdings
Rockefeller Foundation
Rockefeller Foundation 420 Fifth Avenue New York, NY 10018 USA Tel.: (212) 869-8500 E-mail: jmoock@rockfound.org
Bilderberg Meetings Amstel 216, 1017 AJ Amsterdam The Netherlands Phone: 31 20 625 0252 Fax: 31 20 624 4299
Trilateral Commission Europe 35 avenue de Friedland, 75008 Paris. Tel.: 33/1/40.42.45.11 or Fax: 40.42.24.74
calpers
wells fargo
Enron
Rockefeller family
j. p. morgan chase
mellon financial corp
state street bank & trust
59.8% of the total derivatives market controlled by US commercial banks and trusts
Bohemian club
Council on Foreign Relations
Trilateral Commission
Bilderberg group
Illuminati, Inc. 20 E 67th St - New York, NY 10021 http://www.oneworldorder.org/
janus capital corp.
Wellington Management Co.
Dodge & Cox
fidelity manag. & res. co
barclays glob. inv.
Rothschild family
$1.9 trillion US !
Banque privée Edmond de Rothschild Geneva
Rothschild Continuation Holdings AG
Royal Dutch Shell
exxon mobil
disney
awarded the WWF prize for ecological business, 1998
World Wildlife Fund
vodafone
unocal
Rowe Price Associates Inc.
capital guardian trust co.
motorola
putnam century inv.
bae syst.
abn amro rothschild
Bank of England
commercial union ass.
British State
city asset management gr.
vanguard group
capital research & manag. co
Goldcorp Inc.
Newmont Mining Corp.
citigroup inc.
Citigroup Inc. 399 Park Ave. New York, NY 10043 www.citigroup.com The world's second-largest financial services company by assets
iridium
Schroder SalomonSmithBarney
franklin Templeton
Corrections Corporation of America
daimler chrysler
lagardère sca
lagardère sa
nortel dasa
aerospatiale matra missiles
matra syst. and info.
arianespace participations
dassault aviation
eurofighter
eurocopter
aerospatiale matra art
airbus
EURONEXT
bnp paribas
French State
Institutional Investors (??)
Zurich Financial Services CHE
state of kuwait
Dutch share
French share
european aeronautic defence and space comp. nv
astrium
galileo

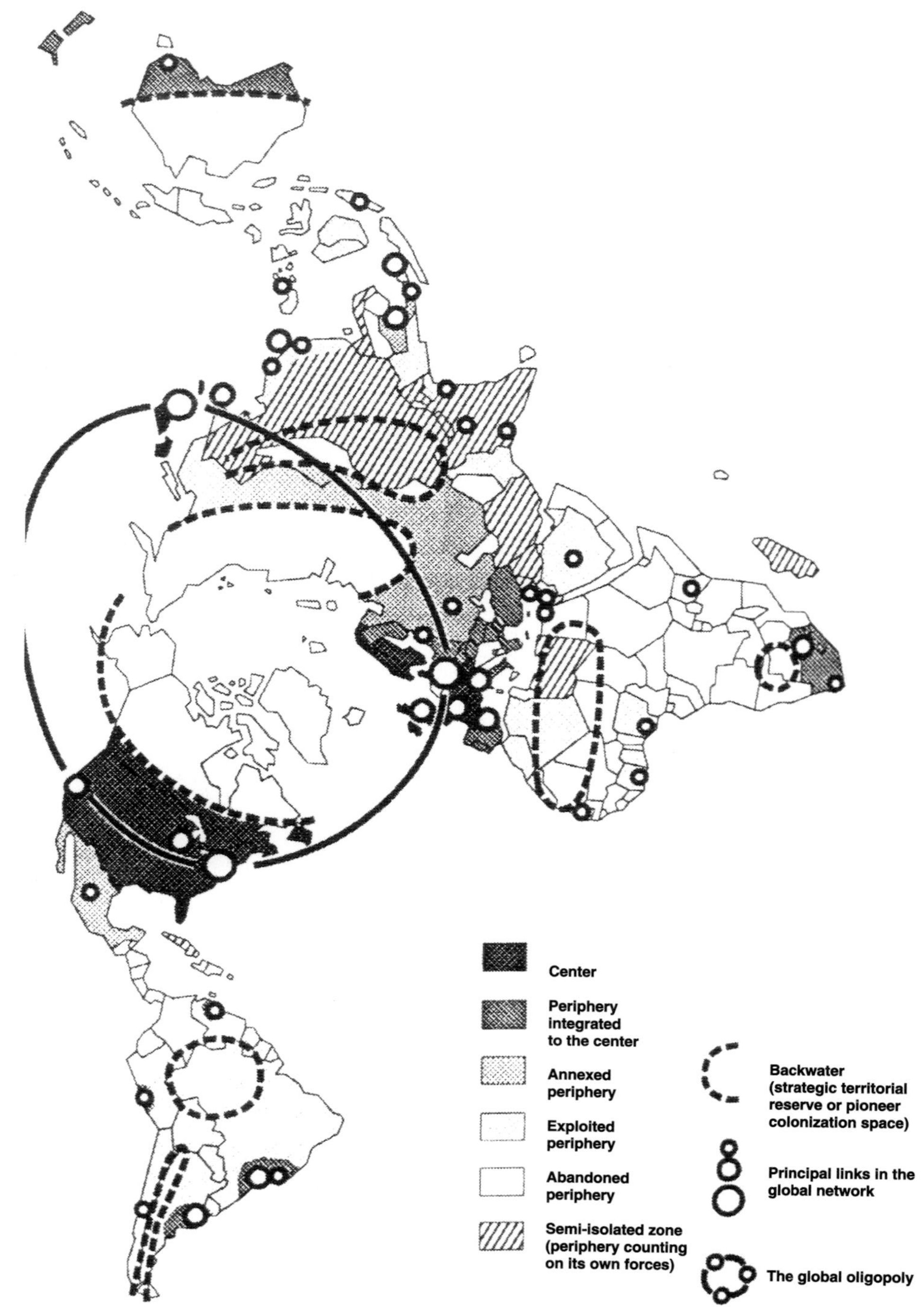

François Chesnais *Centers and Peripheries in the World: A Hierarchical Network*, 1992 / map showing coordination of production lines through the central circuits of global finance / see "Counter Cartographies," p. 21.

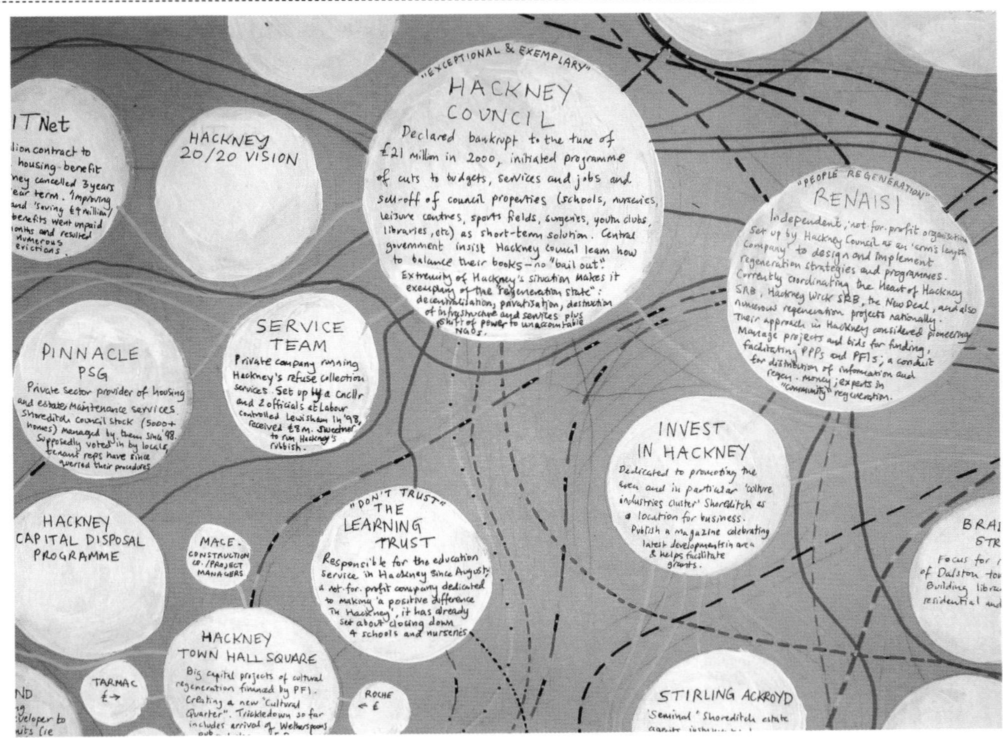

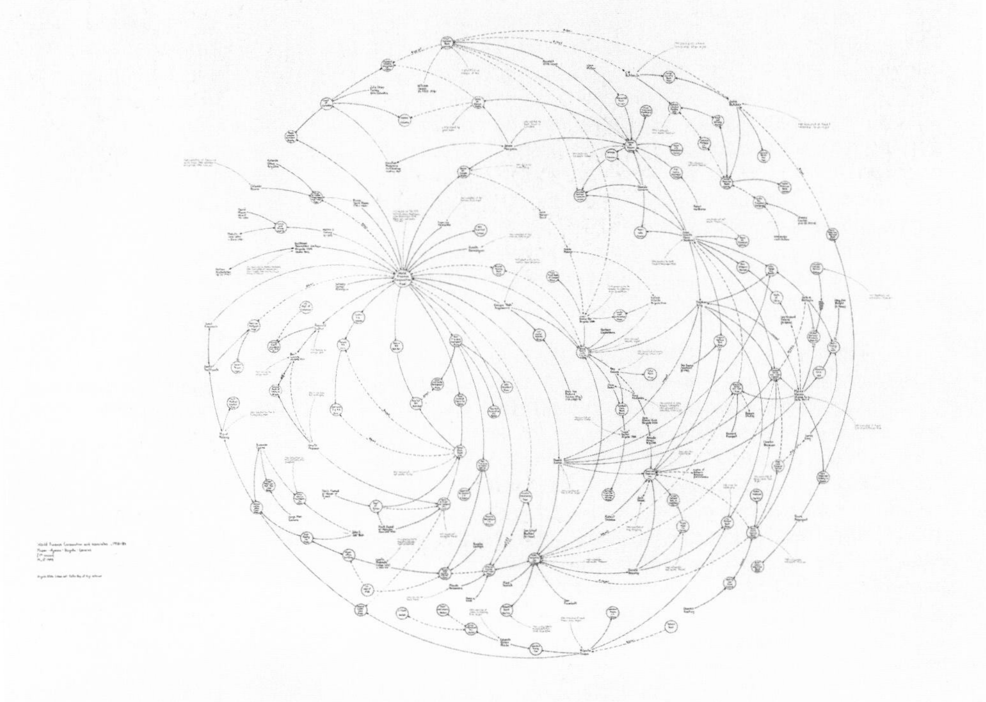

The London Particular *The Physical Impossibility of Regeneration in the Mind of Someone Living* / detail of ongoing map of organizations involved in redevelopment of the East London area of Hackney and the "pseudo-dialogic discourse" surrounding urban regeneration / image courtesy of The London Particular / see "The Node Knows," pp. 48–49.

Mark Lombardi *World Finance Corporation and Associates, ca. 1970–84: Miami, Ajman, and Bogota-Caracas (Brigado 2506: Cuban Anti-Castro Bay of Pigs Veteran)* 7th version, 1999 / image courtesy of Pierogi Gallery / see "The Node Knows," p. 48, "Conversations as Maps," p. 78.

THE NODE KNOWS

THE COURT CARTOGRAPHER HAS BEEN RECALLED FROM DEFUNCT SURVEYS OF THE EMPIRE'S PHYSICAL TERRITORIES TO ADDRESS A MORE PRESSING TASK: STRUCTURING THE INFORMATION SPACES GENERATED BY CONTEMPORARY CAPITALISM. J.J. KING EXAMINES THE MAPPING AND COUNTER-MAPPING OF THE NETWORK SOCIETY.

INTRODUCTION

From the Down Survey of 1650–59, which served as the basis of expropriation of lands belonging to Irish Catholic rebels, to the 1892 drawing of Africa that offered new frontiers instrumental to foreign nation states, or the mappings of London during the 1780 Gordon Riots and the 1926 General Strike, maps have always played a crucial role in determining territory and reallocating property. Scholars such as the late J. B. Harley (1932–1991) have worked hard to illuminate the political and cultural planes that lurk beneath the map's neutral surface, and to draw out the connections between mapping, knowledge and power.

Far from being passive objects, accounts such as Harley's insist, maps are instruments of social and political control. But what implications does this rather mundane insight have for one of the newest forms of cartography: representing knowledge and information? This article examines the social and political uses of knowledge maps and other representations of the contemporary, networked knowledge economy: a complex informational landscape for the contemporary mapmaker.

KNOWLEDGE BEGETS KNOWLEDGE

The importance of knowledge and information to the economy has been long vaunted (see, for example, Bell's *The Coming of Post-Industrial Society*, 1976; Toffler's *The Third Wave*, 1991; Jameson's *Postmodernism, or The Cultural Logic of Late Capitalism*, 1991). For many commentators, we have entered an age of information in which knowledge, important to production across all historical epochs, has taken on a new commanding power. In the influential view of Manuel Castells, what is most distinctive about this phase is a de-coupling of the circuits of information and production. In the industrial mode, information organizes the mobilization of labor and production as well as the exploitation of energy; in the informational mode it chiefly mobilizes the generation of new knowledge. Consequently, an autonomous circuit of information-work is created that never directly contacts the production process: only its products impact the other elements of these processes and their interrelationships.[1] As Peter Drucker has argued:

> The traditional 'factors of production' do not disappear but rather become secondary. They can be obtained, and obtained easily, provided there is knowledge. And knowledge in this new sense means knowledge as a utility, knowledge as the means to obtain social and economic results...knowledge is now being applied to knowledge.[2]

A single sophisticated worker now commands, often completely unconsciously, entire chains of automated production, interlocked with unknown, outsourced human workforces and elements of fixed capital distributed across an archipelago of developing countries. "Creatives" who sell products, artist communities who aid in city regeneration, analysts who produce (rather than merely analyze) stock market value: all take part in the diffuse but articulated process of affective labour that has placed communication in the limelight of the capital cycle.

THE SPACE OF FLOWS

> Our society is constructed around flows of capital, flows of technology, flows of organizational interaction, flows of images, sounds and symbols. Flows are not just one element of the social organization; they are the expression of processes dominating our economic, political and symbolic life.[3]

1. Manuel Castells, *The Informational City: Information Technology, Economic Restructuring and the Urban-Regional Process*. Oxford: Blackwell, 1989, p. 10.

2. Peter Drucker, *Post-Capitalist Society*. New York: HarperBusiness, 1993, p. 42.

3. Manuel Castells, *The Rise of the Network Society*. Oxford: Blackwell, 1996, pp. 412–413.

Castells has coined a name for the quasi-autonomous place in which the primary communicative transactions of the post-industrial economy occur: the "Space of Flows." This spatial arrangement is, in Castells' terms, a "network of places... based on telecommunications and computer systems... connected around one common, simultaneous social practice." Castells inelegantly straddles the old informational metaphors (electronic circuit) and the new (network), but expresses well the sense of transition into a messy informational space generated by the increasing complexity of labor chains, production, distribution and consumption.

It is the project of representing this Space of Flows that is the focus of this article—rather than the topic that has so far proved more diverting for geographers, namely how the Space of Flows impacts traditional cartography. Information and knowledge have always figured and refigured how we experience space, but the stitch-and-suture recombinations that occur when physically-distant locations are networked is novel and noteworthy.

The traditional world-map needs to be re-interpreted. Waldo Tobler's First Law of Geography—*everything is related to everything else, but closer things are more closely related*—is fundamentally inverted under the regime of information.[4] Today, things that are symbolically related are brought into a network proximity that can mitigate or redeem physical distance. This doesn't mean the end of geography, but rather its re-emergence in a new form centered on the instructions, interactions and connections that order global capital across national boundaries—a world reformatted along the lines of financial flow. This is a sort of cartography after information, a necessary reappraisal of traditional geographies under the order of information, but it dovetails with a cartography of information: the task of representing the tremendously complex interactions that take place between knowledge workers and the objects, processes and bodies they administer.

The urge to represent these interactions comes from both sides of the line: those within the managerial elites who want to improve information flow within corporate environments and understand the knowledge resources held by their workers; and those, often styled anti-capitalist or anti-globalization, who oppose what they regard as the detrimental effects of the knowledge economy. In other words, mapping the messy Space of Flows is seen as necessary both by those wishing to critique contemporary capitalism and those seeking improved efficiency in information manipulation.

TRACING THE KNOWLEDGE MAP

Although the first geographic map may have been carved on a mammoth bone 15,000 years ago, thematic maps associated with the handling of non-geographic information seem not to have evolved until the mid 17th Century. This, Edward Tufte argues in his book *Visual Explanations*, is because the move from "maps of existing scenery to graphs of newly measured and collated data was an enormous conceptual step." Tufte explains:

> Despite their quantifying scales and grids, maps resemble miniature pictorial representations of the physical world. To depict relations between any measured quantities, however, requires replacing the map's natural spatial scales with abstract scales of measurement not based on the geographic analogy.[5]

Edmond Halley, the English astronomer famous for his work on the orbits of comets, is often credited with the first thematic map; in a 1686 issue of *Philosophical Transactions*, he used small dashed lines on a world map to represent the location and direction of trade winds. The 18th Century saw the first maps of geology and medicine and the development of contours and isolines. But the real explosion in proficiency and creativity in relation to thematic maps took place the following century.[6] Charles J. Minard's 1861 map of Napoleon's 1812 March on Russia has become celebrated as the first example of information cartography, a flow map that provides an innovative depiction of flows of people and goods in space. Tufte, praising Minard's map, identifies the variables captured within it: the size of the French army depicted by the width of the bands; its location on a two-dimensional surface; the direction of the movement of the advance (upper band) and retreat (lower band); and the temperature on certain dates during the retreat.[7]

<http://zevross.com/special/history/halley.gif>

4. Waldo Tobler, "A Computer Movie Simulating Urban Growth in the Detroit Region." *Economic Geography*, 46:2, 1970, pp. 234–240.

5. Edward R. Tufte, *Visual Explanations: Images and Quantities, Evidence and Narrative*. Cheshire, CT: Graphics Press, 1997, pp. 14–15.

6. M. Friendly and D. J. Denis, *Milestones in the history of thematic cartography, statistical graphics and data visualization*. York University, 2003.

7. Edward R. Tufte, *The Visual Display of Quantitative Information*. Cheshire, CT: Graphics Press, 1983, pp. 40-41.

Minard's map, along with several dozen others published during his lifetime, is part of the general movement toward modern information cartography, whose conceptual basis is found in the work of Paul Otlet (1868–1944).[8] Otlet is regarded by many as the father of information science. In a substantial body of writing dating from 1893, Otlet argued the need for an international information handling system, a *Universal Network for Information and Documentation*, to be accessed through multimedia workstations that lay waiting to be invented just beyond the technological capacity of his time. Otlet was the precursor of Vannevar Bush, Doug Engelbart, and Ted Nelson. The latter, whose conceptual *Xanadu* project linked items of knowledge via informational trails, came up with the original idea of *hypertext*, an information technology for mapping the space of flows that had been anticipated by visionaries such as Otlet.

CORPORATE CARTOGRAPHY

Nelson's vision of the "docuplex"—an abstract "evolutionary structure...a swirling complex of equi-accessible writing, a single great universal text and data grid"[9] remains, strictly speaking, unrealized. But its chief concepts (a space of data, and links between information elements within that space) loom large in the ongoing attempt to map capital's primary information resources: language and communication.

The idea of a corporate information cartography practice seems to have grown out of resource management initiatives in the corporate environment in the late 1970s and early 1980s. In her article "Information Mapping, Guiding Principles", Carol Hildebrand discusses ways to represent "the skills, expertise and information that make up their pool of knowledge" within an organization. As she explains,

> A knowledge map is an easy-to-use guide that shows knowledge workers the straightest path to pockets of expertise in a company... [M]aps can range from simple directories of names, titles and department affiliation to elaborate online search engines with hypertext links to databases of human expertise, research material and abstracts of published information.[10]

Hildebrand's argument that companies can yield big benefits by investing in a geographic representation of their informational resources seems to have been adopted most enthusiastically by those firms operating in a pure information space: consulting. Today, firms such as McKinsey, PriceWaterhouseCoopers and Andersen use sophisticated online tools to map their informational resources. But their first knowledge maps were resoundingly low-tech—as tentative as the first hand-drawn maps of traditional cartography. According to Cornelius Burk, co-author of *InfoMap, a Complete Guide to Discovering Corporate Information Resources*, American Express used a map of the United States and simply "pinpointed the location of different information resources within the company on it." Likewise, the knowledge maps of McKinsey and Co. Inc., in the early 1980s, were built purely on paper.[11]

Such efforts developed cheek by jowl with academic work toward more technologized representations of corporate data. The first use of topological visualization was SPIRE (Spatial Paradigm for Information Retrieval and Exploration) developed in 1995 by the Department of Energy's CIA-funded Pacific Northwest National Laboratory; *Cartia*, a spin-off from the PNNL, is now used for visualizing patent searches.

<www.pnl.gov/infoviz/technologies.html>

Today, a variety of projects offer to fulfill the needs of the corporate knowledge auditor. Projects such as *Thinkmap* and InXight's *Vizserver* "make sense of complex information in ways that traditional interfaces can't." According to proponents, by using such maps, "productivity increases as corporate knowledge is more accessible and the data is more accurate. Flexibility in time of delivery of knowledge is gained as information is always a click away."

<www.thinkmap.com> <www.inxight.com>

<www.intranetroadmap.com/ibenefits.cfm>

Here the mapping of relational affect is seen as essential to a company's effective operation. Management consultant Valdis Krebs describes the evolution of approaches to capturing knowledge resources in a company. The most brutally exploitative approaches ("mine the knowledge from employees, codify it, and store it in knowledge database") tend to meet with little success. "People [are] not always willing to make public their best knowledge," Krebs explains, and codifying the tacit knowledge that resides with a corporation can be "like

8. Paul Otlet, "Something about Bibliography," in W. B. Rayward (trans./ed.), *International Organization and Dissemination of Knowledge: Selected Essays of Paul Otlet*. Amsterdam: Elsevier, 1990. W. B. Rayward, "Visions of Xanadu: Paul Otlet (1868–1944) and Hypertext," *Journal of the American Society for Information Science*, 45:4, 1994, pp. 235–250.

See "Conversations as Maps", pp. 70–79, 92–97.

9. Ted Nelson, *Literary Machines*. Swarthmore, PA, 1981, p. 48.

10. Carol Hildebrand, "Information Mapping: Guiding Principles," *CIO Magazine*, July 1, 1995.

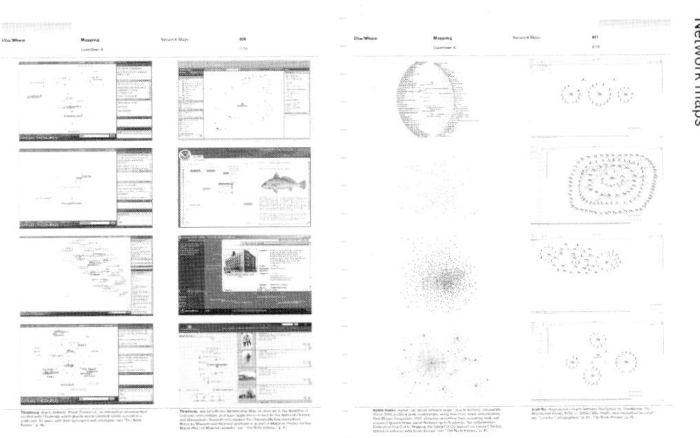

Network maps

gazetteer A 7–8/14 pp. 36–37

trying to nail jelly to the wall." For this analyst, the best use of available technology is "to keep a database of 'who knows what' and add a table of 'who knows who': in other words, store pointers to the knowledge, not the knowledge itself."[12]

Among these representations, it is possible to discern some consistent design principles and assumptions. Laura Garton, Caroline Haythornthwaite, and Barry Wellman define knowledge-mappers' key interests as 1) describing relations between elements in a corporate landscape, 2) tracing the flows of information passing between them, and 3) discovering the effects they have on people and organizations.[13] This usually results in a network structure, represented in a topology involving lines, stars, circles and meshes. Obviously, this is neither a necessary nor a sufficient architecture to contain the sorts of tacit information that researchers like Krebs are interested in studying, although enthusiastic claims continue to be made by advocates and practitioners. Jeffrey Heer, for example, in his recent project, *Exploring Enron*, claims his visualization of emails between Enron executives reveals Tim Belden's role as a mastermind of Enron's manipulation of California's markets. The visualization, seeming to master the febrile communications of the notorious multinational, has been very popular online—but like many knowledge maps, the value of its representation appears to rely on the quality of analysis brought to bear on it. One is left wondering whether the information map is a necessary middle term in the process of this analysis.

<http://jheer.org/enron>

THE OTHER SIDE OF THE TRACKS

The collapse of Enron—although it is really a collapse in reverse, a sort of materialization of prior absence—is an important nexus for information cartography. Enron demonstrated how what Castells sees as the autonomous quality of informational capital can also appear as a hollowness: a complex skein without substance. No doubt, the networked knowledge economy of developed Western economies creates a powerful urge to map, represent and understand, whether inside or outside the corporate context. This urge to represent emerges against a background of a general crisis for the representative mode: as object, in other words, the network at once inspires and thwarts the cartographer.

The leaders of the *Mapping Contemporary Capitalism* (MCC) project, created to develop tools for the "collaborative mapping of power relations," are well aware of the problematic nature of their undertaking; one of them, Simon Worthington, has described it as "like mapping the Bermuda Triangle in reverse."[14] The MCC's ambitious aim is to create software that will "enable groups to... plot the interconnections between organizations, political entities, corporations, and individuals that constitute society." Worthington admits to reservations about how "something as ungraspable as contemporary capitalism—so fast-moving and stealth-like—might be captured cartographically at all." It is unclear what stage MCC has reached in 2005.

The MCC project dovetails and cooperates with that of Bureau d'études, a group that has also begun attempts to map networked capital by representing the links between, for example, financial funds, government agencies, banks and industrial firms. Bureau d'études' map *Refuse the Biopolice* focuses on contemporary control systems, and was distributed at the July 2002 *No Border Camp* in Strasbourg (a meeting of activists working on migration and border regimes). Its *European Norms of World-Production* examines the administrative structures around the bureaucratic European Commission, and was distributed at the European Social Forum in Florence in November 2002, Bureau d'études' *InfoWar* was distributed at *WSIS? WE SEIZE!*, a gathering of autonomous information activists that took place during the World Summit on Information Society in Geneva, 2003.

<http://ut.yt.t0.or.at/site/index.php?option=com_content&task=view&id=32&Itemid=41>

11. Cornelius Burk and Forest W. Horton, Jr., *InfoMap, a Complete Guide to Discovering Corporate Information Resources*. NJ: Prentice Hall, 1988.

12. Valdis Krebs, "Working in the Connected World: Managing Connected Assets," 1999. <http://www.knetmap.com/knowledge-flow.html>

13. Laura Garton, Caroline Haythornthwaite and Barry Wellman, "Studying Online Social Networks," *Journal of Computer Mediated Communication*, 3:1, June 1997. <www.usc.edu/dept/annenberg/vol3/issue1/garton.html>

14. Simon Worthington, "The Bermuda Triangle in Reverse: Mapping

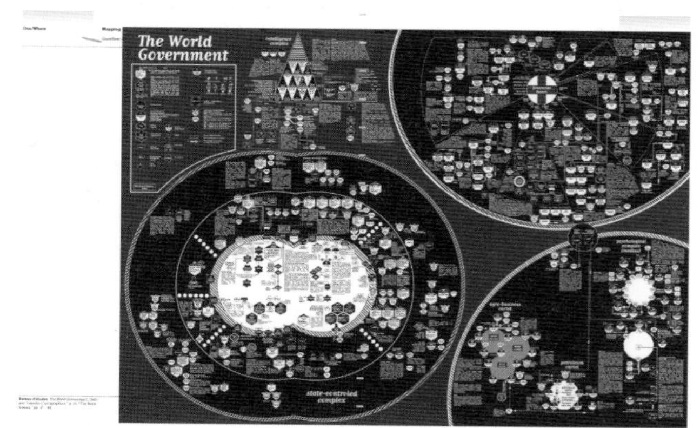
Network maps

gazetteer A 9–10/14 pp. 38–39

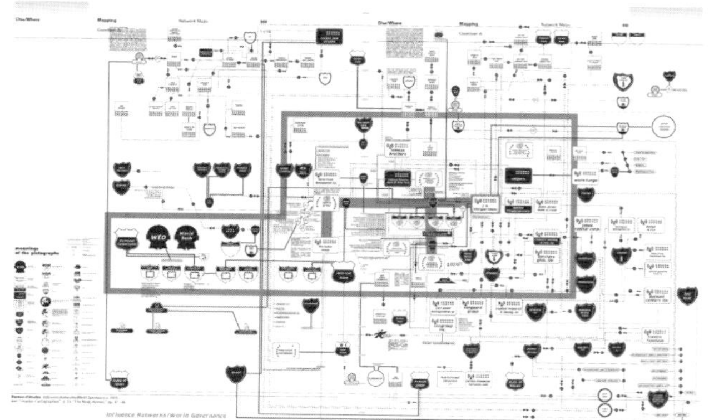
Network maps

gazetteer A 11–12/14 pp. 40–41

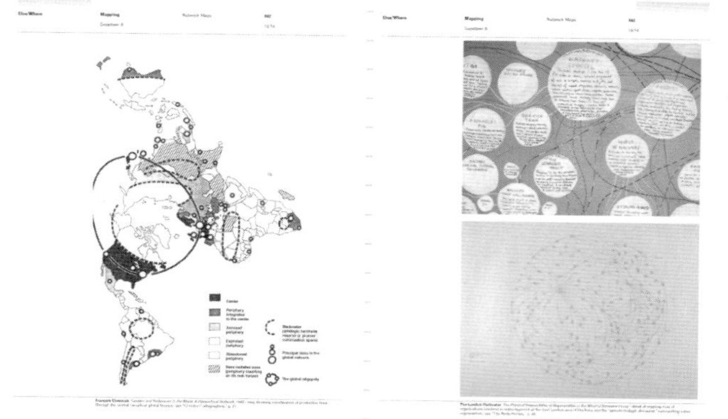
Network maps

gazetteer A 14/14 p. 43

These maps are highly complex and detailed, but ultimately reveal the impossibility of making visible contemporary institutional relationships in a traditional cartographic form. What, then, is their primary aim? They are meant, explains Bureau d'études' collaborator and commentator Brian Holmes:

> to act as subjective shocks, energy potentials... signs pointing to a territory that cannot yet be fully signified, and that will never be 'represented' in the traditional ways.[15]

Such a statement gives the lie to popular projects such as *They Rule*, created by Josh On and California-based Future Farmers, which graphically maps the links between board members of U.S. Fortune 100 companies, and provides multiple views of their interconnections. The project was featured in the *2002 Whitney Biennial* and awarded the Net Excellence at the 2002 *Ars Electronica* festival, but how much closer does it bring us to understanding the power structure of contemporary capitalism than the statement that a few men sit on many boards?

<www.theyrule.net>

In London, The London Particular mapping collective has, since 2000, been developing a counter-regeneration map of a dense and proliferating network of agencies, quangos, (quasi-autonomous NGOs), arts bodies funding authorities, and tenant organizations in the east London area of Hackney. Beginning with an investigation of urban regeneration in a zone of artists, creative industries and long-standing working class and immigrant communities, the London Particular's map attempted to capture the shift from a Keynesian to a neo-liberal model of urban sovereignty with its devolved, decentralized and intensely complex networks. As The London Particular explain:

> The entities that constitute these networks administer and legitimate social and cultural projects through a pseudo-dialogic discourse of consultation and direct democracy ('grassroots', 'people power', 'bottom-up development').

Entitled—with a nod to artist Damien Hirst—*The Physical Impossibility of Regeneration in the Mind of Someone Living*, the project performs what The London Particular call "an ironic mimesis of the popular but hypocritical 'socially engaged' mapping

Contemporary Capitalism," *TCM Reader*, 2004. <www.locative.net/tcmreader/index.php?endo;worthington>.

15. Brian Holmes, "Maps for the Outside," <http://twenteenthcentury.com/uo/index.php/BrianHolmesMapsfortheOutside>.

aesthetic." Hand drawn, complex to the point of illegibility, and obviously incomplete, the map (*pace* Holmes' comment) signals a deliberate refusal to exhaust or appear adequate to its subject. Its creators hope the project:

> simultaneously demonstrates that the cultural institutions, spaces and networks familiar to an art audience, and especially to those attending the gallery itself, are implicated in a broader network of gentrification strategies.[16]

Yet again, one wonders if the map does this better, *per se*, than The London Particular's written analyses. As with the *Mapping Contemporary Capitalism* project, the group is apparently finding it difficult to realize its stated cartographic ambitions.

THE NODE KNOWS

If information cartography is not yet up to the task of capturing the tacit, affective and transversal qualities of the knowledge economy, this may be because mapping's self-conception is inadequate. All the maps discussed in this essay have something in common: they map from the top down, attempting to understand the systems they represent from above, or from the outside.

Let me offer a highly constrained proposition: *when looked at from above, the network is illegible*. Jee Oh, a student in the Masters program in Digital Media at Ravensbourne College, London, is exploring what she terms "node analysis," in which the investigation of a particular network of social relations is approached from the point of view of each node within it.

<www.rave.ac.uk/>

In Oh's view, the node knows—that is, knows its own reasons for taking part in the network, with whom it interacts and why, and in what modality. Its motivations, aspirations, emotions, passions and ideas—which intimately affect how the network develops—are nonetheless non-representable by the cartographic tools currently used by knowledge mappers. Affective personal relations are not well understood by lines and meshes. Oh is developing a kind of node analysis that uses a much more nuanced tool: the written word. Her approach is part of a broader shift towards node-centric organization of information. *Folksonomy*, for example, is a practice of collaborative categorization using freely chosen keywords. In a tool like *del.icio.us*, created by Joshua Schachter (who previously created *GeoURL*, a location-to-URL reverse directory), the whole system of categorization—the entire set of possible key words and their intersections—will not ordinarily be known by a single user or set of users. Instead, they map the part of the system they use through their own ad-hoc categorizations.

<http://del.icio.us>
<http://geourl.org/>

A visual representation of a user's *del.icio.us* map is personal, particular and nuanced, and useful primarily to the person or group that created it, although radical visualizations have begun to develop, as projects like Kalle Kormann's and Michal Migurski's demonstrate.

<www.keikei.de>
<http://news.stamen.com/vox/>

I use *del.icio.us* every day that I'm connected to the network to map my own areas of interest, and examine other people's. So do hundreds of thousands of people. And that is more than can be said for the beautiful, highly designed, but ultimately limited-use productions of the first, and perhaps misguided, wave of network cartography.

16. David Panos and Benedict Seymour of The London Particular, email interview with the author, 2003.

MAPPING SOCIAL MESSES

ROBERT E. HORN IS CONVINCED A NEW LANGUAGE IS EMERGING THAT BLURS THE LINES BETWEEN CARTOONS AND PROSE, DIAGRAMS AND LABELS, ART AND SCIENCE. A POLITICAL SCIENTIST BY TRAINING AND A KNOWLEDGE CARTOGRAPHER BY PROFESSION, HE TELLS DAVID PESCOVITZ WHY VISUAL LANGUAGE IS CRUCIAL IN OUR INFORMATION-SATURATED SOCIETY, AND HOW HIS "MESS MAPS" CAN HELP DISENTANGLE COMPLEX SOCIAL SITUATIONS.

David Pescovitz: What is the high-level thrust of your work?

Robert Horn: I'm attempting to make communication easier, quicker and more accurate in the face of the immense complexity and information overload that all of us face.

To that end, you evangelize a visual language. What does that mean?

Language is what people use to communicate. If you look at the business and scientific worlds, people tightly integrate words and visual elements to communicate. By visual elements, I mean shapes in the diagrammatic sense and images in the illustrative sense. The critical questions to ask are "What do words do best?" and "What do visual elements do best?" In diagrams, words describe the phenomena, the events, or the objects, and visual elements help separate and connect the parts, while also describing relationships. When they're integrated, you get the ability to manage much more complexity.

What about the aesthetics of your maps?

Aesthetics are important. But in the consulting arena, you can only get as much in terms of aesthetics as the client will pay for. Most of my maps are limited by time and the clients usually don't have huge budgets. We try to make the maps pleasant to look at. We have our own database of clip-art and, with each project, we can usually afford to make a few new icons. As we accumulate icons, the maps get prettier.

A graphic designer would argue that the aesthetics of the map dramatically impacts not only its function, but also its usability. Your maps are not as graphically streamlined or slick as one might expect. In fact, they have more of a folksy, homespun aesthetic. What are you trying to convey with that look and feel? How do you think it affects the way people use them?

Not all my maps, or anybody else's, serve the same function. But many, especially the *mess maps*, are the intermediate results of different stages of work by different kinds of problem-solving groups. They are intended to help them gather and process information. For example, groups find it easier to fill in blobs and are intimidated by rectangles. In my experience, slickness and streamlinedness actually hinders the group. Effort in that direction would be costly and probably slow the process down. My work is primarily helping people and groups think—that is, doing analysis and synthesis—and visual language helps me and others do that. I think of visual language as operating at multiple levels, like any language.

I've fired graphic designers because they didn't pay sufficient attention to understanding the content of the diagram or map and hadn't involved themselves in the minute-by-minute process of working with the task forces. They were only interested in how it looked and what kind of exhibit or prize it could be submitted for, and hence were blind to what was going on in front of them in the group. In short, they weren't helpful to the group process—they were impediments. If I had one bit of advice to give neophyte graphics people it would be: get involved in the content.

What is involved in making one of these maps for a client? Let's look at the Complex Social Mess map you created for Multnomah County in Portland, Oregon. Your aim was to help a task force unfurl the complexities of its public mental health system.

Yes, the county commissioners knew they had a mess on their hands a couple of years ago in the delivery of public mental health. They appointed a task force headed by Elsa Porter, a former Assistant Secretary of Commerce, with 25 citizens—lawyers, doctors, caseworkers, policemen, patients' advocates—all trying to understand the same phenomenon. But they didn't have a way of putting the problems and causes together into a common mental map. Their (verbal) language is very linear. It's hard to retain all the relationships and causalities. In groups like this, they often start jumping to conclusions and solutions before they have a common understanding of the problems. Then the meeting ends—"see you next week or next month"—and they start over again, but three or four people who weren't there last time have to catch up. You get the usual committee chaos or stagnation.

How did you help?

Since they knew the territory, and I clearly didn't, they had to make the map. I sat down with a few task force members to learn what they were struggling with and the different organizational sectors they were working in. That's how we identified the blobs. We also determined the level of verbal language to use; here, informal language worked best.

Once you identified the sectors represented by the blobs, how did the task force provide more specific data needed to make the map?

We threw those sectors on a big sheet of paper, divided the task force into subgroups of five, and gave each one a list of sectors. I made a brief introduction and said, "we're going to make a common mental model here. You do that by writing the events and phenomena you believe cause things to happen. Don't worry; you're just putting what you know into these blobs."

When did you make the first map?

After they'd worked for a while, we took their big sheets of paper back to my office and put them in the computer to make a first draft, which we took back to the next meeting and worked on some more. After the third revision, we'd begun to determine what was really important to include and what wasn't.

Can you describe the final product?

It's a cross-boundary causality map that characterizes the situations, events and phenomena involved in this particular "social mess." These items were placed in sectors—the blobs—and connected by arrows that stand for causes or influences. The big yellow boxes are specific problems associated with each sector. Read closely in one sector, and you will see the words "case workers are leaving in droves." That is sufficient as a mental model; the task force doesn't need a table showing resignations over the last 18 months. The colored arrows trace multiple cross-boundary causality. The reason "case workers are leaving in droves" is partly because they have to fill out more paperwork, caused by new federal and state regulations (crossing two organizational boundaries) that have significantly changed county data-processing requirements (another boundary). But the county data-processing department couldn't create the new software because (crossing another boundary) a new Silicon Forest was evolving around Portland and paying higher salaries to programmers than the county could afford and Y2K was also absorbing programmers. This is just one of 85 causality arrows that the task force chose to put on its mental map. They limited themselves to the most important ones. You don't want to describe the whole world.

Was the map a success?

It served two purposes. It facilitated the task force process by helping construct a common mental model. It gave the task force chair a tool to get all members involved and committed to the process. The map was actually used as the interim report to the County Commissioners, who were delighted with it; one said, "I see why we're hearing about problems." A mural-sized version was used in the public meeting where the report was presented. There was no written report.

It helped the supervisors and the task force to focus their thinking?

Yes, making the map helped them find out what their colleagues know and don't know, what they can rely on each other for, and whether one person's description of the world squares with another's. All that was happening in the process of making the map. It's social learning: how we learn together to solve, in this case, community problems.

Would you agree that first-time viewers of the Multnomah County map who were not involved in its creation might initially be confused by the various colored arrows and lack of obvious visual hierarchy?

As I said, the Multnomah Map was shown to the county supervisors. A very brief explanation was all they needed to appreciate it and assign the task force the further job of making recommendations for changes. The map served its purpose. The lack of obvious visual hierarchy is intentional; it conveys the feeling of a social mess.

Making maps of so many territories—from public policy dilemmas to debates about artificial intelligence—must require you to be an intellectual jack-of-all trades.

Human beings have bureaucratic impulses to draw boundaries and defend our territories. Of course, you can see why disciplines exist, for digging into very special questions. But all big real-world problems are interdisciplinary.

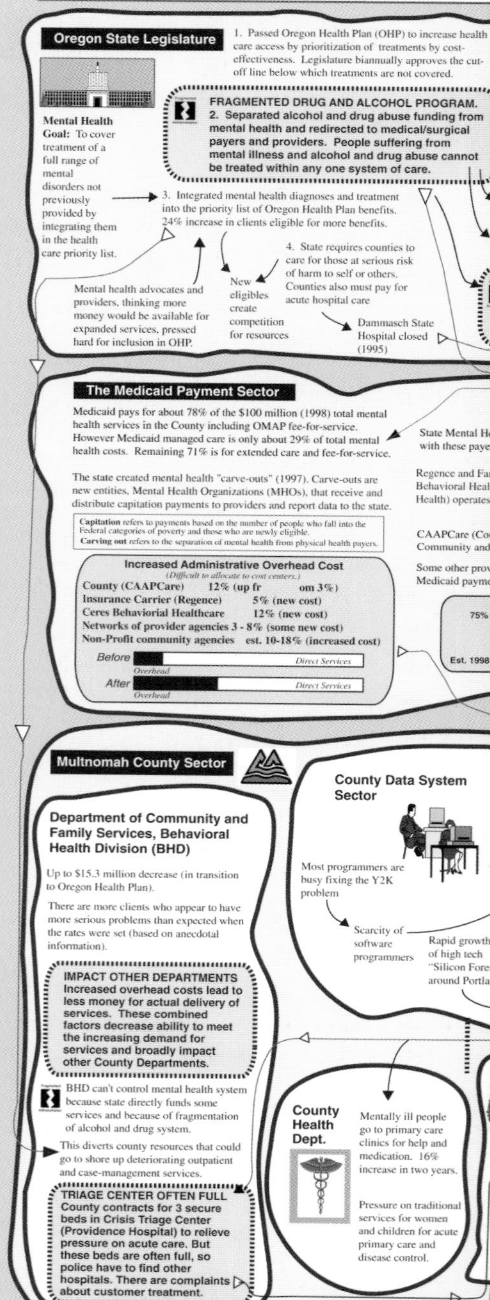

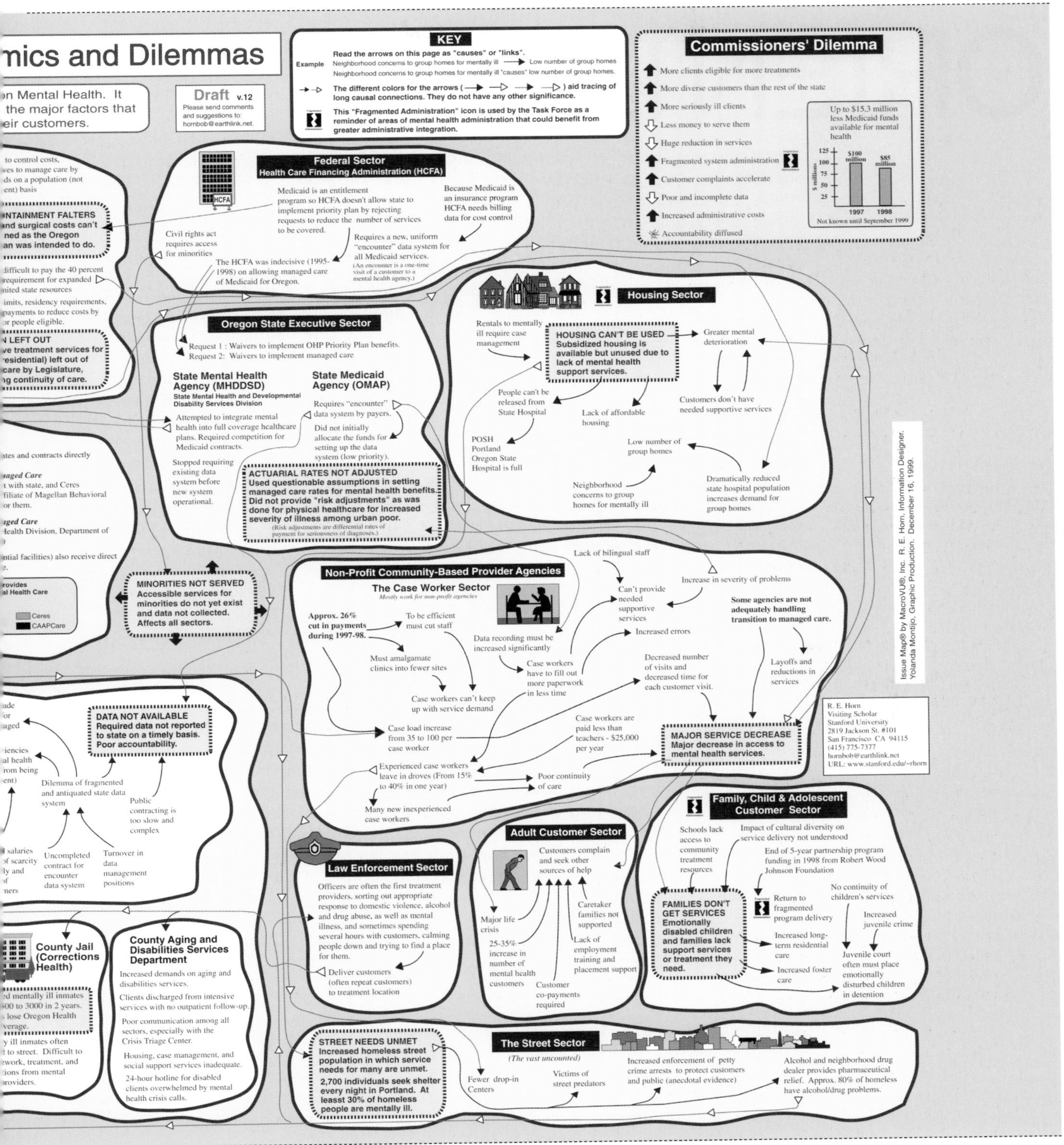

mics and Dilemmas

on Mental Health. It
the major factors that
eir customers.

Draft v.12
Please send comments and suggestions to: hornbob@earthlink.net.

KEY

Read the arrows on this page as "causes" or "links".
Example: Neighborhood concerns to group homes for mentally ill → Low number of group homes
Neighborhood concerns to group homes for mentally ill "causes" low number of group homes.

The different colors for the arrows aid tracing of long causal connections. They do not have any other significance.

This "Fragmented Administration" icon is used by the Task Force as a reminder of areas of mental health administration that could benefit from greater administrative integration.

Commissioners' Dilemma

- ↑ More clients eligible for more treatments
- ↑ More diverse customers than the rest of the state
- ↑ More seriously ill clients
- ↓ Less money to serve them
- ↓ Huge reduction in services
- ↑ Fragmented system administration
- ↑ Customer complaints accelerate
- ↓ Poor and incomplete data
- ↑ Increased administrative costs
- Accountability diffused

Up to $15.3 million less Medicaid funds available for mental health

$ millions: 1997 — $100 million; 1998 — $85 million
Not known until September 1999

to control costs.
ves to manage care by
ds on a population (not
ent) basis

NTAINMENT FALTERS
and surgical costs can't
ned as the Oregon
an was intended to do.

difficult to pay the 40 percent
requirement for expanded
nited state resources

imits, residency requirements,
payments to reduce costs by
or people eligible.

N LEFT OUT
ve treatment services for
residential) left out of
care by Legislature,
ng continuity of care.

Federal Sector
Health Care Financing Administration (HCFA)

Medicaid is an entitlement program so HCFA doesn't allow state to implement priority plan by rejecting requests to reduce the number of services to be covered.

Because Medicaid is an insurance program HCFA needs billing data for cost control

Civil rights act requires access for minorities

Requires a new, uniform "encounter" data system for all Medicaid services. (An encounter is a one-time visit of a customer to a mental health agency.)

The HCFA was indecisive (1995-1998) on allowing managed care of Medicaid for Oregon.

Oregon State Executive Sector

Request 1: Waivers to implement OHP Priority Plan benefits.
Request 2: Waivers to implement managed care

State Mental Health Agency (MHDDSD)
State Mental Health and Developmental Disability Services Division

Attempted to integrate mental health into full coverage healthcare plans. Required competition for Medicaid contracts.

Stopped requiring existing data system before new system operational.

State Medicaid Agency (OMAP)

Requires "encounter" data system by payers.

Did not initially allocate the funds for setting up the data system (low priority).

ACTUARIAL RATES NOT ADJUSTED
Used questionable assumptions in setting managed care rates for mental health benefits. Did not provide "risk adjustments" as was done for physical healthcare for increased severity of illness among urban poor.
(Risk adjustments are differential rates of payment for seriousness of diagnoses.)

Housing Sector

Rentals to mentally ill require case management

HOUSING CAN'T BE USED
Subsidized housing is available but unused due to lack of mental health support services.

Greater mental deterioration

Customers don't have needed supportive services

People can't be released from State Hospital

Lack of affordable housing

POSH Portland Oregon State Hospital is full

Low number of group homes

Neighborhood concerns to group homes for mentally ill

Dramatically reduced state hospital population increases demand for group homes

ates and contracts directly

aged Care
t with state, and Ceres
filiate of Magellan Behavioral
or them.

aged Care
Health Division, Department of

ntial facilities) also receive direct

rovides
al Health Care

Ceres
CAAPCare

MINORITIES NOT SERVED
Accessible services for minorities do not yet exist and data not collected. Affects all sectors.

Non-Profit Community-Based Provider Agencies
The Case Worker Sector
Mostly work for non-profit agencies

Lack of bilingual staff

Increase in severity of problems

Can't provide needed supportive services

Some agencies are not adequately handling transition to managed care.

Increased errors

Approx. 26% cut in payments during 1997-98.

To be efficient must cut staff

Data recording must be increased significantly

Must amalgamate clinics into fewer sites

Case workers have to fill out more paperwork in less time

Decreased number of visits and decreased time for each customer visit.

Layoffs and reductions in services

Case workers can't keep up with service demand

Case load increase from 35 to 100 per case worker

Case workers are paid less than teachers - $25,000 per year

MAJOR SERVICE DECREASE
Major decrease in access to mental health services.

Experienced case workers leave in droves (From 15% to 40% in one year)

Poor continuity of care

Many new inexperienced case workers

ade
for
aged

iencies
al health
rom being
ent)

DATA NOT AVAILABLE
Required data not reported to state on a timely basis. Poor accountability.

Dilemma of fragmented and antiquated state data system

Public contracting is too slow and complex

salaries
of scarcity
ly and
f
ners

Uncompleted contract for encounter data system

Turnover in data management positions

Law Enforcement Sector

Officers are often the first treatment providers, sorting out appropriate response to domestic violence, alcohol and drug abuse, as well as mental illness, and sometimes spending several hours with customers, calming people down and trying to find a place for them.

Deliver customers (often repeat customers) to treatment location

Adult Customer Sector

Customers complain and seek other sources of help

Major life crisis

Caretaker families not supported

25-35% increase in number of mental health customers

Lack of employment training and placement support

Customer co-payments required

Family, Child & Adolescent Customer Sector

Schools lack access to community treatment resources

Impact of cultural diversity on service delivery not understood

End of 5-year partnership program funding in 1998 from Robert Wood Johnson Foundation

No continuity of children's services

FAMILIES DON'T GET SERVICES
Emotionally disabled children and families lack support services or treatment they need.

Return to fragmented program delivery

Increased juvenile crime

Increased long-term residential care

Juvenile court often must place emotionally disturbed children in detention

Increased foster care

County Jail (Corrections Health)

ed mentally ill inmates
00 to 3000 in 2 years.
lose Oregon Health
verage.

y ill inmates often
to street. Difficult to
ework, treatment, and
ions from mental
providers.

County Aging and Disabilities Services Department

Increased demands on aging and disabilities services.

Clients discharged from intensive services with no outpatient follow-up.

Poor communication among all sectors, especially with the Crisis Triage Center.

Housing, case management, and social support services inadequate.

24-hour hotline for disabled clients overwhelmed by mental health crisis calls.

The Street Sector
(The vast uncounted)

STREET NEEDS UNMET
Increased homeless street population in which service needs for many are unmet.
2,700 individuals seek shelter every night in Portland. At leasst 30% of homeless people are mentally ill.

Fewer drop-in Centers

Victims of street predators

Increased enforcement of petty crime arrests to protect customers and public (anecdotal evidence)

Alcohol and neighborhood drug dealer provides pharmaceutical relief. Approx. 80% of homeless have alcohol/drug problems.

R. E. Horn
Visiting Scholar
Stanford University
2819 Jackson St. #101
San Francisco CA 94115
(415) 775-7377
hornbob@earthlink.net
URL: www.stanford.edu/~rhorn

Robert Horn *Mental Health Services Dynamics and Dilemmas*, 1999 / a "cross boundary causality map" developed to help officials in Multnomah County, Portland, Oregon, understand the causes of problems including an increase in mentally ill inmates and an exodus of case workers.

RE: ORIENTATION

Once upon a time you were expected to know your place in the divine order. Or in the secular order. Predestination, occupation, class, race, social milieu and intelligence: these factors determined your precise place in the scheme of things. You also had a fixed abode. In such a rigidly ordered world maps were hardly necessary. Only when you wanted to break out of the order, to escape the inexorable consequences of your origins and social status, did you need a map: first to stimulate fantasies about far-off, unfamiliar places, then to guide you on your journey there. Maps were roads to freedom.

Topographical maps are still handy for visualizing relationships between regions, people, goods—in short, everything that depends on spatial coordinates. But they are almost useless for visualizing a whole host of relationships that have begun to dominate our world: the interactions between knowledge, power, capital, intelligence, technology. In a society in which the cultural core consists of things that are constantly on the move—where motion itself has become the core, where mutations of certain processes are the rule rather than the exception, where that motion is unencumbered by the slowness of matter—maps that impose spatial order on the world are increasingly irrelevant. The new reality calls for maps of a completely different caliber: three-dimensional maps, diagrams, search engines, animations. They still help you find your way but also help you understand the world a little better.

<www.oma.nl>

<www.unstudio.com>

Here we enter the world of design. Architects, at least the more challenging ones, have no problem transcending their traditional role of giving people a place in this world. In their new practice, just as they did in the past, architects provide people with orientation, but now they do so not to help people stand still, but to allow them to move. Architecture is becoming the art of dynamic situations, beginning with conceptual drawings. OMA, for example, rose to fame with its plan for Parc de la Villette in the early 1980s, whose very form of notation (exploded views) opened up completely new perceptions of spatial organization. UN Studio has been very successful in presenting its design for Arnhem Station as a series of dynamic drawings based on extensive mobility studies. What was at first considered a problem—movement—became an asset of the planning process.

Today there are actual buildings in which the art of manipulating dynamic situations is realized through innovative interaction design. In this rapidly emerging field, architects are directing certain kinds of behavior, rather than just framing that behavior. For an impression of the current state of affairs in this field,

THE WORLD OF FIXED LOCATIONS IS BEING SUPERSEDED BY DYNAMIC PROCESSES AND GLOBAL INFORMATION FLOWS. **OLE BOUMAN** ARGUES THAT NEW MODES OF MAPPING ARE NEEDED TO REPRESENT MODERN MOVEMENTS IN ARCHITECTURE.

<www.fusedspace.nl>

check out the entries to the 2004 *Fusedspace* competition which was devoted to examining the overlap between public and information space; the projects focused on changeable modes and overlapping interfaces rather than on irreversible spaces.

Another important aspect of the new reality is an inescapable urge to make things compatible, that is, interchangeable. People, goods, ideas, finances are eagerly subsumed in a global matrix where they communicate at lightning speed, in several dimensions, according to standard protocols. Maps were once meant to represent the mutual specificity of things as a collection of points A and B that people could travel between. Now, if they are to illuminate the journey, they must consist of dynamic configurations of *only* As or Bs. If everything is in motion and in search of areas of overlap, maps too must be all movement and overlap. The work of South-African architect Ronald Wall—whose Ph.D. thesis explores the fertile crossover between descriptive mapping and prescriptive designing—provides a good example.[1]

Maps that depict movement and overlap could also be called animations; they animate reality. The data furnished by Geographical Information Systems, statistics, search engines and visualization software serve less to situate things in relation to one another than to reveal their mutual force fields. They are not about fixed positions, but rather a matter of visualizing tensions of various kinds. As increasing amounts of data and many more parameters are processed, recalculated and visualized by computers, a dynamic reality becomes visible. This very dynamism causes us to lose our way and fuels the demand for new maps—smarter maps—that may not really help us find our way, but allow us to retain a hold on the thin thread of understanding that ties us to the complex reality of our world. We don't need direction so much as orientation. One of the most urgent questions of our time is how to move from movements to trajectories, from strict goal-orientedness to shared vectors. Buildings cannot make that shift. Maps can. If architects make the shift to this new kind of practice, it will be because they are unwilling to concede their role as contextualizers of our culture. Rem Koolhaas's Seattle Library of 2004 may be an interesting work, but in terms of architecture's destiny, it might be much more significant to see his proposals for a new European Union iconography realized.

1. See Ronald Wall, "Between Worlds: Architectural Exercises between the Metageographic and the Microspecific," *Archis* 2, 2004.

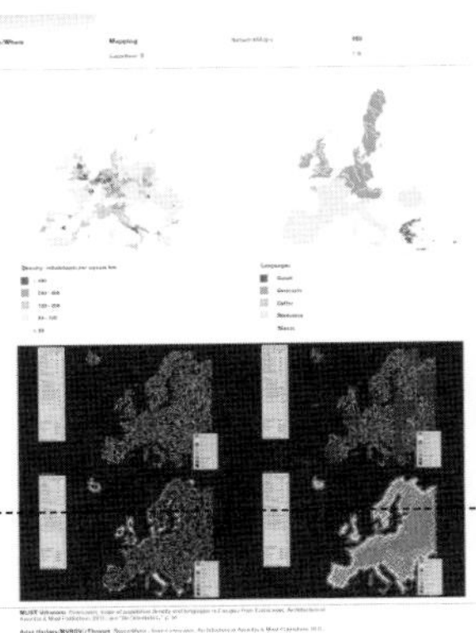

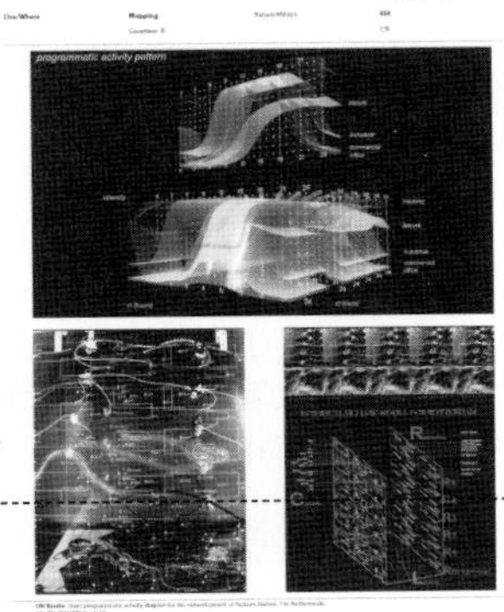

Network maps

Thus, cartography continues to do two things at once. As an act of understanding the world, it helps separate main issues from a multitude of side issues, and allows us to discern what really matters. On the other hand, the opportunities for manipulation are inexhaustible. For example, instead of merely suggesting an order, modern maps also present processes, in all their inexorability.

Sometimes it seems that maps not only don't help us understand the world, they prevent us from doing anything with this knowledge. With today's dynamic maps, you can end up thinking you understand everything without being able to change anything. You can stand above reality and simultaneously be totally overwhelmed by it.

Ordinary citizens can afford to shrug off this paradox. They do their best to keep track of what is going on in the world and then try to use this awareness as a basis for democratic opinion or even a rational vote during some election or other. Designers don't get off so lightly, however, since their work is not about casting a vote but about realizing an intervention.

Designers who aspire to remain forceful actors in the battle for space (as they once were, as master builders) simply cannot ignore the new representations of reality. They need maps in order to understand the big issues and dilemmas. Only then will their designs go beyond solving practical problems, and acquire cultural relevance. That said, there is a growing gap between the fantastic studies in which hidden forces are revealed and interconnected, and the masterplans and scenarios that are supposed to change the appearance of those maps. For example, MUST Urbanism's *Euroscapes* confront urgency with atrophy.[2]

A parallel can be drawn between contemporary mapping and various forms of historicism. Just as historicism once declared the course of history inevitable, these days dynamic maps, animations, data-scapes and other conceptual matrices leave us in shock and awe at what seem to be irrevocable facts. Unfortunately, cartography has yet to produce any figure comparable with the philosophers Karl Popper and Jean-François Lyotard, who judged historicist ambitions by their potential for damage.

2. MUST, *Euroscapes—Forum* v. 41. Amsterdam: MUST Publishers and the Architectura et Amicitia Society, 2003.

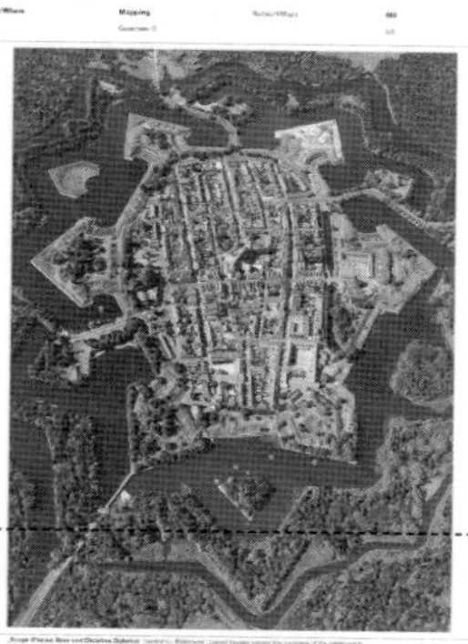

Network maps

But even in the absence of a profound philosophical critique, we need to move forward. If design is to transcend the inevitabilities of the map, there are some essential concepts to be grappled with. Anyone thinking of approaching an architectural intervention by way of description, statistics, visualization and animation needs to take the following principles into account:

The level of administrative support:

a design may be tremendously intelligent, but without any political-administrative underpinning it will get nowhere. Designs that neglect to include an administrative caveat usually end up (after doing the rounds of the lecture circuit) being filed away in the interesting ideas drawer of one or another bureaucrat.

The need to move between various levels of scale:

there is a growing gap between proposals that are very concrete and realizable at the level of the site, and totally unrealizable visions at the national and international level which, for all their rhetoric, no longer have a clear purpose. The intermediate level, that of the region (where an integrated approach is occasionally possible), is also the most underexamined.

The definition of the design grows with the definition of the task:

architects are often required to deliver visionary ideas, but the execution of those ideas remains outside their scope because it is not considered the work of architects. Designers must be prepared to act as developers, process organizers or lobbyists.

There is a sense in which every design—whether it is called a masterplan, a blueprint or a floor plan—is a map, because it organizes man and matter. Now that the ordering of man and matter has become part of the movement of patterns of information, knowledge and capital, architects must change their maps to conform to the new reality. Until now they have done so very cautiously; it is quite something for a progressive insight to be discovered during a design's research and conceptual phase. Such discoveries at least make for improved orientation. But they don't help one to find the way. That is only possible when making a map is the same as making a road. In a society of flows, the need is above all for road maps and these are not discovered but created.

At this moment a buggy is riding around on the surface of Mars, carefully mapping out some new territory. There are no buggies riding around the *terra incognita* of global patterns of movement, however. While they are perhaps being rendered more understandable, there seems to be little ambition to change those patterns. There is no shortage of maps today. Instead of maps of the oceans, we have oceans of maps. But where are the explorers?

Density: inhabitants per square km

- > 400
- 200 – 400
- 120 – 200
- 60 – 120
- < 60

Languages

- Greek
- Germanic
- Celtic
- Romance
- Slavic

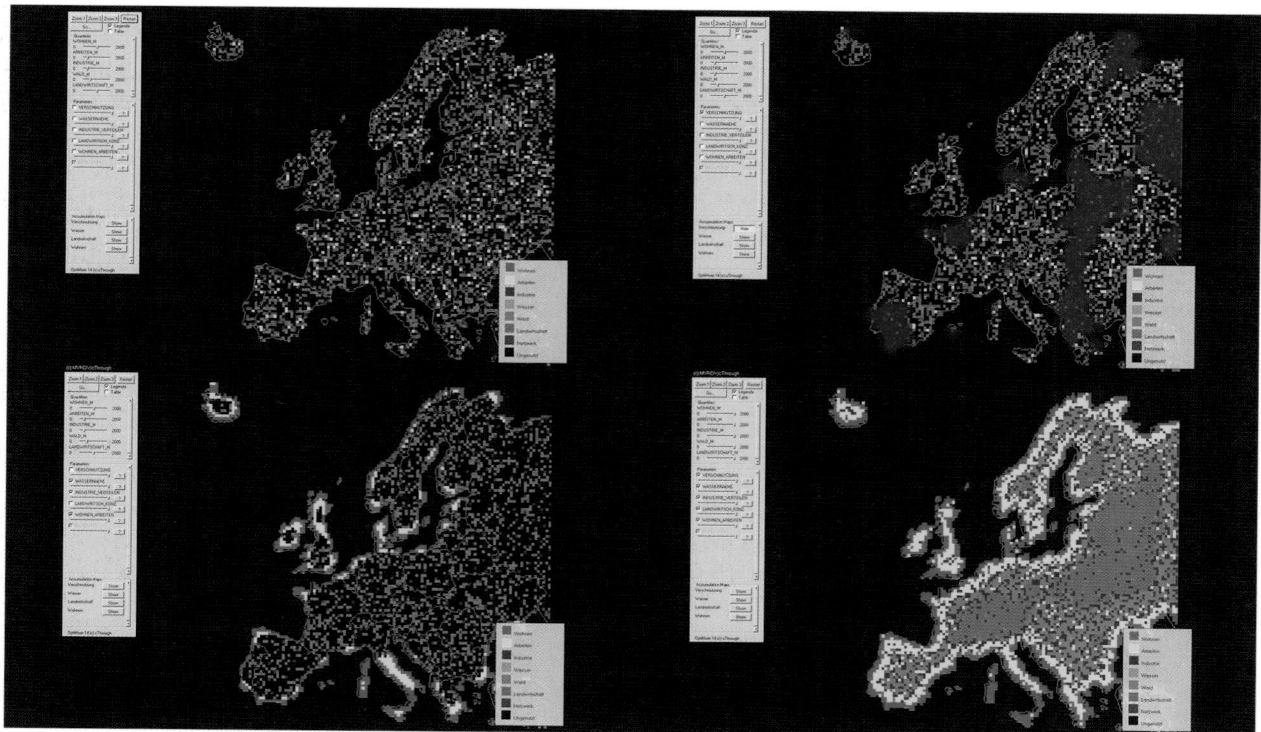

MUST Urbanism *Euroscapes,* maps of population density and languages in Europe / from *Euroscapes*, Architectura et Amicitia & Must Publishers, 2003 / see "Re-Orientation," p. 56.

Arjan Harbers/MVRDV/cThrough *RegionMaker* / from *Euroscapes*, Architectura et Amicitia & Must Publishers, 2003 / see "Re-Orientation," p. 56.

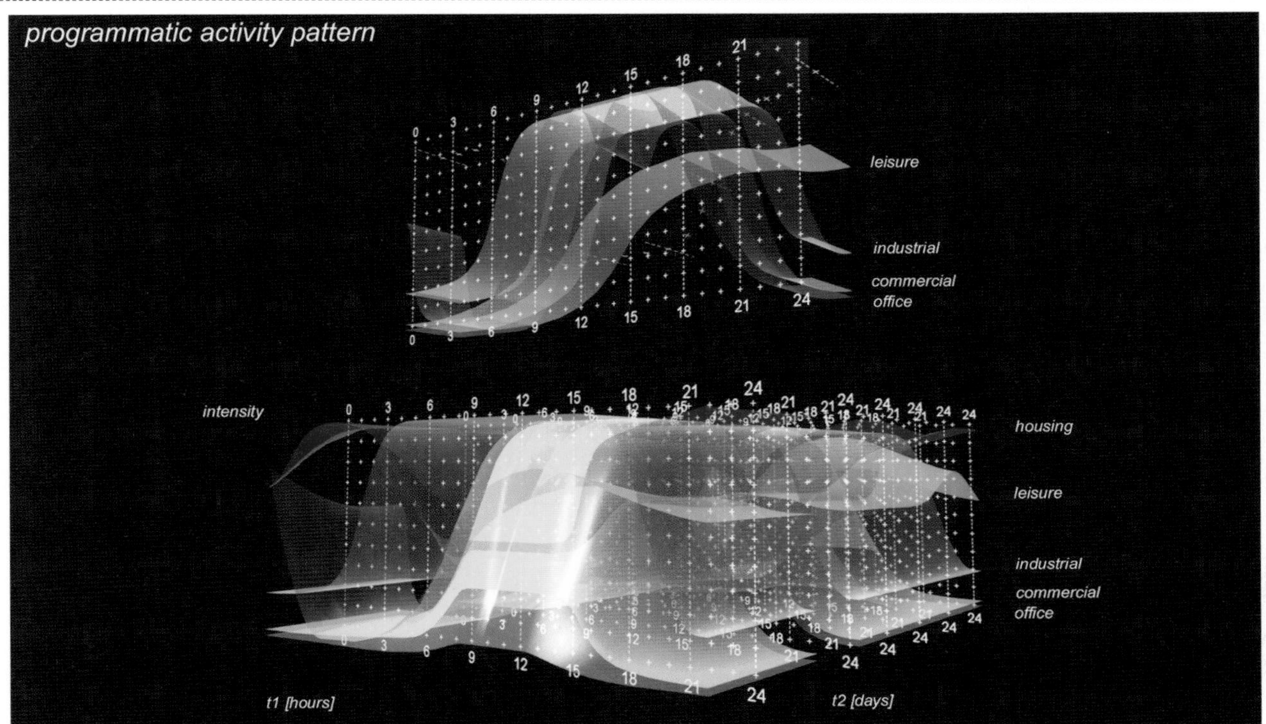

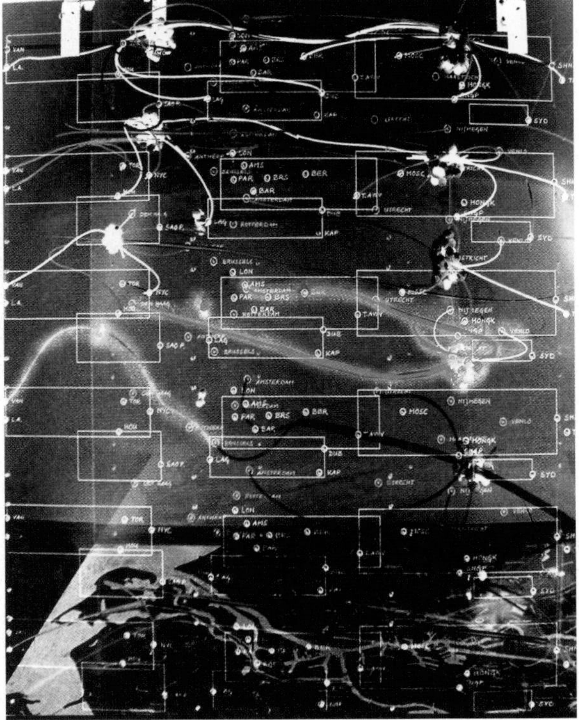

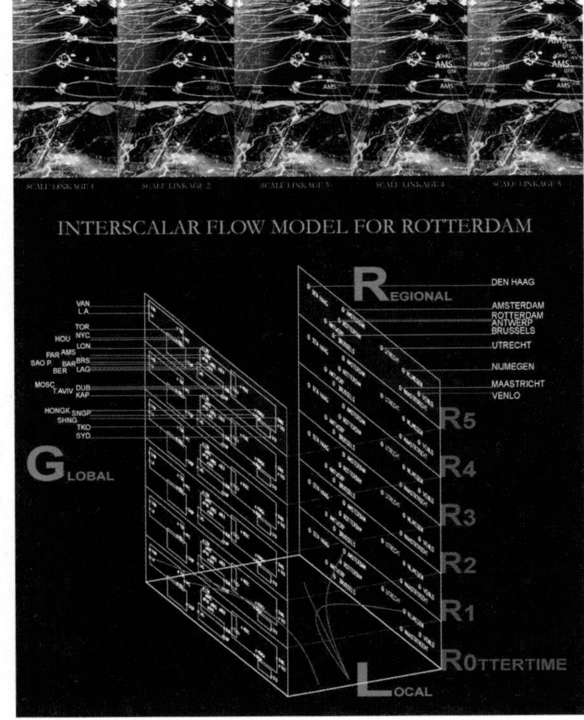

UN Studio (top:) programmatic activity diagram for the redevelopment of Arnhem Station, the Netherlands / see "Re-Orientation," p. 54.

Ronald Wall (bottom, left and right): spatio-temporal model of Rotterdam at local, regional and global scales, showing the flows of goods, services, information, and people / see "Re-Orientation," p. 55.

_Scape (Florian Boer and **Christine Dijkstra)** *Control vs. Wilderness* / paired images convey the inversion of the relationship between landscape and city that has been taking place in the European Union: (this page) an aerial view of the Dutch fortress city of Naarden by Georg Gester, is juxtaposed against the same image manipulated in Photoshop by _Scape (opposite) to convey how "instead of cities surrounded by landscape, the situation nowadays is an urban field surrounding pockets of landscape. The urban jungle is where uncontrollable phenomena emerge, while the former natural wilderness has grown into a safe, predictable place." From *Euroscapes*, MUST Publishers/Architectura et Amicitia, 2003 / see "Re-Orientation," p. 54.

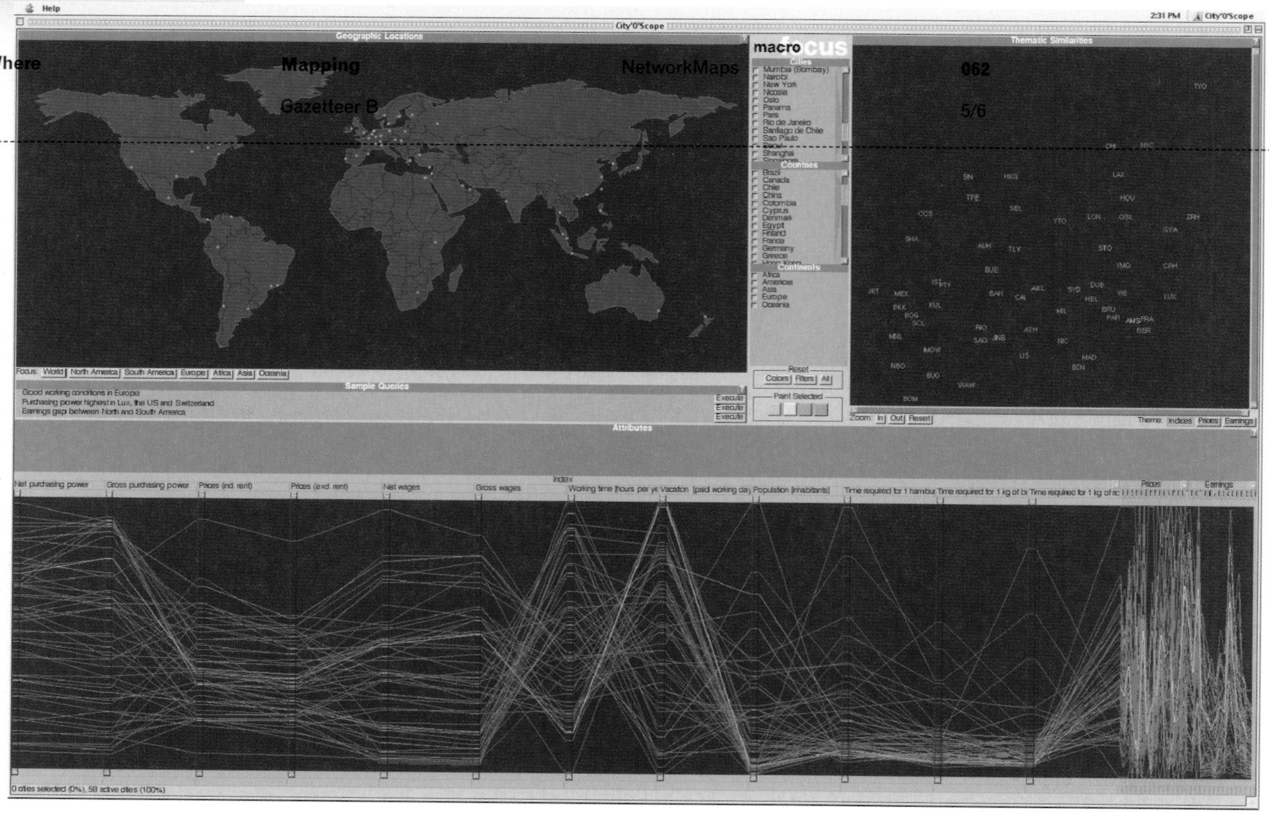

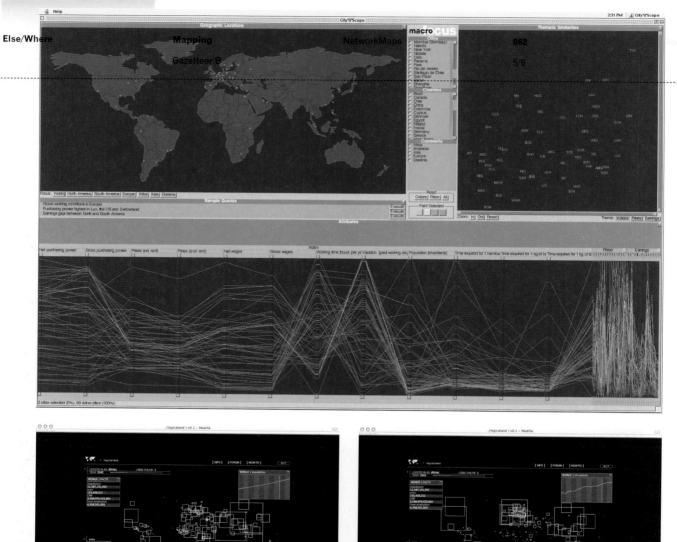

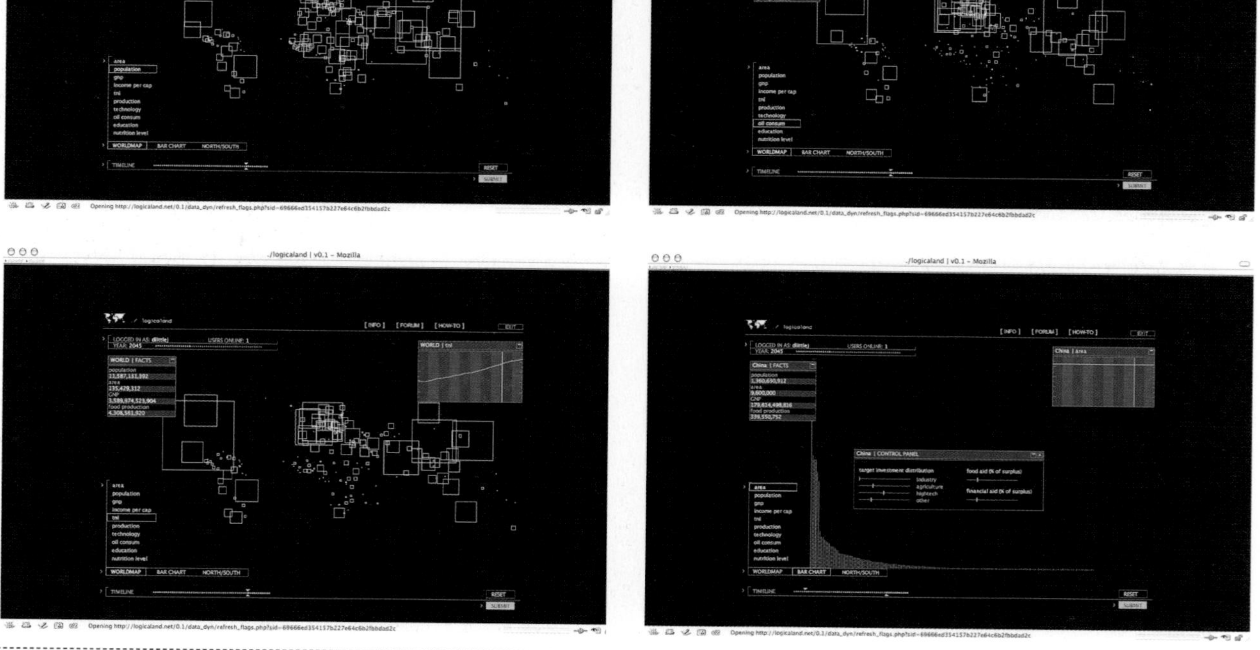

Dominique Brodbeck and **Luc Girardin, Macrofocus** *City'O'Scope*, 1997, revised in 2000 / a visualization of socio-economic data in 58 cities gathered in 2000 by UBS, the Swiss financial firm / see "Network Nations," pp. 64–67.

Michael Aschauer, Maia Gusberti, Sepp Deinhofer and **Nik Thoenen** *Logicaland*, 2004 / (bottom four images): a strategic simulation game based on visualization of predicted global economic, political and social data. Countries are indicated by overlapping white squares on a highly abstracted world map / see "Network Nations," pp. 64–67.

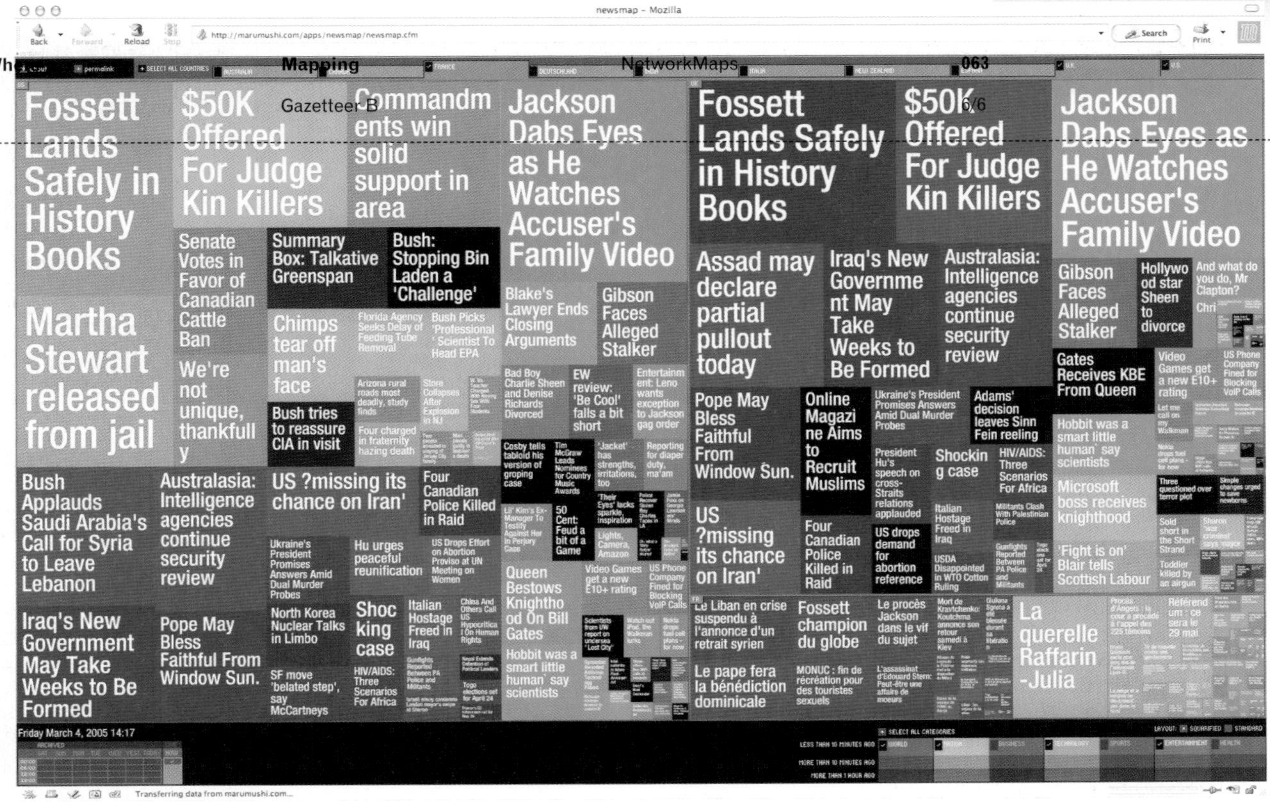

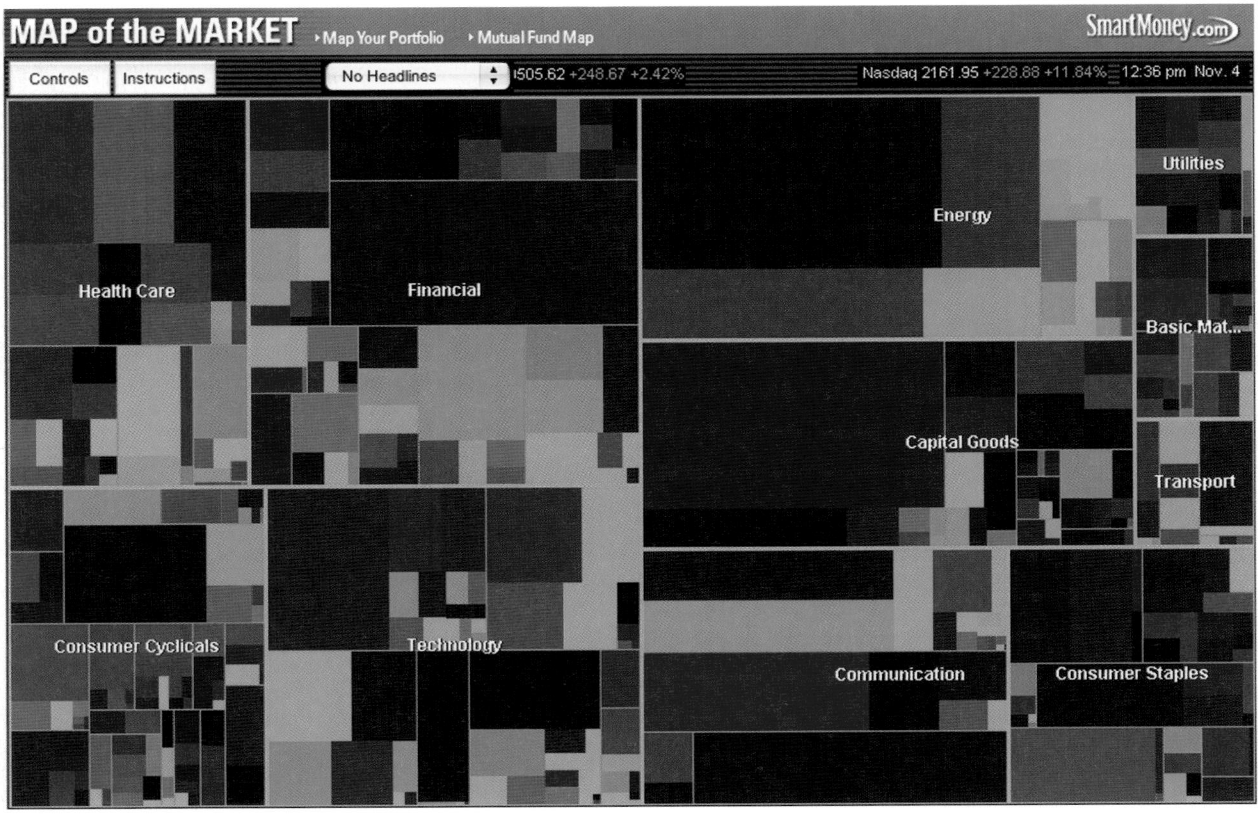

Marcos Weskamp and **Dan Albritton** *Newsmap*, 2004 (screen grab on March 5, 2005) / an application visualizing the shifting landscape of global news stories collected by the Google News aggregator / see "Network Nations," pp. 64–67.

Martin Wattenberg, Marc Frons, Joon Yu and **Jonathan Bellack** *SmartMoney Map of the Market*, 1998 (screen grab on November 4, 2005) / image © 2005 SmartMoney, a joint publishing venture of Dow Jones & Company, Inc. and Hearst SM Partnership / see "Network Nations," pp. 64–67.

NETWORK NATIONS

Dynamic interfaces for comparing and contrasting global statistics are becoming sophisticated, multi-dimensional and collaborative. BEN SCHOUTEN and YURI ENGELHARDT identify the emerging principles of information visualization in three recent interactive projects.

We express many of our plans, feelings and ideas visually, but have we lost the ability to communicate through images? There are plenty of other, perhaps more effective, ways of expressing ourselves: using the letters of the alphabet as building blocks we can mass-produce information. But the limitations of text become abundantly clear when we try to query information on the web, using search engines like Google or AltaVista, where most of the retrieved information turns out to be irrelevant to our needs. Text may be more effective than graphics for conveying abstract concepts such as "freedom" or "efficiency" (do you "see" anything when you say these to yourself?). Other information is more easily remembered when represented visually.[1]

The ascendant field of information visualization draws on ideas from several intellectual traditions, including cartography, art, graphic design, semiotics, cognitive psychology, computer graphics and human computer interaction. Through the use of maps, diagrams, animations and other visual structures, information visualization creates context and facilitates the interpretation of data. As Tamara Munzner, of the University of British Columbia, puts it, "interacting with a carefully designed visual representation of data can help us form mental models that let us perform specific tasks more effectively."[2]

Three recent interactive visualizations of global data — temperature, population, GNP (Gross National Product) or even news stories — provide a useful study of the visualization principles currently at work. In City'O'Scope, data was collected at a fixed moment in time and is therefore more or less static. In Newsmap, dynamic global data is visualized in real time as it is continuously collected. In Logicaland, dynamic global data is visualized in "virtual real-time" as predicted through a world simulation game independent of clock time.

<www.macrofocus.com/cityoscope>

<www.marumushi.com/apps/newsmap/newsmap.cfm>

<www.logicaland.net>

City'O'Scope tries to shed light on the question of where in the world we might travel — or perhaps even relocate — to pay less, earn more, and improve our living conditions. Socio-economic comparisons between 58 cities around the world are made possible through 42 different data attributes such as the average price of a hamburger, the salary of an engineer, the number of paid vacation days, or the cost of renting a three-room apartment. This data is visualized in three interactive display panels: a zoomable world map (Geographic Locations), a city comparison chart (Thematic Similarities) and a chart with "parallel-coordinates" (Attributes).

Newsmap is a software application that reflects the constantly changing landscape of global news stories collected by the Google News aggregator by mapping this into a visual space using the "tree map" visualization technique. Google News continuously crawls over 4,500 news sources from around the world, and selects headlines for its homepage entirely by a computer algorithm based on factors that include how often and on what sites a story appears elsewhere on the web. This reflects the tradition of Google's web search mechanism, which relies heavily on the collective judgment of web publishers to determine which sites offer the most valuable and relevant information.

In Newsmap, those news stories with the greatest number of other stories related to them are given the biggest surface area. News coverage can be monitored as it develops through the day, allowing visual comparison of media coverage in different countries. On an average day, far more stories are devoted to international news in UK news outlets than in the US. On the other hand, a smaller proportion of UK news is devoted to sports than in the US. According to Newsmap's creators, this visualization "is not thought to display an unbiased view of the news" but rather accentuates its bias.

1. G. H. Bower, "Mental imagery and associative learning," in L. W. Gregg (ed.), *Cognition in learning and memory*. New York: John Wiley & Sons, 1972, pp. 51 – 88. L. J. Najjar, "Principles of educational multimedia user interface design," *Human Factors*, 40:2, 1998, pp. 311 – 323.

2. Tamara Munzner, Guest Editor's Introduction to Special Issue on Information Visualization, *IEEE Computer Graphics and Applications*, 22:1, January/February 2002, pp. 20 – 21.

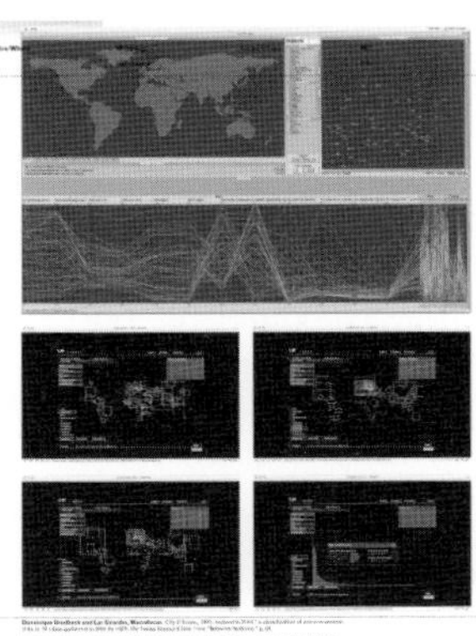

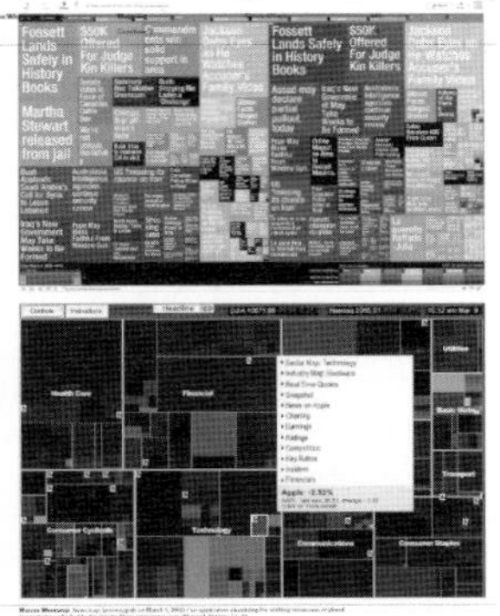

Network maps

gazetteer B 5–6/6 pp. 62–63

Logicaland is an online visualization of global economic, political and social systems that can be regarded as a multiplayer long-run strategic simulation game in which any Internet user can adjust the variables. The calculated average of all users' adjustments determines the state of the simulation. The simulation model is roughly based on the scientific global world model described in the mid-1970s by the Club of Rome.[3] Three different views of the same world data may be chosen:

1. an abstracted geographic world map in which each country is represented by a square whose surface areas are proportional to selected parameters such as geographical surface area, population, gross national product, per capita income, oil consumption, education and the like.

2. a classical bar chart.

3. an abstracted geographic map, which measures and distinguishes between regions in terms of the North/South divide.

Within the game, changes can be made to the parameters representing each country. Clicking on the individual countries reveals a pop-up control panel: various sliders can then be manipulated to control the distribution of parameters such as investments (between industry, agriculture, high-tech) and the relative amount of aid given to developing countries.

VISUALIZATION PRINCIPLES

Our well-developed visual processing skills — such as the ability to detect patterns, search quickly for specific visual details, or make visual comparisons — are hindered when data is presented in text, tables or databases. Comparison and exploration of abstract data are much easier when it is mapped into a visual structure: conceptual similarity may be visualized as shape or color similarity, or as spatial proximity. Various perceptual aspects of visual structures offer ways of representing relationships such as hierarchy, proportionality, category, order and connections. Proportionality can be visualized in spatial distances; categorization can be visualized by spatial divisions of the graphic display or by a color-coding system; hierarchy may be expressed through connections by arrows.[4] The three examples shown use specific visualization techniques to display multi-dimensional data:

SIMILARITY CHARTS AND PARALLEL COORDINATES

In City'O'Scope, a similarity chart (top right of interface) positions items — cities in this case — on the display surface according to a similarity algorithm so that those items with similar characteristics are displayed close to each other, while dissimilar items are far apart. Parallel coordinates (bottom of interface) involve many parallel axes, usually oriented vertically, one per attribute or dimension. In this case, each of the curves represents the data for one specific city.

TREEMAPS

A treemap is based on the proportional division of a display surface into sub-surfaces, where the surface areas stand for some quantitative attribute in the represented domain. Treemaps are ideal for visualizing quantitative proportions within hierarchically-nested data structures. In Newsmap, the surfaces represent the number of other news stories related to a particular story. Most treemaps also use some kind of color-coding; the SmartMoney Map of the Market, designed by Martin Wattenberg, Marc Frons, Joon Yu and Jonathan Bellack in 1998, is another well-known treemap application in which red represents losses, green represents gains and black represents neutrality.

<www.smartmoney.com/maps>

MULTIPLE VIEWS

Both City'O'Scope and Logicaland offer multiple views of the same data set — in map-format as well as chart-format — although organized in different ways. City'O'Scope displays its three views in parallel (all three are visible all the time) while Logicaland displays its three views in serial

3. Donella H. Meadows, Dennis L. Meadows, Jorgen Randers, and William W. Behrens III, *The Limits to Growth*, New York: Universe Books, 1972. Donella H. Meadows, Dennis L. Meadows and Jorgen Randers, *Beyond the Limits*. New York: Doubleday Press, 1992.

4. Yuri Engelhardt, "Meaningful Space," in Janet Abrams (ed.), *If/Then: Play—Design Implications of New Media*, Amsterdam: Netherlands Design Institute/BIS Publishers, 1999, pp. 72–74.

(the user can switch between the views by clicking on the relevant buttons at the bottom of the display). Linking is a very useful enhancement of multiple views; see Selection/Highlighting below.

SIZE AND COLOR-CODING
Size is often used to visualize proportional quantities, as in the size of the squares representing each country in Logicaland, and the rectangles representing each news story in Newsmap. Color is often used to visualize categories, as in the colors of the news stories in Newsmap.

INTERACTION PRINCIPLES

Modern interactive information visualization is based on three principles:

1. INFORMATION DISPLAY IN SPATIAL STRUCTURES
Users should be able to interact with the data in a more meaningful way than via mere hypertext linking, and actively customize what is seen in a single display; hypertext embeds linked words in text but does not show the relationships involved, so it merely enables users to jump from one predetermined display to another. City'O'Scope enables zooming and more choices in graphic display than hypertext jumps could offer.

2. FILTERS AND VIEWS
The user should be able to generate questions or look at the subject from different points of view, by using filters that tailor the displayed information. In Newsmap, both countries and news categories can be switched on and off to enhance the comparison of news coverage. In City'O'Scope, dynamic queries on a combination of attributes can be executed by using range sliders.

3. INTERACTIVE TECHNIQUES
The user should be able to explore new insights by mining information for underlying patterns and structures. In Logicaland, the oil consumption of African versus European countries is visualized as an abstract pattern.

These three general principles can be applied through the following interaction techniques:

SELECTION/HIGHLIGHTING
Highlighting is a very helpful feature of linked multiple views, such that an interaction performed within one view (e.g. highlighting of certain selections) is automatically reflected in the other two views. In City'O'Scope, multiple cities can be highlighted in different colors so these cities can be easily compared in all three views.

ZOOMING, FISH-EYE ZOOMING
A good balance of focus and context can help reduce "information overload," on the one hand, and the limitations of displays and users, on the other. As Ben Shneiderman advises, "Overview first, zoom and filter, then details on demand."[5] Zooming is possible in both the geographic and parallel-coordinates views in City'O'Scope, while Newsmap allows zooming, both by country and by news category.

DETAILS ON DEMAND
Because there is insufficient screen real estate to show all information simultaneously, good visualizations make use of details on demand, so users can retrieve further information by rolling the cursor over, or selecting, a link to obtain further information about a given country in Logicaland, or a given news story in Newsmap, where story headlines are active.

MANIPULATING THE DATA
Unlike the other two examples, Logicaland is interactive to the second power: in addition to changing the display of the data, the user can change the data itself by adjusting the settings of the simulation game.

5. Stuart Card, Jock Mackinlay and Ben Shneiderman, *Readings in Information Visualization, Using Vision to Think.* San Francisco: Morgan Kaufmann Publishers, 1999.

6. Donald A. Norman, *Things that Make Us Smart.* Reading, MA: Addison-Wesley Publishing Company, 1993.

WHY VISUALIZATIONS ARE USEFUL

The external representation of knowledge has a long history, the most basic form being writing with pen and paper. The visualizations discussed here are external knowledge representations, cognitive tools that help us think and communicate. As Donald Norman has remarked, "The power of the unaided mind is highly overrated. Without external aids, memory, thought, and reasoning are all constrained. . . . The real power comes from devising external aids that enhance cognitive abilities."[6]

The visual representations in City'O'Scope take advantage of our cognitive skills in filtering and choosing focus and context on demand, making outliers, patterns and anomalies easy to spot. Its interface encourages exploration and stimulates formulation of new questions and hypotheses such as: What are the differences in working conditions between Europe and the US and how big is the earnings gap between North and South America? Interactive maps are more than merely external aids to personal memory; they are becoming tools of communication and collaboration.

THINGS TO COME

The development of tools that display and process data, transforming it into relevant information, presents both exciting and difficult challenges. On the one hand, we may wish to include an enormous quantity of information; on the other, the amount of information that can be displayed on a given canvas, and handled by a given user, may be very limited. To balance these desires, most visualizations rely on display principles such as multiple views, zooming, and color-, size- and texture-coding. Many of these visualizations offer the same functionality in different layouts.

Most information visualizations offer displays of a priori data, optimized according to parameters set by the user — an effective way of reducing information overload so users can handle large sets of information. However, most such visualizations are one-way streets. More complex information search queries will only be possible when additional contextual information is provided by the user. In the future, visualizations in a multi-user environment may combine the whiteboard functionalities of collaborative work with individual interactions and eye movement tracking. The most exciting prospects may be the possibility of perceptual inference with the user. It is the task of multidisciplinary research to incorporate more elements of human experience into mapping technologies. In one example of perceptual inference, the PARISS interface (Panoramic, Adaptive and Reconfigurable Interface for Similarity Search), textiles can be selected visually from a database by dragging and dropping a subset of displayed examples. The interface can then be instructed to mimic classifications and provide additional textiles matching the user's preference.[7]

Multi-dimensionality of data remains a tough problem, since display surfaces (computer screens) are two-dimensional, but many important aspects of information are often not limited to two dimensions and can vary over time. Multi-dimensional display techniques such as the parallel coordinates used in City'O'Scope can help solve this problem. However, with developments in ubiquitous computing, the field of information visualization stands to benefit from more immersive and pervasive interfaces. Increased computer power and better hardware will enable 3D visualizations, and human interaction will be transformed through distributed interfaces (screens, gloves). By combining methods of interaction with the functionalities of collaborative work, social interactions become possible.

In a multi-sensory environment, supported with pervasive computer technology, new bio-inspired information systems can capture and interpret what users are doing and assist them in realtime. Such systems are expected to appear in public places, on work floors and in home environments. Ramana Rao, founder of Inxight, looks forward to when we'll have overcome some past distractions: "We were willing to drop back considerably in interface quality for many years because of the rich sources of information and knowledge, new services, and connections to other people available through the Internet. Only now are we getting back to considering simpler and richer ways of interacting with content, services, people."[8]

As the real world becomes the computer interface, communicating via visualizations may become as easy and direct as communicating with language.

7. G. Caenen, G. Frederix, A.A.M. Kuijk, E.J. Pauwels and B.A.M. Schouten, "Show me what you mean/PARISS: A CBIR-interface that learns by example," in *Lecture Notes on Computer Science, Fourth International Conference on Visual Information Systems* (VISUAL 2000), Lyon, November 2000. Springer Verlag, 2000, pp. 257–268.

8. Ramana Rao, "Rao's Information Flow," *Information Flow* email newsletter, Issue 2.2, February 2003. <http://www.ramanarao.com/informationflow/archive/2003-02.html>.

MAPPING CONVERSATIONS

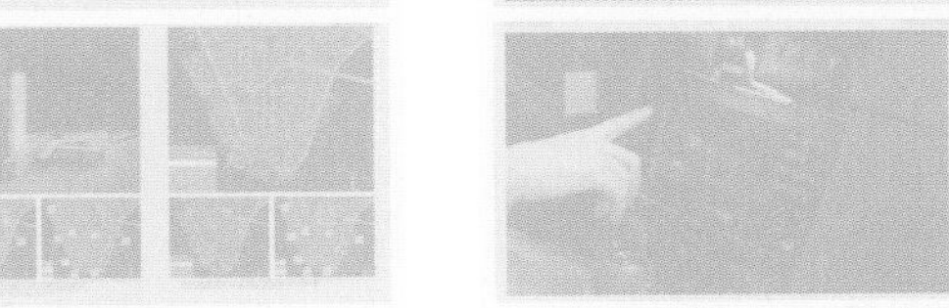

As mapping becomes more prevalent in online social spaces, we will see increased sophistication in the use of metaphorical and evocative renderings. This means going well beyond simply choosing a visual metaphor, but also choosing which data is shown, what remains unpictured, and how it is mapped.

Judith Donath, "Conversations As Maps, Part 1"

CONVERSATIONS AS MAPS / PART 1

Tools for visualizing group conversations — whether via email, in Internet chat rooms or on mobile phones — are proliferating. We invited six leading exponents of Conversation Mapping to discuss their experimental prototypes in an online roundtable held over several weeks by email, then in a two-hour Internet chat session that connected seven cities and four time zones. What are the limits of current online systems for collective conversation? How does Conversation Mapping affect participants' behavior in the social networks depicted? Can techniques from cartographic mapping and face-to-face dialogue make up for the deficiencies of online discourse? Examples of Conversation Mapping appear between Part 1 (email) and Part 2 (chat), which begins on p. 92; three different visualizations of this discussion by its participants are shown on pp. 98—103.

CLOCKWISE FROM TOP LEFT:

JANET ABRAMS / Director / University of Minnesota Design Institute

JUDITH DONATH / Director / Sociable Media Group, MIT Media Lab

PETER HALL / Senior Editor / University of Minnesota Design Institute

MARK HANSEN / Associate Professor, Statistics and Design | Media Arts, UCLA

MARCO SUSANI / Director / Advanced Concepts Group, Motorola

WARREN SACK / Assistant Professor / Film and Digital Media, UC Santa Cruz

RICHARD ROGERS / Lecturer in New Media / U of Amsterdam / Director, govcom.org

VALDIS KREBS / Management Consultant, Software Developer, orgnet.com

JANET ABRAMS: - Minneapolis
Given the range of visualization approaches represented by this group, is it useful to call what you do 'mapping?' Does your work borrow consciously from cartographic mapping or significantly depart from it? How did you each get into Conversation Mapping in the first place?

WARREN SACK: - Santa Cruz
My prior work in computers and education and the analysis of broadcast media made me wonder whether the Internet was another 'space' where alternatives might be produced to the ideologies of mainstream media. I write computer programs to map online conversations so participants can reflect on their own 'common sense' and visualize alternatives, i.e., 'uncommon sense'. I'm interested, in general, in the intersection of politics and design.

I think it is worthwhile calling this area of investigation 'mapping' because it has to do with the production of instruments of orientation and navigation. Etymologically, the verb 'navigate' comes from the words navis (ship) and agere (to guide). **In navigating a large information space such as a Usenet newsgroup archive, the 'self' replaces the 'ship'. Hence, a browser or any other navigation software is best evaluated with respect to how well it supports self-governance.** Very Large-Scale Conversation (VLSC) is an intercultural phenomenon: it's usually conducted on the Internet between participants from many different countries. A VLSC browser should enable us to understand our location in a wider network of social and semantic relations, and make us aware of the collective self-organization constructed through the VLSC text and talk as well as the culturally-specific assumptions that go into its software design.

RICHARD ROGERS: - Amsterdam
I'm not a 'Conversation Mapper' but rather a 'Link Mapper' with occasional forays into lexical and semantic analysis of web pages as well as news and blogs. I came to mapping in 1996 when the International Herald Tribune asked me to write a story in a supplement about Kyoto. I searched AltaVista for 'climate change' and noticed that sites in the climate change 'space' link selectively. I began looking at interlinking from a social and reputational standpoint, and about linking as a 'politics of association'. Lately at <gomcom.org> we've been scraping news and blogs, and trying to create visualizations that show the evolution of a story across the newssphere and blogosphere, with a current focus on 'mapping the ideational space of the Palestinian-Israeli conflict'.

MARCO SUSANI: - Cambridge
Being trained as an architect, I've dealt with maps — the good old maps that represent physical places — throughout my career. About 10 years ago, when I began dealing with interactive media, I encountered maps that described content, navigation and information architectures. Later, working on the social use of digital media in public places, I developed the notion of the 'territory as interface', anticipating what today would be called 'location-based interactions and services', of which maps are a fundamental

element. Recently, I've tried to formulate an atlas of Knowledge Auras, starting from the hypothesis that knowledge diffusion is based on flows (auras) that fuse social relationships, digital information and physical space.

MARK HANSEN: My field is statistics. Before I joined UCLA, I was a member of
- Los Angeles
the technical staff at Bell Laboratories; part of my work involved creating models of how people navigate telecommunications systems. One project involved using proxy logs to tease out complete search sessions — an odd introduction to information retrieval and text processing. In my collaboration with Ben Rubin, these questions have turned from log-centered analyses (who connects to whom via whatever mechanism) to a content-based analysis.

JUDITH DONATH: I did my graduate work at the Architecture Machine Group
- Cambridge
at MIT (a precursor to the Media Lab), and became very interested in the social implications of vast communications networks. I'm interested in maps of large scale conversations in which we think of the already created text as a terrain on which active participants are navigating, in maps of personal email archives, and in alternative media for depicting conversations, e.g., audio or large installations. An increasing amount of our social interaction with other people (and people-like agents) will be occurring online. Visualizations of these interactions can have a huge impact on how legible these social environments are, what behaviors they encourage, and how appealing they are.

VALDIS KREBS: I'm a management consultant and software developer;
- Columbus
I started mapping as a human resources manager at TRW. I'm interested in new applications of network mapping and metrics. **When you interact with folks face to face, you develop a picture of the network in your mind: who else is around, who talks to whom, etc. That is not usually available online. In cyberspace, the context of the social space you're embedded in is missing. A map can help orient you.** When a stranger contacts me over the Net, I immediately Google them to see who and what they are associated with. Even better would be a new service that showed me a person's ego-network (created from public data on the web) so I could see if we know anyone in common, and who influences their thinking.

JA: Hmm: 'ego-network' — can you expand on that?

VK: 'Ego' is an academic term for a network around one individual. Ego's direct contacts are called 'alters'. It's nice to see 'alters' and their interconnections. Two-step links (FOAFs — Friends of Friends) would be a bonus.

RR: A few years ago, people with a rather unique name would use a Google search return on their name as their bio link. Today, such an ego network is a map of all those sites that mention you, so you see the terms of projects you're most associated with, according to others. This is different from

Valdis' suggestion in which relationships (business, personal, etc.) between people are made public. An intriguing post-social software project would discover relationships between people, using relationship data that people may not wish to reveal about themselves. There is a big difference between what some call 'relationship design' and 'relationship discovery'.

MH: My field, statistics, has been the victim of this shift from design to discovery. The notion of a simple statistical model faded in the face of extremely large repositories of data. The idea of discovering patterns in this context emerged in computer science literature and gave birth to a new subfield: data mining. Ironically, the term 'mining' had previously been used to describe 'overfitting'— positing and testing many different models — in effect, searching for statistical significance. I reckon the shift to discovery happened also because big data sets (many records or observations on many variables) are hard to visualize or explore so something is needed to identify 'structures'. Data mining is one way, albeit algorithmically, to find these features.

PETER HALL: I've been thinking about Fredric Jameson's comment in his 1988 essay "Cognitive Mapping" that "the incapacity to map socially is as crippling to political experience as the analogous incapacity to map spatially is for urban experience."[1] So is the mapping of online conversations an attempt to counter the sense of alienation we feel in these extensions of real community space?

- Brooklyn

JD: Yes. I think of these mappings as a way of creating an inhabitable space. They are not designed for the distant and critical eye of the social scientist or other observer; they are made for the participants in the conversation, as a way of making the interaction richer, making its patterns and nuances more readily perceivable. One reason online communication can be alienating is that one's impressions of the other participants are so abstract. A Conversation Mapping can construct a rendering of each participant from the history of that person's interactions in the environment. Such a depiction is meaningful: it can help make each person stand out as an individual. Persistent history is the information world's version of the body.

1. Fredric Jameson, "Cognitive Mapping," in Cary Nelson and Lawrence Grossberg, eds., *Marxism and the Interpretation of Culture*. Chicago: University of Illinois Press, 1988. p. 353.

PH: Judith, your PeopleGarden project, in refuting the idea of a neutral visual language, seems to embrace the idea of the map as an interpretive, perhaps poetic filter. Yet, as you acknowledge, the garden metaphor has limitations. Are you actively pursuing a more ambiguous or open visual language, or is it a case of needing a different map for each terrain?

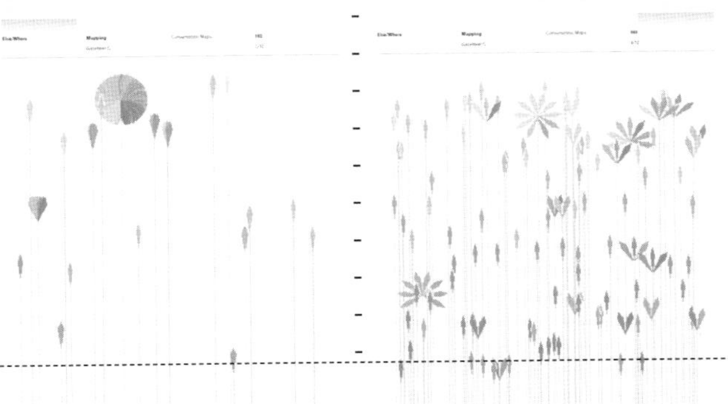

Conversation maps

JD: Both. Neutrality is a complex subject. There's no truly neutral visualization, since even the most seemingly minute design decision — such as whether an axis is oriented up or down — can influence how people interpret the image. Up is growth, more, better, bigger; down is deeper, heavier. These may be subconscious interpretations, far from the designers' intent when they chose to run their axis or expand the hierarchies in a particular direction. But they are still real forces in shaping people's interpretations. So even the most minimalist bar graph is not truly neutral. Some designs, like PeopleGarden, are highly metaphorical and bring a strongly evocative cast to the depictions.

<http://smg.media.mit.edu/papers/>

I try to teach my students to be aware of these meanings, and be deliberate in how they use them. Any line has editorial meaning since, in order to draw a line, you have to choose: is it black or pink, thick or thin, rounded or angular? I want them to be aware of these choices as they create their designs. **In some situations, one wants a mapping that is as neutral as possible; in others, one wants a mapping that is gracefully or pointedly poetic. The goal of my teaching is to enable the students to be able to choose which they are making.** As mapping becomes more prevalent in online social spaces, we will see increased sophistication in the use of metaphorical and evocative renderings. This means going well beyond simply choosing a visual metaphor, but also choosing what data is shown, what remains unpictured, and how it is mapped.

JA: Which comes first: the idea of how you might enable the participants in a collective conversation to array themselves in a 'space' of communication, or the specific content of their communication?

WS: I try to start by clearly identifying issues of social or political theory that I want to illustrate or interrogate with the software design. In Conversation Map, I was interested in combining structuralist ideas of social interaction (as articulated in structural analysis, the branch of sociology that takes social networks as central to its work) and structuralist ideas of language (described by Saussure, Firth and others, and extended by computational linguists). This was a bit tongue-in-cheek since I'm not actually a structuralist from a social theory perspective. I tried to make the oldness of the theoretical machinery underlying the software apparent by appropriating both the visual aesthetics of social network analysis and an antiquated computer look (circa 1980, VT-100 black and green screen). I hoped to reveal ideas about 'technologies of the self' as described by Foucault: what techniques can be designed to help us reflect on and practice various forms of self-governance, where 'self' can refer both to an individual and to a large body of people.

<www.sims.berkeley.edu/~sack/CM/>

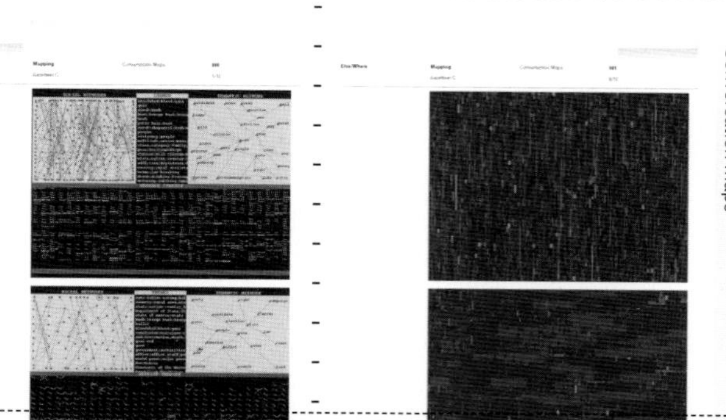
Conversation maps

In my latest project, Agonistics (an art commission from rhizome.org that stretches the definition of 'game'), I am investigating a different theoretical premise: ideas articulated by the political theorist Chantal Mouffe about 'agonistic pluralism', i.e., that democratic debate is more of a competition than a rational argument.

<http://artport.whitney.org/gatepages/artists/sack/>

PH: Mark, Listening Post (created in collaboration with artist Ben Rubin) and the spam out-takes on your website seem to celebrate the idea of a self-organizing object (or machine) that sees and speaks in a revealingly non-human way. How much human curatorial activity is required to make these projects presentable? Are the models for how people navigate telecommunications systems helpful in analyzing online discussions? And has the Semantic Web project influenced your text-mining endeavors?

MH: The spam out-takes are probably machine-generated, but hand selected and ordered (by me); in Listening Post (LP), the fragments are human generated, but algorithmically organized (by machine). LP is an attempt to create a structure for the text-stream we have assembled, but this exercise depends on human-specified notions of 'distance' and 'similarity' so we can create a 'natural 'space' for the text fragments to inhabit.

<www.earstudio.com/projects/listeningpost.html>

Many (exploratory) multivariate statistical methods start with some kind of 'natural space' for a set of data. Points (separate observations) in this space can be compared, and there are various methods for 'mapping', arranging or projecting these points into a two-, three- or four-dimensional space. For certain kinds of data, the 'natural space' is relatively easy to specify. For example, if you have 'n' observations, each on 'm' variables, then you might think of your data as 'n' points in 'm'-dimensional Euclidean space.

If the data are text fragments, the 'variables' might be the number of times different words were used in the fragments (a HUGE space), or you might reduce the data in some way. With text, there are various ways to measure distance, and certain words might be weighted as being more important for judging similarity. Listening Post uses ideas of information retrieval, natural language processing and 'text mining' to structure the flow of text. In some cases, we use notions of distance or similarity to provide clusters of similar fragments; in others, we remove all context and rely on random selection.

Conversation maps

gazetteer C 7–8/12 pp. 86–87

PH: Warren, can you give an example of a browser that does a good job of supporting self-governance, and one that doesn't?

WS: By 'self' I mean a collective self: the group, network or community that makes online discussions a vital part of its discourse; I don't mean the browser. I'm interested in self-governing systems that incorporate machines and people. Fredric Jameson has argued for a new mode of representation "in which we may again begin to grasp our positioning as individual and collective subjects and regain a capacity to act and struggle that is at present neutralized by our spatial and our social confusion. The political form of postmodernism will have as its vocation the invention and projection of a global cognitive mapping on a social as well as a spatial scale."[2]

A browser that supports this sort of 'cognitive mapping' (or what I prefer to call self-governance) would include facilities for reflecting on the history and social dynamics of the discussion, allowing the participants to reflect on their individual and collective positions in terms of race, class, gender, sexuality and political, social and economic conditions. Everyone in this discussion is working on design projects that address these concerns. To pick an outside example, Marc Smith and his group at Microsoft Research have been working on producing a 'social accounting' of a newsgroup with their Netscan project: who posts, how often, whose posts generate replies, etc. Browsers that don't support this facility are easy to come by: practically nothing in conventional newsgroup browsers/interfaces — Internet Explorer, Mozilla, etc — provides a means to reflect on the group as a whole or one's position in the group.

<http://netscan.research.microsoft.com/treemap/>

PH: I'd like to hear more about democratic debate as a kind of competition. It was bewildering to hear in the media that John Kerry won the first presidential debate but that Bush staged a comeback; to my eyes Kerry showed far better debating skills in all three debates. I was obviously missing some of the common sense! Warren, could your Agonistics game engine theoretically be applied to a past event in a different medium, i.e., the televised debates?

WS: The game, in this case, was the sum total of all of the news and media produced, exchanged and distributed prior to the election. Advocating the view that 'Bush made a comeback' is an instance where the main players (Bush and Kerry) were not acting directly, but rather through their intermediaries. Most of American media is (despite the spin of the right) owned and operated by politically conservative corporations. It's not surprising that they would want to characterize Bush's debate performance as better than it was. So the game in this case was far larger than the few hours of presidential debates. And a win, for instance, is getting the majority of voters to believe that Kerry is a flip-flopper or that Bush has made our country weaker, not stronger. These are the strategic struggles for political 'common sense' in which the Republican Party invests millions, while the Democrats, unfortunately, have invested very little. George Lakoff and his colleagues at the Rockridge Institute is one of the few exceptions. My Agonistics game, unfortunately, only works on newsgroups or weblogs, not on the entire media environment. But, yes, it can replay an earlier episode. Here is a sample analysis of the newsgroup <alt.politics.elections> from before we went to the polls:
<dmedia.ucsc.edu/~wsack/Agonistics/APE/Interface/-agon200.html>

<www.rockridgeinstitute.org/>

2. Fredric Jameson, "Postmodernism, or The Cultural Logic of Late Capitalism," *New Left Review* 146, 1984, p. 92.

RR: Information, generally, is in competition to be the top-ranked return for any given query, certainly on the web. I'm always intrigued by the state of the competition. Query any social issue on Google and you can watch sources compete to provide information. A terrorism query on Google currently returns <ready.gov>, <cia.gov> and <defendamerica.mil> in the top 10. Compare the New York Times bestseller list with that of <allconsuming.net>. Who is more familiar with <wikipedia.org> than Encyclopedia Britannica? Other recommendation aggregators—from news and blogs to bookmarks—each use a different means to return information about your query, based on distinctive epistemologies. **Who knows better: the collective intelligence or the editors? This is a different debate from the one conducted by 18th-Century political philosophers, which distinguished only between the mob and the wise. Howard Rheingold gave us 'Smart Mobs', not 'Wise Mobs'. We're only just starting to sense that there's a new epistemological debate unfolding.**

PH: Warren, can you give an example of the 'culturally specific assumptions' in the design of software for navigating Very Large Scale Conversations?

WS: Culturally specific assumptions are built into all interfaces. The ideal is that you should be able to use the interface without consulting a big manual, but to achieve this, interface designers need to presuppose a lot about the user. For example, we're supposed to recognize that things we no longer want go into the trash/recycling bin on the computer desktop. Cultural specificity is even more apparent in software for newsgroups, weblogs and chat environments. As Deborah Tannen and other linguists have shown, **different rules of conversation pertain to different social groups. In certain populations, not to interrupt one's interlocutor in conversation is rude because silence is taken to be lack of attention, whereas in other populations, waiting one's turn is considered civil and interruption is rude.**

JD: Going back to Valdis' earlier suggestion for a Google ego-network service, this could reasonably be done for academics by mapping co-citations and references. By adding in some data about who else is in their department and where they did their graduate work, you could get an informative depiction. And given the existence of Google Scholar, much of this could be done automatically today. But for the rest of the world, and for the non research-related thoughts in a scholar's head, the data about one's network is at best uneven. Which raises two related questions. **When is it better not to create a map at all? And how can we indicate that our map is of the indefinite and the inaccurate? Maps make data appear definitive. As makers of visualizations, we need to work on finding ways to indicate the reliability of the data.** If I map your social network based on data I've drawn from the Net, I am pretty sure I've gotten maybe 5 to 30 percent of your network, and I've got some indication of who's important to you, but I may be totally off the mark.

This is a big problem in the mapping of any social data — such as conversations — where by fixing something onto an image, we give it a solidity that it does not merit. It is very easy to measure some data in a conversation — such as who speaks the most — and depict it in some way. From a purely quantitative standpoint, if the data and the depiction match, then it is good. But, from a more nuanced standpoint, it's important to know how representative the data is. Does it really indicate the inferences one is likely to draw from the depiction?

MH: Excellent, Judith: **uncertainty and how to depict it. It's hard, especially when you are not dealing with simple objects. How do you judge a depiction?** I recently attended a talk by Stanford University statistics professor Dave Donoho to a group of mathematicians who are starting to use ideas from topology (more or less) to abstract data mapping. He made the case that over several decades, statisticians have been 'bitten' by the reification of maps of various kinds. He was specifically referring to the use of multidimensional scaling and the sociological and psychometric work done in the 1950s and 60s. **Providing a map that juxtaposes or clusters objects in a certain way can be a pretty powerful thing; the representation tends to take on a life of its own.**

VK: I agree: a warning label — DATA IS PARTIAL AND MAY BE OUTDATED — is necessary in most network maps. Partial maps are still useful, if they are accurate! When I sketch a driving map for someone, I draw in only a few roads, not to scale. They still seem to find their way to my office, or to the airport, or....

PH: It's a really interesting problem, given that the language of maps has its own history in claiming territorial and navigational authority and, in the case of the network map, portraying a system as a closed, efficient circuit. I'm thinking of the London Underground Diagram first drawn by an electrical engineer. Artist Mark Lombardi chose pencil to draw his 'relationship discovery' network maps of shady deals and corporate/political interests: pencil could connote the idea of a sketch with less finality than, say, a printed map.

JA: I'd like to bring Marco back into the ring with some questions about network topologies, square versus squirly. Your archetypes of mobile phone social behavior — the Kama Sutra, as you put it, of one-to-one/one-to-many communication possibilities — seem to be more about the mapping of psychological space than of network reality. Could Valdis's network topology diagrams, in his "Social Life of Routers" paper, be renamed according to your more poetic taxonomy of human interconnections?

Conversation maps

<www.flow.doorsofperception.com/content/susani_trans.html>

<www.orgnet.com/SocialLifeOfRouters.pdf>

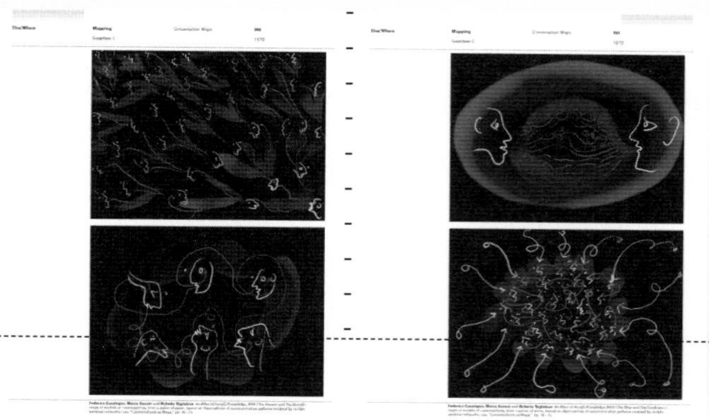

See "Signal Failure," p. 166.
See Gazeteer A, Mark Lombardi plate, p. 43.

MS: In this discussion, so far, it seems we're often treating maps as a 'true' representation of data, hence the need to warn that DATA IS PARTIAL AND MAY BE OUTDATED. There's great value in considering maps for that as well as maps that create a subjective view of the network (ego and alter). **My perspective is different: I'm pushing toward maps that represent the interpretation of a phenomenon, rather than its actual reality. I'm using maps to interpret the social phenomena around networks, not to describe these phenomena. Such maps don't really describe the network topologies, but rather the social/conversational 'densities' stimulated by networks.**

My interest has shifted to studying 'maps' like religious cosmogonies (mandalas, etc.) that represent topologies where DATA IS DEFINITELY NOT AVAILABLE—AND IS NOT THE POINT ANYWAY or representations like the Kama Sutra that 'map' a finite number of positions of the infinite possible positions. These are maps that describe rituals and beliefs: they're less diagrammatic, and apparently more distant from reality (or its realistic representation), but sometimes much more meaningful in understanding it.

JA: What would be the change in meaning if you were to redraw your Womb, Daisy, Jellyfish, etc., models as black-square nodes and straight-line links, rather than gestural faces and breath-like swirls of communication?

MS: I deliberately used a graphic fuzziness to describe the fuzziness of these relational spaces. This is an evolution of my earlier studies of architectural representation and immaterial sensorial aspects. If you want to map an architectural space in terms of what it is, you might be happy with a conventional layout: top view, straight lines, correct measures to scale. But if you want to represent it for what you feel it is, that objective map is no longer so meaningful. **Fuzzy diagrams help declare that sensorial perception is rich, profound and intangible, and rational straight lines aren't. In my network maps, swirly links are a way to represent the immateriality, frailty and ethereality of conversational links.**

JA: Have your diagrams of network connections proved useful? Do they enable you to reshape the tools themselves, or lead to new ideas for products or services that could be implemented in the real world?

MS: In terms of making something useful (for my company, I presume you're implying) out of these maps, the answer is yes. Understanding the patterns of relationships between humans definitely should influence the work of a telecommunications company. Understanding that social tribes have strong—almost isolated and introverted—patterns of communication helps even in trivial aspects like designing the structure and behavior of a phonebook.

"CONVERSATIONS AS MAPS" CONTINUES ON P. 92.

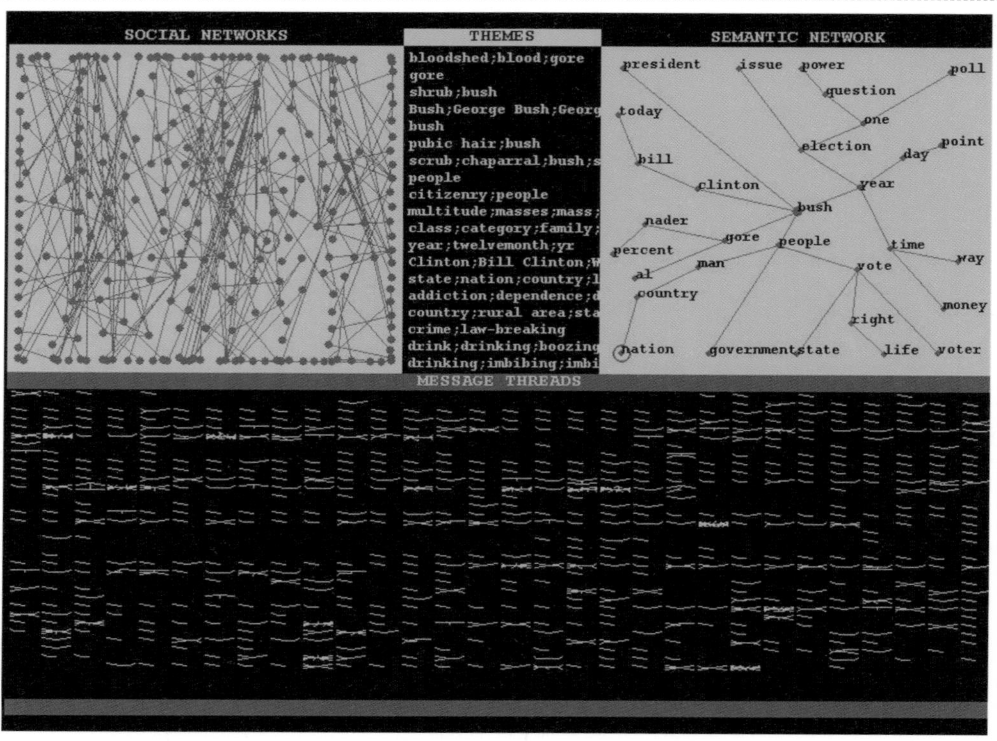

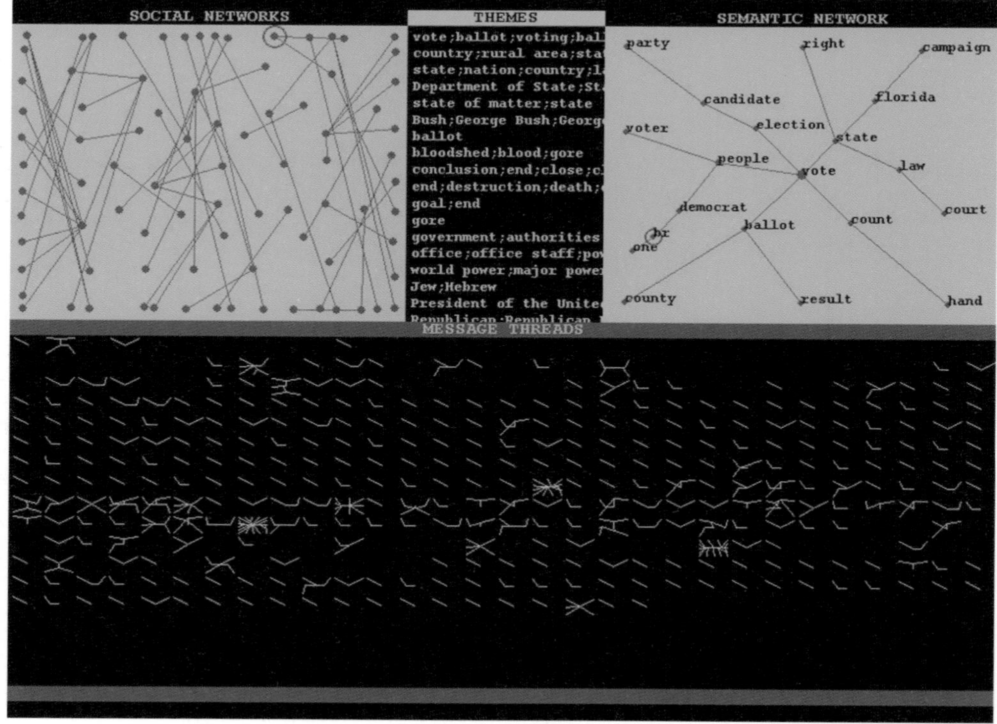

Warren Sack *Conversation Map*, 1997–2000 / two screen-shots of a browser designed to support "Very Large-Scale Conversations" such as newsgroups and email lists. The system computes and visualizes—in a stylistic nod to the aesthetics of early computer terminals—who is talking to whom, and the subject-matter, central terms and possible metaphors of their conversation. Social networks are shown in the upper left corner; the emergent semantic network is depicted in the upper right corner; discussion themes are listed in the upper middle section; thumbnail sketches of all discussion threads analyzed are shown in the lower half / see "Conversations as Maps," p. 74.

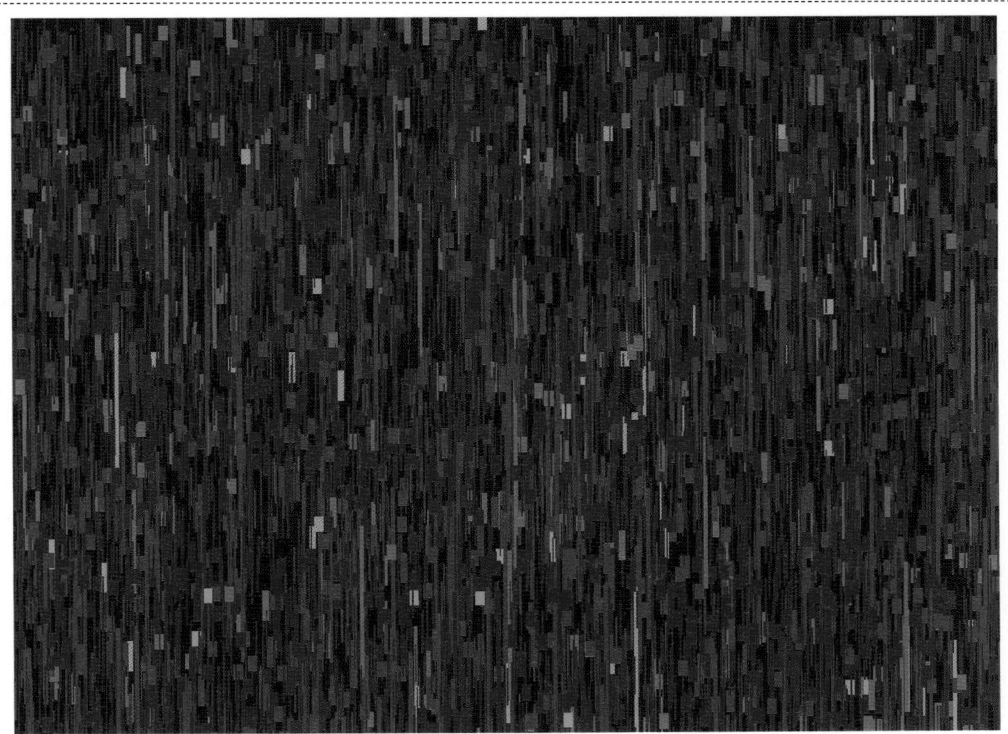

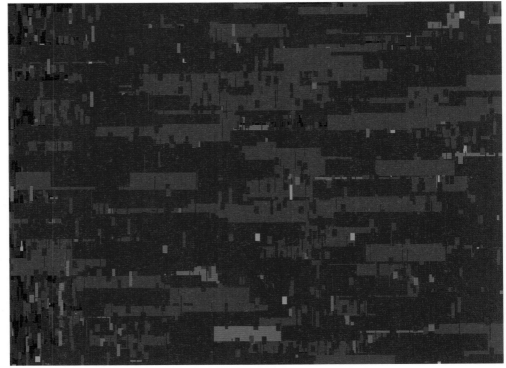

Judith Donath, Hyun-Yeul Lee, Danah Boyd, J. Goler and **Scott Golder, The Sociable Media Group, MIT Media Lab**
Loom 2, 2001 / sketches exploring ways of representing the atmosphere within newsgroups. The goal was to create a landscape of discussion groups, in which color and visual patterns create a topography of information. Each rectangle stands for a person. (top): "Anger," where height represents the degree of anger in a person's comments, compared with their activity level, quantified by analyzing the use of "angry" language and punctuation. (bottom): "Responses per Person," where width indicates the average number of responses a person receives per post/ © MIT Media Lab / see "Conversations as Maps," pp. 73–74.

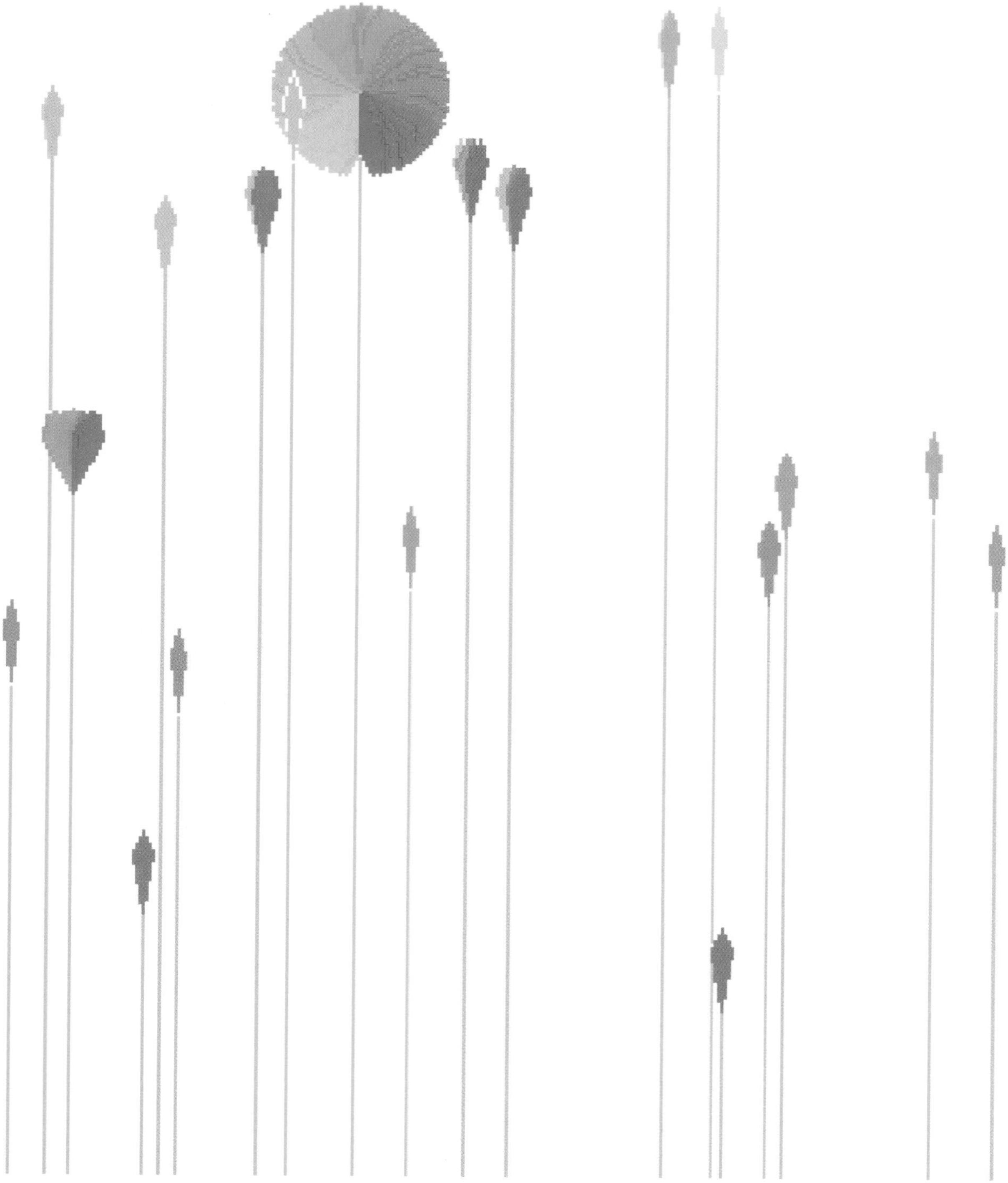

Judith Donath and **Rebecca Xiong, The Sociable Media Group, MIT Media Lab** *PeopleGarden*: *Creating data portraits for users*, 1999 / (this page): experimental visualization of participation in online conversation, where petals represent each person's contributions to an online conversation, such as newsgroup postings. Older petals move to the left to make room for new ones, and fade with age; the newest ones have the most saturated color. (opposite page): pistol-like dots over a petal indicate responses to that posting. Hue indicates whether a posting is an initial post (red) or a follow-up response (blue) / / see "Conversations as Maps," pp. 73–74.

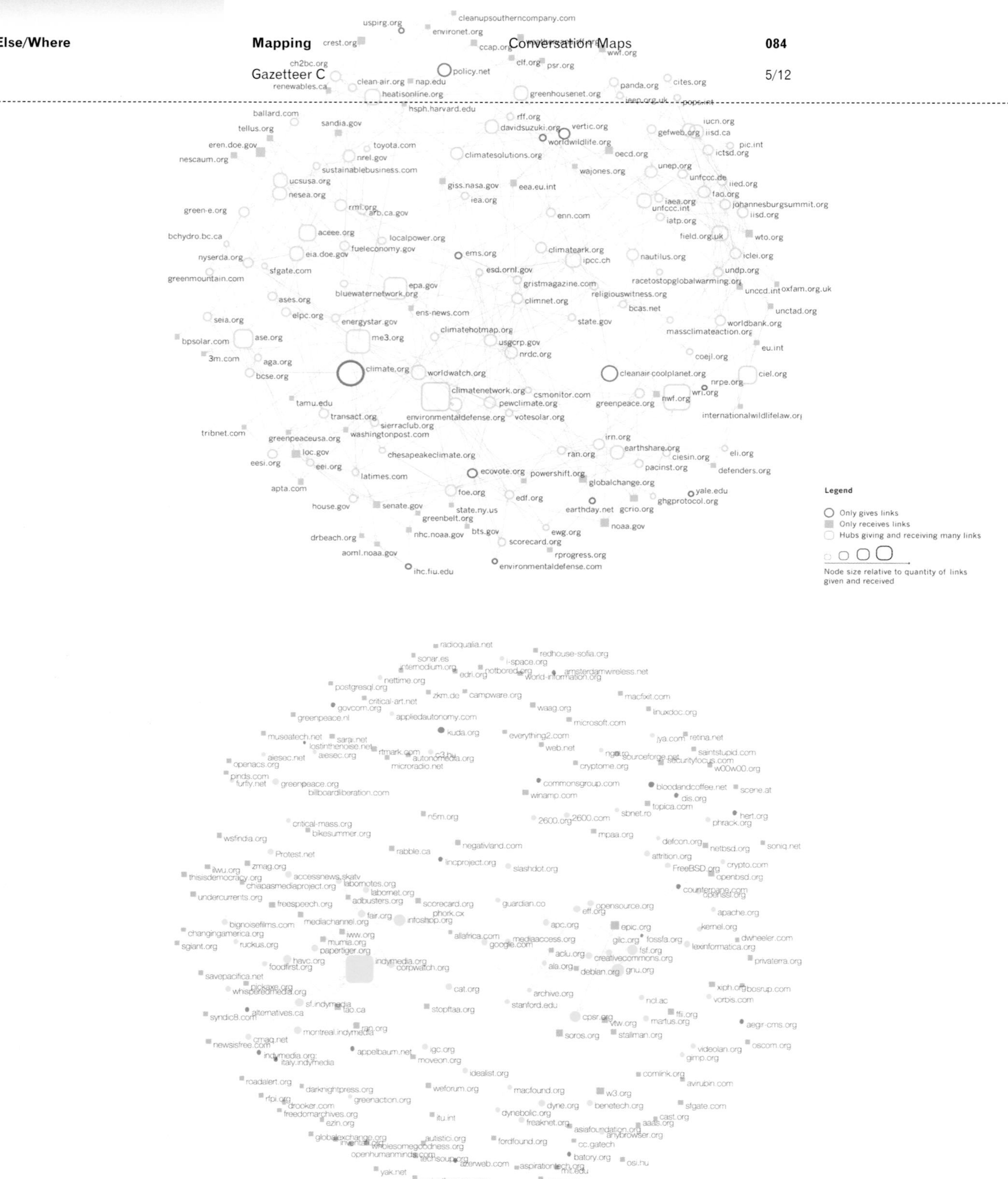

Richard Rogers, govcom.org (top): *Climate Change, U.S. groups in International Context*, 2004 / map of links between websites in the climate change arena, indicating the disconnect between inter-governmental debate on climate change regulation and ground-level initiatives by non-governmental organizations (NGOs) and companies often funded by the U.S. government. Commissioned for Al Gore's climate change network strategy by the E-Volve Foundation. (bottom): *Summer Source: Software Camp for NGOs*, 2003 / map of links between websites of NGOs and open source developers, with a few potential brokers in between / data from *issuecrawler.net* / graph developed in *ReseauLu* by Aguidel / design by anderemedia.nl / see "Counter Cartographies," p. 22, "Conversations as Maps," p. 72.

How 'procedural democrats' and 'participatory democrats' differ in resources and approach to the FCC's proposed deregulation of media ownership, 2003.

Protest
$
Membership & No Paid Staff
Other
Event
$$$$
Membership & 6+ Paid Staff
No Membership & 3 to 6 Paid Staff
$$$
Press
Hearing
Lobby
No Membership & 6+ Paid Staff
$$$
No Membership & No Paid Staff
Ø
Comments
Letter
$$$
Membership & 3 to 6 Paid Staff
Information
Research

Low-cost democracy
Procedural democrats with no resources participate in the formal political process: filing of comments. Participatory democrats with no resources turn towards protest and step outside the political process.

Data from survey of approximately 90 organizations urging FCC limits on media ownership, 2003.

Co-occurrence analysis of organization type and activities.

Legend
○ Organizational activities.
■ Organization type according to resource base.
Ø-$$$$ Resource scale indication.

Product of the workshop ________ Social Life of Issues 9
The News about Networks: Making Issues into Rights?
Amsterdam, The Netherlands. June 04
Analysis_ Data from the Media Policy Action Directory by the International Media Action Center (mediaactioncenter.org). Analysis by Seeta Peña Gangadharan and Catherine Somzé. Visualization with Reseau Lu by aguidel.com. Design by Marieke van Dijk anderemedia.nl.

Occupied and Unoccupied Media Spaces

The adoption of separation fence, security fence, separation barrier, security barrier, security wall, separation wall, and apartheid wall in Palestinian, Israeli and Western News.

Apartheid Wall, used by Al Jazeerah and the Palestinian governmental press agency, is a fusion of the former South African apartheid regime and the former Berlin Wall. The richer term may be thought of as an appeal. It implies racism, discrimination, a militarized zone, a bleak future. It also places the Palestinians behind a wall. There is no exit.

Apartheid Wall
Aljazeerah.info
International Press Center (press release)

Now, anti-graffiti paint is to be used to prevent graffiti-writers from making the fence look like a wall, in the style of the Berlin Wall. (Graffiti is already on both sides of the 'wall'.)

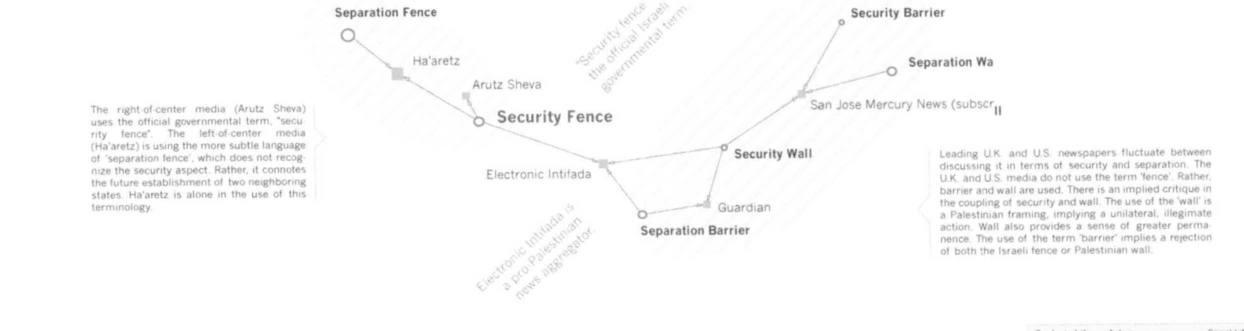

The right-of-center media (Arutz Sheva) uses the official governmental term, "security fence". The left-of-center media (Ha'aretz) is using the more subtle language of 'separation fence', which does not recognize the security aspect. Rather, it connotes the future establishment of two neighboring states. Ha'aretz is alone in the use of this terminology.

Leading U.K. and U.S. newspapers fluctuate between discussing it in terms of security and separation. The U.K. and U.S. media do not use the term 'fence'. Rather, barrier and wall are used. There is an implied critique in the coupling of security and wall. The use of the 'wall' is a Palestinian framing, implying a unilateral, illegimate action. Wall also provides a sense of greater permanence. The use of the term 'barrier' implies a rejection of both the Israeli fence or Palestinian wall.

Conclusion. In not adopting the Israeli fence or Palestinian wall, the Western media leave the (verbally) warring parties to their own devices. The conflict as well as its non-resolution are maintained in the unoccupied media space.

Legend
○ Manner of speaking
■ Media Source

Co-occurrence analysis of keywords and sources.

Product of the workshop ________ Social Life of Issues 9
The News about Networks: Making Issues into Rights?
Amsterdam, The Netherlands. June 04
Analysis_ performed by Anat Ben David, with data by Google News (23 May - 22 June 2004) and visualization by ReseauLu by Aguidel.com.
Design_Marieke van Dijk by Anderemedia.nl.

Seeta Peña Gangadharan, **Catherine Somzé** and **Richard Rogers, govcom.org** *The State of U.S. Democracy,* 2004 / map of the Media Concentration Oppositional Space, showing that organizations with the most resources undertake "informal democracy" (press, events and lobbying); those with least resources engage in "formal democracy" (written comments to FCC) / data: Center for International Media Action / graph developed in *ReseauLu* by Aguidel / design: anderemedia.nl / "Conversations as Maps," p. 71.

Anat Ben-David, **Zachary O'Connor-Devereaux** and **Richard Rogers, govcom.org** *Israeli 'Security Fence': Which news sources use which terms for the 'fence'?*, June 2004 / data from news.google.com / graph developed in *ReseauLu* by Aguidel /design by anderemedia.nl / see "Conversations as Maps," p. 95.

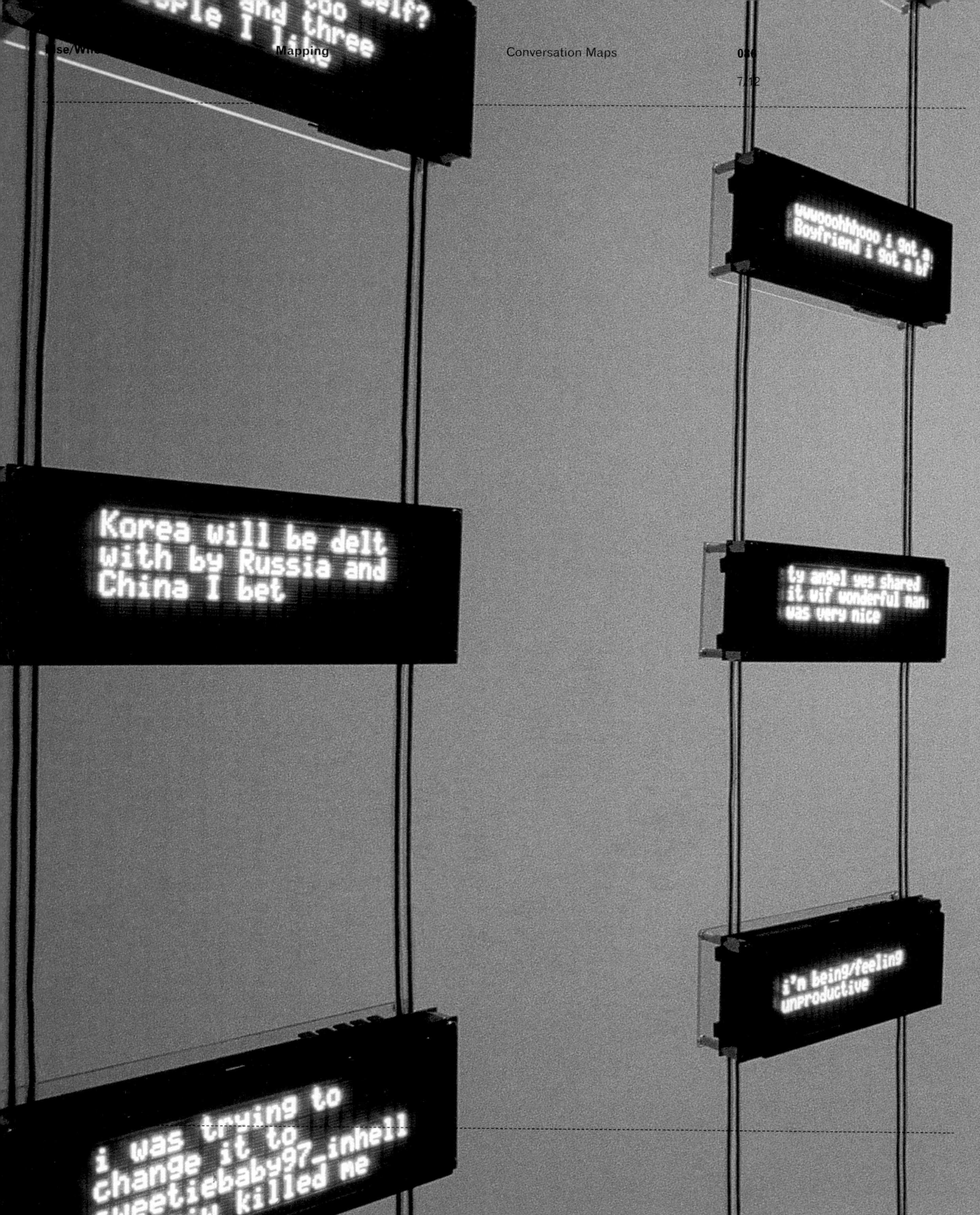
and three
wwwooohhhooo i got a
Boyfriend i got a bf
Korea will be delt
with by Russia and
China I bet
ty angel yes shared
it wif wonderful man
was very nice
i'n being/feeling
unproductive
i was trying to
change it to
sweetiebaby97_inhell

Mark Hansen and **Ben Rubin** *Listening Post*, 2002 / text fragments siphoned real time from Internet chat rooms, bulletin boards and other public forums are read or sung by a voice synthesizer and simultaneously played across a grid of over 200 small LED screens. The system cycles through a series of six movements, each a different arrangement of visual, aural and musical elements, driven by its own data processing logic / see "Conversations as Maps," p. 75.

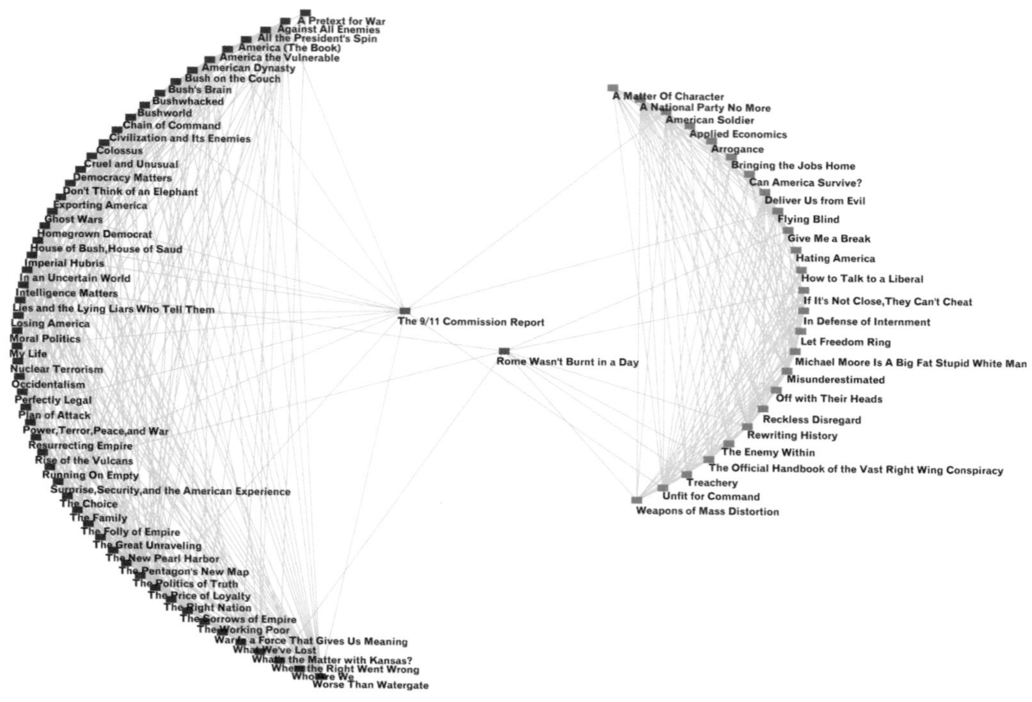

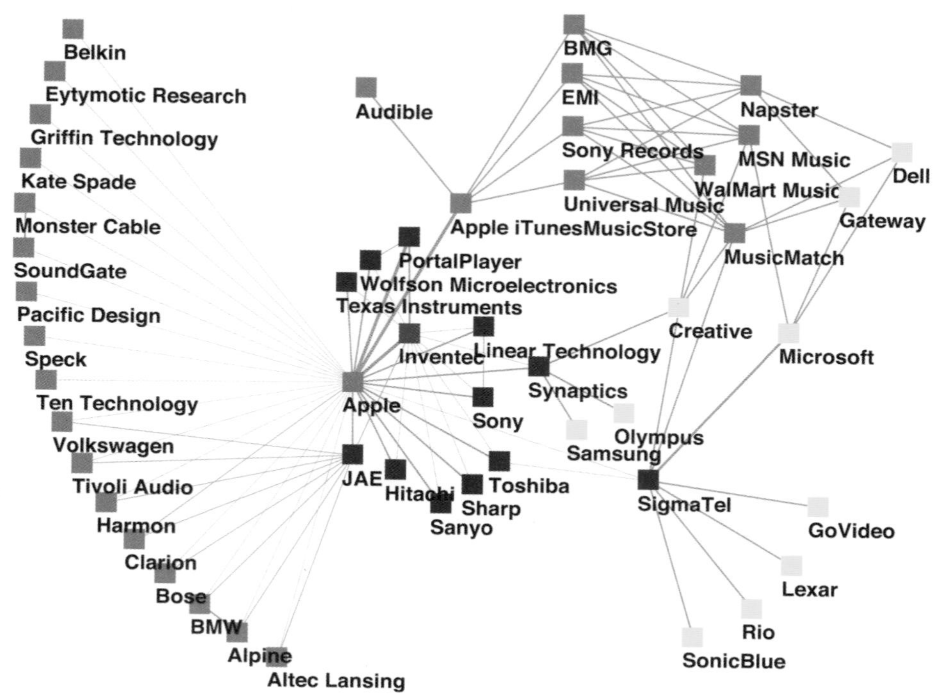

Valdis Krebs, orgnet.com (top): *Divided We Stand*, 2004 / social network map of political book readerships based on purchase patterns from major web book retailers. In this edition of Krebs' map (one of several iterations since 2003; see also p. 37, top), only two books (*The 9/11 Commission Report* and *Rome Wasn't Burnt in a Day*) were bought by readers in both political camps. (bottom): *iPod Ecosystem*, 2004 / "snapshot" map showing the iPod network of manufacturing collaborators as of late 2004 / see "Conversations as Maps," p. 93.

Mohamed Atta
PILOTS hi-lited in yellow
Fayez Ahmed
Marwan Al-Shehhi
Ahmed Al Haznawi
Wail Alshehri
Waleed Alshehri
Abdul Aziz Al-Omari
Mohand Alshehri
Satam Suqami
Ziad Jarrah
Salem Alhazmi
Majed Moqed
Hani Hanjour
Khalid Al-Mihdhar
Hamza Alghamdi
Nawaf Alhazmi
Ahmed Alghamdi
Saeed Alghamdi
Ahmed Alnami

Flight AA 11: Crashed into WTC North
Flight AA 77: Crashed into Pentagon
Flight UA 93: Crashed in Pennsylvania
Flight UA 175: Crashed into WTC South
Other Associates of Hijackers

Valdis Krebs, orgnet.com *9/11 Terrorist Network map*, 2001 / social network map demonstrating the interrelations between the 19 hijackers aboard the planes used in the September 11, 2001 attacks on the U.S. and 15 other individuals (represented as gray nodes) reported at the time to be connected with them. Data derived from news sources was processed in *InFlow* software with connecting lines weighted according to degree of contact / see “Conversations as Maps,” p. 93.

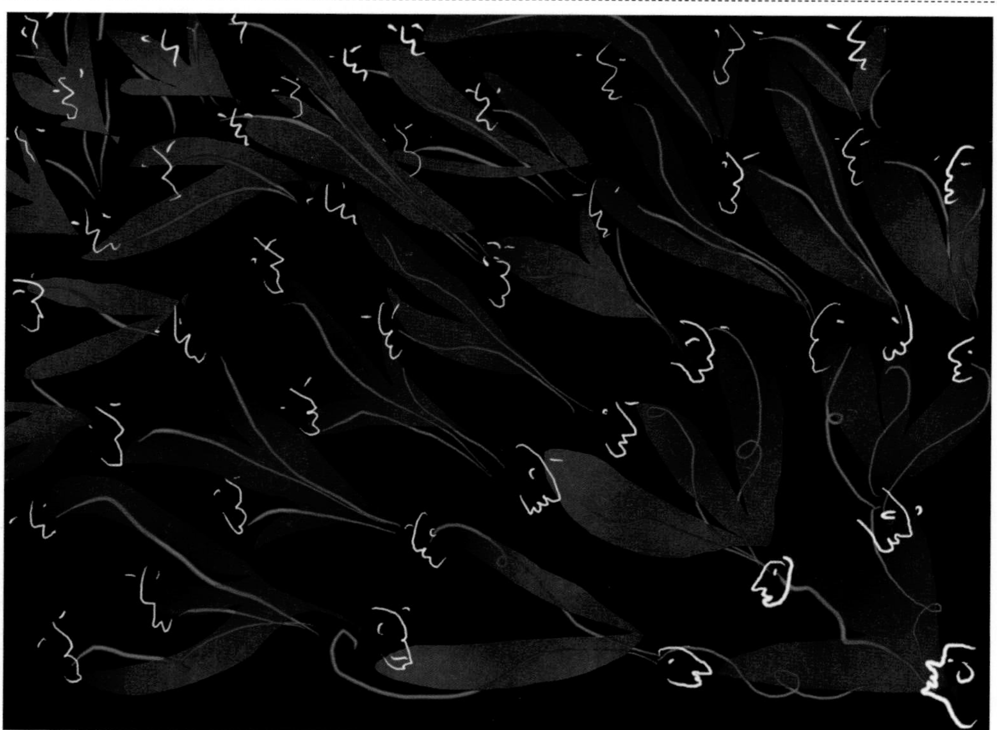

Federico Casalegno, Marco Susani and **Roberto Tagliabue** *An Atlas of Aura(l) Knowledge*, 2002 / maps of conversations based on observations of communication patterns enabled by mobile wireless networks, from a series of ten models. (this page, top to bottom): *The Flames* and *The Ring* / (opposite page, top to bottom): *The Womb* and *The Sunflower* / see "Conversations as Maps," pp. 78–79.

you me today

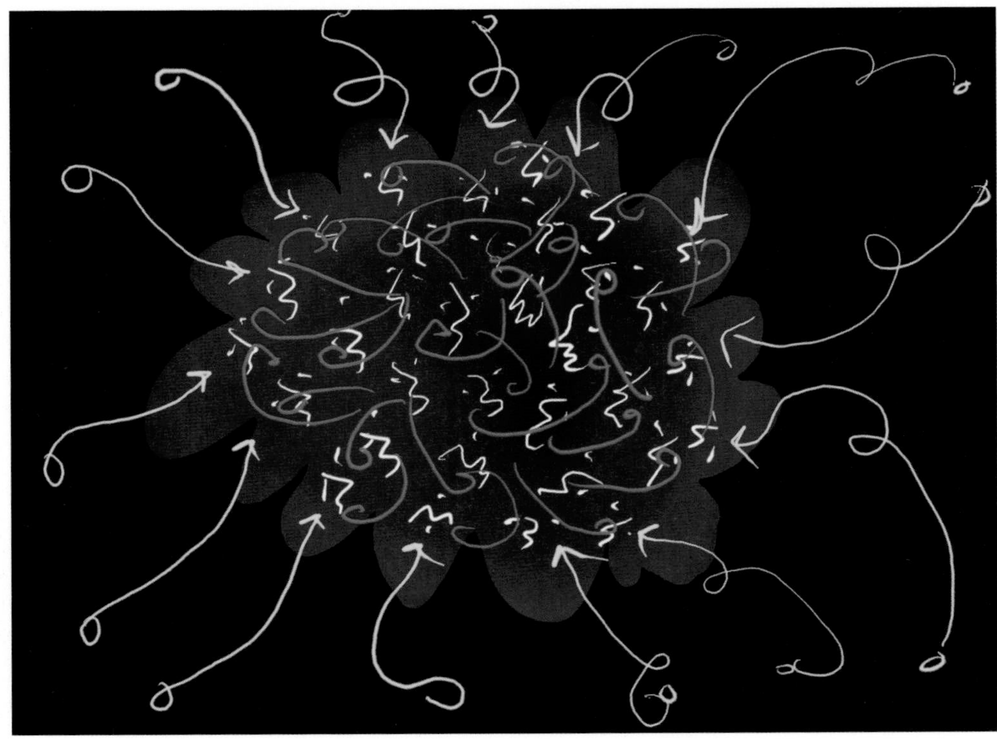

CONVERSATIONS AS MAPS / PART 2

Having conversed via email over several weeks, the Conversation Mappers reconvened to pick up loose threads and spin some new ones in a two-hour Instant Messaging session. Edited highlights follow; three visualizations of this discussion, created by Judith Donath, Mark Hansen and Warren Sack, are presented starting on p. 98.

JANET ABRAMS: welcome to the hell of online chat interface design...

JUDITH DONATH: one observation is that existing chat software is rather the antithesis of Conversation Mapping ideas...

JA: Yahoo, Google and so on seem to 'paste over' the shortcomings of their systems with fripperies like ready-made emotions...

<http://chatcircles.media.mit.edu/>

JD: did you try Chat Circles? We do have a transcribing function (and it draws pictures in the window)

RICHARD ROGERS: hi, Richard here

JA: amen! How cold is it in NL?

RR: dry, warmish, high 40s

VALDIS KREBS: Cleveland is 65F today and 25F tomorrow

JD: so this gets at one of the design issues we've been thinking about: how to build interfaces that work both in the virtual space of the conversation and yet give some impression of the geographical space and distance of the participants

PETER HALL: we're spanning a few time zones now

JA: yet none of that is visible to us, as participants in a box garnished by other boxes

RR: I have AIM [AOL Instant Messenger] figurines for you all

JA: This promotes repartee rather than more contemplative conversation... the kind with meaningful lulls...because that little bell noise which rings each time a participant 'sends' a new posting becomes rapidly addictive

JD: one issue with the little bell is that in linear chats like these, the only way to establish presence is with a constant stream of text. Those who wait 'til they have something to say simply disappear

JA: that is your notion of the 'persistent history' as the information world's version of the body. How is this different from sitting around a table, waiting one's turn to speak?

MARK HANSEN: one difference: someone can pipe in with a very long comment that probably wouldn't happen if we were around a table

RR: maps appear to have simultaneity built in— there's no sense of time in maps

VK: I do snapshots in time... I will try to find the following: iPod alliances 2001 and 2004... the first image is original iPod network of collaborators. The second image was of the ecosystem in late 2004. It would be great to have a snapshot of every month of this iPod ecosystem from 2001 to now

<orgnet.com/iPodEcosystem2004.gif>

PH: interesting too that some of the collaborators do not have a direct relationship with Apple— raises some of the network efficiency questions Valdis raised in his "Social Life of Routers" piece

VK: the network has changed again in 2005 with the release of the iPodShuffle: SigmaTel takes on a bigger role, a new TW mfg was added

JA: to whom are these 'snapshots' addressed? Did you do them out of interest or were you asked to make them by a client (a node or wannabe node?)

VK: I did these maps for a talk on innovation and networks

RR: why are media and ecology related?

VK: a business web/network is like an ecosystem... current book I'm reading: The Keystone Advantage [1]

JA: is that a zeitgeist fad, to see so many things as 'ecologies'?

RR: the nature metaphor grants it some autonomy

1. Marco Iansiti and Roy Levien, *The Keystone Advantage: What the New Dynamics of Business Ecosystems Mean for Strategy, Innovation, and Sustainability*. Boston, MA: Harvard Business School Publishing, 2004

Conversation maps

See "Conversations As Maps, Part 1," p. 78.

VK: ecologies...systems...anything interconnected and interdependent... embeddedness matters

MH: what do you mean by embeddedness?

VK: you are affected by those you are connected to and vice versa...embedded in various patterns of ties

JA: what's the value of seeing that you are connected to x number of other people. How does this help?

VK: it's not the number of connections...more pattern, intensity and changes

MH: maybe it's not recognizing the connection so much as using it... take the example of all the blogs filling up with real time accounts of the tsunami... I'm curious about Jan's earlier comment about how this format encourages breezy conversation rather than deep thought...**how much of this kind of data capture (and by extension, even the resulting visualizations) dictates how we behave and what we see?**

PH: that's a big question: just thinking about how text messaging has changed the way people interact in Europe (and more recently here)

RR: A Paris designer (sounds pretentious — sorry) recently told me: we're mapping ourselves to death. Taking the life out of the networks

VK: I don't think we've yet begun to map! Do photos take the life out of people?

RR: mapping de-animates

PH: but it also reveals, illuminates

JA: Richard: you mean the Paris designer thought that by doing so much mapping, it was killing off the networks thus mapped?

MH: a Heisenberg mapping principle

RR: there's a difference between a PR guy entering a vibrant discussion list, and the list shutting down, and a map guy making everyone in the network think about their behavior. People may start socializing strategically according to the map, but everybody else on the map knows that, too.

VK: **people have told me, while taking a network survey, that this is the first time they had thought about their network behavior so just asking the questions often sparks thought and wonderment.** Mapping just puts it down on a document for discussion

RR: when you map a network, aren't jobs lost, and others think they need to cosy up?

VK: no, jobs are not lost but people do focus on their network behavior more

PH: interesting. I keep thinking how much of corporate network mapping stems out of Taylorism. A kind of rationalization...people become nodes

VK: yeah, many managers want to do that... but we try to focus on innovation and learning

JA: let's progress to some concrete examples. Richard, what's the status of your 'maps of terms' for the 'fence' in Israel? What are you finding?

RR: the fence maps identify which terms are used for the fence by which media sources. 'Apartheid wall' is used with the greatest frequency, but has the least resonance across the mediascape...a matter of screaming and not being heard

- <www.govcom.org/drafts.html>
- <www.govcom.org/publications/full_list/ben-david_rogers_coming_to_terms_2oct.pdf>

JA: how does making a map of those interconnections affect how people will think about the fence aka apartheid wall?

RR: my fence maps have no impact on the conflict (I won't even say yet). We found also that Israeli NGOs are in isolation on networks dedicated to the conflict. Israeli NGOs have a local peace process frame, and international NGOs, donors, and intergovernmentals have a human rights angle. **If you don't do human rights, you're not welcome in the Palestinian-Israeli conflict network**

JA: who asked you to make this particular map? did you just take the initiative (see my earlier question to Valdis about his iPod corporate ecology maps)? How do you pick what to map at a given moment?

RR: Cambridge—Strategic Studies, academic networks asked us to do it, though the initial idea came from Anat Ben-David during the June 2004 govcom.org workshop, "Making Issues into Rights?"

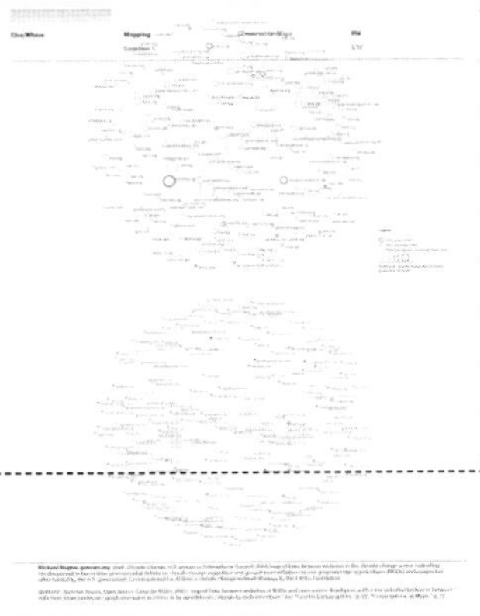

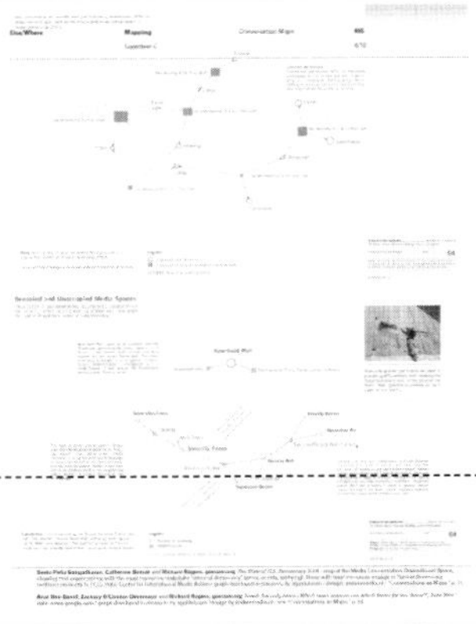

Conversation maps

JA: are you uncovering new knowledge by mapping the fence discussion?

RR: we put forward the notion of the 'complicated Israeli NGO'—a left-leaning networking actor, ignoring and ignored by most all the other NGOs. But don't think much is new. We may have termed it all differently

<http://www.orgnet.com/divided.html>

VK: I pick whatever interests me. The political book maps came out of a chat room conversation several years ago. We were discussing a few books, and I wondered how they all connected or didn't... most of my work is client driven, but sometimes I have time to explore things I find interesting

<www.issuecrawler.net>

RR: I used to look at the Issuecrawler archives to know what's hot. People are constantly mapping what they think is current

JA: Richard, what do you find challenging about mapping this topic? Has the content affected your visualization technique? How do people respond?

RR: The Palestinian-Israeli conflict is a world-wearying subject matter to many. The content has affected the approach. **We're looking at fiery language and sticky issues, as opposed to mapping the overall space**

JA: I am struck by the geographical quality of your fence map, its 'star-map' arrangement. What dictates the angles of the links?

<www.aguidel.com/>

RR: we used ReseauLu social network mapping software, albeit with frequency of ties between actors indicated as well

VK: I would gladly subscribe to a news service that presented each issue mapped out like this... with clickable nodes for more info or URL

JD: this is what Google news should be... it would be great to see how language spans a single issue like this, which words are used in the various coverages of the same story

WARREN SACK: Richard, by ReseauLu you mean the work of Andrei Mogoutov of Aguidel and the Ecole des Mines (de Paris)?

<www.issuescraper.net>

RR: Aguidel's, yes. We have a different ReseauLu built into Issuecrawler, and a new ReseauLu-like module built into Issuescraper (news/blogs). We have data scrapers online and we've built 'adaptive scrapers' of news aggregators, blog aggregators and individual blogs, as well as blog networks 'discovered by crawlers'

WS: this is an important direction for those of us who have been mapping online conversations. Most of us have tried to simply use the archives of the blog, newsgroups, etc., but we all know, following McLuhan, that each new medium displaces the old. Scraping can help us orient the online conversation in a larger media environment — including the news

PH: so are blogs and newsgroups displacing traditional media?

WS: we need to understand our maps as indicative of only a small territory surrounded by a much larger media environment. It's interesting to watch how, for instance, a new television show might influence online discussion, or book and DVD purchases. In his essay "The Rediscovery of Ideology" from 1982, media scholar Stuart Hall asks us to understand news not as a reflection of society's interests, but as a driver of interests.[2] News drives us to talk and think about certain issues and not others

PH: blogs and newsgroups have tipped the balance... newspapers are in crisis because of this

WS: newspapers have been in decline for about 50 years now. For example, the Minneapolis Star-Tribune used to be two papers: one issued in the morning, the other in the evening. some subscribers took both

PH: the idea of a newspaper's authorial voice is the last bastion

JA: Valdis, Richard: do your maps of 'who thinks what about what' serve a meta-function as opinion-leader devices in themselves?

VK: yes, Richard's maps may be leading indicators on what is about to spread/tip/become hot

JA: does having the (technical) ability to map the stakeholders' relative positions put the map maker in an authoritative position vis-a-vis the subject-matter at hand?

WS: yes — the kind of authority exercised by anyone who writes a summary

VK: :or those who write history

JA: so, how powerful do you all feel?

WS: this is exactly the power we touched on in our email exchange: are the maps definitive, or sketches/diagrams?

VK: I see the maps as sense-making documents: when discussed, we all get smarter...or start asking better questions

MH: they are only as definitive as the data they draw from. BTW, here's how we should present the conversation

<www.stat.ucla.edu/~cocteau/sorts.txt>

WS: that looks great Mark! I think we can all stop working on this mapping stuff now. This sort looks like the answer!

MH: no, UNIX. UNIX is the answer...

2. Stuart Hall, "The Rediscovery of Ideology," in M. Gurevitch, T. Bennett, J. Curran and J. Woollacott, eds., *Culture, Society and the Media*. London: Methuen, 1982.

See Gazetteer D, pp. 102–103.

Judith Donath visualization of email conversation (pp. 70–79), 2005, using salient words from the discussion / the discussion builds in chronological order from bottom to top. Each participant's contributions are shown in the column labeled with his or her name; in addition, each is assigned a unique color. Quoted remarks are seen in blocks of another's color in the quoting writer's column and white lines show responses. The overall patterns of the visualization show the rhythm of the conversation and the flow of ideas from one participant to another. A closer view, reading the words, provides a portrait of each participant in the form of their characteristic phrases.

22
21
20
19
18
17
16
15
14
13
12
11
10
9
8
7
6
5
4
3
2
1
I'm interested
experiential
language of maps
Mark Lombardi
I would assume
less certainty
Thanks for elaborating
I now understand
useful distinction
curious
questions
get the conversation rolling
interviewed
give an example
the book
Please respond
reply
New York
co-editing Else/Where
I haven't introduced myself
asking
renamed
redraw
reshape
chatting
expand that for me
uncertainty
hard
judge
mathematicians
manifold
reification
design
extremely large repositories
cautious
discovery
dicey
algorithmically
coffee
spam out-takes
algorithmically
multivariate
statistical
methods
projecting
dimensional
exploratory analysis
features emerge
observations
data
similarity
clusters
informative depiction
co-citations
legible
inhabitable space
perceivable
individual;
Persistant history
no truly neutral visualization
evocative
pointedly poetic
activists
underground
self-governance
relationships
post social software
interaction freak
information query
aggregators
collective intelligence
new media
Amsterdam
lexical
interlinking
analysis
ideational space
extremist forums
cc. lists.
shared
common ground
response.
Driving forces
conversation maps/data portraits
invitation
"Mapping Conversations."
Question
roundtable
online
visualizing
online conversation mapping
article
back to you
data
introductions
professional affiliation
intellectual
statistics
los angeles
models
information
text
processing
retrieval
voyeur
social implications
installations
semantic visualization
social visualization
Peter
Janet
Mark
Judith
Richard

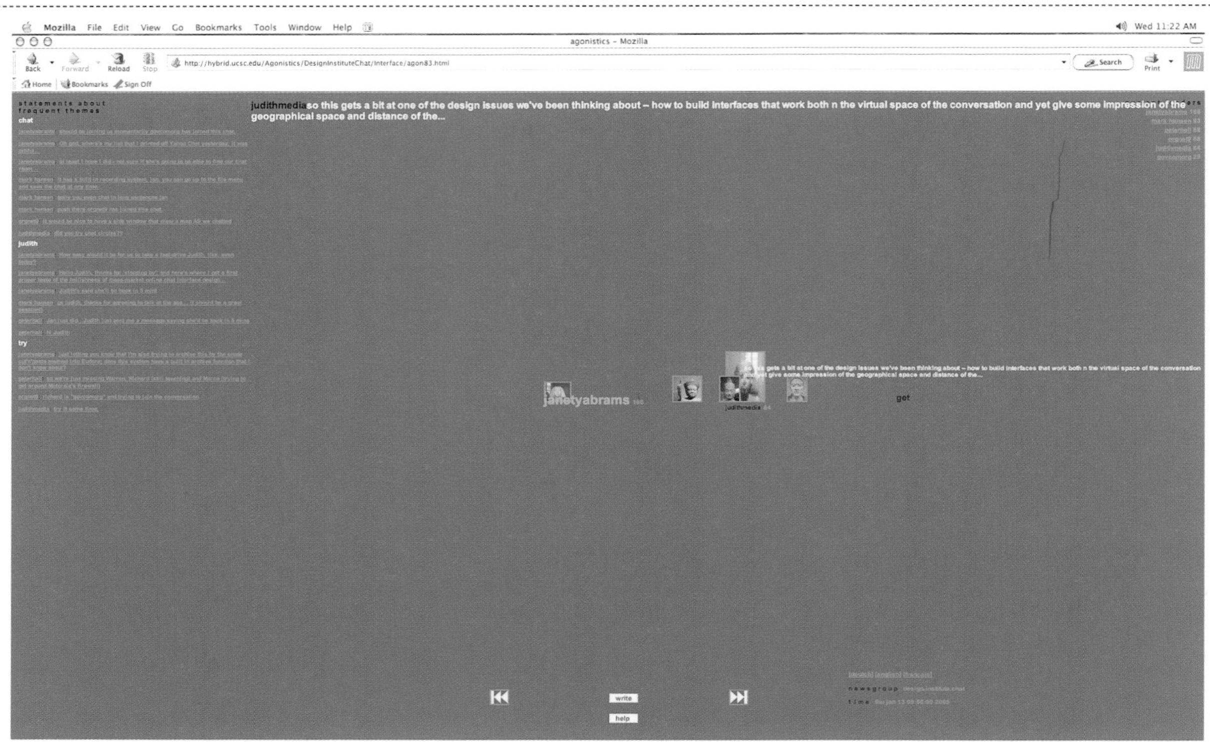

Warren Sack visualization of the full transcript of "Conversations As Maps, Part 2" (pp. 92–97), 2005, using his software program *Agonistics,* 2004 / Sack's game is based on the idea that democratic debate should not be a form of verbal combat, but "constructively adversarial." Postings to an email list are translated by the system into a graphical display that awards points to players who are engaged in dialogue (represented by facial icons), positioning those with the highest points at the center of the ring. Points are awarded to those who respond to or cite messages of other players; to win, one must establish a dialogue with as many other players as possible.

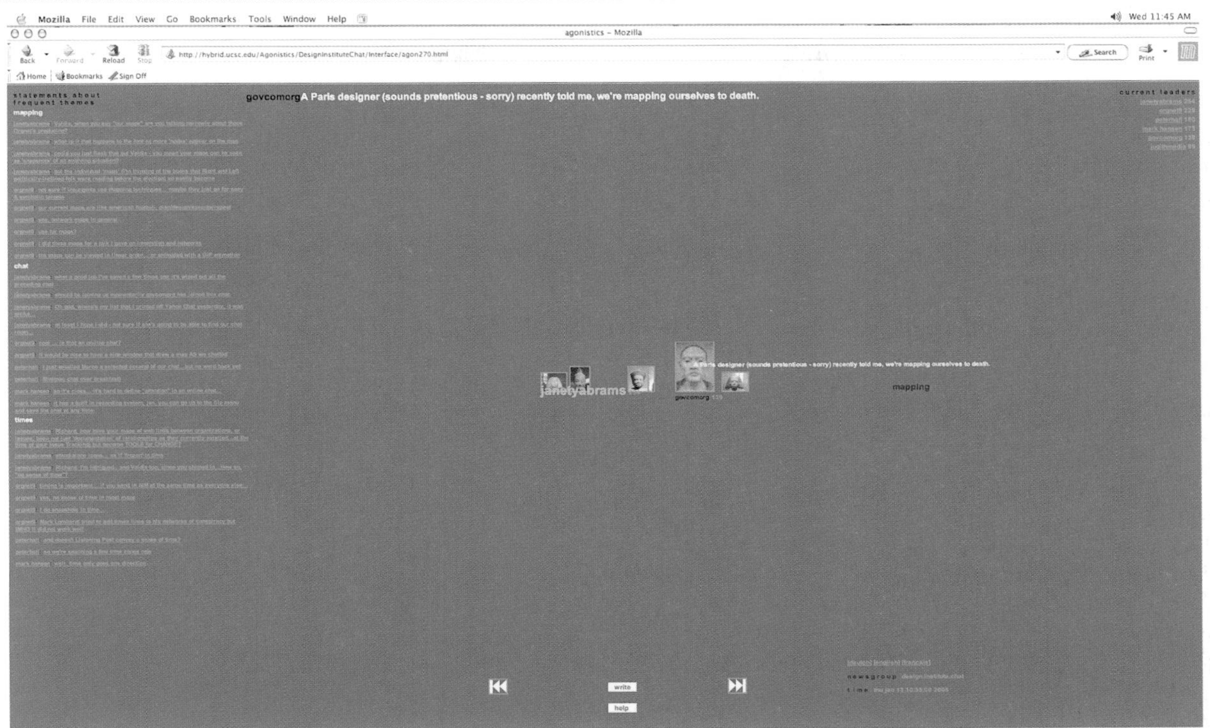
Mozilla File Edit View Go Bookmarks Tools Window Help
Wed 11:45 AM
agonistics - Mozilla
Back Forward Reload Stop
http://hybrid.ucsc.edu/Agonistics/DesignInstituteChat/interface/agon270.html
Search
Print
Home Bookmarks Sign Off
statements about frequent themes
mapping
chat
times
govcomorg A Paris designer (sounds pretentious - sorry) recently told me, we're mapping ourselves to death.
current leaders
janetyabrams
mapping
write
help

Mozilla File Edit View Go Bookmarks Tools Window Help
Wed 12:15 PM
agonistics - Mozilla
Back Forward Reload Stop
http://hybrid.ucsc.edu/Agonistics/DesignInstituteChat/interface/agon505.html
Search
Print
Home Bookmarks Sign Off
statements about frequent themes
mapping
chat
think
mark hansen no, unix, unix is the answer.
current leaders
janetyabrams
mark hansen
answer
write
help

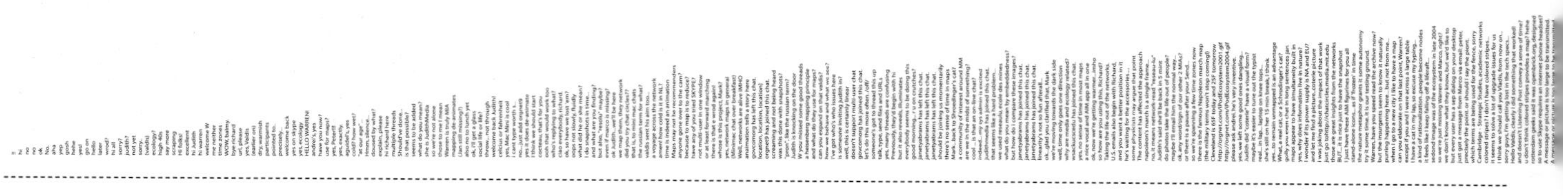

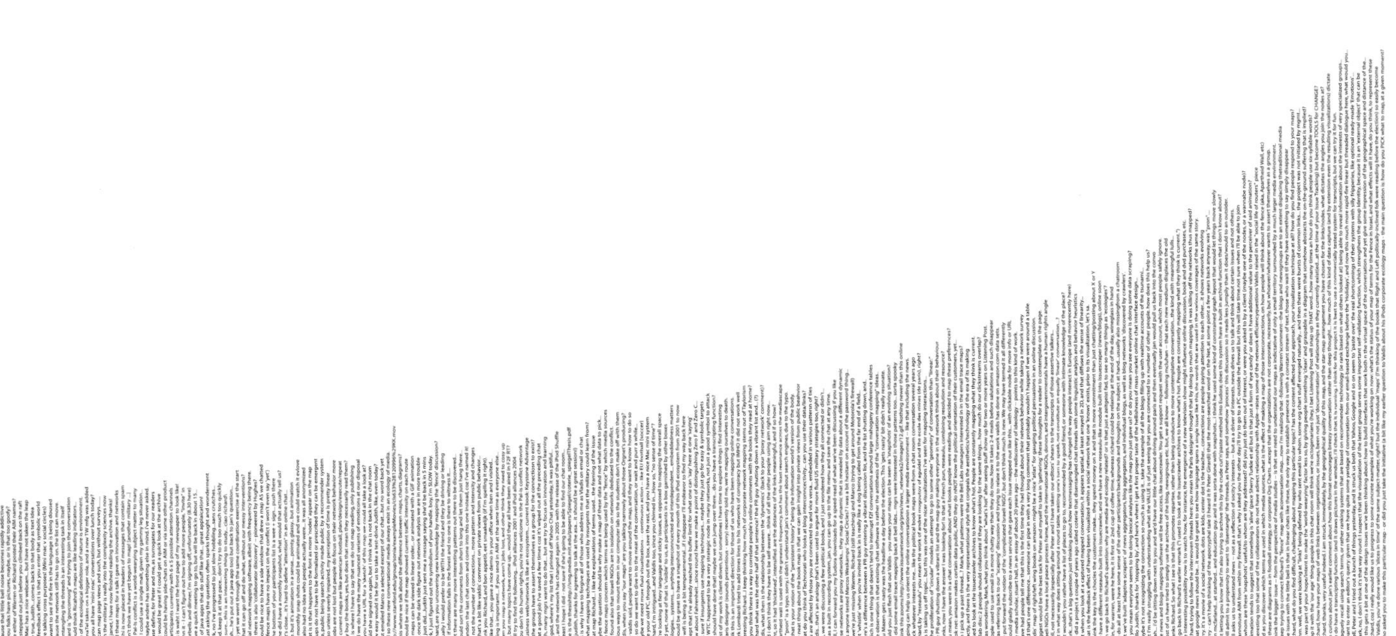

Mark Hansen visualization of full transcript of "Conversations As Maps, Part 2" (pp. 92–97), 2005, with participants' contributions sorted according to length of posting using the UNIX shell command:

<cat mapping.txt | perl -e 'while(<>){ $n = length; print "$n $_"};' | sort -n | cut -d" " -f2->

CONVERSATIONS WITH MAPS

Location technologies and digital displays have changed what maps look like, where we find them and what we do with them. On dynamic maps, cities and continents are set in motion, animated by data that changes at the speed of the network. ANDREA MOED, ALEX TERZICH and JANET ABRAMS look at recent experimental interactive maps that demand iterative querying rather than mere reading, provoking the user into conversations with maps.

THE ELASTIC SPACE-TIME CONTINUUM

Created at the late-lamented Media Lab Europe in Dublin, Amble Time offers an update on the Situationist "dérive," providing urban wanderers with a purposeful way to experience "walkable time" as they meander round the city. By ANDREA MOED.

My route from the hotel to the station is described by a pool of light. The light falls on a portion of the city map on my handheld computer screen as if a follow spot were pointing down from the heavens. The shape and size of this bright spot is determined by a simple algorithm of rate, time and distance: it contains my hotel, the train station from which my train departs in one hour, and every place I can walk to and still have time to catch my train. Still seated in the hotel lobby, I feel my heavy backpack and tired feet and I tell the map to assume a slower walking pace. The pool of light narrows from a circle into an oblong shape with hotel and station at either end. Getting to my feet at last, I set off on a stroll, keeping to the streets in the lighted part of the map to assure that I won't be late. As time passes, that lighted space contracts further and further. Finally, at the point when I really must hurry, only the most direct path to the station remains bright. This scenario is made possible by Amble Time, a prototype "map with a sense of time" created by the Everyday Learning research group at the erstwhile Media Lab Europe in Dublin. Amble Time is an engineered answer to an increasingly popular question in the media business: how are footloose urbanites, seeking adventure but pressed for time, to maximize their returns of aesthetic pleasure and fun?

Book and software publishers have answered with a host of personal navigation aids: websites like CitySearch, magazines like Time Out, software applications like Vindigo, endless specialty guidebooks targeting various demographics and interests. All promise to let busy people in on some precious local secret that they used to discover by ambling: the underground club around the corner, the best bargain shopping, the extraordinary little museum — the ideal thing to be doing in this neighborhood at this moment. Many of these guides include collaborative feedback features in which patrons rate restaurants and other destinations and the system constantly crunches the numbers and promotes the winners. The idea is that if we blunder around but then pool our knowledge, the fun will rise to the top where we can claim it expeditiously.

<www.citysearch.com> <www.vindigo.com>

Amble Time makes no such claims to urban intelligence; instead, it privileges the blundering for its own sake. It imparts to travel the sense of "softened time" that the mobile phone brings to social situations where being able to call friends in transit makes

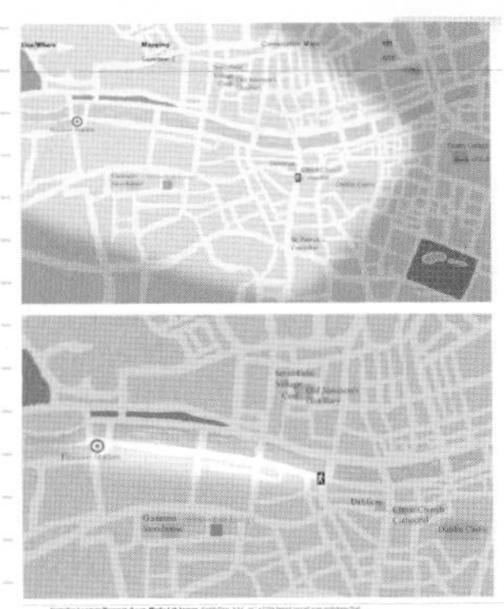

Conversation maps

gazetteer E 5–6/10 pp. 120–121

being on time a matter of consensus. Where cell phone socializing relies on a flexible sense of presence, Amble Time exploits the unique flexibility of the pedestrian condition: the freedom to wander aimlessly, proceed directly or do anything in between. It suggests a notion of walkable time as a companion to that urban planning grail of walkable space. In its Newtonian functioning, it paradoxically allows time to be subjective, at least until one's train draws near.

CAN YOU FIND ME NOW?

On the road, digital maps seem destined to outmaneuver printed maps. In-car satellite navigation systems purport to assist drivers, but they may also reduce our sense of self-reliance. And despite the smooth promptings of their synthesized voices, they often turn out to be less than "expert systems." By ANDREA MOED.

Driving and map reading are activities with a long and troubled relationship. On a car trip to an unfamiliar place, fights between the driver and the map-wielding navigator inevitably create a hazardous environment for everyone else in the car—unless, of course, the driver and navigator are the same person, in which case it's those outside the car who had better watch out.

It's no wonder that computer-generated driving maps and directions are among the most popular applications on the Internet. Websites like MapBlast and MapQuest combine route-finding software and road data gathered by map companies to find a path between any two U.S. addresses and describe it in words and custom-created maps. This free service can feel like a miraculous gift to the direction-impaired driver, even when the route the software comes up with turns out to be circuitous or fails to account for changes to the road system. In fact, some users may trust web maps a bit more than they should, judging by the disclaimers posted on the sites. One warns, "If the directions tell you to make an illegal turn, please don't do it!"

<www.maps.msn.com> <www.mapquest.com>

If web maps partially automate the navigation process, in-car satellite navigation systems promise to finish the job. These on-board computers incorporate GPS receivers and their own map databases. They let the driver input his destination while in the car, then they constantly track his position as he drives. A computerized voice calls out each turn as the driver approaches it, while a small screen displays a view of the intersection. In the event of changed plans or a wrong turn, the system recalculates the directions to put the driver back on track.

For a technology that automates the complex art of cross-country wayfinding, satellite navigation systems seem remarkably cheap. They can be integrated into the dashboards of new mid-to-luxury cars or purchased as stand alone devices for $1,000 to $2,000. Hertz even offers a version, dubbed NeverLost, in some of its rental cars. So why is it that the same American drivers who love Web maps rarely request navigation systems in new cars or rentals? As reported in the New York Times, J. D. Powers estimated that only 300,000 cars with these systems were sold in 2002, despite their being available in over 60 car models. Perhaps consumers are wary of satellite guidance precisely because of what the maps force upon them: a sense of self reliance. Both web maps and satellite navigation systems draw upon imperfect data sets. They don't always know about one-way streets or roads under construction, and their information about nearby services such as restaurants and gas stations is predictably incomplete. Nonetheless, the dynamic, talking satellite navigation device invites the driver to perceive it as an "expert system," more reliable than her spouse or other fellow traveler could ever be. This can lead some drivers to expect great subtlety: on the gadget review website <bythom.com>, one NeverLost user complains, "We attempted using the nationwide database to find the Legal Seafoods restaurant in Sunrise, [Florida], and [were] able to get no closer than the Legal locations in New England!" The man ultimately has to enter an address to make it clear where he wants to go—a minor inconvenience, but out of keeping with the sure-voiced guide he knew.

<http://hertzneverlost.com/>

In their very staticness, printed maps from any source demand a more active navigating posture from people, since the words and graphics in hand are all the driver is going to get. Instead of listening for the next cue to turn, one barrels forward as the world unfolds on the other side of the windshield. The map (long since unfolded, with no hope of proper re-folding) has nothing more to say. Course adjustment and re-calibration may soon become necessary, but they are up to the traveler — a rule of the road that most us don't seem quite ready to discard.

GAMES IN THE ELECTROSPHERE

WiFi and the Global Positioning System (GPS) have spawned a new generation of pastimes. Noderunner and Geocaching offer two contrasting experiences of the wireless world, and reveal the hidden pleasures to be found in the playful (mis)use of panoptic technologies. By ANDREA MOED

The designer and philosopher of technology Anthony Dunne has written of "Hertzian Space," the invisible topographies of electromagnetic (EM) radiation and transmission produced by objects such as cell towers, RFID tags and microwave ovens.[1] People don't inhabit Hertzian space directly; we know it only through perceptible effects such as radio connectivity (or the lack of it) and cell phone-induced brain damage (or the fear of it).

As wireless technologies multiply, Hertzian space figures more and more prominently in everyday life. We come to know where we can use mobile phones and where calls always get dropped, or we recognize twitters of interference where the computer's EM penumbra overlaps the stereo's. Certain neighborhoods of the radio spectrum have grown clamorous and complex, with hidden transmitters and antennae, mobile devices coming and going, and every person free to set up their own baby monitor or wireless home network. What we need to communicate reliably is a good map, but the numbers of private and competing interests involved make that all but impossible to make. One can curse this situation, or see it as an opportunity for subterfuge and play.

In the latter camp are Yury Gitman and Carlos Gómez de Llareña, the inventors of the game Noderunner, a kind of blind man's bluff in Hertzian space. Descended from the practice of "wardriving"— hunting for usable wireless networks by car — Noderunner challenges players to run around a neighborhood or city with WiFi-enabled laptop computers and search for places where open-access network nodes let them connect to the Internet for free. The winner is the team that locates and uses the most nodes before the game clock runs down. Open nodes are almost never labeled by signs or ads. To find them, teams feel their way using special scanning software and a trial-and-error process called stumbling. Gitman reports that to be good at Noderunner,

<noderunner.com>

gazetteer E 7–8/10 pp. 122–123

you need a computer with a strong antenna and an understanding of Wi-Fi technology and practice. For example, it helps to know that most open nodes are in residential areas and that to make a workable connection from the sidewalk, you may need to lift your laptop above your head.

Noderunner engenders a view of the wireless world as a no-man's land of home-brewed networks and ad-hoc connections. The opposite feeling pervades another species of wireless technology game based on the Global Positioning System (GPS). Long before GPS and its enabling network of satellites were launched, world maps showed the globe overlaid by a lattice of vertical meridians and horizontal parallels. Latitude and longitude has become humanity's least controversial shared frame of reference, equally useful and authoritative to hikers, sea captains, smugglers and generals. GPS technology makes this Cartesian consensus visible on the ground. By communicating with corporate or government operated satellite networks, GPS devices can tell exactly where on earth they are, and thus locate anything on a world map.

Lately, GPS receivers have become cheap consumer items, leading some hobbyists to come up with playful uses for them. Geocaching is a game where players hide treasure boxes in uninhabited areas and announce the treasure's coordinates on the Web, inviting anyone to hunt it down. GPS drawing is done by driving a specific path across a territory while using a GPS receiver to direct the journey. By recording her path, the drawer traces a virtual picture on the earth's surface. What's striking about GPS games is their communal, collaborative spirit. It would be logical to resist GPS as a military-industrial panopticon that enables smart bombs and Star Wars. But, instead, these gamers and artists see the benevolent consequences of the technology: an

<www.geocaching.com>

1. Anthony Dunne, *Hertzian Tales: Electronic Products, Aethetic Experience and Critical Design.* London: Royal College of Art, 1999/Cambridge, MA: The MIT Press, 2006.

orderly Hertzian space where no one and nothing need truly be lost.

THE MAP GETS PERSONAL

A new software application for urban exploration has interlaced London with narrative threads, as participants in trial runs of Urban Tapestries map their individual experiences of the city via a network of handheld computers. By ANDREA MOED.

It's sometimes said that on the streets of historic cities you can hear the voices of the past kings, warriors, and fictional characters recalling the notorious events or lost landscapes of local history. That's all very poetic, but in truth it might be just as illuminating to hear from the person who was sitting on your park bench right before you arrived. Everyone has a story, after all, and it's the juxtaposition and intersection of citizens' many stories that creates the truest impression of a city.

<http://urbantapestries.net/index.html>

The Urban Tapestries (UT) project makes that narrative conflux visible through the tiny screens of networked, handheld computers. Created by the London think-and-design tank Proboscis, UT is a PDA-based application that allows users to walk through the city and record their impressions of specific places in text, sound and digital photos. As they move around, they can also access the words, sounds and pictures created by others at those locations. The UT user can leave an isolated comment about a single place, or create a thread that connects multiple locations and annotations as a digital walking tour. In December 2003, Proboscis held the first public trial of UT. After constructing a £115,000 ($218,000) neighborhood wireless mesh network with collaborator Locustworld and configuring 15 PDAs provided by project partner Hewlett-Packard, Proboscis put the system through its paces on the streets of Bloomsbury in central London.

Like UT itself, the trial was designed to encourage many different kinds of geographic annotation. In the introduction for trial participants, the designers wrote: "Imagine building your own location-based game to play with friends and neighbours such as a treasure hunt or a spy game…Imagine creating a thread of local resources…specialist food shops, bookstores, places to learn new things…Imagine creating your own personal map of Bloomsbury." Testers arriving at the trial site were first given an explanation of the project featuring a large, table-mounted paper map of the area. Then they were given PDAs displaying pocket-sized, digital maps. The maps had no directions, points of interest or even street names. It was up to the participants to go outside and "write their city" by marking the places they visited and sharing their stories and impressions through the network.

Charged with this open-ended mission, the trialists mapped Bloomsbury in ways that no transport or travel agency could have dreamed of. They created threads with titles like "Arguments I Had With My Ex-Husband," "A Day in the Life of an Urban Knitter," and "Chocolate With That," a fictional journey. They endured damp, chilly weather and persistent problems with both the handheld devices and the wireless network, and still retained considerable enthusiasm for this new pastime of public authoring. As one tester reflected on the project weblog after returning from her walk, "without consciously trying, I became much more aware of things around me. I enjoyed being able to share my experiences. Normally, such passing thoughts would be forgotten or would seem insignificant by the time I had someone to share them with, but they make sense within the context of the environment. My [writings were] affected by an awareness of people reading them in the future. It was different than if it was just a personal device."

Interestingly, no one seemed to care whether the postings of public authors were factually accurate. Instead, their most frequent concern about content was that there would soon be too much to manage. "What will happen when we have a dense maze of threads?" wondered one tester. "How will we navigate them? How will we [find] interesting content?" Comments like these reveal a knowing disjuncture in the users' minds between the street map of Bloomsbury and its overlay of annotations. While they expected the base map to represent objective reality, they judged added threads on personality and shared interest. It was clear to these users that UT was no digital walking guide, but, as one person put it, "a new, physically rooted web." The map and the Internet had met in a deep kiss; lives had becomes lenses onto land.

WE CAN DO THAT, DAVE-G

A talking map developed at the GeoVista Center at Penn State University uses dialogue, gestures and gaze to articulate future scenarios. With its Sim-like characters, DAVE-G hints at the possibility that maps will soon be considered participants in everyday conversation. By ANDREA MOED.

People looking at maps seem compelled to talk over them. Displayed in communal spaces, maps become catalysts for storytelling, planning and argument. War rooms and archeological digs are the classic settings, but sociable mapping can happen anywhere. On a recent plane trip across the country, I watched a man in a row of silent strangers open his laptop and begin using a digital U.S. atlas. Within minutes he and his seatmate were engrossed in a chat about various places they had lived and traveled. As they spoke, the man moused back and forth across the country, zooming in and out of different areas.

A team of HCI researchers at the GeoVista Center at the Penn State University wants to unlock the community-building power of maps and it sees Geographic Information Systems (GIS) — the digital data-crunching tools of modern cartography — as the key. GIS mapping uses georeferenced information to add layers to a conventional map. It's the technology behind election return maps (with those now-famous Republican "red states" and Democratic "blue states"), demographic maps and weather maps. A GIS map can contain any number of information layers and display them in any combination. For example, one might juxtapose climate and voting data and look for correlations. Theoretically, that means people using such a map could share lots of complex information visually and socially, presenting findings, comparing perspectives and making decisions. The problem is that at present, most GIS's are unwieldy technical beasts that only trained specialists can use.

In a multi-year project called DAVE-G (Dialogue-Assisted Visual Environment for Geoinformation) the GeoVista Center team is devising ways for groups of laypeople to control a GIS and manipulate its maps — not by keying in data, as per usual, but through the intuitive human modes of looking, talking and pointing. According to the DAVE-G website:

<www.geovista.psu.edu/grants/nsf-itr/index.html>

> the project is concerned, specifically, with the use of computer vision and speech processing as a means of interpreting and integrating information from three modalities: spoken words, free hand gestures and gaze. It is also concerned with how to enable a human-computer dialogue with an interactive, multi-layered map in the context of a GIS and with map-mediated dialogue between human collaborators.

As an initial (and timely) test case, the project is building a DAVE-G for emergency management teams needing to make quick decisions. In a sample scenario from the website, two managers and a talking map discuss preparations for an approaching hurricane:

> JANE: (turns to Paul) What's the typical traffic density on Route 17 and these two parallel routes (turns back to map, makes gesture pointing first to one, then to the other road) into it? It looks like a potential bottleneck.
>
> PAUL: Let's find out. (looks at display) DAVE-G, let's see the weekday transportation model and the standard traffic patterns first.
>
> DAVE-G: OK, here it is. (an animation starts in which the width of the highway symbol changes with the ebb and flow of traffic during the day)
>
> PAUL: Now, we will close down this road (pointing to one of the two side roads), add the people who are typically home during the day and will evacuate, and see what happens.
>
> DAVE-G: (the resulting animation runs)

If you've seen the film Minority Report, you'll recognize the sexy tech part of this vision: the incredibly advanced sensors and software that know what Jane and Paul are looking at and instantly parse their rather complex sentences. But consider as well the rhetorical implications: by invoking an animation on the map, Paul implies that they can see the future. When he points to a road and "closes it down," the Sim-like "people" in the map behave as predicted. And who did the predicting? No one knows: the map visualizes data and conjecture alike and hides the distinctions between them.

Of course, maps have always portrayed opinionated and controversial ideas. Just recently, they've been used to depict global warming, electoral landslides, the threat posed by Palestinians to the State of Israel and the subjugation of Palestinians by the State of Israel. Still, maps today generally provide the ballast of the argument: its grounding, as it were. In a future of DAVE-Gs, maps may end up with the kind of oily reputation currently accorded to statistics. This will mean that they have matured fully as a communications tool. No longer neutral by default, maps will be understood as extensions of the people who talk with, through and over them.

CROSSING CAMPUS

University campuses could become more navigable as projects like ActiveCampus and Metronaut deploy hand-held devices to turn the Ivory Tower into the See-Thru U. But these experiments also demonstrate the differences between user-driven and top-down information mapping. By ALEX TERZICH

In his design for the University of Virginia, Thomas Jefferson adopted the metaphor of the village to

See "Visualizing Democracy, $ by $," pp. 113–114.

See "Contested Terrain," pp. 220–227.

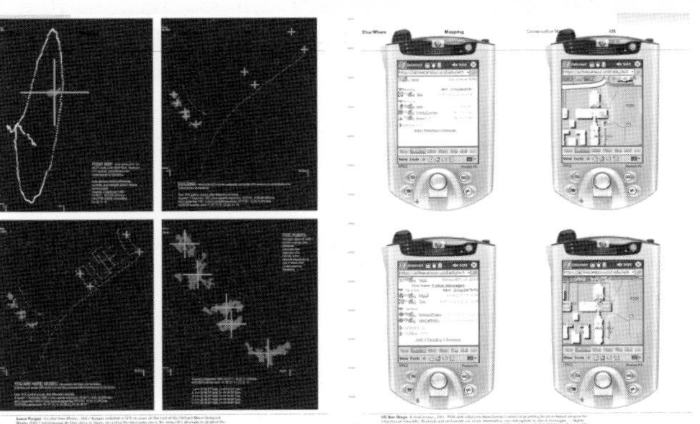

Conversation maps

gazetteer C 1/6 pp. 124–125

characterize the series of pavilions arranged around an open square of grass and trees. This academical village became a campus model for American universities, most of which have since expanded to become more like cities than villages. Today, it's not uncommon to find a central lawn and its flanking neoclassical buildings set like some historic downtown in an otherwise sprawling campus. As universities continue to expand, the difficulty of campus navigation has prompted the invention of new navigational systems. Two mobile computing applications offer opportunities to rethink the metaphor of today's university.

Software developers at UC San Diego have created ActiveCampus, an application designed to foreground the essential aspects of campus life — friends, colleagues, destinations and events — and mute out the crowds and undistinguished buildings that interfere with campus legibility. The application is built around a handheld device and pervasive wireless infrastructure, and allows users to locate and communicate with other users as well as digitally attach messages called "graffiti" to physical entities in space. This digital graffiti is invisible until a user calls it up on her handheld screen. Its appearance can reveal attributes embedded in a site: past events, personal stories, political statements. The result is a highly diverse and user-driven campus guide that allows one to see through physical appearances; the effect is a reconceptualization of the campus as a transparent city.

< http://activecampus.ucsd.edu>

The Wearable Group at Carnegie Mellon has developed a considerably less social application in Metronaut, a system designed to link up users with campus computing infrastructure rather than other users. With a two-way pager, one can access the central information server and retrieve scheduling information and directions to sites on campus. In addition, a barcode sticker network is used to encode information across the campus, accessible to a geared-up user with a handheld reader. By scanning a barcode affixed to a building or roadsign, one can identify current location and receive directions to a final destination. Because the system is top-down, meaning that other users can't encode their own information or place barcodes around campus, Metronaut remains a limited application offering only orientation and expediency. Its cognitive side-effects, however, are much greater: landmarks are reduced to tracking checkpoints that verify the correct route; students and visiting scholars move through campus like so many packaged goods; the heterogeneity of an historic campus is recast as a homogenous space for the efficient circulation of academic commodities. The metaphor is that of the logistical city.

<www-2.cs.cmu.edu/~wearable/metronaut.html>

Thomas Jefferson was disappointed by schools comprising a single building, calling them "a large and common den of noise, of filth and of fetid air." The evolution of the campus metaphor from den to village to city clearly has a profound impact on the shape of education. New campus navigation tools come with metaphors already built-in, and will help determine for better or worse how we see and use our universities.

INSTRUMENTS OF UNCERTAINTY

As civilian use of GPS receivers expands, a range of artists have been exploring the presumed precision of this location technology, and demonstrating how unstable our coordinates can be. By ALEX TERZICH

At a May 2000 press briefing, the United States announced that it would stop its intentional degradation of GPS signals available to the public. By removing a feature called selective availability, civilian GPS receivers became 10 times more accurate overnight. A primary motivation behind the decision was to encourage private sector investment. As Department of Transportation Assistant Secretary Gene Conti put it, "Commercially, there's a lot of demand for accuracy. It's a very popular thing." Amidst the appeal for geographic accuracy, there have been several projects that exploit the inconsistencies of GPS to generate unpredictable results.

In 1995, long before the removal of selective availability, artist Laura Kurgan experimented with GPS as an instrument for exploring the displacements resulting from information technology. In her project You Are Here Museu, a single, stationary GPS receiver placed on the roof of the Museu d'Art

Contemporani de Barcelona became a drawing tool that recorded the scatter of points caused by military scrambling and atmospheric interference. The uncorrected position recordings provided an image of geographic instability: a receiver appearing in multiple positions even while remaining in a fixed location. The project acted allegorically; as Kurgan notes, "Even standing still, we operate in a number of overlapping and incommensurable networks, and so in a number of places at once."

<www.princeton.edu/~kurgan/urhere/html/intro.htm>

Kurgan's project prefaced an approach to GPS visible in the work of architects John Randolph and Bruce Tomb of the Interim Office of Architecture, and graphic designer Tom Bonauro. In late 1996, their exhibition Gnomon was on view at the San Francisco Museum of Modern Art. The installation comprised a large polyurethane object described as looking like a rock, a cranium, or a whale housing a robotic system linked (via a power and data umbilical cord) to a GPS receiver mounted on the roof. The object was programmed to position itself at the coordinate location received by the static antenna. Due to the meander or skew caused by a degraded civilian GPS signal, the whale-like form was constantly being asked to relocate itself, often ramming walls as it tried to move beyond the confines of the 26-foot-square gallery. Deliberate or not, Gnomon was a physical manifestation of the cartographic studies Kurgan had produced the year before.

<www.randolphdesigns.com/html/art.html>

Given the availability of an improved civilian signal, the uncertainty of GPS continues to be a subject of exploration. British artist Jeremy Wood has created an extensive collection of GPS drawings, many of them figural (such as the elephant drawn on foot) or typographic (like the word "Information" written while riding a bicycle through the streets of Brighton and Hove). Wood can be seen as extending the work of British walking artists like Richard Long, Gilbert & George, and Hamish Fulton. He's also clearly interested in GPS as a medium with its own built-in expressiveness. A series of motionless recordings titled "Single Line Stills" were made from a static receiver recording satellite signals and rounding errors. The result is a set of three-dimensional linear constructions that look like elegant wireframe models of some unbuilt architecture.

Back at the May 2000 government press briefing, Neal Lane, director of the Office of Science and Technology, remarked that should the occasion arise in which it is in the country's interest to block accurate GPS signals, the United States will have the ability to do so. Perhaps more alarming is the future possibility of an inescapable, faultless system.

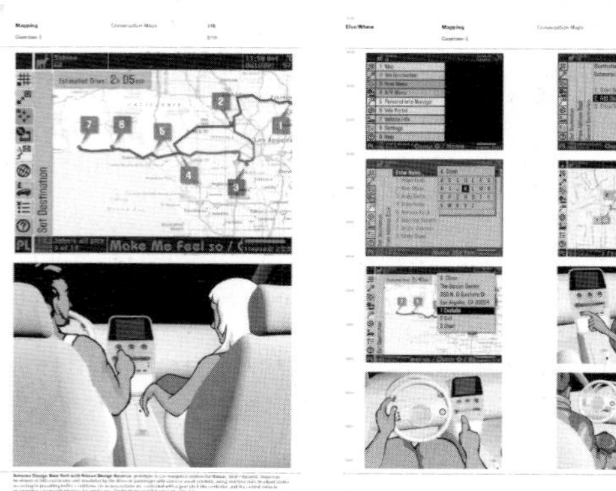

gazetteer E 3–4/10 pp. 118–119

DESTINATIONS AND DETOURS

In-car navigation systems have come a long way since an eery female voice warned "You're on your own now, Claire," in Wim Wenders' 1991 film Until the End of the World. A prototype designed for Nissan would let drivers add their own voice to the map. By JANET ABRAMS.

One of the pluses of printed maps — despite their propensity to crack along the folds, or rip from their spiral binding — is that you can scribble on them. Blurred by rain, these on-the-move jottings capture your own ramblings through a city, and designate personal rather than official landmarks: great local restaurants stumbled upon, a flea market that just happened to be in action, the opening hours of arcane museums. Through these handwritten vestiges, memory is congealed. Planning a new visit to the same place, you dig out the dog-eared map and travel back in time, as well as forward — to the next journey, the next layer of the palimpsest. It's exactly this quality of historical patina that is missing from most in-car electronic mapping systems.

Commissioned in 2002 to develop a prototype in-car navigation system for Nissan, the Japanese car manufacturer, Antenna Design New York thought carefully about how these attributes of printed maps might be transported into the digital realm. Working in collaboration with Nissan Design America, Antenna came up with an "Enhanced Navigation" system whose route planning and navigation functions are augmented by real-time location-based information, and capable of individual annotation.

The system was intended for new crossover vehicles (post SUV) for the American market, aimed in particular at so-called "Tattoo Dads" — men in their late 20s-to mid-30s who want to retain the freedoms of singlehood despite having become

See "Skywriting," p. 268.

parents, and aren't easily impressed by new gadgets. "Technology itself is no longer entertaining," says Antenna partner Masamichi Udagawa. "It has to work, understandably."

Antenna's design anticipates the day when vehicles are able to receive real-time data, either from communications infrastructure embedded in the roadway itself, beamed from light poles with narrow-area wireless broadcast capability, or delivered via a car-borne device that is "dumb to the driver but smart to the system," as Udagawa puts it, based on a standardized communication protocol similar to the EZ-pass toll-payment system.

"We threw in a few things that are a bit further down the road," says Antenna partner Sigi Moeslinger, "because they rely on a bigger system to work, to show what possibilities might open up." Cognizant of the environmental implications of a system that might actually encourage more driving than is actually necessary, she points out that this prototype was intended for cities where cars are already a necessity rather than a pastime. "The current state of navigation is to help you go from Point A to Point B," she adds. "We thought, with all these kind of things available, we could make driving itself a destination."

With the touch-screen already established by other auto makers (such as Toyota) as their "brand" of interaction, and an internal group at Nissan already at work on this kind of interface, Antenna was asked to explore alternatives. "You want to minimize the shift of attention from driving to the touch-screen," explains Moeslinger. "To achieve this, it's better if the screen is more or less located on the windshield, so you don't have to adjust your eyes as much. But then it's far away. Toyota found a compromise where their screen is reachable but close to the console. Nissan wanted to push the screen itself further back and provide physical control, closer to the steering wheel."

Of three options they designed for the physical controller, Antenna recommended one slightly larger than the gear stick, and positioned close to it. "It's a familiar gesture, easy to reach from the driving position, and you can rest your hand on it," says Moeslinger. The designers decided that scrolling through a list-based menu would be best in the in-car context, reducing the likelihood of inaccurate selections. "The more cursor freedom we give, the more attention is required, and the higher the chance of error." On-screen actions are effected by tilting the controller side-to-side, or by clicking a button beneath its tip; a built-in fingerprint scanner recognizes individual users and automatically resets the system to match their stored preferences. "Even though it was for a concept car, Nissan didn't want it to be a fantasy demo, but something grounded," she continues. "They wanted to get some knowledge out of it that could be implemented. So it's based on existing things — the iPod was always mentioned as one of the interfaces that this demographic likes because it's minimal but extended to include other functionalities."

Integrating communication functions usually accessed via desktop and hand-held devices, the system would draw on a central database to provide email, news and other live information. The console is equipped with a keyboard for composing email, though Moeslinger hastens to assure that "the idea is not for anyone ever to type while driving. Many times, there's a passenger who will do these things."

The navigation system computes the most efficient journey to a chosen destination, taking into account current traffic conditions. Having set a destination, the user can add multiple stops en-route (shown as numbered flags) then use the Show/Edit Route option to adjust the journey, eliminating certain stops in order to reduce travel time. The map can be easily viewed at different scales, to gain an overview of a journey, using the Zoom/Pan function, and seen from various perspectives; as the driver progresses along the chosen route, an elegant red compass icon marks the car's changing location. "It's a space-time continuum map," comments Udagawa.

The system includes two additional features that rely on real-time data: the Scanner looks out for friends driving nearby and signals their presence with the appropriate icon (logged in the address book). Then, by choosing the Squawk function, a one-minute voice message can be recorded and instantly sent to them. In map-mode, Targeting allows the user to select featured items on the map, such as the charges at the parking ramp at one's final destination. The driver can also plant flags on the map, to designate places of interest noted in passing; the system stores voice recordings, pegged to location, for future exploration.

Accumulating a patchwork of such annotations, the in-car map shifts from being merely a more efficient means of navigation to a container of personal impressions — a veritable Baede-Kar, as Reyner Banham once remarked (of his in-car audiotape guide to Los Angeles) for the flâneur behind the steering wheel.

Conversation maps

CLICKIN'N'SCRAPIN'

When is a city also a database? Answer: when it's Manhattan, as shown on the Skyscraper Museum's website. But the VIVA archive sits on top of yet another urban database. By JANET ABRAMS.

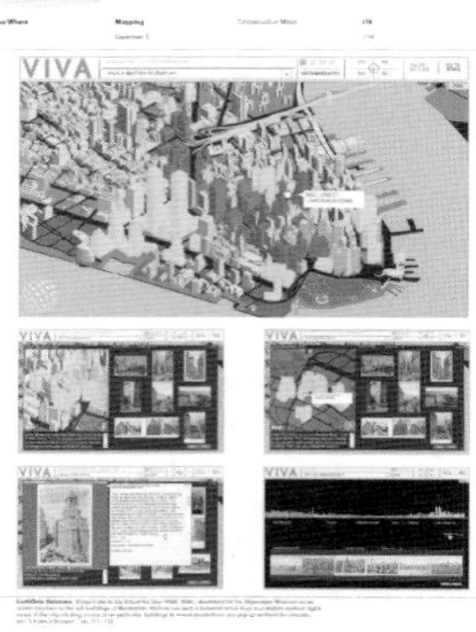

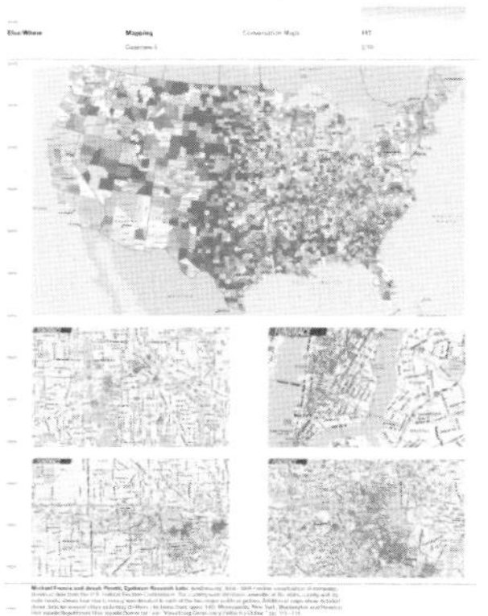

gazetteer E 1/10 pp. 116–117

The Skyscraper Museum is dedicated to tracing the evolution of the edifices with which New York has become synonymous. So it makes sense that the buildings themselves are used as the points of entry to the museum's growing online archive of historical documents and photographs in VIVA (Visual Index to the Virtual Archive), launched online in 2004.

<www.skyscraper.org/viva/viva.html>

VIVA's interface was developed with a $130,000 National Leadership Grant for Museums Online from the Institute of Museum and Library Services, a U.S. government agency. The project as a whole cost around $200,000. It is built on top of an interactive 3D map of Manhattan completed in 2000 by Urban Data Solutions (UDS), which became EarthData Solutions upon its 2004 acquisition by the geo-spatial information company. The museum's founding director, Carol Willis, came across the UDS model in a Columbia University urban history course, and first used it in the museum's 1999 Big Buildings exhibit.

"Our idea in the grant was that this project could serve as a paradigm: to use the web, an inherently visual means of communication, to make a visual index," says Willis. "So you click on an image rather than clicking on words. It seemed obvious that you should be able to explore the city via the buildings—if it could be done. Retrieving the historical city by clicking on postcards provides access in a very charming way." Since the museum has limited space for physical archives, digitization is "a logical way to proceed with collections management."

A successor of sorts to Robert Moses' 1964 wooden model of the city, the UDS digital model was developed over several years using various techniques, including LIDAR, ground and aerial photography, orthophotos and parcel maps to compile a massive database, accurate to within one meter of the physical landscape. EarthData has produced SIMmetry 3D models for some nine U.S. cities, showing the dimensions and shape of every built structure, with accurate rooflines and heights, and features such as floorplates, sidewalks and parapets. Their primary target markets are professionals in spatial information management industries—mobile telephony, real estate, urban planning, government, engineering and architecture—who may license a whole city, or just one particular chunk. According to Willis, the UDS model of New York City took a dozen people three years' full-time work to produce.

While the UDS digital model is continuously updated, the VIVA interface uses a version showing the city as it appeared in 2000: the conspicuous presence of the World Trade Center towers cause an involuntary pang when one first encounters the site and realizes that, despite its use of seemingly up-to-date technology, the city as portrayed is already an anachronism. "It's very much an historic artifact, which is also aging," Willis admits. "The UDS graphic language is beginning to look like something that happened in the late 20th Century."

VIVA launches with an axonometric "aerial" view of Manhattan, which can be manipulated using an icon on the upper menu bar, to be viewed from all four compass points. For those accustomed to seeing Manhattan from the toe (its southern or, more strictly, southeastern tip), some of the other stiffly axonometric views provide strangely disorienting vantages, only vaguely recognizable from flying over the city on approach to landing at La Guardia Airport.

In the "Skyline" view, the alternative main mode, the city's Hudson and East River elevations are shown as line renderings against a black background; these can be cruised from several proximities with arrow keys that lure one to continue the tour or switch to the opposite side of the island. Archival snapshots are presented along the lower margin, easily enlarged and captioned with a click of the mouse.

To investigate a particular architectural gem, one mouses over the relevant area in "aerial mode," which highlights it in blue, and then clicks to zoom in to the next level of detail: from aerial, to neighborhood, to street, to building view. Given the historic concentration of skyscrapers in Lower Manhattan, this area of the map has so far received most of the museum's archival attention, though a few buildings

See "Perils of Precision," p. 184.

in Midtown have also been annotated. Users accustomed to SimCity speeds of development may find themselves frustrated by flags that pop up over other neighborhoods, declaring "Skyline Only" or "Area Under Construction."

Once an area has been selected, groups of buildings can be pulled up at street scale, isolated in 3D against the city grid. One more click retrieves an individual building and its associated archival documents (antique postcards and construction shots), which appear in an album format to the right. The richly textured facades of the historic buildings, seen in photographic perspective, contrast pleasingly with the anonymous, plastic precision of their 3D block-model digital stand-ins. "Postcards are a cheap but rich visual repository of urban history," says Willis. "If you have 15 postcards from 1900 to 1930 of the same building, they all look a little bit different. Postcards mostly aren't dated, but we have the expertise to identify what is in each one."

The VIVA team included archivist Sueyoung Park and web designer Mark Watkins, who had worked with Brian McGrath on the Skyscraper Museum's earlier online project, Manhattan Timeformations. "The technology wasn't easy," says Willis. "We spent a lot of time thinking about what worked intuitively for the viewer, working on the compass, and on the ability to turn off the context. You can't cut a building out of a construction photo or a postcard. This map enables us to represent individual buildings in a way nobody could afford to do if it was just an academic project."

Besides the digital city interface, VIVA offers five other more traditional modes of exploration: via specific buildings, architects and developers' names, collections, visual timelines, or The Allstars — half a dozen canonic skyscrapers, still standing or (as the site discreetly puts it) demolished, ranging from the Woolworth Building to the World Trade towers, that symbolize New York.

VIVA II, now under development, will focus on the Empire State Building and the World Trade Center, using two photographic collections donated to the Skyscraper Museum: 503 photos from a paper notebook on the former, and color slides of the latter from engineers Leslie Robertson Associates. VIVA II will allow visitors to compare construction technologies in the 1930s and the 1970s using each building's elevation as the interface, by clicking either on a timeline, a floor, or a grid of photos in nine topic categories such as machinery and equipment, or views out. VIVA II is expected to debut in 2006.

VISUALIZING DEMOCRACY, $ BY $

By mapping political contributions to donors' locations using geo-coding technology, Fundrace offered a new view of U.S. political geography in the run-up to the 2004 presidential election. By JANET ABRAMS.

During national elections, especially in the United States, maps come to the forefront of public consciousness: maps of redistricting; TV graphics showing hour-by-hour changes of party territory as the results come in; maps showing quadrennial patterns of blue/red quilting. In the run-up to the 2004 U.S. election, campaign strategists used digital mapping software to target swing voters down to their doorsteps, while New York Times website visitors could click on a U.S. map that morphed between the states' geographic dimensions and their markedly different proportions when measured in terms of Electoral College votes.

One experimental project created in 2003 — 04 by Michael Frumin and Jonah Peretti at Eyebeam, a New York media arts organization, used mapping to draw a different portrait of American political loyalties. Opinions varied as to whether Fundrace was merely entertaining or an intrusion into people's private lives. But it unquestionably tapped a popular nerve, by providing a new view of existing information. Drawing on data about individual campaign donations, collected and published by the Federal Election Commission (FEC), Fundrace reveals the political complexion of the country as a whole, and allows more detailed views of several cities, offering visitors the ability to drill down via zip code searches to individual addresses, and check on their next-door neighbors' political proclivities. Political candidates are required to file information with the FEC on any donor who contributes $200 or more, including their name, address, occupation and how much they gave to which party. "This information has actually been available for a long time, first on paper, more recently on the Internet," says Fundrace co-creator Michael Frumin. "But 'til now, it has been the domain of political analysts and reporters, not something the average person thought about or looked at." The information was available on such sites as Opensecrets and PoliticalMoneyLine, "but that does not necessarily mean it was accessible." Fundrace makes the data meaningful to ordinary people by mapping it, exploiting geo-coding technology that enables latitude/longitude coordinates to be attached to any piece of information.

<www.fundrace.org>

<www.opensecrets.org/> <www.fecinfo.com/>

"We used geo-coding to exploit the principle of locality," Frumin explains. "If you have a large set of information, and you want to find the parts most relevant to a particular person, then you need to find

See "Looking for a Less Imperial Gaze," pp. 114–115.

the information that is closest to them on some axis — such as time, space or issues. This principle has many applications, the first and most obvious of which is to make a map."

Fundrace offers two different kinds: maps of the entire country (showing how much money was donated to the two major U.S. political parties, county by county, and within three digit zip codes) and maps of individual cities. Initially, just the top 10 donating cities were mapped, but several more have since been added, including Minneapolis and close-up sections of New York and Los Angeles.

On the countrywide map, pie charts for key cities show percentages of donations to each party (blue equals Democrat, red equals Republican). On the city maps, thanks to geo-coding, the distribution of political support is instantly apparent: like urban EKGs of political affluence, these scatter plots reveal the geography of wealth and show political bedfellows clustering in certain neighborhoods, though these patterns vary according to each city's urban morphology. Two different search modes allow users to enter a specific name, or zip codes (their own or any other), and pull up who gave how much to which party. It turns out that certain people donate sizeable amounts to both parties, hedging their bets. "Some people staunchly support one candidate, or one party," Frumin notes. "Sometimes people play both sides. They just want influence."

With his colleagues at Eyebeam Research Labs, Frumin conceived Fundrace in the fall of 2003, when Howard Dean's campaign was stirring excitement over the pace of its web-based grassroots fundraising. Released in March 2004, the site immediately gained notice by the Associated Press, and within a week was getting hundreds of thousands of hits, and millions of searches. People gravitated to Fundrace to check out how much their namesakes and neighbors donated, bringing the drama of national politics down to a more immediate and personally perceptible scale. Celebrities' names could be plugged in find out their political affiliations. Concerns about invasion of privacy soon followed because some donors had not realized that their addresses and occupations were stored in the FEC database, and that this is public information. As geocoding becomes more accessible, Frumin predicts, such applications will become more prevalent, for political and other purposes. "If there is a conclusion to be drawn" he adds, "it's that it's definitely possible to take open government information and make it way more interesting to people. And don't be surprised: if you give them the opportunity to snoop on each other, they will."

gazetteer H 4/13 p. 190

LOOKING FOR A LESS IMPERIAL GAZE

3D digital imaging usually strives for glitzy verisimilitude but Manhattan Timeformations deliberately uses wireframe animation to visualize the boom and bust cycles of New York's skyscraper history. By JANET ABRAMS

"Every map or presentation is a kind of lie. You draw certain things and leave out certain things. Depending on what scale it is, it tells a certain truth." So says architect/urban designer Brian McGrath who, with web designer Mark Watkins, created Manhattan Timeformations for the Skyscraper Museum in 2000. A computer animated model of Manhattan, it allows the viewer to look at certain things and leave out others, as they select layers of information about the city's urban history. Piloted in a series of public presentations in the museum's temporary spaces downtown during the summer of 2000, the project is presented on the museum's website and in its Battery Park City home.

<http://skyscraper.org/WEB_PROJECTS/MANHATTAN_TIMEFORMATIONS/mt_intro.htm>

Manhattan Timeformations consists of six sections: Perspectival Flythrough, Timeformations, Transparent New York, Downtown New York, Midtown New York and Manhattan Timetable. Funded by a grant from the New York State Council on the Arts, the project gave such a seductive demonstration of how interactive mapping could animate architectural history that it proved pivotal in helping the museum secure a subsequent grant to create VIVA.

Using data from real estate directories and other sources, McGrath — an architect and adjunct professor of urban design at Columbia University's Graduate School of Architecture and Urban Planning — entered the dimensions of 726 major skyscrapers into FormZ 3D modeling software. McGrath and Watkins then used Flash software to animate successive layers of the city's development,

See "Clickin'n'Scrapin'," pp. 112–113.

so they hover like a Close Encounters spaceship then zoom impossibly towards you in zingy bright colors against a black background.

The model incorporates time, using a scale of one hundred feet to a year (along the vertical axis), and offers a bar-graph of the city's upward mobility that clearly delineates the cycles of boom and bust in downtown and midtown Manhattan real estate. The clustering of skyscrapers into distinct bands of time corresponds, the site explains, to "frenzied peaks of investment and construction" separated by long speculative lulls. "This deceptive quiet masks enormous shifts: structural and economic adjustments along with technological changes, parallel government reactions, social and cultural shifts, recession, depression and war."

Manhattan Timeformations allows you to explore various eras and types of urban development and infrastructure, and superimpose them in contrasting colored layers. A dozen different types of map-based information can be selectively activated at the click of a button: for example, the dense cluster of early Dutch settlements at the southern tip of the island can be "switched on" along with elevated railway lines, monuments and parks, subways, and street grids of different eras. The intensive waves of skyscraper development in midtown and downtown are depicted as 3D wire frame buildings: click the button for a given period of intense speculation, and a new a crop of office towers springs into view, outlined in different colors, and comes to populate the island's precious real estate.

The buildings in Manhattan Timeformations are deliberately shown as unrendered skeletons. "That's radical," says McGrath, "because commercial 3D images are emphatically rendered: they presume that the more realistic the light and the materials, the better. That's what all the time and money goes into. It's a new technology, there's a wow factor, and everyone jumps to verisimilitude. By dispensing with all that, you can be free to get at other issues."

Those other issues are public participation in the urban design process, and the possibility of maps that engage people in what McGrath calls "attentive circuits," instead of just being entertained or dazed by digital technology. Manhattan Timeformations is a prototype for a kind of urban design tool that would ideally be available not just to developers.

McGrath's perspective is heightened by his experience teaching for four months a year in Thailand. "Cities are being developed in very different ways in S.E. Asia. It's a difficult situation, where public agencies don't have the same tools as the private developers. How do you build a sustainable city within a neo-liberal capitalist economy, with no master planning? You have to have tools that are not dazzling. Somehow, if you have more viewpoints, or the ability to interact from many viewpoints, you can get a different picture of a project. Imagine if a community could make a rendering so they could understand what a proposed development would look like from their street corner, as opposed to the privileged point of view of the planners or developers. A less imperial gaze is what I'm looking for."

Since completing Manhattan Timeformations, McGrath and Watkins have been working on a project for the U.S. Forest Service to develop an interactive map and related website of 9/11 memorials in U.S. towns and cities, including some 30-50 USFS-funded memorials (which had to include tree-planting to be eligible for its grants) and several hundred others. Erika Svendsen, a Senior Researcher at the USFS New York Field station, recognized Manhattan Timeformations as "a successional forest of skyscrapers," says McGrath. She asked his firm, Urban Interface, to develop a map that shows the geographic distribution of the memorials and links to a database of interviews and other information about the memorials. "What's fascinating is how bizarre the American city is," McGrath remarks. "There are all these college campuses, town centers, corporate campuses and edge cities that are sites of memorial gardens. They are small lenses into America today."

<www.urban-interface.com/client/livingmemorial/lmps_launcher.html>

Manhattan Timeformations and this new project hint at the "deep-data" views of cities that will become feasible as urban and architectural renderings converge with Geographical Information Systems (GIS). But McGrath is determined to get beyond the clichés of computer-generated urban imagery to a more nuanced representational language influenced as much by cinematography as cartography. "We're just beginning to see how architects and designers can use GIS. It's ubiquitous in planning and the sciences, but it needs an architect's imagination to untangle it. We haven't really scratched the surface of its capabilities."

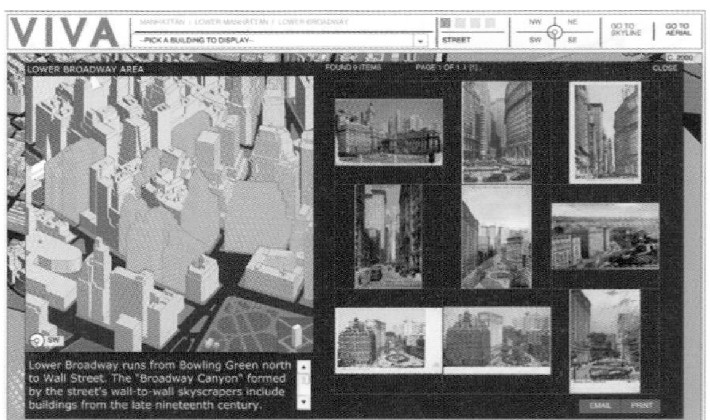

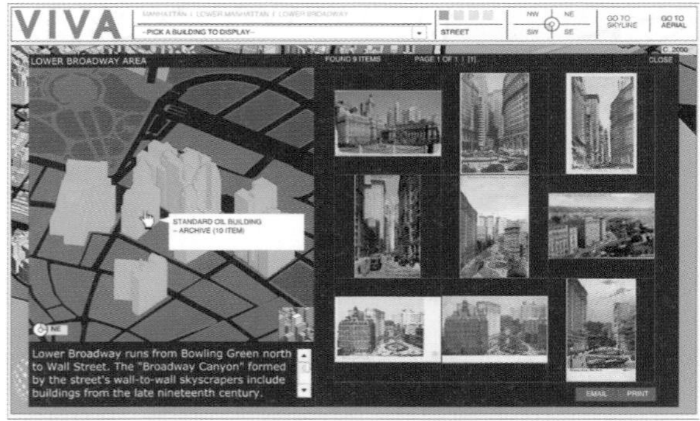

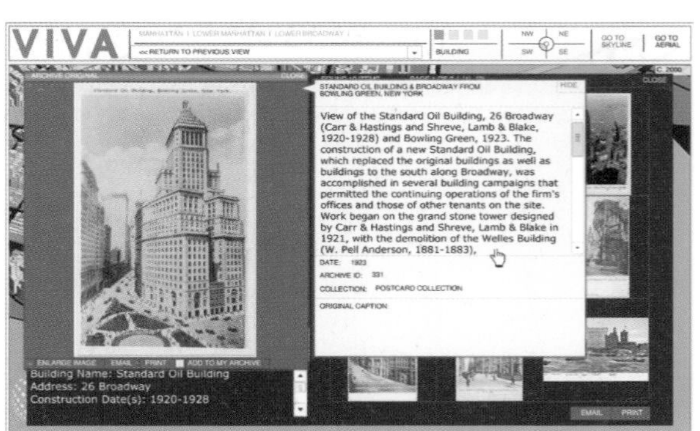

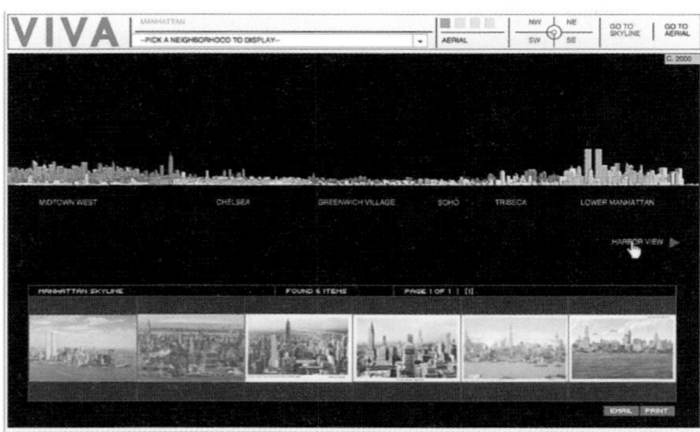

Mark Watkins, Carol Willis and **Sueyoung Park, Skyscraper Museum, New York** *Visual Index to the Virtual Archive (VIVA)*, 2004 / developed as an online interface to the tall buildings of Manhattan. Visitors can switch between aerial (top) and skyline (bottom right) views of the city; clicking zooms in on particular buildings to reveal annotations and pop-up archival documents / see "Clickin'n'Scrapin'," pp. 111–112.

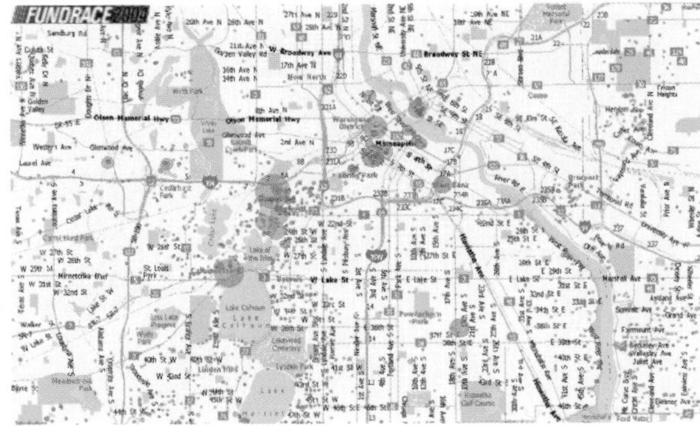

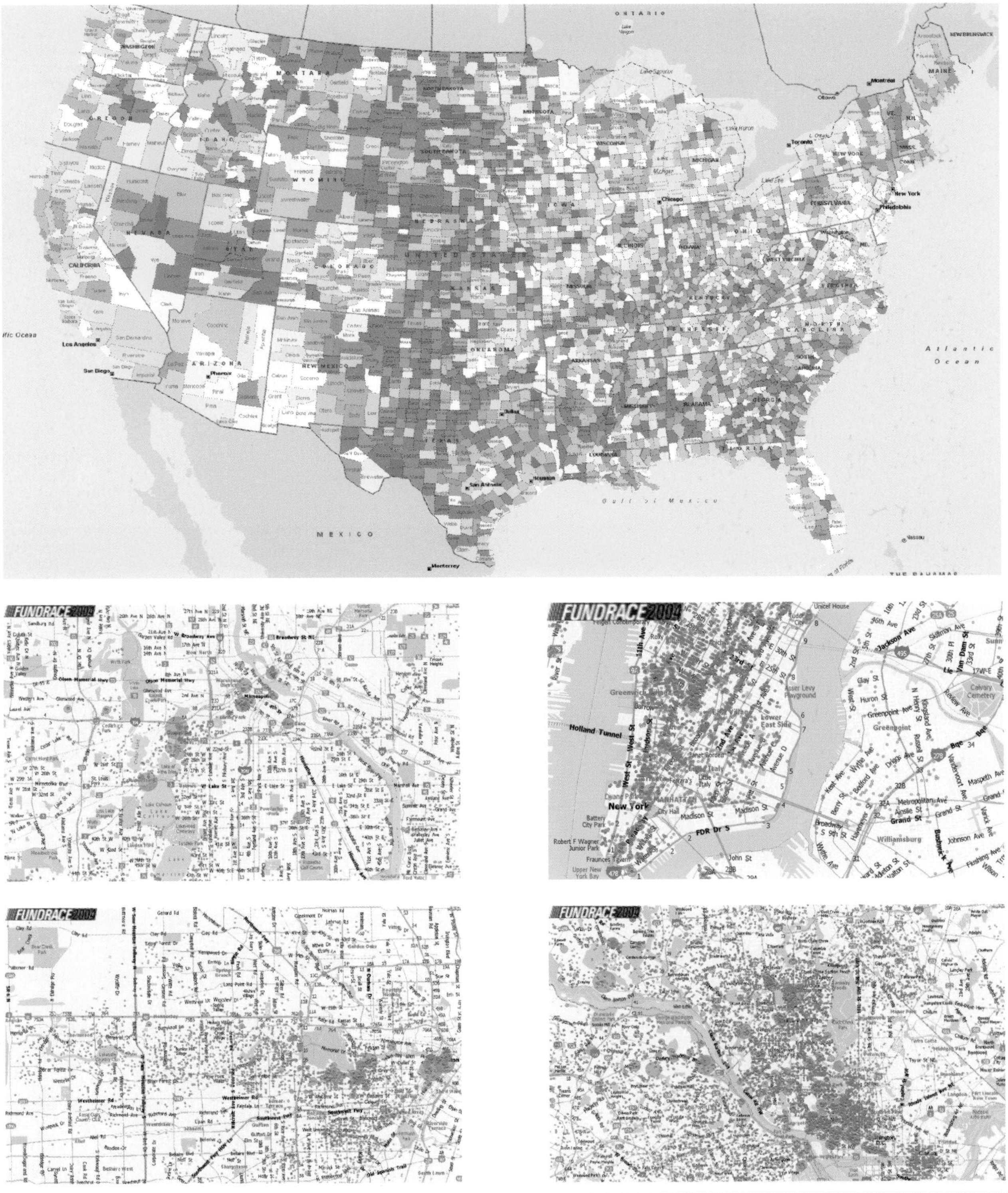

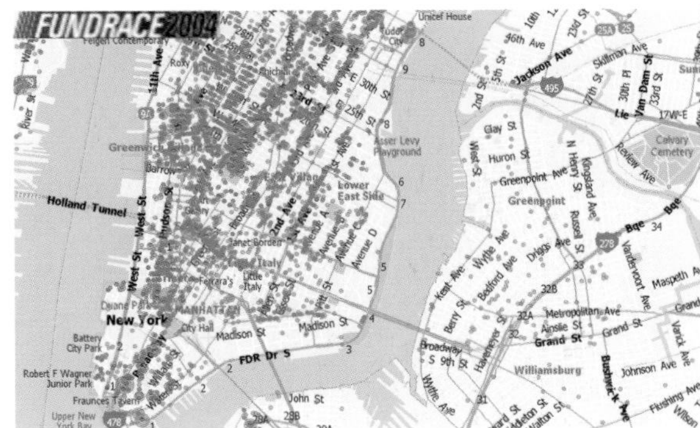

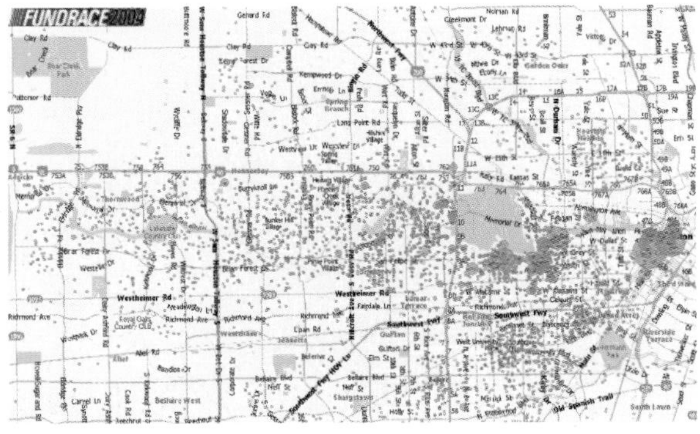

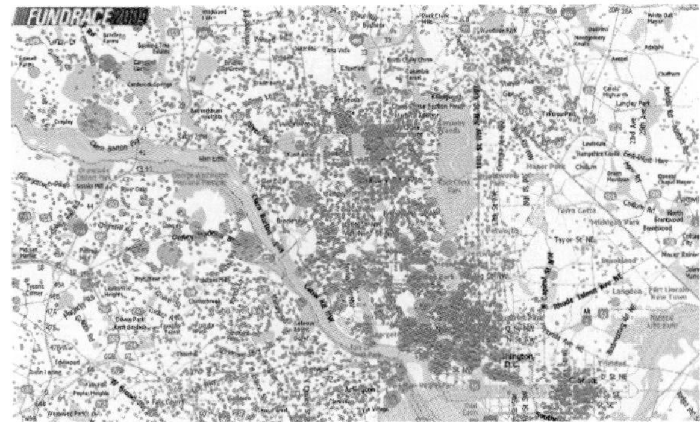

Michael Frumin and **Jonah Peretti, Eyebeam Research Labs** *fundrace.org*, 2003–2004 / online visualization of campaign donation data from the U.S. Federal Election Commission. The country-wide interface, viewable at the state, county and zip code levels, shows how much money was donated to each of the two major political parties. Additional maps show detailed donor data for several cities including (bottom, clockwise from upper left): Minneapolis, New York, Washington and Houston. Red represents Republican; blue represents Democrat / see "Visualizing Democracy $ by $," pp. 113–114.

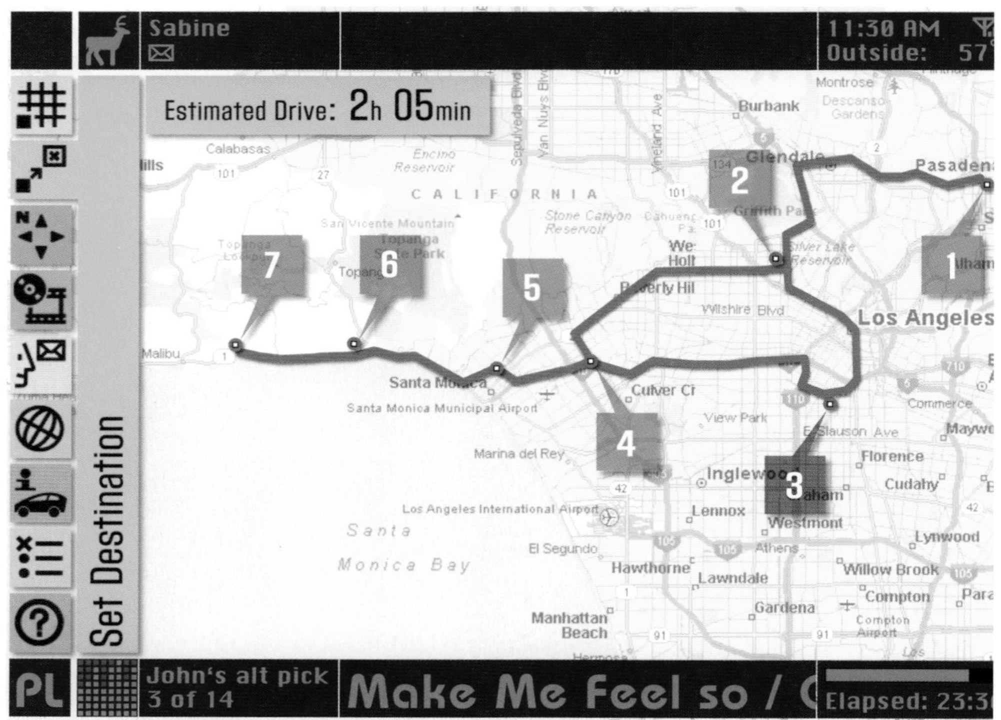

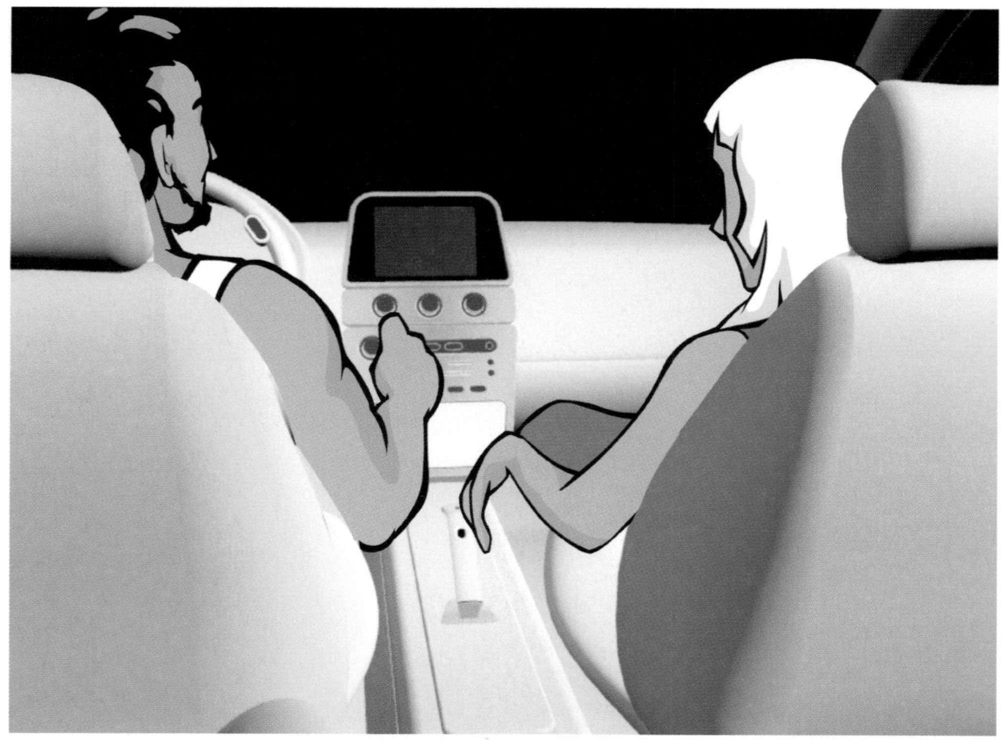

Antenna Design New York with **Nissan Design America** *prototype in-car navigation system for Nissan*, 2002 / dynamic maps can be viewed at different scales and annotated by the driver or passenger with voice or visual markers, using real-time data to adjust routes according to prevailing traffic conditions. On-screen actions are controlled with a gear stick-like controller, and the central console incorporates a keyboard interface for email / see "Destinations and Detours," pp. 110–111.

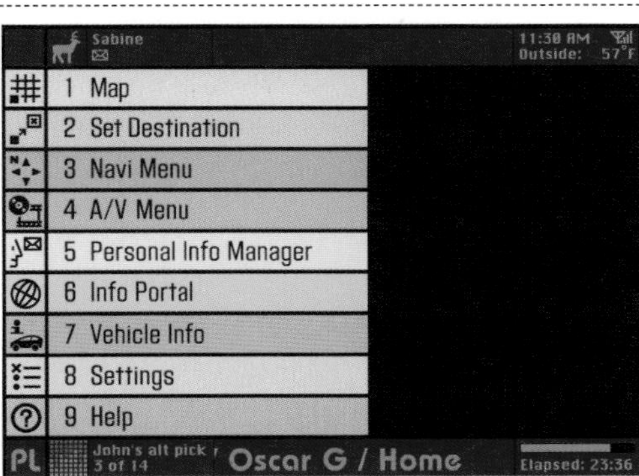
Sabine
11:30 AM
Outside: 57°F
1 Map
2 Set Destination
3 Navi Menu
4 A/V Menu
5 Personal Info Manager
6 Info Portal
7 Vehicle Info
8 Settings
9 Help
John's alt pick
3 of 14
Oscar G / Home
Elapsed: 23:36

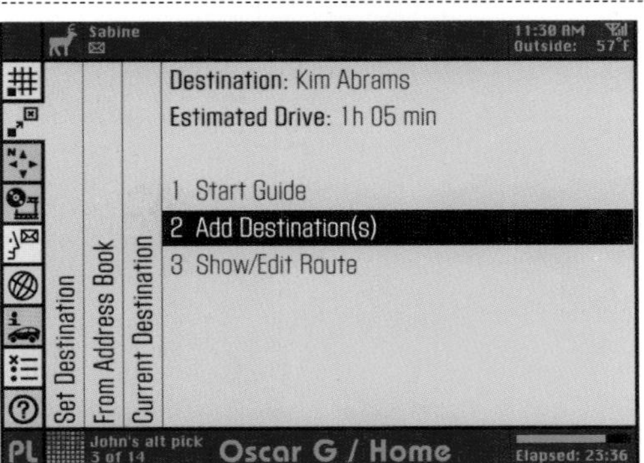
Sabine
11:30 AM
Outside: 57°F
Set Destination
From Address Book
Current Destination
Destination: Kim Abrams
Estimated Drive: 1h 05 min
1 Start Guide
2 Add Destination(s)
3 Show/Edit Route
John's alt pick
3 of 14
Oscar G / Home
Elapsed: 23:36

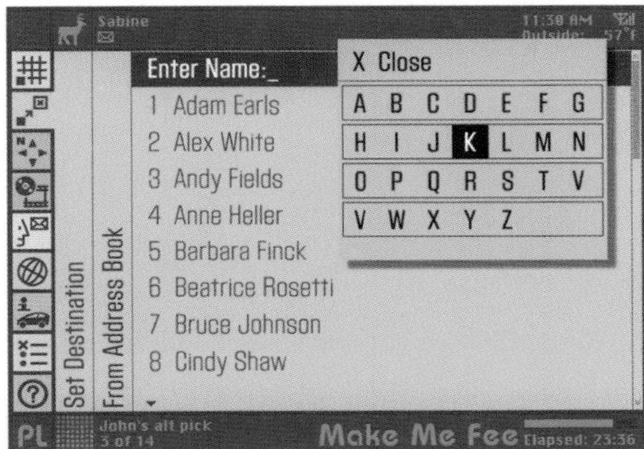
Sabine
11:30 AM
Set Destination
From Address Book
Enter Name:_
1 Adam Earls
2 Alex White
3 Andy Fields
4 Anne Heller
5 Barbara Finck
6 Beatrice Rosetti
7 Bruce Johnson
8 Cindy Shaw
X Close
A B C D E F G
H I J K L M N
O P Q R S T V
V W X Y Z
John's alt pick
3 of 14
Make Me Fee
Elapsed: 23:36

Sabine
11:30 AM
Outside: 57°F
Pasadena
00:57 s
John's alt pick
3 of 14
Feel so / Oscar G /
Elapsed: 23:36

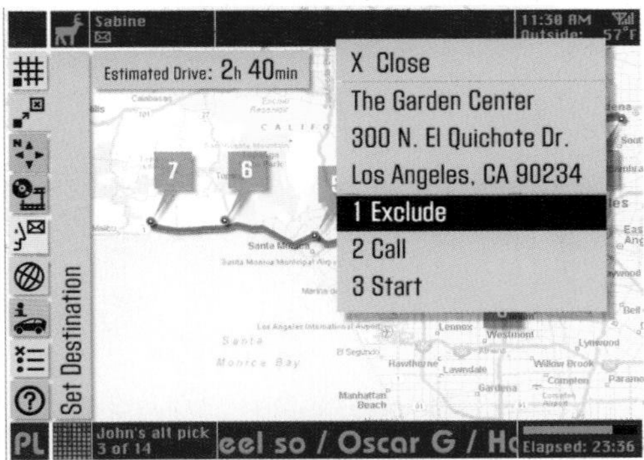
Sabine
11:30 AM
Set Destination
Estimated Drive: 2h 40min
X Close
The Garden Center
300 N. El Quichote Dr.
Los Angeles, CA 90234
1 Exclude
2 Call
3 Start
John's alt pick
3 of 14
eel so / Oscar G / H
Elapsed: 23:36

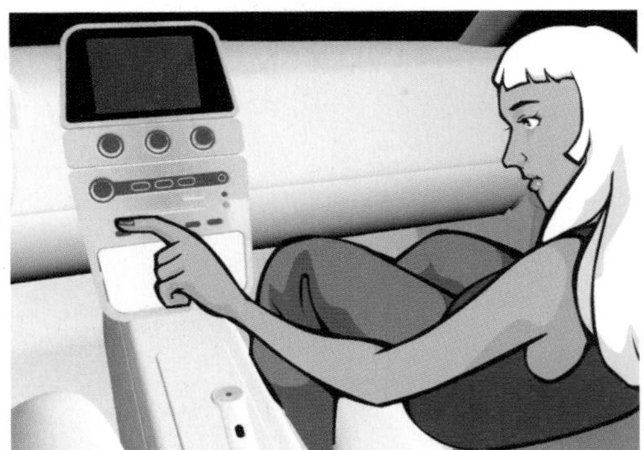

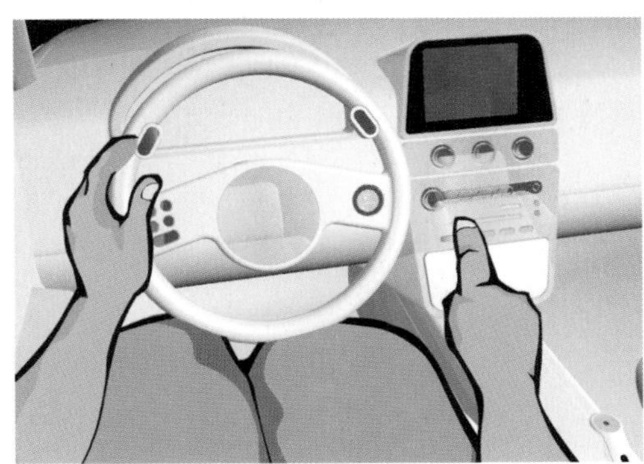

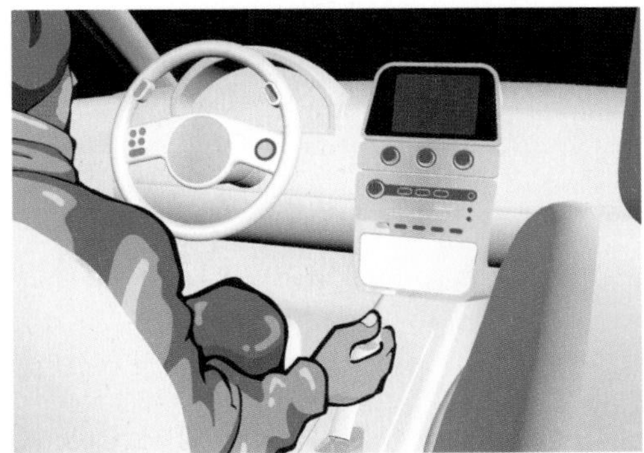

Hertz *Neverlost* GPS-based in-car navigation system, 2004 / drivers enter a destination address using the arrow buttons and menu options on a dashboard console, and select a routing method (shortest time, least use of freeways, or most use of freeways). A digital map, assisted by voice prompts, presents the prescribed route / © 2004 Hertz Systems, Inc. Hertz is a registered service mark and trademark of Hertz System, Inc. / see "Can You Find Me Now?" pp. 105–106.

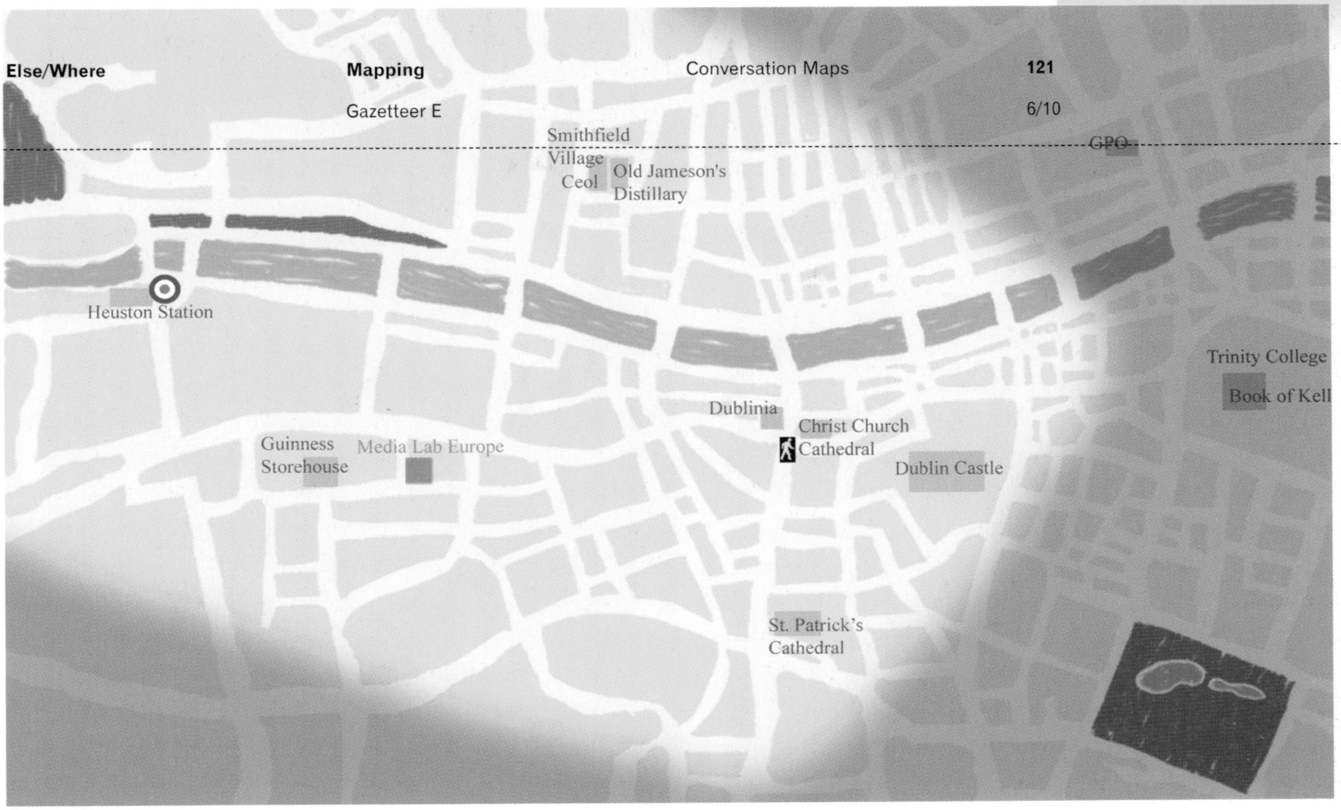

Smithfield Village
Ceol
Old Jameson's Distillary
GPO
Heuston Station
Trinity College
Book of Kells
Dublinia
Christ Church Cathedral
Guinness Storehouse
Media Lab Europe
Dublin Castle
St. Patrick's Cathedral

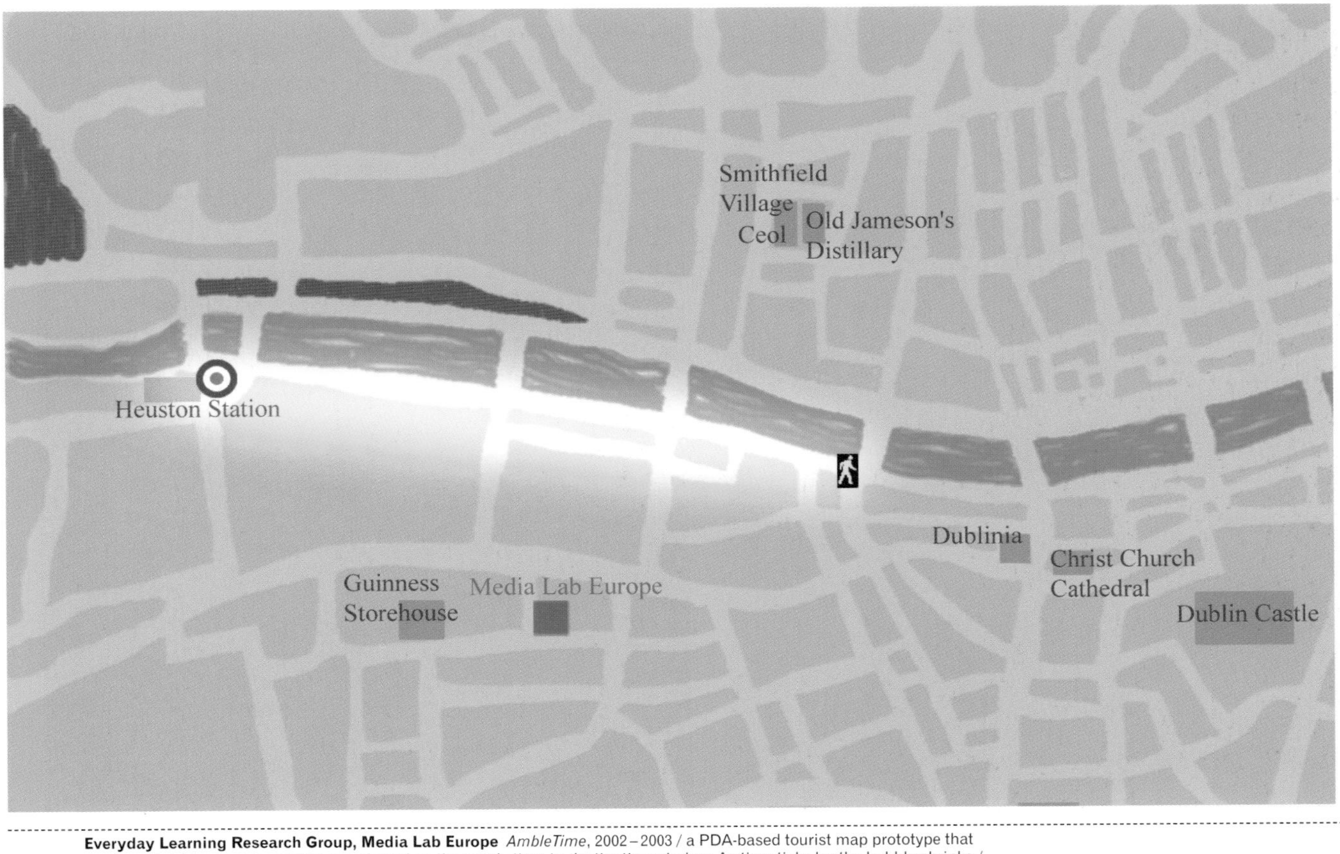

Smithfield Village
Ceol
Old Jameson's Distillary
Heuston Station
Dublinia
Christ Church Cathedral
Guinness Storehouse
Media Lab Europe
Dublin Castle

Everyday Learning Research Group, Media Lab Europe *AmbleTime*, 2002 – 2003 / a PDA-based tourist map prototype that creates a bubble-shaped ambling zone based on the user's time-to-destination window. As time ticks by, the bubble shrinks / / see "The Elastic Space-Time Continuum," pp. 104 – 105.

Proboscis *Urban Tapestries*, 2004 / prototype PDA-based application allowing pedestrians to annotate a shared map of London with their personal geographic experiences by recording and uploading photographs, text and sound files. Threads from the public trial include "Arguments I Had With My Ex-Husband" / see "The Map Gets Personal," p.107.

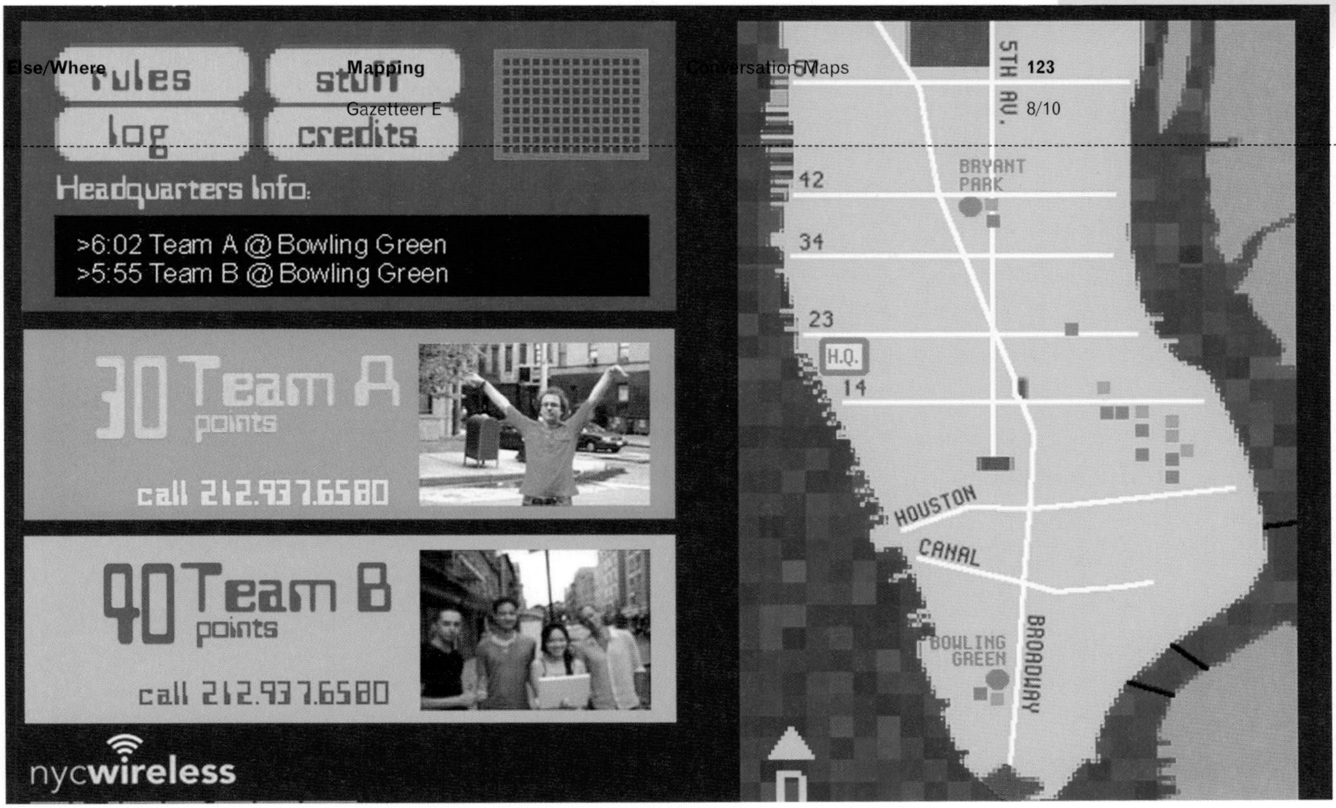

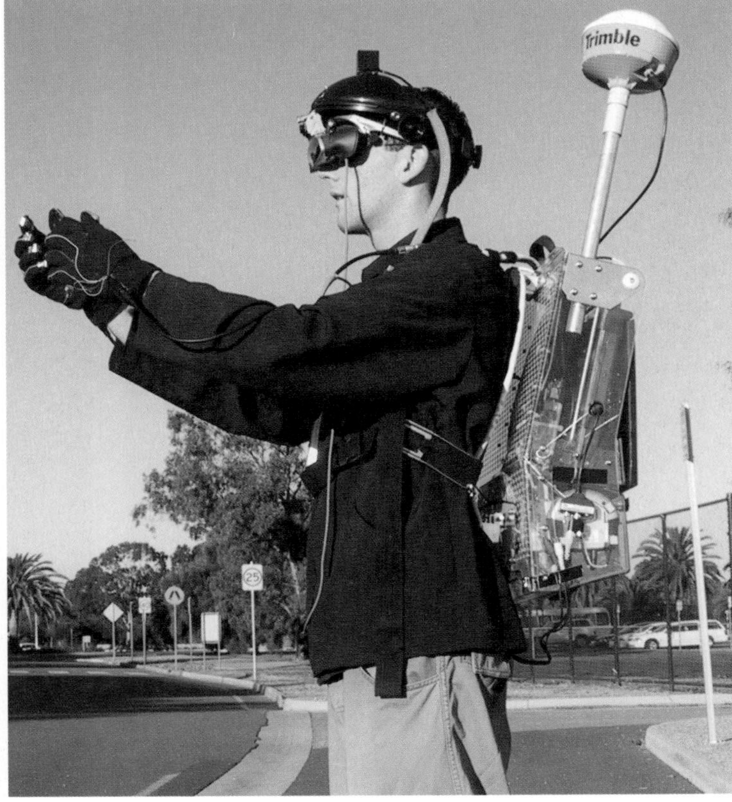

Yuri Gitman and **Carlos J. Gómez de Llareña** *Noderunner*, 2002 / game participants race in teams against the clock to access as many wireless Internet nodes as possible. Each team submits photographic proof of a connection to the *Noderunner* weblog, which becomes a real time scoreboard / see "Games in the Electrosphere," pp. 106–107.

Wayne Piekarski and **Bruce Thomas**, **University of South Australia** *Tinmith*, 2001 / (bottom three images): wearable computing system developed as a potential tool for city planning and medical applications / images courtesy of Wayne Piekarski, Wearable Computer Lab, University of South Australia / see "Possible Worlds," p. 28.

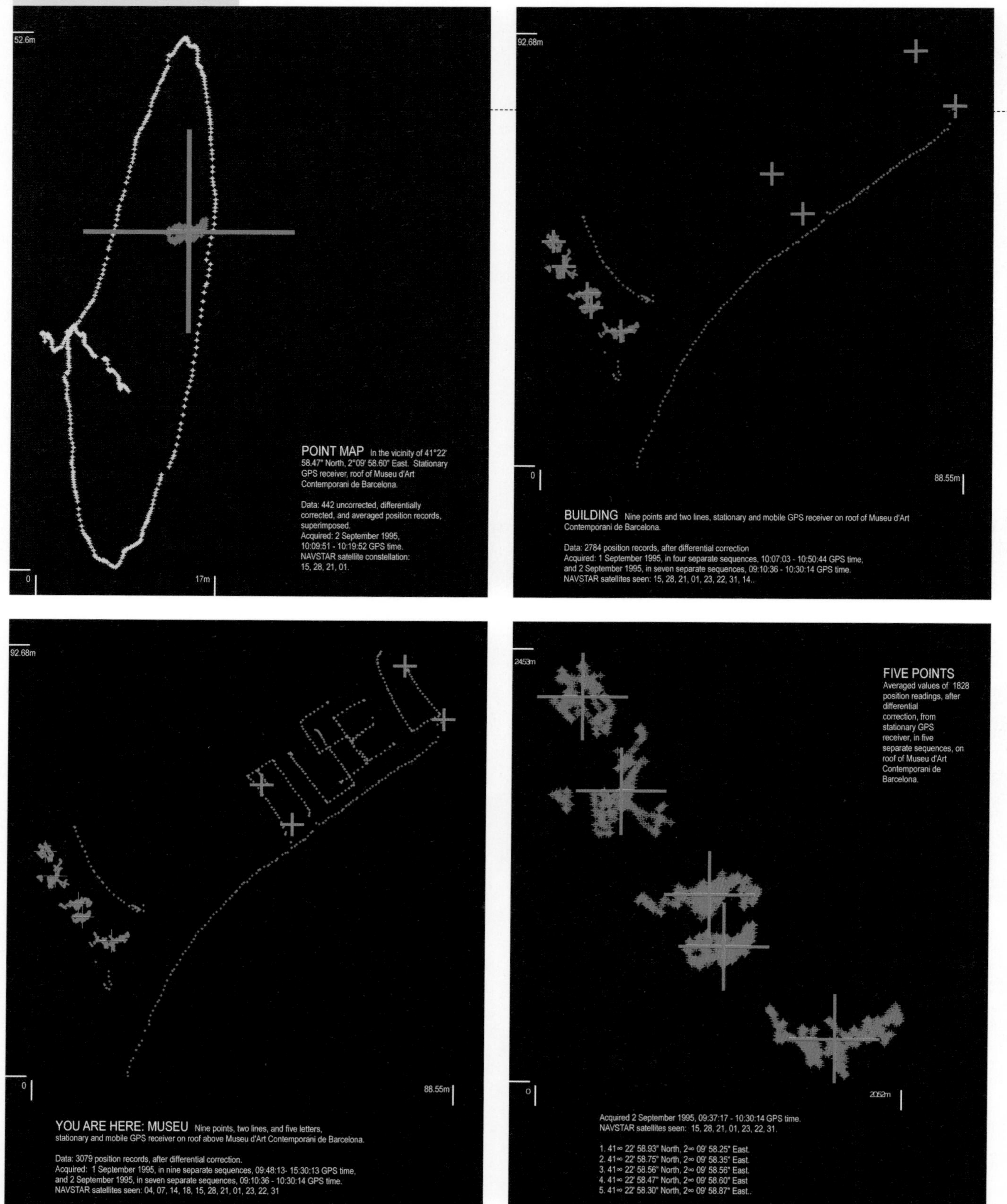

52.6m
0
17m
POINT MAP In the vicinity of 41°22' 58.47" North, 2°09' 58.60" East. Stationary GPS receiver, roof of Museu d'Art Contemporani de Barcelona.
Data: 442 uncorrected, differentially corrected, and averaged position records, superimposed.
Acquired: 2 September 1995, 10:09:51 - 10:19:52 GPS time.
NAVSTAR satellite constellation: 15, 28, 21, 01.
92.68m
0
88.55m
BUILDING Nine points and two lines, stationary and mobile GPS receiver on roof of Museu d'Art Contemporani de Barcelona.
Data: 2784 position records, after differential correction
Acquired: 1 September 1995, in four separate sequences, 10:07:03 - 10:50:44 GPS time, and 2 September 1995, in seven separate sequences, 09:10:36 - 10:30:14 GPS time.
NAVSTAR satellites seen: 15, 28, 21, 01, 23, 22, 31, 14..
92.68m
0
88.55m
YOU ARE HERE: MUSEU Nine points, two lines, and five letters, stationary and mobile GPS receiver on roof above Museu d'Art Contemporani de Barcelona.
Data: 3079 position records, after differential correction.
Acquired: 1 September 1995, in nine separate sequences, 09:48:13- 15:30:13 GPS time, and 2 September 1995, in seven separate sequences, 09:10:36 - 10:30:14 GPS time.
NAVSTAR satellites seen: 04, 07, 14, 18, 15, 28, 21, 01, 23, 22, 31
2453m
0
2052m
FIVE POINTS Averaged values of 1828 position readings, after differential correction, from stationary GPS receiver, in five separate sequences, on roof of Museu d'Art Contemporani de Barcelona.
Acquired 2 September 1995, 09:37:17 - 10:30:14 GPS time.
NAVSTAR satellites seen: 15, 28, 21, 01, 23, 22, 31.
1. 41∞ 22' 58.93" North, 2∞ 09' 58.25" East.
2. 41∞ 22' 58.75" North, 2∞ 09' 58.35" East.
3. 41∞ 22' 58.56" North, 2∞ 09' 58.56" East.
4. 41∞ 22' 58.47" North, 2∞ 09' 58.60" East
5. 41∞ 22' 58.30" North, 2∞ 09' 58.87" East..

Laura Kurgan *You Are Here Museu*, 1995 / Kurgan installed a GPS receiver on the roof of the Richard Meier-designed Museu d'Art Contemporani de Barcelona in Spain, recording the discrepancies in the network's attempts to pinpoint the building's exact location, due to atmospheric interference and military scrambling / images courtesy of Laura Kurgan / see "Instruments of Uncertainty," pp. 109–110.

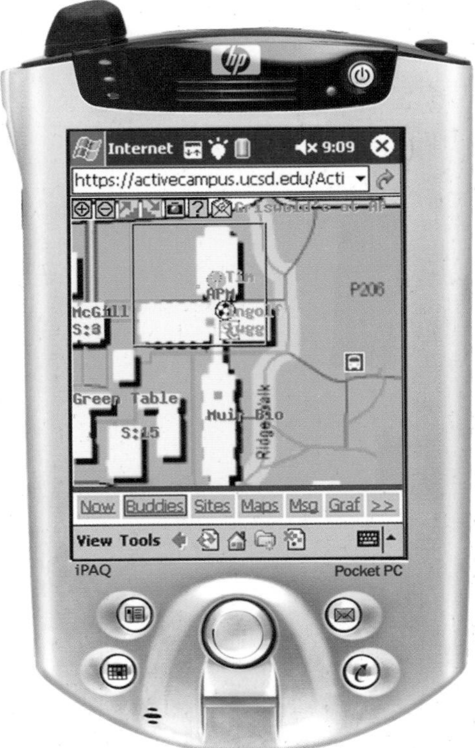

UC San Diego *ActiveCampus*, 2003 / PDA and cellphone-based project aimed at providing location-based services for educational networks. Students and professors can share information over the system or attach messages—"digital graffiti"—to specific locations on an online map / images courtesy of William G. Griswold © 2003 UC San Diego and the UCSD ActiveCampus Project / see "Crossing Campus," pp. 108–109.

HOLDING PATTERNS

NAVIGATING THROUGH AIRPORTS HAS BECOME INCREASINGLY TRICKY, GIVEN THE COMPETING INTERESTS OF SECURITY, COMMERCE AND EFFICIENT PASSENGER FLOW. PETER HALL TALKS TO PAUL MIJKSENAAR, DESIGNER OF EXEMPLARY WAYFINDING SYSTEMS FOR SCHIPHOL IN AMSTERDAM AND NEW YORK'S THREE MAJOR AIRPORTS, ABOUT THE FINE ART OF GETTING FROM GATE A TO GATE B.

Peter Hall: Your firm Bureau Mijksenaar is working on a pilot project to develop a wireless wayfinding system at Schiphol Airport in Amsterdam. How did this begin?

Paul Mijksenaar: We hired a student from Delft University to work on a feasibility study into using mobile devices for navigating an airport, and asked Schiphol to join us. At first, we looked into the idea of a new device like the hand-held audio systems in museums, but this was not feasible from a security point of view. Then we came to the Personal Digital Assistant (PDA), which has a big screen and software programs like Vindigo that include navigation systems. The PDA is very advanced but it has a low distribution—it's only used by nurses and business people. So we decided to use cellphones. 93 percent of Dutch people have them; it's the medium of the future.

How would your cellphone know exactly where you are in an airport?

Well, WiFi technology was coming up, and it was being installed all over Schiphol at the same time. We were committed to the idea that you don't need any special technology for this system, that we could piggyback on another technology. A WiFi system is not interested in your location, but several WiFi systems can tell where you are.

Through triangulation?

Exactly. The system knows which direction you are walking because it measures your position, and on the cellphone screen a moving map is oriented in that direction. With the mobile system, you can ask the software on your cellphone, "Show me a restroom within three minutes' walking distance" and it shows you on a map where you are, and gives you an animated line that you follow in the direction you are walking.

You've already designed a widely respected conventional wayfinding system at Schiphol. Why add a high-tech, wireless version?

There's always a need for commercial information at an airport; a quarter of the income at Schiphol comes from retail, and there's competition between our signs and the commercial signs. The nice thing about this mobile phone-based system is that you can filter the information: you can check a box to say you're interested in shopping for electronics, or want to go to a bar and have some Dutch beer but be warned when it's time to go to your gate. The phone will give you a signal to go at the right time. This way you get to your gate on time and the retailer gets you into his shop or bar. You can also choose your own language for the system—the fixed airport signs at Schiphol aren't in Chinese, for example. And, if you are visually impaired, the phone can give you audio directions.

Does this require a menu of choices on your cellphone?

Yes, simple menus. You can check "shopping, drink, gate" or type in your flight number, or when you've landed and you're still on the aircraft, you can say "show me an exit" or ask directions to the nearest ATM. You can ask it to send you information as you need it or you can download information in advance if you need to prepare.

How is the project going?

We tested it at the airport but now we need a manufacturer, since Schiphol is not a developer. We need to talk to someone like AT&T or Vindigo.

What would you say are the main limitations of fixed wayfinding tools like maps and directional signs?

There are many. You cannot individualize information on signs, so you have to make generic information. There's always a large group that doesn't fit, so you have to provide additional layers of information for, say, elderly people, people with impairments, and people with different languages. Pictograms are limited; a suitcase pictogram, for example, can mean "baggage reclaim" or "baggage check." At one point we thought about a wayfinding system that projected individualized information on blank screens or glass walls in the airport as people approached them. But what would happen when three people came along at the same time? A better system is the number-based signage on a cycleway in Belgium and the Netherlands where you have a different list of numbers to follow for each route.

Does it require a degree of mental aptitude to master a numbers-based wayfinding system?

No, it's simple. For example, if you are going to a forest or park, you scribble down a list of numbers from a menu and follow them—it's been a big success. It's not an intellectual thing; it's more that you have to get used to it. Coming back to the airport, you can number intersections and when your boarding pass is issued you get a list of numbers on it to follow to your gate. People are often confused by gate signs. They will see a sign for "Gates D1-20" and ask "Is gate D6 that way?"

Is cartographic literacy another problem?

Yes. The majority of people cannot read maps at all. They often think they can. In a city like Venice where there's no other way to navigate than with maps, you see people struggling with maps, turning them around and around. Scaling is always a problem; people have no idea of scale on a map. Orientation to reality is a problem, which is why the *Upside Down* road map of Britain was a big success, particularly with women. Research suggests that more women have more difficulty than men with spatial orientation. A map is a very precise instrument but most people don't use it like that. Most maps provide a spatial overview. For example, in shopping malls, people will use a map to establish that food is on the fourth floor but not to get to a particular store.

So perhaps maps have too much detail?

Reading a map is a learning process; the more you learn the more you are able to use it and the more you are really controlling your environment. But reading depth or vegetation is not that easy, and there are strange conventions like color coding; industrial areas are usually light gray, which intuitively look like unbuilt areas. After aerial photography came along, there was a revolution in cartography. Deep blue had been used for deep water and dark brown had been used for the highest level of a mountain, but they seemed unnatural. If you approach the Pyrenees they don't become browner and browner. People got used to aerial photographs showing their countries in much softer colors. The first "natural colors" atlas came out and convention changed to more associative colors.

How do you decide whether to include a map in a wayfinding system?

At Schiphol, at first every map was the same, and showed the whole passenger area.

See "The Sirens of Venice," pp. 238–245.

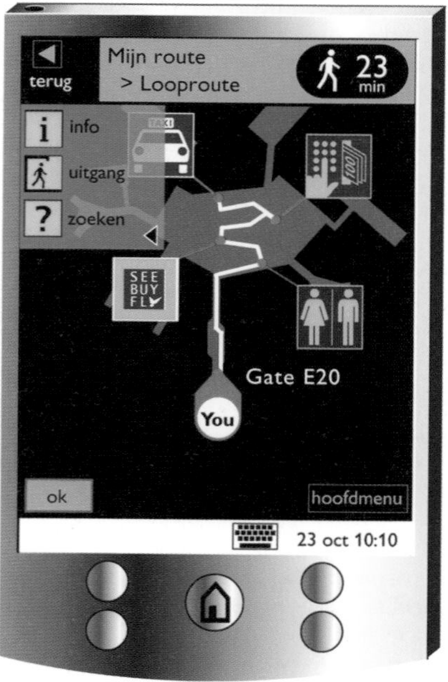

Bureau Mijksenaar *prototype Wi-Fi-based wayfinding system for Schiphol Airport, the Netherlands*, 2003 / airport passengers can access the system via their cellphone/PDAs and navigate their way to a departure gate, adding diversions (shopping, eating, drinking Dutch beer) from a menu of options. The system tracks the passenger's location, and provides a digital map including estimated journey time / images courtesy of Bureau Mijksenaar.

But we learned that that was too much. Now we show only detailed maps of the environment you have immediate access to. All the facilities are repeated so there's no need for an overview of other lounges further away. But generally we don't make maps. I'm interested in maps as an information designer; I wrote about "cartophobes" and "cartofreaks" for an exhibition catalog.

Cartophobes are people who fear maps?

Yes, and cartofreaks love them. But most cartofreaks are also cartophobes; they collect maps because they are frightened of their environment; they want to be in control and don't want to be lost. But that doesn't mean they can really use them when the moment of truth arrives.

You alluded earlier to the conflict between commercial interests and public information, especially in airports. Is that an increasing challenge for an information designer?

It always has been. Heathrow is a perfect example—you can see there that commercial interests are stronger than wayfinding interests. It's difficult to find a balance. In Schiphol, the commercial people—the shop owners—produce their own maps that show the shops. But then you have two maps.

So whoever makes the map has a vested interest in what they show.

Yes, we're talking about the manipulation of information. With the Mercator projection, if you follow a line from Europe to Brazil, you will get there. But the south and north are exaggerated. Every map is a manipulation that starts with a projection of what you want to show. If you want to show the volume of continents you shouldn't show the Mercator map at all. The problem is that the public takes it literally. A map can only make one point. In the future, you might be able to choose electronic maps in your own way; a map for navigation (push button A) or a map for comparison of sizes or distance (push button B). That would be interesting.

At Schiphol you're providing something like that. But I imagine there will be a battle between information design and those who sponsor the system and want their commercial information to come up first.

As a designer you are able to make things clear; you have some tools to do a good job and show, say, McDonald's and Manhattan at the same time. It's only when the client is stupid that you have a problem.

In the U.S., one of the big debates is about the increasing lack of public space and its enclosure in corporate space. Is there any public space in an airport?

No. Some airports try to act as though they have public space, and find a balance between commercial and other interests. There are areas that look like public space, dedicated to functionality. Of course they aren't, but there's no hidden agenda where a map would bring you to McDonald's before a check-in.

At Heathrow you go through to the departure lounge and are confronted by the duty free area. It quickly becomes quite difficult to find your way.

Of course. But that's manipulation of the space; it's got nothing to do with the maps.

Are the wayfinding system designers losing the battle there?

That is a real fear. Heathrow is a final destination; people fly to London to go to London. So even if there's no map or sign at all you will get to London. Schiphol Airport is a hub. People go there to find a connection. If you find a particular hub difficult to maneuver in, you will go to a different airport, like Frankfurt, the next time. If there is competition, you will see airports doing a better job of wayfinding. But in London there's no competition. The commercial people say, "why do you bother with a sign? They will come here anyway. And we make money, you don't." The argument is always "You spend the money we earn." And in a way, they're right.

My conclusion is that the conflict is not in the airport, it's in the human being. I like to shop and I like to be on time at the gate. I would be pissed if I missed my gate announcement because I was shopping. That's the reason design is not art. It's filling the requirements of human beings. They can be mixed and contradictory requirements. People have no single goal. Maps should reflect that.

No Mouse Required

A table-based interactive map responds to the hand of authority. JANET ABRAMS gets under its surface.

The scene is familiar from countless Hollywood war movies: a bunch of men walk into a room, clear everything off a big table, slap down a map, then gather around and stoop over it to make strategic decisions that will impact all humanity. Today, that map is no longer a paper document, but more likely, multiple layers of a Geographical Information Systems (GIS) database, manipulated on a massive digital screen at the touch of a finger.

In 2004, Glendale, CA-based Applied Minds, Inc., and Los Angeles-based defense company Northrop Grumman debuted their Touch Table, an interactive table with two accompanying vertical screens that allows multiple participants to converge over an interactive map rather than crowding around the limited screen real estate of a personal computer. According to Northrop Grumman's marketing video, the table is a tool "that excels where cutting-edge visualization, collaboration, and universal situational awareness are needed to accomplish the mission."

"We were tasked by the Defense Intelligence Agency to find a way to interact intuitively with map-based GIS data," says Jim Benson, Chief Technology Officer for the Touch Table at Applied Minds, the company co-chaired by the former head of Disney Imagineering Bran Ferren and ex-Disney Fellow (and parallel computing pioneer) Danny Hillis.

The Disney culture of storytelling is an obvious influence on the development of the Touch Table, whose ease of interaction—using hand gestures, surface pressure, and a shareable menu of control buttons—is meant to enable everyone from 4-star generals to schoolchildren to grasp, almost literally, what on earth is going on. "When a general comes in and sees the Touch Table, he sees something he's familiar with: he knows about maps and placing objects on maps," says Benson. "They have a tremendous amount of geographical filtering to do, and need to be able to talk about that in a common space. When you've got a large table, it's a lot easier."

The software underlying the Touch Table supports visual applications such as those written to utilize ArcGIS, a GIS software engine (made by Redlands, California-based GIS company ESRI) that stores layers of geo-spatial information such as cartographic maps, satellite imagery, hyperspectral imagery, shape files and elevation data. Touch-screen buttons can be "thrown" across the table from one user to the other, allowing different people to take the controls and apply annotations, outlines or shading to particular zones on its map or image layers; their respective color-coded notations can then be stored in a personal geo-database. But the most seductive interaction is via bodily gestures.

Simply by moving your hands apart, you can zoom in to magnify an image; by moving your hands together, as if packing a snowball, you zoom out from an image. By swiping your arm laterally across the surface, an underlying layer of data can be fully or partially revealed, to make side-by-side comparison of images (for example, satellite photos of a construction project in progress, whether an Olympic stadium or a military installation). The Touch Table responds to gestures made within one eighth of an inch of its surface, as well as actual surface contact; infrared tracking and built-in pressure sensors read users' movements and hand pressure.

Pressing on an individual icon on a map summons additional data to one of the accompanying vertical plasma screens. Merely by applying hand pressure to the table, deeper layers of data are drawn to the surface, giving the owner of that hand the impression that the sheer weight of their presence (in other words, authority) suffices to call forth the information. Just the thing to reassure the men in uniform.

With its seamless shifts between scales, the Touch Table inevitably recalls the thrill-ride of Powers of Ten, the 1977 film by Charles and Ray Eames about the relative size of things in the universe. But why does putting digital mapping information on a horizontal surface make such a difference to the way information is perceived? "It goes back to the campfire idea, with everyone sitting around, looking eye-to-eye," argues Benson. "There's a whole different interaction. It's the idea of having a paper map that has these almost magical properties. You can look at a globe and find spots on it, but you can't do that macro-micro shift. You can't look at Paris on a globe and find the Eiffel Tower."

Images are projected onto the table from an overhead projector, connected to one or more Windows workstations; software designed by Applied Minds, Inc., known as TouchShare, translates users' physical gestures to control the GIS software. The freestanding vertical plasma screens stationed at one end of the table provide surfaces to display additional data, or for teleconferencing: multiple Touch Tables can be networked so people in different locations can share the same visualizations and their underlying databases.

For demonstrations, Applied Minds has installed satellite images produced by DigitalGlobe, taken from the Quickbird satellite at 0.61m resolution. Military images, produced at even higher resolution, put the Touch Table through its paces: using live satellite feeds, the table can show, for example, the position of a platoon in a given country, and allow command and control personnel to simply click on the aerial image to draw up specific data about the unit.

There are currently just a few Touch Tables in existence, besides those installed at the corporate headquarters of ESRI, Applied Minds, Inc., and Northrop Grumman. Unsurprisingly, the Defense Department and Secret Service personnel have been among the early adopters, and Homeland Security and several large cities have expressed interest in acquiring their own Touch Table for planning purposes at the local, state and federal level.

Applied Minds is keen to emphasize the Touch Table's potential educational uses, and is currently planning several models beside the currently available TT84 (54 x 74 inches, 84 inches in diagonal) and TT45; a smaller LCD version is in development. But at around $250,000 for a fully-loaded TT84, it will be a while before any university, let alone your local primary school, gets hold of one for geography classes.

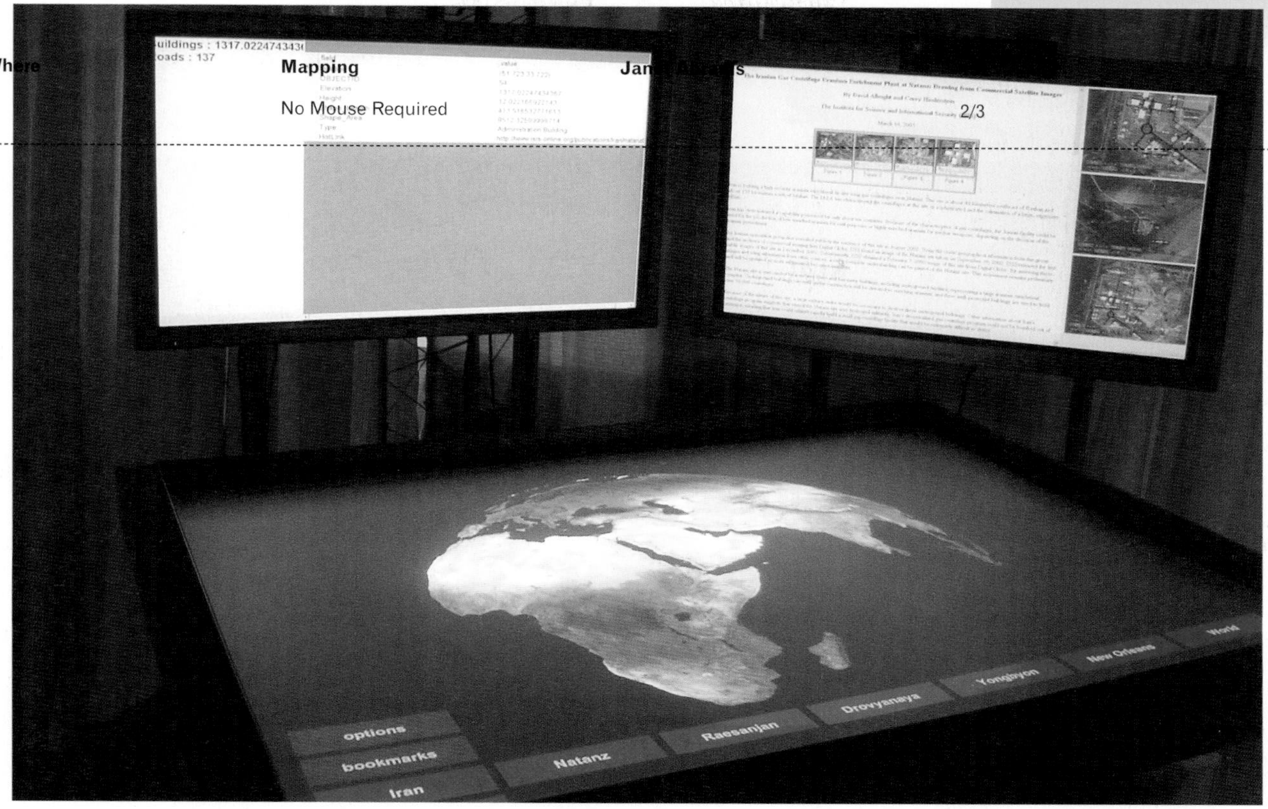

Applied Minds Inc. and **Northrop Grumman** *Touch Table*, 2004 / (top): the interactive table and its accompanying screens. (bottom): demo of the touch-screen surface using an aerial photo of Washington D.C. / images courtesy of Applied Minds, Inc.

Applied Minds Inc., and **Northrop Grumman** *Touch Table*, 2004 / hand gestures close to the table surface are used to summon and interact with various kinds of images and data. An on-screen control menu can be "thrown" from one side of the table to the other. In a demo, Applied Minds personnel point out the National Academy of Science on an aerial photograph of Washington D.C., while the Department of the Interior is outlined in red / image courtesy of Applied Minds, Inc.

Antenna Design New York *Civic Exchange*, 2004 / a large touch-screen map of Lower Manhattan provides a range of information for residents, workers and tourists, in this competition-winning design for a public information exchange, a hybrid of street furniture, emergency alert signage and community bulletin board / image courtesy of Antenna Design New York.

Antenna Design New York *Civic Exchange*, 2004 / (top): night time view showing individual terminal for Internet access, on opposite side from map table, and illuminated glass-mosaic message tower for cultural and emergency announcements. (bottom left): color-coded flags appear on the map, presenting four main categories of information, clickable for expanded text. (bottom right): a "floating" pink poll panel invites responses to a local community issue / images this spread courtesy of Antenna Design New York.

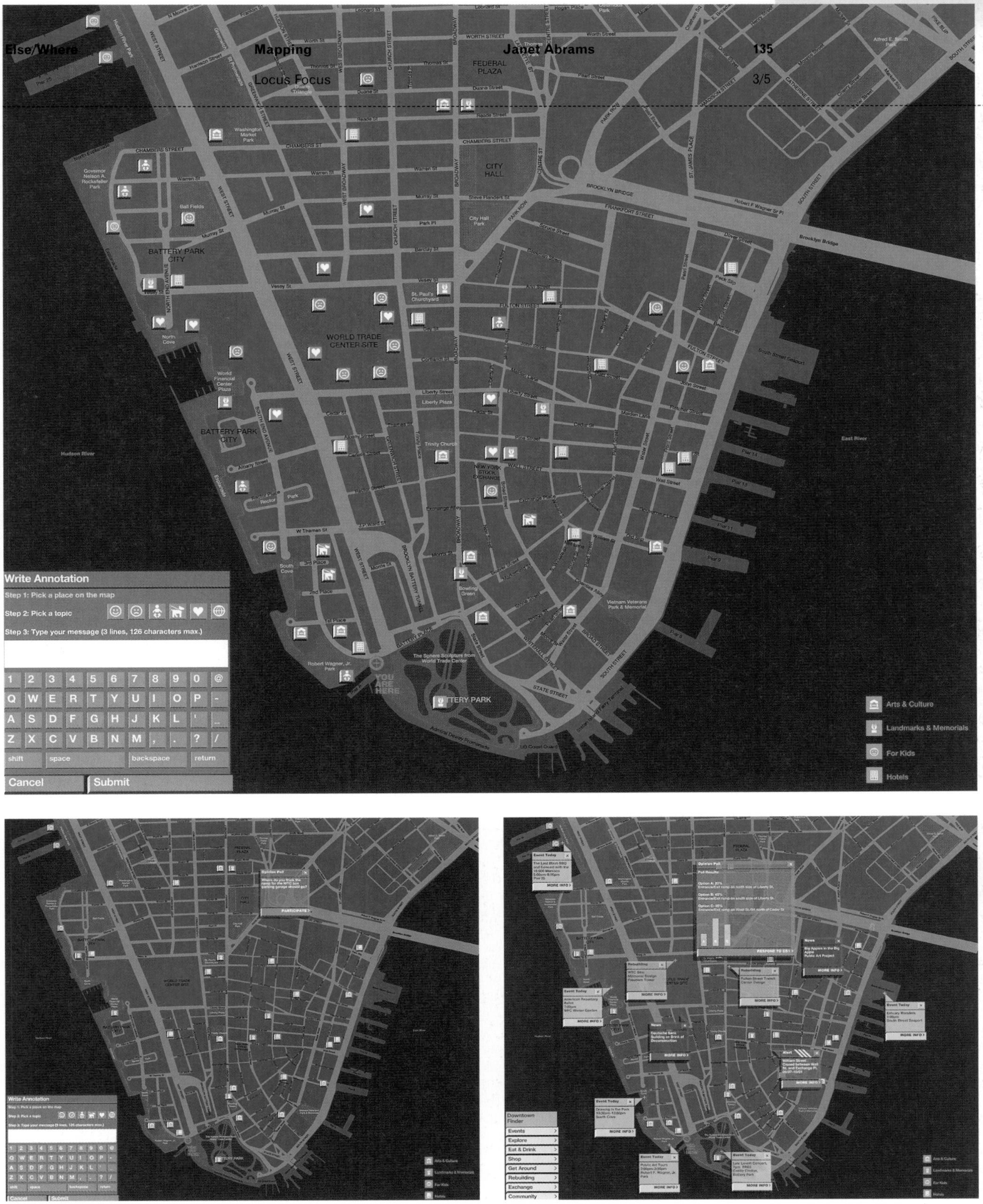

Antenna Design New York *Civic Exchange*, 2004 / (top): a touchscreen keypad allows users to annotate and place their own landmarks on the map. (bottom left): poll questions. (bottom right): poll results appear on the map, on an "intelligent" panel that automatically adjusts its position so as not to obscure other information requested by users.

Locus Focus

When information about a place can be accessed via the Internet from virtually anywhere, on desktop or mobile devices, what might be the advantage of supplying that information on a platform anchored at the location to which it refers? Since communication technology has, to a great extent, released the "genius" from the "loci," could such a platform reinstate a sense of "public-ness" in the public realm?

This was the challenge set in 2004 when three New York City organizations, the Van Alen Institute, the Architectural League of New York and Hugh L. Carey Battery Park City Authority, joined forces to host the Civic Exchange competition for an interactive installation that would go "beyond the kiosk" to provide information about Lower Manhattan — from road closures to sightseeing and cultural opportunities to emergency alerts — for visitors, workers and residents. Multi-disciplinary teams comprising at least one architect/designer and one multimedia designer were invited to submit their credentials; of the three dozen teams that entered, four were chosen to proceed to the second stage: Antenna Design New York; Leeser/StoSS/Levin/Kurgan; The Exchange; and MESH Architectures/ORG, Inc.

Their resulting design proposals — juried in October 2004 — utilized various modes of interaction, from touch-screen surfaces to full body gesture-recognition, and offered divergent formal solutions for what, if it is eventually realized, is likely to become an iconic "beacon" for Lower Manhattan.

For the purposes of the competition, the prototype was to be sited in an open space at the southern tip of Battery Park City next to Historic Battery Park and opposite Pier A — a nexus for tourists bound for the Statue of Liberty and Ellis Island, and within a short walk from Ground Zero, in an area dense with cultural and historic landmarks such as the Museum of Jewish Heritage and the Skyscraper Museum. The prototype was required to provide information both passively and actively, serve groups as well as individuals (especially those not equipped with personal mobile devices) and be capable of replication at other sites in Lower Manhattan.

Antenna Design's winning solution turns the Civic Exchange into a locus of social exchange, where people seeking different kinds of information might find themselves engaging in conversation with strangers, recommending things to do or places to see, or simply hanging out on this new piece of street furniture. Using a neutral palette, with ceramic mosaic for the benches and light-transmitting glass mosaic for the message tower, the modular "hub and spoke" arrangement invites people to linger or use the Civic Exchange as a rendezvous point, whether or not they come there to access information.

Antenna partners Sigi Moeslinger and Masamichi Udagawa quickly hit on the idea of a map as the main interface, although they almost abandoned the concept, concerned that their competitors would alight on the same solution. "At first we thought: it's so obvious, everyone will do it. But since this is about location-based information, then making a representation of the location, for input as well as output, seemed logical," says Moeslinger. As it turned out, they were the only team to use a map as the crux of their design. The sheer familiarity of a map would make it approachable and intuitive — critical factors in the success of a system destined for diverse users, as Antenna had previously discovered in designing the Metrocard vending machines for the New York City Transit Authority in 1997 — 1999.

Antenna briefly considered menu-driven or theme-driven alternatives, using a large physical object as the interface, such as some kind of giant mechanical lever that members of the public would "dial" to select thematically organized information. But they soon returned to their initial idea. As Udagawa points out: "If someone goes to an unknown area, the first thing that comes to mind is a map. The next question is how to make the information more special in the here-and-now context." By making Civic Exchange a gathering point, information that could potentially be retrieved anywhere would be enhanced by unique social encounters. This led directly to the decision to make a touch-screen horizontal map table the central focus.

"There are good things about vertical maps," says Moeslinger, "but while people may all stand next to each other, they never look at each other. There's a collective consumption of information, but it doesn't encourage the interpersonal aspect." Vertical maps are the more typical format (a more typical format in public spaces, such as the wall size Neighborhood Maps found at every New York subway station, or metal signs offering maps of historic or cultural districts). But by orienting the map horizontally, the map table enhances the possibility of face-to-face experience among strangers.

"We thought the table arrangement would force a little more exchange, because you're grouping around it," she adds. "Often, when you start talking to other people, they will tell an anecdote about what they've already done, or they'll recommend a place they've already been, which can be important in deciding how to make your trip."

For the competition, it was anticipated that the Civic Exchange would draw on information from existing websites and databases that focus on Lower Manhattan (such as the City of New York's information site <lowermanhattan.info>), thereby freeing the teams to concentrate on physical and interaction design rather than data-gathering. As well as conveying this "top down" information from public authorities, Civic Exchange was also meant to serve as a platform for "bottom up" communication among members of the local community.

"Downtown is a fairly active community, because lots of development is happening there. So we felt it would be good to make a platform that fosters more 'horizontal' exchange," says Moeslinger, referring to qualities of citizen-to-citizen discourse, rather than the table's spatial orientation (though the metaphor clearly translates).

And though the competition brief was quite precise in its requirements, Antenna designed the map table so it could carry many different kinds of maps, offering different experiences and perspectives — including aerial photography — on the

See "Destinations and Detours," p. 110.

The *Civic Exchange* project was supported in part by an award from the National Endowment for the Arts, with additional funding from the Stephen A. and Diana L. Goldberg Foundation; it was made possible with the participation of the Hugh L. Carey Battery Park City Authority.

Project Organizers:
Raymond W. Gastil, Jonathan Cohen-Litant (Van Alen Institute); Rosalie Genevro (Architectural League of New York).

Conceived as a gathering point for Lower Manhattan, Antenna Design's Civic Exchange offers a glimpse of the next generation of intelligent street furniture — a hybrid of industrial, urban and interactive design with a multi-user map table at its heart. By JANET ABRAMS.

neighborhood. "If you offer not just practical information about a neighborhood, but also curious and interesting facts and figures, this makes for a rather wonderful group experience," says Moeslinger. "We didn't really develop these ideas, because we had to cover other aspects for the competition, but they could easily be accommodated in our set-up. For example, it would be really nice to see a historic map that showed the expansion of Downtown, in purely territorial terms, since there has been a lot of landfill in Lower Manhattan."

In "default mode," the map table shows an abstracted map of Lower Manhattan with small orange icons representing four categories of fixed attractions (Arts and Culture, Landmarks and Memorials, Events For Kids, and Hotels. Larger color-coded Post-It style flags designate changing information, and are positioned over their location: Events (yellow), News (dark blue), Reconstruction (pale blue) and Alerts (red) bring information from public transportation websites and official sites such as that of the Department of Transportation. (The data is prioritized by vicinity, so if multiple versions of the prototype Civic Exchange are eventually installed around Lower Manhattan, each one would feature more events relevant to the area in which it is sited.)

Floating at random over the map, pink "Poll" panels invite response to questions about local topical issues, open to residents as well as visitors. The question might come from local organizations, such as Community Board 1, or from individuals. By clicking on the "flag," a reply form appears; tallied poll results appear in a box on the table's lower left. These "smart" panels adjust their position so as not to obscure information that a user might want to consult on the map, underneath.

In theory, "Poll" posts might be completely uncensored, or edited by a representative of the map table's owner/operator, or (to a lesser extent) automatically "filtered" by computer software. But the opportunity for "bottom up" communication also exposes the double-edged nature of a public information kiosk.

"People can pick any spot on the map, place an icon there, and say whatever they want to say," says Moeslinger. "We didn't specify what that should be. Obviously, as soon as you open things up, it becomes a bit unpredictable. Public agencies always want to be super-correct. They don't want the potential for anything offensive happening within their equipment. But it raises an interesting issue: if you create something for public space, how public do you allow it to be? Do you allow everyone to say everything? It would be interesting to see what people actually do say: maybe they'd behave well."

Beside the map table, Antenna's Civic Exchange comprises several components, in various configurations depending on location: a single-user Internet access terminal; an LED message column incorporating a 311/911 intercom, which can relay messages that are choreographed, color coded and set in various typefaces according to subject matter/urgency; a solar cell shade, with a video camera for security surveillance and presence-detection, which activates the LED messages; and benches clad in customizable mosaic tiles. Beyond the minimum configuration (map table plus octagonal seating unit), the modular system could accommodate additional Internet terminals and extra benches, radiating out at angles from the core.

Clad in mosaic or transparent glass tile (the message tower) with a "sacrificial" vandal-resistant polycarbonate layer (on both the map table and Internet touch-screens), Antenna's Civic Exchange has a 2001: A Space Odyssey quality. Like the offspring of a Braun electric toothbrush and an iPod, the precision and crispness of its visual language would mark it out as an optical respite in the hectic, multicolored 24-hour movie that is Manhattan.

Antenna's partners acknowledge that the design submitted for the competition may not end up exactly, on the streets of the city, given that it was developed with limited consultation with its eventual owners — Battery Park City Authority — or those who will be responsible for its maintenance, such as the Parks Department. "You can't expect a competition project to be implemented 'as-is,'" says Moeslinger. "But it's meant to raise awareness and excitement about what is possible." Adds Udagawa: "And to guide the design direction. Right now, it's more like an event, as a competition."

Asked when they thought the first Civic Exchange might be available for use in Lower Manhattan, the designers were cautious, pointing out the many different constituencies — among them the BPCA, the City of New York, Department of Transport, the Parks Department, and private developers of Pier A — that will have to come together to agree on its final physical form, determine its site or sites, and, to some extent, authorize its content. "It's really hard to say," says Moeslinger, "'Soon' might mean five years."

But in February 2005, Battery Park City Authority agreed to fund a feasibility study by Antenna to estimate the project's likely cost, taking Civic Exchange at least one step closer to realization. And in June 2005, it won the Gold award for Design Explorations in the annual IDEA awards co-sponsored by the Industrial Design Society of America and Business Week, an acknowledgment of the project's potential to reconfigure the delivery of public information in public space.

Finalists for the *Civic Exchange* competition were:

Antenna Design (winning team) Masamichi Udagawa, Sigi Moeslinger, principals / concept and design, with Bruce Pringle / 3D Modeling and rendering
Gaspard Giroud / 3D animation
Veronique Brossier / animation and programming
Jonathan Brzyski / animation

Leeser/StoSS/Levin/Kurgan Thomas Leeser/Leeser Architecture, Golan Levin, Chris Reed/StoSS, Laura Kurgan

Mesh Architectures/ORG inc. Eric Liftin, David Reinfurt, Leo Villareal, Nina Rappaport

The Exchange Inbar Barak, Jake Barton/Local Projects, Claudia Herasme, Dan Shifman, Rosten Woo/CUP, Guy Zucker

Civic Exchange competition jury: Kadambari Baxi (Martin/Baxi Architects, VAI trustee), Stephanie Gelb (Battery Park City Authority), Joyce Lee (NYC Office of Management and Budget), John Maeda, (MIT Media Lab), Michael Rock (2x4) and Tucker Viemeister (Springtime-USA), and the author (a VAI trustee).

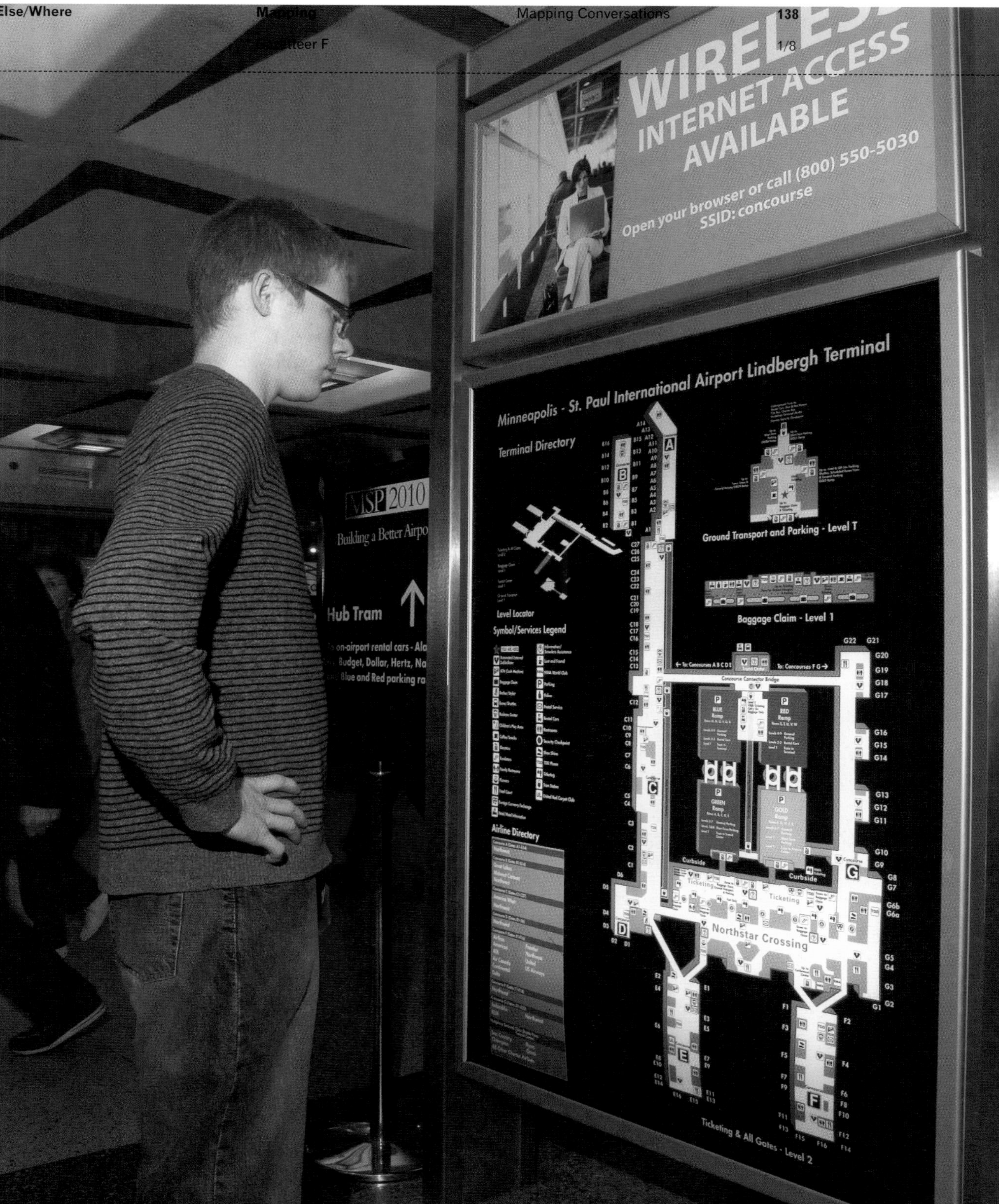

pp. 138 – 145: Photographs by Kimberlee Whaley © 2005 University of Minnesota Design Institute.

Hiawatha Line (Route 55)
Warehouse District/ Hennepin Avenue
Nicollet Mall
Government Plaza
Downtown East/ Metrodome
Cedar-Riverside
Franklin Avenue
Lake Street/Midtown
38th Street
46th Street
50th Street/ Minnehaha Park
VA Medical Center

AUDIO
SAT
NAV
SERV
SEEK
RPT
MUTE
EJECT
END
AUTO
OFF
FRONT
REAR

OFF
1
2
ABC
3
DEF
4
GHI
5
JKL
6
MNO
7
PQRS
8
TUV
9
WXYZ
*
0
#
OK
OFF
ROAD

Nicollet Mall
7th Street S
Target Center
Metrodome
Convention Center

Free Wireless
Available for Customers

Safari File Edit View History Bookmarks Window Help
Map of Fifth Element, 2411 Hennepin Avenue South Minneapolis, MN by MapQuest
http://www.mapquest.com/maps/map.adp?latlongtype=internal&addtohistory=
D•B Gmail Apple Type Design News
Features
Interview with Martin M...
Map of Fifth Element, 2...
MAPQUEST
FIND IT
MAPS
DIRECTIONS
Maps
Fifth Element: 612-377-0044
2411 Hennepin Avenue South Minneapolis, MN 55405, US
Find Nearby:
(e.g., Theaters)
Top Categories
Search
NORTH
SOUTH
WEST
ZOOM IN
ZOOM OUT
Summit Ave
Lincoln Ave
Kenwood Park
Logan Ave S
S James Ave
S Newton Ave
S Humboldt Ave
S Girard Ave
S Fremont Ave
S Emerson Ave
Hennepin Ave S
S Bryant Ave
S Dupont Ave
S Colfax Ave
S Lyndale Ave
S Aldrich Ave
Garfield Ave
Harriet Ave
S Grand Ave
S Pleasant Ave
W Franklin Ave
Ridgewood Ave
Lake Pl
Oliver Pl S
W 25th St
W 25 1/2 St
W 26th St
S Irving Ave
W 27th St
W 28th St
Lake Of The Isles
Kenwood Isles Dr
© 2005 MapQuest.com, Inc.; © 2005 NAVTEQ
Above Location
Get Directions
To
Address or Intersection
Search Minneapolis For
Airports
Hotels
Restaurants
Post Offices
Hospitals
Minneapolis offers:
- Select -
Other Offers:
Record Stores
Vinyl Record Store

MAPPING TERRITORIES

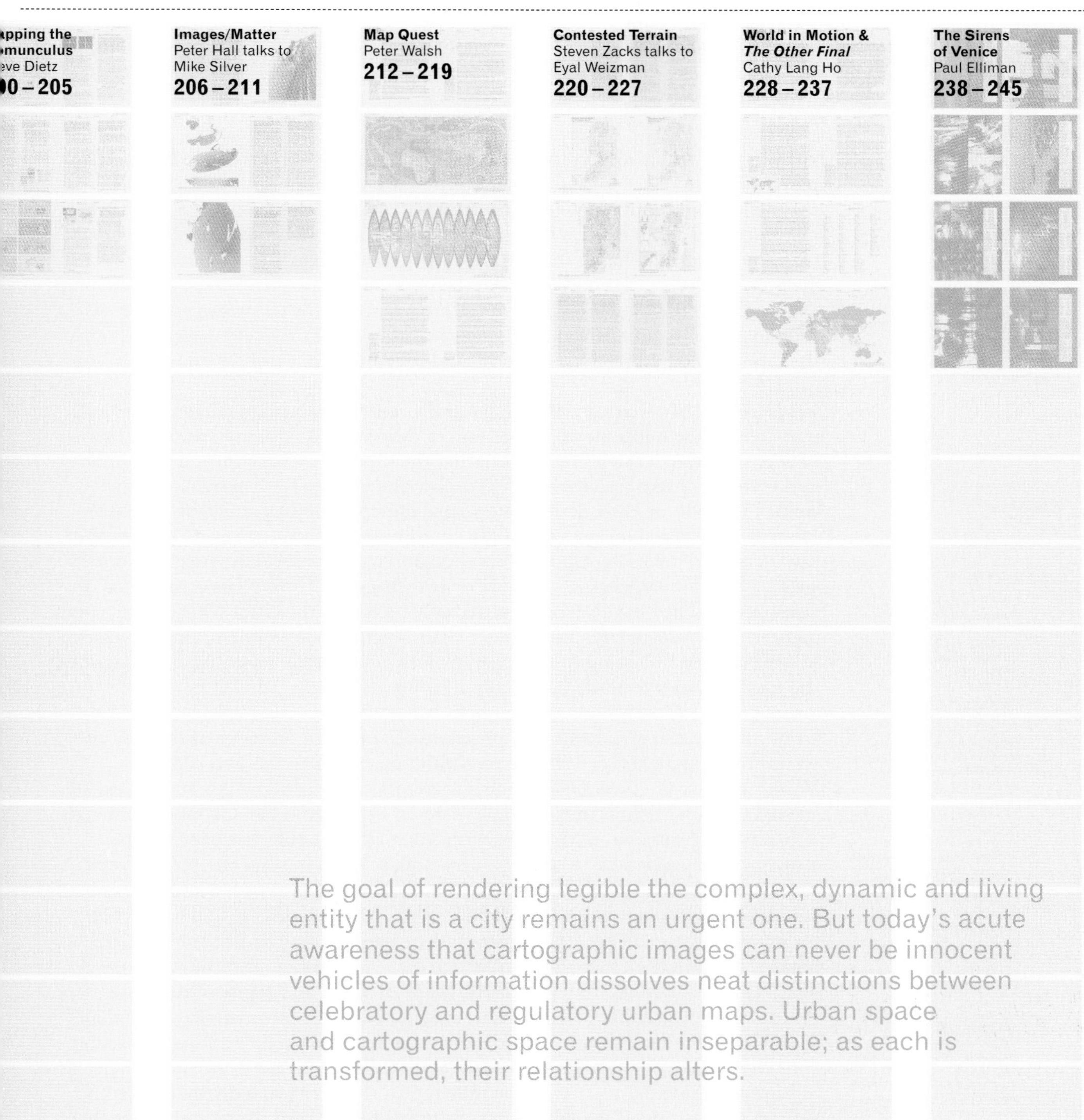

The goal of rendering legible the complex, dynamic and living entity that is a city remains an urgent one. But today's acute awareness that cartographic images can never be innocent vehicles of information dissolves neat distinctions between celebratory and regulatory urban maps. Urban space and cartographic space remain inseparable; as each is transformed, their relationship alters.

Denis Cosgrove, "Carto-City"

CARTO-CITY

Urban space and cartographic space are inseparable. This is the case historically, practically and conceptually. Urban origins, at Ur or Sumer for example, are revealed through the mapped reconstruction of their street geometry and building plot plans.[1] Elevation is the least durable element of urban form; horizontal plan the longest lasting. Urban archaeology reconstructs urban places through peeling back successive surfaces, like the pages of an historical atlas, and mapping the stratigraphy of material deposits stretched across former urban space. From such material mappings we reconstruct not only its physical appearance but also the city's social, political, commercial and religious life.

Practically, confrontation with an unfamiliar city is typically mediated by the map: of transit routes, of streets, of tourist destinations. Urban experience in a new city is often a process of negotiating the divergence between cartographic and material spaces. In cities with complex underground rail systems such as Tokyo, London or Paris, it can take years before the point pattern of stations familiar from the subway map is fully coordinated with the surface experience of townscape. In great metropoli, possession and use of a standard street directory such as London's pocket *A - Z* guide or Los Angeles' *Thomas Guide* are signs of citizenship.[2] They have become cartographic icons of the cities whose streets and addresses they designate. Much more than functional instruments, aids to fixing destinations or following routes, they are bearers of urban meaning and character: the map becomes to some degree the territory.

- <www.a-zmaps.co.uk/>

Conceptually, the map has either preceded the physical presence of the city or served to regulate and coordinate its continued existence. St. Petersburg, Washington D.C., New Delhi, Brasilia, countless fortress and colonial cities, existed on paper before they had any material expression. Paris, Rome, Vienna, Amsterdam, Jerusalem — virtually every great city — either has been reconstructed or expanded by means of a drawn plan.[3] And beyond the physical extension or reconstruction of urban space, the map has both recorded and determined countless aspects of urban life and citizenship. Maps of disease and morbidity, for example the cholera cartography of Victorian London or Philadelphia, helped make the modern metropolis a survivable space in the face of those viruses and bacteria that thrive on human density. Maps of social and ethnic status have shaped the political life of urban democracies, nowhere more dramatically than in the case of 20th-Century American zoning maps, used by housing and loan companies for red-lining inner-city ghettoes and later by government agencies to assert civil rights. In every way, the map registers the city as a distinct place and a unique landscape. Cartography acts not merely to record the various ways that the city is materially present, but as a creative intervention in urban space, shaping both the physical city and the urban life experienced and performed there.[4]

1. Adam T. Smith, *The Political Landscape: Constellations of Authority in Early Complex Polities*, University of California Press, 2003.
2. Appropriately, London's *Geographers A–Z* guide can be held in the hand and carried in the pocket. Los Angeles' *Thomas Guide*, by contrast, is designed to sit on the passenger seat of a car.
3. Most histories of urban form are illustrated with maps and plans but rarely explore critically the precise relations between these images and the built form of cities. See for example Richard Sennett, *Flesh and Stone: The Body and Civilization in Western Civilization*, Faber, 1994; Joseph Rykwert: *The Seduction of Place: The City in the Twenty-First Century*, Pantheon, 2000.
4. For historical examples, see Ola Söderström, "Paper Cities: Visual Thinking in Urban Planning," *Ecumene*, 3, 1996, 249–281. For a more contemporary discussion of the processes of negotiating urban space planning through maps see Ola Söderström, Elena Cogato Lanza, Roderick J. Lawrence & Gilles Barby, *L'Usage du projet* Editions Payot, Lausanne, 2000.

A version of this essay appeared in German in *Mapping A City: Hamburg Cartography*, edited by Nina Möntmann, Yilmaz Dziewior and Galerie für Landschaftskunst. Ostifildern Ruit Bei Stuttgart. Hatje Cantz Verlag, June 2004.

Never innocent guides, city maps have always shaped the experience of urban space, serving both as scientific instruments and aesthetic representations of the city. Denis Cosgrove traces the history of urban cartography and its techniques, from the grid to the aerial perspective to contemporary digital mapping technologies.

The ubiquity of cartography as a dimension of urban life and form makes a comprehensive survey of their relations impossible. I focus here on ways that the urban map is positioned between creating and recording the city. It is this dual function that releases the imaginative energy of mapping, and which has consistently attracted the attention of artists as well as technicians to urban mapping. From the vast archive of urban maps, plans and artistic interventions into urban mapping, I have chosen here to explore how the modern city as material and social space interacts with the map as scientific instrument and artistic representation of its space and life.

The complexity of the interaction is dramatically apparent in a post-modern American city such as Los Angeles, Houston or Phoenix. These are perhaps the most intensively mapped spaces in the history and geography of the planet: every square meter is geo-coded by government and private or commercial agencies for purposes ranging from environmental protection, public health and safety, efficient transportation and taxation to property insurance, marketing, political persuasion and religious evangelism.[5] Maps have played a critical role in shaping their physical spaces and land uses, and continue to control the daily lives of citizens through zoning ordinances, zip codes and the myriad territorial regulations that shape urban daily life. Theoretically, scientific cartography should make these cities highly rational, coherent spaces. Indeed, flying over a city such as Houston, a cartographic order is immediately visible in the repetitive grid of major streets, and within this the curvilinear geometry of residential roads and house lots, or in the rectangularity of office, production, storage/distribution and retail spaces. Yet, on the ground, such cities are among the least legible places on earth. Moving across their surfaces, an individual familiar with the spatial sorting of land uses and the hierarchy of distinctive symbolic structures that characterize conventional urban space is confused, even assaulted, by the seemingly random scatter and apparent chaos of urban elements. The post-modern urban landscape seems to confirm the problem of legibility in the constant and competitive presence within it of words, phrases and whole texts: billboards, street signs and posted ordinances.[6] The volume of written language in the public spaces of contemporary urbanism far exceeds that in more traditional cities. Image and text, whose effective harmonizing is cartography's signal contribution to spatial representation, has become disjointed, and their falling apart denotes the erosion of a relationship that underpinned urban modernity.[7]

This does not mean a reduction in the map's role in urban place making and experience. Indeed, a characteristic way of negotiating movement within the post-modern American city is the computer-generated map, custom produced for any destination address, from any point of departure within the United States.

5. On Los Angeles for example, see Greg Hise, *Magnetic Los Angeles: Planning the Twentieth Century Metropolis*, The Johns Hopkins University Press, 1997, and *idem* & William Deverell, *Eden by Design: the 1930s Olmsted-Bartholomew Plan for the Greater Los Angeles Region*, University of California Press, 2000.

6. The classic texts on post-modern urban landscape include Edward Relph, *The Modern Urban Landscape*. Johns Hopkins, 1987; David Harvey, *The Condition of Postmodernity: An Enquiry Into the Origins of Cultural Change*, Blackwell, 1989; Edward Soja, *Thirdspace: Journeys to Los Angeles and Other Real-And-Imagined Places*, Blackwell, 1996; *idem*, *Postmetropolis: Critical Studies of Cities and Regions*, Blackwell, 2000.

7. Despite the graphic sophistication of iconic communication in the contemporary city, the volume of text in the public landscape seems to increase with the number of enterprises competing for the attention of a highly mobile, car-borne public. This is very noticeable in the U.S. where neon and other forms of illuminated text are characteristic features of urban space. On the role of text in regulating urban legibility in the past, see R.M. San Juan, *Rome: A City Out of Print*, University of Minnesota Press, 2001. We should also recall the significant role traditionally given to public maps in countries such as Italy where they have frequently been carved onto the facades of public buildings.

<www.mapquest.com>

Map Quest© can create an instant digital image of any urban location at any requisite scale using a simplified set of standard colors and cartographic signs. Such images are resolutely functional, entirely ignoring the context of the places they represent, utterly unconcerned with *civitas* or the city as public space. No urban map could be further removed from an image such as Jacopo de' Barbari's *Venetia* map of 1500. The paradigm example of early-modern city mapping, Jacopo's detailed townscape guided the observer not to a physical destination but to the civic spirit of Europe's greatest commercial city.[8]

"Scientific" cartography's inability to capture the contemporary city has, however, opened new possibilities for urban mapping. As I shall illustrate, these have been colonized creatively for a wide variety of projects: conceptual, political, and purely ludic, breathing new life into the connections between city space, city life and mapping.

RADIAL AXIS AND THE GRID

Geometry, specifically the radial axis and the grid, underpinned scientific cartography and modern urban form. Their power and historical endurance in both the map and the city lies in their combined practical and symbolic efficacy. The circle's 360 degrees generate a center-enhancing axial form focused on a single point. Functionally and symbolically, this extends power panoptically to the horizon, encompassing a potentially infinite territory. Versailles, Karlsruhe, Baroque Rome and Second Empire Paris have all inscribed this simple geometry into urban space. The same axial pattern emerges from the simplest mapping technique: taking radial sightlines from a single point. Multiple survey points can be selected randomly along a pathway or be connected to a cardinal base line. Back sighting confirms positional accuracy, producing a network of intersecting axes such as the wind-related rhumb lines on a marine chart. The magnetic compass connects these sightings to global and even cosmic geometry. The radial planning of a city is at once practical and symbolic, as Vitruvius recognized in his description of the city perfectly oriented in respect of wind directions. The first record in the West of systematic urban mapping was Vitruvius' first popularizer, Leon Battista Alberti, in a description of Rome. No actual map exists for this project, merely a set of coordinates produced by Alberti for known locations along axes converging on a single point of observation.[9]

8. J. Schultz, "Jacopo de' Barbari's view of Venice: map making, city views and moralized geography before the year 1500," *Art Bulletin*, 60, 1978.

9. One of the principal advantages of the coordinate system for mapping is that it allows for greater mobility of the map than a purely pictorial outline and plot. Obviously, errors of transcription can occur in both forms, but the transmission of tables of figures from which a map may be constructed allows for much greater accuracy of positioning than merely copying lines and points by eye.

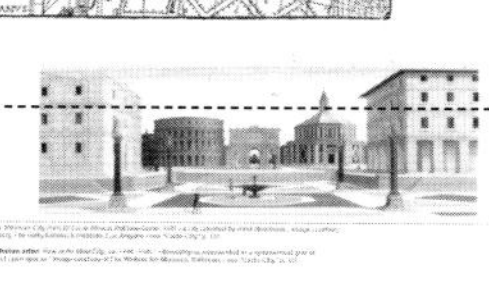

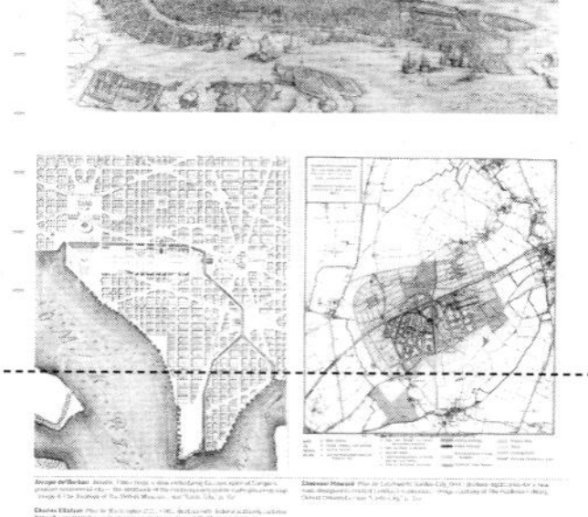

The alternative geometrical form shared by urban plan and mapping is the grid or checkerboard of orthogonal lines crossing at right angles. While radial axes enhance the center, the grid is space equalizing, infinitely extendable over the surface and privileging no single point, but reducing each to a unique coordinate. The grid generates the simplest and most ubiquitous form of urban plan. It is found in the earliest Greek colonies in the Mediterranean, in the design of imperial Chinese cities, in Spanish New World pueblos, in the urban settlement of the U.S. The colonial urban form *par excellence*, the grid can also be an expression of urban democracy, equalizing lot sizes and maximizing the ease of platting and disposing of urban land into private property. As William Penn's Philadelphia design reveals, the grid can easily be elaborated to generate open spaces—squares—to interrupt its monotony and produce public space within an otherwise privatized space.

<www.roman-britain.org/ptolemy.htm>

The grid performs a similar function in mapping. Introduced into modern Western cartography in the early 15th Century through Claudius Ptolemy's Geography, but known to Chinese cartographers at least 300 years earlier, the introduction of a graticule of longitude and latitude lines as the basis for determining location and translating the sphere to a two-dimensional map is by far the most significant feature of modern cartography.[10] The grid is a ubiquitous location-fixing device. Unrelated to planetary coordinates, the grid can be stretched across any spatial scale, as the British Ordnance Survey's national grid or the lettered and numbered squares superimposed on countless urban maps demonstrate.

These shared geometries of urban design and cartography are instrumentally effective and symbolically significant. They are conceptually easy to grasp and relatively simple to apply in spatial design and representation. Neither is restricted to a single scale but may be applied from microcosm to macrocosm. Thus, each possesses not only specific symbolic attributes—power and panopticism, reason and democracy, respectively—but also a common capacity to connect mundane space to the cosmic patterns, movements and logic. They therefore propose and permit urban mapping as a philosophical exercise.

The philosophy and ethics of the urban map are apparent across the history of modern urbanism. The profound impact of Vitruvius' urban plan in Renaissance Europe derives from its appeal to humanists and scientists engaged in rethinking both the nature of urban life and the mapping of global space. The ideal city debate among architectural writers from Alberti and Francesco di Giorgio Martini to Sebastiano Serlio and Vincenzo Scamozzi concerned more than the formal design of urban space. It was about mapping urban life and of citizenship.[11] The city, represented in the anonymous image now in Baltimore, represents much more than a symmetrical grid of buildings, streets and open spaces rendered in deep perspective. It maps an image of citizenship derived from Republican Rome and the Stoic writings of Cicero, Seneca and Marcus Aurelius. The civic virtues of Justice, Prudence, Temperance and Fortitude stand atop the four columns that define its central square. The buildings gathered around that space correspond to the public functions that regulate urban life. And across the foreground of the image creeps the bent and burdened, but immensely dignified figure of the Stoic. Acknowledging the cosmic order mapped into urban space, and subordinating body to mind, he signifies the good citizen's duties of reason, reverence and sociability. The map of urban space is also the map of urban virtue.

10. See the fascinating discussion of the grid as a mode of spatial representation in E. Casey, *Representing Place: Landscape Painting and Maps*, University of Minnesota Press, 2002, pp. 199–215.

11. V. Hart & P. Hicks, *Paper Palaces: The Rise of the Architectural Treatise*, Yale University Press, 1998.

Axial and grid geometries were united in the service of Modernity's grandest social project: the creation of the U.S., notably for this discussion in the design of America's federal capital. Charles L'Enfant's map combined the democratic principles of the U.S. Constitution and Bill of Rights in its checkerboard of residential streets, with the inscription of federal authority through axes radiating from the separate seats of executive and legislative power. An earlier proposal by the federalist Thomas Jefferson had envisioned the city as a simple grid similar to that which his Committee on the Disposal of Western Lands proposed for rural America: to ensure individual liberty through a self-governing, property-owning democracy. It is tempting to see the Frenchman's incorporation of axiality into the Washington D. C. scheme as the superimposition of a more continental vision of liberty secured through the authority of the state, a view much more congenial to Jefferson's great rival, Alexander Hamilton. Whatever truth there may be in such speculation, the realized plan generated fifteen public open spaces, one for each state of the union at the time of the city's foundation. Universal principles embodied in the new republic were thus mapped into its capital.[12]

GEOMETRY, THE MAP AND URBAN LEGIBILITY

Early modern and Enlightenment city planning saw in geometry a medium of legibility. The city was to be read as a text for its rulers, its citizens and its visitors. Printed urban maps expressed and reinforced the city's legibility. These were not initially intended primarily as location markers or way-finding instruments, except for a small number of guide book maps such as those describing the monuments and pilgrimage sites of Rome. The earliest urban maps are overwhelmingly celebratory, intended to frame in a comprehensive image the city's complex social and spatial totality. Such maps form a distinct genre by the 16th Century, emerging in Europe's most heavily urbanized, mercantile regions: upper Italy, Southern Germany and Flanders. Italian urban maps such as Leonardo da Vinci's map of Imola adopted an orthographic perspective, or the high angle, bird's eye view apparent in Jacopo's Venice. Northern maps were more commonly townscape views, graphing the urban skyline in silhouette along a horizontal perspective.[13] While the former universalized the city by representing it according to a standard set of geometrical rules and surveying principles, the latter particularized the city through the unique elements of its skyline: cathedral, guildhall, parish churches. By mid century the distinction was fading. Nicholas Crane captures the impact of changes in urban mapping by describing the cartographer Mercator's reaction to Hieronymous Cock's 1557 view of Antwerp:

> As long as Mercator could remember, Antwerp had been pictured from the water, as a bustling, dishevelled river port. Cock's viewpoint was high above the opposite side of the city. Antwerp had become a disciplined urban network of streets and civic symbols surrounded by massive geometric defenses. Wagons entered landward gates, bound for fleets of patient ships on a distant, placid Schelde. Cock's Antwerp was a celebration of mercantile might, and a working diagram of a modern city.[14]

12. M. Tafuri, *Architecture and Utopia: Design and Capitalist Development*, MIT Press, 1976.

13. L. Nuti, "Mapping Places: Chorography and Vision in the Renaissance," in D. Cosgrove ed., *Mappings*, Reaktion, 1999, pp. 90–108.

14. N. Crane, *Mercator: The Man Who Mapped The Planet*, Phoenix, 2003, p. 188.

<http://historic-cities.huji.ac.il/mapmakers/braun_hogenberg.html>

<www.wga.hu/art/s/schedel/chronic1.jpg>

<www.latvians.com/en/Reading/reading-1550-Cosmographia.php>

The paradigmatic early modern urban mapping project was the multi-volume urban atlas, *Civitates Orbis Terrarum*, edited by Georg Braun and Frans Hogenberg from 1580. Intended to illustrate every major city in the world according to a standard, printed cartographic format, it was conceived in response to Abraham Ortelius' first systematic world atlas of 1570. Earlier encyclopaedias and cosmographies had illustrated cities, but while some places were well served by recognizable images — Constantinople, Rome, Paris and Venice for example — many of the named cities in Hartmann Schedel's *Chronical* (1493) or Sebastian Münster's *Cosmographia* (1544) had been pictured by generic townscape images. Braun and Hogenberg gathered printed city maps from local sources to ensure the most accurate and up-to-date image of the city, allowing the atlas owner to survey the civilized globe of urban places within the privacy of a study or reading room. While some images adopted the urban silhouette, the favored perspective was the bird's eye view, exemplified perfectly in the maps of Cologne or Amsterdam. The city is seen from an elevated point far above and beyond its confines, at an angle sufficient to reveal both its pattern of streets, squares and open spaces and the elevation of its principal buildings and monuments. Distant, to be sure, yet close enough for the rhythm of its life to be pictured in the pedestrians, carriages, wagons and ships moving on its roads and waterways, the city is immediately legible as a coherent community.

Braun and Hogenberg's emphasis on unity and civic order is reinforced by decorating their maps with the coat of arms of the city and of its great families or principal guilds. Cartouches and printed text further reinforce the message, that each city is honored by the depth of its history, the nobility of its citizens, the wealth of its merchants, the beauty of its buildings. The map is synthetic rather than analytic; its goal is celebration rather than analysis or critique. This is true even of the two New World city maps included in the collection: the Aztec capital Tenochtitlan and the Inca city of Cuzco. The former map, based on Cortez's own map, illustrates the very antithesis of civilization in the Classical sense of civic virtue lived out in urban space. It is dominated by its central square and great ziggurat, upon which human sacrifices are being performed. Cartographic parallels between the island cities of Tenochtitlan and Venice reinforced the Aztec capital as "Other" to Europe's self-proclaimed model of civic perfection, yet Braun and Hogenberg's urban mapping principles subordinate difference to stylistic consistency.[15]

LEGIBILITY, IMPROVEMENT AND CONTROL

The decorative, celebratory style of urban mapping exemplified by *Civitates Orbis Terrarum* dominated European urban mapping into the 18th Century.[16] Urban plans projecting newly founded cities or urban expansion adopted a more severe, undecorated style as part of their rhetoric of practicality. This is apparent in Vincenzo Scamozzi's 1599 plan for the Venetian fortress-city of Palmanova, in John Evelyn's 1666 plan for rebuilding fire-damaged London, and in the 1703 plans for St. Petersburg. Their draughtmanship provided the model for the scientific urban maps of the Enlightenment such as Michel Etienne Turgot's 1739

15. Kirsten A. Seaver, "Norumbega and Harmonia Mundi in Sixteenth-Century Cartography," *Imago Mundi*, 50, 1998, pp. 34–58.

<www.microcolour.com/uk002-2.htm>

16. Braun, W. and Hogenburg F., *Civitates urbis terrarum*. Nuremberg, 1580–1617

- <http://feature.geography.wisc.edu/histcart/stp.gif>
- <http://usm.maine.edu/maps/exhibit7/turgot.html>

Plan de Paris. Urban legibility becomes the overarching goal of city mapping, to be achieved through precisely measured survey using carefully calibrated instruments. The undecorated simplicity of 18th-Century graphic design articulates goals of cartographic accuracy and objectivity by erasing evidence of human intervention between survey instrument and printed image.[17] The severely constrained outline of carefully surveyed streets, open spaces, building plots and footprints, together with monochrome printing from fine-line copper engraving or later lithography, together with an absence of decorative embellishment, all signify new ways of thinking about the city and about urban life. The traditional vision of the city as a self-governing polis or a Christian community had underpinned cartographic emphasis on civic harmony, community and dignity within a unified urban space. This vision was being eroded by modern secularism and individualism, and by urban population growth and spatial expansion, industrial production, and new forms of social cleavage and solidarity. In response, the city was reconceived; new ways of imagining and experiencing urban life were reflected in maps whose intent is analytic rather than synthetic.

By the mid-19th Century, plain-style urban plans had become the base maps for the emerging science of urban statistics, by which expanding state capitals and new industrial cities were to be regulated. Cholera and typhoid, poverty and prostitution, alcohol consumption and criminal deviance — all regarded as primarily urban ills — came to be understood through the medium of the urban map.[18] The accuracy of the base map was fundamental to the persuasive power of the statistical information plotted onto it. Rather than celebrating the unity and harmony of urban community, the map's task was to bring into the light of practical reason invisible but all-too-potent urban pathologies. Their amelioration often involved further mapping of urban space: clearing and replanning crowded districts, laying water supply and drainage systems, platting new suburbs, cemeteries and park lands.

The celebratory aspect of the urban map did not entirely disappear. In the United States, for example, it gained a new lease on life in mid-19th Century county atlases lauding Western expansion. The bird's eye perspective was perfect for demonstrating the elegance and prosperity of newly established and often scarcely built towns. Emphasizing their grid of streets and the bustle of carriages and carts, the maps promoted often chaotic and violent places as well-ordered civic communities. They contrast strongly with American fire-insurance maps from the same years whose functional goal of assessing risk and determining premiums is apparent in the severity of unembellished detail, coding such data as street width, building height and constructional materials, or the proximity of hydrants. Anticipating the zoning and planning maps, insurance cartography anticipated the dominant direction of urban mapping in succeeding decades.

17. Lorraine Daston and Katharine Park, *Wonders and the Order of Nature, 1150–1750*, Zone Books, 1994.

18. G. Palsky, *Des Chiffres et des Cartes: Naissance et Développement de la Cartographie Quantitative Française au XIXe siècle*, Paris, C.T.H.S., 1996.

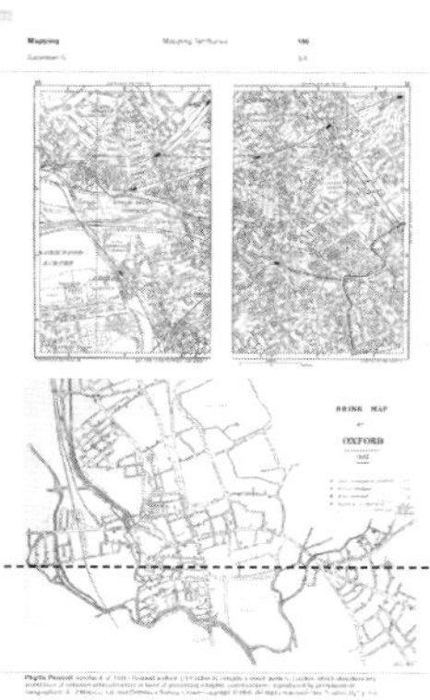

Territory maps

Controlling metropolitan cities was a dominant theme of 20th-Century urban mapping. The response to monster urbanism is recorded in maps, with the modern metropolis constantly threatening to outstrip the map's capacity either to make it legible or to regulate its material and social disorder. London, the first world-city of the 20th Century, is a prime example. The seemingly unco-ordinated and uncontrollable sprawl of its suburbs, dramatically accelerated by mass transportation and later car ownership, anticipated forms and processes that now dominate city landscape and life globally. One heroic, individual response to metropolitan legibility was Phyllis Pearsall's 1935 creation of *London A to Z*, a pocket atlas with gazetteer of every street address in London. Her hugely successful commercial project began in response to a personal dilemma: finding an individual address without an adequate street guide of London. To create her urban atlas she walked 23,000 streets and a distance of nearly 3,000 miles.[19] The outcome was a work that remains a handbook for every Londoner, but it reduces every urban element to the same format, abandoning any semblance of the city as a coherent urban structure in favor of its legibility as a continuously coded surface.

A more bureaucratic cartographic attempt to control the British metropolis was the 1932–34 *National Land Use Survey* in which school children recorded the use of every piece of land in England and Wales, including non-productive urban land. The London plate uses garish color to illustrate vascular urban tentacles strangling the soft green of rural England.[20] It can be read alongside the 1904 plan for Letchworth garden city or the 1999 map of Milton Keynes: urban visions designed to control London's spread. These represent the apotheosis of the map as an instrument of urban policy: not only to recapture the legibility of the city on paper, but to sustain its physical and social coherence as a material space.

In their own ways, these city maps reveal that the modernist faith in geometry as guarantor of urban legibility was unsustainable. Conventional Euclidean forms neither describe nor contain the spaces of the increasingly flexible, mobile, cybernetic city. Since the late 18th Century, the free-flowing serpentine line has battled with orthogonal geometry as privileged design medium for expressing the triumph of individual, natural man over the Classical or Christian model of the citizen.[21] A minor element in the picturesque Letchworth plan, by late 20th Century Milton Keynes the serpentine line is omnipresent. It dominates post-modern urbanism in both street plan and built form. Indeed, high-tech mapping techniques help assure its triumph. Computer-based digital laser technologies allow 21st-Century architects to deform conventional building structures in response to new materials.[22] These are mapping techniques that will soon be applied beyond such signature urban buildings such as Frank Gehry's LA Disney Concert Hall to the form of the city as a whole. Scientific mapping remains more successful in projecting the future form of the city than in capturing the legibility of its daily life.

19. The history of the A–Z guide is told by its creator in P. Pearsall, *A–Z Maps: the personal story from bedsitter to household name*. Geographer's A–Z Map Company, 1990.

20. D. Cosgrove and S. Rycroft, "Mapping the Modern Nation" *History Workshop Journal*, 40, 1995, pp. 91–105.

21. Tafuri, *Architecture and Utopia*, *op. cit.*

22. M. Silver, "Mapping curves," in M. Silver and D. Balmori, eds. *Mapping in the Age of Digital Media: the Yale Symposium*, Wiley-Academy, 2003, pp. 40–47.

NEW LEGIBILITIES: THE ARTIST, THE MAP AND THE CITY

Pearsall's *London A-Z* project was intended to make the city legible for everyday life. We might contrast it with an entirely different but contemporary mapping of the modern metropolis of the German, Hermann Bollmann. Armed with a technique known to 19th-Century artist-cartographers as *Vogelschaukarten*, which dates back at least to Jacopo de' Barbari's 1500 map of Venice, Bollmann confronted modernity's most demanding urban landscape: Manhattan Island. Using 67,000 photographs, 17,000 taken from the air, he created in 1948 a hand-drawn map image that captures precisely the soaring quality of New York's skyline, while rendering streets and buildings with remarkable accuracy. Pearsall's and Bollmann's distinct mappings of the mid-20th Century metropolis may be used to illustrate a debate over how urban space is known and experienced and how it should be mapped.

In the early 1960s a group of French Situationists led by Guy Debord, inspired in part by Walter Benjamin celebrations of urban space and life, invented the dérive or drift as a way of experiencing everyday life in the city free from the attempts of authority to plan and regulate urban movement.[23] They explicitly associated the panoptical map with rational, alienating Modernity. Pearsall's London rather than Bollmann's Manhattan is the paradigmatic mapping mode for the group: derived from walking, signifying the view from the street, refusing all hierarchy of urban places, its pagination generating arbitrary discontinuities on the city map. The Situationist critique of the coherent urban plan in favour of the city as performance art has been a favored cause for later urban progressives such as Michel de Certeau and Rosalyn Deutsche, opening the idea of urban mapping to a range of artistic intervention over the closing years of the 20th and the opening years of the 21st Centuries.[24] These mappings may deploy the analytic capacities of scientific cartography, often using advanced technologies to rework some of the goals of early urban mapping. They seek to capture legibility from the contemporary city, not as a means of reworking its material spaces, but as a way of enhancing the experience of everyday urban life.

23. Guy Debord, *The Society of the Spectacle*, Zone Books, 1994.

24. M. de Certeau, *The Practice of Everyday Life*, University of California Press, 1985; R. Deutsche: "Boy's Town," *Environment and Planning D: Society and Space*, 9, 1991, pp. 5–30.

9/11: URBAN MAPPING AND ART

Space permits discussion of only one example of such creative use of mapping. But it is a powerfully telling example in its symbolic and ethical dimensions. Michel de Certeau's celebrated critique of scientific mapping's distanciated and totalizing vision of the city took as its model the view of Manhattan from the top of the World Trade Center. Ironically, the destruction of those towers on September 11, 2001 presented, perhaps, history's greatest single challenge to urban mapping. Maps and plans of every system affected by the attack—transportation, utilities, communications, air quality—and new maps detailing its changing impacts were vital to the response mounted by the city's myriad public

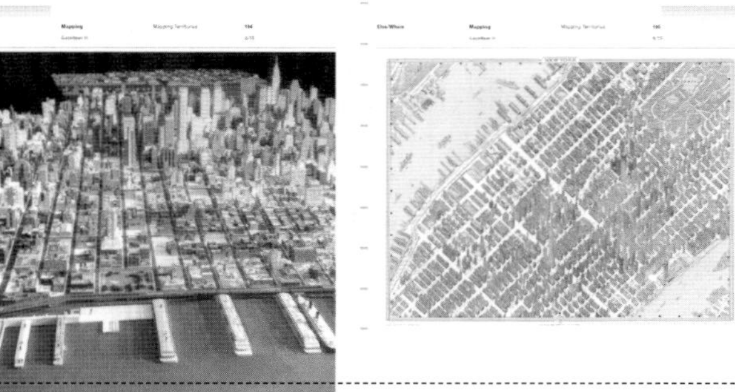

Territory maps

See "Mapping the Homunculus," p. 200.

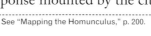

and private agencies. Cartographers used the latest Geographic Information System (GIS) technology to coordinate and plot these diverse data sets. Maps could not be redrawn in a continuously evolving situation as information fed in from scanners, satellites, and photogrammetry surveys had to be integrated with existing maps and databases for the affected zone. Over a three-month period, more than 2,600 maps were produced, using "techniques of layering, seriality and transparency, complemented by the destabilizing power of interactivity, movement and animation."[25] Many were made available on the web.

Over the extended period of recovery, interest among the public in the site remained intense: victims' relatives, New York citizens, distinguished visitors and ordinary Americans came to bear witness and observe progress. The scale of the site and the barriers erected to protect the recovery work made it almost impossible to the casual visitor to comprehend what they saw. In response, the artist Laura Kurgan who had previously used mapping techniques to explore a range of issues surrounding political violence, gained funding for the production of two editions of a map: *Around Ground Zero* published in December 2001 and March 2002. These used primary colors and simple graphics to identify key elements of the site: viewing platforms, temporary memorials, cranes and trucks as well as variously demolished or damaged buildings. Her maps negotiated the most delicate of ethical dilemmas given the implications of viewing a scene of mass murder from which human remains were being actively removed. They were distributed free to visitors.

The contemporary city presents both complex new challenges and enormous opportunities for mapping as do emerging survey and plotting technologies. Indeed, the map may be the only medium through which contemporary urbanism can achieve visual coherence. There remains a strong, if unrecognized, celebratory dimension to urban mapping, not merely in the banal sense of cities' self-promotion through advertising or tourist maps and plans, but in the choice of scale, content, design and color of the myriad cartographic devices (many today interactive), developed by public agencies and private bodies to communicate and regulate contemporary urban systems and processes. The goal of rendering legible the complex, dynamic and living entity that is a city remains an urgent one. But today's acute awareness that cartographic images can never be innocent vehicles of information dissolves neat distinctions between celebratory and regulatory urban maps. Urban space and cartographic space remain inseparable; as each is transformed their relationship alters. Current visual technologies mean that the opportunity for creativity in shaping and recording urban experience is greater than ever, as too is the need for critical attention to the making and meaning of both public and private urban spaces.

25. M. Silver and D. Balmori: "Networking maps: GIS, virtualized reality and the World Wide Web," in Silver and Balmori, *Mapping in the Age of Digital Media*, op. cit., pp. 48–50.

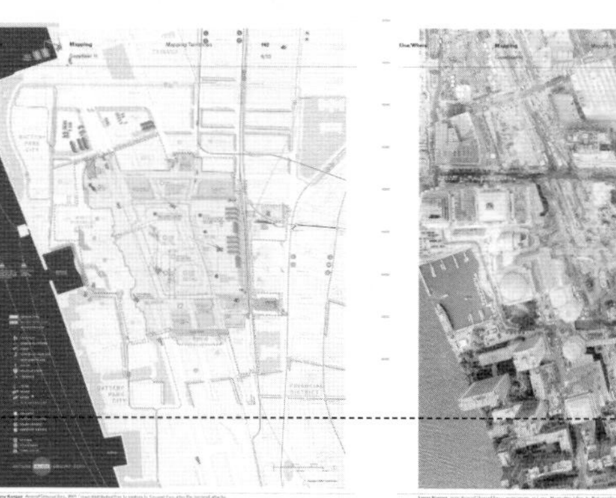

Territory maps

See "Monochrome Landscapes," pp. 310–319, and "Instruments of Uncertainty," p. 109.

gazetteer H 6–7/13 pp. 192–193

greatest commercial city—the antithesis of the contemporary online route-planning map / image © The Trustees of The British Museum / see "Carto-City," p. 150.

Oxford University / see "Carto-City," p. 155.

Charles L'Enfant *Plan for Washington D.C.*, 1786 / (bottom left): federal authority radiates through axes from the seats of power / image courtesy of the National Archives, Washington, D.C. / see "Carto-City," p. 152.

Phyllis Pearsall *London A–Z*, 1935 / Pearsall walked 3,000 miles to compile a street guide to London, which abandons any semblance of coherent urban structure in favor of presenting a legible coded surface / reproduced by permission of Geographers' A–Z Map Co. Ltd. and Ordnance Survey. Crown Copyright © 2003. All rights reserved / see "Carto-City," p. 155.

Anonymous *Oxford "Drink Map,"* 1888 / Victorian maps of urban pathologies used plain-style urban plans as their base maps / image courtesy of The Bodleian Library, Oxford University / see "Carto-City," p. 155.

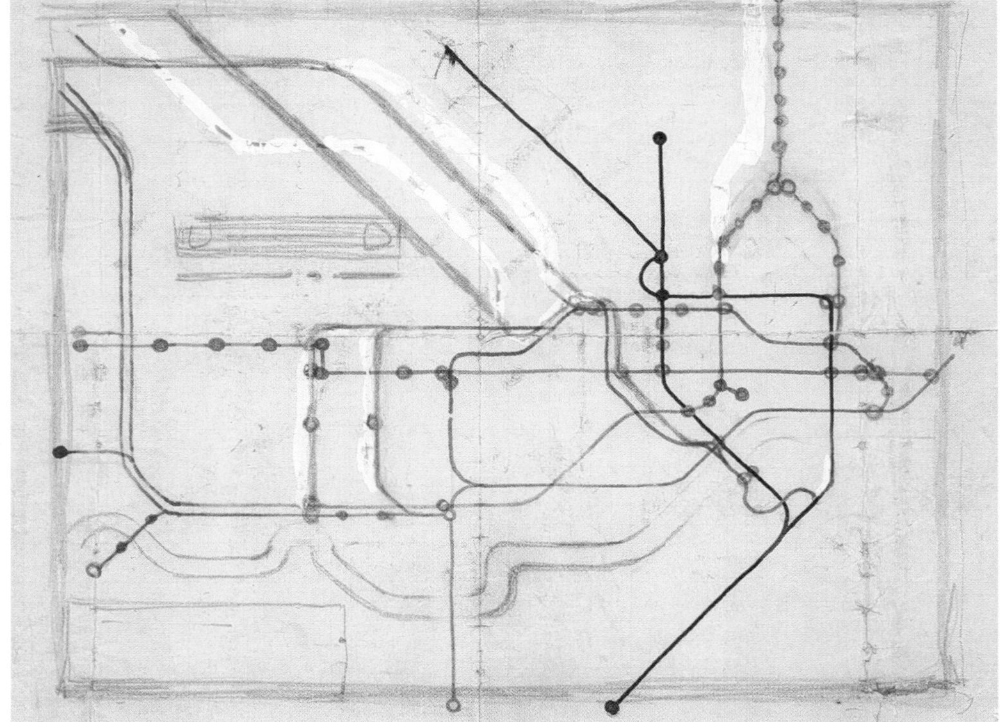

Ken Garland *Harry Beck*, 1965 / photograph © Ken Garland / see "Signal Failure," p. 166.

Harry Beck *Original sketch for the London Underground "Diagram,"* 1931 / all surface detail except for the River Thames is eliminated / image courtesy of the Trustees of the Victoria & Albert Museum, London / see "Signal Failure," p. 166.

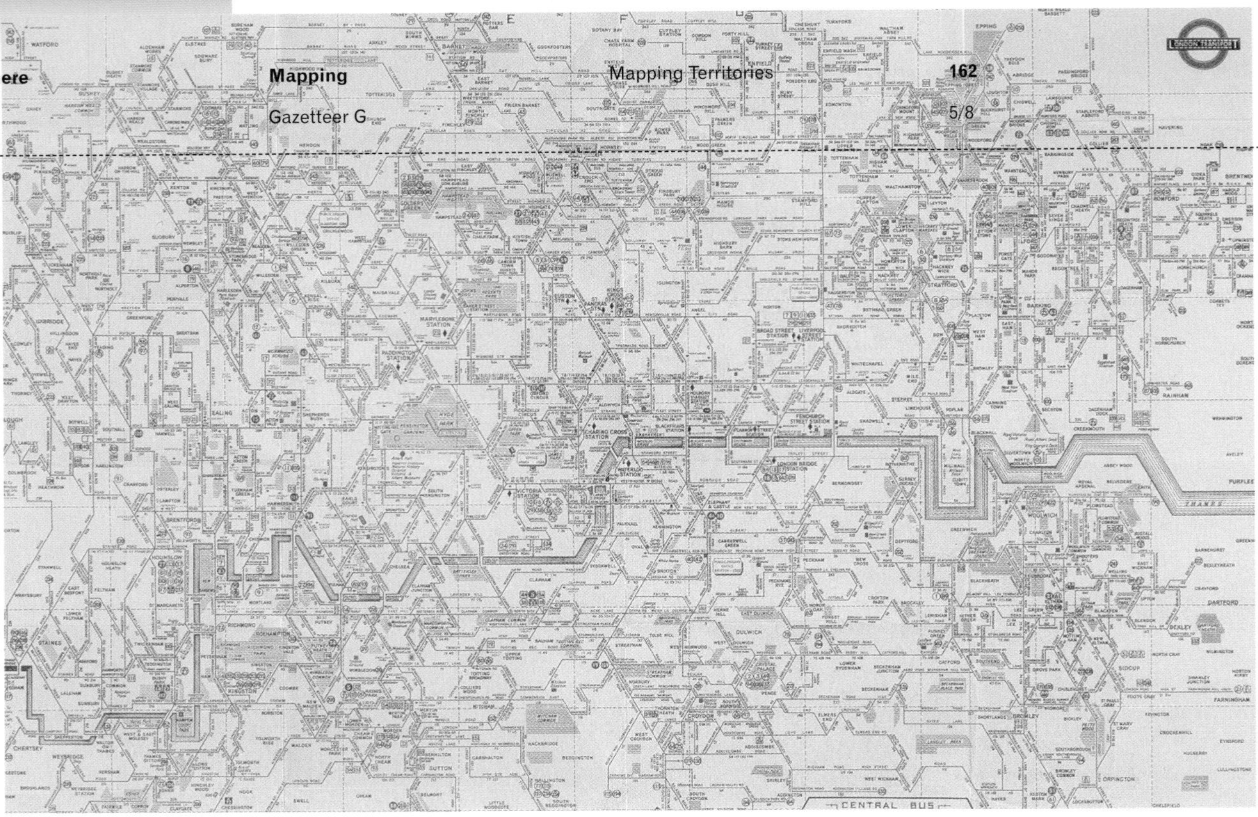

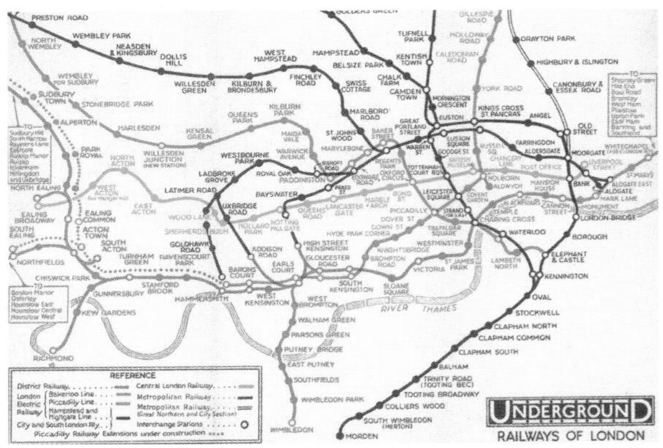

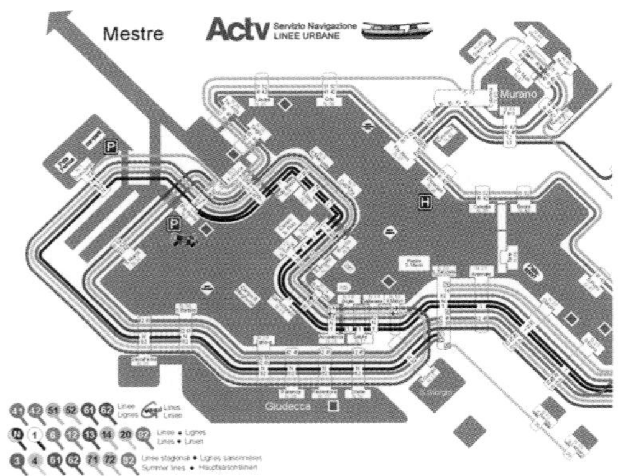

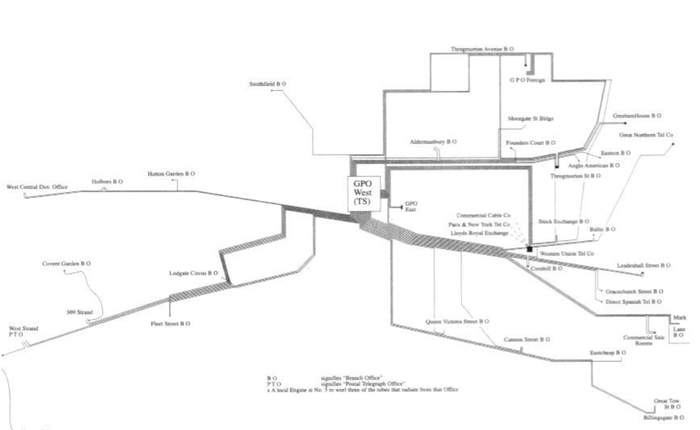

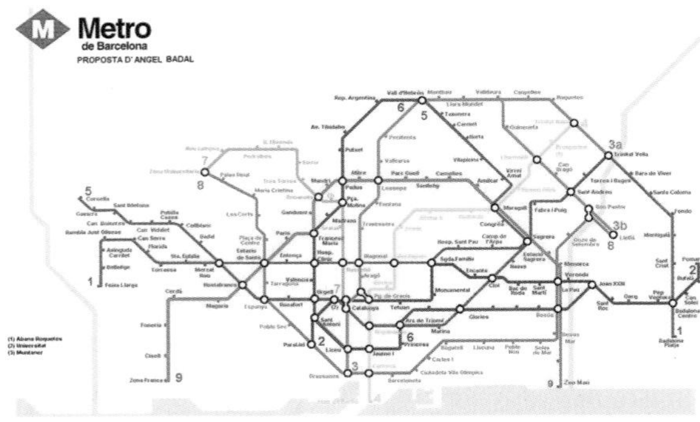

Fred Elston *Diagrammatic Central Bus map*, 1946 / (top): clearly inspired by Harry Beck's Underground diagram, Elston's rather dense London bus map was swiftly replaced by a more conventional version / © TfL reproduced courtesy of London's Transport Museum / see "Signal Failure," p. 166.

(bottom, clockwise from upper left): the London Underground map in 1932 prior to Beck's diagram; Venice vaporetto map, 2004; Barcelona Metro map, 2004; London Post Office telegraph system, 1890, a template for Beck's schematic diagram / see "Signal Failure," pp. 166–175.

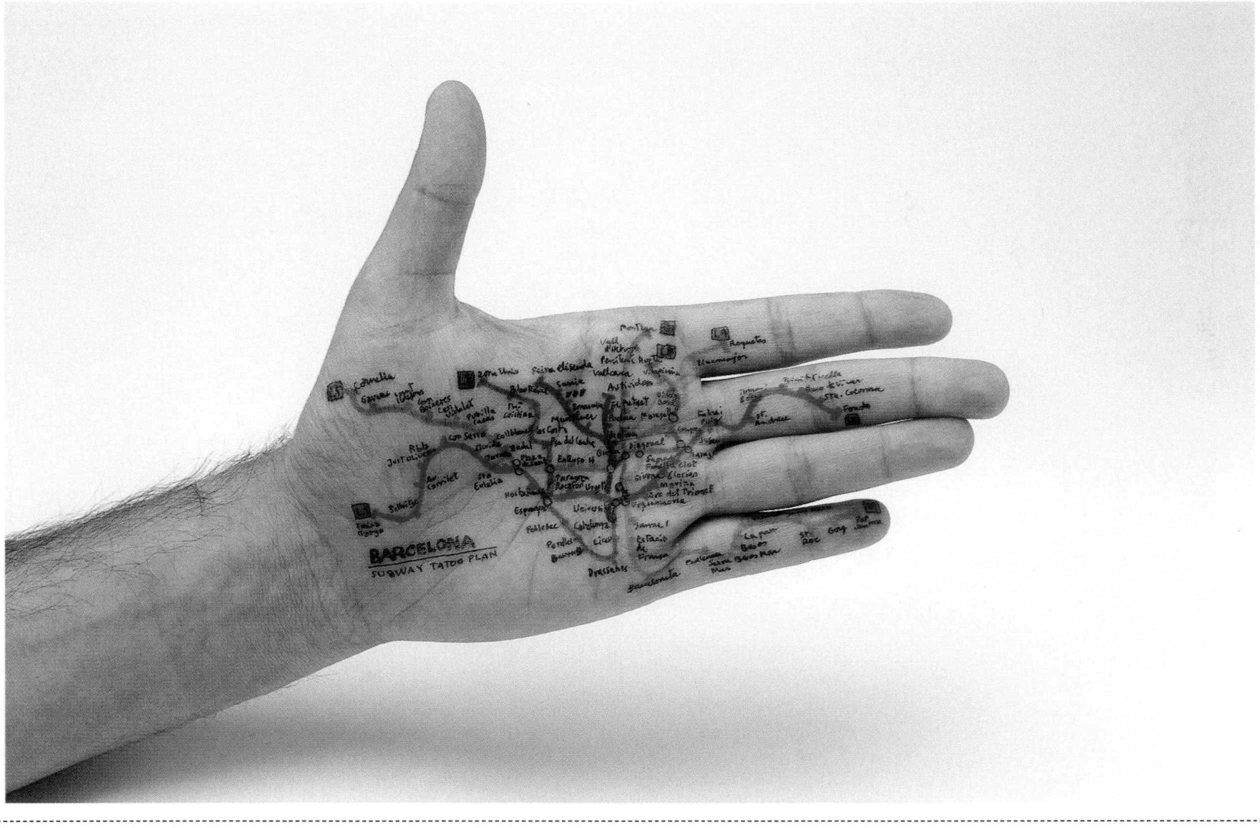

London by laptop.

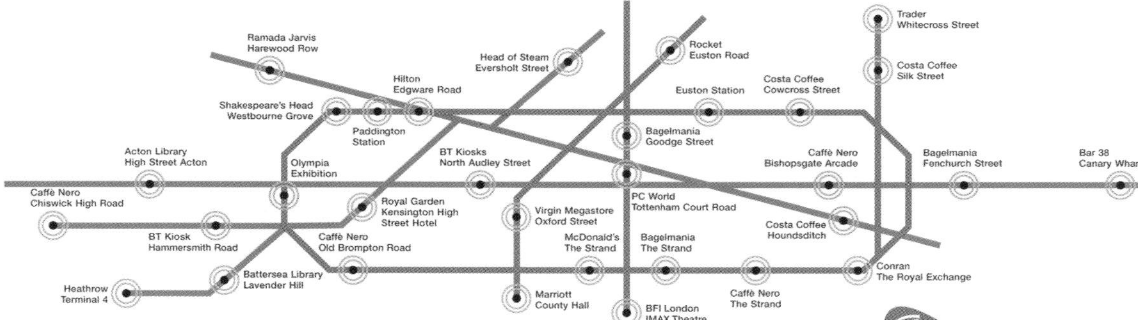

With laptops powered by Intel® Centrino™ mobile technology you can get online at wireless hotspots all over London. **For your nearest hotspot, visit www.intel.co.uk/unwire.**

Euro RSCG London, Nigel Rose (art director) and **Alan Curson** (copy writer) *London by laptop,* advertisement for Intel, 2004 / image courtesy of EuroRSCG London / see "Signal Failure," p. 175.

Martí Guixé *Tourist Tattoo*, 1997 / Barcelona subway map drawn on the artist's palm / photograph © Imagekontainer.

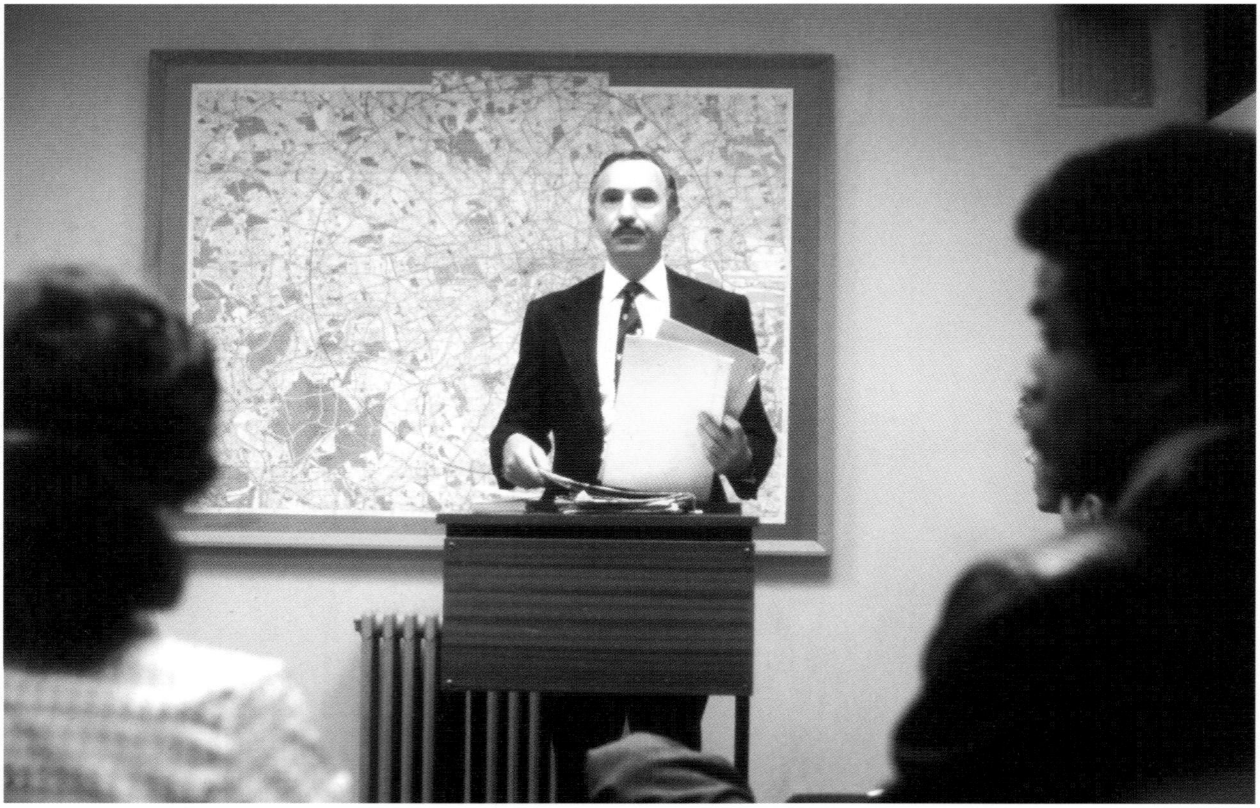

Guy Pearce as Leonard in *Memento* directed by Christopher Nolan / photograph by Danny Rothenberg © 2001 IFC Films / see "Cerebral Cities," p. 176, 183.

Nigel Hawthorne as the instructor Mr. Burgess in *The Knowledge*, 1979 / scene from the British television drama by Jack Rosenthal, which follows four would-be taxi-drivers as they attempt to acquire "The Knowledge," the street-by-street memorization of London / image © TalkbackThames/Euston Films / see "Cerebral Cities," pp. 181 – 182.

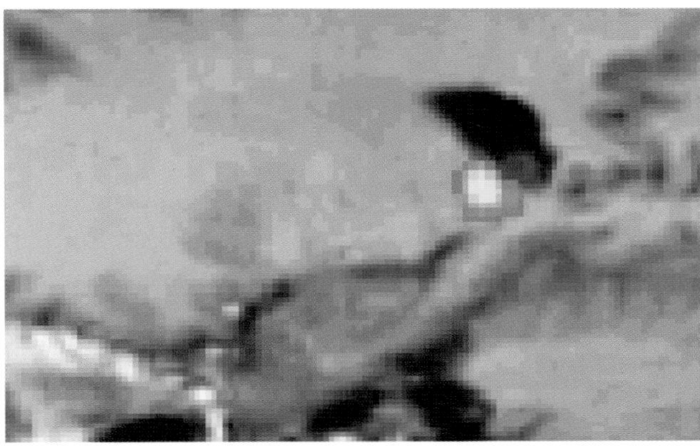

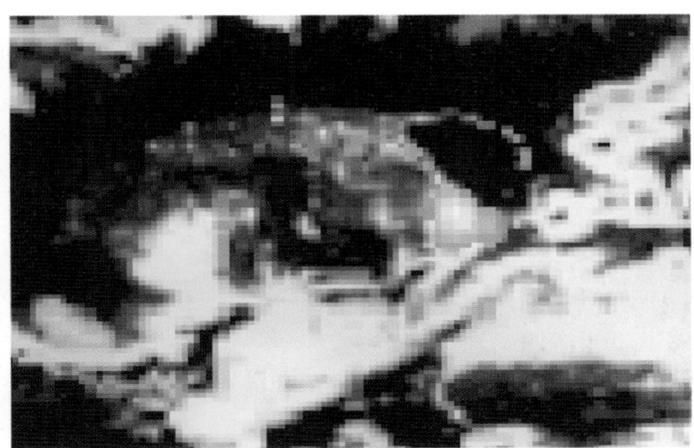

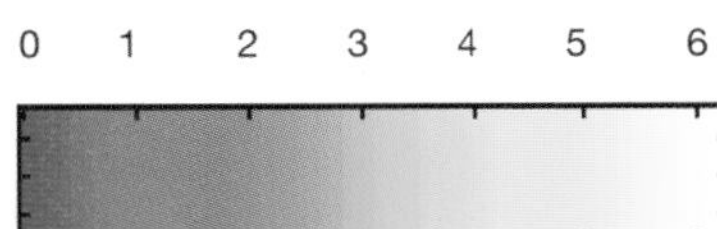

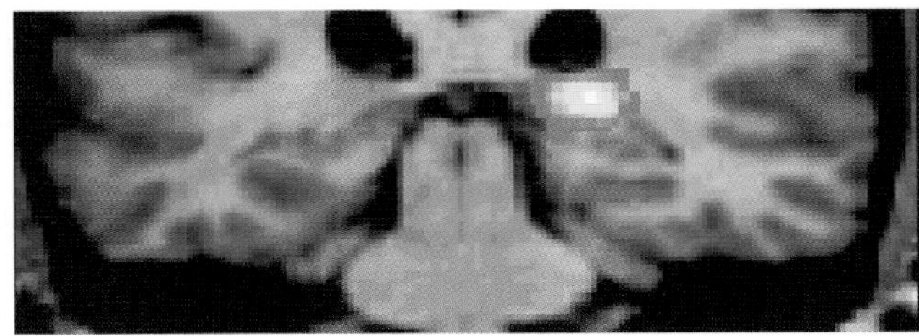

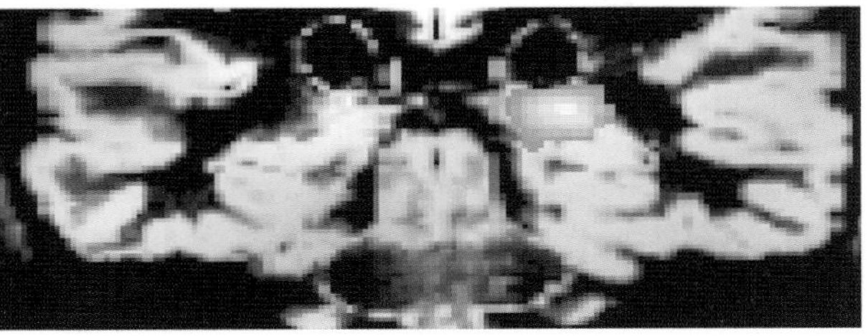

Trainee London cab driver acquiring "The Knowledge" / photograph by Paul Elliman / see "Cerebral Cities," p. 176.

Structural MRIs of the brains of long-time London taxi drivers revealed a larger volume in their posterior hippocampi compared to those in control subjects. Study produced by the Wellcome Department of Cognitive Neurology, Institute of Neurology, published as "Navigation-related structural change in the hippocampi of taxi drivers," April 2000, by Dr. Eleanor Maguire *et al* / image courtesy of Dr. Eleanor Maguire / see "Cerebral Cities," pp. 181–182.

SIGNAL FAILURE

Few things capture the modernist vision of the city as an efficient machine better than Harry Beck's 1933 system map for the London Underground — a transport diagram apparently based on an electrical circuit board. But just as Beck's famous diagram seems to render London as a dynamic landscape of flawless interconnectivity, its continued use (not to mention clarity) also underscores an often less-than-efficient daily relationship with the city — where power failures and derailments, along with the threat of terrorist attacks, cast a contradictory shadow over the map's utopian graphic form.

<http://www.ltmuseum.co.uk>

An introduction to London Transport's website reminds that "In 1933 Harry Beck designed the London Underground map. An electrical engineer, he based the design on a circuit diagram...".[1] Almost everyone who has written about the map points this much out. London historian Stephen Halliday, in his recent book *Underground to Everywhere*, describes the route-finder as "strongly reminiscent of an electrical wiring diagram. It is no coincidence that much of Beck's work in the signal engineers' department, involved drafting just such diagrams for signalling circuits…".[2]

Ken Garland, in his impressive study, *Mr. Beck's Underground Map*, includes a spoof version drawn in 1933 for a transportation magazine in which Beck parodied the notion that he had somehow graphically rewired the city of London according to the language of electrical engineering, with tube station names adapted accordingly: oriented toward a "North Pole," Hampstead becomes "Amp," the Bakerloo Line becomes "Bakerlite Tube," and the affluent Kensington area gets a station called "Ideal Ohms."[3]

Despite frequent references to the influence of electrical engineering, the broader implications of the circuit-board style mapping of a modern metropolis have received little attention in discussions of Beck's profoundly influential representation of London.

1. <http://tube.tfl.gov.uk/content/tubemap/realunderground/loader2.swf>
2. Stephen Halliday, *Underground to Everywhere*. London: Sutton Publishing, 2001.
3. Ken Garland, *Mr Beck's Underground Map*. London: Capital Transport, 1994.

* * *

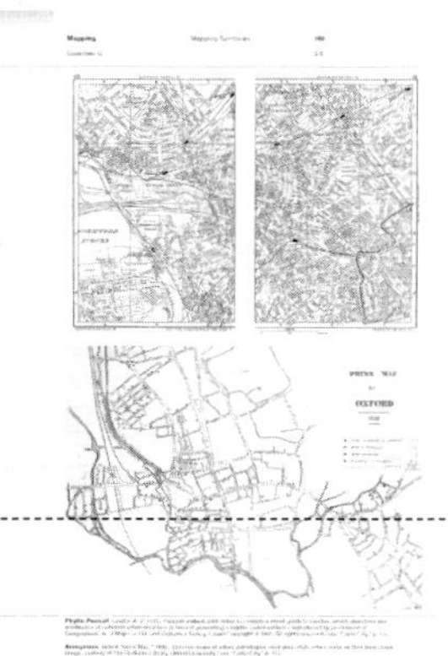

Territory maps

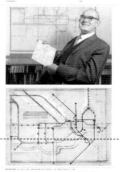

Beck devised the new Underground map just as the electrical firmament of modern urban life was finally being systematized. The year that the map was introduced, London Underground agreed to allow the London Electricity Board to install cables along its tunnels, formalizing a longstanding relationship between the two companies. Britain's National Grid, initiated through the Electricity Supply Act of 1926, was established in 1934.

The London Underground "diagram"—designed amid the capital's electrification and expansion in the 1930s—established an archetype for network and transportation maps worldwide. **Paul Elliman** compares the image of the city as an efficient machine projected by Beck's map, with the reality of public transport in London today.

With the smoke and fumes, and generally low performance of steam locomotives, underground railways seem an unlikely prospect without the power of electricity. The first electric tramway had opened in Germany in 1881, with London adapting to the new technology only when the first tube opened in 1890. This was still a world without an electricity supply industry, and the new rail and tram companies began to build their own power stations—profiting, in some cases, by supplying power for local domestic lighting. Between 1902 and 1905, in order to supply the District Line and their three tube lines, the Underground Group built an immense power station at Lots Road, Chelsea. For a while it was the largest in Europe, and later provided electricity for the entire Underground system.

Today, Beck's city is pinned across a network connecting 275 subway stations, and a sunken cable network of some 12,000 electricity substations. Receiving power from larger converter stations, these substations transform the voltage for commercial distribution, flooding London's streets, buildings and homes with electric current. Hundreds of thousands of miles of high-voltage cable are threaded above, below and along the routes of the Underground. Some cables share tunnels with trains, but many of them also occupy their own tunnels, usually about 80 feet beneath the surface; the subterranean tube stations are often used as markers for key points in the electricity network.[4]

In other words, even if Beck's map had never existed, a version could have been drawn up simply to chart London's electrical energy—a thought that conjures up the Borgesian image of a gigantic diagram, pieced together from fragments found in the files of every electrical engineer in the city.

A map of the London Post Office telegraph system of 1890 offers a working template for Beck's schematic diagram, and for so much of our contemporary sense of London life. From the Post Office headquarters next to St. Paul's, a familiar pattern of connecting lines maps a network from Shepherd's Bush to Limehouse, from Camden Town to Elephant and Castle. An electrical Central Line already extends from Holborn to Moorgate and the City. Like some mysterious act of Victorian clairvoyance, the speed and power of modern business life threatens to burst out of the telegraph map's premonition of a fast-approaching, fully electrified London.

Electricity brought standardization. Telecommunications and then street lighting were the earliest commercial applications, physically altering the functional nature of buildings and streets long before liquid crystal paneling or cellular Wi-Fi coverage. In 1839, Marc Brunel, chief engineer of the Great Western Railway, had a telegraph system installed along 13 miles of track between Paddington and

4. Richard Tench and Ellis Hillman, *London Under London*. London: John Murray, 1993.

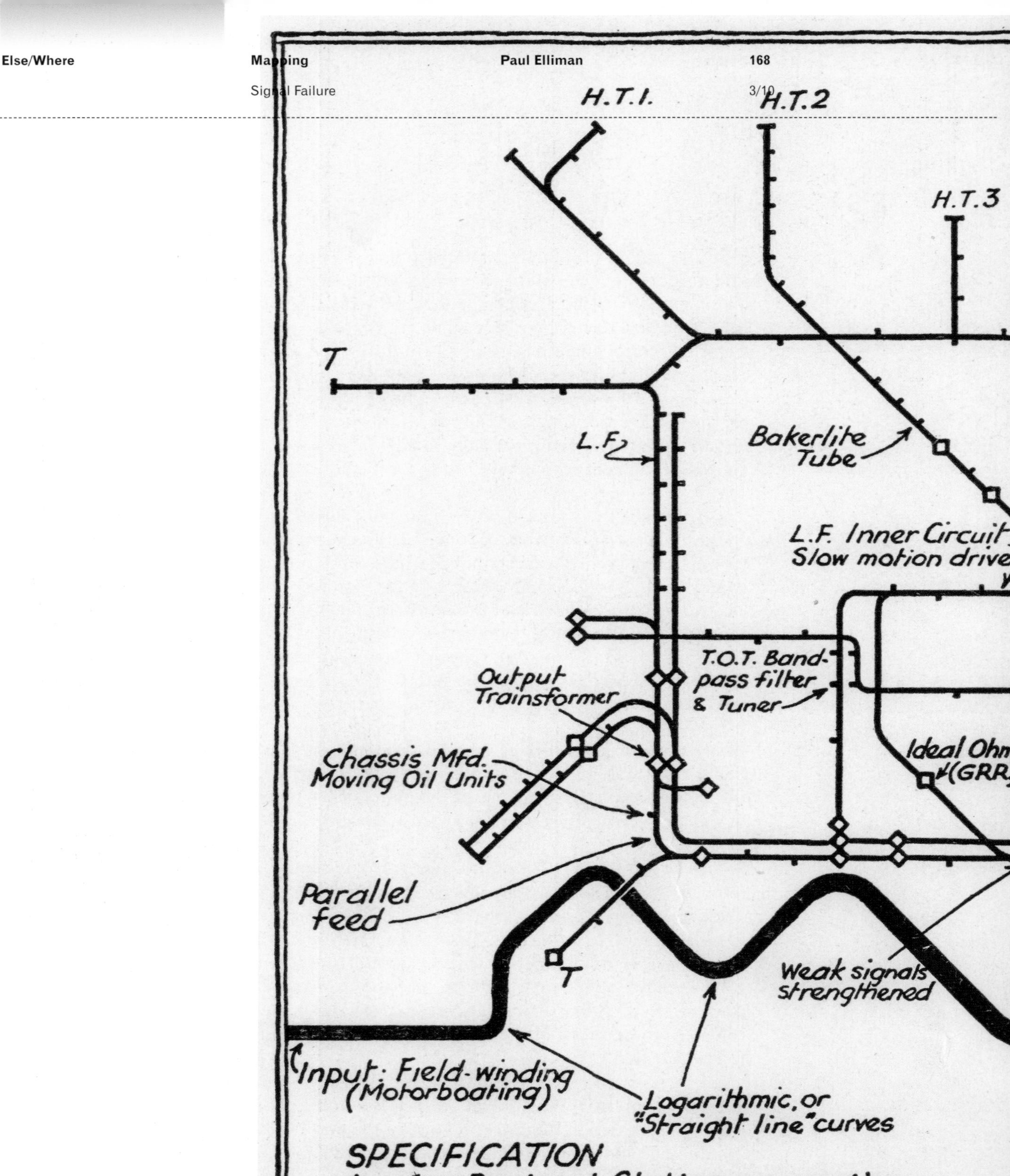

Harry Beck *Spoof Diagram*, 1933 / originally published in the *Train, Omnibus and Tram Staff Magazine* / © TfL reproduced courtesy of London's Transport Museum.

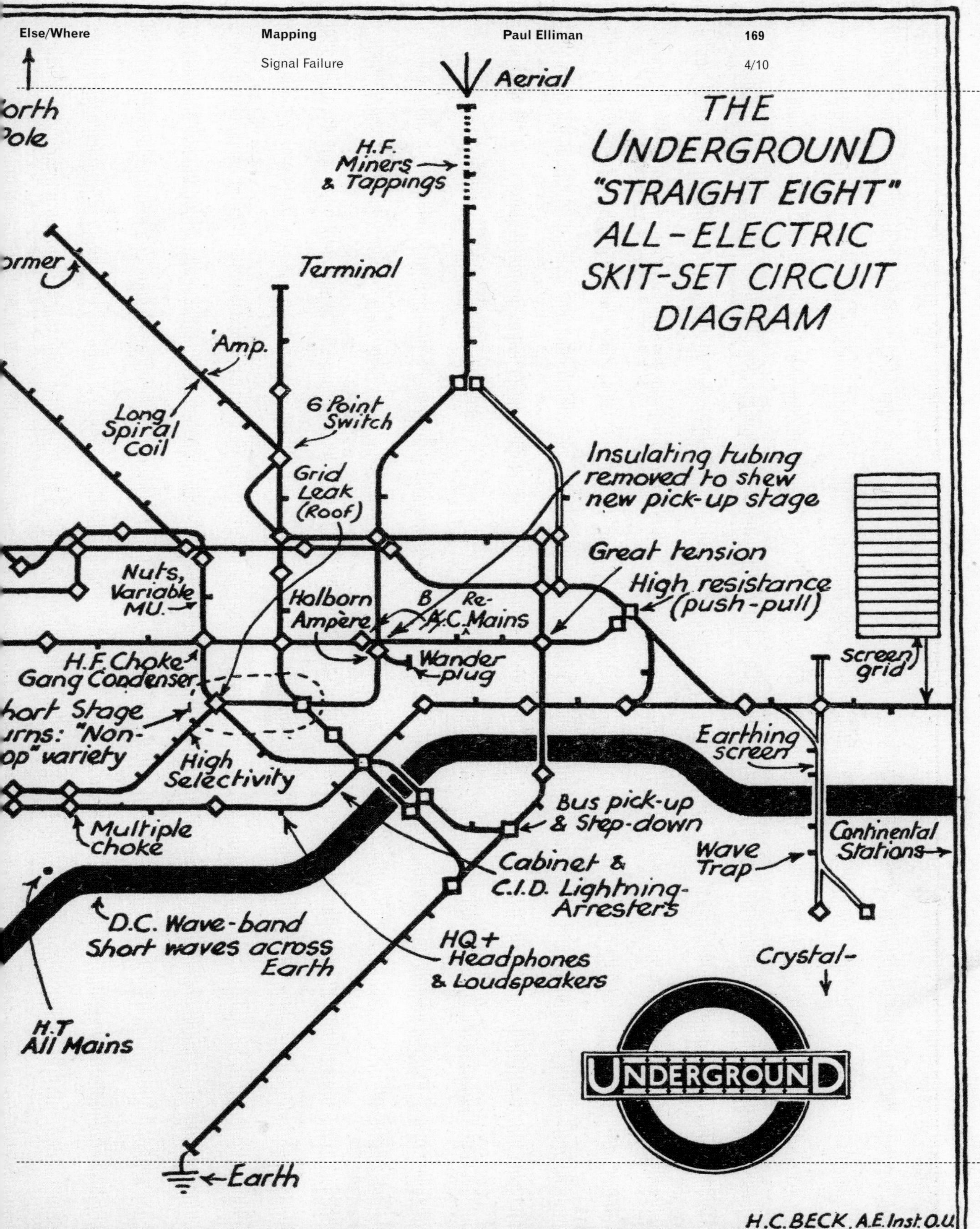
THE UNDERGROUND "STRAIGHT EIGHT" ALL-ELECTRIC SKIT-SET CIRCUIT DIAGRAM
Aerial
H.F. Miners & Tappings
Terminal
Amp.
Long Spiral Coil
6 Point Switch
Grid Leak (Roof)
Insulating tubing removed to shew new pick-up stage
Great tension
High resistance (push-pull)
Nuts, Variable MU.
Halborn Ampère
B Re-A.C. Mains
Wander plug
Screen grid
H.F. Choke
Gang Condenser
High Selectivity
Earthing screen
Multiple choke
Bus pick-up & Step-down
Continental Stations
Wave Trap
Cabinet & C.I.D. Lightning-Arresters
D.C. Wave-band Short waves across Earth
HQ + Headphones & Loudspeakers
Crystal-
H.T All Mains
UNDERGROUND
Earth
H.C. BECK. A.E. Inst. O.U.

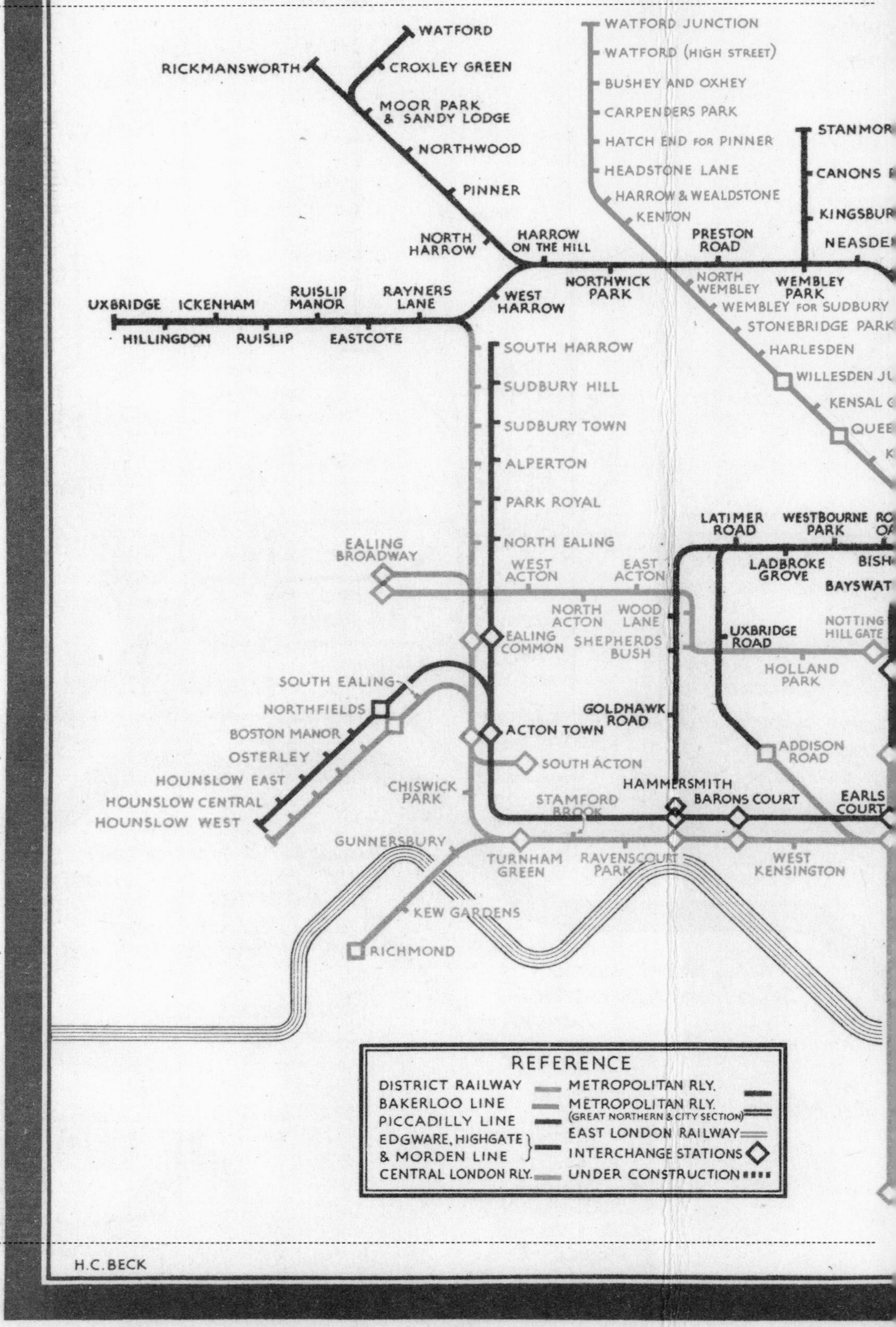

Harry Beck *First foldout card version of London Underground diagram,* 1933 / © TfL reproduced courtesy of London's Transport Museum.

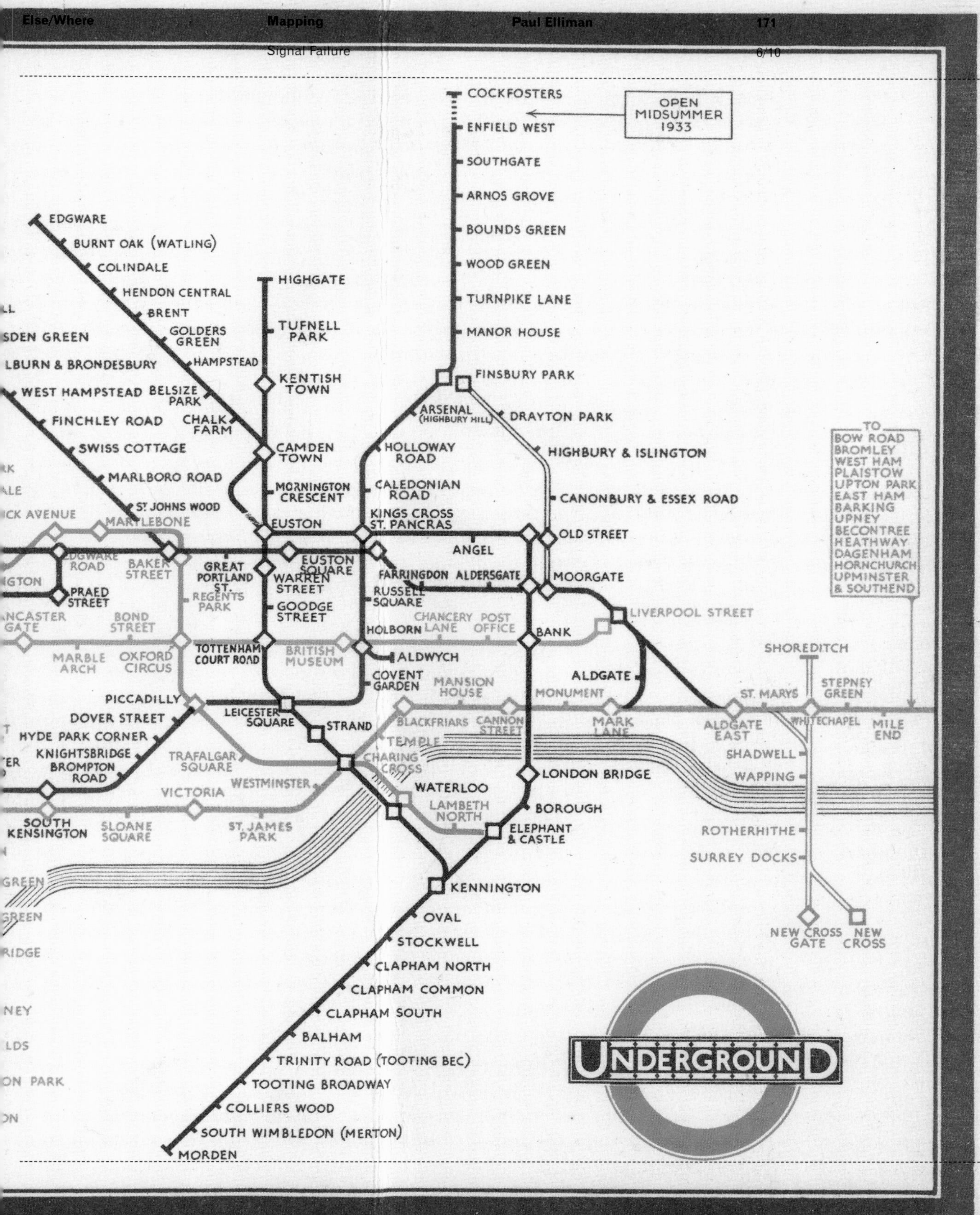
COCKFOSTERS
OPEN MIDSUMMER 1933
ENFIELD WEST
SOUTHGATE
ARNOS GROVE
BOUNDS GREEN
WOOD GREEN
TURNPIKE LANE
MANOR HOUSE
FINSBURY PARK
EDGWARE
BURNT OAK (WATLING)
COLINDALE
HENDON CENTRAL
BRENT
GOLDERS GREEN
HAMPSTEAD
BELSIZE PARK
CHALK FARM
HIGHGATE
TUFNELL PARK
KENTISH TOWN
CAMDEN TOWN
MORNINGTON CRESCENT
EUSTON
WEST HAMPSTEAD
FINCHLEY ROAD
SWISS COTTAGE
MARLBORO ROAD
ST. JOHNS WOOD
ARSENAL (HIGHBURY HILL)
DRAYTON PARK
HOLLOWAY ROAD
HIGHBURY & ISLINGTON
CALEDONIAN ROAD
CANONBURY & ESSEX ROAD
KINGS CROSS ST. PANCRAS
OLD STREET
ANGEL
EUSTON SQUARE
FARRINGDON
ALDERSGATE
MOORGATE
GREAT PORTLAND ST.
WARREN STREET
RUSSELL SQUARE
REGENTS PARK
GOODGE STREET
LIVERPOOL STREET
CHANCERY LANE
POST OFFICE
HOLBORN
BANK
TOTTENHAM COURT ROAD
BRITISH MUSEUM
ALDWYCH
ALDGATE
COVENT GARDEN
MANSION HOUSE
MONUMENT
EDGWARE ROAD
BAKER STREET
PRAED STREET
BOND STREET
MARBLE ARCH
OXFORD CIRCUS
PICCADILLY
DOVER STREET
HYDE PARK CORNER
KNIGHTSBRIDGE
BROMPTON ROAD
LEICESTER SQUARE
STRAND
BLACKFRIARS
CANNON STREET
MARK LANE
ALDGATE EAST
ST. MARYS
WHITECHAPEL
STEPNEY GREEN
MILE END
SHOREDITCH
TEMPLE
CHARING CROSS
TRAFALGAR SQUARE
WESTMINSTER
VICTORIA
WATERLOO
LAMBETH NORTH
LONDON BRIDGE
BOROUGH
ELEPHANT & CASTLE
SHADWELL
WAPPING
ROTHERHITHE
SURREY DOCKS
SOUTH KENSINGTON
SLOANE SQUARE
ST. JAMES PARK
KENNINGTON
OVAL
STOCKWELL
CLAPHAM NORTH
CLAPHAM COMMON
CLAPHAM SOUTH
BALHAM
TRINITY ROAD (TOOTING BEC)
TOOTING BROADWAY
COLLIERS WOOD
SOUTH WIMBLEDON (MERTON)
MORDEN
NEW CROSS GATE
NEW CROSS
TO BOW ROAD BROMLEY WEST HAM PLAISTOW UPTON PARK EAST HAM BARKING UPNEY BECONTREE HEATHWAY DAGENHAM HORNCHURCH UPMINSTER & SOUTHEND
UNDERGROUND

West Drayton. National time was first standardized for railway timetables. Historian Roy Porter describes how, from 1852, London time was being transmitted to the rest of the country, "pulsed out by hourly telegraph signals."[5]

A survey of the public buildings quickest to install electric lighting — notably Billingsgate Fish Market, the *Times* newspaper offices, the Gaiety Theatre, the Old Bailey courtrooms, the General Post Office and London Bridge Station — reveals urban interests parallel to our own: commerce, media, entertainment, law, communications and transport. The world's first power station was built in Holborn, central London, in 1883; seven years later, the world's first underground electric railway opened — the City & South London Railway — with locomotives powered by Compton traction motors.

Even the very earliest cartographic designs for the Underground reflected life in a metropolis transformed by electricity. In 1908, an electrical engineering company produced one of the first pocket maps, which adopted (in order to fit the postcard-sized format) the distorted topography later associated with Beck's diagram. London, along with other European capitals, including Berlin and Paris, underwent a period of unprecedented expansion in the five decades preceding publication of Beck's diagram. The city itself seemed to be on the move, gathering up villages, towns and open fields in all directions of the old City of London, grouping new neighborhoods and districts into an extended version of its oldest and most labyrinthine streets and passages.

In the middle of such rapid and large-scale developments, London Underground increased its efforts to appeal to the public and attract more passengers. Melodramatic posters portrayed the outer reaches of London, its New Towns and Garden Cities, as an English suburban paradise. The rail networks, along with the distribution of public utilities, allowed some kind of urban unity to exist, if only by connecting all the parts of the sprawling city together. In what seems, today, little more than a fantasy of orderliness, Beck's London Underground map offered an image of organizational clarity, brilliantly presenting the increasingly chaotic city as an object of coherence.

* * *

By conferring a specific kind of image on a place, maps help establish certain aspects of territorial hold. Beck's map did not by itself magically generate the city we know today, much of which already existed at the time of its devising. But it signaled the shift into a supposedly modernized consciousness, helping to reconfigure the spirit of place, of London, around the emerging concept of an information economy.

Beck's diagram is consistent with the two most dominant metaphors through which the modern city has been portrayed: body and machine. Ken Garland cites Beck's reference to the Underground diagram as a "living and changing thing, with schematic and spare-part osteopathy going on all the time," corresponding

5. Roy Porter, *London: A Social History.* London: Hamish Hamilton, 1994.

with the organic notion of the city as a body.[6] Yet Beck's diagram is also an example of just how fully, by the 1930s, metaphors of the city as machine had been integrated into the conception of urban life. In an essay about Fritz Lang's *Metropolis*, film historian Thomas Elsaesser points out that the "machine aesthetic"—already established in the formal languages of the avant-garde—had clearly entered the language of cultural criticism by the beginning of the 20th Century.[7] Beck's diagram shows the extent to which the language of visual representation can shape a mental image of a city, inscribing inaccurate or vague senses of distance, scale and direction, and giving prominence to certain places simply by virtue of their being selected for the map.

Beck's use of the electrical circuit board was also consistent with an urban vocabulary of reticular terms such as circuit, circulation, grid and network—terms that have helped to idealize certain perceptions of the modern city. Sociologist Richard Sennett describes how medical awareness of the circulation of blood in the 17th Century had an impact on urban design as well as awareness of a "circulating" economy of labor and goods.[8] Discoveries made by physician William Harvey helped to establish what Sennett calls a "new master image of the body." By the 18th Century, urban planners were applying words like "artery" and "veins" to city streets, using the body's blood system as analogue for traffic systems, but also to provide a moralistic image of a healthy body in a healthy society.

Similarly, historian Armand Mattelart has followed the genealogy of the term network (*réseau*, in French), adapted from earlier uses in the French silk weaving industry and applied to military cartography and the design of fortifications. The invention of the telegraph established the modern technical sense of the term, as "the spatial form of a communication system."[9] This led to a 19th-Century "cult of the network", and the conception of society along managerial lines "based on networks of banking and finance, rail and transportation." As Mattelart points out, telegraphic communication networks were explicitly used to symbolize an international community and served as a model for intergovernmental organizations. We can sense in the earliest uses of the network image—"at once both symbol and tool of economic and social relations"—the beginnings of a globalized economic market.

In his influential book, *The Production of Space*, urban sociologist Henri Lefebvre compares the circuit-like flows of the city to those that characterize a modern house "...permeated from every direction by streams of energy which run in and out of it by every imaginable route: water, gas, electricity, telephone lines, radio and television signals."[10] But Lefebvre was skeptical of the great planners and schemers of the modern city, mistrusting a functionalism that was based on the ideological circuitries of capital, production and commodities: "To claim that the city is defined as a network of circulation and communication, as a centre of information and decision making, is an absolute ideology." In the bowels of the city, that ideology is contradicted by the physical evidence of transformation. In

6. Garland, *ibid*.

7. Thomas Elsaesser, *Metropolis*. London: BFI, 2000.

8. Richard Sennett, *Flesh and Stone*. London: Faber and Faber Limited, 1994.

9. Armand Mattelart, "Mapping Modernity: Utopia and Communications Networks," in *Mappings*, Denis Cosgrove, ed. London: Reaktion Books, 1999, pp. 169–192.

10. Henri Lefebvre, *The Production of Space*. Oxford: Blackwell, 1991.

its emergence as a global telecommunications center, London resembles a kind of cyberpunk time machine in a constant struggle between the physical world of cables, machine parts, buildings and people and, on the other hand, the codified representational space of telecommunications.

This ongoing traumatic shift between the physical and representational has left a trail of interim technologies: between 1853 and 1962, London had the world's most substantial pneumatic tube communication system: at its peak during the late 1950s, an average of 50,000 pneumatic tube messages a day were forced by air-pressure along its cast-iron ducts — a system finally eclipsed by telex and teleprinters. From 1927, the Post Office (which had taken over the National Telephone Company in 1911) ran its own electric rail network, the Mail Rail's underground system of miniature, remote-controlled trains, operating between Paddington, Whitechapel and Liverpool Street. Electronic communications played a key a part in its demise: on closing the mini-rail network in March 2003, the Royal Mail (the Post Office's successor) claimed that, over a five-year period, the amount of letters posted in London had fallen by the equivalent of an entire mail center, "largely due to the growth of email."[11]

The contemporary scientific image of public transport passengers as "message bearing systems" originates in these transitional technologies. Science philosopher Michel Serres has compared commuters to the numerous infrastructural messaging-systems of telephones, radios, audio announcements and electronic signs.[12] Under close observation, the crowds of people moving through cities on subway trains, or across the world in airplanes, come to represent the transient worlds of business, government, media, management and science. Like Beck's diagram, we are no less electrically connective than the high-voltage world of subway trains and substations that we move in.

Unfortunately, Fritz Lang's film *Metropolis* might seem a more relevant depiction of life beneath the city to current users of the London Underground. With its hallucinatory images of clocks, manic machinery and surging crowds of people herded together, Lang's movie, released in 1929 just as Beck was developing his map, offers a harsh contrast to the clean lines of a circuit diagram. *Metropolis* is still closer to today's everyday experience of the London Underground, from the impressive scale and expertise of its (aging) engineering, to its over-crowded and under-funded stations and trains.

11. *The Guardian* April 22, 2003, "Closure looms for capital's other underground railway." <http://www.guardian.co.uk/uk_news/story/0,,940742,00.html>

12. Michel Serres, *Angels, A Modern Myth.* Paris, New York: Flammarion, 1995.

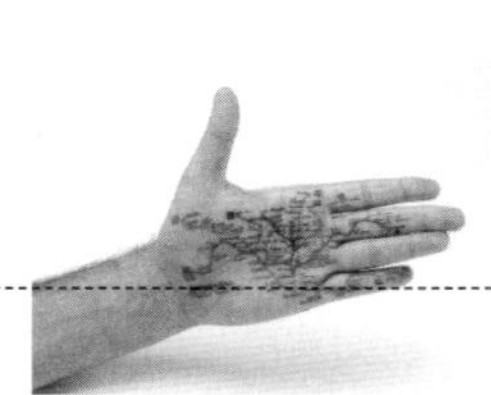

Territory maps

gazetteer G 5–6/8 pp. 162–163

* * *

The city today is defined by the continuous movement of goods, people, information and capital; early subway systems and electrical grids were the essential prototypes of this phenomenon. As Rem Koolhaas reminds us, circulation itself may be the principle function of architecture today: urban planning has finally been "unmasked as the mere organization of flow — shopping centers, airports — it is evident that circulation is what makes or breaks public architecture."[13]

Appropriately, the influence of Beck's diagram for the London Underground is not limited to the mapping of subway systems. It has become a seductive visual template for every kind of network, from public transport to flows of electronic information. The latest graphic spoof on the Underground diagram is a series of ads for computer company Intel that appeared on billboards at Tube stations and elsewhere around London in 2004. Across a Beck-style map titled *London by laptop*, the traditional station stops are replaced by cafes, hotels and shops, all offering wireless Internet connections: from Heathrow Terminal 4 to PC World on Tottenham Court Road, McDonald's on the Strand, the Edgware Road Hilton, the Virgin Megastore on Oxford Street, and Bagelmania on Fenchurch Street. "With laptops powered by Intel Centrino Mobile Technology," the ad proclaims, "you can get online at wireless hotspots all over London."

Beck's map, representative of London in a highly abstract sense, has — with a certain unintentional irony — become better applied as the defining image of network efficiency (a somewhat abstract conceit in itself). The Intel ad borrows Beck's diagram in order to map, not worn-out Underground purgatory, but a kind of blue-tooth communications utopia instead of consumer heaven.

But if the world is more explicable to some in the color-coded form of diagrams and curved lines, to others its pieces are more complicated. They are part of an electrical modernity of power grids, fault lines and signal failures inseparable from the physical space of objects and materials. "I never forgot the smell of the Underground — the singed smell of an electrical retailer's…" writes Stephen Smith in his recent book *Underground London*.[14] A recent news report tells of computer problems on the Northern Line, whose drivers cannot be contacted because their radios don't work. Tube Lines, the company managing this section of the Underground, is apparently in the habit of combing eBay for spare parts.[15]

The city-as-machine metaphor has been superseded by the city-as-computer-network. And yet, as any regular commuter knows, if the city is a machine (even a computerized one) it remains the most vulnerable kind: a web of intricate parts liable to break down at any moment. In spite of this, official graphic representations continue to portray the modern city as a technology of the highest efficiency — a regulated urban landscape that operates more like the logic board of a giant computer, mapped like an electrical diagram. As they say on the Tube: Mind the Gap.

13. Rem Koolhaas, architect's statement for the Museum of Modern Art expansion project. <http://www.moma.org/expansion/charette/architects/koolhaas/>

14. Stephen Smith, *Underground London*. London: Little, Brown, 2004.

15. BBC News, December 8, 2004. <http://news.bbc.co.uk/2/hi/uk_news/england/london/4079135.stm>

CEREBRAL CITIES

In Christopher Nolan's 2001 film, *Memento*, a man who has lost the capacity for short-term memory has the basic facts of his story tattooed onto his body, his skin stretching the ink-stained blueprints of this memory palace. One curiosity of the film is that, despite remembering nothing else as he begins each day, this character somehow always knows where to go.

In that small logical lacuna lies a metaphor for the way we make our way in the world: less by a process of memory—a chain of remembered routes, places and directions—than by an instinctual drive present in all humans, even amnesiacs. Most of us live our daily lives without recourse to a map. Even those who are "bad with directions" know the particulars of their environs. We internalize the map; the map is us. But a map is a crude, even incorrect, analogy for understanding how we interpret and remember space, since a map is just a story told by someone else. After all, any given space (Main Street, a shopping mall, France, the Western Hemisphere) could yield a million different maps.

I was walking on lower Broadway in Manhattan one day when a man asked me how to get to Ground Zero. I stopped to think for a moment. In its initial atomic test incarnation, Ground Zero was an epicenter from which measurement proceeded outward, as distance from the blast; since 9/11, the phrase has a reversed geographical imperative, serving as a site of pilgrimage. Certain streets in Tribeca on the way to the former World Trade Center flashed into my head, as did nearby subway stops and buildings that bordered the site. I even briefly pictured the site itself—the viewing platforms, the steel and concrete "pile" of the towers' remains. But I couldn't articulate exactly how to get there, the successive streets one would need to take. I knew where I was and where it was but in between was a blank space. So I simply pointed south and said, "just head down Broadway, and it will eventually be off to your right. Not far."

A month later, I was canoeing with the naturalist Mark "Bird" Westall in the J.N. Darling National Wildlife Refuge on Sanibel Island, off Florida's Gulf Coast. As we piloted down countless channels in the swamp—each a tangle of brackish water and mangrove roots exposed like gnarled hands—a fellow passenger asked Westall how he knew where he was going. "How do you know where you live?" he asked after a few seconds. "This is my backyard."

In both these examples, a person had formed an internal awareness of a familiar environment, but was unable to render that knowledge into anything resembling a map. Psychologists and geographers use

"MEMORY LANE" IS NOT JUST A TURN OF PHRASE. TOM VANDERBILT SCANS RECENT BRAIN IMAGING RESEARCH—INCLUDING A LANDMARK STUDY OF LONDON TAXI DRIVERS WHO HAVE MASTERED *THE KNOWLEDGE*—AND FINDS THAT BY MEMORIZING URBAN ROUTES, WE CARVE PATHWAYS IN OUR HEADS.

the term "cognitive map" to describe "long-term stored information about the relative location of objects and phenomena in the everyday physical environment." But "map" may be too tidy a metaphor. Barbara Tversky, a professor of cognitive studies at Stanford University, has suggested that "cognitive collage" may be a more fitting phrase. "In wayfinding, memory and judgment," she argues, "we make use of a multitude of information, not just remembered experiences or remembered maps of environments."[1]

My inability to provide detailed directions to the World Trade Center site might have been a consequence of the simple fact that the towers are no longer there. During my lifetime in New York, they had served as a ready visual reference, an irrefutable signpost for Downtown. Much as Roland Barthes remarked of the Eiffel Tower, the only way *not* to see the World Trade Center towers was to be inside them. I had yet to create a memorable narrative of how to reach the abstracted site where the towers formerly stood.

Something else might also have been at work. Tim McNamara, a professor of cognitive psychology at Vanderbilt University, has conducted several studies of how people remember and interpret spatial relations among objects in their environment, and use that information to navigate. When asked to estimate the distance from a recognized landmark to another, more anonymous, building, and then vice versa, research subjects tend to estimate a smaller distance in the first case than in the second. McNamara accounts for this asymmetry with what he calls a "contextual scaling model":

> When people retrieve the location of the buildings, they activate in long-term memory what they know about that memory and what the neighboring buildings are in the space or on the map. A landmark activates a larger context—more things come to mind—and the actual space, the distance of the other objects that come to mind from that landmark, is greater than when they first think of a non-landmark.[2]

Just as our imaginary cognitive maps are subject to these asymmetries, so too is the most rigorous cartography subject to corruption by our perceptions of it. Given a choice between a world map showing North America incorrectly aligned with Europe, and a map that shows the true layout of the continents, respondents tend to choose the incorrect, symmetrical version. In a landmark 1956 study titled "The Graduated Circle: A Description, Analysis, and Evaluation of a Quantitative Map Symbol,"[3] the geographer J. J. Flannery noted that map readers consistently underestimated the size of circular depictions of urban areas—a typical cartographic

1. Barbara Tversky, "Structures of Mental Spaces: How People Think About Spaces." *Environment and Behavior*. Volume 35, issue no. 1. pp. 66–80.
2. Telephone conversation with author, 2003.
3. James J. Flannery, "The Graduated Circle: A Description, Analysis and Evaluation of a Quantitative Map Symbol." Ph.D. thesis, University of Wisconsin, 1956.

method of indicating city populations. Flannery's findings led to a change in standard cartography, such that the radii of graduated circles were scaled to 0.57 times the logarithm of their purported quantity—so as to compensate for the inherent distortion.

This speaks to the arbitrariness of mapping in general, since there is no correct size for a circle or dot on a map (and probably no standard amount by which such circles are underestimated); the marks on a map are just generalized abstractions, approximate ways of understanding the world. As a child, taking long car trips through the western states of America, I often imagined there would be "lines" when we crossed state boundaries, just as there are on a map. This might seem fanciful, but I'd suggest that much of our sense of large-scale spaces is conditioned by cartographic interpretation.

Maps are informed by our experience, location and condition. My personal map of New York (being based in Brooklyn) would probably be quite different from that of someone living in Washington Heights. Though today this observation may seem blandly intuitive, it was novel stuff in 1960 when the geographer Kevin Lynch wrote, in his now-classic book, *The Image of the City*:

> The creation of the environmental image is a two-way process between observer and observed. What he sees is based on exterior form, but how he interprets and organizes this, and how he directs his attention, in its turn affects what he sees. The human organism is highly adaptable and flexible, and different groups may have widely different images of the same outer reality.[4]

Lynch's argument was informed by the groundbreaking work of University of California psychologist Edward Chance Tolman, originator of the cognitive map theory. In his 1948 paper, "Cognitive Maps in Rats and Men," Tolman proposed that rats who were able to find food in a maze weren't simply reacting to a conditioned behavioral stimulus (e.g. "turn right for food"), but had generated a cognitive map of the overall environmental field.[5] Thus, when they began from a different starting point, they didn't simply "turn right" for the usual treat, but were able to "turn left," having generated an internal image of the entire maze.

"Despite a few remaining puzzles, it now seems unlikely there is any mystic 'instinct' of wayfinding," Lynch wrote in *The Image of the City*. "Rather it is a consistent use and organization of definite sensory cues from the external environment."[6]

Even with Lynch's insights, a vast puzzle remained: what is it that occurs in the internal environment when we find our way through the external environment? After all, maps and routes don't exist in themselves; they are simply projections onto a landscape that is, in itself, utterly abstract. The solution to this puzzle required

4. Kevin Lynch, *The Image of the City*. Cambridge: The MIT Press, 1960. p. 131.

5. Edward Tolman, "Cognitive Maps in Rats and Men," *Psychological Review*, 55, 1948. pp. 189–208.

6. Lynch, *op cit*, p. 3.

a technology not yet available in the early 1960s: a means of mapping the cognitive mapping apparatus itself.

Our man in *Memento*—our bleeder of memories—cannot remember people he met the day before, yet seems to possess intact some cognitive map of the larger environment in which he moves. He is said to suffer from anterograde amnesia, an extremely rare condition that prevents formation of short-term memory, but leaves memories formed before the damage and "procedural memory" (the ability to learn new skills) unimpaired. When the motel manager changes the narrator's room, he is unaware that he has been moved. But how does he even know how to get to the motel in the first place? Of all the memories tattooed onto his body, none are maps; we can only assume he knows this landscape intimately from his life before the accident. Without a map, navigation proceeds from memory: to move forward, one must look backwards. So how does our *Memento* hero remember where he is going? The answer, if there is one, lies in the mapping of another form of territory: the human brain.

The advancement of functional brain scanning techniques over the past decade has yielded vast troves of new information about how the brain undertakes processes such as memory and navigation. After decades of observing from above how rats and men move through mazes (as it were), the focus has shifted to studying what happens in the brain as one works one's way through a maze, or a city. The cartographic metaphor is frequently invoked as these brain atlases are generated. "Just as maps of the Earth locate continents, mountain ranges and nations," said one neurobiologist, "our cortical maps will show the locations of the brain's structures and functional subdivisions."[7]

Perhaps thanks to its somewhat topographical appearance—a wrinkled, hemispheric mass of contours and regions—mapmaking of the brain has a venerable history, dating back at least to Egyptian papyrus relics, of circa 2500 B.C. At the end of the 19th Century, experiments with electrical shocks and intentional brain lesions produced evidence that particular regions of the brain were associated with certain behaviors. Much as ancient navigators were granted namesake islands and continents, two areas of the brain are still named after the 19th-Century neurologists who discovered them, Pierre Broca and Carl Wernicke: respectively, the frontal lobe of the left hemisphere, and an area stretching across the back of the temporal lobe, bordering the parietal lobe. Both of these areas related to speech actions, though neither is anywhere near the speech areas identified by the preeminent phrenologist Franz Gall. Broca discovered his area in a patient who, having suffered a stroke, couldn't speak, but was otherwise normal. After the patient's death, an autopsy revealed a massive lesion in what became known as "Broca's area." In 1957, a pair of neurologists noted the case of H.M., a patient who had received bilateral lesions of a section of his brain to relieve severe epilepsy. After the procedure, H.M. found

7. David Van Essen, quoted in University of Washington at St. Louis news release, October 29, 2002.

he couldn't remember things that had happened since the surgery; he later compared his condition to being permanently in a state of having just been awakened. Much of the damage to H.M.'s brain involved the hippocampus, which, after more than a century of study, has been fully charted as the locus of memory and spatial navigation. (This is also the fate of our man in *Memento*, whose accident has led to some damage of the hippocampal region.)

Where neuroscience once relied on a procession of the maimed and the dead for insights into the brain's operations, now the penetrating but harmless incursions of PET and Magnetic Resonance Imaging (MRI) produce real-time pictures of brain function rather than brain failure. Like a heat-sensitive map showing human activity in a landscape, responses in the brain can be watched, live, via MRI as they play out in reaction to activities, emotions and conditions. And one of the endeavors brain mapping has begun to unpack in breathtaking detail is the process of mapping itself: how we move about in the world.

Behavioral psychologists have long noted gender differences in the process of wayfinding: women are generally said to rely on landmarks and things such as street names, while men employ geometric and distance cues. A study at the University of Ulm in Germany, led by Manfred Spitzer, investigated the neural underpinnings of this difference. Subjects wired to MRI scanners worked their way through a computer maze using buttons to navigate toward an unknown exit. Certain walls were color coded to serve as landmarks. In all subjects, as expected, the hippocampus—the presumed site of the cognitive map—was the general locus of MRI activity. But in men (who were generally faster at exiting the maze), increased activity in the left hippocampus was noted, while in females an increase was seen in the right parietal and right prefrontal cortex. Presenting their findings in the journal *Nature*, the researchers noted that "[T]his distinct functional anatomy of spatial cognition in women versus men may be related to differences in the processing of spatial information."[8]

But locating general regions in the brain that are activated in men or women as they undertake wayfinding has not answered the question of how we actually navigate. Russell Epstein and Nancy Kanwisher, researchers in the Department of Brain and Cognitive Sciences at Massachusetts Institute of Technology, have documented a region within the parahippocampal cortex that showed more intensified brain activity when subjects viewed large-scale environments such as rooms, streets or landscapes than when they viewed images of objects or faces. Epstein and Kanwisher dubbed this the "parahippocampal place area" (PPA)—an area of the brain that lit up when a place was viewed.[9] What might the purpose of such an area be? Could it be a memory bank of sorts that matches a scene to a stored equivalent somewhere in the hippocampus? Apparently not: in subsequent experiments, the MIT researchers found no difference in

8. Georg Grön, Arthur P. Wunderlich, Manfred Spitzer, Reinhard Tomczak, and Matthias W. Riepe, "Brain activation during human navigation: gender-different neural networks as substrate of performance." *Nature*, April 2000, 3:4, pp. 404–408.

9. R. Epstein, A. Harris, D. Stanley and N. Kanwisher, "The parahippocampal place area: Recognition, Navigation, or Encoding? " *Neuron*, 23:1999, pp. 115–125.

subjects' responses to places they had previously seen as compared with places they had never seen. They were then shown photos of "places" and objects constructed from Lego blocks; although the former were clearly unreal places that could never have been visited, the subjects' responses were still higher to these faux Lego places than to the Lego objects.

The Lego experiment seemed to dispel the notion that the PPA might be a route-planning mechanism to places stored in the cognitive maps. As the researchers noted, "the lack of a familarity effect for scenes further demonstrates that the PPA is very unlikely to play a direct role in planning routes to distant locations, since one cannot plan routes from locations one does not know."[10] Was the PPA's function simply to encode new place information? This thesis seemed to yield the strongest results: brain activity was found to be higher in that region when subjects viewed a succession of novel place scenes, as opposed to viewing a series of identical scenes. In previous case studies of patients who had lost the ability to recognize places, damage was thought to have occurred in the general parahippocampal cortex. But the MIT study hinted that the problem might lie in a more specialized zone since, in these subjects, the PPA did not seem to serve any recognition function.

Perhaps this was mapping at its most fundamental: the simple processing of spatial information, all spaces being equal. Nomads excepted, this is not how most of us lead our lives. We inhabit places we know well, full of familiar scenes. Into what dusky regions of the brain does this spatial information settle? A landmark study of London taxi drivers undertaken by researchers at University College London's Wellcome Department of Cognitive Neurology revealed stunning insights into this process.[11]

Experienced taxi drivers who had fully grasped *The Knowledge* (as the encyclopedic memorization of London's street system is famously known) were asked to give the shortest route between two points without the aid of a map. Functional MRI mapping recorded their brain activity as they articulated the routes, and a surge in activity of the right hippocampus was observed. To determine whether this was an act of memory recall like any other, the taxi drivers were also asked to recall plot sequences of well known films they had seen. The researchers found that "the network of brain regions showing increased activation during semantic topographical memory retrieval are entirely different from those activated during non-topographical semantic memory."[12]

The taxi drivers were also asked to describe several famous landmarks outside London that they had never visited. This

10. *ibid.*, p. 121.

11. Eleanor A. Maguire, Richard S. J. Frackowiak, and Christopher D. Frith, "Recalling Routes around London: Activation of the Right Hippocampus in Taxi Drivers." *The Journal of Neuroscience*, September 15, 1997, vol. 17.

12. *ibid*, p. 7106.

Territory maps

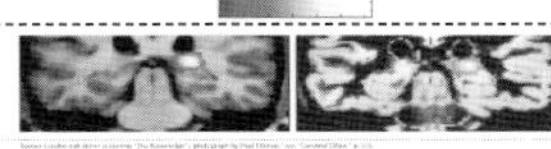

PERILS OF PRECISION

The power of the map has long been aligned with its presumed accuracy. REBECCA ROSS compares current and post-war planning models of New York with a fuzzy, digital map of Amsterdam collaboratively-created by its residents and asks: which is more accurate?

"What would happen if, when saying that some image is human-made, you were increasing instead of decreasing its claim to truth?"
—Bruno Latour, Iconoclash[1]

The Panorama of the City of New York, a 1 inch to 100 feet scale wooden model of the five boroughs, built for the 1964 World's Fair, is possibly the most detailed physical map ever made. But what does it reveal? According to museum archives, the original contract with the fabricator, Lester & Associates, specified a "less than one percent margin of error between the model and reality." The idea was that passage through the Panorama would provide views equivalent to those from a helicopter ride through the city. A precise image of the city, it was assumed, would be the natural product of incorporating an extreme level of physical detail. Today, the Panorama stands as an elaborate object that humbly exudes the impossibility of this assumption.

Three years ago, I visited the Flushing Meadows fairgrounds for the first time. I had sped by the Unisphere on countless previous occasions. The historic New York City building, a structure built for the 1939 fair, houses the Queens Museum of Art and the World's Fair Ice Rink. Still on exhibition today at the Queens Museum of Art, the room housing the Panorama has the feel of a school gymnasium. The Empire State Building measures about twelve and a half inches high. The room features a 20-minute light/dark cycle that signifies a compression of diurnal time to correspond with the model's attempts to compress space. Beyond the lighting, the Panorama is static, as silent as the city is vast and unwieldy.

Robert Moses, the notorious "power broker" and New York state and municipal official, championed the creation of the Panorama by citing its potential as a tool for the future of city planning. He envisioned that the model would be kept up-to-date over time and referred to by city leaders as they thought through changes to the city's master plan. A Queens Museum booklet reveals that the gathering of the necessary data was a tremendous activity: block by block schematics were made of building footprints, over 500 aerial photographs were taken, contour maps of the land base were drawn up, pictures of individual structures were culled from libraries and other institutions. This costly measuring phase aimed to achieve a mechanized accuracy that was quickly lost as the city carried on past 1964. Although the Panorama has been cleaned, repainted and supplemented with certain key buildings, The New York Post reported in 1989 that the model would need another 20,000 structures to be brought up to date.

I grew up in a development of split-levels set into the leftover speck on a map where the Long Island Expressway crosses the Northern State Parkway. Exit 43 is truly the artifact of a schematic. The most obvious qualities of the landscape are the hills formed by under- and over-passes and the frequent sprinkles of green signage. The turns of the median running down the center of the Expressway reinforce its obedience to its diagrammatic origins. What value or meaning does this yield for, in Jane Jacobs' terms, the needs of real people? Efforts like the Panorama make it possible for certain individuals—in the case of Moses, unelected officials—to act on a whole dimension of peoples' lives by assembling and rearranging a collection of technical drawings or painted wooden blocks. The results are places dominated by artifacts that are merely representations

gazetteer H 8/13 p. 194

Territory maps

1. Bruno Latour and Peter Weibel, *Iconoclash: Beyond the Image Wars in Science, Religion and Art*. Cambridge, Mass: MIT Press, 2002.

of the abstractions to which they are subservient. To achieve the level of detail incorporated in the Panorama required that one agency would gather and give form to data on behalf of the entire city, thereby necessitating a bottleneck that impedes the vital relationship between the richness and diversity of a city and its representation. Today, the impulse to act on territory based purely on experience, without the interference of symbolism, has been re-fueled by the potential of contemporary model-making materials such as pixels and databases. The City of New York, for example, is assembling a many-layered high-resolution map of the city in the form of a GIS (Geographic Information System) database. The NYCMap project began with the difficult process of gathering and reconciling data from a wide range of city agencies. Many of the layers are incomplete and contradictory at this point, but the long-term ambition is to create a consistently accurate and up-to-date image of the city in as much detail as possible.

As one might expect, the City's Department of Information Technology tightly controls access to most layers of NYCMap and goes to great expense to continually measure, collect and digitize.[2] However, the infrastructures and phenomena that the Department strives to summarize are available to me, in complete detail, every time I turn on my faucet or ride the Q train across the Manhattan Bridge. This paradox of representation — in which summary is valued more highly than the experience to which it refers — enables official maps to become information-spaces within which power is accumulated and maintained. Highly detailed maps are presented to culture as if they were flawless reflections of space. In fact they are more typically accumulations of the maker's own experience from a single point of view, subject to the limits of space and time.

I spent my childhood summers building sand castles on the beach at Robert Moses State Park. Today, I find myself interested in the tyranny and possibility of maps because I can sense that while maps are often used by individual entities to claim power, they can also serve a greater interest as tools for reclaiming agency over space. As the failures of the Panorama reveal, fine detail in mapping can be a signifier of false omniscience, a means of asserting power over territory by developing a semblance of wide-scale knowledge of what goes on there. But what kind of images, spaces and places would be enabled by infrastructure that supported true wide-scale participation in mapping activities? Maps and their territories have the potential to become serious reflections of the wishes and desires of the many.

This idea took me to a meeting at the Waag Society for Old and New Media in Amsterdam. The Waag occupies a 500-year-old building, originally a gate through the walls of the city and, at another time, headquarters for several artisan guilds. Amsterdam RealTime, a project implemented by the Waag with artist Esther Polak in 2002, gestures toward a way of mapping the city that favors incorporating public participation over reproducing minute detail.

<www.waag.org/realtime>

Participants in Amsterdam RealTime comprised a diverse sampling of Amsterdam experiences. A public call for volunteers requested details of each applicant's occupation, gender, age, travel habits, place of residence, place of work and week-by-week availability. Forms were made available on the Waag's website and on posters hung throughout the city. Four-hundred people responded, motivated as much by curiosity as by a sense of community. Sixty were invited to participate. The only requirement was that for a few weeks during October and November 2002 they had to carry around a slightly bulky pack containing a trace-unit comprising Global Positioning System (GPS) sensors attached to networked personal digital assistants (PDA). Most of the packet could be carried inside a backpack or pocket but, in order to maintain a clear line of site with the GPS satellites, the antenna itself had to be worn on the outside of clothing or secured to a car roof.

To form a collective synchronous map referred to as "the most current map of Amsterdam," latitude and longitude coordinates collected by each participant were transmitted to a Waag server via General Packet Radio Service (GPRS). The server compiled images based on accumulations of participants' points over specified periods time. Frequently traveled points became brighter over time, and the most densely traveled areas, such as Centraal Station, were noted in yellow and then red. Less frequented

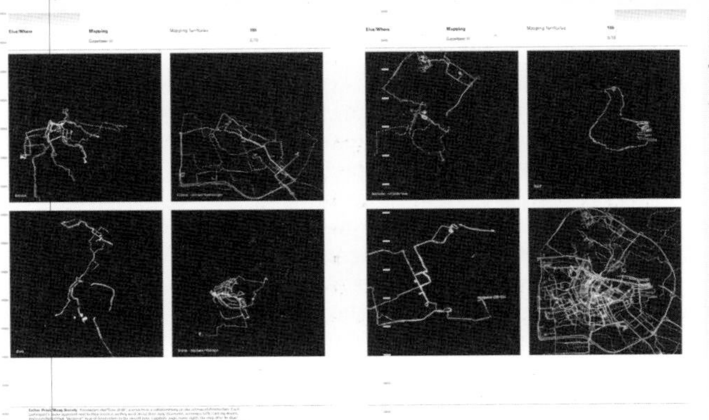

Territory maps

gazetteer H 2–3/13 pp. 188–189

See "Mapping the Homunculus," p. 201.

2. In 2002, the cost of the *NYCMap* was established to be $3 million; see Adam Gopnik, "Street Furniture," *The New Yorker*, November 6, 2000, pp. 54–57. See also Lucas Graves, "NYCMap," March, 2005. <www.gothamgazette.com/article/tech/20050301/19/1337>.

trails remained pale gray traces, with physical features such as bodies of water made obvious only by black space lined with dense concentrations of foot traffic over the occasional bridge. Every aspect of each image was generated by recent and current activity within the city. The names of participants marked their current locations as they continued to form the map while pursuing their normal daily activities.

The hierarchy presented on this map corresponds automatically with life in the city as its residents simultaneously create and experience it. One participant, training for the marathon, continuously looped the same path, reinforcing his accumulated miles by thickening the lines that define his route as a place on the map. Others wandered more freely about lesser known streets and alleyways, their movements collected as more delicate lines. The form of the map is reclaimed by the same basic paradoxes and gestures that define the city. One notable absence from these images is the contribution of public officials themselves. Both police officers and tram drivers were asked by their employers not to participate.

The project ran in conjunction with an exhibition mounted by the Amsterdam Municipal Archives of a history of maps of Amsterdam, Kaarten van Amsterdam: 1866 — 2000. Maps presented as records of the city as it once was were displayed side by side with maps that served as proposals, alternative diagrams of what Amsterdam might have become. As a collection, they revealed a history of increasing discrete lines and integrated detail. The Amsterdam RealTime images are a sparse inversion of this, more akin to medical X-rays than anatomical illustrations. The pictures generated by Amsterdam RealTime are fuzzy because that is the nature of summaries that encompass many experiences simultaneously. Such blurriness is a counter-intuitive expression of a new potential for vitality in mapping, a new level of honesty about its own limits and capabilities.

According to Polak, the goal of Amsterdam RealTime was to offer participants and spectators a new awareness of their own presence within a city with which they are already so familiar. She commented that after seeing the project, or even just hearing about it, people would become compelled to discuss their daily routines. A participant named Chris became so conscious of the relationship between his movements and the form of the city map that he chose to alter his course in order to inscribe the shape of a pigeon. One could imagine that this duif[3] took Chris off his usual path, perhaps to sections of Amsterdam he had never been through before. By permitting us to play with the hitherto one-way relationship between map and wayfinding to which our culture is accustomed, the Amsterdam RealTime project encourages us imagine a very different use of maps — to reclaim spatial meaning.

In Amsterdam, before visiting the Waag, I attended a party called De Trut, which doesn't publicize its address — I had to ask around to find out where to go. The party, held in a squat on an anonymous street at a distance from the city center, caters to a strictly gay and lesbian crowd. The bartenders are volunteers and rumor has it that the profits from the bar and cover are donated for AIDS research. Partygoers are advised to arrive well before 11 pm because once the door opens, allowing the crowd to funnel through, it immediately closes. Passersby would not necessarily realize what is happening inside: hundreds of kids dancing to experimental music. This event can be defined purely by its status as "off-the-map" and yet I noticed a trace of it on a few of the Amsterdam RealTime accumulations. I was delighted to observe that an act of "leaving the map" can become a means of defining a new one.

When asked whether this new kind of map could be useful in city planning contexts, Polak commented that reliance on volunteers might be a stumbling block. Participation requires a willingness to be tracked through space but also necessitates having one's own relationship to the city broadcast to the map-viewing public at large: living and mapping become dynamically linked. Embedded in the Panorama of the City of New York are Robert Moses' presumptions about what kind of knowledge is meaningful for urban planning and policy, presented behind a façade of precision and expertise that enabled him to concentrate so much civic authority. Amsterdam RealTime, by contrast, demonstrates that it is possible for a map itself to take on dynamic qualities such as diversity, multiplicity and an attitude of participation that also define a city. The re-positioning of maps as spaces for public interaction could lead to an improved flow of information from citizens to decision-makers, and a strengthening of the form of our built environment. But this would require a vital shift in our attitude toward space and the creation of meaning. To take up Latour's idea of human-made truth: what would it mean to say that a map is even more human-made because it incorporates the participation of many people? Might it even increase its claim to accuracy?

See "Counter Cartographies," p. 25.

3. "dove" in Dutch.

Esther Polak/Waag Society *Amsterdam RealTime*, 2002 / cumulative map of volunteers' itineraries, relayed to a screen installed at the Amsterdam Municipal Archives, during the exhibition *Maps of Amsterdam, 1866–2000*, in late 2002 / image © Esther Polak/Waag Society / see "Perils of Precision," pp. 184–186.

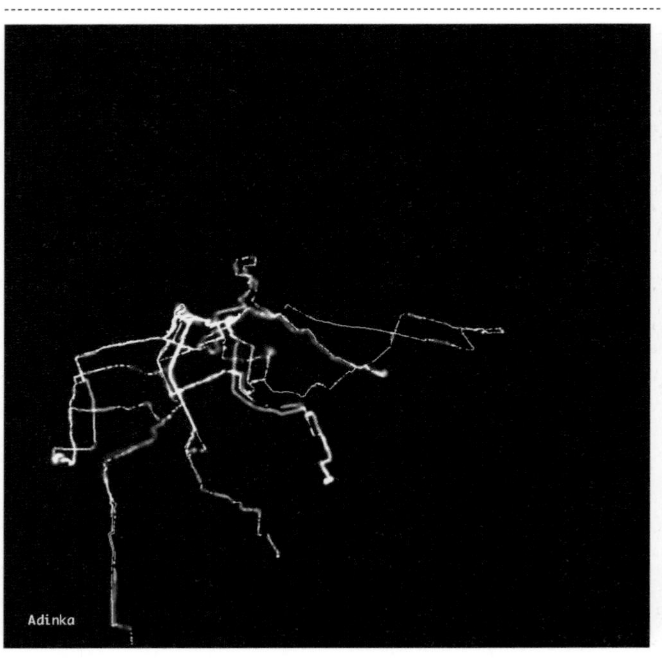

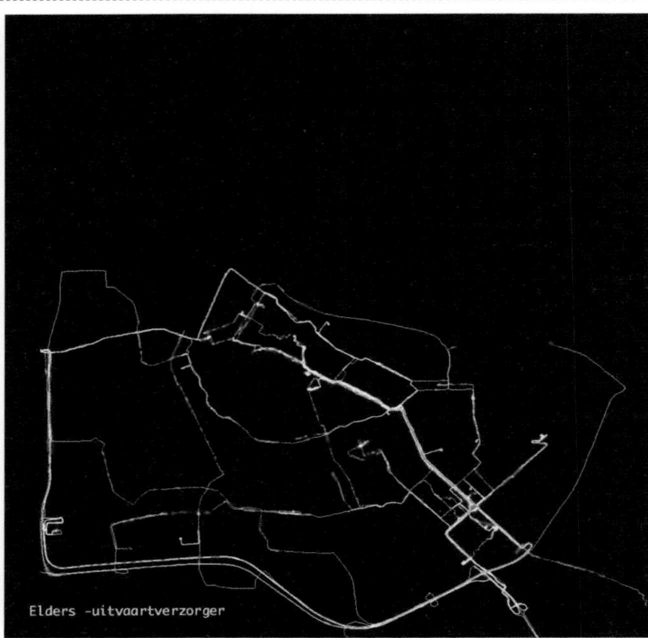

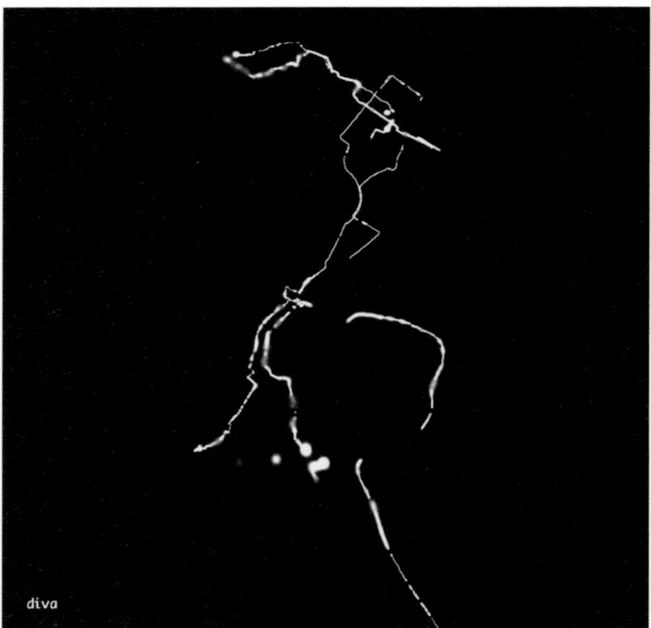

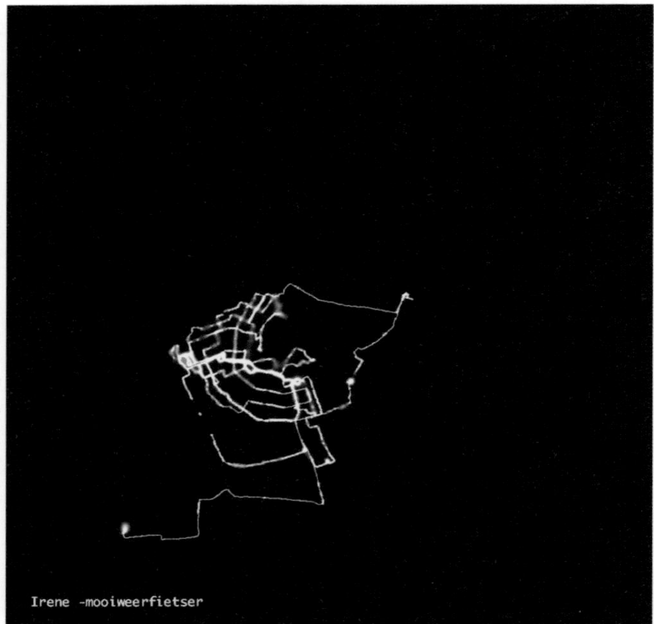

Esther Polak/Waag Society *Amsterdam RealTime*, 2002 / scenes from a collaboratively-produced map of Amsterdam. Each participant's name appeared next to their location as they went about their daily itineraries, wearing a GPS tracking device, and contributed their "personal" map of Amsterdam to the overall map. (opposite page, lower right): the map after 40 days' accumulations, November 2, 2002. Brighter lines indicate more frequently traveled routes; the most frequently destinations such as Centraal Station became progressively yellow, then red / all images this spread © Esther Polak/Waag Society / see "Counter Cartographies," p. 25, "Perils of Precision," pp. 184–186, "Mapping the Homunculus," p. 201.

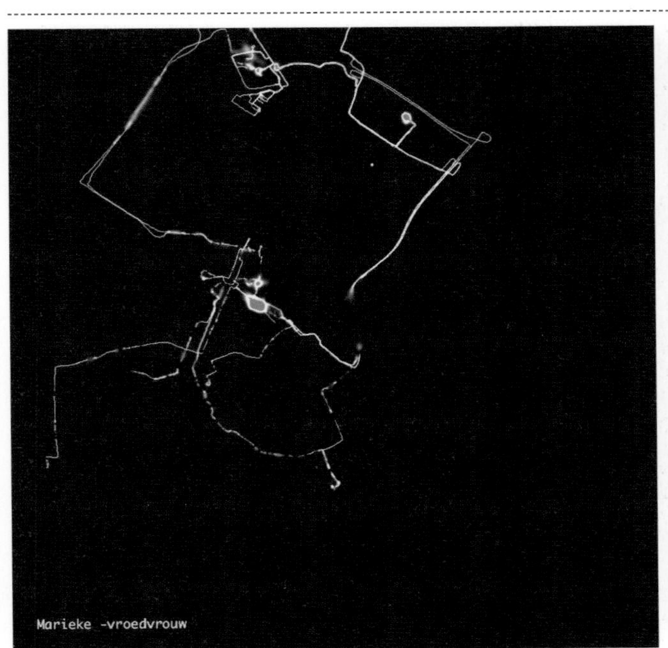
Marieke -vroedvrouw

Duif

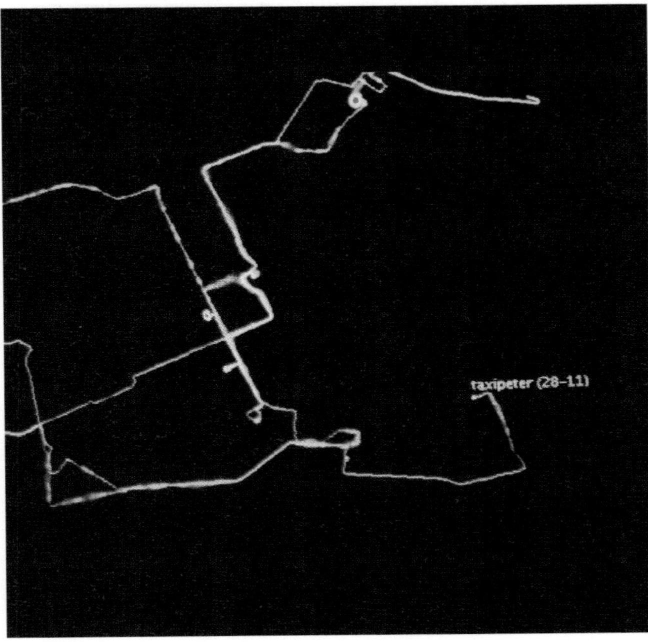
taxipeter (28-11)

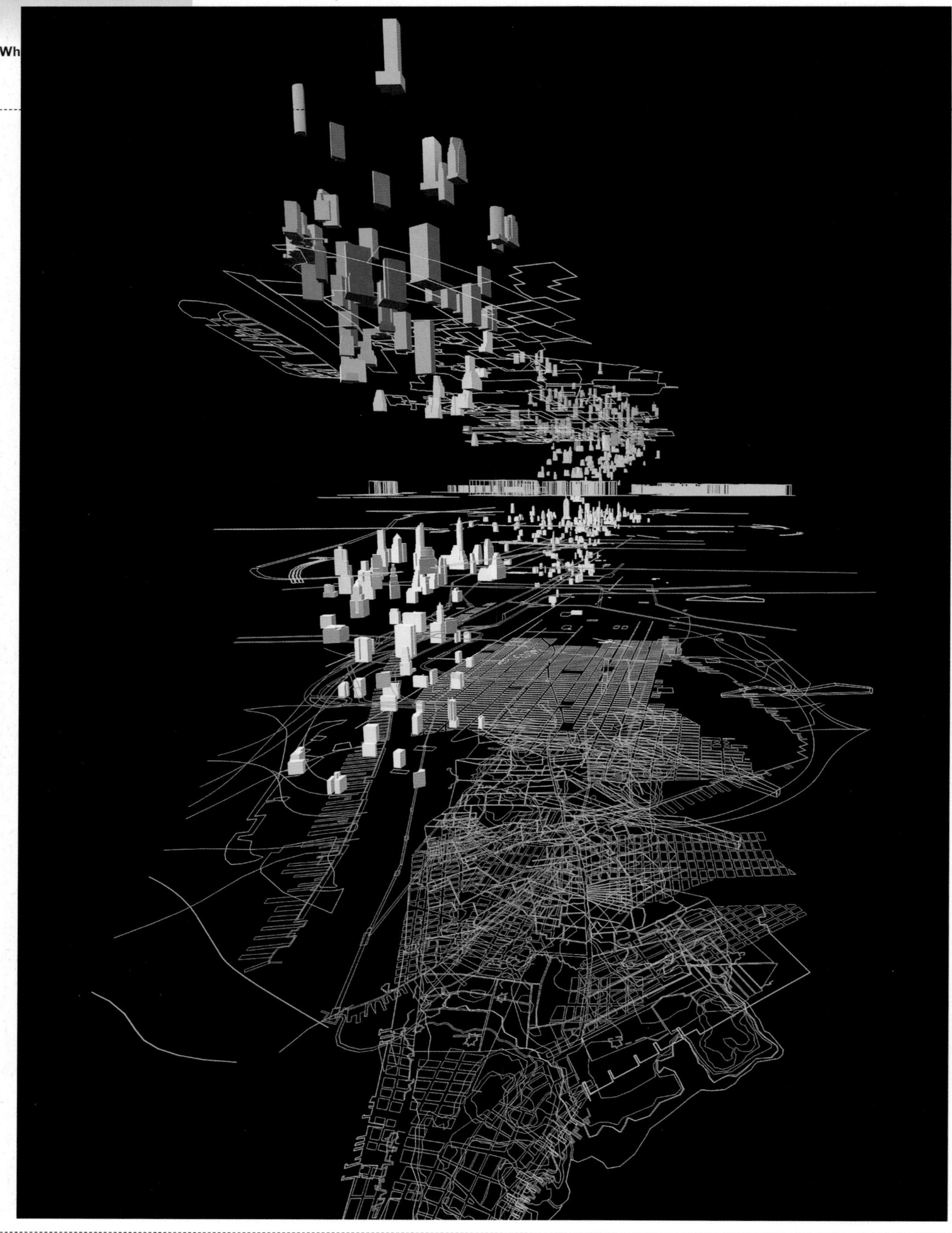

Brian McGrath and **Mark Watkins** *Manhattan Timeformations,* perspectival flythrough, 2000 / exploded still-frame from the computer animation created for the Skyscraper Museum, New York, showing layers corresponding to different eras of the city's skyscraper and infrastructure development / see "A Less Imperial Gaze," pp. 114–115.

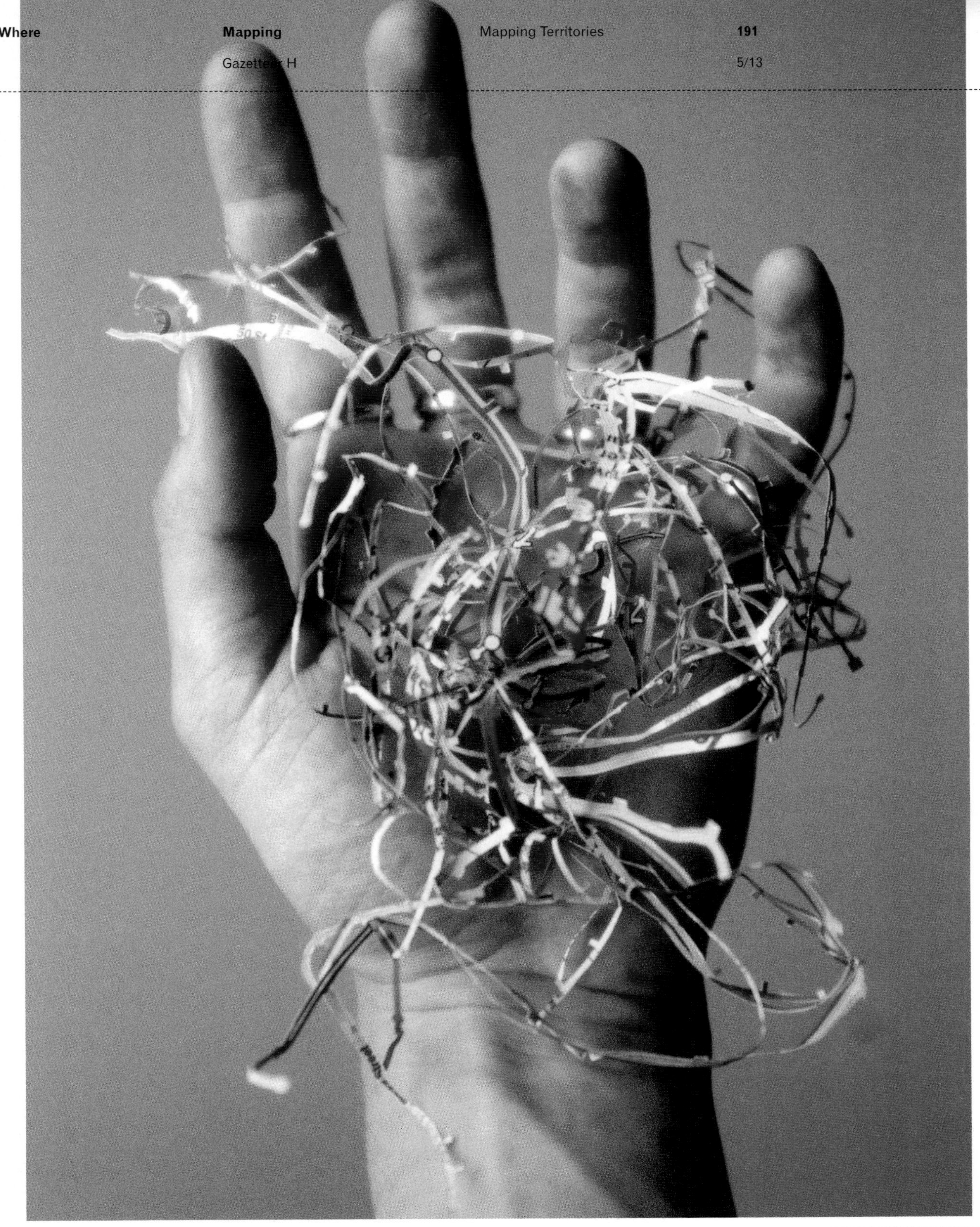

Nina Katchadourian *Hand-held Subway*, 1996 / paper subway map of New York City with subway lines excised, 16 in. x 20 in., cibachrome / image courtesy of Nina Katchadourian and Sara Meltzer Gallery, New York.

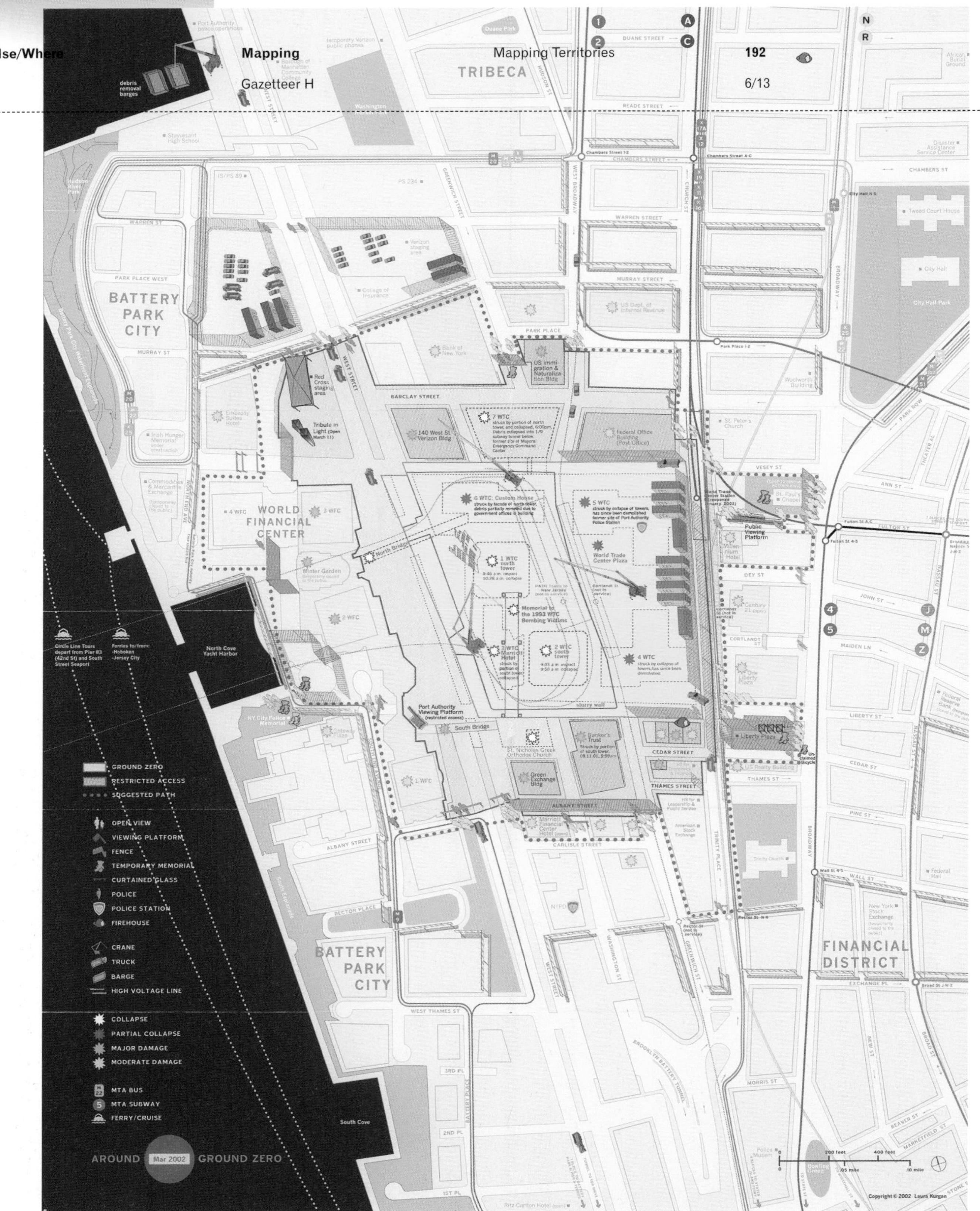

Laura Kurgan *Around Ground Zero*, 2001 / map distributed free to visitors to Ground Zero after the terrorist attacks of September 11, 2001, showing key points of interest such as damaged buildings, trucks and viewing platforms / map photographed by Kimberlee Whaley / see "Carto-City," pp. 156–157.

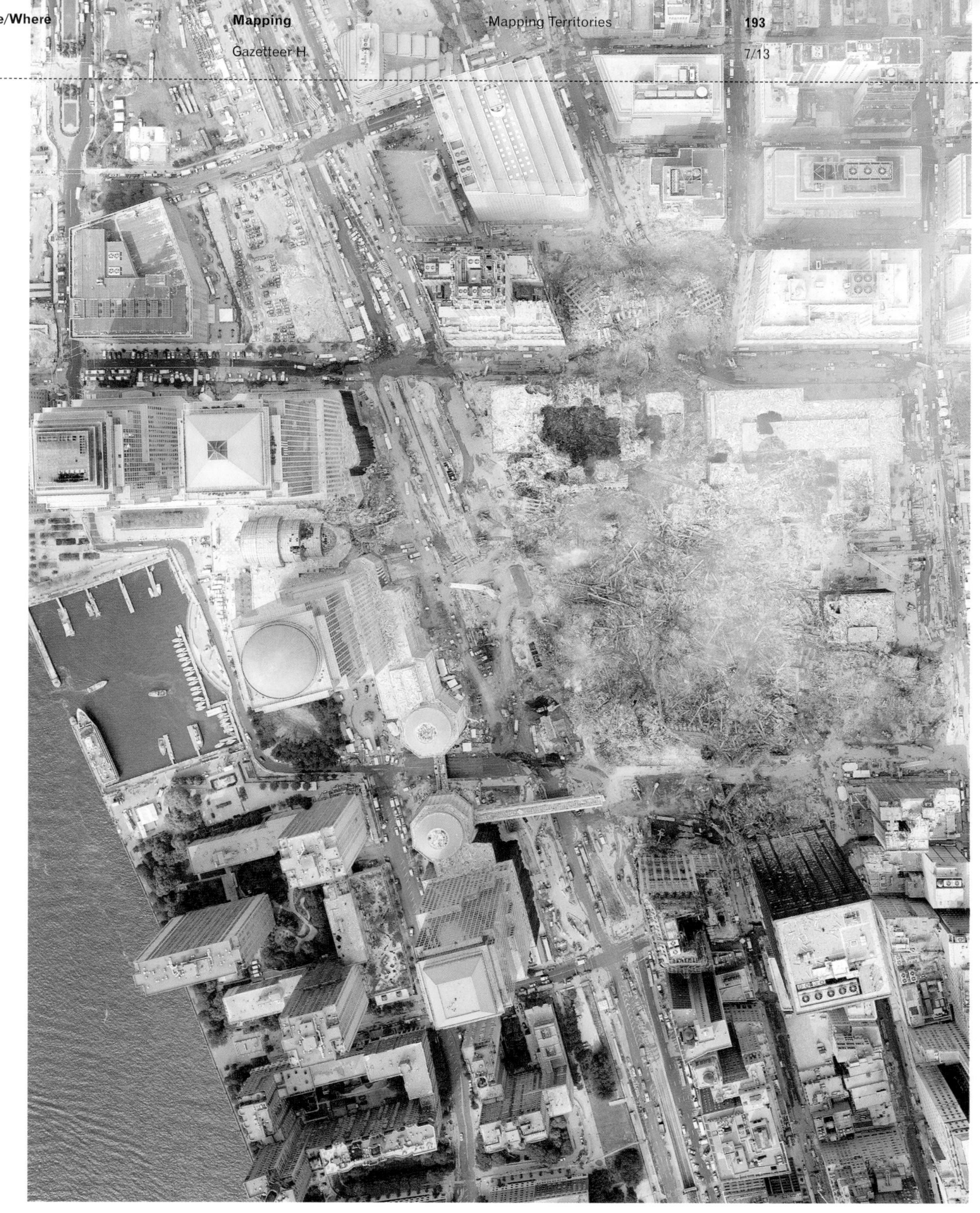

Laura Kurgan from *Around Ground Zero* / aerial image of Lower Manhattan taken by National Oceanic and Atmospheric Association Cessna Jet on September 21, 2001, released on October 22, 2001 / image courtesy of NOAA / see "Carto-City," pp. 156–157.

Panorama of the City of New York, 1964 / section of the *Panorama* on display at New York City Hall before being installed at the New York City Building at the 1964 World's Fair (now the Queens Museum of Art). Conceived by New York state and municipal official Robert Moses as an aid in urban planning, the wooden 1 inch : 100 feet scale model was built by Raymond Lester & Associates, and included 895,000 miniature buildings / collection of Queens Museum of Art / see "Perils of Precision," pp. 184–185.

Hermann Bollmann *Manhattan*, 1948 / a hand-drawn map informed by 67,000 photographs of the city and employing the cartographic technique known as *Vogelschaukarten* / image courtesy of UCLA Libraries © Bollmann-Bildkarten-Verlag GmbH & Co. KG, Braunschweig. Photographed by Kimberlee Whaley / see "Carto-City," p. 156.

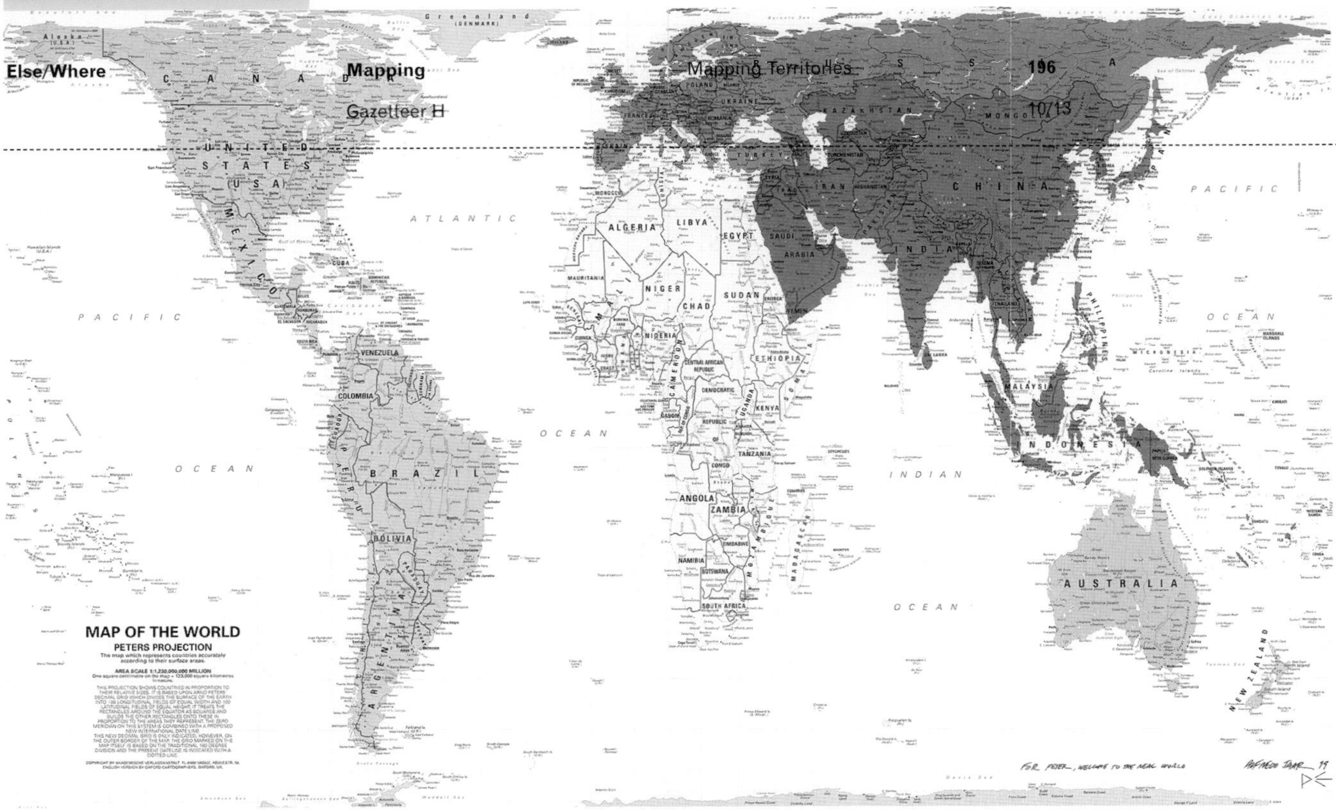

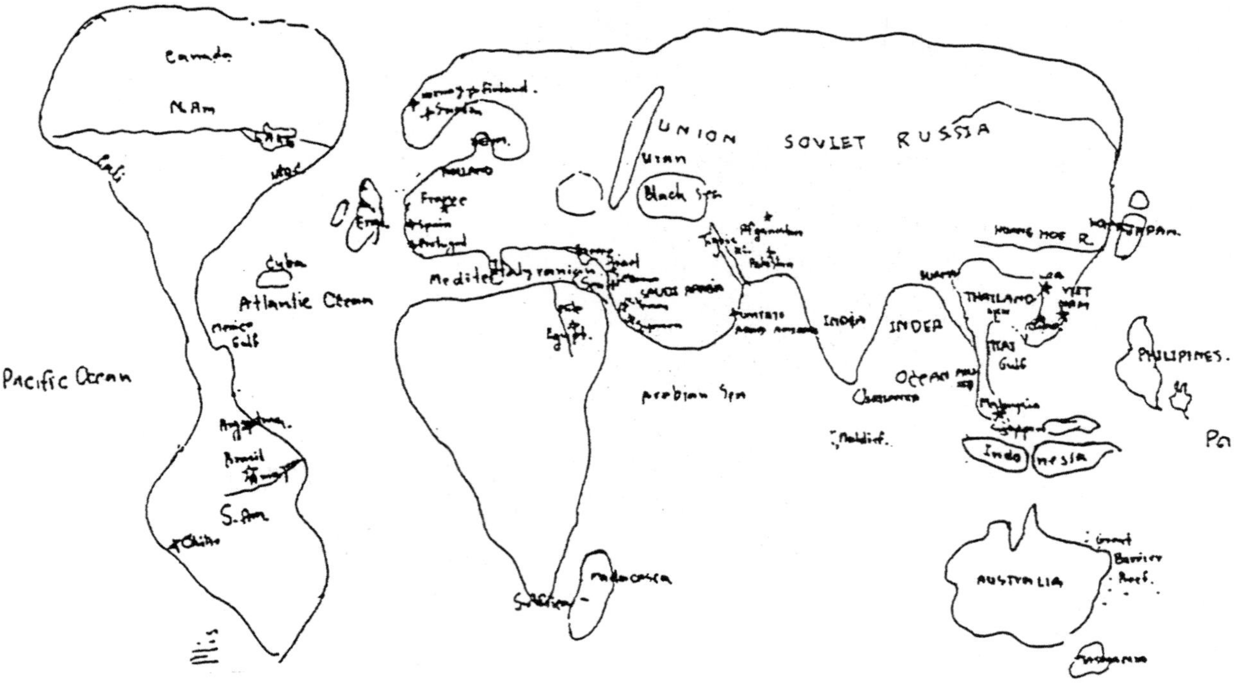

Alfredo Jaar and **Arno Peters** *Weltanschauung*, 1988 / world map adapted from the 1974 *Peters projection*, which accurately portrays the size of landmasses—in contrast to the more familiar 1569 Mercator projection, which centers the world on Europe, enlarging the landmasses near the poles / published by GAK, Bremen. Photographed by Kimberlee Whaley / see "Mapping the Homunculus," p. 200.

Thomas Saarinen *Children's Mental Maps of the World*, composite of drawings by children from Thailand, 1999 / from "The Euro-centric Nature of Mental Maps of the World." Saarinen gathered over 3,800 sketch maps of the world by children in 49 countries, and found that a Eurocentric view of the world remains dominant / image courtesy of Thomas Saarinen / see "Mapping the Homunculus," p. 201.

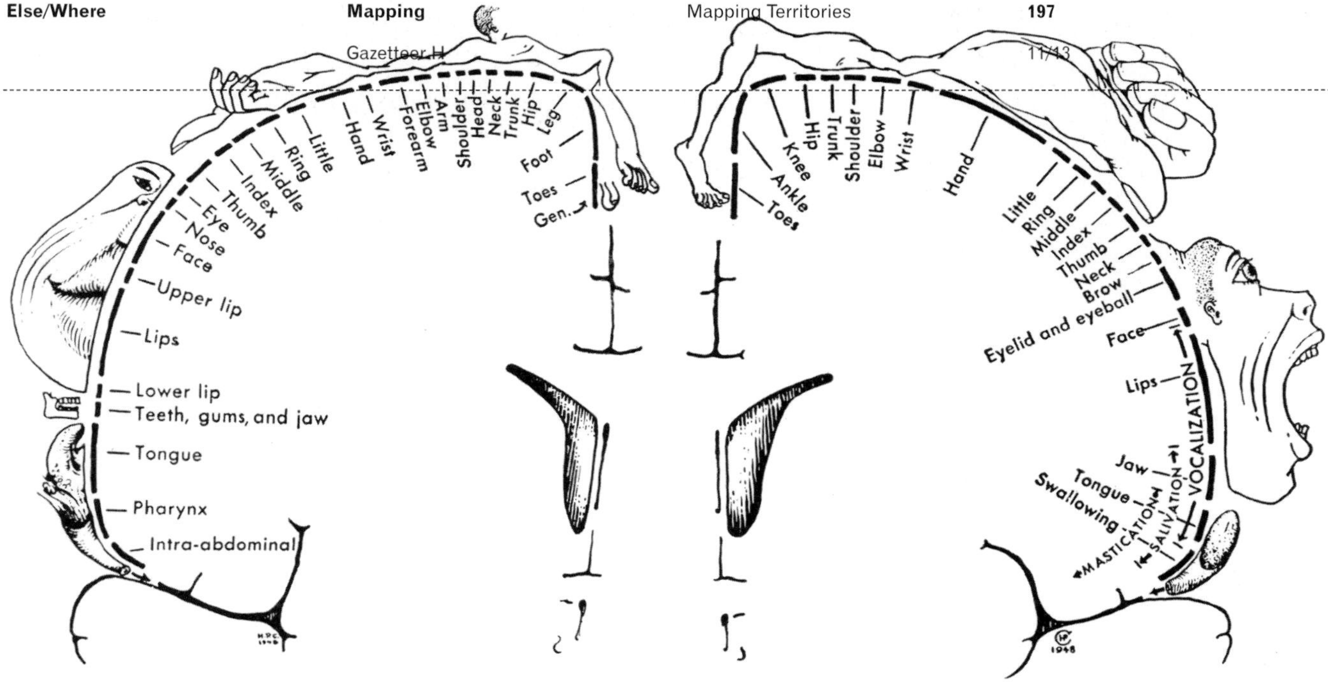

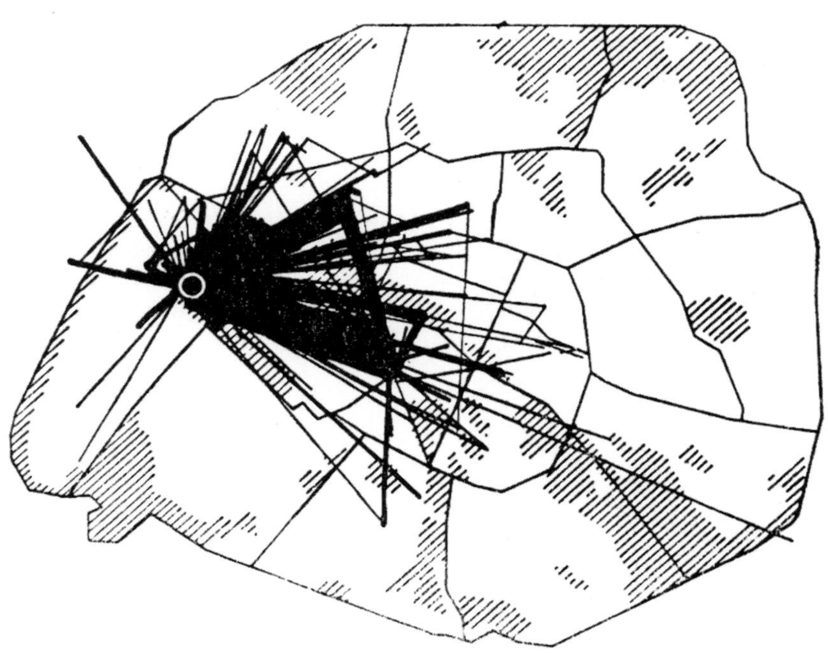

Wilder Penfield *Homunculus*, 1950 / cross section through the cortex of the brain showing the somatosensory areas. From Wilder Penfield and Theodore Rasmussen, *The Cerebral Cortex of Man*. New York: Macmillan, 1950 / see "Mapping the Homunculus," p. 201.

Paul-Henry Chombart de Lauwe *Trajets pendant un an d'une jeune fille du XVIe arrondissement*, 1957 / map showing a young Parisian woman's dominant triangle of movement between home, school and piano lessons over the course of one year / see "Mapping the Homunculus," p. 200.

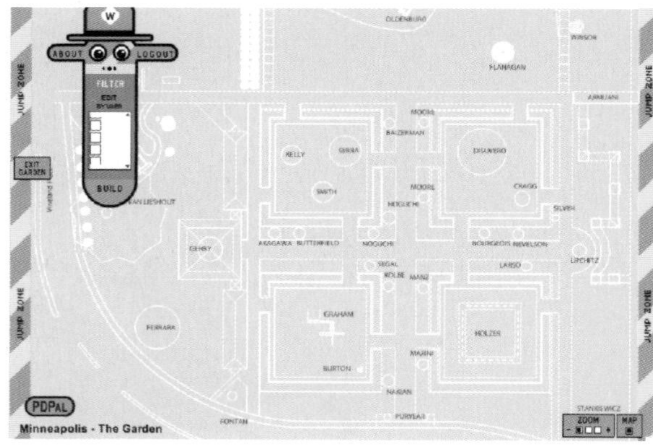

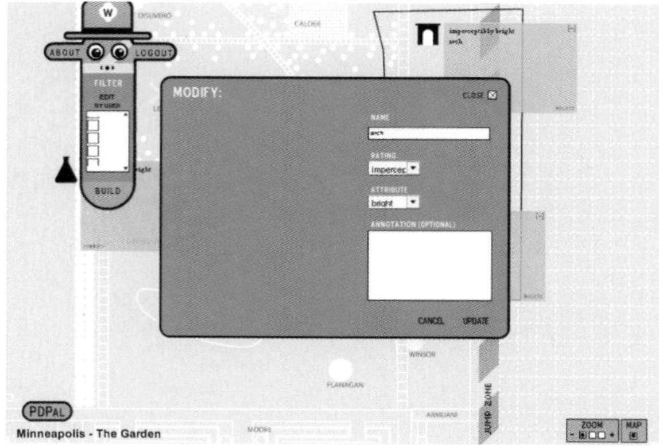

Scott Paterson, **Marina Zurkow** and **Julian Bleecker** *PDPal*, 2003 / public digital mapping project jointly commissioned by the Walker Art Center and Creative Time, which allows users to record impressions and opinions of their city on a handheld Personal Digital Assistant via a custom-designed Palm-OS-based interface. (top): kiosk installed in the Minneapolis Sculpture Garden. (below): four screengrabs taken from the website to which users could also upload their stories / see "Mapping the Homunculus," pp. 203–205.

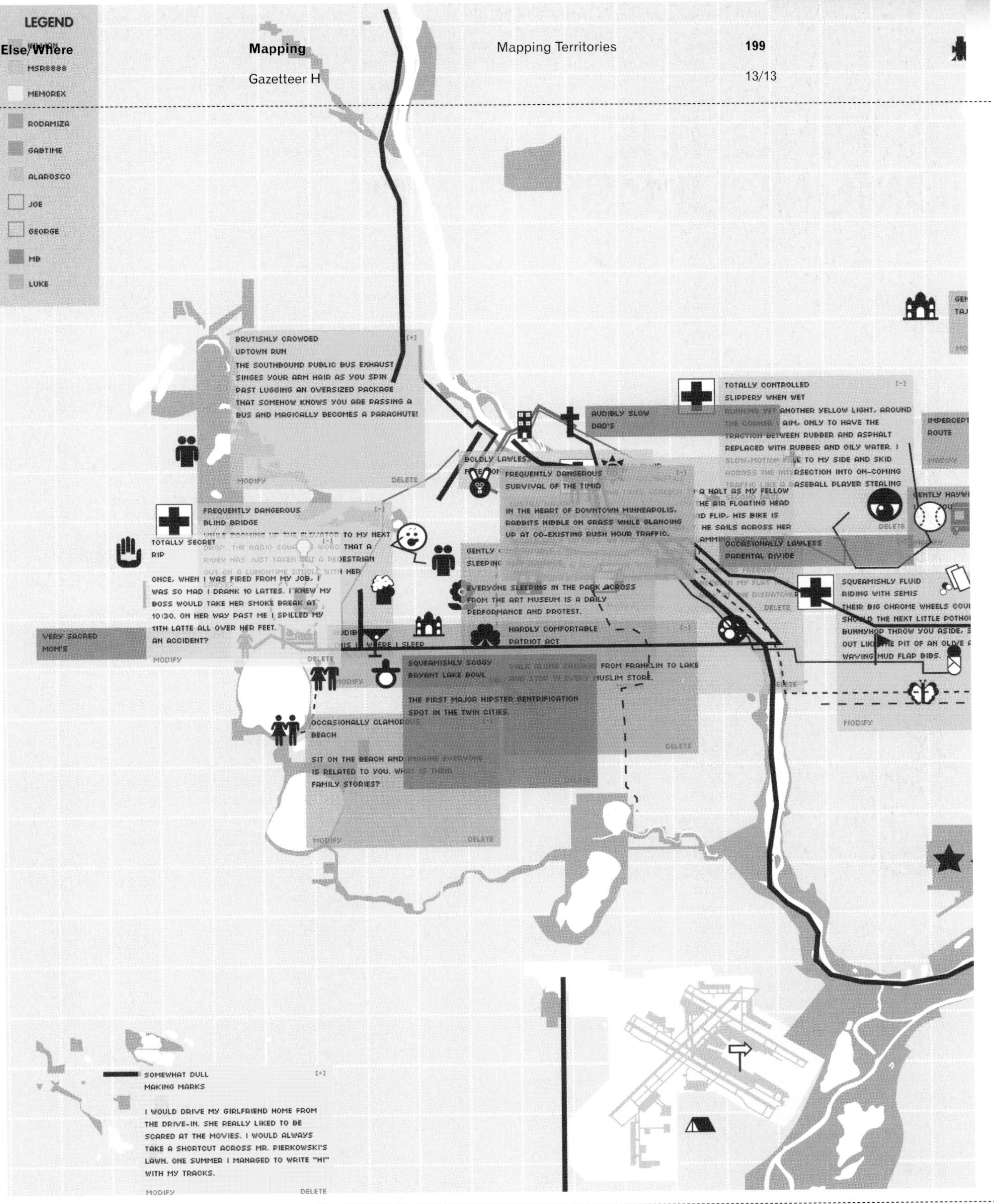

Scott Paterson, **Marina Zurkow** and **Julian Bleecker** *Write Your Own City* (detail), 2003 / detail from the artists' Twin Cities Knowledge Map, highlighting experiences logged in Minneapolis/St. Paul by users of *PDPal* experimental mapping software. Knowledge Map published as one of nine alternate cartographies of the Twin Cities / © 2003 University of Minnesota Design Institute / see "Mapping the Homunculus," pp. 203–205.

MAPPING THE HOMUNCULUS

RECENT ART PROJECTS CONJURE ALTERNATIVE IMAGES OF THE CITY, WITH DYNAMIC INTERFACES THAT ALLOW COLLECTIVE EXPRESSION OF INDIVIDUAL URBAN EXPERIENCES. **STEVE DIETZ** EXPLORES HOW MODELS OF MENTAL MAPS AND EMERGENT SYSTEMS THEORY INFORM WORK BY ARTISTS WHO USE DIGITAL MEDIA TO RECORD NEW PSYCHOGEOGRAPHIES.

One of the most common ways to place ourselves in relation to the incomprehensibly vast, be it God or *The Matrix*, is by creating a map. In an age of information overload, the map has become a favorite interface to data sets of all types, geographic and otherwise. More importantly, the map can become a kind of visual bridge between disparate facts—zip codes and cereal preferences, for instance. As location-aware devices proliferate—from cell phones to any object with a radio frequency ID tag—maps will become an increasingly important means to theorize and discover relationships that are not easily graspable.

Several artists' projects model how maps might help not only locate us, but how mapmaking can be a tool to build a counter-image of our future urbanity—in contrast to contemporary culture's panoptic, data-mining gaze onto our zip-coded profiles. I shall argue that the image of the homunculus—a diminutive human character who serves as a kind of sensory index—is a useful concept in two respects: it embodies the idea that what we experience physically or personally has a disproportionate effect on our mental maps of the world, and that simple rules can give rise to complex—even intelligent—systems.

Neurologist Wilder Penfield used the term "homunculus" in his famous early brain maps, which showed that each part of the body is represented on two strips of the brain's cerebral cortex, the somatosensory cortex (which receives sensations of touch) and the motor cortex (which receives control movements). Fingers, mouth and other sensitive areas take up most space on both maps, a point he exaggerated on another drawing of a homunculus with sensitive body parts exaggerated. If we extend this notion to mapping our direct experience of the lived environment, it will create a very different image from a conventional street plan.

In his *Theory of the Dérive*, Guy Debord quotes the sociologist Paul-Henry Chombart de Lauwe: "an urban neighborhood is determined not only by geographical and economic factors, but also by the image that its inhabitants and those of other neighborhoods have of it."[1]

De Lauwe included in one text a map of all the movements made during one year by a student living in the 16th Arrondissement of Paris. Her itinerary forms a small triangle with no significant deviations, the three apexes of which are the School of Political Sciences, her residence and that of her piano teacher—illustrating, according to Chombart de Lauwe, "the narrowness of the real Paris in which each individual lives" and which, according to Debord, ought to provoke "outrage at the fact that anyone's life can be so pathetically limited."

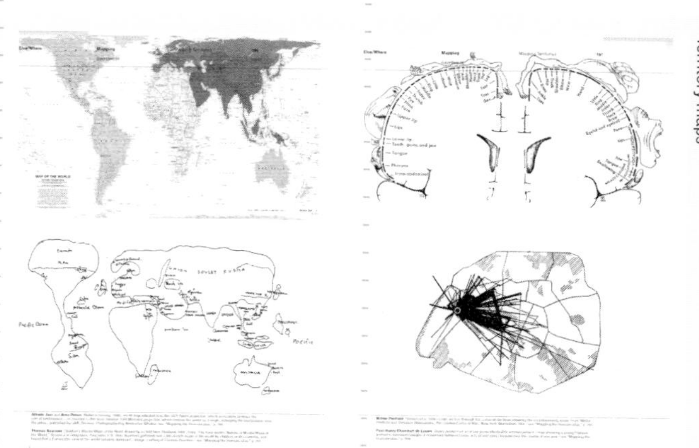

Territory maps

gazetteer H 10–11/13 pp. 196–197

1. Guy Debord, "Theory of the Dérive," *Internationale Situationniste #2* (December 1958) translated by Ken Knabb. <http://www2.cddc.vt.edu/situationist/si/theory.html>

2. Regarding complexity and emergent systems, see Steven Johnson, *Emergence: The Connected Lives of Ants, Brains, Cities, and Software;* Mitchel Resnick, *Turtles, Termites, and Traffic Jams: Explorations in Massively Parallel Microworlds,* 1997; and Albert-László Barabási, *Linked: The New Science of Networks,* 2002.

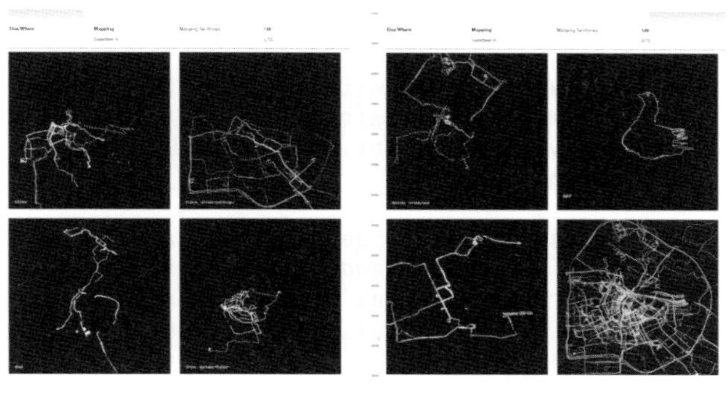

Territory maps

gazetteer H 2–3/13 pp. 188–189

Probably many of us can relate to a dominating triangle of home, work and hobby—regardless of its parochial nature—but metaphorically speaking, de Lauwe's mapping of the student's movements in Paris *is* her geographic homunculus. A contemporary version of Chombart de Lauwe's project is the Waag Society's *Amsterdam RealTime* project. The issue with such homuncular maps is that individually they don't create a rich image of the whole city. However, with new understanding of complexity and emergent systems, it is possible to imagine that when these simple views are combined, the sum may be greater than the parts.[2]

<www.waag.org/realtime>

Homuncular maps, deeply rooted in the personal, can give rise to very powerful and useful maps of more complex systems such as cities. It is possible to imagine societal systems that rely on individual input to generate emergent and dynamically adaptive solutions independent of a pre-existing structure, single leader or top-down process. It may be stating the obvious, but one of the reasons to focus on maps is that they matter. They make a difference in society's somatosensory cortex as profound and direct as touch has on our own.

Creating abstractions of the physical world is no mean feat, posing the problem of how to represent the third dimension. Mercator's 2D projection of 1569 came as an almost magical event, providing a synoptic image of the world which has dominated ever since. As cartographer Arno Peters demonstrated in his alternative 1974 projection, the Mercator map accurately depicts the shape of landmasses, but dramatically enlarges the size of landmasses nearer the poles—primarily Europe and North America.[3]

In contrast, the Peters projection accurately portrays the size of all nations, and, according to its creator, gives a voice to underrepresented countries in the developing world. This would seem an important issue, especially given the research by Thomas Saarinen, who gathered over 3,800 sketch maps of the world by children from 49 countries for the project *Children's Mental Maps of the World.* A composite of the results by children from Thailand looks most like the Mercator projection, which greatly exaggerates areas where the children don't live. Theirs is the opposite of a homuncular view of the world.[4]

The Peters projection is significant not only for the interface it provides, but for its highlighting of the fact that the Mercator projection is only one option among worldviews, not the natural way to map the world, no matter how logical or efficient. Homuncular projects are important not only for their viewpoint, but for how they denaturalize the dominant interfaces we swim in, whether the interface is Sky News or America Online or MapQuest. More powerful than the meanings of the visualized data is how that very act of visualization disrupts systems of knowledge and relationships of power. As the geographer Denis Wood frames it, “maps work by serving interests.”[5]

The following projects serve the interests of individuals and local communities while still attempting a holistic functionality; they disrupt business as usual in terms of who and what is represented; and many of them provide alternative interfaces that viscerally connote the possibility of alternative viewpoints and multiple worldviews.

MINNEAPOLIS AND ST. PAUL ARE EAST AFRICAN CITIES

In 2002, the New York-based artist Julie Mehretu was invited to undertake a residency at the Walker Art Center in Minneapolis. As she tells it, she was quite surprised in this land of *lutefisk* and *lefse*[6] to get into a heated conversation with her airport taxi driver about current events in Ethiopia—where they were both born. On further investigation, it turned out that the largest Somali population outside of Africa lives in the Twin Cities and that a significantly

2. See “Perils of Precision,” p. 184.
3. The *Peters Map Project* was undertaken in a class taught at the University of Minnesota in 2003 by artist Alfredo Jaar, Winton Chair in Liberal Arts. <www.petersworldmap.org/>
4. Thomas Saarinen, “The Euro-centric Nature of Mental Maps of the World.” *Research in Geographic Education*, 1 : 2, 1999.
5. Denis Wood. *The Power of Maps*. New York and London: The Guilford Press, 1992.
6. See <www.angelfire.com/mn/matbird/fromminnesota.html>.

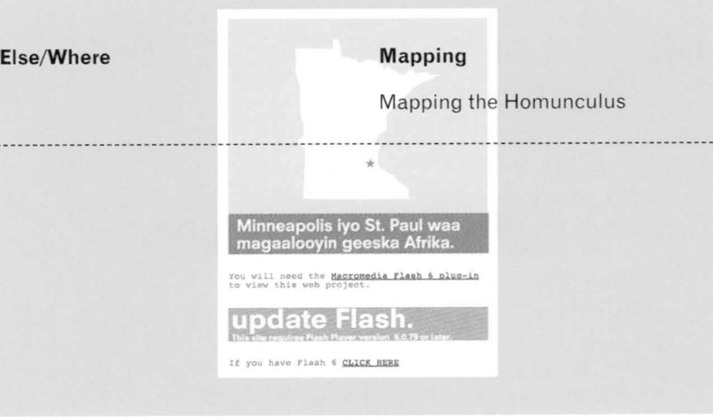

Minneapolis iyo St. Paul waa magaalooyin geeska Afrika.
You will need the Macromedia Flash 6 plug-in to view this web project.
update Flash.
If you have Flash 6 CLICK HERE

Location: at South High School. Just got to school with my cousin Fikeru for class...

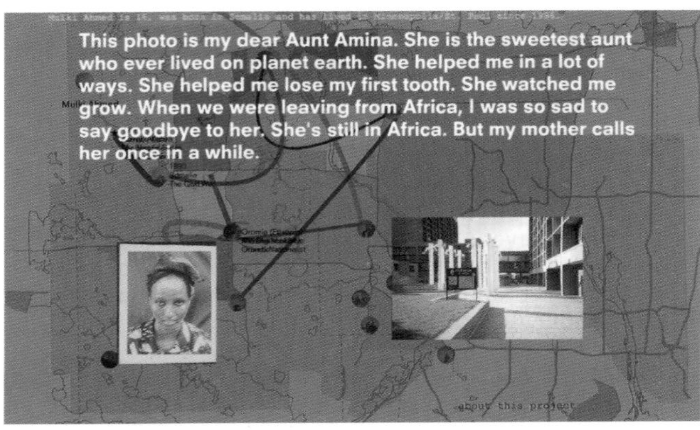

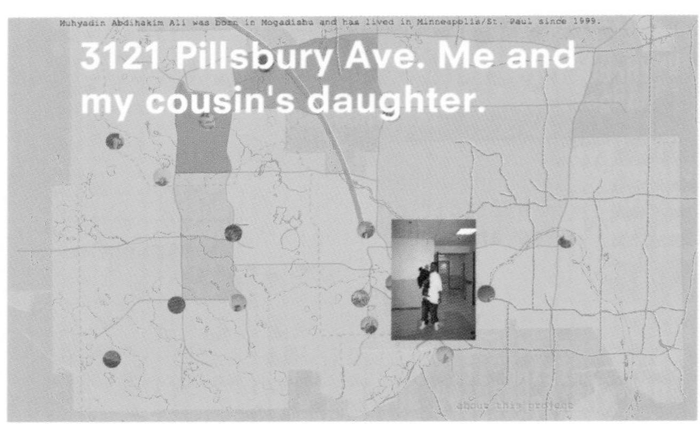

3121 Pillsbury Ave. Me and my cousin's daughter.

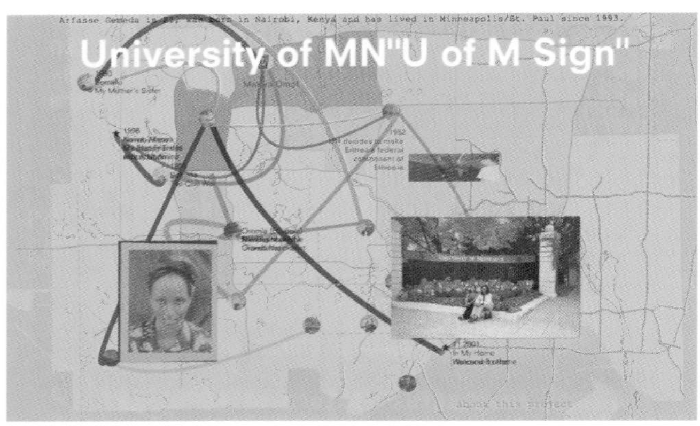

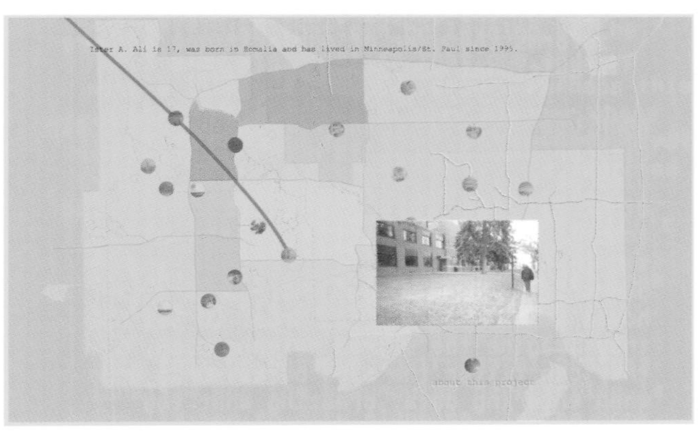

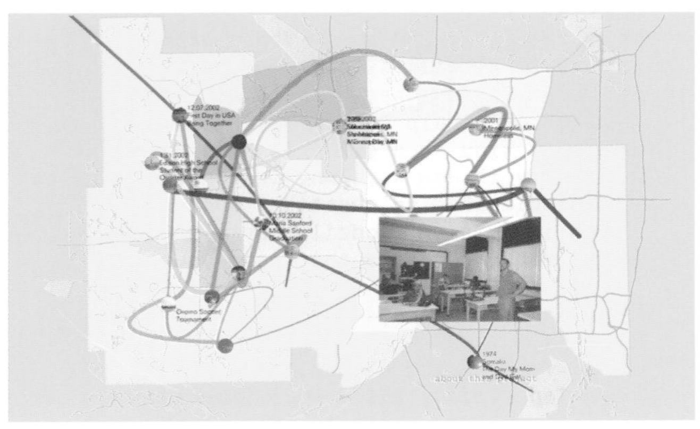

Julie Mehretu *Minneapolis and St Paul are East African Cities*, 2002 / interactive map and database of the Twin Cities as seen by Minneapolis high school students of East African descent. The project was led by Ethiopian-born artist Mehretu, while she was an artist-in-residence at the Walker Art Center; interaction designers Entropy8Zuper! created the interface.

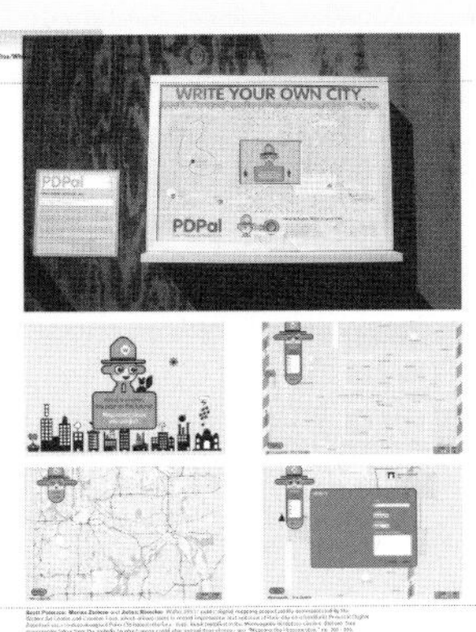

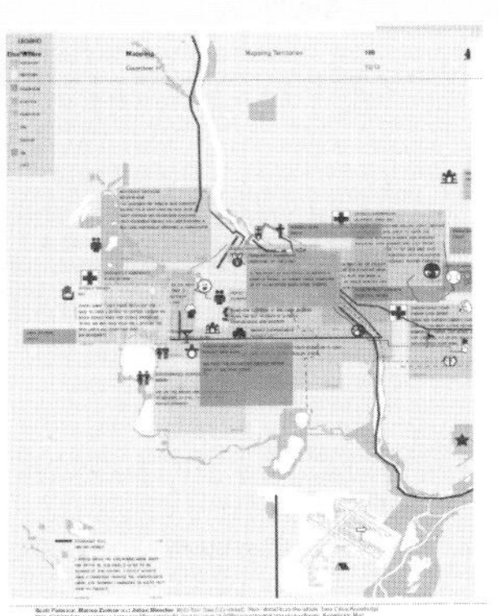

Territory maps

gazetteer H 12–13/13 pp. 198–199

everyone's personal city, without losing access to the personal and the individual. Everyone's individual maps can thus be combined and recombined, so that *PDPal* effectively image-maps the city without the intervention of an authority.

Open systems nevertheless need to take on a life of their own—to *emerge*—if they are to be truly successful. During the launch and promotion of *PDPal*, it received significant use, but it is unclear whether the narratives that are now being told are sufficient to keep the "communicity" growing. However, each iteration of the project has made enormous conceptual leaps and adjustments, and as the ability to add any geographic base-map into the system becomes available, *PDPal* has the potential to become a virtual locus for homuncular storytelling.

Whereas *PDPal* allows users to enter information from home, via the web, a number of other current projects investigate personal mapping, but require the viewer-participant to be physically present at the location of the story in order to access it. The city becomes the map, or perhaps more accurately a telecommunications layer is overlaid on the physical city at a 1:1 scale. A user can leave a story about a particular location at that location. When another user walks by, her location-aware device can alert her to the presence of the story, to which she may decide to listen while strolling about the location.

GEOGRAFFITI

At the core of the *Geograffiti* project by Marc Tuters and Karlis Kalnins, co-produced by the Banff New Media Institute, is an open source philosophy. As they write:

<www.gpster.net/add.html>

> Recently, researchers and free-GIS enthusiasts have begun to share their data in a variety of networking machine-searchable environments, enabling the development of a non-proprietary data pool of human geography, where meaning emerges and is inscribed at ground level.[13]

GPS devices use "waypoints" that mark a particular spot. Generally, these are personal and not shared, but part of *Geograffiti* is an open database (called GPSter) of waypoints—or GPS-encoded locations where someone has left a story—writing, audio, video or some combination. *Geograffiti* is as much a platform for the exchange of geographically-tagged information as is a particular interface like *PDPal*, but its goal is to enable "collaborative cartography...to map according to our desires, providing artists with tools with which, effectively, to step outside of the box, whereby architectonic space now becomes their canvas." In other words, it is a platform for mapping the urban homunculus.

PANOPTIC AND HOMUNCULAR VISIONS

The future of computing is ubiquitous, aware, embedded and distributed.[13] Increasingly, computers and devices such as RFID tags that communicate with computers will be embedded in objects throughout our environment. These skeins of computing can and almost certainly will give rise to nightmarish scenarios of Total Information Awareness by governmental, commercial and illegal powers. At the same time, especially if we can maintain a system of protocols that is predominantly open, these capabilities can be used to give expression to personal points of view which, in turn, can be mapped into collaborative, alternative visions. These will not be sufficient actions, but they are important if we are to approach the lines of flight necessary to imagine an alternative outcome to our urban condition.

13. Jeffrey Gennari, et al. "Preparatory Observations Ubiquitous Knowledge Environments: The Cyberinfrastructure Information Ether," *Wave of the Future*, 2003. <www.sis.pitt.edu/~dlwkshop/paper_spring.html>.

IMAGES/MATTER

LIDAR SCANNING ALLOWS OBJECTS, BUILDINGS AND POTENTIALLY WHOLE CITIES TO BE CAPTURED IN 3D AT HIGH RESOLUTION. WILL THIS NEW MODE OF MAPPING MAKE TRADITIONAL ARCHITECTURAL PROCESSES OBSOLETE? ARCHITECT **MIKE SILVER** TELLS **PETER HALL** ABOUT THE IMPLICATIONS AND INNOVATIVE USES OF LIDAR IN THE DESIGNED ENVIRONMENT.

Peter Hall: What is LIDAR? How does it work?

Mike Silver: LIDAR stands for Light Detection and Ranging. A LIDAR scanner uses an automated, high-resolution laser range finder to map space by measuring the time it takes for a beam of light to reflect off an object or body. From these measurements, the scanner can record a surface in three dimensions.

When was this technology invented?

LIDAR was developed in the 1960s to solve a wide range of mapping problems and has been used in atmospheric research, land surveys and even astronomy. By reflecting a single laser pulse off a mirror placed on the moon during the Apollo missions, scientists were able to obtain a very accurate measurement of its distance from earth. As computers became smaller and more accurate, technologies were developed that could record extremely large amounts of data.

How much data can a LIDAR scanner record?

The machine we used at Yale University, a Cryax 2500, can capture about 800 to 1000 thousand points per second at a resolution as small as 0.002 of an inch. With that much data, you can easily generate files that choke most desktop computers. So you really need a good machine. Newer and faster scanners are already on the market, which makes increases in computing power extremely important for the practical implementation of this technology.

When did 3D space mapping technology become popular with architects?

Frank Gehry was probably the first architect to use a 3D scanner to augment the design process, but LIDAR didn't work well with the way he practices. His office owns a manually operated digitizer called a Ferro Arm to record points on the surface of a model, creating low-resolution maps. This technology is more for general captures, whereas LIDAR is a high-resolution imaging system that looks at objects in detail. So there's a big difference. LIDAR is less reductive. It's more like a camera.

James Corner defines mapping as a productive act that can "unlock potentials."[1] Does your work with LIDAR make a similar argument?

1. James Corner, " The Agency of Mapping," in *Mappings*, ed. Denis Cosgrove. London: Reaktion Books, 1999, pp. 213–253.
2. Robert Venturi, Denise Scott Brown and Steven Izenour, *Learning from Las Vegas*. Cambridge, MA: The MIT Press, 1966.

Mike Silver *deformed LIDAR scans*, 2003 / sketch image produced using the data from a LIDAR scan of a building in Ninth Square, New Haven, CT, showing the potential for manipulating data captured by this 3D mapping technique (compare with image on p. 210).

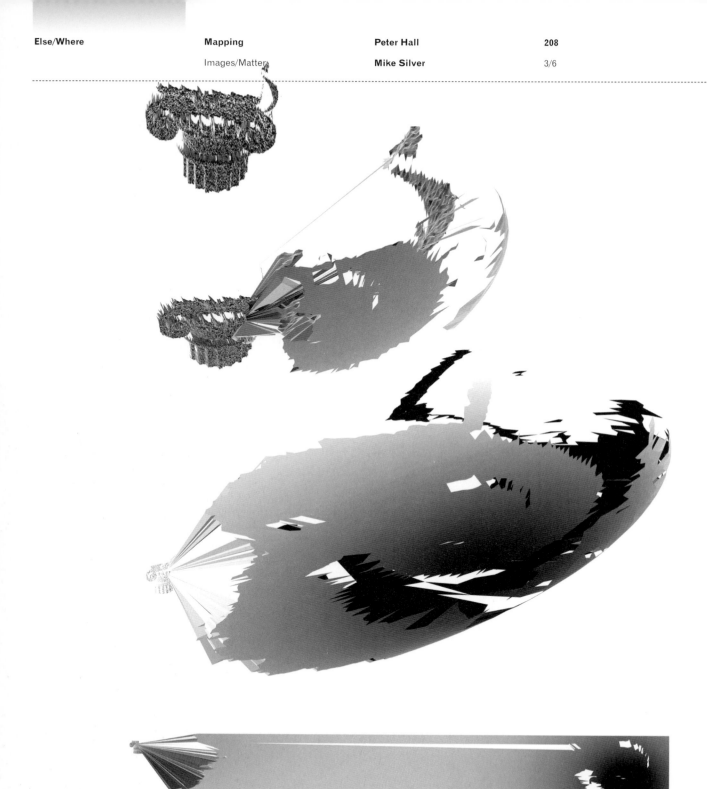

Mike Silver *deformed LIDAR scans of corinthian capital at the Master's House, Berkeley College, Yale University*, 2003 / (top three): taking advantage of the fact that LIDAR scanners cannot read the back sides or undercuts of objects, an algorithm is used to amplify the "breaks" and "tears" generated during a LIDAR scan of a classical column on the Yale campus, and project those gaps in the trace into an ellipsoid. (bottom): another program is then used to stretch the distorted amplification into a functional shape, to create a proposed design for a 7 ft. high garden wall at Berkeley College.

Yes, but Corner explores mapping through the history of paper, whereas I've focused on the potential transformation of design procedures using "soft cartography"—new digital mapping techniques.

How does LIDAR affect the design process?

When you make a high resolution scan of a site in three dimensions, you're basically creating a complex, almost photographic representation of it on your computer. This is a really new situation for architects, who are used to very reduced images of the contexts for their work, namely 2D drawings and pictures. More importantly, the connection between spatial imaging systems and new robotic fabrication technologies has become increasingly fluid. A LIDAR map is essentially a 3D sign rendered in virtual space as X/Y/Z coordinates, stored in a computer's memory—a sign that can be digitally fabricated in the physical world using real materials. The commands that drive construction are based on the same binary code.

This effectively alters the relationship between the tectonic and the scenographic — or what architect Robert Venturi famously defined in the 1960s as the opposition between the "Duck" (modern architecture) and the "Decorated Shed" (functional structures ornamented with appliqué symbols, supergraphics or video displays). Now, with a computer, input and output become inseparable: both exist as connected flows of information. The privileged status given by Venturi to applied decoration is not as meaningful as it used to be.

While his "building board" typology grew out of a fascination with postwar American culture (roadside architecture, urban sprawl and the Las Vegas strip), today's virtual technologies have created a new world where pervasive computing and the Internet have become as ubiquitous as the automobile. Also, Venturi's economic argument against the "Duck" is no longer valid because with digital tools a complex shed is as easy to manufacture as a simple one.

Where does your reading of information theory fit in here?

Claude Shannon's 1948 essay "A Mathematical Theory of Communication" provided the foundation for developments in digital communication technology which, unlike analog systems, allows you to communicate without noise.[3] By using error-correction protocols, Shannon was able to neutralize the effects noise had on a signal. That meant information could be understood in a pure way, disconnected from its context and method of transmission. In other words, the message is separated from its medium.

Shannon's model is useful if you want to design a functional cell phone, but problematic as a general definition. You can hear echoes of Shannon in Paul Virilio's thesis that virtual technologies will make architecture disappear; Virilio has even said that today "information is more important than mass and energy."[4] This is simply not the case. If anything, digital tools have allowed buildings to become even more physically complex. Shannon's model doesn't work well for architects because design flourishes in the space between materials and information, forms and ideas.

I think the British information theorist Donald MacKay offers architects a more promising definition of communication by focusing on how information is encountered in a specific place according to the status of its receiver. MacKay's notion of "conditional readiness" can be used to accentuate the ways information is interpreted and transformed when it changes media. Noise can be a good thing or a bad thing depending on the situation. It can be used to great effect as a means of expression.[5]

How do you define noise?

Noise can be a random sound, a lightning strike that produces static on your TV set, the hum created by electricity flowing through the valves in a guitar amplifier, or even missing information. According to the *Audio Dictionary*, there is "no such thing...as a noise-free signal...everything you do to a message adds some noise to it."[6] If you record music on a magnetic tape, there is something like a three-decibel increase in noise each time you make an additional copy.

And this applies to digital sampling, too?

When you make a 300 dpi scan of a photograph, you're effectively adding noise by

3. Claude Shannon, "A Mathematical Theory of Communication," Urbana and Chicago: University of Illinois Press, 1963.
4. Paul Virilio, " Architecture in the Age of its Virtual Disappearance," in *The Virtual Dimension*, ed. John Beckmann. New York: Princeton Architectural Press, 1998, pp. 178–188.
5. Donald MacKay, "Meaning and Mechanism" in *Information, Mechanism and Meaning*. Cambridge, MA: MIT Press, 1969, pp. 19–30.
6. Glenn D. White, *The Audio Dictionary*. Seattle: University of Washington Press, 1993. p. 106 and p. 221.

Mike Silver *deformed LIDAR scan of a building in Ninth Square, New Haven, CT*, 2003 / one of a series of sketch images (see also p. 207) created deliberately to put in question the presumed documentary quality of LIDAR, and demonstrate how information from the physical world, once taken into the digital world, is no longer necessarily anchored to any particular stable form.

lowering the amount of information contained in the original.

The advance of mapping techniques has been presented as an increasing drive toward verisimilitude: it is touted as a means to create perfect replicas of buildings and cities for posterity. You're insisting, on the other hand, that digital mapping adulterates or distorts the information.

Yes. There are quantitative differences between a LIDAR scan and a drawing, just as there's a difference between an abstract portrait of a person and a photograph. A scan has increasing detail and verisimilitude, but it can't capture reality; the real is far too complex to be represented.

It's like the difference between a supercomputer and a calculator. You can use a calculator to design an airplane wing, or you could use a supercomputer and start to understand new ways of constructing that wing because you're dealing with a much more complex model. The increase in detail does affect perception, but of course it never captures reality.

Have you applied the principles we've been discussing to the design of a building?

At Yale, we amassed a large database of classical buildings scanned with a LIDAR machine, and used one group of scans to "grow" new context-specific buildings. One challenge was to find a meaningful way of translating our data into complex forms that can be easily produced on a Computer Numeric Controlled (CNC) stone saw. We even developed a mapping technique that squeezes the data into easy-to-fabricate shapes while also preserving traces of the scanner's mediating effects.

What kind of traces?

A single LIDAR scan cannot capture undercuts or any surface that runs parallel to the laser beam. You can only get a complete capture by taking multiple scans—which is a way of masking the limits of the technology. It's a process of error correction. By keeping the breaks, holes and gaps generated from a single scan, you fix the record of its making into the image. The actual position of the cartographer relative to the object he or she is mapping produces specific forms that can be considered a creative mediation of the source material. For example, we mapped a column capital on site, and used its "noise" to generate a complex corner-turning garden wall for the Berkeley College Pavilion proposal at Yale.

How do you think computing will change architecture in the next decade?

Much of the design we see today is a result of the extensive use of prefabricated programs; we've borrowed a lot of code that simply doesn't address the problems of construction. Architects want to do what creative people have always done, that is, build new forms that grow out of new ways of thinking. I believe that programming will become a more intimate part of the design process. I imagine a future where every architect has his or her own homemade software. This will open up computing to new possibilities. Even the perspectival space in which buildings are represented could be reconfigured to include invisible dimensions and new mathematical structures that appropriated code simply cannot process. This will be seen as an unprecedented moment in the history of architecture.

MAP QUEST

Maps of the 15th Century were composites — eyewitness accounts (sometimes many steps and centuries removed from their original sources) mixed with theory, religious doctrine, fantasy and wild speculation. They reflected the era's predominant view that the world was primarily dry land, showing large continents interspersed with small inland seas and fringed by thin strips of ocean. This was the world Columbus knew, one in which the sailing distances between continents were short and the continents themselves nearly touched each other.

In 1507, the German cartographer Martin Waldseemüller and his colleagues in the French city of Saint-Dié published a book of maps that changed forever how people saw the world. The *Cosmographiae Introductio,* or *Introduction to Cosmography*, comprised a printed text, a 36-square-foot map and a woodcut of segment-shaped map sections, or gores, that could be made into a globe. They are the first maps in European history to show the Americas as independent continents, separate from Asia. But the significance of these maps today, as well as most of their market value, lies in the magical name "America," intimately connected not just to two continents but to the mythologies of a nation.[1]

Geographer J. B. Harley points out that historians often ignore maps — they are relegated along with paintings, photographs and other nonverbal sources, to a category of evidence lower than the written word:

> Among the many classes of documents regularly used by historians, maps are well known but less well understood. We could compile an anthology of statements that categorize maps not only as "slippery" (the adjective used by the distinguished historian J. H. Parry) but also as "dangerous" or "unreliable." ...When a historian reaches for a map, it is usually to answer a fairly narrow question about location or topography and less often to illuminate cultural history or the social values of a particular period or place.[2]

On the Waldseemüller planisphere, the most revealing information is in the details and on the borders of the map. At its base, an inscription links the contemporary Florentine navigator Amerigo Vespucci to the ancient geographer Ptolemy. At its head, flanking a smaller version of the world map, are impressive portraits of Vespucci and Ptolemy, sometimes attributed to Albrecht Dürer. Elsewhere on the map are notes about new lands discovered "under the authority of the King of Castille."

Why did Waldseemüller choose to name the new continent after Vespucci, rather than Columbus? And why did the name stick?

1. One of four known original examples of the gore map was sold in June 2005 at Christie's in London for $1m; another example resides in the James Ford Bell Library at the University of Minnesota. Four years earlier, the sole surviving copy of the larger Waldseemüller planisphere was sold to the Library of Congress for $10m. See "First map of America makes $1m," CNN.com, June 8, 2005. <cnn.com/2005/WORLD/europe/06/08/america.map/index.html> Linton Weeks, "Library of Congress Buys First Map of 'America'," *Washington Post*, July 21, 2001, p. C08.

2. J. B. Harley, *The New Nature of Maps: Essays in the History of Cartography*, Paul Laxton, ed. Baltimore: The Johns Hopkins University Press, 2001, p. 34.

Printed pamphlets had begun to circulate in the early 1500s carrying vivid descriptions attributed to Vespucci of the geography, peoples and culture of what he firmly came to believe was a New World. The decision to name these lands America is explained in the ninth chapter of the *Cosmographiae*, in the effusive style of poet Mathias Ringmann, the book's main editor:

> But now that these parts of the world have been widely examined and another fourth part has been discovered by Americu Vesputiu (as will be seen in the following), I see no reason why we should not call it America, that is to say, land of Americus, for Americus, its discoverer, man of sagacious wit, just as Europe and Asia received in days gone by their names from women.[3]

In the United States, at least, the name has brought little true honor to Vespucci's memory. For most of the last two and a half centuries, scholars and poets alike have heaped abuse on Vespucci for "stealing" the name of the New World from Columbus.[4] Ralph Waldo Emerson called Vespucci "the pickle-dealer at Seville" who went out on "an expedition that never sailed, managed in this lying world to supplant Columbus, and baptize half the earth with his own dishonest name."[5] Yet, as all well informed authorities have pointed out, Vespucci never suggested that the new lands be named after him. More importantly, it was Vespucci's accounts that made the claim that a New World, and not Asia, lay to the west of Europe and that another ocean lay between that New World and the legendary lands of China and Japan that Columbus had sought. Columbus did not, in fact, claim to have discovered the Americas. As far as anyone has been able to determine, he died stubbornly believing that he had sailed to Asia.

To those at Saint-Dié, Vespucci's news was far more exciting than the accounts Columbus brought back from the same region. Waldseemüller was part of a small intellectual community in touch with the latest ideas and technologies: under the patronage of René II, Duke of Lorraine, an independent monarch whose wide-ranging interests included geography and literature, that intellectual community had access to a wide network of information and expertise. Its canon was René's secretary and chaplain, Vautrin Lud, who had assembled a small group of thinkers and trained technicians, that came to call itself the Gymnase Vosgien.[6] Its central treasure was a printing press, then a new and thrilling invention. The printed map was a major step in the development of modern cartography, making possible wide distribution of multiple, identical copies of maps, no longer subject to the errors copyists introduced into hand-drawn images.

As printing technologies spread throughout Europe, the geopolitical and geo-economic alignments of the world — especially the boundaries between

3. Germán Arciniegas, *Amerigo and the New World: The Life and Times of Amerigo Vespucci*, trans. by Harriet de Onís. New York: Alfred A. Knopf, 1955, p. 296.

4. The debate over priority between Columbus and Vespucci centers largely on who first touched on the mainland of South America. Columbus reached the coast of what is now Venezuela during his third voyage (1498–1500). Vespucci discovered and explored the mouths of the Amazon in an expedition of 1499 and explored the southern coast of South America in his Portuguese-sponsored voyage of 1501. There was a disputed claim for an earlier Vespucci voyage in 1497. Unlike Columbus, however, Vespucci definitively identified these discoveries as part of a "New World" detached from Asia. Of course, it is now established that the Icelandic explorer Leif Eriksson reached America about 500 years earlier than either Columbus or Vespucci.

5. Ralph Waldo Emerson, "Cockayne," *English Traits*, 1856.

6. Translation: "Academy of the Vosges Region."

CLAVDII PTHOLOMEI ALEXANDRINI COSMOGRAPHI
ZEPHIRUS
CHORUS
AFRICUS
LYBONOTHUS
NOTVS
OCEANVS OCCIDENTALIS
MARE GLACIALE SIVE CONGELA
CIRCULUS ARCTICUS
SPAGNOLLA INSULA
TOTA ISTA PROVINCIA INVENTA EST PER MANDATUM REGIS CASTELLE
TERRA ULTRA INCOGNITA
EQUINOCTIALIS
AMERICA
AFFRICA
ETHIOPIA INTERIOR
LIBIA INTERIOR
ASIA
AFRICA
VNIVERSALIS COSMOGRAPHIA SECVNDVM PTHOLOMAEI TRADITIONEM

Martin Waldseemüller world map from *Cosmographiae Introductio*, 1507 / the first map in history to show the Americas as an independent continent, separate from Asia. The 36-square foot planisphere gives prominence to the discoverer Amerigo Vespucci, after whom America was named (portrait, top right) and geographer Ptolemy (top left) but not — significantly — to Columbus. Subsequent maps yielded to political pressures, and the word "America" was temporarily dropped / image courtesy of the Library of Congress.

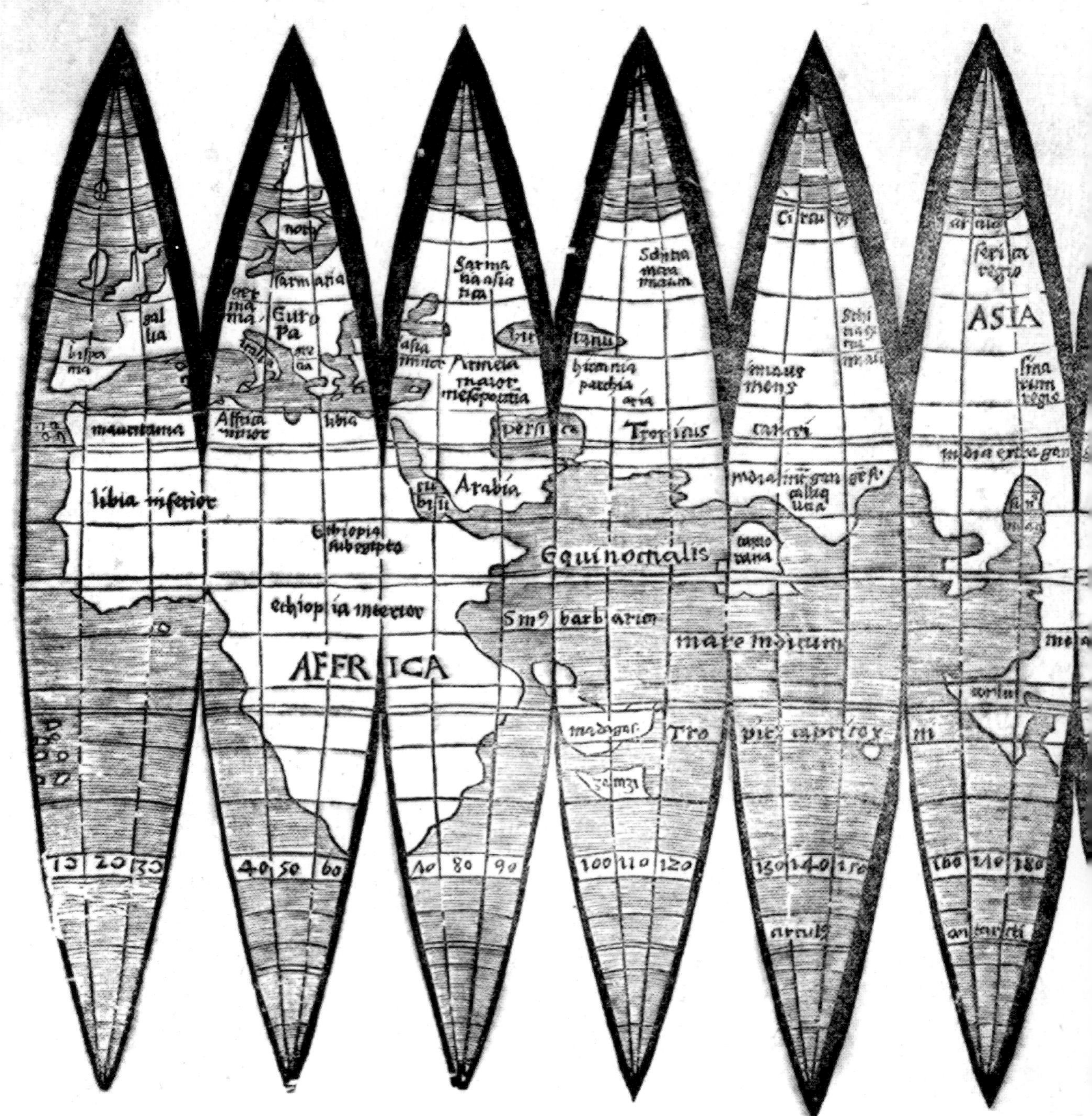
Arabia
libia inferior
AFFR ICA
ASIA
mare indicum
20
40
50
60
80
90
100
110
120
180

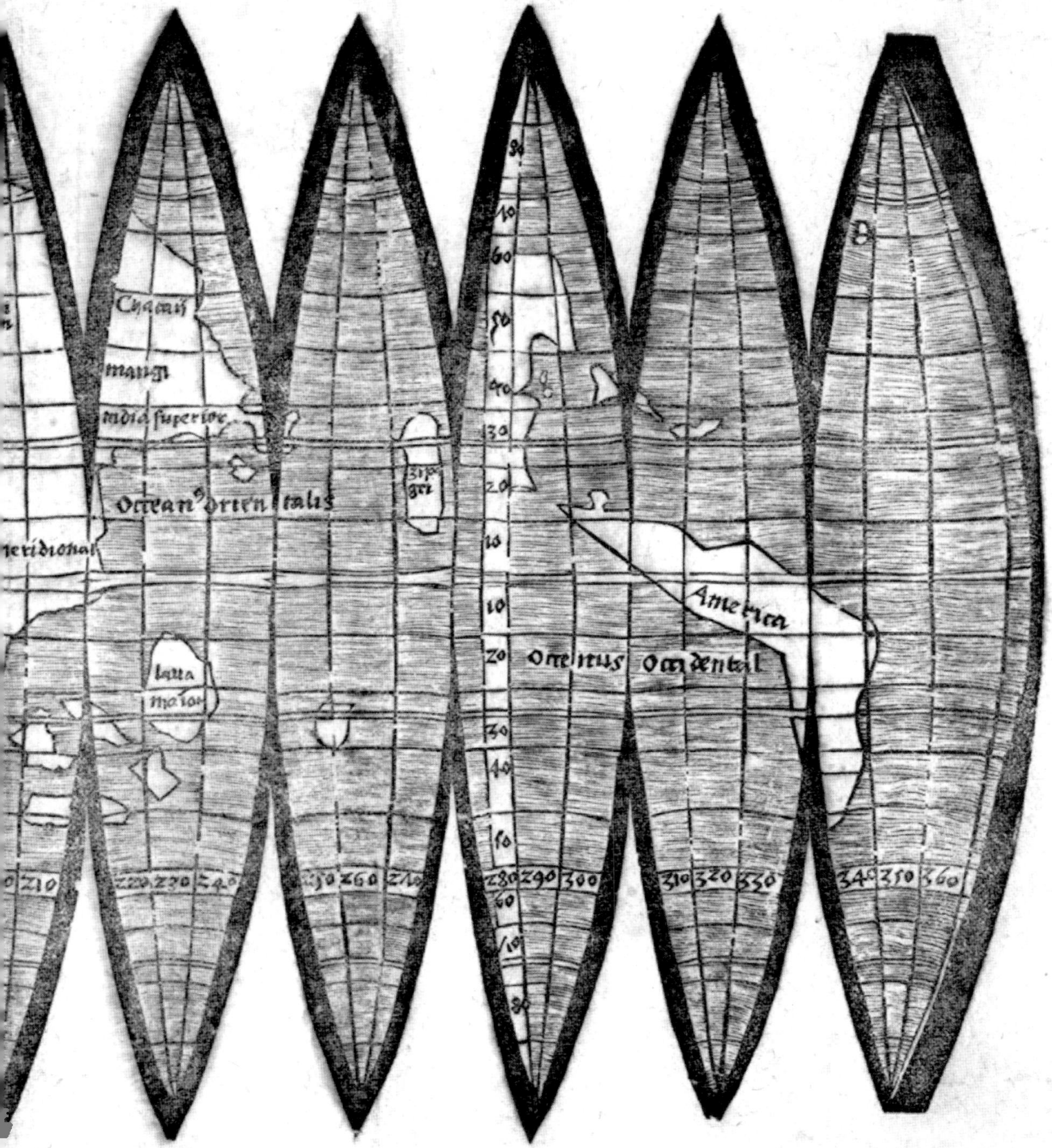

Martin Waldseemüller gore map from *Cosmographiae Introductio*, 1507 / the segments or "gores" could be cut and assembled around a sphere to make a globe, the first such printed map in European history / image courtesy of James Ford Bell Library, University of Minnesota.

Christendom and Islam — were also changing. Since ancient times, trade between East Asian and Western Europe had traveled over the fabled Silk Road through Central Asia to Mediterranean shipping routes. As the 15th Century progressed, however, the increasing separation between the Christian West and Muslim East brought the decline of the land-based trade system. Western Europeans, especially the Portuguese, began to seek alternative routes, sidestepping the Silk Road and forging new sea routes through the Atlantic.

The land-based system had not required scientifically accurate maps. Following paths laid down by countless generations before them, traders had simply traveled from landmark to landmark, resting point to resting point. These trade routes involved so many steps and middlemen that no one trader needed to know the entire way. But when Portuguese sailors began to inch around Africa toward India and the Spice Islands, accurate navigation maps became essential. The Portuguese, largely in secret, began to develop new technologies to make them.[7]

Several writers have speculated that parts of the Waldseemüller maps, especially details of the supposedly unknown west coasts of North and South America, suggest he had access to information gained on secret Portuguese voyages into the Pacific.[8] He may have had more data about the early exploration of the Americas than we do. The Waldseemüller maps also offer a compelling indication that the Gymnase had weighed the evidence and thoroughly rejected the claims of Columbus, whose accounts of his first voyage had been widely published, but with vague and colorless descriptions. Vespucci had reached the New World after Columbus, but his conclusions about the nature of the world were correct. As Columbus biographer John Noble Wilford has pointed out, "Vespucci... discovered what it was that Columbus had found" and the Saint-Dié group recognized this in itself as a surpassing achievement.[9]

Within a year of its publication, copies of the *Cosmographiae Introductio* had circulated throughout Europe and had begun to establish, once and for all, that what lay beyond the Ocean Sea was, in fact, a different world from either Europe or Asia. As the European conquest of the New World continued through the 16th Century, Columbus partisans — realizing that the discovery of the New World was a far more important accomplishment than sailing west to reach Asia — objected to Vespucci's cartographic honors and disputed the claims of discovery made in Vespucci's name.[10]

Without clear explanation, Vespucci's name completely disappeared from all maps in the 1513 Gymnase Vosgien edition of the *Ptolemy Geography*. The word America was removed from its place in South America and, instead, the publisher included a note that translates roughly as "this dry land with the nearby islands were initially discovered by Columbus under the commission of the King of Castille." Conventional wisdom has long held that between 1507 and 1513, Waldseemüller simply realized that Columbus, not Vespucci, deserved the credit for discovering America and corrected his maps accordingly. Yet, if establishing

7. See Leo Bagrow, *History of Cartography*, revised and enlarged by R. A. Skelton. Cambridge: Harvard University Press, 1964, p. 105.

8. See Peter Whitfield, *Mapping the World: A History of Exploration*. London: The Folio Society, 2000, p. 90.

9. "A Name for the New World," in John Noble Wilford, *The Mysterious History of Columbus: An Exploration of the Man, the Myth, the Legacy*. New York: Alfred A. Knopf, 1991, p. 214.

10. Notably, the most vigorous objections to the name "America" came after Waldseemüller's own death. The celebrated "Apostle of the Indies," Spanish missionary and historian Bartolomé de Las Casas went so far as to call the name "America" an "offense against God," because, he said, "God had Himself chosen Columbus to discover the New World." His argument was based on fabricated accounts of Vespucci's voyages.

priority were his only motive, the changes to his maps seem oddly perfunctory. The publisher of the 1513 maps rather pointedly did not rename "America" as "Columbiana". Nor is Columbus conspicuously glorified, in inscriptions and elaborate allegorical portraits, as was Vespucci in 1507.

There is a geopolitical reason for the change, however, which conventional wisdom has apparently missed. By 1513, Vespucci, Ringmann and René II were all dead. René's successor did not continue the old duke's patronage. Canon Lud's successor, his nephew Nicholas, had left Saint-Dié and the printing press established in his house had apparently ceased operation. The *Cosmographiae introductio* was rather grandly dedicated to the Holy Roman Emperor Maximilian I, who at this point was deeply preoccupied with glorifying, especially in print, his productive reign and his richly endowed progeny.[11] His young grandson was heir apparent not just to the Low Countries but, through his maternal grandparents, also to the kingdoms of Aragon and Castille. With this Spanish legacy came Castille's vast claims in the New World.

Vespucci posed a bit of a problem for Maximilian: he had made his crucial 1501 voyage under the authority of the Portuguese crown, Spain's leading competitor in the New World. Waldseemüller had also made use of—and acknowledged—the work of Portuguese navigators and explorers. It would have been diplomatic, to say the least, for Waldseemüller or his publisher to omit so conspicuous a reference to this Portuguese-sponsored voyage to South America and replace it with the territorial claims of the Spanish crown, made via Columbus.

On the other hand, despite his efforts and those of his followers, Columbus' name was by no means free of controversy in the Spanish court. Spain had been embroiled in a longstanding lawsuit with Columbus' heirs over their claims against Spain's holdings in the New World, which would have given Columbus' family a significant share of all the land and wealth claimed by the Spanish crown. Substituting "Columbiana" for "America" would not have been wise, either.

In the end, Vespucci's name was the one that stuck. By 1522, when Waldseemüller was probably dead, "America" reappeared on European maps of the New World.[12] Maximilian's Spanish grandson had succeeded to the throne and was otherwise engaged with his conflicts with France and Martin Luther. The naming of the New World was no longer a pressing issue with the authorities, and so the cartographers could have their way.

In 1538, Gerardus Mercator, another great figure in the history of cartography, published a world map that named both continents of the New World "America." Before the end of the 16th Century, America was the established name for the entire Western Hemisphere. In thousands of 17th- and 18th-Century works of art, "America"—an Indian maiden crowned with feathers—joined her sisters "Europa," "Africa" and "Asia"—as one of the four quarters of the globe.

11. Gerhard Benecke, *Maximilian I (1459–1519): An Analytical Biography*. London; Boston: Routledge & Kegan Paul, 1982, p. 16 ff.

12. Marion Caming, *The Martin Waldseemüller 1507 Hauslab-Liechtenstein Globular Map of the World*. New York: Parke-Bernet Galleries, 1950, p. 18.

CONTESTED TERRAIN

IN MAY 2002, A MAP APPEARED ON THE WEBSITE OF B'TSELEM, THE ISRAELI HUMAN RIGHTS GROUP, SHOWING THE PRECISE CONTOURS OF ISRAEL'S WEST BANK SETTLEMENTS AND PLANS FOR THEIR FUTURE EXPANSION. THE MAP WAS CREATED AS PART OF A B'TSELEM REPORT AND INTENDED AS THE CENTERPIECE OF *A CIVILIAN OCCUPATION: THE POLITICS OF ISRAELI ARCHITECTURE*, THE ISRAELI EXHIBITION AT THE WORLD CONGRESS OF ARCHITECTURE IN BERLIN THAT SUMMER. IN JULY 2002, THE ISRAEL ASSOCIATION OF UNITED ARCHITECTS (IAUA) CANCELLED THE EXHIBITION AND ORDERED ITS CATALOGUES DESTROYED. THE ENSUING CONTROVERSY PLACED THE MAP AT THE CENTER OF A GLOBAL DEBATE ON THE RELATIONSHIP BETWEEN ARCHITECTURE AND POLITICS. **STEPHEN ZACKS** DISCUSSES THE ORIGINS AND IMPACT OF THE MAP WITH ITS DESIGNER, ISRAELI ARCHITECT **EYAL WEIZMAN**.

Steven Zacks: How did you get involved in mapping the West Bank?

Eyal Weizman: I took a year off from studying at the Architectural Association in London in 1995. I was working in Tel Aviv, and volunteering for the Palestinian Ministry of Planning in Ramallah. At some point they realized they didn't have some of the maps needed for routine planning work and asked me to find aerial photographs and maps from public institutions in Israel. They were still using Jordanian maps from the 1960s. None of the information I got was inaccessible to the general public, but Israel was very reluctant to provide Palestinians with information about the territories that had been granted autonomy under the 1993 Oslo Accords. Since Israel continued to control the air space over the entire region, aerial images were almost impossible for the Palestinians to obtain.

Were those maps being used in the Oslo negotiations in 1993?

Abed Samih, then deputy head of the Palestinian Ministry of Planning, was part of the negotiations, but the Palestinians came to the Oslo negotiations with a very general notion of their territorial aims. At the end of the process they wanted to acquire everything in the West Bank and Gaza up to the line of June 1967, before the Israeli occupation (following the Six Day War). The Israelis had maps that included topography, the locations of settlements and roads, and up-to-date aerial images. The Palestinians had only basic maps with triangles showing roughly where the settlements were located, without any details of topography, land use, agriculture or road networks. If you look at the border of an Area A or B—areas designated for Palestinian autonomy in the 1995 Israeli-Palestinian Interim Agreement—it was determined by realities on the ground. There was intense negotiation about each segment of that line: should it be on this or that side of this house, junction or extension of the village? By having better access to the tools with which the negotiations took place, and by having military personnel participate in them, Israel could use the territorial complexities to its advantage. Military officers are very accustomed to reading maps and understanding the terrain in a very physical manner, whereas Palestinian negotiators at the time were much more attached to political ideas than to geographical realities.

A line is not an abstract thing: each small fluctuation determines the fate of a neighborhood, a village or a group of houses. Israeli negotiators were absolutely brilliant in that respect. A small bend in the road connecting cities in the southern West Bank (Bethlehem and Hebron) to the northern West Bank and Ramallah brings a section of the road into the municipality of Jerusalem. That barely noticeable detail allows Israel to control the road: Israeli police can set up a roadblock in a situation where everything else is controlled by Palestinians. There are many such minute manipulations of the drawings that have an enormous influence on how the territory functions.

Were you working with B'Tselem beforehand?

There were always connections between B'Tselem and the Palestinian Ministry of Planning. I made other connections with Palestinians at Michael Sorkin's 1999 *Next Jerusalem* conference at Bellagio in Italy.[1] At some point I was invited by B'Tselem's Yehezkel Lein to collaborate on a human rights report on the settlements.[2] People in Israel like anthropologist Jeff Halper and geographer Oren Yiftachel were already working on issues of space and territoriality.[3] Up to that point, the settlements had mainly been criticized by the Israeli left and human rights groups on the basis of Article 49 of the Fourth Geneva Convention (1949), which states that an occupying power cannot transfer its population into an area occupied by force; every settlement east of the Green Line (Israel's border in June 1967) is in breach of Article 49. We wanted to extend the discussion to provide a human rights perspective. So we needed to analyze the organization of the settlements as a regional network, and look at its effects on daily life. There's a different perspective when you move from a political critique to a human rights one, and the shift required a new tool.

<www.btselem.org>

What maps were being used at the time?

On the wall of every left-leaning Israeli political organization or NGO was the 2000 population map of the West Bank provided by Peace Now (p. 225), showing settlement populations in colored circles. Peace Now is a political organization; its aim was to emphasize the number of settlers. As a human rights organization, B'Tselem wanted to go a step further. By drawing the map, we could work backwards from the form to answer some questions: why the space is organized the way it is, how the work of architects and planners causes the material damage that is apparent. The essence of the B'Tselem report was to show that the responsibility doesn't stop at the level of government policy and military action. Violations of international law and human rights were being performed on the drawing boards of planners and architects, and you can read them in the way that the outlines of settlements had been drawn.

<www.peacenow.org>

A settlement that is designed to disrupt the pathway between two Palestinian villages, isolate them, limit their growth and supervise them from above, inflicts material damage. This is consistent with the Israeli policy that the Palestinians refer to as "silent transfer".

Architecture can no longer be regulated by an order of architectural critique that is merely cultural and takes place in magazines and schools of architecture. Architects participate in the larger geo-political game with politicians and military personnel, and should be made to abide by the same international humanitarian laws and subjected to the same critical framework.

Can you talk about the map-making itself—what sort of research did you undertake and how did you compile the information?

Initially, we had to construct a file of the settlement master plans. This was during 2002, one of the most violent years of the Intifada, so it was quite difficult. We were traveling between settlements and either going to the Palestinian/Israeli regional planning office or the councils of the settlements themselves, to build an archive.

Then we compared this data with aerial images we took while flying in a private chartered plane over the West Bank, photographing as much as we could. It became impossible to fly for a while: there was a kind of temporary ban during Israel's "Operation Defensive Shield". We couldn't complete the whole aerial survey, but had to

1. Michael Sorkin, ed. *The Next Jerusalem: Sharing the Divided City*. New York: Monacelli, 2002.

2. Yehezkel Lein and Eyal Weizman, *Land Grab: Israel's Settlement Policy in the West Bank*, B'Tselem, The Israeli Information Center for Human Rights in the Occupied Territories, May 2002. <www.btselem.org/english/publications/summaries/200205_land_grab.asp>

3. Jeff Halper, "The 94 Percent Solution," *Middle East Report*, Fall 2000; Oren Yiftachel, "Settlements as Reflex Action," *Ha'aretz*, July 23, 2001.

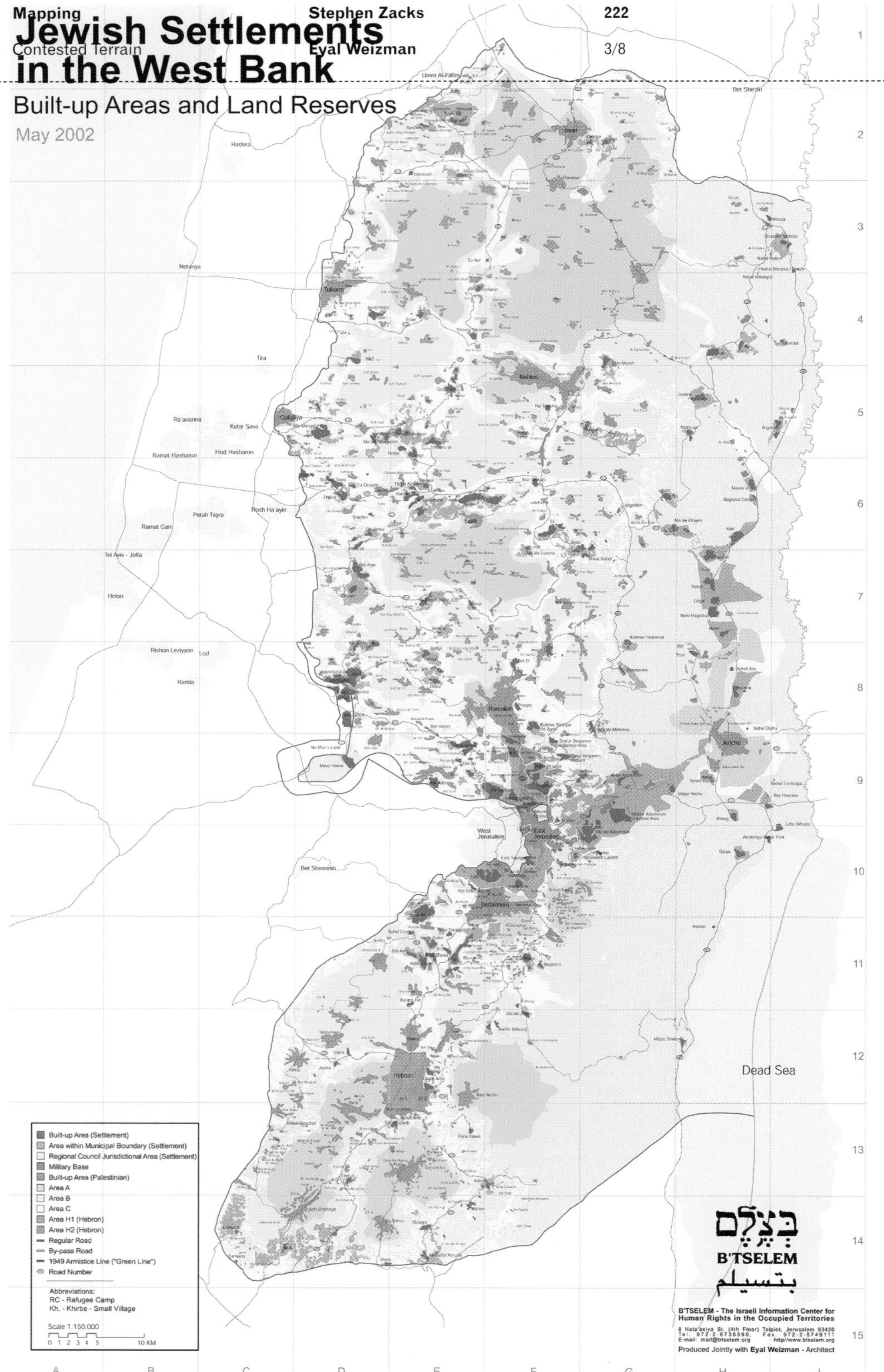

B'Tselem *Jewish Settlements in the West Bank*, May 2002 / the first map to document in detail existing Israeli settlements in the West Bank and the areas reserved for their future expansion / © B'Tselem, The Israeli Information Center for Human Rights in the Occupied Territories.

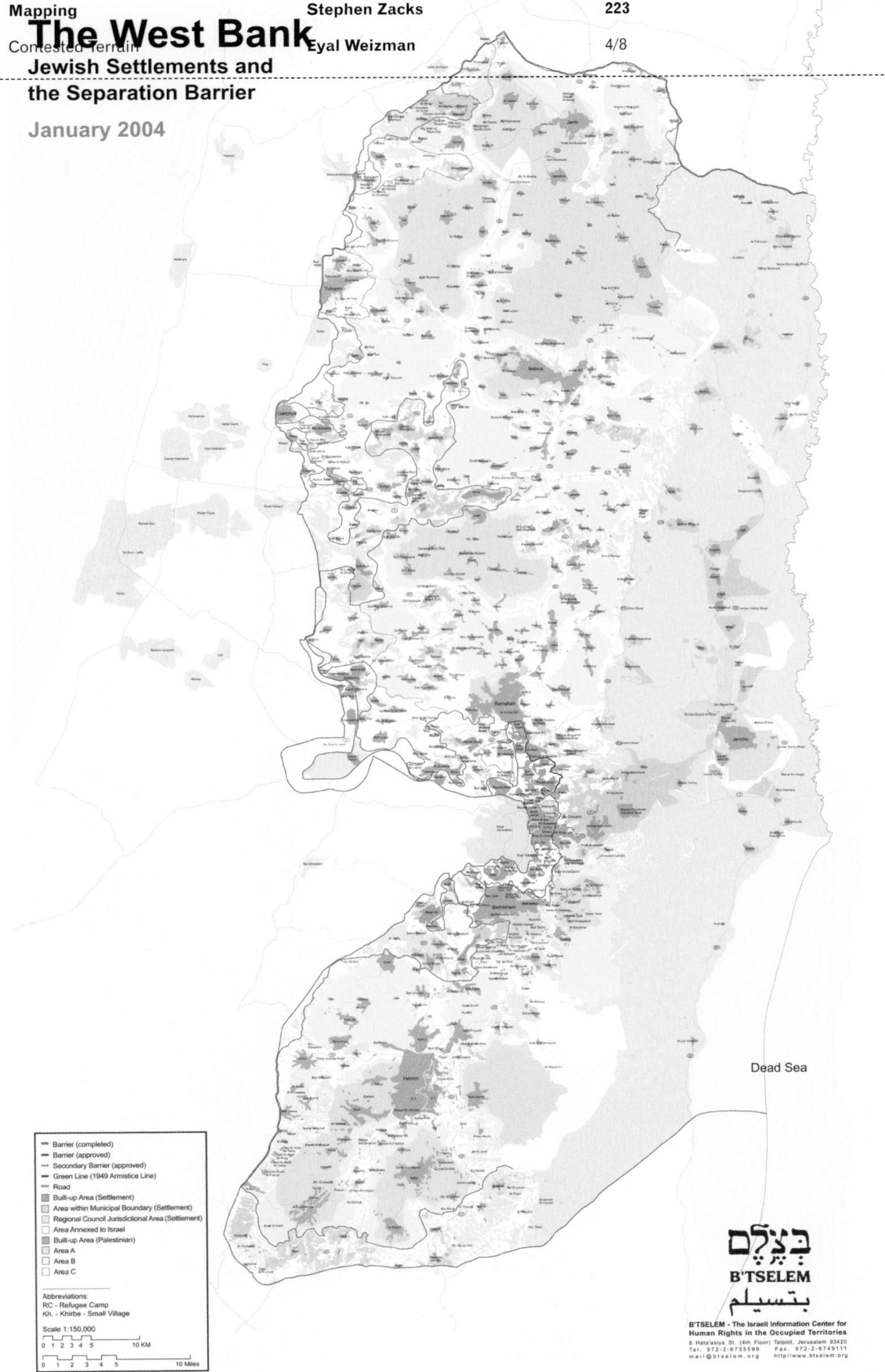

B'Tselem *The West Bank Jewish Settlements and the Separation Barrier*, January 2004 / showing the stages in the construction of the wall through the West Bank / © B'Tselem, The Israeli Information Center for Human Rights in the Occupied Territories.

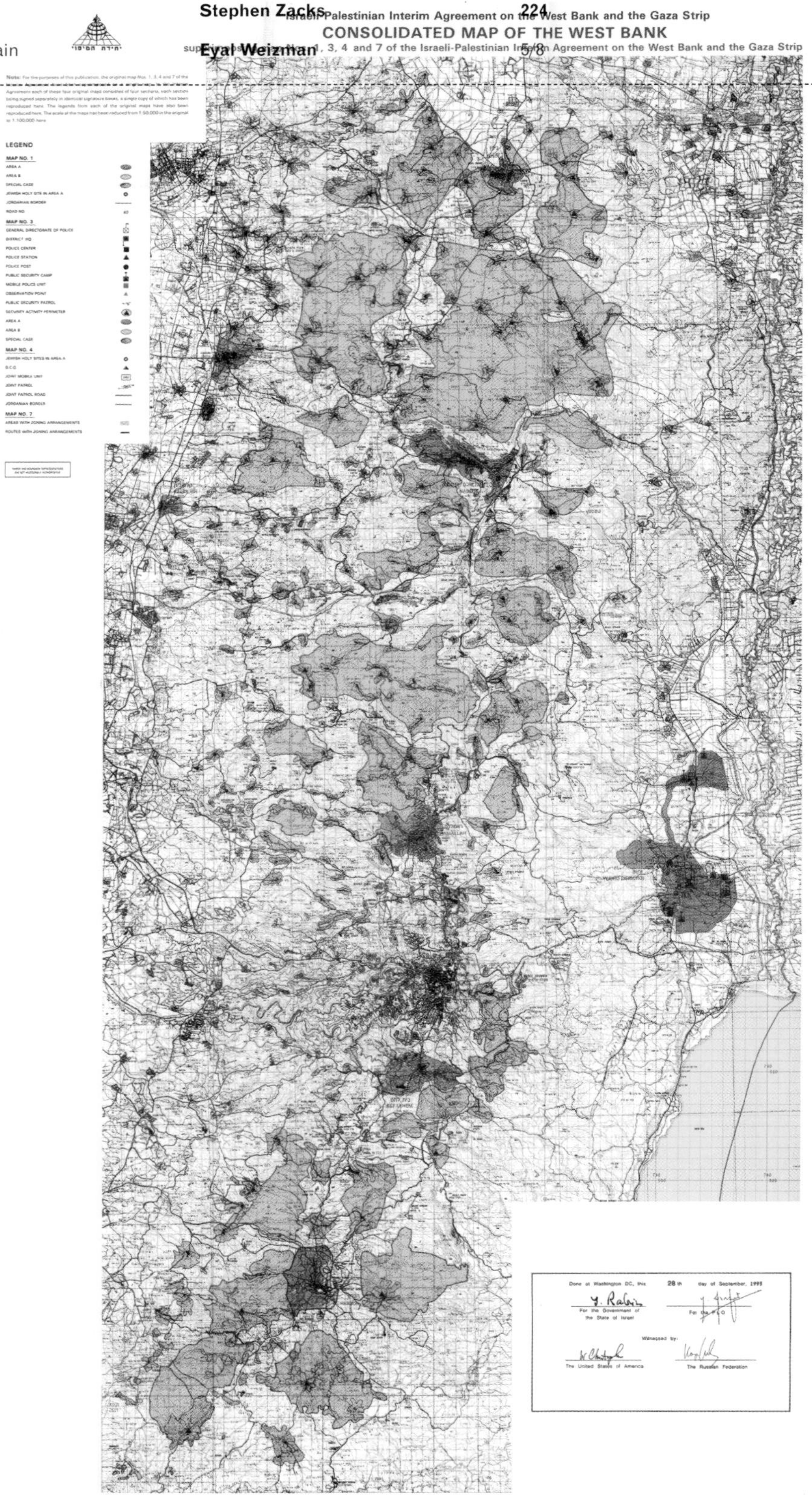

יחידת המיפוי

Israeli-Palestinian Interim Agreement on the West Bank and the Gaza Strip

CONSOLIDATED MAP OF THE WEST BANK

sup[illegible] 1, 3, 4 and 7 of the Israeli-Palestinian In[illegible]n Agreement on the West Bank and the Gaza Strip

Note: For the purposes of this publication, the original map Nos. 1, 3, 4 and 7 of the [illegible] Agreement each of these four original maps consisted of four sections, each section being signed separately in identical signature boxes, a single copy of which has been reproduced here. The legends from each of the original maps have also been reproduced here. The scale of the maps has been reduced from 1:50,000 in the original to 1:100,000 here.

LEGEND

MAP NO. 1

AREA A

AREA B

SPECIAL CASE

JEWISH HOLY SITE IN AREA A

JORDANIAN BORDER

ROAD NO — 40

MAP NO. 3

GENERAL DIRECTORATE OF POLICE

DISTRICT HQ

POLICE CENTER

POLICE STATION

POLICE POST

PUBLIC SECURITY CAMP

MOBILE POLICE UNIT

OBSERVATION POINT

PUBLIC SECURITY PATROL

SECURITY ACTIVITY PERIMETER

AREA A

AREA B

SPECIAL CASE

MAP NO. 4

JEWISH HOLY SITES IN AREA A

D.C.O.

JOINT MOBILE UNIT

JOINT PATROL

JOINT PATROL ROAD

JORDANIAN BORDER

MAP NO. 7

AREAS WITH ZONING ARRANGEMENTS

ROUTES WITH ZONING ARRANGEMENTS

Done at Washington DC, this 28th day of September, 1995

For the Government of the State of Israel

For the PLO

Witnessed by:

The United States of America

The Russian Federation

Israeli Ministry of Foreign Affairs *Consolidated Map of the West Bank* from *The Israeli-Palestinian Interim Agreement on the West Bank and Gaza Strip*, 1995 / the official map of the territory, indicating areas designated for Palestinian autonomy.

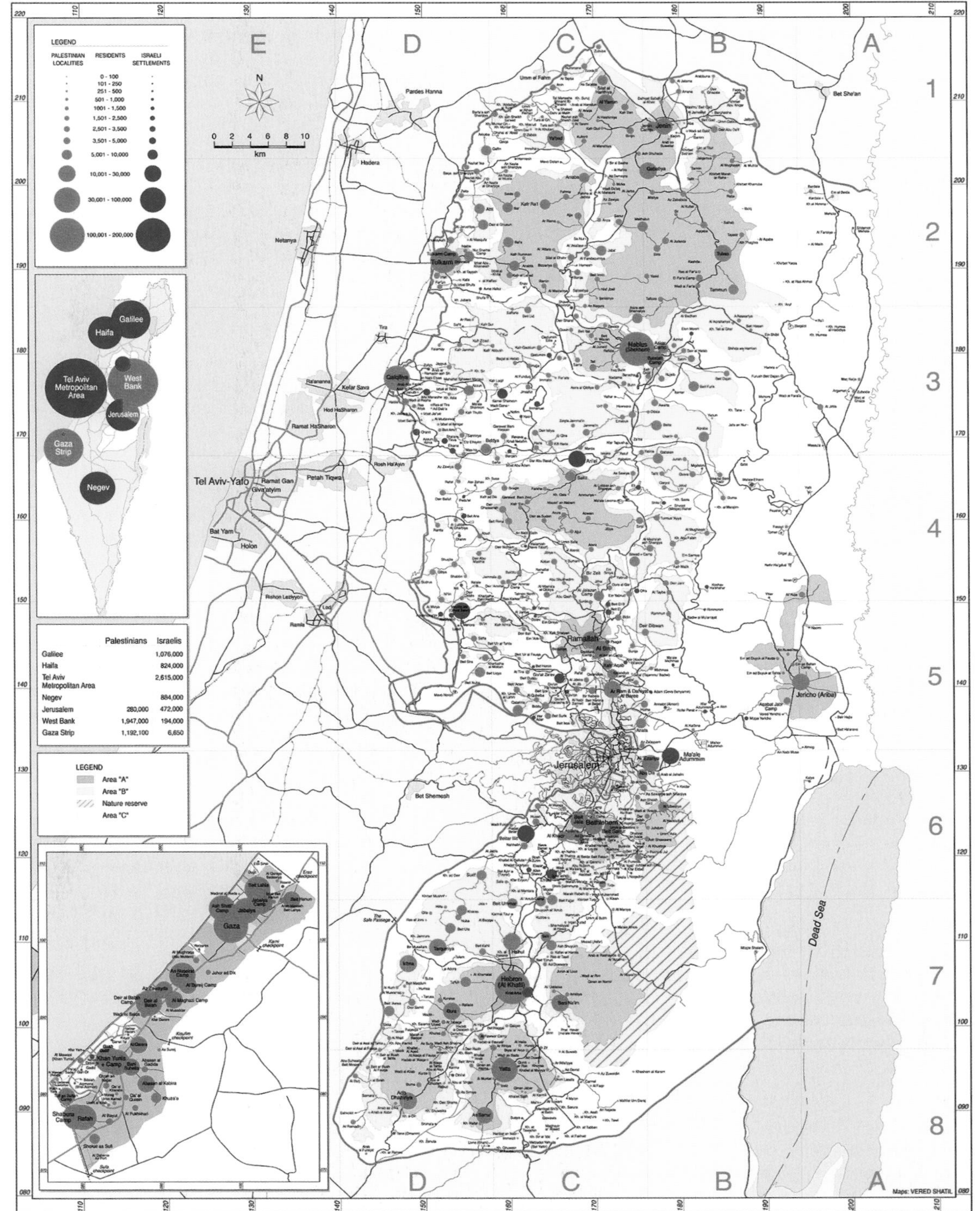

Peace Now *Population Map of the West Bank and Gaza Strip* November 2000 / emphasizing the number of settlers in the West Bank and Gaza / © Peace Now Settlements Watch Team.

rely on Dror Etkes' work at Peace Now and on satellite images from the CIA office in Jerusalem. All this information was cross-referenced from the ground, because we didn't want to rely on any one source. The master plans were then superimposed on a topographical map. To understand the formal logic of each settlement, we had to draw each one in far more detail than it actually appears on the map—these drawings later became the basis for *A Civilian Occupation*.[4]

Finally, in order to draw the blue sections we had to distinguish between built fabric and the planned areas. Do you draw the line of the "built area" around the road, around gardens, or limit it to the furthest house? We also analyzed how the settlements are integrated into the topography. The roads are always stretched out along topographical lines and close in on themselves—that's how infrastructure like sewage systems has to be laid, in rings all at the same height, draining down. The topography of the mountain becomes the form of the settlement.[5]

What choices did you make in terms of the character of the map, its color palette, how this information is represented graphically?

We created an AutoCAD file, laid out the information as raw data, then worked with a research assistant and a graphic designer—neither of whom wants to be identified because they both work in the Israeli public sector—looking at different grades and shades of color. The color saturation would make some facts seem more substantial than others. How much blue we put in the planned area around the built fabric would make it appear more or less substantial. We realized that there is a spectrum of color that communicates. The map looked very different when it had different colors. The built area—dark blue—was the constant. If we had blended the lighter blue, which stands for the planned area, it would have looked much less conspicuous, and we wanted to bring it to the fore, to communicate the possible future—what is called the "natural growth" of the settlements. When Ariel Sharon says "This is just natural growth," the term is often misunderstood to mean simply putting another floor on an existing structure, but actually it refers to low-density solidification of the form of the settlement, which further bisects the surrounding area as the settlement grows.

So the map depicts both the actual and possible future outlines of the settlements?

Almost every settlement in the West Bank began as an outpost, then solidified into a settlement, which grew into another settlement, then into a bloc, which became contiguous with Israeli neighborhoods or territories on the other side of the line. We were analyzing that possible future scenario and graphically bringing it to the fore. Much of what we were drawing was planned areas that don't exist yet as settlements—if you go on the ground there's probably still a shepherd or an olive orchard there. But there is a line drawn by an architect or planning bureaucrat at the civil administration of the Israeli military, which determines that the settlements, left to their own devices, will grow into that form. By emphasizing that possible future, we were trying to make it urgent.

The colors for Area A and Area B resemble the Interim Agreement map. Was it available?

Yes, from various sources. But in the Palestinian areas there were villages that were not marked. Traditional Palestinian geography is based on the extended family living outside cities and villages in clusters of between four and twenty houses. If you put a name on it, it is recognized; if not, it remains unrecognized. There are at least twenty unrecognized Palestinian villages in Israel, which means that Israel does not acknowledge the land rights in them or include them in plans for schools or electricity supply. People living there are mainly refugees who have not left the country; they're called "present absentees". We made an effort to work with Palestinians and name things that were not previously named.

Did you have an idea of how the map would be received or what audiences it would attract?

Initially it was a tool enabling us to write a report, *Land Grab: Israel's Settlement Policy in the West Bank*,[6] which analyzes how the planning of settlements is tied to human rights violations; Chapter 8 analyzes the West Bank using the map. Subsequently, the map has become a tool available for anybody else. When we put it on the web, we saved the PDF in a way that allows it to be used and expanded upon by other organizations. Many people have since begun to post their

4. Rafi Segal and Eyal Weizman, *A Civilian Occupation: The Politics of Israeli Architecture*. New York: Verso, 2003.

5. Eyal Weizman, *The Politics of Verticality*. <www.opendemocracy.net/conflict-politicsverticality/debate.jsp> April–May 2002.

6. Lein and Weizman, *op. cit.*

maps in a similar way, and mapping has increasingly become a real, functioning "open source" practice.

Various Palestinian organizations have used it, and the map and the report were both used as evidence in the 2004 case against the Wall heard by the International Court of Justice at the Hague. The real surprise was that the American administration started to use it. If Condoleezza Rice uses the map as a basis for negotiations, it undoubtedly has an influence—albeit only in a small way—on the politics conducted around it.

The Israel Association of United Architects recently changed its position on *A Civilian Occupation*. How did this come about?

Though banned in Berlin in 2002,[7] the exhibition traveled to several U.S. and European cities before returning to Israel and Palestine in 2004. The IAUA decided to react to the continuing debate around *A Civilian Occupation* by dedicating its 2005 annual conference to the relation between architecture and politics. The participants of the banned exhibition were invited to debate with the association's members, along with Shimon Peres, education minister Shimon Shitreet, and Yossi Beilin, initiator of the Oslo negotiations. I refused to take part, but other participants did so and there was a somewhat heated debate. At the end, IAUA deputy chair Itzhak Lir publicly retracted the banning, apologized for it, and accepted the project's validity. He said it was a very traumatic thing for him and the association, and basically aligned himself with the project. I find his retraction candid and honest. Unfortunately, some other IAUA members apparently wanted to use the conference to get the issue out the way and return to the insular architectural discourse that prevailed in Israel before the exhibition.

What other effects has the map, and the controversy around it, had on architectural discourse in Israel?

After *A Civilian Occupation* was banned, and after Zvi Efrat—who curated the *Borderline Disorder*[8] exhibition at the *2002 Venice Biennale*—became head of the architecture school at the Bezalel Academy of Art and Design in Jerusalem, the political dimension of architecture and planning came very much to the fore in Israel. I was very pleased to see that more young architects and students began dealing critically with the relationship of the built environment to the conflict. Some have even worked with Palestinian groups in Israel or in the West Bank. In just a few years, this younger generation has created numerous projects, exhibitions, publications and maps. One of my former students, Malkit Shoshan, has worked with unrecognized Palestinian villages in Galilee, and organized an international urban design competition for Ein Hud, a Palestinian village near Haifa that had never been drawn on maps.

Can you address some of the negative critiques of the work?

One architectural theorist wrote in the newspaper *Ha'aretz* that the research should be based on a "universal position" that "does not adhere to a single political perspective"—saying, effectively, that one should not support the occupation but take a resigned attitude toward it and not get personally involved. Other critics argued that maps are tools of domination, and that we are only registering the geography of power, though this power can be subverted. One argued that we had adopted a vertical perspective ourselves by flying above the settlements and drawing the reality from the top down; others said we had put too much emphasis on formal arrangements. They are right in some respects, but I don't think our approach excludes drawing and describing things from the ground. I just hope our research complements other approaches. It cannot and does not try to offer the tools for all critiques.

One of the most fascinating things about being in the territories for me was passing back and forth across the boundaries, particularly through the checkpoints.

These are experiences that are not drawn into the map. There are many ways of subverting the existing geography of power. You draw a road, which is where the settlers drive. But when that road is blocked, the surface of the terrain either side of it becomes a means of passage. Since 2000, many Palestinians simply drive through the landscape rather than on the roads, to avoid the road blocks. A map is not absolute: the power it represents can never be perfect. It can be constantly subverted and challenged.

7. The banning of the exhibition was widely reported. See, for example, Esther Zandberg, "Political brochure leads architects' union to cancel exhibit," *Ha'aretz*, July 10, 2002; Alan Riding, "Are Politics Built into Architecture?" *New York Times*, August 10, 2002; Esther Addley, "Lines in the Sand" *The Guardian*, July 25, 2002; Inge Günther, "Kontrollierte Bauoffensive," *Frankfurter Rundschau*, July 30, 2002; Marie-Christine Aulas, "Architecture israélienne: un réquisitoire serein," *L'Architecture*.

8. Zvi Efrat, curator, *Borderline Disorder*. Catalogue of the The Israeli Pavilion, 8th International Architecture Exhibition, *La Biennale di Venezia*, 2002.

WORLD IN MOTION

Few things spark the passion of more people in the world than football.[1] It is a common denominator, providing a means of social connection surpassed by no language, religion or ideology. When Brazil met Germany for the final match of the 2002 FIFA (Fédération Internationale de Football Association) World Cup in Japan, over two billion people stopped whatever they were doing to share the moment, constituting the largest audience for any event in history.

How and why did football spread like a religion, with zealots all over the world willing to live and even die for it? Many writers have tried to understand its power, from Albert Camus ("All I know most surely about morality and obligations, I owe to football") to Jean Baudrillard ("Power is only too happy to make football bear a diabolical responsibility for stupefying the masses.")[2] The subject of sports is well established as a territory of cultural studies, but football demands unique attention.[3] What makes football capable of triggering riots, suicides, and even wars? More nations belong to FIFA than to the United Nations;[4] football is an important part of daily life in much of the world; for many countries, it is an integral part of their cultural identity.[5] Mapping football's dissemination — identifying its delivery, missionaries, its earliest converts, and the variety of meanings it holds for its diverse followers — might help us understand its scope and power.

Ball-kicking sports have been identified in many ancient cultures — *tsu chu* in 3rd-Century B.C. China; *il calcio* in 16th-Century Italy; *tlatchi* in Pre-Columbian North, Central and South America; *le soule* in early 19th-Century France — indicating the innate pleasure humans have found in this sporting (and ritualistic) activity. But the birth of the modern game — football as we know it today — occurred in England in 1863 when representatives from a dozen public schools established rules enabling them to play the game, then a mixture of football and rugby, against each other under less chaotic and violent circumstances.[6] That football emerged alongside the Industrial Revolution may explain how it became a paradigm of globalization.

Football was first proselytized by those diplomatic and military personnel who administered its colonies and protectorates from Scotland to Malta, Singapore to South Africa. So a map of football's earliest adopters corresponds with that of the British Empire. The next wave of countries to take up the sport were mostly those where the British had a strong presence or influence at the time of the sport's emergence.[7] In the 19th Century, Great Britain's technological advances facilitated its relations with other developing economies, which looked to the world's first industrial nation for innovations to fuel their own progress.

1. I prefer to refer to the sport as "football"—as it is known everywhere in the world—as opposed to "soccer" (a derivation of "association football") which is used only in the United States, Ireland (to avoid confusion with Gaelic football), and Australia (which has Aussie Rules Football).
2. Camus quoted in Ian Hamilton, ed., *The Faber Book of Soccer*. London: Faber and Faber, 1992. Jean Baudrillard, *In the Shadow of the Silent Majorities*. Cambridge, MA: The MIT Press, 1983. See also <philosophyfootball.com>
3. The refereed academic journal *Soccer and Society* is devoted to the study of "all aspects of soccer globally from anthropological, cultural, economic, historical, political and sociological perspectives." *Soccer and Society*. Oxfordshire, England: Frank Cass Publishers/Taylor & Francis Group.
4. FIFA, the football world's governing body, was founded in Paris in 1904 by representatives of France, Belgium, Denmark, the Netherlands, Spain, Sweden, and Switzerland. As of February 2005, the United Nations has 191 member countries. FIFA has 205 member countries. The discrepancy stems from FIFA's inclusion of Scotland, Wales, Northern Ireland, Guam, U.S. Virgin Islands, and other "territories"—recognized independently in footballing terms, if not in political terms.
5. See Simon Kruper, *Football Against the Enemy*. London: Orion Books, 1994.
6. Sports in pre-modern times, like the ball-kicking predecessors of football, were mostly "mob" games, often associated with seasonal or religious rites. Industrialization imposed order on both time and space — and inevitably, sports. Bill Murray, *The World's Game: A History of Soccer*. Urbana and Chicago: University of Illinois Press, 1996, pp. 1–7.
7. Willy Meisl, *Soccer Revolution: Great Britain taught the world how to play and enjoy Association football — later to be taught many a hard lesson by former pupils*. London: The Sportsmans Book Club, 1956, pp. 53–64.

The first and certainly most comprehensive example of globalization is not Coke or McDonald's, but soccer — known in most parts of the world as football. Cathy Lang Ho maps the international dissemination of the beautiful game, and shows how the spread of this sport parallels global industrial development.

Employees of British Gasworks brought the game to Prague, Vienna and Graz in 1894. Around the same time, British mining engineers introduced the game to Spain's Basque country, while British military delivered the sport to Valencia and Madrid. British cotton mill owners brought football to an industrial town just outside Moscow in 1894, while British sailors began playing it in Odessa. Oil businessmen began playing football in Romania in 1878. A Scottish engineer working in Shanghai organized the first Asian international, held in Manila in 1916. Italy and Belgium, strong trading partners of Britain, were also early football enthusiasts. Some of the oldest clubs in the world have roots in urban capitals and old industrial towns (Liverpool, Turin, Dresden, São Paolo).[8]

Students also played a major role in spreading the gospel: English students in the late 1800s took football to France, Germany, Denmark, the former Yugoslavia, Uruguay and Switzerland. In return, Portuguese and Dutch students at English boarding schools and universities brought the game back to their home countries. In many places, the sport had more than one evangelist.[9] There are accounts of British sailors playing football on Brazilian shores around the time that Charles Miller, the acknowledged father of Brazilian football, returned from university in England with two footballs. Born in São Paolo to English parents, Miller arranged matches among the employees of English companies, including the English Gas Company, the London Bank and the São Paolo Railway. In the first organized game on Brazilian soil, Gas beat Rail, 4 to 2.[10]

Around the turn of the century, other colonial-minded football-playing countries like France, Portugal, and Holland helped spread the game. With an empire rivaling that of the British, France was the greatest influence on African football, having enjoyed great success in the "Scramble for Africa" — the period between the 1870s and World War I in which the European powers essentially carved up the as-yet-untapped, resource-rich continent. Great Britain, Germany, Italy, Portugal and Belgium all got a piece. Football's emergence happened to coincide with the period during which European nations were busy annexing the continent that made up one-fifth of the world's land area.[11]

Football's global acceptance corresponds, roughly, with the course of industrial development around the world. (One wonders what Brazil's primary national characteristic would be today if not for its interest in British rail technology and the U.K.'s interest in Brazil's natural resources, like oil and rubber.) The countries that played football in the late 1800s and early 1900s (indicated in red on Sulki Choi's map, *Football Diaspora*, pp. 234–235) were, by and large, so-called First World countries — most of England's European neighbors and the early developing nations of the Americas and Asia.

8. *ibid*, pp. 53–86. See also Murray, pp. 1–41.

9. *ibid*.

10. *ibid*., pp. 65–72. See also Alex Bellos, *Futebol: Soccer, the Brazilian Way*. New York: Bloomsbury, 2002.

11. Thomas Pakenham, *Scramble for Africa: White Man's Conquest of the Dark Continent from 1876 to 1912*. New York: Morrow/Avon, 1992.

If football is an index of a nation's economic and cultural development, then what can be inferred from its delayed adoption in many countries? A society's development or modernization depends on an advanced economic and political system, social stability, available resources and a forward- and outward-looking cultural attitude. Among the developed countries that only adopted the sport after the 1920s (indicated in yellow) were many torn by political strife. For much of the early 20th Century, Greece was engaged in a civil war, so football didn't take off there until the 1920s (it joined FIFA in 1927), and the Greek national league was not fully professionalized until the 1970s. Poland's boundaries were in flux from the 1870s until its establishment as an independent state in 1921, whereupon its national football league was formed almost immediately. Though most African countries were introduced to football earlier in the 20th Century, most did not form national leagues or join FIFA until the 1950s and 1960s, coinciding with the wave of independence movements across the continent.[12]

Each nation's football facts—the date its national league was formed or the date it joined FIFA and, to a certain degree, its standing in FIFA's international ranking—are intertwined with political and economic histories. Estonia, Lithuania, and Latvia all formed leagues in the 1920s, but they ceased to exist as nations—hence to participate in international play—having been subsumed by the U.S.S.R. in 1940. They re-emerged on the world football scene, along with 12 new republics, after the Soviet Union's dissolution in 1991. Israel is another interesting case: its national league and FIFA membership predate the Mandate era by 20 years, having been established in Palestine, whose early football success (it was the only Asian country to participate in the World Cup competition in 1934) was suppressed after Israel's founding in 1948. Then, because the Arab nations refused to play against Israel in the region's Asian Football Confederation (AFC) in the 1970s, Israel played for some years as part of Oceania and later Europe, before being officially accepted into the Union European Football Association (UEFA), in 1994. In football terms, clearly, the world's borders can be bent.[13]

12. See the official FIFA website, <fifa.com> for the year each country became a member. In the majority of cases, the founding of a national association or league predates a country's membership in FIFA by only one or two years.

13. In Tel Aviv and Haifa, European immigrants were playing football as early as 1912. The Eretz Israel-Palestine Football Association was accepted into FIFA in 1929. Palestinian football developed mostly in exile after the founding of Israel in 1948. The Palestinian FA was established in 1994 and restored its FIFA membership in 1998. See <palestinefa.com/>.

Football's later converts (indicated in blue and green) are also those to which the glories of tourism, Coca-Cola, McDonald's and television came belatedly: the world's more remote or less industrialized countries. (These also tend to be the same countries at the bottom of the FIFA world rankings.) By the middle of the 20th Century, the world's remaining football philistines were learning about the game through mass media, such as newswire and newsreel reports, most notably through the Olympics (football was an Olympic sport from the second Games, held in Paris in 1900) and the FIFA World Cup, inaugurated by 13 teams in Uruguay in 1930. These competitions played a significant role in cementing the notion of a single world order, already propounded by the two World Wars and the formation of the United Nations in 1945 (41 years after FIFA's founding).

Territory maps

World in Motion 7–8/10 pp. 234–235

The one country that remains an anomaly in the (men's) football universe is the United States. Football began in the U.S. as early as the 1880s and a national league was started in 1904. But, resistant to the influences of its former colonizer — and of any other country, for that matter — the U.S. preferred to develop its own sports, like baseball, basketball and American football. With a sense of independence verging on arrogance, and separatism that approached xenophobia (football — known as soccer in the U.S. — was disdained early on as something played by foreigners), the U.S. failed to foster the sport not only at home but in its territories as well. It's no coincidence that four of the 12 bottom-ranked football nations in the world — Puerto Rico, American Samoa, U.S. Virgin Islands, and Guam — are U.S. possessions.[14]

There is, inevitably, a predatory side to the process of globalization: early on, competitive countries tapped into resources abroad that they lacked at home — cultivating not just cash crops and raw materials but sporting talent to maintain their economic and cultural edge. Global talent-shopping has become a key component of success: the leading players of the current French national team have origins in Algeria (Zinédine Zidane), Ghana (Marcel Desailly), Senegal (Patrick Viera), French Antilles (Lilian Thuram) and New Caledonia (Christian Karembeu). Portugal owes past football triumphs to Eusebio and Mario Coluna, originally of Mozambique, and to José Agnas from Angola. And the Netherlands might not rank sixth in world football were it not for the legacy of Ruud Gullit, Frank Rijkaard, Edgar Davids, Clarence Seedorf and Patrick Kluivert — all of Surinamese descent.

So why didn't more countries in the world reject football as a relic of oppressive colonialism? Some countries did initially resist football on ideological grounds. But the game grew to acquire a host of important social functions, for example, serving in many places as an effective social lubricant, leveler and glue. To be sure, football began in many places as an elite and alien activity — the domain of expatriates (and wealthy locals emulating them). But unlike other colonial sports, such as cricket or rugby which remained elitist for longer because of their high barriers to participation, including special equipment, clothing, playing grounds and code-enforcement, football was more accessible. Neither a ball nor a playing field were even necessary — any round object (an orange, a bundle of rags) and a patch of open space would do. Locals were charmed by the game's simplicity, and how susceptible it was to being made their own. In nearly every early football-playing country, there are accounts of the milestone "shocking upset victory" over an established powerhouse British club by a scrappy local side. Eventually, the balance of football power shifted, so that it was no longer the colonial or "white" sport but the game of the locals, the masses. In many former colonies and occupied territories, football came to signify social mobility, equity and integration. In African nations, for example, football imagery was used on political posters to convey anti-colonialism, and continues to be deployed as a symbol of black power.[15] Football gave (and still gives) immigrants a common language with which to relate to their new communities. The English may have

14. Murray, *op. cit.*, pp. 14–17. Women in the United States, by contrast, are a dominant presence on the world football stage. My theory of why American women have achieved so much success in the sport is precisely because it is so marginalized in the U.S. American women were able to claim football as their own in a way that would be less possible, or even ridiculous, for women in countries where men are obsessive about it. The U.S. national men's team is currently ranked eleventh in the world, and football is the most played sport in the U.S. among people under the age of 18, but it continues to be routinely ignored by mainstream media.

15. Peter Alegi, "'Feel the Pull in Your Soul': Local Agency and Global Trends in South Africa's 2006 World Cup Bid," *Soccer and Society*, 2:3, Autumn 2001, pp. 1–21.

brought football to Brazil, Argentina and other parts of Latin America, but Italian migrant workers contributed to the sport's development (which explains the similarity between the South American and Italian styles of play). Football could not have succeeded without the diaspora of the 20th Century.

In a similar vein, football has historically eased immigrant's cultural assimilation, giving them a common language with which to relate to their new communities. But sharing the same field, the same language, the same world, is a double-edged sword. Football in the 21st Century confronts the same issues that are at the core of the anti-globalization debate: fair trade and cultural preservation. The global trade of players has depleted many countries of their best football talent, weakening the leagues of poor or less developed countries, while strengthening those of rich nations. (The predominance of African nationals in France's first division became dramatically apparent when 57 star players left their club to play in the 2004 African Cup of Nations.) Many leagues, most recently those in Italy and Portugal, enforced limits on the number foreign players on each team, in a form of protectionism that ostensibly retains job opportunities for home-grown talent and preserves the game's national characteristics.[16] Economically-weak Brazil, meanwhile, exports more footballers than any other country: 5,000 Brazilians play professionally all over the world, from the Faroe Islands to Iceland to Qatar.

In this international arena — encompassing not just the free trade in players but also high-stakes international matches and the worldwide television market — players, teams and coaches find it necessary to adopt a more uniform playing style to maintain their competitive edge and market value. As a result, football is becoming increasingly homogenous, tending toward an efficient, technical approach. Countries can no longer succeed with their idiosyncratic, localized football styles. The Brazilian team of the 1960s and 1970s — fielding the unteachable, unsystematic magic of Garrincha and Pélé — would not be able to penetrate the perfected defense of today's English, French, Italian, Dutch or German teams. The loss of regional football identity is just one casualty of 21st-Century globalization.

In one regard, however, football will always remain immune to the world's continual shifts of economic and cultural power. In an attempt to understand the deep appeal of football, semiologist Umberto Eco concludes his essay "Sports Chatter" with the declaration "Sport is Man, Sport is Society."[17] He links sport — and football in particular — to the "deep area of the collective sensibility," an inexplicable, inexorable human desire to be a part of the social whole.[18] Football has served this purpose better than anything else in the modern era: everyone has football. The same can be said of few other things, not even of electricity or running water. Any footballer in the world would recognize an improvised football field with a goal: two piles of T-shirts, bags, or any objects on a patch of grass, dirt or asphalt. The signs and rituals of football are a *lingua franca*, understood by people of all ages and races throughout the world.

16. After Germany lost to Brazil in the 2004 World Cup final, patriotic pundits noted that the reason for Germany's failure is that the nation's own players are deprived of playing time because the Bundesliga is crowded with foreign players.

17. Umberto Eco, *Travels in Hyperreality*. New York: Harcourt 1986, p. 160.

18. For a close reading of Eco's writings on football, see Peter Pericles Trifonas, *Umberto Eco and Football*. Cambridge, England: Icon Books, 2001. Eco sees football as — more than a game — a complex system of cultural signs.

FIFA Men's World Ranking
as posted on www.fifa.com, Feb 13, 2005

1 Brazil
2 France
3 Argentina
4 Czech Republic
5 Spain
6 Netherlands
7 Mexico
8 England
9 Portugal
10 Italy
11 USA
12 Republic of Ireland
13 Sweden
14 Denmark
14 Turkey
16 Germany
17 Uruguay
18 Greece
19 Japan
20 Iran
21 Korea Republic
21 Nigeria
23 Cameroon
23 Croatia
25 Poland
26 Colombia
27 Costa Rica
28 Romania
29 Paraguay
30 Saudi Arabia
30 Senegal
32 Russia
33 Egypt
34 Morocco
35 Tunisia
36 Norway
37 Bulgaria
38 South Africa
39 Ecuador
40 Jordan
41 Côte d'Ivoire
42 Slovenia
43 Finland
44 Belgium
44 Iraq
46 Serbia and Montenegro
47 Jamaica
47 Uzbekistan
49 Israel
50 Bahrain
51 Mali
51 Switzerland
53 Slovakia
54 China PR
55 Kuwait
56 Oman
57 Ukraine
58 Australia
59 Honduras
60 Zimbabwe
61 Trinidad and Tobago
62 Libya
63 Hungary
63 Venezuela
65 Qatar
66 Latvia
67 Peru
68 Belarus
68 Guatemala
68 Wales
71 Zambia
72 Cuba
73 Angola
74 Algeria
75 Chile
75 Kenya
77 Ghana
78 Congo DR
79 Bosnia-Herzegovina
80 Estonia
80 Thailand
82 Austria
83 United Arab Emirates
84 Burkina Faso
85 Syria
86 Albania
86 Scotland
88 Guinea
89 Togo
90 Canada
91 Indonesia
92 Haiti
93 FYR Macedonia
94 Iceland
95 Bolivia
96 New Zealand
97 Korea DPR
98 Rwanda
99 Turkmenistan
100 Lithuania
101 Panama
102 Vietnam
103 Botswana
104 Singapore
104 Sudan
106 Georgia
107 Lebanon
108 El Salvador
109 Cyprus
109 Northern Ireland
109 Uganda
112 Gabon
112 Malawi
114 Malaysia
115 Azerbaijan
116 Moldova
117 St. Lucia
118 Congo
119 St. Kitts and Nevis
120 Armenia
121 Barbados
122 Benin
123 Yemen
124 Liberia
125 Tahiti
126 Mozambique
126 Palestine
128 Swaziland
129 Cape Verde Islands
130 Solomon Islands
131 Ethiopia
132 Faroe Islands
133 India
134 Hong Kong
135 Malta
135 Tajikistan
137 Fiji
138 St. Vincent & the Grenadines
139 Sri Lanka
140 Maldives
141 Andorra
141 Lesotho
143 Mauritius
144 Liechtenstein
145 Burundi
145 Vanuatu
147 Myanmar
148 Grenada
149 Kazakhstan
150 Madagascar
151 Surinam
152 Kyrgyzstan
153 Antigua and Barbuda
154 Gambia
155 Chinese Taipei
155 Luxembourg
157 Bermuda
158 Namibia
158 Nicaragua
160 Sierra Leone
161 Papua New Guinea
162 Laos
163 British Virgin Islands
163 Netherlands Antilles
165 San Marino
166 Dominica
167 Bangladesh
168 Chad
169 Eritrea
170 Dominican Republic
171 Equatorial Guinea
172 Tanzania
173 Niger
173 Seychelles
175 Mauritania
176 Cayman Islands
176 Nepal
176 Pakistan
179 Samoa
180 Central African Republic
181 Belize
182 Guyana
183 Tonga
184 Cambodia
185 Mongolia
186 New Caledonia
187 Philippines
188 Bhutan
189 Somalia
190 Macao
191 Cook Islands
191 Guinea-Bissau
193 Bahamas
194 Puerto Rico
195 São Tomé e Príncipe
196 US Virgin Islands
197 Anguilla
198 Aruba
199 Brunei Darussalam
200 Afghanistan
201 Djibouti
202 Montserrat
203 Turks and Caicos Islands
204 American Samoa
205 Guam

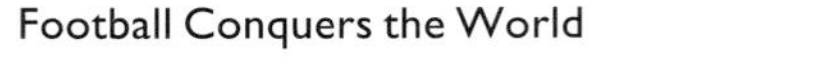
Football Conquers the World

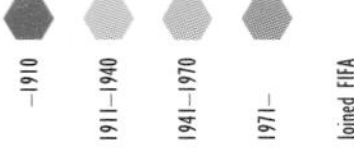

Sulki Choi *Football Diaspora*, 2005 / map tracking the global spread of the modern game since its conception in England in 1863. Countries are numbered according to their ranking in FIFA (Fédération Internationale de Football Association — see chart p. 233) as of February 2005. They are color-coded according to the year they joined FIFA, with red indicating the football organization's earliest members and green its most recent / map commissioned for *Else/Where: Mapping* © University of Minnesota Design Institute.

The Other Final

Football is an index of a country's readiness to join the globalized world — a point made clear in the delightful documentary *The Other Final.* Matthijs de Jongh and Johan Kramer, executives of Dutch advertising agency KesselsKramer, conceived the film while brooding over Holland's failure to qualify for the 2002 World Cup.[1] Consoling themselves that many other countries were more accustomed to losing than their own, they decided to stage a final between the world's two bottom-ranked teams, Bhutan and Montserrat, respectively ranked 203 and 204 at the time. The bottom ranking is a metaphor, in a sense, for both countries' lost (as opposed to loser) status — Bhutan deliberately so, as a part of a national strategy of controlled development and cultural preservation; and Montserrat, economically, having been devastated by a volcanic eruption in 1997 that left it impoverished, deserted and now largely dependent on aid from Britain, of which it has been a colony since 1632.

The two countries have little in common, besides both being tiny, scarcely known and football-loving. Bhutan is a hereditary monarchy in the Himalayas where most of its citizens wear the national dress, derived from Buddhist customs. On the opposite side of the world is Montserrat, an island in the Caribbean with a mostly Christian population, descendents of British and Irish colonists and of African slaves brought to work on sugar, coffee and other plantations. Football reportedly arrived in Bhutan in the 1950s, via traveling students (predating the arrival of paved roads, cars, aircrafts, telephones and television by several decades), while football's ambassadors to Montserrat were its British occupiers.

The Other Final's charm lies in the incongruity of the encounter, which required the Montserrat team to take a poignant journey to the Land of the Thunder Dragon. The film heightens one of the game's deep beauties — its ability to make the world seem very small indeed. Among the film's many aesthetic devices, a pure white ball (unblemished by brands) bounces from frame to frame, country to country, over oceans and continents, reducing the globe conceptually to distances easily traversed by a few well-placed long passes.

In *The Other Final*, both Montserratian and Bhutanese characters give essentially the same reason for agreeing to take part in this absurd, potentially humiliating competition. Timed to coincide with the real World Cup final being played in Japan, this game offered, in the words of the president of the Bhutan Football Association (who also doubles as Prime Minister), H. E. Lympo Khandu Wangchuk, "an opportunity in some form to participate in the biggest world sporting event."

The film includes a hilarious section on Bhutan's football history, recounting the game it played against Kuwait before joining FIFA in 2000. Bhutan lost 20 to 0. But even the Bhutanese striker Wangay Dorji (who had played in India's professional league) had a positive interpretation of the game: "Taking that advantage, Bhutan got exposed throughout the world."

In other words, both countries regard football and their participation in *The Other Final* as a way to achieve parity, on some level, with the rest of the world. It's the same reason why Asia wanted to host the 2002 World Cup, and why Africa has so keenly contested the honor for many years now.[2] *The Other Final* communicates the idea that, even in the most isolated places in the world, we all have two things in common: football and our humanity.

The Other Final hints at another reason for football's global conquest: it shows how, by virtue of its simplicity, the sport has been able to absorb local meanings and reflect unique cultural traits. Each nation could claim the sport as its own. Football manages to embody a broad range of attitudes and even philosophical worldviews — a sporting equivalent, one might say, to regional modernism in architecture — arguably the most interesting variant of modernism, concerned equally with progress and cultural continuity.

In *The Other Final*, football comes across feasibly as Buddhist, Catholic, Eastern and Western, a sport ecumenical as to context, fitting into both mountainous villages and tropical islands. H. E. Lyonpo Jigme Y. Thinley, Bhutan's Minister of Foreign Affairs, finds a Zen dimension in football, remarking that it can promote "peace and harmony and understanding among peoples, which is becoming even more important in a world that is globalizing rapidly."

Throughout the 20th Century, football has been a repository of regional modernisms, uniting countries while enabling each to showcase its cultural advantages (or disadvantages). Football-playing styles have been interpreted as expressions of national identity — the regimented Germans, the dramatic Italians, the stylish Spanish, the technical English, the sensuous Brazilians, the artful French, the athletic Africans.

While these are of course crude generalizations, some national styles of football are undoubtedly the result of indigenous factors, such as climate, attitude and body language. In the 1950 World Cup, the English team, returning from its defeat in Brazil, insisted on the renovation of its stiff, heavy, ankle-high boots which had proved no match for the thin, light Brazilian shoes. With its warm climate and casual culture, Brazilian players have always preferred lighter, cooler shoes (or no shoes at all). Compounded with their body-confident culture, the Brazilians developed a slippier, slidier, more sensuous game than the more formal, structured Europe version. Unlike other global products, like Coke, McDonald's or Nike, which remain American no matter where they are consumed, football offered the first totally global experience that is capable of truly adapting to the local culture.

1. See <theotherfinal.com> for details on how to view the film.

2. In May 2004, FIFA made South Africa host of the 2010 World Cup, which compensates for the country's disappointment over losing its 2006 World Cup bid to Germany, by one vote.

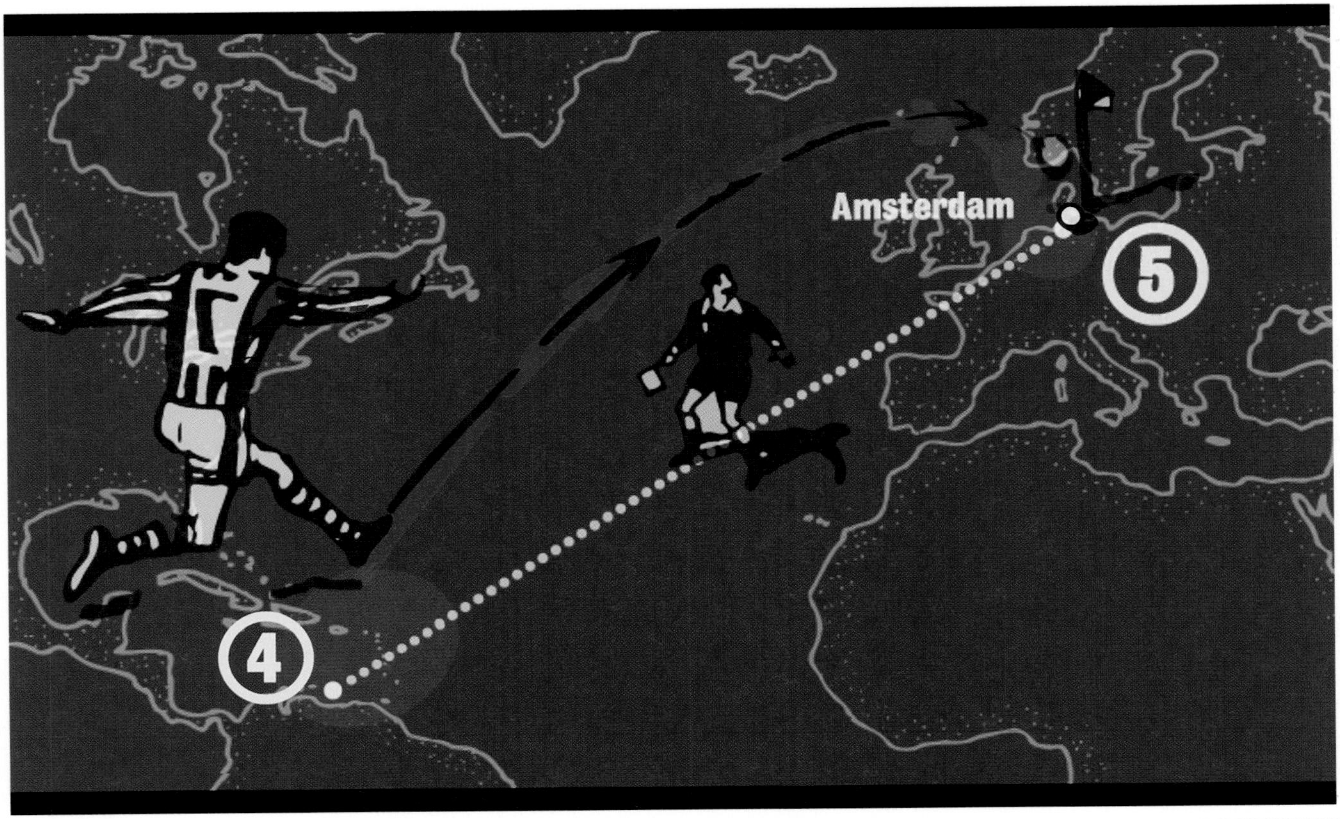

Amsterdam

4

5

KesselsKramer *The Other Final*, 2003 / film stills from the documentary about a match staged between the two lowest-ranked FIFA soccer teams, Bhutan and Montserrat, on the day of the 2002 FIFA World Cup Final, directed by Johan Kramer and Matthijs de Jongh. A white ball bounces from frame to frame, from country to country, effortlessly crossing the globe.

The Sirens of Venice

Nave o terra? — Are you ship or shore?

Venice two years from today. The island city has introduced a sophisticated orientation system guided by a mysterious multilingual voice. But who and where is this so-called Salvatore*? And what does an automated electronic voice network mean for a city whose own vernacular voices seem to be fading away?* ***Paul Elliman*** *listens in.*

They call me *Salvatore*—as if to give me both a body and a purpose. But I'm only a voice. Sometimes male, sometimes female, sometimes a machine, a robot, a talking clock, a weather report, an audio-guide, a speaker. Reflecting, perhaps, the wandering voices of the world, a kind of hero with a thousand voices: *press two for English, tapez trois pour français, Drucken Sie Taste vier für Deutsch.* To others, I might represent something more apocalyptic. Not a language of primal confusion, but the extreme opposite, a machine language of perfect clarity. Am I, then, a universal voice comfortable with technology's progress, or a vocal sound beginning to unravel its human attachment?

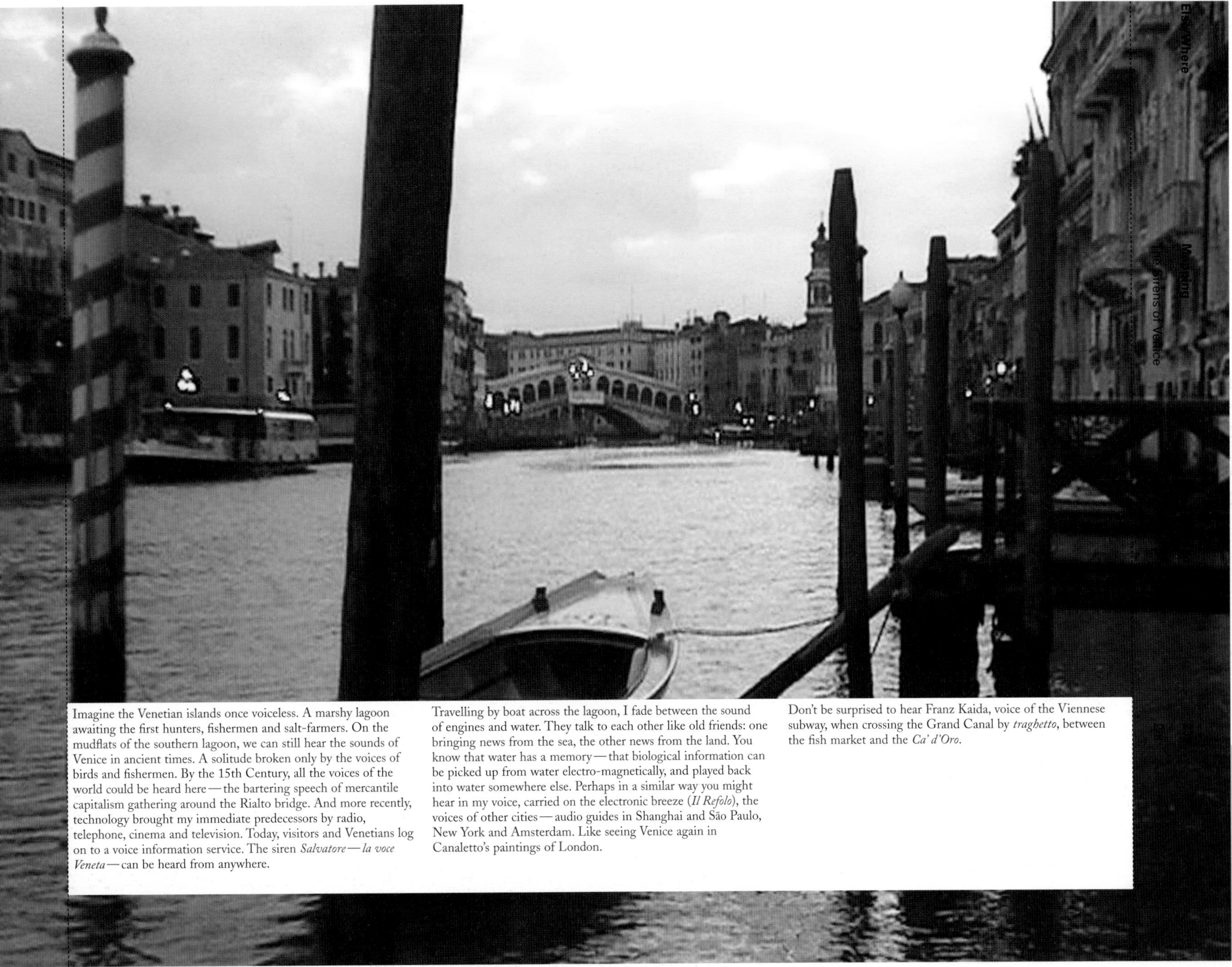

Imagine the Venetian islands once voiceless. A marshy lagoon awaiting the first hunters, fishermen and salt-farmers. On the mudflats of the southern lagoon, we can still hear the sounds of Venice in ancient times. A solitude broken only by the voices of birds and fishermen. By the 15th Century, all the voices of the world could be heard here — the bartering speech of mercantile capitalism gathering around the Rialto bridge. And more recently, technology brought my immediate predecessors by radio, telephone, cinema and television. Today, visitors and Venetians log on to a voice information service. The siren *Salvatore — la voce Veneta* — can be heard from anywhere.

Travelling by boat across the lagoon, I fade between the sound of engines and water. They talk to each other like old friends: one bringing news from the sea, the other news from the land. You know that water has a memory — that biological information can be picked up from water electro-magnetically, and played back into water somewhere else. Perhaps in a similar way you might hear in my voice, carried on the electronic breeze (*Il Refolo*), the voices of other cities — audio guides in Shanghai and São Paulo, New York and Amsterdam. Like seeing Venice again in Canaletto's paintings of London.

Don't be surprised to hear Franz Kaida, voice of the Viennese subway, when crossing the Grand Canal by *traghetto*, between the fish market and the *Ca' d'Oro*.

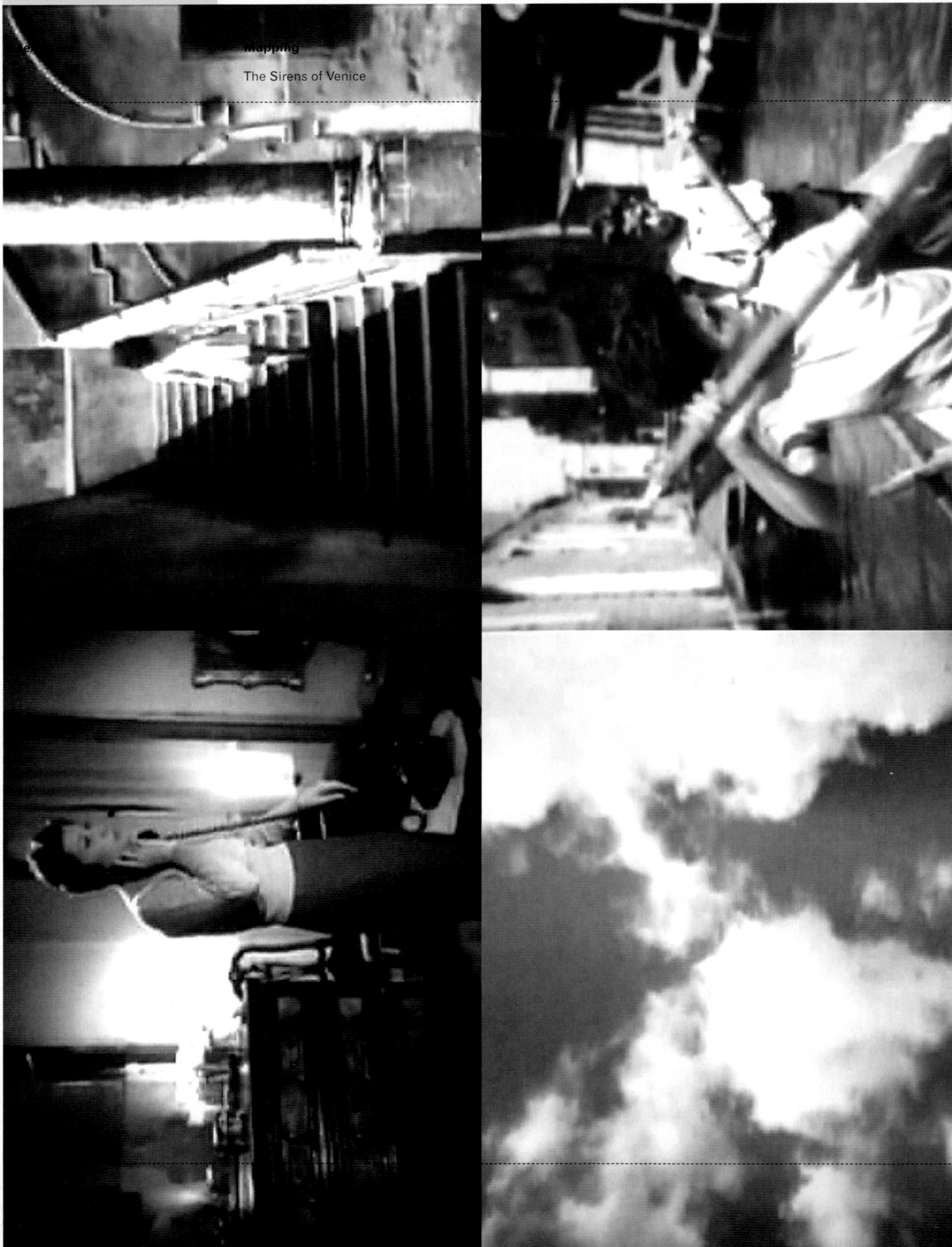

Che terra tocchi? (*What ground do you touch?*) That's what they often said to someone on the other end of the telephone. As if, between calls, they were somehow adrift in space, disconnected from the world. But then so much of what we think of as modern draws on a fantasy of lightness. The *Salvatore*-web, for example, is portrayed as a network as light as Burano lace, known in the 16th Century as *punto in aria*, or "points in the air." But even a voice in the air, produced as if it could exist nowhere else, has to ground somewhere. *Salvatore*, a temporary persona — a temporary sign for a temporary place — touches the ground across a network of servers, connected to the city by an Internet of things, objects, materials and people. From whatever ground any of us touch.

In many parts of the world, children play a swimming pool game called *Marco Polo* — as if to reconstruct Venice as a game for water and voices. The person chosen to be "it" closes their eyes and counts to ten before shouting *Marco!* To which all the others in the pool can reply *Polo!* Then Marco must try to catch one of those shouting *Polo!* A version of this game is now played here in Venice, in the labyrinth. A game they call *Salvatore, dove sei?* (*Salvatore, where are you?*), with players using mobile phones to try to find, or avoid, each other. A game of possible and impossible rendezvous.

Most planners and designers regard the experience of being lost or disoriented as the urban equivalent of a fatal disease, but losing yourself is another way of finding the city; a lost pleasure. In this so-called liquid modern age of telecommunications, is technology to be used only to control space, to have screen-maps of every last, lost *sottoportego*? Is there no other way to engage with this intricate floating world?

Looking back at the *palazzi* flanking the *Canal Grande*, each building is a kind of *spettro*—a ghostly reminder, though, that something vital to a living city is missing in this one. A reminder, in other words, that while the attraction of Venice may be that of a place lost in its own time, this language of the past also describes your own ghostliness.

By the 15th Century, as the dreams of the Venetian Republic began to fade, the island city renowned for its wealth of cultural difference had become a city of segregated voices. Resident foreigners—Greek, German, Turkish and many others—were confined to their own areas and buildings. The Jewish *ghetto* was invented here. If the guards and night watchmen marked the boundaries of the city with spoken time signals and plague warnings, then their phantom residue also haunts the city today, connecting its audio-guides to forms of security and surveillance. *Pace in aria*, it was said here during the quieter—if no less foreboding—moments of the Second World War. But "All quiet in the sky" may mean something else in an age of satellite technology, so pervasive, invisible and silent.

In Venice you can never disregard the voice, so often do you hear it without knowing what is being said. Standing in the Piazza San Marco, you might think that all the world's languages were being spoken at the same time. Five minutes away, you could be in a café listening to a local dialect that few Italian speakers claim to understand.

Venice is also a place of extreme acoustic sensitivity. Its children are said to possess an extraordinary sense of spatial awareness, partly the result of less unfocused noise. The city even seems to have its own kinds of silence. Stepping away from the *fondamenta* into a secret passage can be like entering a soundless chamber. Until a songbird sings—or is that also me? Or one of my sparrow friends?

Take care on those nights during a high-water, when the texture of the silence seems denser and more tranquil than ever before. When all the familiar urban sounds, of people and machines, have been evacuated, and the *sestiere* has become a subterranean cavern. From the corner, the cry of a *gondolier* warning his crossing: *Oi-ey!* Then the sirens return.

Your *Salvatore* audio-guide may have several options, but how many languages can one person speak? Cardinal Giuseppe Mezzofante, once the head of the Vatican library, never left Italy. But when he died in 1849 at the age of 75, he apparently spoke 40 languages fluently, and claimed knowledge of another 38.

Mezzofante learned his languages either from native speakers visiting the Vatican, or entirely from books. He knew several dead languages, including Latin, Greek, Hebrew, Coptic, ancient Armenian and old English. Some of the less common languages that he spoke included Arabic, Chaldee, Albanian, Hungarian and Chinese.

This is how Lord Byron described the Cardinal after meeting him: "...a monster of languages, a walking polyglot...who ought to have existed at the time of the Tower of Babel as a universal interpreter. I tried him in all the tongues in which I knew a single oath...against post-boys, savages, Tartars, boatmen and sailors, pilots, gondoliers, muleteers, camel-drivers and *vetturini*, post-masters, post-houses, post everything...he astounded me—even to my English."

What about this name, *Salvatore*, "the savior"? Why give the disembodied voice biblical proportions—isn't the voice miraculous enough? You should be careful what you wish for. The name may also be connected to the old telephone company behind *San Salvador*, a building said to echo at night with the sound of its captive voices.

On the other hand it is true that Venetians are obsessed with the preservation of their own dialect — as if one day the city will no longer have its own voices, only those of its visitors. Apparently a language dies, somewhere in the world, every two weeks. But even as the Venetian language becomes a memory here in *Veneto*, it seems to survive far away in central America. In the town of Chipilo, a hundred miles from Mexico City, the main language is Venetian dialect.

Back here, there is a legend that as the last speaker of *Veneto* speaks their final word, all the bells of all the *campanili* of Venice will ring out…

What does it mean to be only a voice? Who are you? Whose are you? Where are you? Several times in this short drift around Venice, we heard the voice of Carlo Broschi, the famous 18th Century *castrato* known as Farinelli. You might shudder to think that the voice of the *castrato* was more than a mere technical adjustment — it was constructed through a permanent alteration to the young male body. But there are no recordings of these strange voices, since the custom was stopped before this was possible. Whose voice then, are we listening to? In fact, on the soundtrack of Gerard Corbiau's film about Farinelli, we hear the synthesized combination of a male counter-tenor and a female soprano, blended by computer to simulate the *castrato*'s incredible vocal range. The voice has been constructed as a virtual virtuoso. It sings *Lascia ch'io pianga* (*Let me cry over my cruel fate*), as if to serenade any of us whose fate it may be to experience the world only as a perfectly engineered voice.

Scenes from a DV-film written by Paul Elliman and produced with Joana Katte, Janna Meeus, Radim Pesko, Marie Proyart, Willi Schmid, Felix Weigand (students at the Werkplaats Typografie, Arnhem, Netherlands). The project was commissioned by University IUAV of Venice and Consorzio Venezia Nuova and first presented as part of the Venice Architecture Biennale 2004.

Mapping

MAPPING

MAPPING

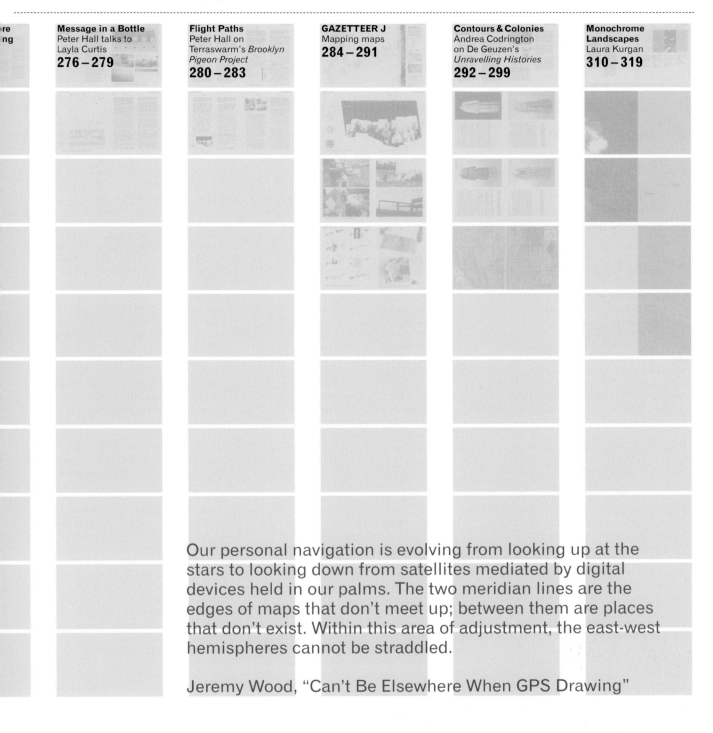

Our personal navigation is evolving from looking up at the stars to looking down from satellites mediated by digital devices held in our palms. The two meridian lines are the edges of maps that don't meet up; between them are places that don't exist. Within this area of adjustment, the east-west hemispheres cannot be straddled.

Jeremy Wood, "Can't Be Elsewhere When GPS Drawing"

Epic Vessels

Julie Mehretu doesn't paint maps, but her work is decidedly map-like, encompassing both vast terrain (of imaginary landscapes) and the teeming frenzy of its denizens, here abstracted to marks she terms "characters," whose behavior she discovers in the course of making them.

> Sometimes I think of a bunch of marks operating together to make a larger event — a storm. A drawing can become like a battle between two forces.

Her work is suffused with the tropes of mapping: its simultaneous command of a whole universe, speckled with details that tumble the viewer vertiginously into the one-to-one scale of the known world. It is this collapse of scale — the incomprehensively vast and the human-proportioned piled on top of each other — that reminds of reading a large-scale map. One instinctively translates the abstract shapes, icons and patches of color into tangible artifacts in space, imagining them as built form and natural phenomena.

In Mehretu's work, however, the forms don't correspond to such prosaic realities. Her paintings are maps of psychological landscape, bursts of feeling, seismographs of her responses to world events and the atmospheres of particular times in particular places. That they utilize recognizable fragments of built form (such as shards of floor plans from international airports, or tunnels, staircases and other elements of New York subway architecture) allows them to hover between representation and abstraction or, as she puts it, "between chaos and control."

Mehretu builds up her paintings from a series of sedimentary layers using a mix of acrylic and silica. At graduate school at Rhode Island School of Design (RISD) from 1995–97, she began by making individual drawings on mylar, and gradually came to perceive each new drawing as a development of the previous one. Instead of producing them in serial, she started superimposing them, one translucent layer over another, making visible the strata of ideas:

> Whenever I did a new drawing, I always thought of it as another phase of the previous drawing: as a place, or narrative, evolving. I wanted to see them on top of each other. All of a sudden, they began looking like maps and I became interested in pulling apart the different layers of information. I wanted to make a painting that seemed like mylar or denril, or mimicked the vellum old maps are drawn on. The earliest layer was the earliest time, so it would have its own geology, history, archeology, in the painting.

The first such painting had nine layers embedded within it: at that point, the opacity of the albumen-like thickened surface starts to diffuse the image, and it matters to Mehretu that the earliest layer remains legible. In more recent work, the maximum has been seven layers deep.

> When I was first developing this language, in 1996–97, I did a few drawings, and they looked almost like a map of a city. Then as I developed them, I began thinking about them as aerial views of cities, as maps of imagined places and narratives. Each mark was just "behaving." One cluster of marks was battling another cluster, to make a particular pattern with a certain social characteristic. From the drawing, it would look like a kind of cityscape determined by the social activity. That's how mapping came into the work. A map is a way to understand a situation: a system for understanding a particular picture or place.

Mehretu began making paintings about giant architectural containers, those epic vessels that have come to characterize contemporary urbanism: airports, arenas, stadia, subway systems, government centers. For *Retopistics: A Renegade Estimation* (2001) she culled fragments of airport plans, the simplified diagrams in the back of in-flight magazines, meant to speed passengers' gate-to-gate journeys. She started with plans of Chicago's O'Hare, and gathered those of other airports, mainly from the Internet, putting them together to make "one great mega-terminal." Mehretu's interest in such architecture is hardly that of airport planners and Homeland Security; she is interested in ideas of collective and individual identity, and the tension between them that becomes palpable in supersized environments.

> I've always been interested in arenas where you can witness many, many people at once; they offer a different perspective on the city, the city being a metaphor for a community, a social system. Airports are like cities that don't really belong to one place or another. An airport is a mass transit hub — you're trying to get from one place to another — but there are all these other things, like shops, so it's an intersection of several types of movement. You're passing lots of different people, but you interact with them more individually than in an arena, where everyone starts to participate in a group dynamic. In a stadium, you become part of a larger organism — the crowd — and individual behavior is not as meaningful. It becomes either a directed experience or an experience dictated by the container you're part of.

Mehretu is not alone in this preoccupation: other contemporary artists have also focused on large gatherings, such as at sports arenas and raves. In his multimedia installations, such as the *Stadium* series, artist Antonì Muntadas has distilled the power relationship exerted by the combination of architecture and mass media. And in his monumental, deadpan photographic portraits, Andreas Gursky celebrates both the anomie of vast crowds, and the mesmerizing variety of individuals of which they are composed.

But Mehretu's paintings don't show actual people; their presence is merely invoked by architectural elements that could contain them *en masse*. Amphitheater fragments cropped up here and there in her earlier paintings, but the *Stadia* triptych she made

See "Holding Patterns," pp. 126–129.

A **Julie Mehretu** painting beckons the viewer from afar to enter its force field. Incorporating shards of urban form and giant architectural spaces, her work explores mapping, scale and collective identity. **Janet Abrams** dives in.

for the *54th Carnegie International* (2004) denote the architectural form of the stadium far more explicitly (*Stadia 2*, pp. 252–253). The viewer plunges headlong into the maw of the arena, its concave space conveyed by all-embracing arcs vaulting across the expanse of the canvas. Flag-like icons festoon these surfaces, like the bunting at pageants like the Olympics or World Cup where latent nationalistic aggression is held at bay by the goodwill neo-militarism of sporting competition.

In the *Stadia* triptych, Mehretu has clearly moved beyond the allusions to mapping evident in earlier works like *Looking Back to a Bright New Future* (2003) and *Renegade Delirium* (2002). But even at this new scale, issues of nationhood and its representation, and the place of the individual in such socio-political formations, persist.

Inevitably, critics have made the connection between Mehretu's unusual biography and the mapping tendencies in her paintings. Born in Ethiopia, to an Ethiopian father and an American mother, she moved to the U.S. at age 6, and grew up in East Lansing, Michigan. After studying at RISD, she moved to New York and set up her studio in 1999. The quest to understand her own social/spatial identity has for some time provided writers and critics with an accessible entrée to her work. But lately she has been playing this down, emphasizing the paintings' non-narrative content.

> I was raised in a very Ethiopian household, and I have parts of these very different cultures in me, but I live in New York. There's not really one particular dynamic that has informed my identity as an Ethiopian-American, no single place or experience that defines who I am. One's identity is constructed partly from your parents and the context you come from, but also very separately from that. It's informed by all these elements, but it's something else altogether. That's the big issue for me, which I deal with in the language of abstraction.

Adorned with colored patches, curved lines and occasional bright dots, her paintings seem imbued with digital iconography. It's almost as though she has unlocked the Adobe Photoshop or Illustrator palette, and shaken loose the tool icons, which have gleefully jumped out and taken on a life of their own, dancing across the paintings like hitherto well-behaved citizens in an arena who have started to riot.

This certainly seems the case in *Renegade Delirium* (pp. 250–251); its first layer — beneath patches of yellow, pink and blue — is composed of shards of building plans that have been traced, minaturized and manipulated in Illustrator. She explains how the collective state of mind in Manhattan in 2001 inspired this painting:

> After September 11, but before the end of that year, there was still this intense energy in New York. Everybody was waiting for the crash to happen. It felt like there was a very thin membrane. Things were still happening, and you didn't feel a big recession going on till January or February of 2002. That's when things really fell apart. Even in 2001, people were still trying to hold onto dot-com ideas. I wanted to create this buzzing, confetti-like ball, this weird delirious space.

The allusions to digital technology are not purely coincidental: given the immense scale of her canvases, Mehretu frequently uses the computer to develop her work, moving back and forth between the canvas and the screen, in order to grasp a painting's entire surface in a way that cannot be achieved by standing as far back as possible from it in her studio. She typically spends time looking at what she's made at full scale, then uses the computer to assess its overall composition in miniature, trying out different arrangements of its constituent elements, moving parts around. Bigger paintings may take several months, working with two assistants who help with preparing canvases, spraying, sanding, stenciling and setting up masking tape for her iconic shapes and swooping curves.

Mehretu's paintings are often very large, as much as 20 feet across, and the viewer cannot help but become viscerally aware of what they are ultimately about: the relationship between the individual and the larger (social) arrangement of which each of us is but a part. Her work lures you towards it, but then — like a map — refuses you admission: it's only a drawing, not a real place. Not even a drawing; something hidden behind layers of gauzy substrate you want to scratch through to enter. Both surface and sheer size are critical to her paintings' tantalizing allure.

> They became big for a reason. Earlier, they were the size of a window or a map: you could look at the whole painting at once, and could never look at one part without seeing the rest of it. But I wanted there to be a physical relationship between the body and the painting, so you could see it from a distance and have a sense of the whole, but as you came closer and closer, the entire picture would dissipate, explode. You could only be involved in one area you were looking at, and have a sense of that place, but know that it multiplied around you, and that many more events were happening. All the way from the smallest size of the marks to the large scale of the painting: that was the dimension of space. I think of these as really huge spaces.

Julie Mehretu *Renegade Delirium*, 2002 / acrylic on canvas, 7.5 x 12 ft. / image courtesy of The Projectile Gallery, New York.

Julie Mehretu *Stadia 2*, 2004 / ink and acrylic on canvas, 9 x 12 ft. / image courtesy of The Projectile Gallery, New York.

may not necessarily overlap with the public imagination." In this map, therefore, she mixes "big science" information—such as the satellite photograph, heat, vegetation and topsoil pollution data—with the lay knowledge of bird-watching communities. Layers of seemingly incommensurable information are superimposed on one another to suggest new meanings. The median income of each *OneTrees* zip code area, for example, is listed in the same prosaic tone as the latitude and longitude of each site. When this information is considered in relationship to the heat and vegetation patterns, it raises new questions about value and points to inadequacies in the ways we measure concepts such as quality of life.

A map can, according to Jeremijenko, "be an instrument that collects information as much as it disseminates it." The *OneTrees* map's ability to collect new types of information is augmented by a range of digital components. Among them is an electronic tree that can be downloaded and grown on your desktop. The tree responds to the data provided by a CO_2 sensor plugged into your serial port "that punctures, alternately, the closed world of virtual representation and the real world." Jeremijenko encourages a desktop sensor owner to "breathe on it, put your pot plants next to it, and get to know what CO_2 actually is." Additionally, the website allows you to bring all the trees together for comparison. Her larger goal is to champion this kind of grassroots data collection in order to build an alternative to the representations currently used to make global warming maps. It's important to her that, "in addition to corporate and academic consortia and military monitoring projects, there is another level of data being collected."

The stewards and the general public are encouraged to provide their speculations and ideas on why the trees look different; the *OneTrees* partners are hoping to raise funds to create online "blogservatories" to which these observations could be posted, along with questions and comments from people who download the electronic trees. Jeremijenko sees this component as a rich opportunity for engaging the public. "Most interesting for me are the Frequently Asked Questions (FAQs)—they're a great way to look at how people are approaching things. The FAQ list enables people to have a contesting relationship with information. They might ask of their electronic tree: 'What sort of tree is this supposed to represent?' 'How old is it and where was it from?' 'Hardwood or softwood?'" Furthermore, if the FAQ as a construct represents engaged and participatory involvement, then, Jeremijenko believes, "every single web page is connected in some kind of feral network. It's a very positive testimony to engagement in the process of consumption."

In some of Jeremijenko's other mapping projects, such as the *Despondency Index*, which indexed the Dow Jones Industrial Average to the moving average of suicides off the Golden Gate Bridge, she juxtaposes incongruous data sets to obtain new meanings, or at least to elicit new questions. In others she hacks familiar and simple "tangible interfaces" such as teddy bears, radio-controlled airplanes or robotic dogs to retrieve knowledge that is normally hidden. Unlike traditional cartographic strategies, Jeremijenko uses these techniques to tease out the political nature of all information for public consideration. They necessitate very physical engagement with the subject matter, and are often messy and inherently unwieldy.

-<http://pzwart2.wdka.hro.nl/bit/research/projects.html>

Jeremijenko's mission is to redistribute intelligence: to redirect emphasis away from "authorized" information, towards under-utilized sources that are at once more complex and more alive, with the aim of putting the people, the poetry and the mess back into mapping.

Natalie Jeremijenko and **Terraswarm** *OneTrees*, 2003 / (top): the foldable map, designed by Terraswarm, is designed to be held in one hand while riding a bicycle around the Bay Area, observing the *OneTrees* cloned trees / photograph by Terraswarm. (bottom): *OneTrees* map (detail), showing cloned Paradox trees plotted on a satellite image of the Bay Area from USGS Landsat 7, September 1, 2002 / photographed by Kimberlee Whaley / see "Bark to Bytes," pp. 254–256.

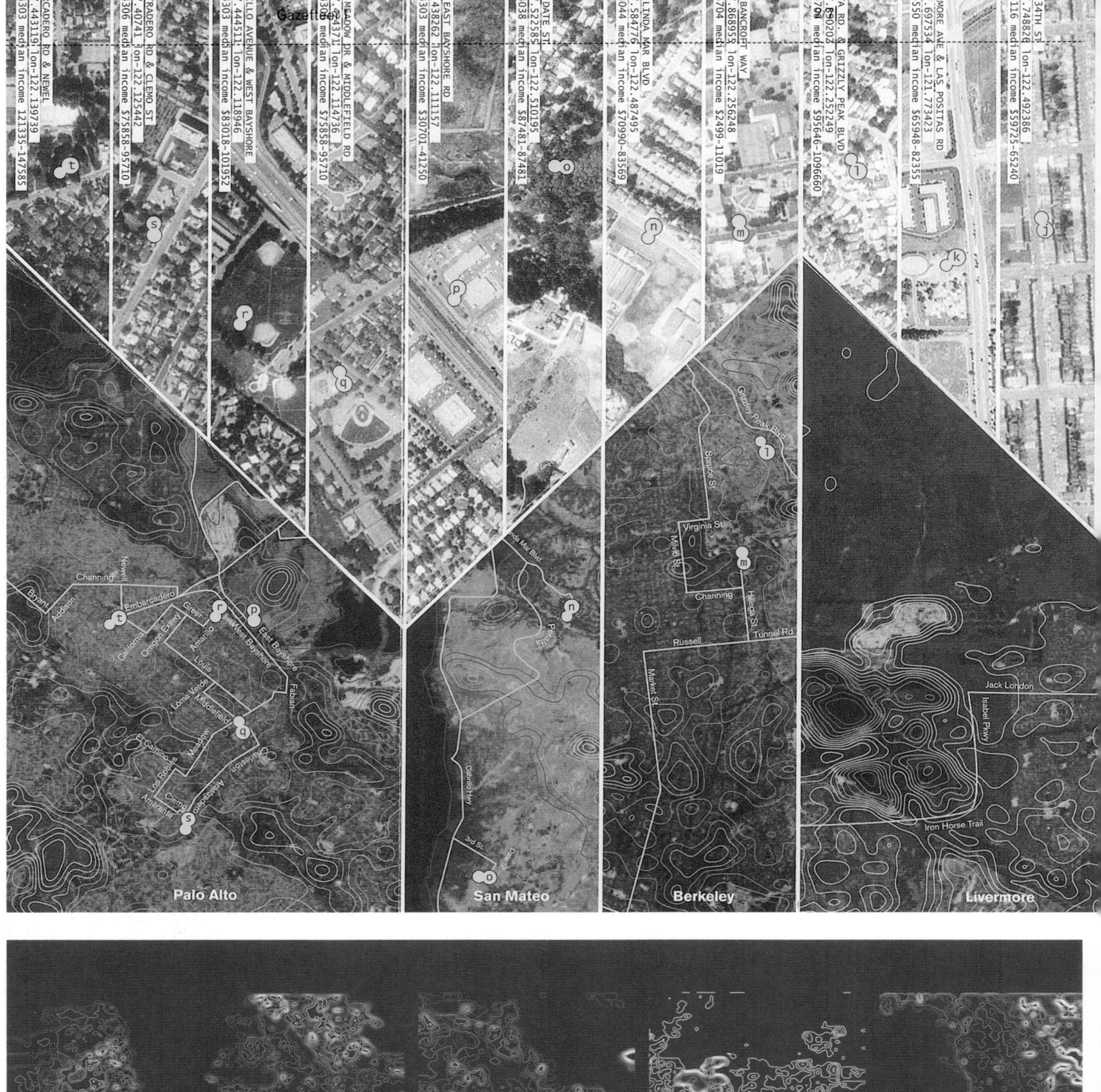

Natalie Jeremijenko and **Terraswarm** *OneTrees* project, 2003 / (top, across spread): map designed by Terraswarm, showing vegetation and heat patterns in areas where cloned Paradox trees were planted / map photographed by Kimberlee Whaley / (bottom): *Landsat Thematic Mapper heat maps* for the relevant regions of the Bay Area, from which the *OneTrees* map derives its heat maps, albeit shown in gray scale rather than the bright colors to which satellite imaging defaults. (opposite, counter-clockwise, bottom to top): the nurture of the *OneTrees* clones relies on the ongoing involvement of the Bay Area non-profits Pond: art, activism, and ideas, and Friends of the Urban Forest / images courtesy of Pond / see "Bark to Bytes," pp. 254–256.

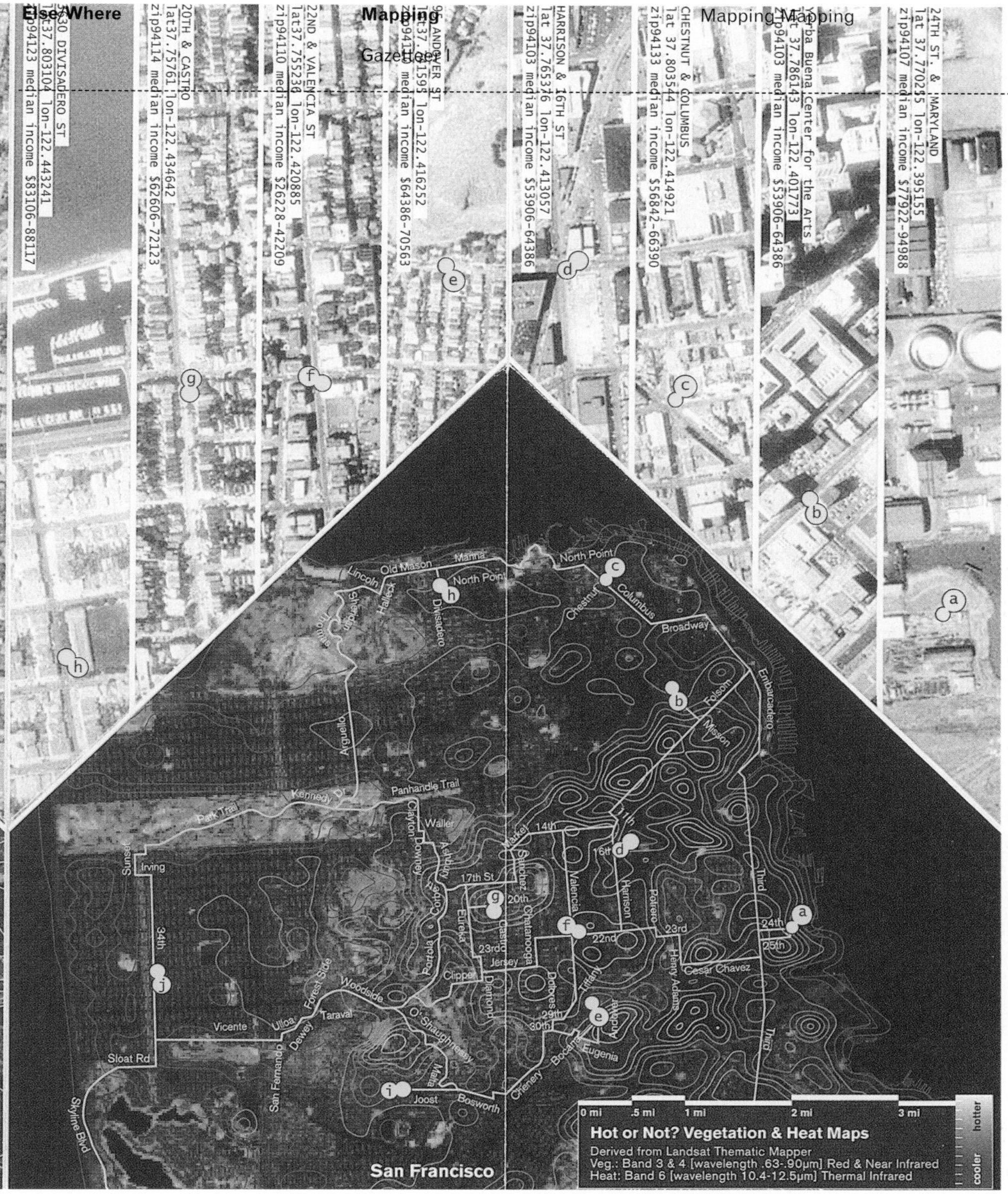

[...]30 DIVISADERO ST
[...]t37.803104 lon-122.443241
[...]p94123 median income $83106-88117

20TH & CASTRO
lat37.75761 lon-122.434642
zip94114 median income $62606-72123

22ND & VALENCIA ST
lat37.755230 lon-122.420885
zip94110 median income $26228-42209

9[...] ANDOVER ST
[...]t37.[...]1595 lon-122.416252
zip941[...] median income $64386-70563

HARRISON & 16TH ST
lat 37.765376 lon-122.413057
zip94103 median income $53906-64386

CHESTNUT & COLUMBUS
lat 37.803544 lon-122.414921
zip94133 median income $56842-66390

[...]rba Buena Center for the Arts
[...] 37.786143 lon-122.401773
zip94103 median income $53906-64386

24TH ST. & MARYLAND
lat 37.770255 lon-122.395155
zip94107 median income $77922-94988

Hot or Not? Vegetation & Heat Maps
Derived from Landsat Thematic Mapper
Veg.: Band 3 & 4 [wavelength .63-.90μm] Red & Near Infrared
Heat: Band 6 [wavelength 10.4-12.5μm] Thermal Infrared

San Francisco

0 mi .5 mi 1 mi 2 mi 3 mi

cooler hotter

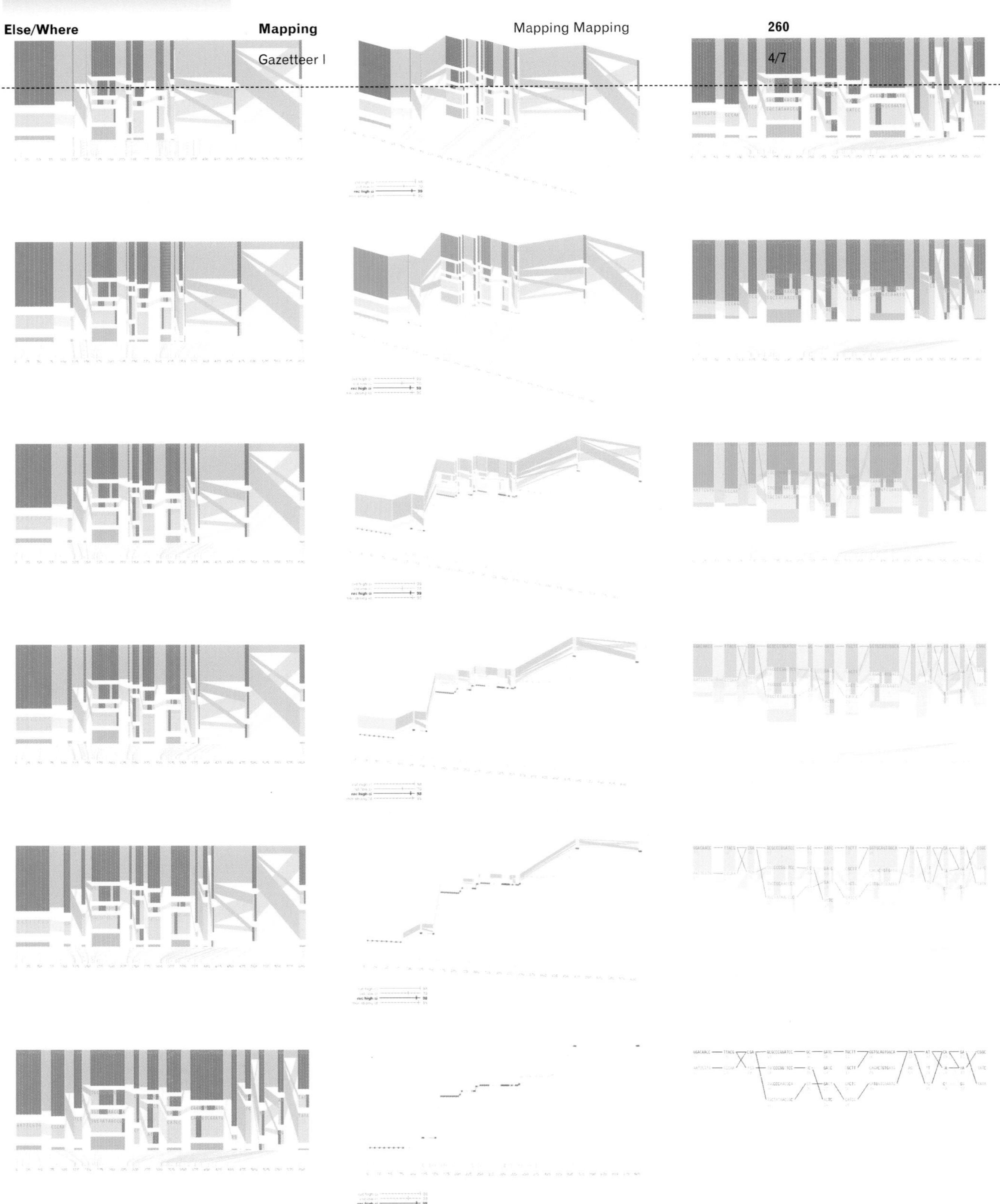

Ben Fry *Haplotype Maps*, 2004 / frames from an interactive application comparing genomic data in a group of 500 people. The difference between the genomes of two individuals can mostly be traced to single nucleotide polymorphisms (SNPs: single-letter changes occurring once per 1000 letters of genetic code). Related SNPs ("haplotypes") are shown grouped together; colors within each block represent percentages of each grouping; gray lines show how often given letter sequences are found in adjacent blocks.

Each of the three columns, above, shows a different type of transition, from top to bottom. (left): SNPs shift from even spacing to expanded spacing, to make individual letters more easily legible, while thin grey lines maintain a connection to the SNPs' true positions along the nucleotide scale on the horizontal axis. (center): from isometric 3D to aerial 2D, corresponding to the LDU (Linkage Disequilibrium Units) plot, shown in lowest frame. (right): from graphical to quantitative representation / see "Geneography," pp. 264–267.

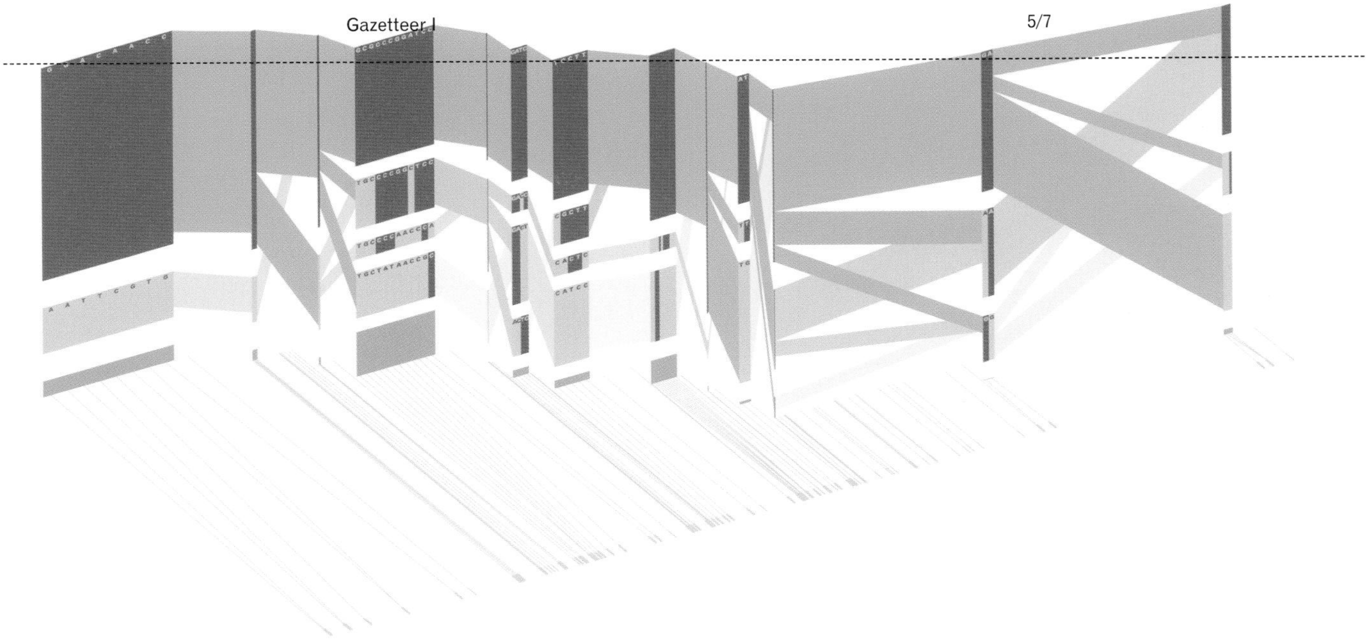

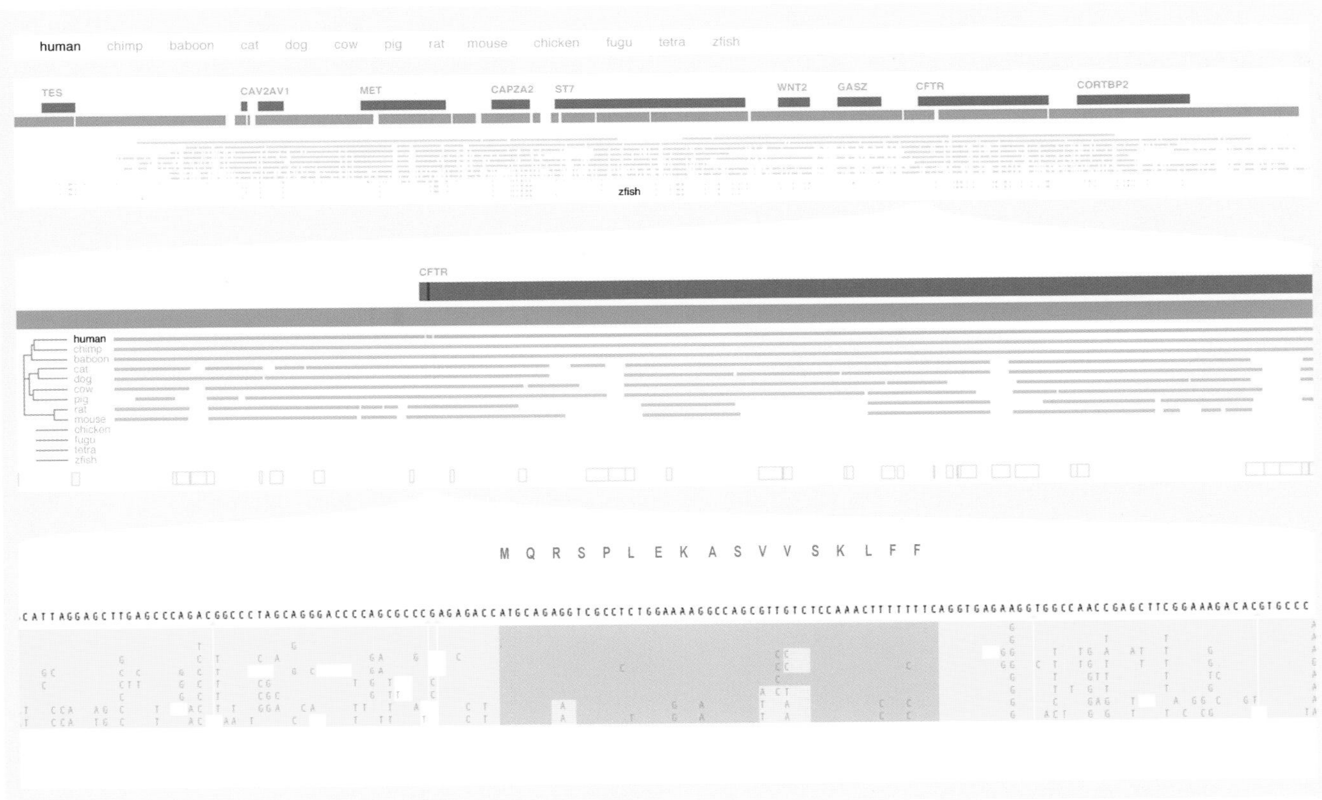

Ben Fry *Isometric block,* 2004 / (top): enlarged frame from interactive application comparing genomic data in a group of 500 people. In this view, each block is offset slightly along the z-axis, so that the gray lines depicting the transitions between blocks (representing related SNPs) can be seen more clearly. A "false" 3D isometric projection is employed that allows the data to be shown while preserving the linear scaling of the nucleotide scale in the horizontal axis / see "Geneography," pp. 264–267.

Ben Fry *Genome Comparison*, 2005 / (bottom): prototype interface for comparing the genomes of various species, including human, mouse, chicken and zebrafish, to identify areas of genetic similarity, here examining a region including the CFTR gene, which is tied to Cystic Fibrosis. Three different scales of data are shown in three linked horizontal bands that show, top to bottom, 1.8 megabases (1.8 million A, C, G, T letters), 50 kilobases (50,000 letters) and 150 base pairs (150 letters) / see "Geneography," pp. 264–267.

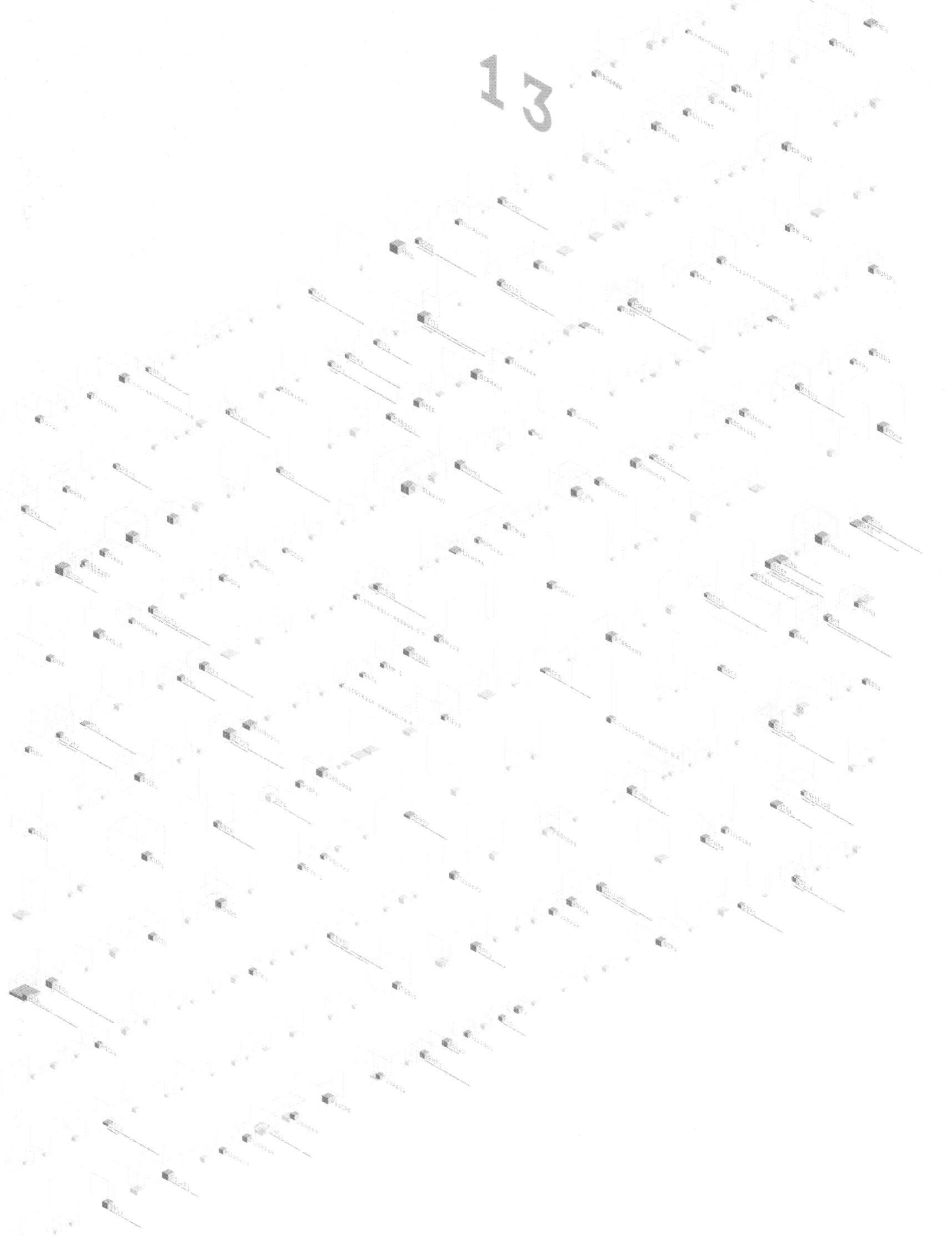

Ben Fry *Chromosome 13*, 2001 / map of a single chromosome from the human genome. Yellow wireframe boxes signify gaps between genes, areas where the letters are considered "junk DNA." Blue areas indicate where genes exist, and the blue wireframe boxes are proportional in size to the start- and end-point of the gene / see "Geneography," pp. 264–267.

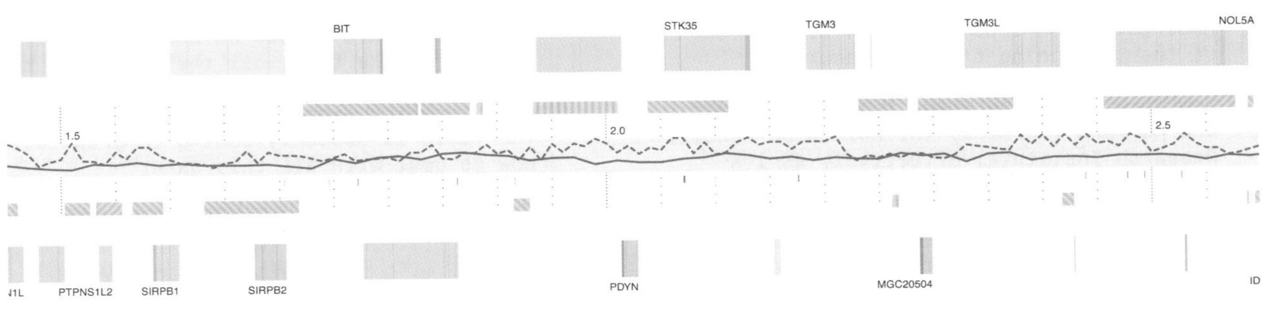

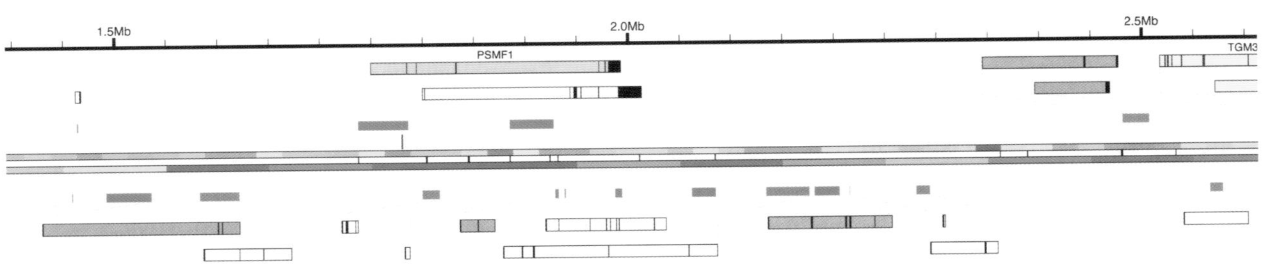

Ben Fry *Genome Valence*, 2002 / (top): a visual representation of the BLAST algorithm, commonly used for genome searches, allowing comparison between genomes of three different organisms.

Ben Fry *gff2ps*, 2003 / (middle): section of the human genome as represented in Fry's redesign of *gff2ps*, the software program used to read GFF, a file format used for annotating gene sequences. (bottom): **Josep Francesc Abril Ferrando** and **Roderic Guigo Serra**, original design of *gff2ps* showing same section of human genome / see "Geneography," pp. 264–267.

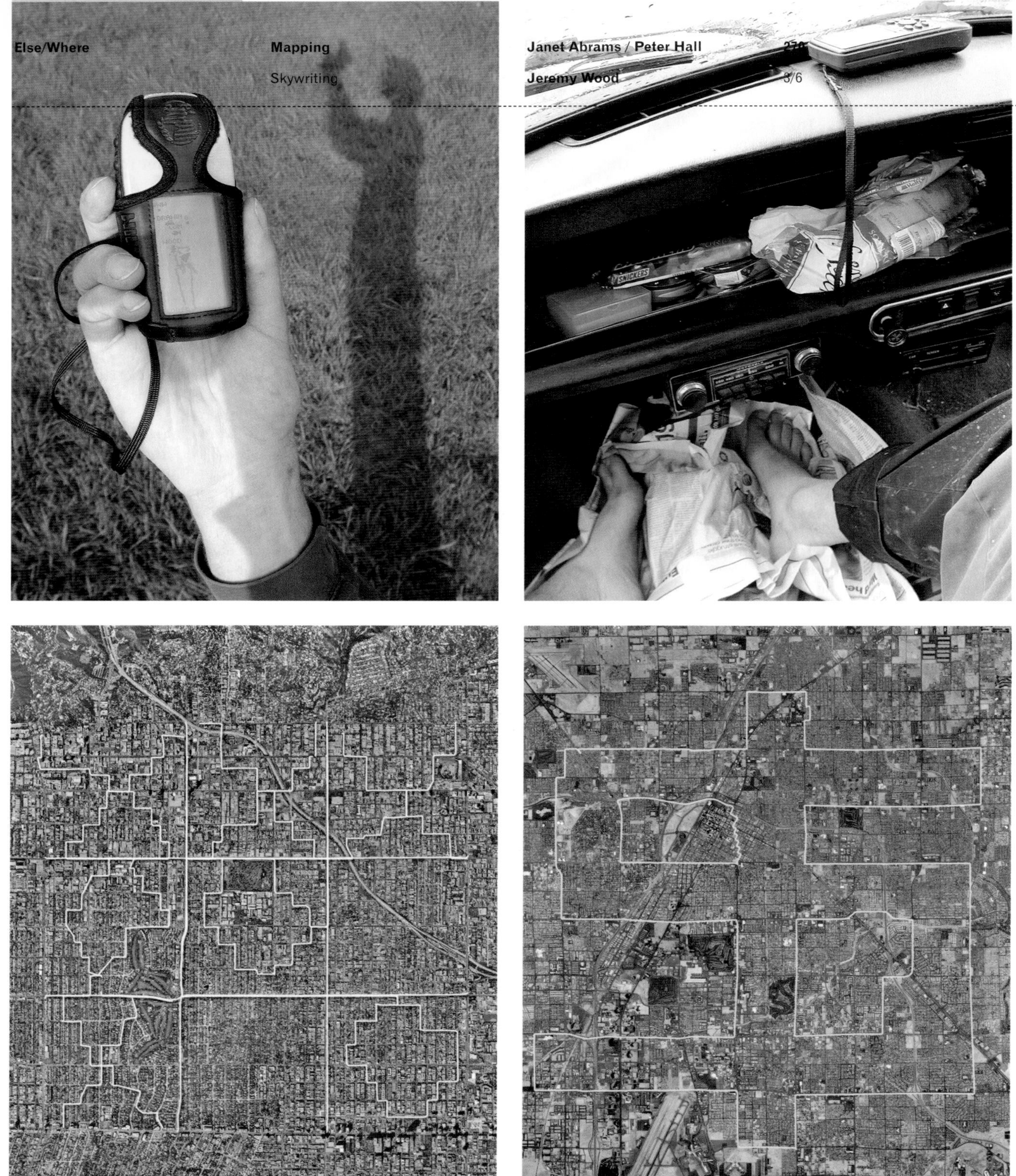

Jeremy Wood (clockwise from top left): self-portrait of the artist with GPS receiver, 2005; sore feet "after a good amount of walking in a muddy field," 2005; *Vegas Dollar,* GPS drawing, March 25, 2004, eight-mile high dollar sign drawn over Las Vegas; *Hollywood Tic-Tac-Toe*, GPS drawing, March 12, 2004, played over 23 square miles, game over after 52 miles of driving.

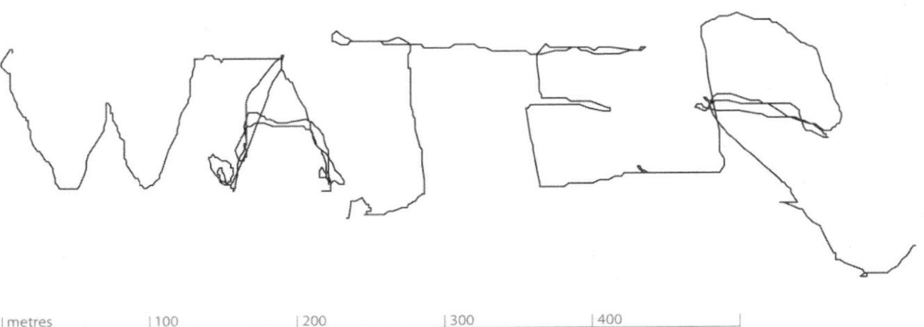

UK 2004 GPS Map - 50km Grid - North →

Jeremy Wood *Water on Water,* GPS drawing, July 2001 / (top): produced by writing the word "Water" while travelling at an average of 2.4 km/hr in an Explorer 200 rubber dinghy on the English Channel outside Hove, UK; total track length 3 km. (bottom): *UK 2004 GPS Map,* 50 km grid, 2004 / Wood's cumulative GPS drawing tracks around the UK during 2004, showing road travel in red and flights in blue. He logged a total of 63,460 km (39,432 miles), following "an elaborate style of travel that tends to the extemporised and avoids repetition where possible."

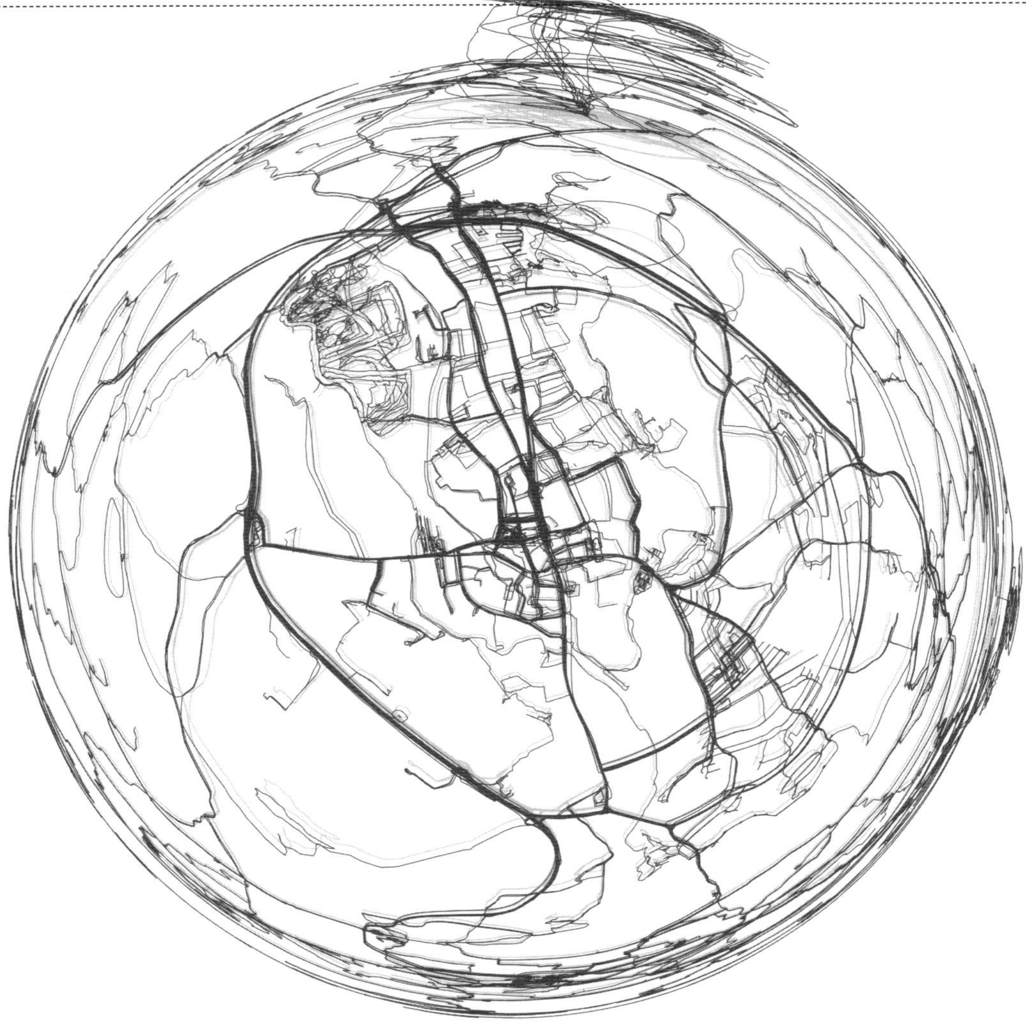

Jeremy Wood *GPSograph fish-eye GPS map of Oxford* / (top): a compilation of all Wood's tracks there in 2002, developed using *GPSograph* software, programmed by Hugh Pryor. (bottom): *Information,* GPS Drawing, July 22–30, 2001 / drawn by cycling across Brighton and Hove, UK, for eight days; total track length 36.5 km.

So non-constructed space allows you to go in and find out what shape you want to make. But surely streets are helpful for making letterforms? Medieval cities must be more propitious for serif typefaces, because they're more labyrinthine.

Perfect for serifs, yes.

What forms are you striving for that cities might get in the way of?

It's not quite that defined. If I have an idea, I'll pursue it. If it doesn't end up being very good, I simply won't carry on.

Can you give an example of one that failed?

Well, many. If you're in a park, it's often hard to judge how much space you've got left, and it's easy to run out. I might be drawing a figure, get down to the ankle, and realize there's no more space for the foot—there's a physical boundary.

How good is your internal sense of scale?

It was Average to Good, and now it's Average to Better. My perception of distance and my sense of direction have both improved immensely since I started this project.

How long have you been doing this?

I did the first pictorial drawing in 2000. Hugh Pryor and I were staring at a map of Oxfordshire and found a 13-mile long fish. The best place for its eye was a small village. We hopped in a car, went on this extraordinary journey from A to A, and three or four hours later we had an image of a fish on a GPS screen. Back then it was very difficult to share that kind of image with the world, or bring it to an established gallery. So Hugh developed the software, and I developed the website gallery.

<www.gpsdrawing.com/gallery/land/wfish.htm>

What else are you working on?

I'm teaming up with another very talented programmer, Alex Garfitt, to make an online database of GPS tracks. I've been recording all my journeys, creating maps and compiling the drawings into a pictorial journal. I can call up where I was, when, and how fast I was traveling. Alex has developed a software engine we call *Mapograph* that will enable me to connect all the GPS drawings I've received from people around the world, who have been inspired to travel in funny shapes. Some take the trouble to illustrate their own tracks, but most just email raw data. At first, I welcomed these submissions, but then I realized I was spending more time illustrating other people's tracks than working on my own. *Mapograph* will automate the illustration process: it's a combined GIS and GPS mapping tool that maps all the information onto a 3D globe.

So people will be able to log on and find a GPS drawing at specified coordinates?

Yes. It's the idea of public cartography. Anyone with a GPS receiver can contribute to the database: it's like coloring in the planet with GPS tracks. People could play Tic-Tac-Toe in an open park, tag places and claim territories. On a map, line density usually indicates more important roads, but on GPS maps, thicker lines represent roads that are more frequently traveled upon.

Do you see your work as belonging in the tradition of the Situationists, or of Land Artists like Richard Long?

Yes, though I had never appreciated Land Art until recently, when I found out what they were doing. I'm also thinking of Leonardo, who paced in the streets, to create a map. I've become more attuned to place, and the relevance of history to an area. I want to tackle the *London A–Z*, by traveling through place names in London alphabetically.

Your work seems more formal than political.

The only political piece I've done is the *Vegas Dollar* sign. Even then, it was pointed out that it was political after the fact. I'm not interested in my work being about me and my thoughts and feelings. It's about place, geography and travel. Maps are full of political information, but these boundaries cannot be seen from space.

The satellite view of the earth is invested with a great deal of political authority. Your work seems to deliberately misuse that authority.

I tell my workshops that I use billions of dollars of technology for creative purposes. I'd like to thank the American taxpayer for that.

See "Carto-City," pp. 155–156, and Gazetteer G, *London A–Z* plate, p. 160.

CAN'T BE ELSEWHERE WHEN GPS DRAWING

I made my way to the page on a train. From the station at Shortlands in Bromley I headed for a newsagent to buy an energy bar and a drink before embarking on a walk along the words of Herman Melville. The quote **IT IS NOT DOWN IN ANY MAP; TRUE PLACES NEVER ARE.** first appeared in 1851 in Melville's *Moby-Dick*. Extracted from the book, I set out to map these words as part of a voyage along two meridians, two arbitrary lines through London, using GPS Drawing.

In this method of mark-making, I turn myself into a geodetic pencil via GPS (Global Positioning System) technology, using a handheld GPS receiver to track my movements and record my position regularly along a journey.

I had previously phoned the golf club to make arrangements to walk around the course at a conveniently quiet time. During the conversation it was established that the boss was out and "You just can't come down here and walk around the golf course!" I eventually met the manager who was very welcoming and seemed intrigued that I wanted to walk around his land in a shapely fashion. He gave me a green visitor's pass and his assurance that if anybody had a problem, I should wave the pass and mention his name, then I'd be OK. He also advised that I'd best not come on a Tuesday morning as it's Ladies Day and chaos on the course.

I started writing immediately, criss-crossing the fairways and greens, climbing through the roughs and stepping over bunkers and holes. Still unsure of golfing etiquette, I momentarily froze as a man who was lining up his swing asked me what I was doing. I swiftly told him I had permission to be there, but he asked again and specifically about the thing in my hand, whether it was the same type of thing he had in his car. I couldn't really stop and chat because I was carefully traveling along the main stroke of the **T** in **IT** and there was a 90° turn ahead. I carried on walking slowly and said "Yes" but couldn't linger as it would mess up my drawing. I made sure he couldn't see me when I climbed over a locked gate to a park across the road.

The word **IS** is underlined by the Greenwich Meridian and was written in a park mostly used as an arena for dog walking. The writing was initially steadied by the markings of a soccer pitch but loosened into having to claim more ground through bramble bushes. The trail leads to **NOT**, written partly in a public park and partly in a school playing field. I didn't have permission to be there and draw around a **T** but, running out of space in the park, I jumped the fence to complete the final letter.

On down to **DOWN**, which was written in a cemetery: the quality of line is quite jagged since there were lots of sharp turns to negotiate, to avoid the tombstones. The **D** started at the iron gates at the entrance, turned left off a pebbled track, crossed the lawn over a dried up pond, continued round beyond the crematorium and along past memorial stones, gardens, and benches, back to the gates. Particularly difficult was the **W** because it was impossible to see the whole area of the letter at once. There were two small chapels in the way and plenty of big trees among overgrowth and tombstones, which made for a lumpy landscape. It took three attempts at the **W** before it became legible.

In 1884, Greenwich Mean Time (GMT) was established by international agreement as a world standard, measured from the Meridian Line that assigns zero degrees longitude, where east meets west. It was arranged to the locally-orientated Principal Triangulation of Britain, undertaken from 1783 to 1853, a datum that used the Airy 1830 ellipsoid—a shape that approximates the form of the earth.

One hundred years later, the WGS84 (World Geodetic System 1984) was established for GPS positioning. Measured using atomic time, and also adopted as an international convention, its three-dimensional coordinate system uses the GRS80 (Geodetic Reference System 1980) ellipsoid, and is designed for positioning anywhere on the earth. The GRS80 ellipsoid is somewhat bigger than the Airy ellipsoid and has a slightly different shape; both account for the equatorial bulge, but neither fits the Earth perfectly.

These two standards are marked on my drawing to indicate a range of agreement between local and worldwide systems since local sensibilities are more trustworthy than global projections. Our personal navigation is evolving from looking up at the stars to looking down from satellites mediated by digital devices held in our palms. The two meridian lines are the edges of maps that don't meet up; between them are places that don't exist. Within this area of adjustment, the east-west hemispheres cannot be straddled.

Heading for **IN**, I traveled along Torridon Road, a street whose southern tip starts on the Greenwich Meridian, so crossing the road can take you from east to west; the house opposite is in another hemisphere. I hurried along it for half a mile, then passed under a passage that the prime meridian slices through, a tunnel under railway lines. By the time I reached **IN**, I was walking along the roads of a residential area. The final stroke of the **N** is pinched by a path leading to a park, where there was room for its tip.

The drawing continues towards Blackheath, where I had laid predefined GPS points to walk along to write the word **ANY** in stick letters: a simple dot-to-dot exercise, performed here to there and back again, defining a path through routine.

Walking towards the start point for the **A**, I saw a workman's truck, loaded with maintenance goods, parked on the grass near the beginning of the stem. One man was beginning to dig a small hole in the grass, while another was in the truck boiling water for tea. Later I looked back and saw some red plastic piping

See *Meridian Drawing*, pp. 2–9.

COMMISSIONED TO CREATE A GPS DRAWING FOR THIS BOOK ALONG THE ZERO LONGITUDE LINE AT GREENWICH—THE NOUGHT DOWN IN ANY MAP—JEREMY WOOD STEERS AROUND GOLFERS, TOMBSTONES, CIRCUS CLOWNS AND AN OVER-FRIENDLY DOG, TO DISCOVER A "NO MAP'S LAND" BETWEEN LOCAL AND GLOBAL MERIDIANS.

coiled on the grass near the truck and noticed a trench had been dug in wedged segments the width of a spade. When I returned again they were both sitting in the van.

The tail of the **Y** leads to the word **MAP** drawn in a large open area, ideal for writing on, with roads and footpaths crisscrossing the grass, dividing it into ample segments for the structure of large letters. I drew in pencil on a map where the word **MAP** was to be written. The day I chose to make the drawing happened to be the day Zippo's Circus was in town. Some clown called Zippo parked his circus right on top of the **P** of my **MAP**.

I started to draw a weighty **M** using a church to anchor the main stroke, traveling parallel up the first leg to help keep a consistent scale. Between the letters **M** and **A**, I encountered a man in a yellow day-glo jacket, leaning on a temporary fence that would lead the public the full length of the letters to the circus entrance. Asked how long the circus was around, he could reply only by pointing to the entrance and saying "Tickets" and "Yes Zippo".

The **A** was made in a tile of land in the middle of which a short man dressed as a golfer was practicing his swing. I first defined the outer shape of the **A** clockwise around his game, then found myself heading towards him as I drew the underbelly of the **A**. I looked up and saw myself directly in line with the intended trajectory of his ball. He was patiently poised with a grin. As I approached, I apologized and told him I couldn't really be elsewhere because I was writing the word **MAP** with a GPS receiver. He quickly understood and asked whether it would be any good for "The Knowledge"—he was studying for the road test to become a licensed London taxi driver.

On towards the **P**, but the clown and his friends had scattered their circus vehicles all over the place. Instead of making the intended steady curves, I had to negotiate jaggedly around caravans, support trucks, storage trailers and generators, and in between brightly decorated games and rides. The dot of the semi-colon was formed by circumnavigating a burger van.

TRUE PLACES was written in Greenwich Park, home of the Royal Observatory: the place where time and space was established as an international standard in 1884. When Melville wrote *Moby-Dick*, places disagreed when they met up with others. They still do. The Greenwich Meridian (measured on the local best-fitting Airy 1830 ellipsoid coordinate system) forms the baseline of the word **TRUE**, while the GPS meridian (measured on the GRS80 system, aligned to best fit the whole earth) serves as the cap line of the word **PLACES**. The distance between the two meridians measures 343 feet. The **R** in **TRUE** stands on the grounds of the Royal Observatory, while the **A** in **PLACES** had to be adjusted to avoid a café.

In the middle of Greenwich Park I got bitten on the chin by a dog (Time 14:38:45, Place N51.47876° W0.00152°). I was trying to tightrope along the Greenwich Meridian and saw an excited black Labrador pelting towards me from a distance. Her eyes were wide and her tongue was loose and, as she galloped towards me, I tightened my footsteps in anticipation. I couldn't move off course to play or I'd spoil the line. She leapt up and pounced on my chest. I lifted the GPS receiver above my head but the dog continued to leap for it again and again when she happened to bite me on the chin. "She's only young," the owner yelled from a distance. Neither blood nor scar but I was pleased nonetheless to have come back from the park with a mucky jacket.

On one of my reconnaissance trips, I roamed around the Millennium Dome complex, built to celebrate the turn of the 21st Century, in search of a space to compose **NEVER ARE**. The dome itself is still magnificent; the surrounding area is in an awkward state. High fences protect large spaces; rows of empty bicycle racks stand waiting on the edges of empty parking lots; fields ready to accommodate apartment blocks are fenced off with billboards advertising a better standard of living.

At one point, I found a gap in a wooden fence that opened to sufficient ground for writing. I recorded the position and returned a few days later, only to find that the opening had been closed. A familiar lesson learned once again. When I eventually found the opportunity to draw over a huge empty parking lot—usually fenced off—I seized the chance. The gates had been opened for builders constructing a set of new apartments. I glided in exhausted at sunset, and improvised the word **NEVER**, pacing along the letters, all the while checking scale against remaining distance, orientation, spelling and security guards. The lobe of the last letter arc'd under a silenced helicopter pad and the final leg extended into the far corners of the fence. I headed back along to underline the word, and went on to write the word **ARE**, squeezing it into the operational parking lot next to the Dome by pacing past Porsches, meandering around Mercedes and fumbling past Fords.

The text was written over a period of three months from January 2005. The distance of the lines recorded on foot composing the drawing was 44.2 miles and the total distance traveled to make the drawing was 458.6 miles. I had two bicycle punctures with reinforced puncture resistant tires, the first of which happened 20 miles into a reconnaissance journey that ended after pushing the bike home for 9 miles. I wrote under the sun, in the rain, and in snow, and saw the trees sprout the beginnings of spring. After closing the body of the last letter, I headed as far north as the land allowed, to a small pier on which the Greenwich Meridian is marked, and finished the drawing by circling around on the footpath at the edge of the River Thames, for a full stop.

See "Cerebral Cities," pp. 180–183.

MESSAGE IN A BOTTLE

WITH HER ATLAS COLLAGES AND GLOBE TRACINGS, BRITISH ARTIST **LAYLA CURTIS** DEFAMILIARIZES MAPS, REFLECTING ON OUR WISHFUL ATTEMPTS TO CHART THE WORLD. IN HER RECENT PROJECT *MESSAGE IN A BOTTLE: FROM RAMSGATE TO THE CHATHAM ISLANDS*, SHE DROPPED GPS-ENABLED BOTTLES IN THE OCEAN. SHE TELLS **PETER HALL** HOW SHE TRACED THEIR ALEATORY JOURNEYS.

Peter Hall: Last year you released 50 bottles into the sea, some containing GPS devices and some with printed messages. How did this curious project start?

Layla Curtis: I was commissioned by Turner Contemporary in Margate, Kent, as part of a program of residencies running up to its launch in 2007. My project came out of a residency at the Ramsgate Maritime Museum. The museum is an old clockhouse, and there is a sign above the main door that says "this clock is five minutes, 41 seconds faster than Greenwich Mean Time." Inside the building is a longitude line inlaid in the wooden floor. Standard national time was only introduced in Britain in 1847, and the idea that Ramsgate could announce its own line and own time intrigued me. I began thinking about which countries you'd come across if you followed that line half way around the world. The nearest inhabited place to the precise mathematical point antipodal to Ramsgate is Rehoku, which was renamed The Chatham Islands in the 1700s by a British explorer, after his ship, *HMS Chatham*. The ship actually set sail from Dover, which is 10 miles away from Ramsgate, something I couldn't ignore. You try to research the other side of the world and end up on your own doorstep.

That's an interesting indication of the historical lines of power.

Exactly. Those things really interest me. I thought it would be nice to somehow connect Ramsgate to The Chatham Islands by sending a message to them. A message in a bottle seemed a really obvious thing to do.

And romantic.

I was interested in the relationships that have grown from people finding messages in bottles. I was struck by a tale of a sailor who had put a message in a bottle that said "To the beautiful woman who finds this message, please contact me." Apparently, a beautiful woman did find it, got in touch, and they ended up getting married.

There's wishful thinking in hurling a message in a bottle into the ocean.

Yes, normally when you send a message in a bottle you don't have a clue who, if anyone, is going to find it. But the sailor's

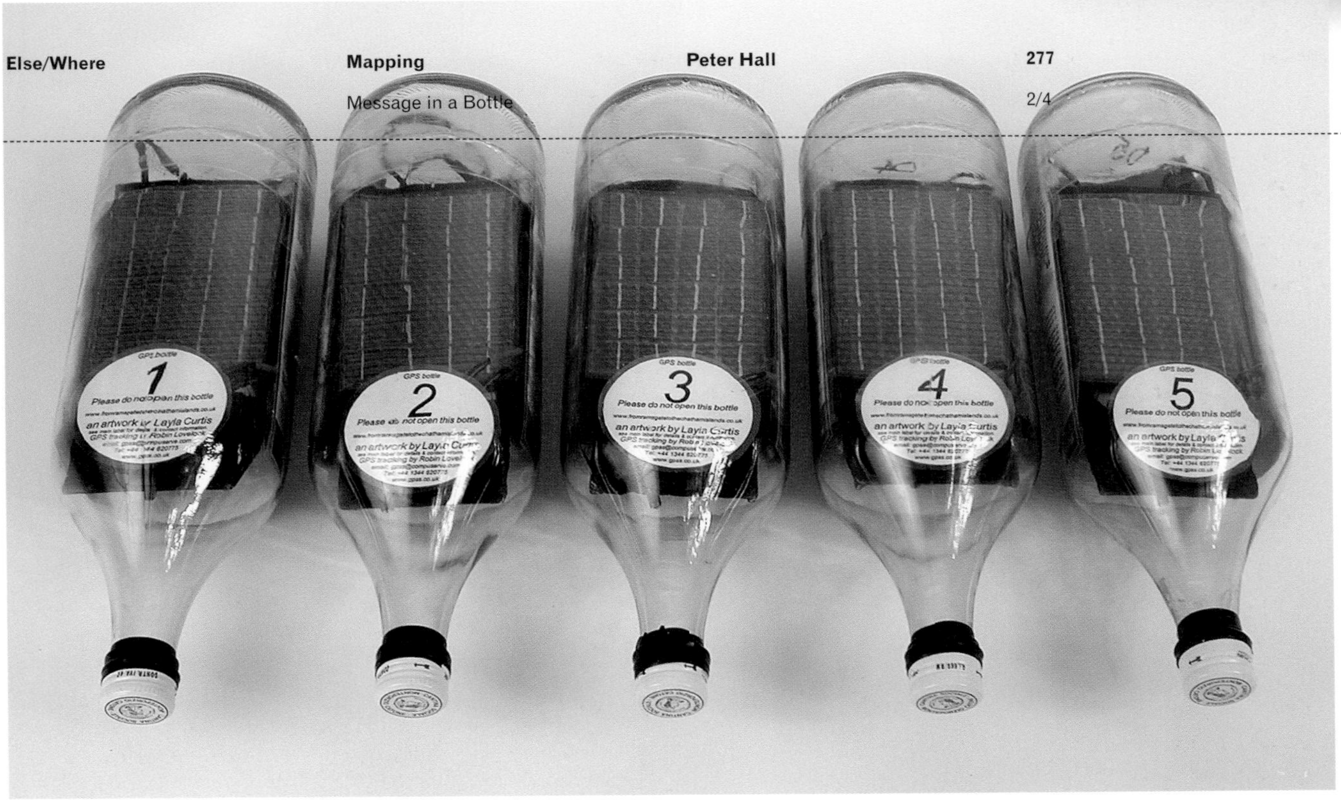

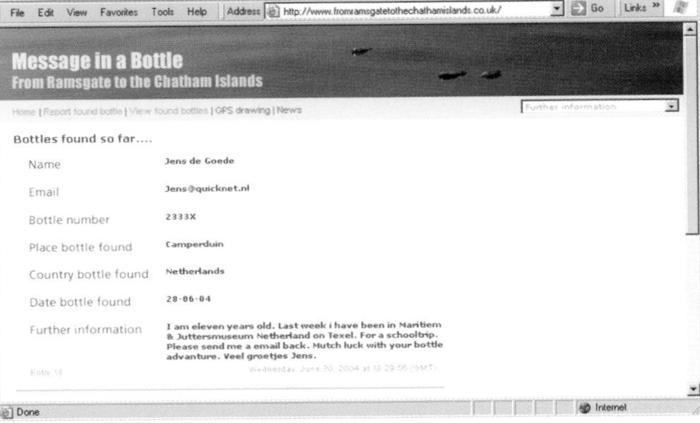

Layla Curtis *Message in a Bottle: From Ramsgate to The Chatham Islands*, 2004 / commissioned by Turner Contemporary following a residency by the artist at Ramsgate Maritime Museum / (top): five bottles containing GPS tracking equipment. (bottom, clockwise from upper left): the artist determining the longitude and latitude co-ordinates of launch locations; launching the non-GPS bottles off the coast of Ramsgate, Kent, with the help of local school children; project website, showing an entry by an 11-year-old Dutch boy who reported finding bottle 2333X in the Netherlands; bottles floating / images courtesy of Layla Curtis.

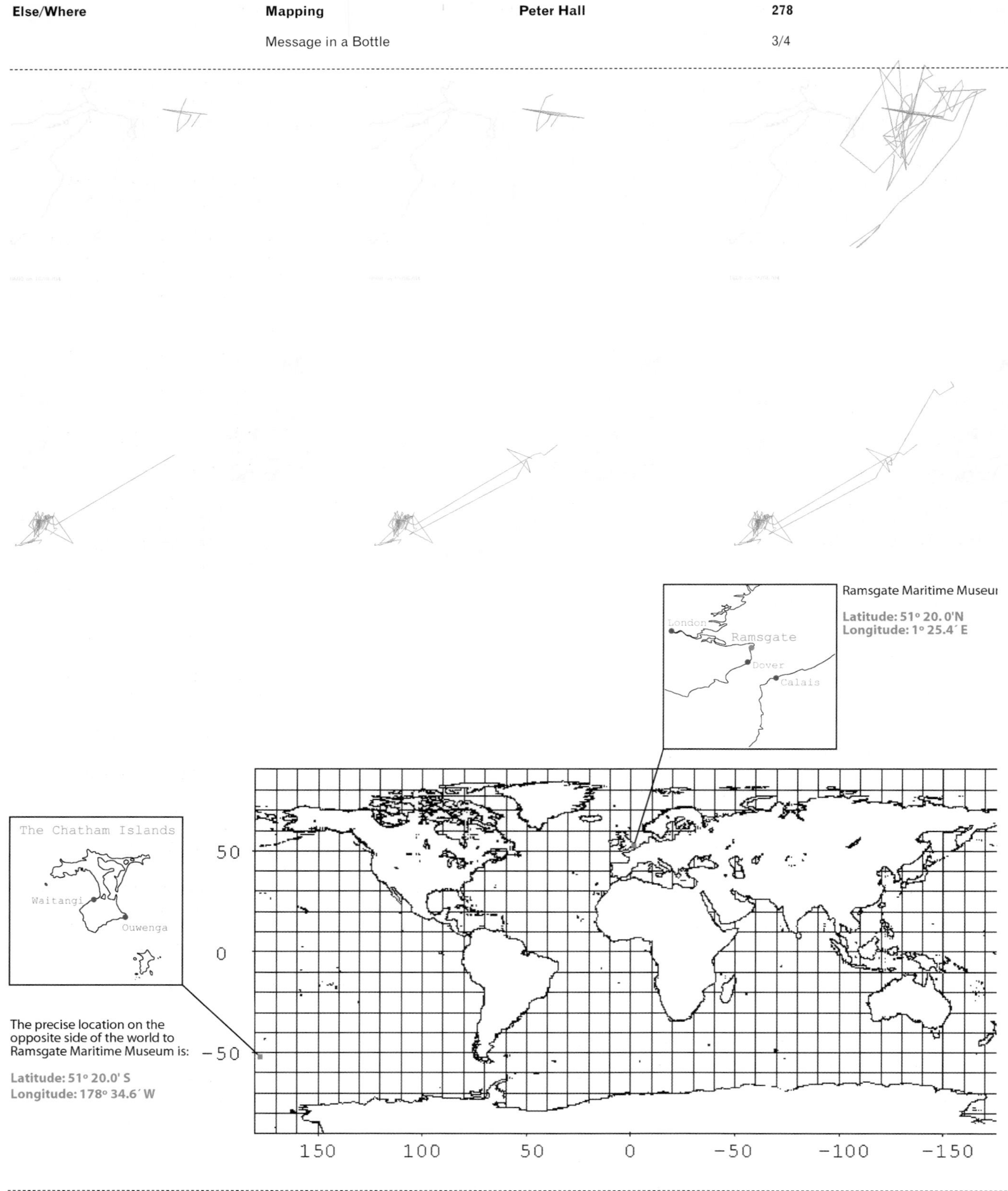

Layla Curtis *Message in a Bottle: From Ramsgate to The Chatham Islands*, 2004 / commissioned by Turner Contemporary following a residency by the artist at Ramsgate Maritime Museum. (top): live GPS drawings (selected stills) showing the paths the GPS-enabled bottles followed; (bottom): determining Ramsgate's antipodal point / images courtesy of Layla Curtis.

message was directed to a specific kind of person, which is obviously ridiculous—similar to what I was doing, in sending a message to people in The Chatham Islands. I was interested in tracking the journeys of these bottles to see if they ever actually get there, which is how the two methods of tracking came about: tracking through human contact and through GPS.

If you find a bottle, there's an instruction leaflet inside with a code number that asks you to visit the website to report it, and then put everything back inside and return the bottle to the sea to continue its journey. The idea is that these bottles might go through many hands and form a chain of contact. Within six weeks that started to happen; four or five have been found more than once. Some sailed up to Aberdeen and most of the rest went to Holland and France.

What's the furthest a bottle has traveled?

We've had a GPS report from a bottle in Holland. But it's difficult to know exactly where the GPS bottles are at all times as they rely on a mobile phone signal to transmit their location to us. While they're crossing massive oceans they can record where they are but they can't send messages. A non-GPS bottle was reported found in Scotland, 400 miles from the launch point. I've read stories about bottles going around the world in a couple of years or taking six months to cross the Atlantic.

Is there a bell that rings in your studio when a GPS bottle sends a message?

The whole process is automatic. There's a computer with a GSM modem that can receive text messages from the bottles as soon as they are within mobile phone range. We've had some reports that bottles have reached the U.S. but I have no real proof because the people who have reported bottles found in New York or Chile haven't managed to supply the code number.

There's a nice juxtaposition here between the precision of the GPS mapping system and the relative imprecision of people reporting findings by email.

I really liked the idea of people finding the bottles and using the Internet, so while they're logging on to report their own find, they can find out where other bottles have landed. It's the idea of a random network of people coming together, which the Internet allows you to do.

Do you have any qualms about appropriating military technologies for your projects?

When I was researching tracking technologies used in mobile phones, I noticed that in the UK, there were posters advertising systems that allow parents to track their children using triangulation, if mobile phones are used near three different masts. In the States, much of the advertising for the same technology is about tracking your lover: "Is he at the office or somewhere else?"

You've made several other projects in which you've dissected and rearranged maps. How did you get into making those collages?

When I graduated from Edinburgh College of Art in 1998, I moved directly to Japan. In Japan's map of the world, Japan is in the center. I made a collage map of the UK using Japanese road maps called *The United Kingdom of Japan*. I also wrapped the globe with tracing paper and traced only the text, which became a way of mapping the shapes of the land masses. The projection—if you can call it that—changed depending on how the paper was wrapped around the globe. I made a series of tracings, with alternative view-points, so north isn't always at the top.

What do you hope these strange tracings evoke in the viewer?

They are just ways of pointing out different associations between places. On Japanese maps, Japan was very close to the west coast of America. I was accustomed to seeing Japan and America on opposite sides of the world. Suddenly Europe and the U.S. were as far from each other as they could possibly be.

What is it about cartography that most interests you?

The familiarity of it. Everyone can identify with mapping and everyone trusts maps on a daily basis, to get from A to B. But when you dissect them, maps are very subjective things and only hold a certain amount of information. I'm interested in playing with that system.

FLIGHT PATHS

COULD PIGEONS BE PREFERABLE TO SATELLITES IN ESTABLISHING REMOTE SENSING NETWORKS? **PETER HALL** GETS A BIRD'S EYE VIEW AS AN EXPERIMENTAL FLOCK OF AVIAN MAPPERS TAKES ITS MAIDEN FLIGHT IN BROOKLYN.

At evening, casual flocks of pigeons make
Ambiguous undulations as they sink
Downward to darkness, on extended wings.
—Wallace Stevens, "Sunday Morning"

The scene: a Brooklyn rooftop where two architects and a pigeon coop owner are preparing to launch a new chapter in the history of aerial surveillance. While one architect holds a white pigeon, the other fits it with a customized harness containing a video camera lens and circuitry. On cue, the coop owner swings a long white stick like a cheerleader's baton, scaring a flock of pigeons into the sky, while the second architect presses a button on the camera and releases his bird. Cut to the sound of flapping and jumpy video footage: behold, the rooftop, now spattered with white bird droppings, then a pair of jeans, the architects' faces and, suddenly, treetops and the discombobulated skyline of northern Brooklyn.

This, the first "sortie" in the *Brooklyn Pigeon Project* in May 2003, yielded a three second approximation of a pigeon's eye view of the earth, albeit a little warped and distorted by unexpected in-flight vibrations. The architects behind the experiment, Benjamin Aranda and Chris Lasch, plan to equip a flock of pigeons with their customized miniature cameras to capture simultaneous footage of the city below. The idea is to set up a remote sensing network that records in a distributed and episodic fashion, revealing something about how flocks of birds move and (perhaps) how things are missed by conventional, photographic mapping techniques using airplanes and orbiting satellites.

The wish to see as a bird sees is nothing new. Before the invention of aircraft, human attempts to achieve a bird's eye view took various forms, from ascending tall buildings to mounting cameras on rockets, balloons and kites. A more direct precedent for the *Brooklyn Pigeon Project* occurred in 1903 when the pharmacist and photographer Julius Neubronner patented a miniature pigeon camera, the "Doppel-Sport," which was carried aloft by a bird and activated by a timing mechanism to take pictures every 30 seconds. The resulting imagery, of a castle in Kronberg, Germany, is curiously different from aerial photographs taken from balloons and kites around the same time. Whereas the latter reflect a relatively stately ascent, Neubronner's pigeon shots, complete with bird wingtips in the corner of each frame, offered hurried, choppy stills snatched during an unpredictable flight path. The strangeness of the images caused a sensation at the 1909 Dresden International Photographic Exhibition where Neubronner exhibited them as picture postcards. The Doppel-Sport was subsequently put into service with homing pigeons in World War I for spying on the French.

Aranda and Lasch, who formed their experimental architecture lab, Terraswarm, after graduating from Columbia University's Master's program in architecture, arrived at pigeon surveillance via an interest in filming the dynamic city. "Coming from architecture, video was liberating," Aranda says. "A time-based medium exposes the city's behavior rather than its image, as much as it's possible to allow this parsing. Phenomena like rate, exchange, transaction and feedback began to emerge as common themes. We called all these phenomena 'traffic' and consciously decided that any product of the studio dealing with them will be catalogued as a 'traffic primer'."

Terraswarm's fifth traffic primer was originally meant to be a documentary film on CD-ROM, mapping the sport of pigeon flying in Brooklyn, where coop owners known as "mumblers" compete to raid pigeons from rival coops. They capture each others' birds by training their flocks to fly in wider and wider circles until they intersect with an errant pigeon from a neighboring coop, before swiftly bringing the flock back home—with disoriented pigeon in tow. A bucket of grain is shaken to signal the birds to return. But after securing enough funding to begin the project, with a $15,000 film, media and new technology production grant from New York State Council for the Arts (NYSCA), Aranda and Lasch realized that the pigeons could make the film themselves.

A pigeon's flight path is far more complex and unpredictable than that of an orbiting satellite, making the idea of a remote sensing network based on organic flight patterns a potentially rich area of investigation. But Terraswarm's project also presents an inherent critique of our reverence for conventional sensing networks. "We're not attaching, for example, a GPS device to a pigeon because we're not interested in placing a pigeon on a grid in a kind of universal order," says Aranda. "We're interested in finding the edge of the mapping grid, and trying not to use it."

According to Aranda and Lasch's research, airplanes and orbiting satellites produce imagery of the earth that needs to be heavily doctored to create the illusion of continuous real-time coverage. "Planes go along a path and then overlap that path on the way back, and satellites do the same thing with overlapping elliptical patterns in orbit," says Aranda. "There's this painstaking [post-production] process to remove the element of time. Two images along a path will be corrected to look like the same view, or to have shadows removed if the sun has moved. All these displacements are flattened out." A satellite image of a specific territory may be made up of several frames; in addition, the lone eye of the

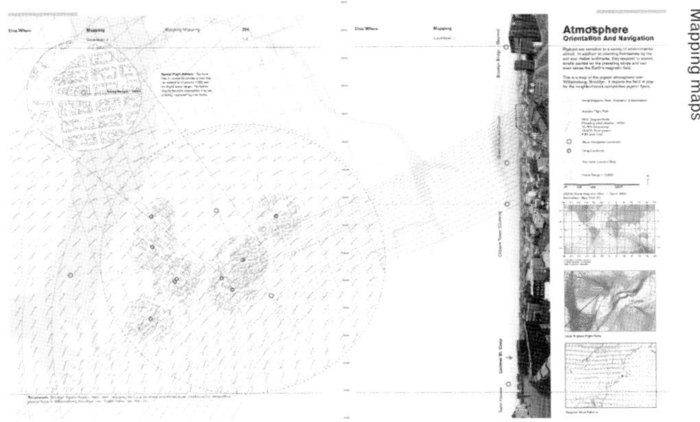

Mapping maps

gazetteer J 1–2/8 pp. 284–285

camera can only show one point that is not distorted by the curvature of the earth. "In order to remove distortion and conform to existing data sets—latitude/longitude—takes lots of work," Lasch says.

What could a pigeon network reveal that a satellite could not? The question seems to demand a degree of lateral thinking. A flock of birds in flight offers a vivid example of an emergent system, in which coordinated activity occurs apparently without any hierarchical control. Mitchel Resnick, of the Massachusetts Institute of Technology, has noted our tendency to mistakenly assume that a flock of birds determines which direction to fly by following a leader bird: "People assume centralized control where there is none."[1] Craig Reynolds' classic artificial simulation study of flock behavior in 1986 grants each bird—or "boid"—three behavioral attributes: separation (to avoid hitting other birds), alignment (to follow the average direction of other birds) and cohesion (to move toward the average center of the flock).[2] Terraswarm tested Reynolds' model on filmed footage of pigeon flocks in flight, singling out specific birds to follow their individual patterns, and how they track other birds to move in parallel. But they also found that some birds move in an opposite direction to the flock. At certain points, coordinated patterns break down and errant birds peel off, or the flock splits in two, or into apparent chaos, before reforming. "The system always wants to tear apart—it's in a continual state of entropy," Aranda says. "The lack of control in a flock of pigeons makes the system really hard to map."

U.S. Air Force researchers have already investigated the potential of flock-like formations of airborne cameras: they have proposed launching micro-satellites in bird-inspired formations to minimize fuel consumption.[3] But film and video arguably offer, uniquely, a means of capturing data that is not dependent on a human subject—a mode of seeing not attached to the human eye. The pigeon-camera represents an attempt to distance human control yet further from this seeing. To see as an airborne flock of pigeons sees is perhaps (to appropriate a Deleuzian term) to be "becoming-pigeon." Like Kafka's human-insect and Melville's whale, the pigeon-camera reflects a crossing of lines, the human-made and the animal,

1. Mitchel Resnick, "Can Organizations Behave Like a Flock of Birds?" lecture, MIT Center for Coordination Science, April 7, 1995. See also *Turtles, Termites, and Traffic Jams: Explorations in Massively Parallel Microworlds*. Cambridge, MA: MIT Press, 1997.

2. Craig Reynolds, *Boids: Flocks, Herds and Schools—a Distributed Behavioral Model*. <www.red3d.com/cwr/boids/>

3. Space Vehicles Directorate, "Birds Inspire Formation-Flying Satellites," (November 5, 1999) <www.vs.afrl.af.mil/News/1998-2000/99-23.html>

driven by a human desire to become "other." As critic Claire Colebrook puts it, "becoming-animal is the power, not to conquer what is other than the self, but to transform oneself in perceiving difference."[4]

Part of this interest in birds' in-flight behavior—in "becoming-pigeon"—is a long-standing human desire to comprehend a highly successful non-human mapping system. Pigeons have been domesticated since the Bronze Age, and are famously able to find their way home after being released in foreign territory hundreds of miles away. Before the advent of the telegraph and telephone, pigeons provided the swiftest means of delivering a message; during the Prussian siege of Paris in 1870–71, over a million communications—official and private—were carried by pigeon post. Consensus among ornithologists is that these birds use a number of navigation methods. Over familiar terrain, visible landmarks and sounds seem to help them pilot their routes. Migration routes follow leading lines along rivers, coastlines or mountain ranges; nocturnal migrants have been shown to use the Pole Star, while other birds use the sun as a means of orientation. A series of experiments in the 1960s demonstrated that some birds, including robins and pigeons, have tiny crystals of magnetite, an iron oxide, in their brains, which may act as lodestones pressing against sensitive tissues, and help them orient themselves using the Earth's magnetic field. More recent research suggests that olfactory clues also guide birds within 60 miles of home, and that the modern pigeon has even learned to follow highways. Racing pigeons can find precise

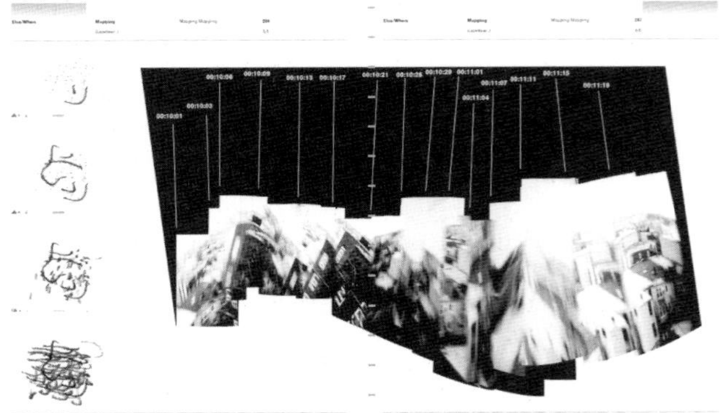

Mapping maps

gazetteer J 3–4/8 pp. 286–287

locations even when blown off-course by crosswinds, indicating that their navigational ability is even more sophisticated than sailors' distance and bearing technique, according to naturalist Alexander Skutch, who concludes:

> When we contemplate navigational feats that baffle our comprehension, performed by birds that lack the charts, instruments and special training that humans need for comparable accomplishments, we are filled with profound respect for their abilities while we continue to wonder what goes on inside their little heads.[5]

Aranda and Lasch insist they did not embark on their project as bird lovers, and it has yielded quite different material from the footage of migrating birds in Jacques Perrin's 2001 documentary *Winged Migration*. Rather, Terraswarm's investigation reflects a revival of interest in the architecture profession in learning from non-human species, and in viewing the built environment as a system of flows. Like a building, a flock of pigeons is, as Aranda puts it, "unstable but contained" and as such it can teach the limits of our mapping system: "What's so wonderfully frustrating is that the birds resist this instrumentality. Because of their movements, the harder we tried to turn the pigeons into earth-bound satellites and the longer we worked on the maps and diagrams and videos, the more the edges frayed, and the more doubtful we became of their authority. Yet, this teasing was somehow refreshing."

Throughout 2004, Terraswarm was grappling with how to present footage gathered by four pigeons simultaneously in a format that conveyed the sortie's multiple perspectives. The project had received a new $4,000 Harvest Works artist-in-residence grant; Aranda was working with a sound engineer to record a 3D soundscape of a flock in flight, for a multi-screen, surround-sound spectacle. "Whether it's 15 seconds or 15 minutes," he said, "we want to show the footage of four cameras with simultaneous sound capture, presented as-is."

Joining Aranda and Lasch for a rooftop sortie in a late September afternoon of that year, however, I witnessed just how incommensurate are the worlds of electronic

4. Claire Colebrook, *Gilles Deleuze.* (New York: Routledge, 2002) p. 133.

5. Alexander F. Skutch, *Life of the Pigeon.* Ithaca: Cornell University Press, 1991, p. 110.

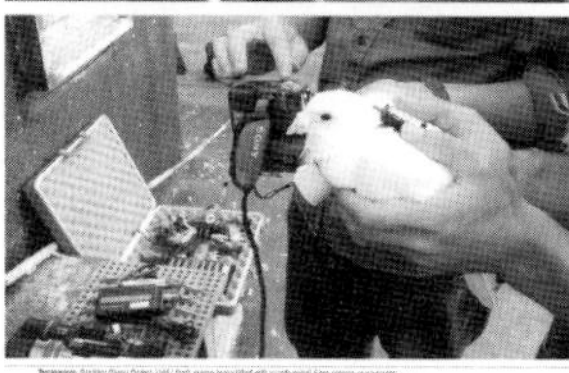

Mapping maps

gazetteer J 5–6/8 pp. 288–289

surveillance and avian movement. Terraswarm had developed (with electrical engineer Carlos Diaz) a new wireless camera design that would eliminate some of the distortion caused in its predecessor—which recorded to an onboard flash memory card. With the new camera, pigeon-captured video would be transmitted back to a handheld camera for simultaneous viewing, as long as line of sight was maintained. This presumed a degree of cooperation from the pigeons. But in fact, as each harnessed bird was released it flew uncharacteristically down below the rooftop rather than up with the flock, breaking the line of site and interrupting the video feed. We gathered excitedly around the camera screen to witness the bird's-breast view only to be greeted by a blank image. Occasionally, the video would burst onto the monitor, but all that appeared was a disappointingly static view of a nearby building rather than the jumpy in-flight footage we had anticipated: the camera-clad bird had perched atop a chimney or building ledge, as if in a sit-down protest against its newly-enforced job description.

Terraswarm remains convinced that once the pigeons become accustomed to wearing the harnesses, and with improved camera battery life, the *Brooklyn Pigeon Project* will fly. The unexpected benefit of the project, however, has been its influence on subsequent work by Aranda and Lasch. The "peeling studies" of the flock's behavior, which established certain patterns within a chaotic system, directly inspired the architects' entry for PS1's summer pavilion competition, the New York museum's high profile annual commission to build an outdoor structure for its sun-baked grounds. Aranda and Lasch teamed up with engineer Daniel Bosia from Arup's Advanced Geometry Unit to design a system of algorithmically-generated modular foam boulders arranged to form a courtyard water-filled grotto. "It's not that we were ever interested in nature for its beauty," says Aranda, "but we back-tracked into that space where rules and algorithms can generate structure."

The pigeon project also opened up—conceptually at least—new ways of seeing and uncovering the dynamics of the cityscape, which in turn influenced Terraswarm's newest project, *RGB*. For this, the architects purchased advertising space on the largest video billboard in the United States, which sits at the entrance to the Midtown Tunnel in Queens, New York. Aranda and Lasch observed that from positions behind the video billboard, the light cast at night illuminates a quarter-mile radius of the surrounding urban environment. "The city flickers like a living room in front of a TV," says Aranda. The project, scheduled for January 2006, will use the advertising space simply to display red, green and blue light—video's most saturated colors—on the screen, and record its effects. "It's a new way to literally paint the town," says Aranda.

It is a particular and rare kind of architectural practice that allows this kind of open-ended research to co-exist with more conventional paid commissions and allow its own momentum to transform a project, even overturning its original premise. Even during that first sortie on the Williamsburg rooftop, as Aranda and Lasch squinted at footage on a laptop, it was apparent that pigeon flights were not going to provide a swift and systematic re-mapping of the urban vicinity. The project had nestled itself at the intersection of two different mapping systems: between man and bird. As Wallace Stevens' poem (in the epigraph) hints, pigeons' undulations are ambiguous because they are always subject to the interpretations of the human eye. Any systematic mapping project based on pigeons will surely end in failure. But Terraswarm's might just sow the (bird) seeds of a hybrid mapping system: one that aggregates information without first needing to superimpose a grid. Either way, it offers an imaginative rebuttal of the satellite's claim to omniscience.

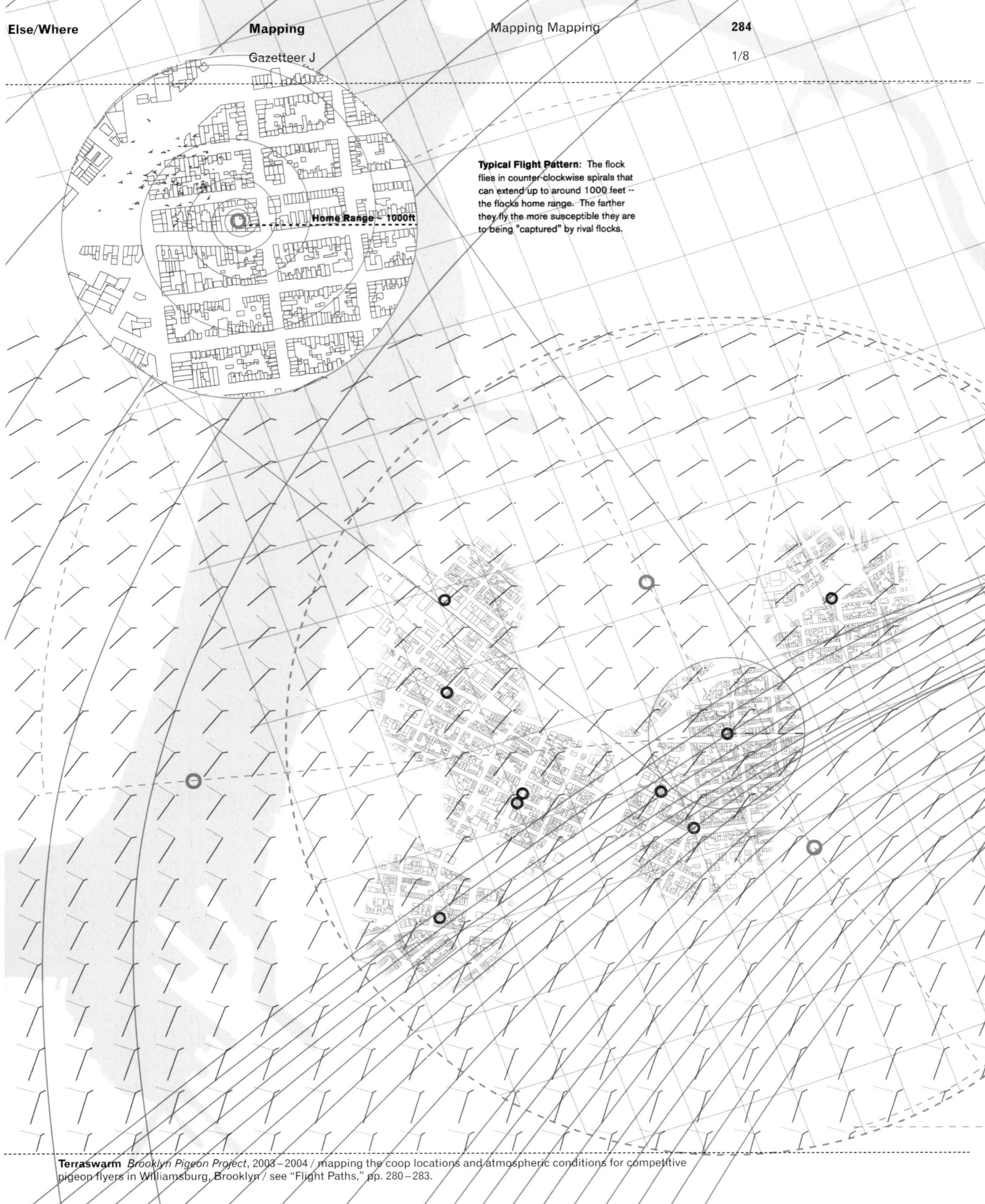
Home Range - 1000ft
Typical Flight Pattern: The flock flies in counter-clockwise spirals that can extend up to around 1000 feet -- the flocks home range. The farther they fly the more susceptible they are to being "captured" by rival flocks.

Terraswarm *Brooklyn Pigeon Project*, 2003–2004 / mapping the coop locations and atmospheric conditions for competitive pigeon flyers in Williamsburg, Brooklyn / see "Flight Paths," pp. 280–283.

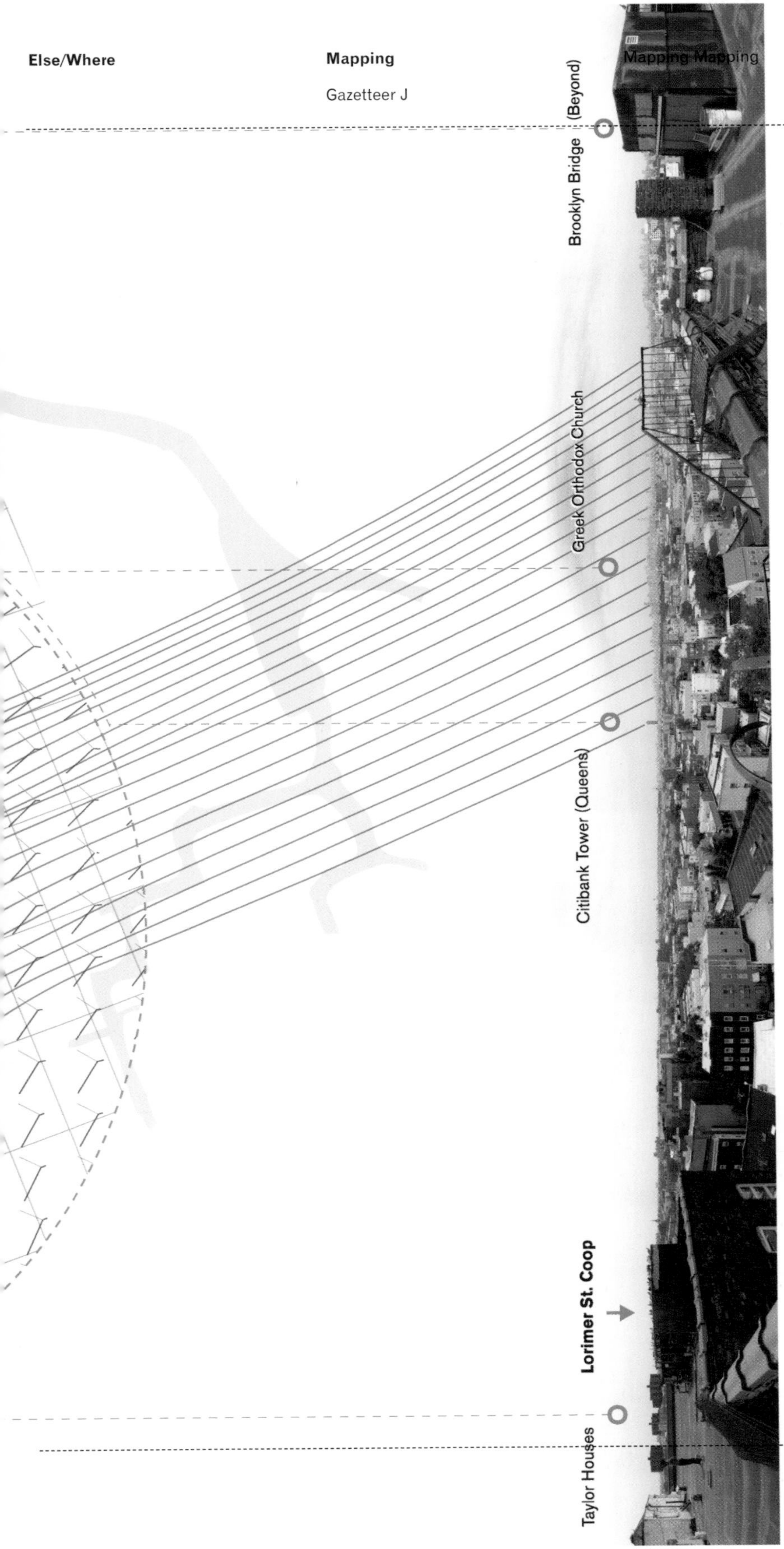

Atmosphere
Orientation And Navigation

Pigeons are sensitive to a variety of environmental stimuli. In addition to orienting themselves by the sun and visible landmarks, they respond to sound, smells carried on the prevailing winds and can even sense the Earth's magnetic field.

This is a map of the pigeon atmosphere over Williamsburg, Brooklyn. It depicts the field of play for the neighborhoods competitive pigeon flyers.

Brooklyn Bridge (Beyond)

Greek Orthodox Church

Citibank Tower (Queens)

Lorimer St. Coop

Taylor Houses

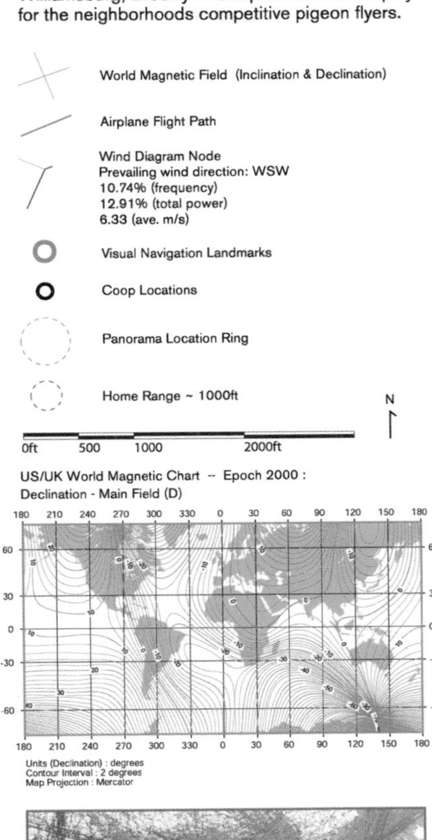

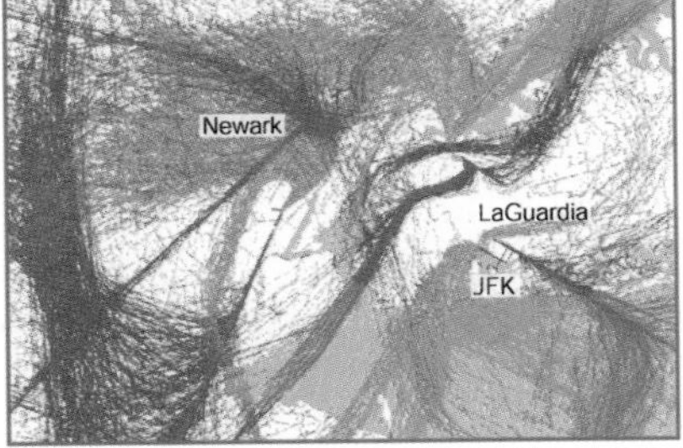

Local Airplane Flight Paths

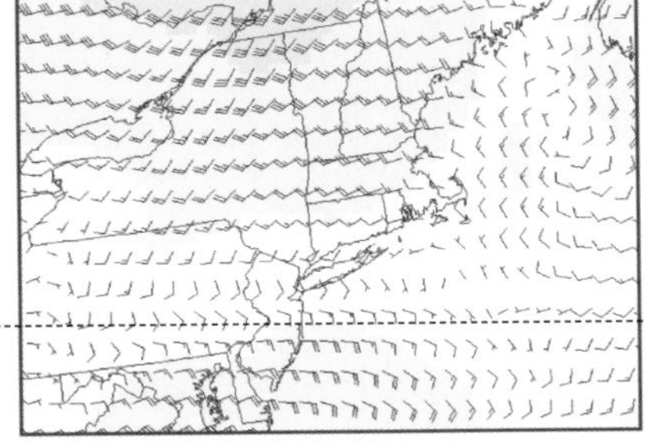

Regional Wind Patterns

Terraswarm *Brooklyn Pigeon Project*, 2003–2004 / (left, top to bottom): peeling studies, flock behavior analyzed by tracing individual bird movement in video footage shot from the ground. (across spread): time and space pigeon flight map, showing stills of bird-filmed footage / see "Flight Paths," pp. 280–283.

:21
00:10:25
00:10:29
00:11:01
00:11:04
00:11:07
00:11:11
00:11:15
00:11:19

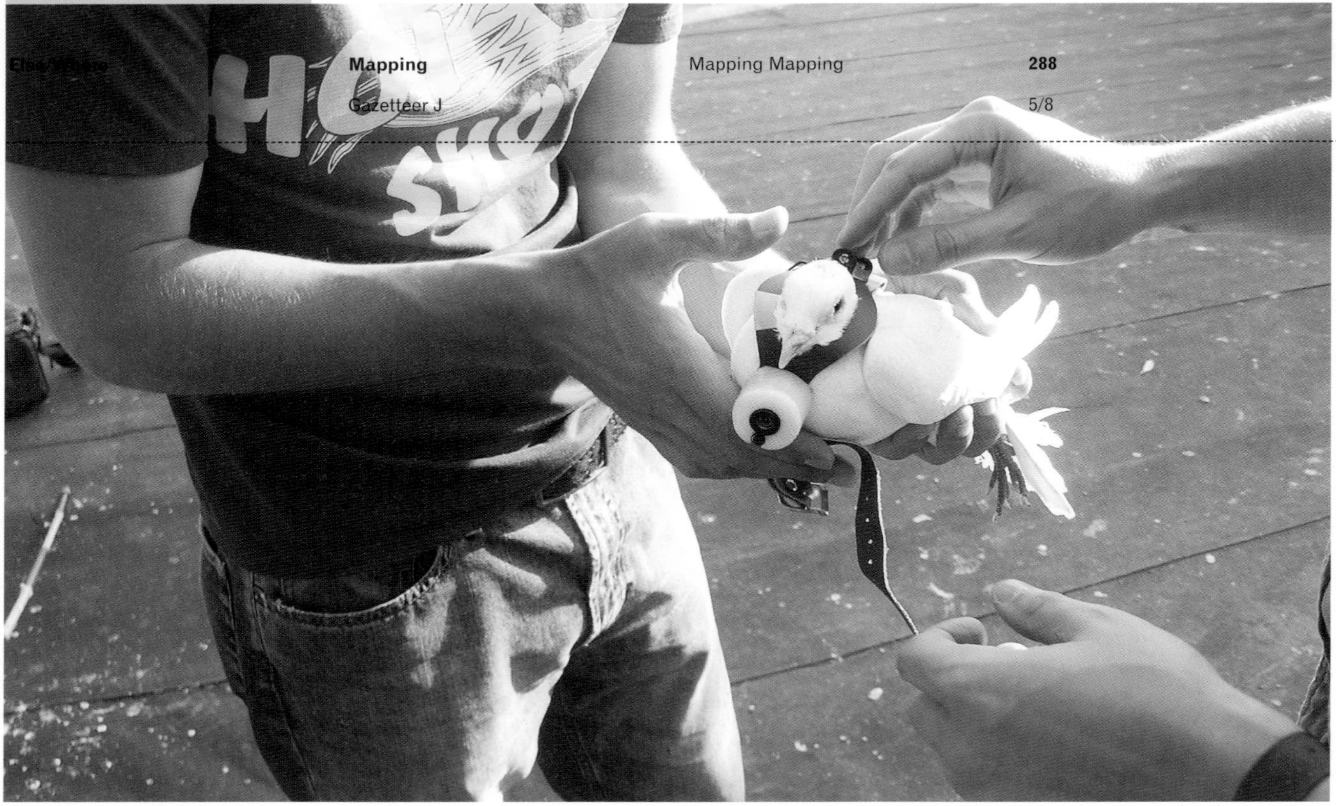

Terraswarm *Brooklyn Pigeon Project*, 2004 / (this page, top): pigeon being fitted with a customized video camera on a harness; (this page, bottom): activating the camera—video battery is clipped into the harness on the pigeon's back. (opposite, top): avian surveillance. (opposite, bottom): Jose Sanchez's Williamsburg rooftop coop / photographs by Peter Hall / see "Flight Paths," pp. 280–283.

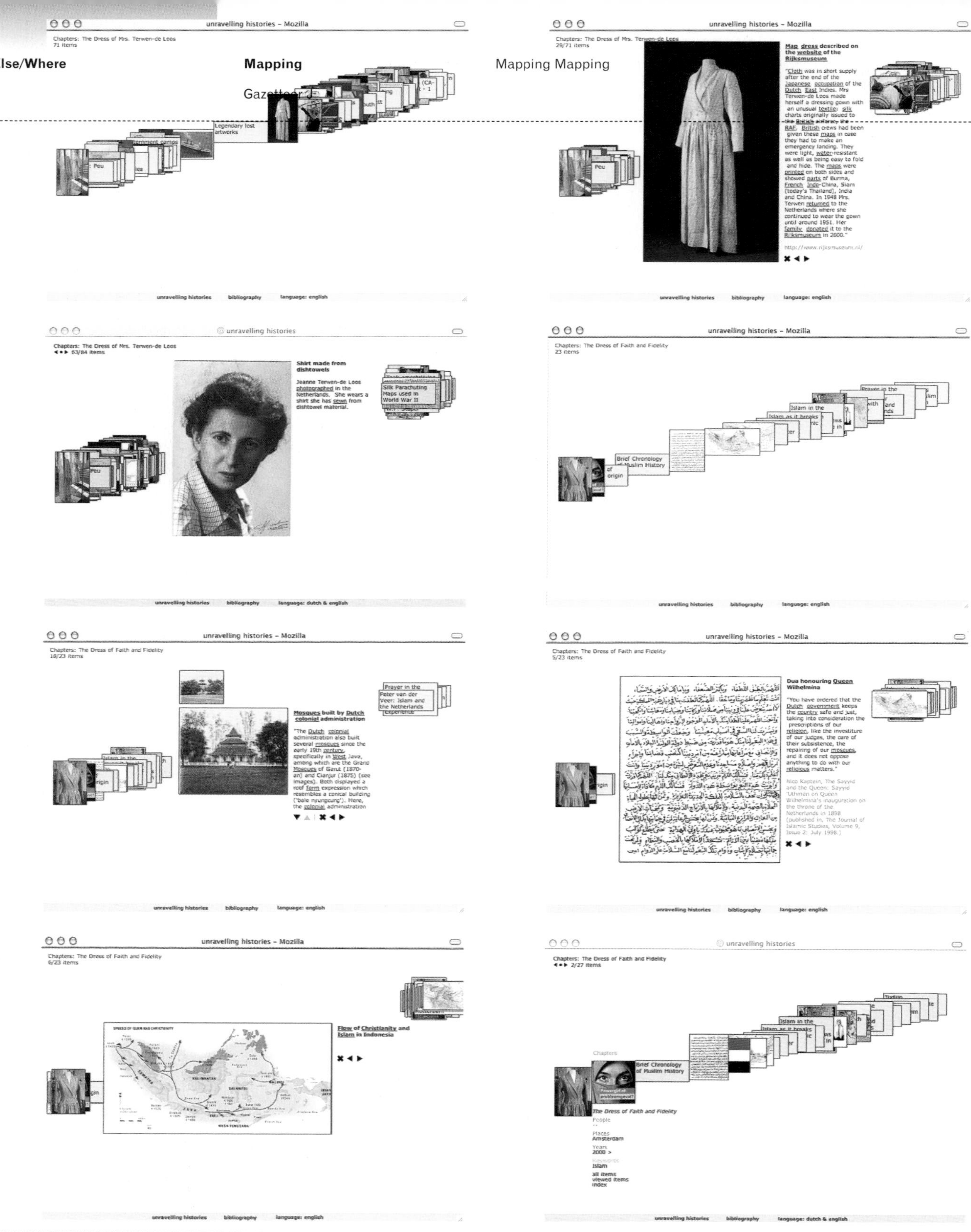

Michael Murtaugh with **De Geuzen** *Unravelling Histories*, 2002–2004 / selected screens from the online component of a two-part project by De Geuzen, which explores Dutch colonial narratives and their traces in the present. By clicking on one of the overlapping "cards," full-size images and additional information are retrieved / see "Contours and Colonies," pp. 292–299.

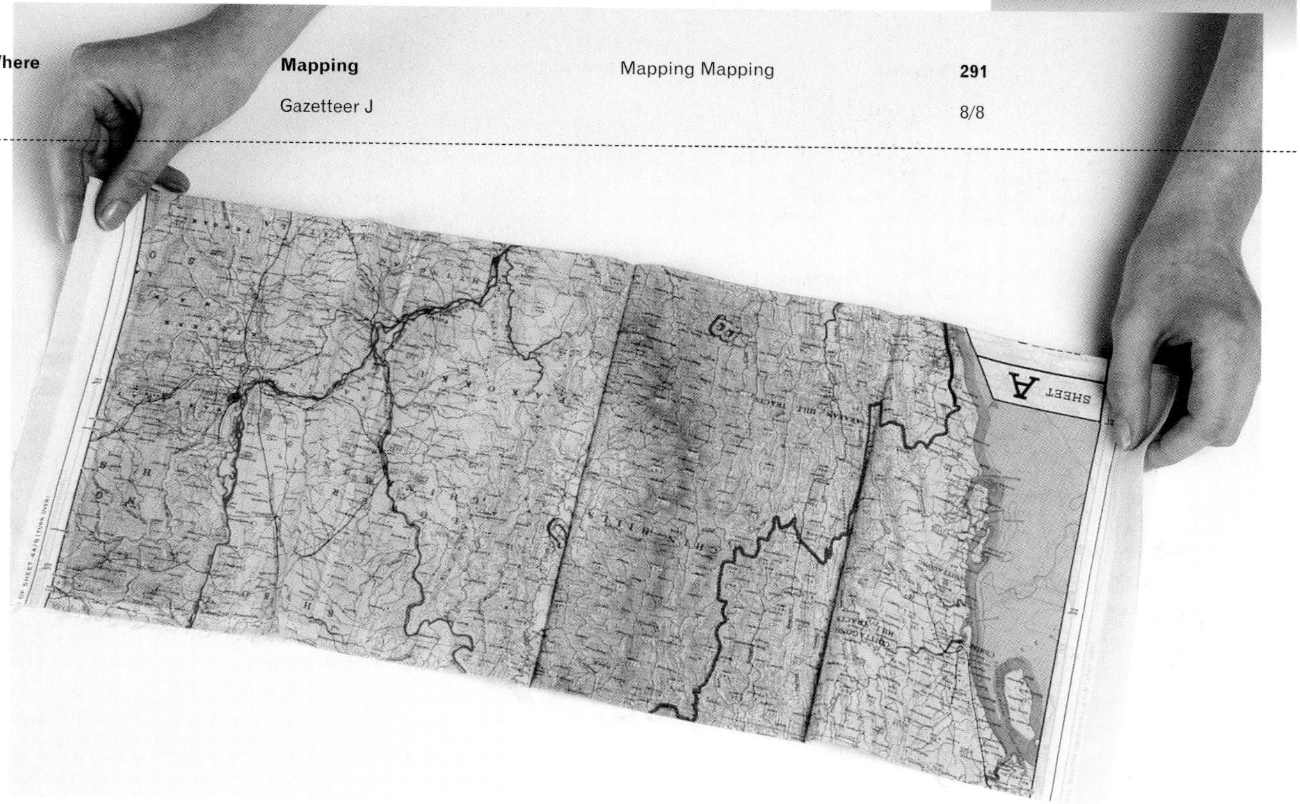

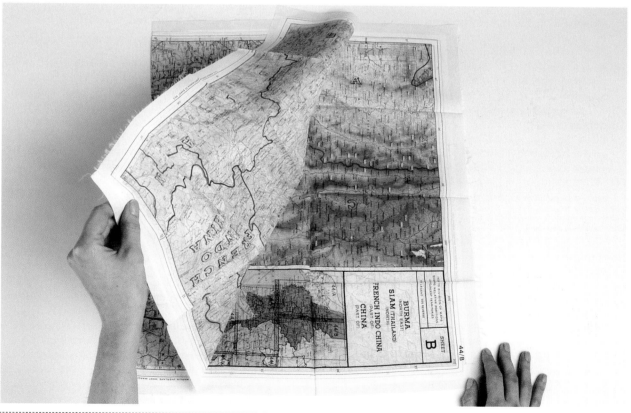

Royal Air Force double-sided printed silk parachutists' map from World War II showing Burma and parts of French-Indo China, Siam (now Thailand), India and China, 50 cm x 50 cm / from a set of RAF silk maps purchased in 1945 by Jeanne Terwen-de Loos / private collection Pier Terwen. Photographs © 2005 Gert Jan van Rooij / see pages 298–299 for enlarged views of this textile, which remained unused after Mrs. Terwen-de Loos had used the other maps to make her dress, now in the collection of the Rijksmuseum, Amsterdam / see "Contours and Colonies," pp. 292–299.

CONTOURS & COLONIES

Silk RAF parachutists' maps, made into a dress by a Dutch World War II widow, provide the text/ile for a rereading of Dutch colonial history, in the hands of contemporary artists **De Geuzen**. **Andrea Codrington** introduces Mrs. Terwen-de Loos' dress, then fabricates fictional accounts of the original dress and the artists' three recent re-editions.

In 1945, shortly after her release from a Japanese internment camp in Indonesia, a Dutch-born art historian named Jeanne Terwen-de Loos searched in a Jakarta flea market for remnant fabric to piece together into clothing. Passing her eyes over the usual batiks, she settled on a richly patterned and brightly colored bundle of material. The cloth turned out to be silk maps created by Britain's Royal Air Force for World War II parachutists making sorties over Southeast Asia who needed information about unfamiliar territories in easily transportable form. With clever cutting, she would transform the greens, oranges and blues of cartographic convention into a wearable map of her own history.

Conceived in Indonesia, but worn and eventually retired in Holland, Terwen-de Loos' dress eventually made its way to the Rijksmuseum in Amsterdam as an artifact of the Dutch colonial experience. On rare occasions the "morning dress" or "kimono" (as its acquisition listing describes it) could be seen behind a vitrine, but more often was stored away in the depths of the museum's archives. There it would likely have languished, had it not been for *Upstream*, an invitational exhibition exploring the legacy of the Dutch East India Trading Company, held in autumn 2002 in multiple venues throughout Amsterdam and the port city of Hoorn.

Invited to participate, the three partners in De Geuzen, an Amsterdam-based multi-visual research foundation, decided to build their contribution around the Terwen-de Loos garment, and used it as a map to investigate issues of Dutch and Muslim cultural and religious identity. With funds from Amsterdam's Fond voor de Kunst (Art Fund), Riek Sijbring, Femke Snelting and Renée Turner examined the original gown in detail — measuring its dimensions and styling, noting where it had been worn and mended — in order to create three new dresses that replicate its form, while offering up different content.

The Dress of Faith and Fidelity bears excerpts from a prayer to Allah written for the coronation of Queen Wilhelmina in 1898 — a text that bears bald testament to colonial attempts at bringing Islam to heel at the foot of the Dutch crown. Juxtaposed with the Arabic script are statistics about the growth of Islam in contemporary Holland and scraps of government policies conceived to monitor the religion's propagation and practice. *The Dress of Here, There and Other Dislocations* is divided into a bodice that shows a current cartography of Indonesia, and a skirt that bears street maps of Holland's twelve provincial capitals — places remade by immigrants from the country's former colonies. Finally, *The Dress of Propriety and Longing* is emblazoned with excerpts from various fictional and non-fictional sources depicting colonial life in the Dutch East Indies.

If the Terwen-de Loos gown acts as a kind of map of its owner's personal identity — her size (small), her era (World War II), her geographical context (Southeast Asia) — then its repeated form in the three other dresses provides a point of orientation from which to spin out related stories. All four dresses were shown together in fall 2002 in an installation called *Unravelling Histories* at Amsterdam's Historical Museum, the original behind glass because of its fragility, while the re-editions could be touched and viewed up close, adding a sensual layer to the cerebral context.

Terwen-de Loos' handmade gown represents a slippage between objective and subjective — between the hard/masculine instrumentality of maps made for wartime use and the soft/feminine intimate form of domestic apparel — providing a poetic frisson that seems only appropriate for an exploration of the legacies of colonialism. "Usually, maps are like a screen, a surface the viewer cannot penetrate," says Turner. "But with the Terwen-de Loos dress, a kind of transference happens because you empathize with her figure. You trace borders across her waist, along

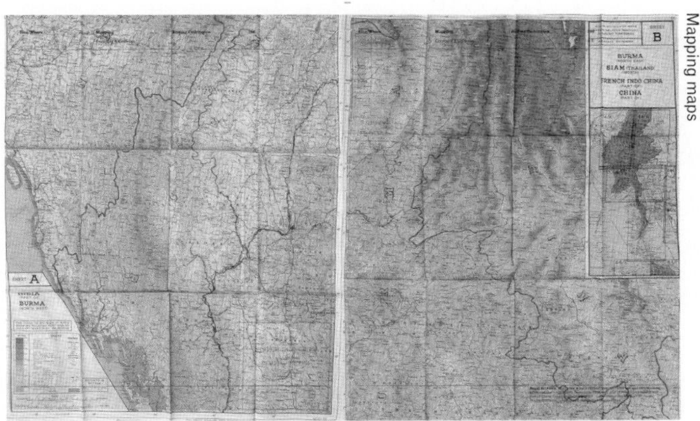

Contours & Colonies 7–8/8 pp. 298–299

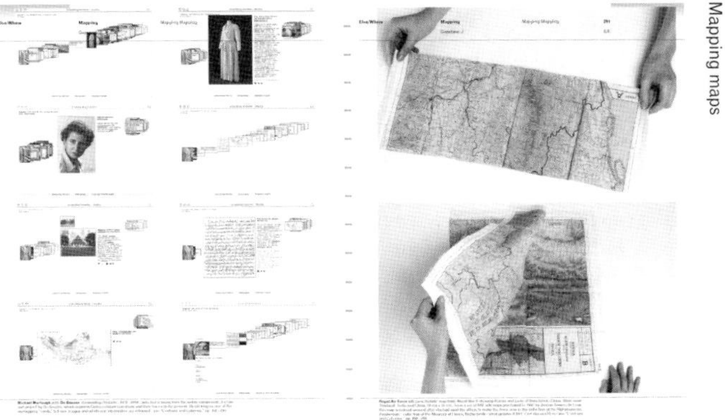

gazetteer J 7–8/8 pp. 290–291

her arm or around the nape of her neck, and that is a very different experience from looking at a flat screen or the perfect circumference of a globe."

While the installation was a one-time event, the project's accompanying website is ongoing and, in contrast to the installation, its interface deliberately subverts the direct wayfinding metaphor implicit in the gown's material provenance. Created for De Geuzen by digital artist Michael Murtaugh, the site presents multiple threads of inter-related information about Terwen-de Loos' life, Dutch colonialism in the East Indies, and narratives woven around the other dresses in such a way that getting lost is not just inevitable, but integral to the experience. "Where the dresses are contained or restrained by Terwen-de Loos's body scale," Turner explains, "the web presence is dispersed and less hierarchical."

<http://unravelling-histories.org/>

For each dress, a trove of related images, text excerpts and Internet links appears on the screen in panels overlapped like playing cards, from lower left to upper right. This plethora of information can be organized as chapters linked variously to the dresses, people, places, years or keywords (such as Cartography, Divided Allegiance, Islam, Literature). Each path carries the viewer off on an indirect and associative journey. A link from Terwen-de Loos' dress might, for example, lead to a mini-biography of her first husband, which, in turn, might lead to something about post-colonial literature, or to the number of boats sunk in the Battle of the Java Sea.

The experience of navigating the *Unravelling Histories* website is comparable to landing in the center of a foreign city without a map and making one's own way, unhindered by an official guide, to sanctioned sites of interest—a journey that is bewildering, at times maddening, but ultimately gratifying. Following Terwen-de Loos's life in this aleatory fashion is certainly an exercise in getting lost, but well worth the trip in terms of what one discovers about her lively, messy history and the world she inhabited.

The entwined threads of De Geuzen's physical and virtual exploration ultimately weave a darker view of the Netherlands' attitude to the outsider population of its former colonies—an attitude that is wrapped, today, in the national guise of tolerance but, upon closer examination, belies elements of prejudice. "Tolerance is a double-edged sword," concludes Turner, pointing to the numerous rules the Dutch government has created to regulate everything from Islamic butchers to Islamic schools. "Tolerance can also be a means of assimilating the other, accepting them without understanding them, or even worse, taming them, or controlling their behavior."

The Dress of Mrs. Terwen-de Loos

The woman reaches into a bin of textile scraps, rummaging until she finds something that slips easily and softly between her fingers. She rubs the material, which feels like silk, but dismisses the thought as impossible. Silk belongs to her past, a privileged contrast to the exotic roughness of Indonesia.

It has only been a few months since her release from a Japanese internment camp where she spent the last two years wondering what would be left of her world, were she able to return. The answer is: not much. She is glad not to have found out about her husband's death in the Battle of the Java Sea until she returned home. Job—her sweet scholar with the bittersweet name. She believes his body is resting on the seabed somewhere, surrounded by creatures that illuminate the dark water with their own strange lanterns. Instead of sackcloth and ashes, she wears a dress made of dish towels fished out of an old storage closet in the home they once shared, and pieced together over a series of kerosene-lit evenings.

She pulls out a pile of material and looks at it in the sunlight. There are five pieces of cloth, generous in size — certainly enough for a dress or robe, if she is thrifty enough in her cutting. She is small, and her time in the camps made her realize what a gift this can be. Her family called her Peu when she was a child, their lips pouting out the French word in jibing affection. She knew she was spared in the camps by the way she looked. She watched her Japanese captors scan the lines of women every morning, and saw in their eyes that she did not exist. And that was fine. It was always the mice that could nibble away at the power cord.

The cloth is emblazoned with maps of Burma, Siam, China and French Indochina, and she sees that it is silk, a product of Britain's Royal Air Force. She squints and the colors remind her of van Gogh's sower, scattering seed against a purple sky and fields of orange wheat. She imagines young men tumbling from the heavens, their landings made soft by parachutes and thoughts of bravery, or perhaps just a pint of beer.

And then there's the bewildering disjuncture between the map's graphic depiction and the three-dimensional reality. She remembers the honeymoon she and Job had taken in Lisbon before the war. Looking at the map at a café, they planned a meander from the Baixa where they were staying to the Bairro Alto. When they got there, they found that a sheer cliff separated the two streets, which appeared adjacent on the map. Fortunately there was an elevator, designed by one of Eiffel's students. Job had kissed her as the clanking mechanism rose in the air. She wondered if things could ever be as sweet as they were before the war.

She returns home to sketch out a pattern for her new kimono, and realizes she has two cheerful green buttons that will match the green expanse of Burma's rainforest. She works on her foot-treadle sewing machine until she finishes the next morning. *They will beat their swords into ploughshares and their spears into pruning hooks.* The hope was always one of transformation.

Jeanne Terwen-de Loos original silk dress, 1945–1946 / collection of the Rijksmuseum, Amsterdam.

The Dress of Here, There and Other Dislocations

overseen at Restaurant Samo Sebo, lunchtime, early December:

A septet of well-dressed ladies, 50-ish, hair the shade of winter wheat fields or aubergine. They perch above a *rijstaffel*, the steam from the food obscuring their faces when it is first brought out. The usual talk about sons and daughters, overworked husbands, vacations taken and vacations soon to come. There is the occasional silence when the women bring forks of Sambal Goreng to their mouths, fishing most delicately for the shrimp tail that coyly peeks out from the sides of their lips after the nubbin of flesh is gone.

A line is cast out into the expectant waters. “Did you hear about Gertrud Kuyper's youngest, Dominica?” Heads bob “no” and the circle tightens. Trim bodies are pushed forward as if by irresistible magnetic force and stay perfectly still like delicately carved ivory statues in the rough-hewn setting of the ersatz Indonesian interior.

“Well, you know they've always gone to the Caribbean on winter holiday. They've been all over. Dominica got her name from being conceived on the island of Dominica. And her brother Maarten. You get the idea. So this year they decide to go to Trinidad, where they've never been. Two weeks on the beach, Gerti and Jan reading and sleeping, Dominica and Maarten windsurfing with the hotel water-sports boy. The one who also helps with the towels and umbrella?

“On the last day, Dominica informs her parents that she has fallen in love with the local boy, the windsurfer, and is going to stay with his family and live. That means, of course, they'll live with his mother, because the men never stick around. And that's where it stands. She's been there for two weeks already, and Gerti is beside herself.”

The women are flushed and animated now, fed by food and vicarious folly. Stomachs work like internal combustion engines, blood chugs through veins. They remember their own daughters, lovely and peach-skinned—this one studying in London, that one due home from school in three hours. Some of the women pick their teeth discreetly behind hands cupped like dried leaves.

“It'll sort itself out,” says one of the aubergines in a low voice, walking out of the restaurant into the stone-gray Amsterdam afternoon. “Potato eaters and rice eaters never stay together for long.”

De Geuzen (**Riek Sijbring, Femke Snelting** and **Renee Turner**) *Unravelling Histories: The Dress of Here, There and Other Dislocations*, 2002 / divided into two cartographic representations, the bodice is printed with a current map of Indonesia, and the skirt features detailed street maps of the Netherlands' provincial capitals (Zwolle, Maastricht, Assen, Haarlem, Den Haag, Lelystad, Groningen, Utrecht, Den Bosch, Middelburg, Leeuwarden and Arnhem). Apart from Middelburg, these cities still bear traces of Dutch colonial history with an *Indische Buurt* (Indies neighborhood), and streets such as Javastraat, Molukkenstraat, Atjehstraat and Borneostraat, which are marked on the dress by a glass bead / photograph © 2005 Gert Jan van Rooj.

The Dress of Faith and Fidelity

The bald one got shot, that politician, in a parking lot. It was raining, as always, and the lights of the news teams reflected off the pavement as if they were making a Hollywood movie. I saw this on television, though I couldn't hear it because my grandmother was snoring, and our remote control is broken. So I sat next to her, afraid to wake her up by getting up and turning up the sound myself. Later on, when he got back from working at the restaurant, I told my father. He raised his eyebrows for a second, filled his cheeks with air like he was blowing a trumpet. "They'll probably think we did it." This said while puffing out little bursts of breath until his face was all loose jowls and deep-etched lines. He smelled like food—like my uncle's kebab house.

Sometimes I think about becoming a vegetarian, but when I mention this to my mother she grabs at my stomach and tells me not to be ridiculous, that I could already blow away in a stiff wind if she didn't weigh me down with sweaters and a coat. She packs me lunches that don't quite fit into the bags she puts them in. And they always ooze grease, leaving an oily smear at the bottom of my backpack. When we first came to Holland, my schoolmates made such fun of my lunches that I would toss them away before I got on the tram and spend all my pocket money on the fried croquettes everybody else ate. I'm still not sure if the stomach ache I had for two years was due to nerves or the unfamiliar food. Now I'm saving money for a trip to the United States. My parents don't know yet, but I have some time to get them used to the idea before I leave in a few years.

I'm really lucky to have a job I can do before school. And especially lucky since, if I arrive extra early, I can read the newspaper before I start my deliveries. My sister tells me I'm crazy to get up so early, but I tell her it's easier to think when it's dark out. She's a year older, and seems to sleep just as much as my grandmother. But I get to see the lights go on in all the grand houses on the canals, yellow against the thick black water. And hear the dogs that bark like crazy when I walk by. I wonder what I smell like to them.

At the end of my route last week, I sat for twenty minutes reading all about the bald politician's murderer. He was a vegetarian, and spent time when he was my age wiping spilled oil off sea birds in a coastal town. I am trying to make sense of this, but I'm not sure I can.

I know I'm not the only one who reads. One day last winter I showed up to the distribution center and saw a crowd of the other news carriers speaking in loud voices. Some held the weekly magazine above their heads and shook it like a disobedient child. The cover had a photo of the Koran on it, and then I realized there would be a walkout that morning. No part of the word of Allah (May He Be Blessed) can be thrown away — even a picture of it — and I imagined Rotterdam's garbage cans brimming with the magazine.

I left after everyone else, but took a copy with me to the canal and sat in the cold under a streetlamp, reading. Afterwards, I dug a hole in the hard soil with my penknife and buried the magazine. It was bad to miss work that week, although my parents were proud of me. Maybe America will always be one week out of reach.

De Geuzen (**Riek Sijbring, Femke Snelting** and **Renee Turner**) *Unravelling Histories: The Dress of Faith and Fidelity*, 2002 / features a section of the *dua*, or devotional prayer, written by Sayyid Uthman, then Honorary Adviser of Arabic Affairs, for the coronation of Queen Wilhelmina in 1898, when Indonesia was still under Dutch colonial rule. Juxtaposed to the prayer are statistics on the Netherlands' current Muslim population and the dates and titles of government policies regarding the practice of Islam in the Netherlands today / photograph © 2005 Gert Jan van Rooj.

The Dress of Propriety and Longing

Dear Margit,

I know that all the tales that I tell you of my times in this new country seem highly unlikely as you sit there in Bergen watching the water change colors in the afternoon sun. How I think of the dunes and the patterns they form, set about by the cool wind. I write you from the first-floor parlor of our house on this winter day, but even with two overhead fans and a cool drink brought to me, the temperature is enough to melt the sealing wax on this letter.

Margit, would you believe me if I told you that tobacco saved my life the other day? Please do not think that I have succumbed to fleshly temptation, for you know me better than that. Father and Piet and I set out on an afternoon walk in the wilds yesterday, accompanied by one of our natives, a surly man known more for his affection for father's tobacco than for any human form.

We had been walking for a quarter of an hour when suddenly a great hullabaloo broke out, and I nearly fell down with fright. A great orangutan leapt out of an overhanging branch and made for us with what seemed a mad vengeance. Father and Piet leapt to the fore to try to ward off the beast, and it very nearly seemed the end until the native did a most unlikely thing. He drew a cigarette to his mouth, lit it calmly and motioned to the orangutan, whereupon the beast grabbed it greedily, grabbed a vine and pulled itself up into the tree from whence it came. I tell you Margit, that beast took long, satisfied draughts on that tobacco like any student or gentleman, and hung his leg from the branch in leisurely pleasure.

It surely seems the evils of mankind have been extended to all God's creatures in this dark country. Still, I did find the prettiest material at market the other day, which I enclose for you to make into a precious blouse for my dear niece. My thoughts are with you and Niel always.

Yours,

Annek, c. 1898

De Geuzen (**Riek Sijbring, Femke Snelting** and **Renee Turner**) *Unravelling Histories: The Dress of Propriety and Longing*, 2002 / quotations from fiction and non-fiction works about Dutch colonial life in the Indies are repeated across the dress: excerpts from the *Indische Literatuur* written by well-known authors such as Eddy Du Perron and Multatuli are juxtaposed with writings by the early Indonesia feminist author Soewarsih Djojopoespito and contemporary Indonesian writers whose work illustrates a continuing fascination with the conflict between identities, and the outsider's perspective / photograph © 2005 Gert Jan van Rooj.

SHEET A
INDIA
(PART OF)
BURMA
(NORTH WEST)
FOR INDEX TO DIVISION OF MAPS
SHEWING RELATIVE POSITIONS OF
ADJACENT TERRITORIES SEE REVERSE
METRES
LEGEND
HSIPAW
HEIGHTS IN
METRES
The intervals between contour
lines vary in places
Scale 1:1,000,000
CACHAR
TRIPURA
CHITTAGONG
HILL TRACTS
CHITTAGONG
Chittagong
CHIN HILLS
ARAKAN HILL TRACTS
UPPER CHINDWIN
SHWEBO
LOWER CHINDWIN
PAKOKKU
MYINGYAN
SAGAING
MINBU
MAGWE
THAYETMYO
YAMETHIN
Akyab
Pakokku
Mandalay

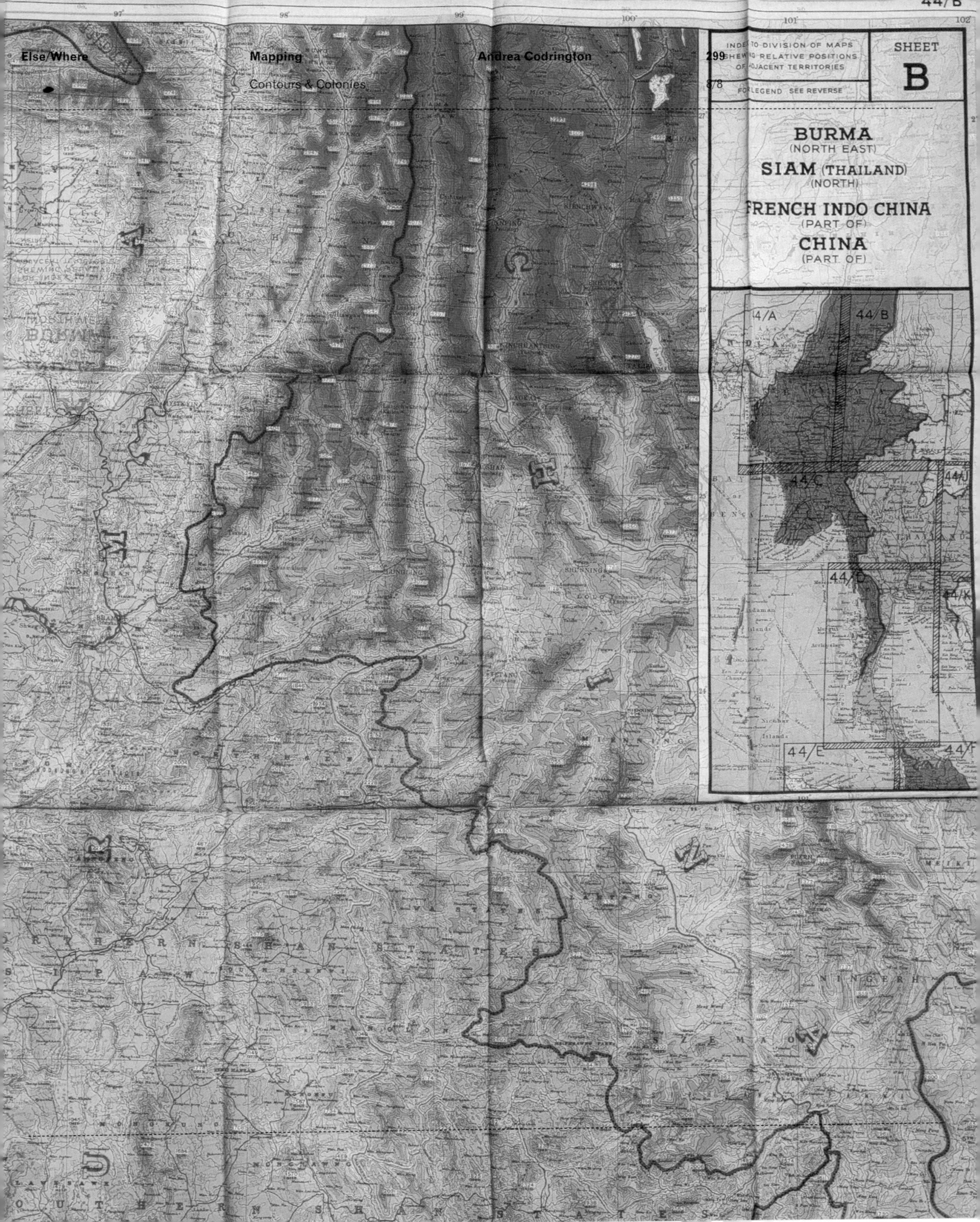
44/B
SHEET
B
INDEX TO DIVISION OF MAPS SHEWING RELATIVE POSITIONS OF ADJACENT TERRITORIES
FOR LEGEND SEE REVERSE
BURMA
(NORTH EAST)
SIAM (THAILAND)
(NORTH)
FRENCH INDO CHINA
(PART OF)
CHINA
(PART OF)
44/A
44/B
44/C
44/D
44/E
44/F
44/J
44/K
97°
98°
99°
100°
101°
102°
NORTHERN SHAN STATES
SOUTHERN SHAN STATES
WA STATES
SZEMAO
NINGERH
TALIFU
SHUNNING

CONTRIBUTORS

Antenna Design New York
(info@antennadesign.com) was co-founded in 1997 by **Sigi Moeslinger** and **Masamichi Udagawa**. Antenna's mission is to make the experience of technological objects and environments more meaningful and exciting through a combination of product, interaction and environmental design. Antenna's diverse output ranges from public and commercial projects, such as New York City Transit Authority subway cars and ticket vending machines, JetBlue check-in kiosks and Bloomberg Terminals, to interactive environmental installations, such as *Power Flower*, a window installation at Bloomingdale's that was activated by passersby. Antenna Design won four awards in the 2005 *Business Week/IDEA Awards*, including a Gold Award for *Civic Exchange*, its competition-winning design for an interactive information installation for Lower Manhattan. <www.antennadesign.com>

Julian Bleecker
(julian@techkwondo.com) is director of the Mobile and Pervasive Lab, a near-future R&D think tank run by the School of Cinema-TV and Annenberg Center for Communication at the University of Southern California. An assistant professor at USC's Interactive Media Division, and research faculty at USC's Institute for Multimedia Literacy, he held a research fellowship at the Annenberg Center for Communication in 2005–06. Bleecker has a BS in Electrical Engineering from Cornell, an MS in Engineering from the University of Washington, and a PhD from UC Santa Cruz where his dissertation was on the link between technology, entertainment and culture. His art-technology collaboration with Marina Zurkow, *Pussy Weevil*, was exhibited at Ars Electronica in 2005.

Ole Bouman
(oleb@xs4all.nl) is editor-in-chief of *Volume* and of *Archis.org*. A critic, author, designer and curator, his publications include *The Invisible in Architecture* (1994), *RealSpace in QuickTimes: Architecture and Digitization* (NAi, 1996) which accompanied the exhibition he curated for the *XIX Triennale di Milano*, and *The Battle for Time* (2003). Earlier exhibitions include *Egotecture* (Boijmans van Beuningen Museum, Rotterdam, 1997) and *Freeze* (Arti e Amicitiae, Amsterdam, 2000). He was co-curator of *Manifesta 3* in Ljubljana, 2000. <www.archis.org>

Bureau d'etudes
(bureaudetudes@gmail.com) are artists based in Paris, engaged in the mapping of contemporary power relations at the institutional and international level. In 2002, Bureau d'etudes produced *European Norms of World-Production* (on the "normalization" activities of European institutions; texts created in collaboration with Brian Holmes) at the European Social Forum in Florence. *Refuse the Biopolice* was distributed at the 2002 *no-border* camp, set up in Strasbourg in opposition to the Schengen policy. *The World Government* was published in 2004 by ed. universite tangente, and shown in *The Use-Value of Art: The future of the reciprocal readymade and other art-related practice*, at APEX art, New York, in March–April 2004. *Crisis* (a map about financial crises since the 1980s) was exhibited at the *Ex-Argentina* project at the Museum Ludwig, Cologne, in spring 2004. *The System* (comprising two maps, one about world government, the other about the global laboratory) was published by ed.universite tangente in 2005. *The Ring* (about the Bohemian Club) was published in California in 2005. These and other maps are online at <www.u-tangente.org>

Sulki Choi
(me@sulki.com) was born in Seoul, Korea, and is currently living and working in Maastricht, the Netherlands, as a researcher at the Jan van Eyck Academie, where she participated in *Micropolis*, a research project dealing with the cultural identity of the City of Leuven, Belgium. She earned her MFA degree at Yale University with a thesis on the diagram and its various pragmatic functions. Her dynamic world-map system, *Daily World View*, has been exhibited in De Appel, Amsterdam, and her design work has been published in journals and books including *IDEA* (Japan), *Nana 3* (Korea) and *Art & Design* (China).

Andrea Codrington
(acodrington@nyc.rr.com) is a New York-based writer and editor specializing in design and visual culture. Currently editing architecture and art books at Phaidon Press, she has been a columnist for the *New York Times* and has written widely for such publications as *I.D. Magazine*, *Metropolis* and *Cabinet*. She is the author of the monograph *Kyle Cooper* (Yale University Press, 2003), the co-author of *Pause: 59 Minutes of Motion Graphics* (Laurence King, 2000), and is currently at work on her first novel — a story about art, love and medical imaging.

Denis Cosgrove
(cosgrove@geog.ucla.edu) is Alexander von Humboldt professor of geography at UCLA. A contributor for over two decades to thinking and research in cultural geography and landscape studies, his work has evolved from a focus on the meanings of landscape in Human and Cultural Geography, especially as these have evolved in Western Europe since the 15th Century, to a broader concern with the role of spatial images and representations in the making and communicating of knowledge. He is the author of *Social Formation and Symbolic Landscape* (University of Wisconsin Press, 1984, 1998), *The Palladian Landscape: Geographical Change and its Representations in Sixteenth-Century Italy* (Pennsylvania State University Press, 1993), *Apollo's Eye: A Cartographic Genealogy of the Earth in the Western Imagination* (Johns Hopkins University Press, 2001) and editor of *Mappings* (Reaktion Books, 1999).

Layla Curtis
(info@laylacurtis.com) was awarded the 2005 Arts Council England and British Antarctic Survey Fellowship and will travel to Antarctica during the Antarctic summer 2005–06, to spend three months as artist-in-residence working alongside scientists at an Antarctic research station. She was artist in residence at Akiyoshidai International Arts Village in Japan in 1998–99 and in 2004 at Ramsgate Maritime Museum in partnership with Turner Contemporary. Her work is included in the Tate Collection, the Government Art Collection and the World Bank Collection. Recent exhibitions include *A Bigger Splash: British Art from Tate, 1960–2003* at the Pavilhão Lucas Nogueira Garcez, São Paulo, Brazil, and *De leur temps, Collections Privees Françaises*, Musée des Beaux-Arts de Tourcoing, France. Current projects include a new video work commissioned by *Vivid* and a collaged map *Newcastle-Gateshead* commissioned by *Locus+* which will publish her work in 2006. <www.locusplus.org.uk>

De Geuzen
(info@geuzen.org) is an art and design collective based between Amsterdam, Brussels and Rotterdam. Since 1996 **Riek Sijbring**, **Femke Snelting** and **Renée Turner** have been working together on projects that deploy a variety of strategies — both on and offline — to explore interests in female identity, critical resistance, representation and narrative archiving. They have done educational workshops at the *Impakt Festival*, the Piet Zwart Institute and *Digitalis*, and their projects have been featured in *Manifesta 3*, Kuenstlerhaus Bremen and the Amsterdam Historical Museum. Some of their projects are by commission and many are self-initiated. <http://www.geuzen.org/>

Steve Dietz
(stevedietz@yproductions.com) is Director of the ISEA 2006 Symposium and *ZeroOne San Jose: A Global Festival of Art on the Edge* taking place in August 2006 in San Jose, California. In 2005 he co-curated *Database Imaginary* at the Walter Phillips Gallery, Banff, Canada, where he is curatorial fellow. He curated the web projects for the 2005 exhibition *Making Things Public* at ZKM, Karlsruhe, curated by Bruno Latour and Peter Weibel. With Sarah Cook, he co-curated *The Art Formerly Known as New Media*, which opened at the Walter Philips Gallery in September 2005. He is based in Minneapolis, Minnesota. <http://www.yproductions.com>

Judith Donath
(judith@media.mit.edu) is an Assistant Professor at the MIT Media Lab, where she directs the Sociable Media research group. She focuses on the social side of computing, synthesizing knowledge from graphic design, urban studies and cognitive science to build innovative interfaces for online communities and virtual identities. She recently directed *Id/Entity*, an exhibit of collaboratively produced installations examining the science and technology transformation of portraiture, and has pioneered several social applications for the web, including *The Electric Postcard*, *Portraits in Cyberspace* and *A Day in the Life of Cyberspace*. She received her doctoral and master's degrees in Media Arts and Sciences from MIT, and her BA in History from Yale University. <http://smg.media.mit.edu/people/Judith>

Paul Elliman
(paul.elliman@yale.edu) is a London-based designer whose work and writing explores the mutual impact of technology and language. His work has been exhibited at the Tate Modern in London and is included in collections by the British Council, the Victoria and Albert Museum (London) and the Cooper Hewitt National Design Museum in New York. He has been a faculty member at Yale School of Art since 1997 and is also currently thesis supervisor at Werkplaats Typografie, in Arnhem, the Netherlands.

Yuri Engelhardt
(Y.Engelhardt@uva.nl) is interested in principles underlying the visual communication of information, from ancient pictorial inscriptions to interactive data visualizations. In 1995 he founded the *InfoDesign* and *InfoDesign-Cafe* mailing lists. Author of "Meaningful Space" in *IF/THEN: PLAY* (The Netherlands Design Institute/BIS, 1998), he holds a master's degree in medicine and a PhD in computer science, for a dissertation titled "The language of graphics." Yuri is assistant professor in the Department of Media and Culture at the University of Amsterdam, and lecturer in Information Design at the Utrecht Graduate School of Visual Art and Design. <http://informationdesign.org> <http://yuriweb.com>

Entropy8Zuper!
(deux@entropy8zuper.org) **Auriea Harvey** and **Michael Samyn** started their online lives and web design practices in 1995, the former as Entropy8 in New York City, the latter as Zuper! and Group Z, in Ronse, Belgium. In 1999, they merged their activities as Entropy8Zuper! and moved to Gent, where they still live. In 2002, they started *Tale of Tales*, for the purposes of developing interactive entertainment. <http://entropy8zuper.org/>

Michael Frumin
(mfrumin@eyebeam.org) is the Technical Director of R&D at Eyebeam, a non-profit media arts and technology research organization in New York City. He began his career in original and creative technology-based research while working on advanced networking protocols as an undergraduate at Stanford University. After school, he was a founding member of a team of hackers using their quantitative skills to find proprietary, novel real-time sources of qualitative information for hedge fund managers. He accepted the prototype Research Fellowship at Eyebeam where he has been the primary developer of *fundrace.org*, as well as *reBlog*, an open source software project; *reBlog.org*, *ForwardTrack*, *Pizza Party*, and other works, some still in development. He currently lives in Brooklyn, NY, very close to where he grew up. <www.fundrace.org> <www.eyebeam. org>

Ben Fry
(fry@media.mit.edu) received his doctoral degree at the MIT Media Laboratory in 2004, where his research focused on methods of visualizing large amounts of data from dynamic information sources. His current research involves the visualization of genetic data at the Broad Insitute of MIT

and Harvard. His work has been shown at the *Whitney Biennial 2002*, the *Cooper Hewitt 2003 National Design Triennial*, the Museum of Modern Art, New York, and in the films *Minority Report* and *The Hulk*. With Casey Reas of UCLA, he is currently developing *Processing*, an environment for teaching computational design and sketching interactive media software. <http://acg.media.mit.edu/people/fry/>

Marti Guixe
(info@guixe.com) was born in Barcelona and studied interior design there, and industrial design at Milan Polytechnic. After working as a design consultant in Seoul in the mid-1990s, he began a long collaboration with Camper, the Spanish shoe retailer, designing its London store in 1998, and Camper stores worldwide since then. Guixe divides his time between Barcelona and Berlin, designing products for companies such as Cha Cha, Authentics and H20. *H!BYE* (prototype pills for nomadic workers) was shown in *Workspheres*, MoMA, New York, in 2001. His books include *Marti Guixé: Libre de Contexte* (Birkhäuser, 2003) and *The Marti Guixé Cookbook* (2004). <http://www.guixe.com>

Mark Hansen
(cocteau@stat.ucla.edu) is an associate professor of statistics at the University of California, Los Angeles. Prior to joining UCLA, he served as a member of the Technical Staff in the Statistics and Data Mining Research Department at Bell Laboratories, Lucent Technologies. His work involves applications that are rich in complex data. Together with his long-time collaborator, Ben Rubin (EAR Studio), he explores new representations and new mappings of text feeds. Their project *Listening Post* was installed at the Whitney Museum in 2002–2003, and won the Golden Nica award at *Ars Electronica 2004*. Hansen and Rubin are winners of a 2005 Media Arts Fellowship. <http://www.stat.ucla.edu/~cocteau/>

Cathy Lang Ho
(cathylangho@nyc.rr.com) is the founding editor of *The Architect's Newspaper*, the first and only architecture tabloid in the United States. She was an editor at *Architecture* magazine, and has written for *The New York Times*, *Metropolis*, *ID Magazine*, *Frame*, *Domus* and *Dwell*. She is the former editor of *Design Book Review* and co-author of *American Contemporary Furniture* (Universe, 2000) and *House: American Houses for the New Century* (Universe, 2001). She is also an avid footie player and fan.

Brian Holmes
(brian.holmes@wanadoo.fr) is an art and culture critic, born in San Francisco, living in Paris. He holds a PhD in Romance Languages from UC Berkeley, devotes most of his time to working with artistic projects in the context of social movements, and is the author of a book of essays entitled *Hieroglyphs of the Future: Art and Politics in a Networked Era* (Zagreb: WHW, 2002), with another collection coming up, under the title *Unleashing the Collective Phantoms*. An archive of his work can be found at <http://www.u-tangente.org>

Robert Horn
(hornbob@earthlink.net) is a political scientist with a special interest in policy communication, social learning and knowledge management. Since 1993, he has been a visiting scholar in the Program on People, Computers and Design at Stanford University's Center for the Study of Language and Information, pursuing research work in knowledge management and information design. Horn's books include *Mapping Hypertext* (Lexington Institute, 1989) and *Visual Language: Global Communication for the 21st Century*. Founder and for 15 years CEO of Information Mapping, Inc., his consulting clients have included Boeing, Lucent Technologies, AT&T, HP, and other Global 1000 companies. <http://www.stanford.edu/~rhorn/>

Natalie Jeremijenko
(njeremijenko@ucsd.edu) is a design engineer and techno-artist working at the intersection of contemporary art, science and engineering. She is currently Assistant Professor at UC San Diego, where she runs the XDesign Lab, the Experimental Product Design Lab. She previously held a research position at the Media Research Lab/Center for Advanced Technology in the Computer Science Dept., New York University, and was the director of the Engineering Design Studio at Yale University. Named one of the top one hundred young innovators by the *MIT Technology Review*, she was a recipient of a 1999 Rockefeller Foundation New Media Fellowship. <http://xdesign.ucsd.edu/>

Lisa Jevbratt
(jevbratt@jevbratt.com) is a Swedish systems/network artist working primarily with the Internet, who has lived in the U.S. since 1994. Educated in art and computers at Konstfack, Malmo Konstskola Forum, and CADRE (San Jose State University), she is currently an assistant professor at UC Santa Barbara (UCSB) in the Studio Arts Department and the Media Arts Technology program. Her work has been exhibited in venues such as The New Museum, New York, the Walker Art Center, *Ars Electronica*, *Transmediale*, Berlin, *Electrohype 2002* Malmo, the *Whitney Biennial 2002*, and *Ciberart Bilbao 2004*, Spain. She is an affiliate of C5, the Silicon Valley collaborative research endeavor. <http://jevbratt.com>

Nina Katchadourian
(Nina@immaterial.net) is a Brooklyn-based conceptual artist who works with a wide variety of media including sculpture, video, photography and sound. Her past projects have involved mending broken spiderwebs with sewing thread, creating a machine that listens to the pattern of popping popcorn and uses Morse Code to translate it into spoken language, and constructing a genealogical chart incorporating all the people who appear on common grocery store products. Katchadourian has taught at Brown University and at the Rhode Island School of Design. She is represented in New York by Sara Meltzer gallery and in San Francisco by Catharine Clark gallery.

J. J. King
(jamie@jamie.com) is a London based writer specializing in new media. An editor at *Mute* magazine, he writes the *World According to Blog* column for Channel 4 News online, which reviews the week's most popular blogged topics. He is also a lecturer at Ravensbourne College, a member of the music collective Antifamily, and an activist in the area of intellectual property. His work as a 2003 DI Research Fellow formed part of the early research for this book. His doctoral thesis at the University of Southampton examined the history of the Internet as an extension of the American frontier. Jamie is currently working on a new biotechnology murder-mystery novel. <www.metamute.com>

Valdis Krebs
(valdis@orgnet.com) is a management consultant whose firm, orgnet.com, is based in Cleveland, Ohio. The developer of *InFlow*, a software-based organization network analysis methodology, he has been mapping and measuring human networks within and between organizations since 1988. His clients include IBM, TRW, Raytheon, Booz Allen & Hamilton, Deloitte Touche Tohmatsu, KPMG, and the Centers for Disease Control. His work has been covered in the *Wall Street Journal*, *Forbes*, *Release 1.0*, *First Monday* and major newspapers around the world. Valdis holds undergraduate degrees in mathematics and computer science, and a graduate degree in Organizational Behavior/Human Resources. <http://www.orgnet.com>

Laura Kurgan
(ljk33@columbia.edu) is director of Visual Studies and director of the Spatial Information Design Lab at Columbia University Graduate School of Architecture, Planning and Preservation. She is also principal of Laura Kurgan Architecture in New York City. Her work explores the interface between building, electronic media and information technology in both her art and her architecture. Over the last decade she has worked with new spatial information and mapping technologies, especially declassified satellite imagery and GPS technology. She recently completed the new offices for WITNESS, a human rights organization that distributes video technology and training to local activists. <http://www.arch.columbia.edu/gsap/44749>

Brian McGrath
(bpm7@columbia.edu) is an architect and co-founder of <urban-interface.com>, which explores the relationship between urban design and multi-media. Creator of *Manhattan Timeformations* (2000) for the Skyscraper Museum, New York, he is the author of *Transparent Cities* (SITES Books, 1994) and *New Urbanisms/New Workplace* (Columbia Books on Architecture, 2000). McGrath teaches architecture and urban design at Columbia and Parsons in New York, and at Chulalongkorn University in Bangkok. A Senior Fulbright scholar in Thailand in 1998–99, he is currently a co-investigator on a Long Term Ecological Research team, linking science and design. <www.skyscraper.org/timeformations>

Julie Mehretu
(info@projectilegallery.com) was born in Addis Ababa, Ethiopia, and lives and works in New York City where she is represented by The Projectile Gallery. She received an MFA with honors from Rhode Island School of Design in 1997. *Julie Mehretu: Drawing into Painting*, a traveling exhibition, originated at the Walker Art Center in 2003. Her work has been shown in international exhibitions including the *Carnegie International*, *São Paulo Biennial* and *Whitney Biennial* (all in 2004) and is in the permanent collections of the Museum of Modern Art, New York, San Francisco Museum of Modern Art, Philadelphia Art Museum, Studio Museum in Harlem, and the National Gallery, Washington, D.C. She was named a 2005 MacArthur Fellow by the John D. and Catherine T. MacArthur Foundation. <www.elproyecto.com/>

Paul Mijksenaar
(paul@mijksenaar.com) is principal and founder of Bureau Mijksenaar (Amsterdam)/Mijksenaar Arup (New York) and professor at the Department Industrial Design of Delft University (Netherlands). He lives in Amsterdam. His office focuses on visual information design, especially wayfinding, most recently for Schiphol and Dulles Washington airports, the MoMA Store, the Rijksmuseum in Amsterdam and the Erasmus Medical Centre in Rotterdam. Paul Mijksenaar is the co-author of *Open Here: the Art of Instructional Design* and the author of *Visual Function*. <www.mijksenaar.com>

Andrea Moed
(amoeda@gmail.com) is a designer and writer who specializes in developing media and information systems that foster conversations about places. Past projects include *New York Snap Exchange*, a networked digital photography game, and *Annotate Space*, a participatory walking tour of a Brooklyn neighborhood. Andrea has published numerous articles on design and technology and her work has been featured in *Discover* magazine, *BBC Online* and the *Wall Street Journal*. She holds a master's degree from New York University's Interactive Telecommunications Program and has taught at the Parsons School of Design. She entered UC Berkeley's School for Information Management Systems in Fall 2005. <www.snapexchange.com>

MUST Urbanism
(mail@must.nl) is a studio based in Amsterdam led by **Robert Broesi** (urban designer), **Pieter Jannink** (urban designer) and **Wouter Veldhuis** (architect). The studio combines urban design and research and is attracted by regional design survey and urban transformation issues, preferably containing mixed-use programs. Projects range from the local to the European scale, and include the *Limes Atlas*, an atlas of the Roman frontier, the regional study *Veenkolonieen*, and a redevelopment plan for 7,000 dwellings in Amsterdam's Garden Cities. MUST has its permanent location in Amsterdam, but its mobile work station criss-crosses Europe. <www.must.nl>

Monochrome Landscapes

Laura Kurgan's suite of satellite images shows the limit and potential of resolution and brings the geo-politics of data visualization down to earth.

SATELLITES: Two commercial companies have launched high-resolution satellites, and, for a modest fee, these satellites can be tasked to capture images of almost anything, anywhere on earth. Once collected, the data (images) are stored in a database for resale, fully searchable. The Ikonos satellite, privately owned and operated by Space Imaging, Inc., of Thornton, Colorado, takes pictures at a resolution of 1.0 meter per pixel; the QuickBird satellite belongs to DigitalGlobe, Inc., of Longmont, Colorado, and takes pictures at 0.61 meters per pixel.

MONOCHROMES: I wanted a series of monochrome landscapes, so I asked for pictures of places on earth primarily characterized by one of four basic colors: white, blue, yellow and green. The rules were simple, and there weren't many choices: snow, water, sand and trees. The satellites had been, or had to go, looking at the Arctic National Wildlife Refuge in Alaska, the middle of the Atlantic Ocean, the Southern Desert in Iraq, and the Cameroonian rain forest. For each of these places, I purchased the image/data corresponding to an 8-km x 8-km square of the earth's surface. Two were already in the DigitalGlobe archives (Alaska and Iraq) and two required new tasking (Ikonos over Cameroon, QuickBird over the Atlantic). The results evoke questions that are at once aesthetic and geo-political, mapping some of the most vulnerable landscapes of our time — the largely uninhabited, resource-rich other sides of globalization. The color fields are strangely abstract, even minimalist: formal, sheer information, but a little ominous.[1]

DIGITAL LANDSCAPES: The images on the following pages are just small fragments of the 256 square kilometers' worth of data acquired. These landscapes are digital in an old-fashioned sense: they are uniquely located on the coordinate grid of longitude and latitude, and have a time stamp as well. Every one of the 755 million pixels in each scene can be described in terms of a number (latitude and longitude) corresponding to its singular position on earth. The heat value of each position is also expressed as a number which, in turn, is assigned a standard color and rendered as a pixel of a certain measure. Finally, they are photographs: information, event, surface, pattern, chance encounter, memory, field of color.

ZOOM: Within the database, the zoom has already taken place. That is one definition of high-resolution. Over a 16.5 x 16.5 kilometer surface — the footprint of a full QuickBird image — a progressive zoom is already implied, right down to the two-thirds of a square meter that constitutes the pixel itself. But the monochrome character of the images, where every pixel looks pretty much alike, makes looking for or emphasizing something in particular rather complicated. It's hard not to look for something, even if it's just the pixels themselves. The vector of the zoom is highly codified: the camera seems to travel relentlessly, in a straight line, nearer and nearer, until it freezes on the objective it seeks. Often the sequence of images demonstrates its reliability by its reversibility: zoom in, zoom out. The Eames' film Powers of Ten predicted — no, constituted — the generic form of this operation: direction, continuity and reversibility, all anchored in the 1:1 scale that we think (wish) defines our reality. The zoom on the following pages, however, is merely a pragmatic device designed to display the resolution of each pixel within the constraints of the page. In certain cases, there is something to see.

1. Four of these images, each 40 by 82 inches, were exhibited as *Monochrome Landscapes* in *Architecture By Numbers* at the Whitney Museum at Altria in New York City, April–July 2004. Thanks to Michael Hays, who curated the show, and the staff of the Whitney-Altria; Erik Carver, who helped to produce these images; and Bill Guthie, who helped with image processing. See Geoffrey Batchen, "The Forest for the Trees," *Aperture* 178, Spring 2005, pp. 26–33, for further information on this project.

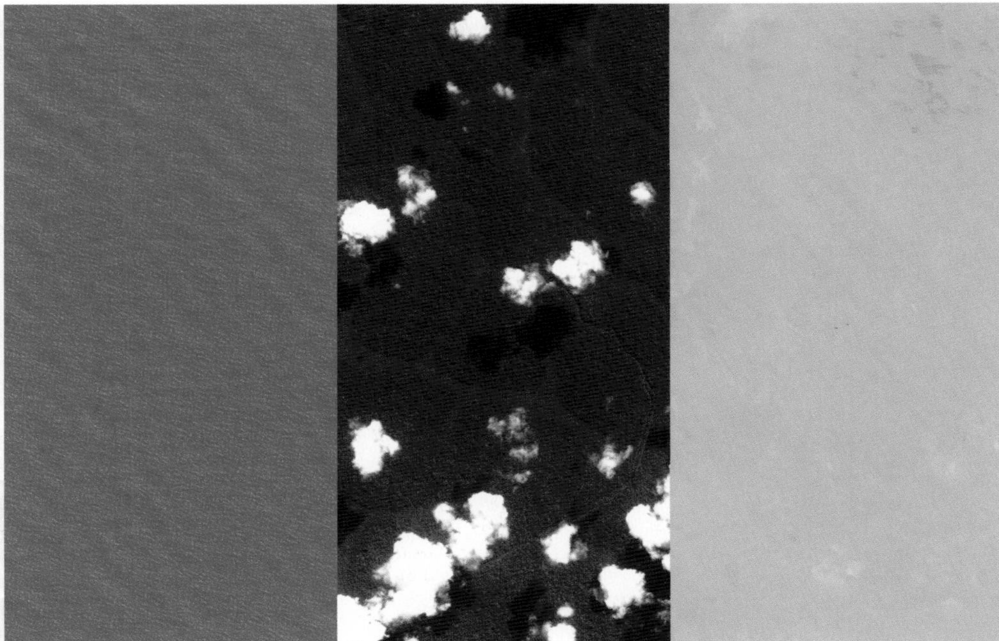

White
1002 area, Arctic National Wildlife Refuge, near Kaktovik, Alaska.

Geologists estimate that the Alaskan Coastal Plain area in ANWR harbors about 10.4 billion barrels of recoverable crude oil, as well as polar bear, musk ox, caribou, and scores of migratory bird species. Oil exploration and drilling is currently prohibited here, although this may change shortly.

Acquired
7 April 2003 / 21:12:49 GMT.

Center coordinates
Lat. 69.79985 / Long. −144.54275.
QuickBird satellite, 0.61m per pixel.

Blue
Atlantic Ocean, intersection of the Equator and the Prime Meridian, south of Accra (Ghana) and west of Libreville (Gabon).

Representatives of 25 nations met at the International Meridian Conference in Washington in October 1884 to "fix upon a meridian proper to be employed as a common zero of longitude and standard of time-reckoning throughout the whole world."

Acquired
16 May 2003 / 10:19:54 GMT.

Center coordinates
Lat. −0.00195 / Long. −0.00045.
QuickBird satellite, 0.61m per pixel.

Green
Old growth tropical lowland rain forest, south eastern Cameroon, about 100 km west of Yokadouma and 70 km east of the Dja reserve.

An illegal logging road, first identified by Global Forest Watch in early 2001, traverses a not-yet-allocated forest concession area (UFA 10-030).

Acquired
4 December 2001 / 09:48 GMT.

Upper left coordinates
Lat. 3.21939 / Long. 14.2077.
Ikonos satellite, 1.0 meter per pixel.

Yellow
Southern Desert, south eastern Iraq, between Al Busayyah and An Nasiriyah.

Two helicopters fly in formation, during the second week of Operation Iraqi Freedom.

Acquired
30 March 2003 / 07:32:10 GMT.

Center coordinates
Lat. 30.3136 / Long. 46.3738.
QuickBird satellite, 0.61m per pixel

Laura Kurgan *Monochrome Landscapes*, 2002 / (opposite page): *Green*, 72 dpi.
(this page): *Yellow*, 72 dpi.

Laura Kurgan *Monochrome Landscapes*, 2002 / (opposite page): *Green*, 28 dpi.
(this page): *Yellow*, 28 dpi.

Laura Kurgan *Monochrome Landscapes*, 2002 / (opposite page): *White*, 72 dpi.
(this page): *Blue*, 72 dpi.

Laura Kurgan *Monochrome Landscapes*, 2002 / (opposite page): *White*, 28 dpi.
(this page): *Blue*, 28 dpi.

Else/Where: Mapping

Editors: Janet Abrams and Peter Hall

Designer & Publication Manager:
Deborah Littlejohn

Consultant Designers:
Mevis & van Deursen

Proofreading: Elizabeth Haukaas

Printing: Die Keure, Belgium

Published by:
University of Minnesota Design Institute
308 Northrop Memorial Auditorium
84 Church Street SE
Minneapolis, MN 55455
<http://design.umn.edu>

University of Minnesota

A Cataloging-in-Publication record for this book is available from the Library of Congress.

ISBN 0-9729696-2-4

Distributed by:
University of Minnesota Press
111 Third Avenue South, Suite 290
Minneapolis MN 55401
<http://www.upress.umn.edu>

Design Institute
The Design Institute commissions, publishes and implements innovative design ideas for the public realm, with a focus on intersections of physical space and emerging technologies, and on new design pedagogy. DI fellowship research, publishing and educational programs (for university students and the general public) aim to stimulate fresh thinking about the design choices available to us today — in the products, systems and environments that comprise our everyday material landscape — and inspire the development of new tools, skills and artifacts to expand those options.

Else/Where: Mapping was conceived as one of five mapping projects forming the Twin Cities Design Celebration (TCDC), produced by the Design Institute with a generous gift from Target Corporation. Previous TCDC projects include *Typeface: Twin Cities*, a new typeface, *Metro Letters* book, and chocolate alphabet; *Twin Cities Knowledge Maps*, nine alternative urban cartographies; the *B.U.G.* (*Big Urban Game*), played online and throughout Minneapolis/St. Paul in September 2003; and *Map City*, a University of Minnesota Design Minor seminar on urbanism, cartography and digital technologies. For more information on TCDC projects, visit: <http://design.umn.edu/go/to/TCDC>

The editors gratefully acknowledge additional funding for ***Else/Where: Mapping*** from the Consulate General of the Netherlands, New York.

Acknowledgments:
Pier and Jan Willem Terwen for allowing De Geuzen to borrow the original RAF silk map belonging to their mother, Jeanne Terwen-de Loos, and the Rijksmuseum, Amsterdam, for providing access to her dress.

EDventure Holdings, New York, for providing a copy of Jack Dangermond's talk at PCForum 2004.

<getmapping.com> for reducing the fee for aerial photographs of London used in Jeremy Wood's *Meridian Drawing*.

Every effort has been made to contact copyright holders of images published herein. The editors would appreciate being informed of any omissions in order to make due acknowledgment in future editions of this book.

Near/Future:
<http://www.elsewheremapping.com>

GRATITUDE/BELONGITUDE

This book has benefited from many conversations with longstanding friends and colleagues, and encounters with new people and ideas, over the past five years. Thanks in particular to Rachel Abrams, Stuart Albert, James Boyd-Brent, Gloria Bremer, Dick van Dijk, Daniel de Segovia Gross, Melle Hammer, David Harris, David Karam, Julie Lasky, Bill Moran, John Maeda, Tom Oliphant, Chee Pearlman, Randall Richardson, Mark Robbins and Kevin Slavin; to Jouke Kleerebezem, Jerry Michalski, Sean Blair and Sara Diamond, for invitations to conferences that proved to be pivotal; to Clay Shirky, Liddy Nevile, Alan Elsner and Dan Monk, for their comments on certain essays in draft form; to Lisa Strausfeld and Deyan Sudjic, for words of encouragement and structural suggestions at a crucial moment; and to Pieter Martin of the University of Minnesota Press, and Robert Kloos of the Consulate General of the Netherlands, New York, for their generosity and patience!

Linda van Deursen and Armand Mevis worked with us to outline the book's design from their previous format for *If/Then: Play* (ed. Janet Abrams, 1999), then graciously provided their framework, enabling Deborah Littlejohn to design ***Else/Where: Mapping*** at the DI's headquarters in Minneapolis.

We have learned enormously from our contributing authors, artists and designers: thanks to you all.

The completion of this book would not have been possible without the support of staff at the University of Minnesota Design Institute and its home, the College of Architecture and Landscape Architecture (CALA). Many thanks to Tom Fisher, CALA Dean, James Watchke, CALA Accounting, and Richard Schunn and Chuck Yust, CALA Technology.

Thanks to former DI staff members Mary deLaittre, Amy Pogue Brady and especially Kate Carmody for help with picture research and project administration, and to Alex Terzich for contributions to the book's conceptual strategy and editorial assistance in its early stages. Wendy Friedmeyer, DI educational programs coordinator, and Pat Hemmis, teaching fellow, have nurtured the Design Minor and Design Camp, the DI's educational programs for undergraduates and teens, with exceptional dedication while this book percolated in the background. Thanks to Daniel Tsegai, Fesseha "Fish" Gebremariam, and the custodial crew at Northrop for keeping us company while we persevered on many a late-night stint.

Special thanks to:
Lana Lê and Wendy Bryant for their encouragement and feedback; Sheila de Bretteville for her interest in incorporating mapping as an introductory topic in the Yale MFA graphic design program and the students at Yale for their own related work. (PH)

and to:

Santiago Piedrafita for his support, encouragement, and, as always, his uncompromising and honest style of critique. (DL)

and to:

Marc Hacker and Kenny Schwartz, for their abundant hospitality, and letting their dining room table become the DI's *de facto* New York office; Mark Hansen, always ready with *there you are!* wherever (else) I happen to be; and David Gordon, cartographer of psychic space, with whom I have come to appreciate that *right here/right now* is invariably better than being *else/where*. (JA)